Over Fifty

*The Resource Book
for the Better Half of Your Life*

Over Fifty

The Resource Book
for the Better Half of Your Life

Tom and Nancy Biracree

HarperPerennial

A Division of HarperCollins*Publishers*

For our parents,

Bill and Val Biracree
Jerry and Gloria Dobkin
Norman and Betty Goodfellow

Your love, devotion, and positive example inspired this book and provides inspiration in our lives every day.

And, as always, for *Ryan.*

First HarperPerennial edition published 1991

Designed by Joan Greenfield

Library of Congress Cataloging-in-Publication Data
Biracree, Tom, 1947-
      Over 50 : the resource book for the better half of your life / Tom and Nancy Biracree — 1st HarperPerennial ed.
            p.   cm.
      Includes index.
      ISBN 0-06-271501-1 — ISBN 0-06-273000-2 (pbk.)
      1. Middle aged persons—United States—Life skills guides.
      2. Aged—United States—Life skills guides.   I. Biracree, Nancy.
      II. Title.   III. Title: Over fifty.
HQ1059.5.U5B47   1991
305.24′4—dc20   90-55490

91 92 93 94 95 CC/HC 10 9 8 7 6 5 4 3 2 1
91 92 93 94 95 CC/HC 10 9 8 7 6 5 4 3 2 1 (pbk.)

Contents

S E C T I O N   T W O :
YOUR HEALTH
123

CHAPTER 15   Mental Health   229

SECTION FOUR:
LIVING A RICH, REWARDING LIFE
309

Introduction

The idea for this book, the first comprehensive resource book for adult Americans, emerged from our research for a previous book that presented a statistical portrait of life in the United States. Our research explored the lifestyles, love lives, family lives, career attainments, housing choices, and leisure time activities of Americans in different demographic groups. The more research we did, the more we came to see that the lives of Americans who were no longer children progressed through two separate stages, each with its own set of attitudes and priorities: early adulthood and full or mature adulthood.

The dominant characteristic of early adulthood is the quest to acquire in all areas of life. From the time we move out on our own, we strive to find a rewarding career, romantic partners, a spouse, a family, possessions, a house, a place in society, and, ultimately, a sense of self. Because America has, in the recent past, been youth-oriented, the lifestyle and concerns of this stage of life has dominated our culture, from soap operas to supermarket book racks.

That domination, however, is in the process of changing as the first of the "baby boomers" reach full or mature adulthood. The predominant characteristic of this second stage of adult life is the transition from the need to acquire to the emergence of a deep, fundimental sense of self-acceptance. If you are an adult, you find yourself less interested in obtaining more material possessions than in deriving more satisfaction from what you have. Comfortable with who you are, you are much less motivated by peer pressure and more interested in sharing your experience and knowledge with others. You are forward thinking and you constantly seek more involvement with life. Contrary to popular belief, numerous studies have shown that you are happier, more adventurous, and have more enthusiasm than people in early adulthood. Even though your life isn't problem-free, you have developed a practical, pragmatic method of attacking those problems.

Recognizing that your needs, interests, and attitudes were different spurred our interest in creating a brand new tool, a book that included nearly every important resource you might need in every area of life, along with the information necessary to make best use of those resources. For you and 65 million other adults, this book will serve as:

- A gateway to new experiences and choices—we have assembled resources that will help you get more fulfillment out of life. For example, you can:

  Start your own business

  Take advantage of the latest health and fitness information

  Find an exciting education-travel program

  Get a higher return on your investments

  Play hundreds of golf courses for free

  Find a sales outlet for your arts and crafts

- A consumers guide to products and services—in this book, you will find resources and information to help you purchase and protect the highest quality products and services. For example, you will be able to:

  Obtain the best banking services

  Locate the least expensive automobile insurance

  Find the best health care at the right price

  Save money on your federal, state and local taxes

  Quickly solve a warranty problem on your new car

- A manual for dealing with the problems and crises of life—this book includes detailed information on thousands of resources to help overcome obstacles and deal with difficult conditions. For example, you will be able to:

  Find financial and emotional support while caring for an ill parent, spouse, or other relative

  Adapt your home environment to meet your special needs

  Resolve a problem with Social Security or Medicare

  Locate special travel programs, if you're disabled

  Join a support group after the death of a spouse

- An almanac of opportunities to share your knowledge and experience with others—much of the joy of adult life comes from giving rather than taking. Using this book, you can:

  Find a rewarding volunteer opportunity

  Make the wisest use of your charitable dollars

  Pass on your vital family heritage to your children and grandchildren

  Obtain a part-time job that makes use of your experience

By exploring this book, you will find hundreds of ways to make better use of your time and money, to increase your involvement with others, and to derive more intense satisfaction out of life in the decades to come.

Your Personal Finances

The tremendous increase in the average life span has made the subject of personal finance and retirement planning of great importance to everyone. If you're just turning 50, you have, on the average, more than one third of your life ahead of you.

Financial security is one of the two most important factors—the other is good health—in making those years the happiest time of your life. By financial security, we don't mean being wealthy. Rather, financial security means assuring ourselves of sufficient income to cover housing, food, transportation, medical care, and the other necessities of life, with some money left over to help us enjoy the increasing number of leisure hours we'll have as we get older.

The good news is that studies have shown that financial security has become an attainable goal for the vast majority of older Americans. The most dramatic evidence is the decline in the number of people age 65 and older who have incomes below the official poverty level, as defined by the U.S. Census Bureau:

- In 1959, 33% of Americans age 65 and older lived in poverty
- In 1969, 25% of Americans age 65 and older lived in poverty
- In 1988, only 12.6% of Americans age 65 and older lived in poverty, a rate lower than the poverty rate of all Americans

Of course, not being officially poor doesn't mean that most retired Americans live as comfortably as they would like or are free from financial worries and problems. But having sufficient income and other resources, such as equity in a home, means that financial security is an attainable goal.

Attaining that goal requires financial planning. Many Americans avoid that subject completely because it sounds complicated; for the same reason, many others pay exorbitant fees and commissions for information, services, and financial products.

Many elements of financial planning, however, involve paying closer attention to the details of one's financial life. In this section of the book, we'll outline a plethora of information and resources that will help you accomplish three major financial objectives:

- Evaluate your current financial situation, examine your spending and saving habits, and plan for the future
- Protect the assets, income, and resources you presently have by maximizing your return on your investments and adequately preparing for problems and emergencies
- Drastically reduce what you pay for financial services, products, and information, such as banking services, insurance, and credit

Much of what we'll talk about in this section of the book is sometimes called "retirement planning." Retirement, however, is only one of a number of important transitions in life, all of which can be eased by a lifelong process of paying attention to your finances and projecting future financial needs. Financial planning pays rich rewards to all of us, regardless of how old we are.

CHAPTER 1

ORGANIZING YOUR FINANCES

No doubt you've already experienced some of the basic elements of money management and financial planning. But these activities become more important at age 50 and beyond. Even if you are in your peak earning years, there will come a time when your income will be reduced. And with every year comes an increased chance of illness or other unexpected problems.

The first step in gaining control of your finances is organizing your financial records to:

- Calculate your net worth
- Itemize your monthly income and expenses

DETERMINING YOUR NET WORTH

Your net worth is the result of subtracting what you owe from what you have. Your assets might include:

Cash
Bank balances
    Checking
    Savings
    Certificates of deposit
Savings bonds
Bonds
Life insurance cash value
Mutual funds

Other investments
Retirement plans
Private pension funds
Profit-sharing plans
Market value of home
Other real estate
Equity in a business
Cars
Household goods
Collections
Debts others owe you

Your liabilities might include:

Current bills

Mortgage debt

Credit card and installment debt

Taxes due

Debts owed others

Some of this information, such as the balances in your bank accounts, is readily available. Other information, such as the current value of your home, your business, or stamp collection, probably requires some investigation.

You can take a simple ledger sheet or a pad of paper and compute your net worth. However, we recommend the worksheets and information from the following sources:

Handbook: *Managing Your Personal Finances*
Contains: An extremely valuable and useful three-part series on personal finance and financial planning prepared by the Extension Service of the U.S. Department of Agriculture. The three parts are:
1. The Principles of Managing Your Finances ($3.25)
2. Financial Tools Used in Money Management ($1.50)
3. Coping with Change ($1.75)
These sections are hole-punched to fit a three-hole binder, so that the many worksheets included are removable for your calculations

From: Superintendent of Documents
Government Printing Office
Washington, DC 20402
Stock Number 001-000-04484-2
(202) 783-3238

Booklet: *Your Financial Plan*
Cost: $1.25
Contains: A very readable and informative introduction to financial planning. Contains worksheets
From: Money Management Institute
Household International
2700 Sanders Road
Prospect Heights, IL 60070

Book: *Looking Ahead to Your Financial Future*
Cost: $9.95 (check payable to "Prep Project")
Contains: A very useful 70-page guide to financial planning written for working women, but useful for any reader. Contains worksheets
From: Prep Project
Long Island University
Southhampton Campus
Southhampton, NY 11968

Book: *Finances After 50: Financial Planning for the Rest of Your Life*
Cost: $10.95
Contains: Readable 200-page guide to all aspects of financial planning, with easy to use worksheets, prepared under the auspices of the United Seniors Health Cooperative, a nonprofit consumer group
From: HarperCollins*Publishers*

CALCULATING YOUR MONTHLY INCOME AND EXPENSES

These excellent resources also provide worksheets for determining what you make and spend each month. Your income may include:

Wages and salaries

Interest

Dividends

Proceeds from sales of assets

Rents on property

Profits from business

Repayment of personal loans

Your expenses fall into one of two categories. *Fixed expenses* are those that you have to pay in specific amounts at specific times. Some, such as rent, mortgage payments, utility payments, and taxes, you either pay monthly or they are deducted from every paycheck. Others, such as insurance payments or car registration fees, are payable quarterly or annually. A list of common fixed expenses includes:

Rent

Mortgage payments

Maintenance fees

Taxes

Utilities

Garbage pickup and other home services

Installment payments on credit cards, car loans, etc.

Insurance payments

Transportation expenses

Membership dues

Contributions to churches and other charities

Tuition and other education expenses

Subscriptions

Savings and investment

Flexible expenses vary from week to week or month to month. These include:

Food eaten at home

Restaurant meals

Clothing

Laundry and dry cleaning

Purchase of furniture and appliances

Household maintenance and repair

Home improvements

Household supplies

Household help

Gifts

Vacations

Health expenses (not covered by insurance)

Personal care

Entertainment

Recreation

Miscellaneous, such as stamps, tobacco, etc.

An accurate assessment of how your income compares with your spending normally requires tracking your spending over a period of months. One publication that can help you do this is :

Handbook: *The Consumer's Almanac*
Cost: $1.00
Contains: Calendars of every month, with worksheets to record income, fixed expenses, and variable expenses. This valuable publication also lists the goods and services that normally go on sale every month, as well as providing a wealth of other financial and consumer tips
From: Central Order Desk
American Financial Services Association
1101 14th Street, NW
Washington, DC 20005
(202) 289-0400

If you have a personal computer, you can purchase software that will help you compute your net worth and your monthly cash flow. Most programs also balance your checkbook, track your savings and investments, update your net worth and cash flow, compare actual spending with your budget, help compute insurance needs and costs, and assist in tax preparation. Some of the best-known programs, available in almost all software stores, are:

Program: *Andrew Tobias's Managing Your Money*
Versions for: IBM and compatibles, Apple, and Macintosh

Program: *Dollars and Sense*
Versions for: IBM and compatibles, Apple, and Macintosh

Program: *Quicken*
Versions for: IBM and compatibles, Apple, and Macintosh

Program: *Sylvia Porter's Personal Financial Planner*
Versions for: IBM and compatibles, Apple, and Commodore

Program: *MoneyMate*
Versions for: IBM and compatibles,

Program: *MacMoney*
Versions for: Apple and Macintosh

BENEFITING FROM YOUR NET WORTH AND CASH FLOW STATEMENTS

These statements are the basis for both your short- and long-term financial planning. After you complete them, you should have a good idea of how effectively you've been managing your money. The next step is establishing some financial priorities. You'll need to:

- Establish a comfortable level of savings sufficient to meet foreseeable short-term emergencies
- Protect your retirement income and establish a solid retirement plan
- Use credit wisely
- Maintain comprehensive insurance coverage

- Trim your taxes and tax preparation expenses
- Develop a diversified investment program
- Plan your estate

Fortunately, both the financial industry and all levels of government realize how important this process is to every American age 50 and over. During the last two decades, financial information, services, products, programs, and protections directed partially or completely to this age group have dramatically increased in number and in quality. In the following pages, we will present these invaluable resources, all available to help you establish your priorities.

BEFORE MOVING ON . . . BUDGETS AND FILING SYSTEMS

Once you've assembled all of your important financial papers and information, you should

take the time to accomplish three tasks basic to managing your finances:

- Create and follow a budget
- Create a vital papers or estate file for your spouse and heirs
- Create a financial filing system

How to Create and Follow a Budget

You should have a written budget, even if you haven't established any firm long-term goals. A budget makes it easier to:

- Prevent impulse spending
- Decide what you can and can't afford
- Increase dollars for savings
- Make decisions about major purchases
- Protect against problems and prepare for emergencies

All of the resources we have discussed thus far help in creating a budget. Two additional resources that are especially useful in budgeting and setting financial goals are:

Booklet: *Budget Blueprint*
Cost: $1.00
Contains: Simple budgeting worksheets and information prepared by the Credit Union National Association
From: Your local credit union

Book: *Dollar Watch: The Personal Financial Organizer*
Cost: $19.95 plus $3.00 postage and handling
Contains: A much more complete financial planner that is very easy to use
From: Datamax
132 Nassau Street
New York, NY 10038
(212) 693-0933

How to Create a Vital Papers File for Your Spouse and Heirs

Well-meaning people create nightmares for their spouses and heirs because they've neglected to leave information as basic as the location of their wills and safe deposit boxes, information on prepaid funeral plans and plots, existence and policy numbers of insurance policies, and a wealth of other valuable information.

Creating an estate file is a vital task not only for yourself, but for your older parents, in-laws, or other relatives. This estate file should include:

- Names, addresses, and telephone numbers of accountants, tax preparers, lawyers, financial planners, stockbrokers, and other people important to an estate
- A list of all savings and investments, including bank accounts, stocks, bonds, mutual funds, investment real estate, along with account numbers and approximate value
- A list of all debt, with account numbers and the names and addresses of creditors
- A list of important papers, such as income tax returns, birth and marriage certificates, military discharge papers, automobile and home titles, etc., with the location of the papers
- Complete information about safe deposit boxes, with inventories of the contents of each box

A valuable workbook that will make this task easier is:

Workbook: *Your Vital Papers Logbook*
Cost: $6.95 (AARP member price $4.95) plus $1.75 postage

From: AARP Books/Scott, Foresman and Co.
1865 Miner Street
Des Plaines, IL 60016

How to Set Up a Financial Records Filing System

You should set up a filing system to keep your financial records organized, and we recommend you create the following file folders:

- *Banking:* Monthly statements, canceled checks, deposit slips, and a list of all accounts
- *Credit:* All credit agreements, charge slips, and monthly statements
- *Employment and business expenses:* Pay stubs, information on employee benefits, copies of expense reports, and any other business-related records
- *Contributions:* Receipts, correspondence, logbook of expenses you incur as a volunteer, and all other records relating to charitable contributions
- *Pension plans and IRAs:* All documents related to your retirement accounts
- *Insurance:* Copies of policies, invoices, claims, and a copy of home inventory
- *Investments:* All records related to stocks, bonds, mutual funds, and other investments
- *Medical and dental:* List of doctors and other medical professionals you've seen, a copy of medical records, bills, inoculation records, and health insurance claims
- *Residence:* Copies of lease, rent checks, copies of mortgage papers, mortgage statements, home maintenance receipts, home improvement records, utility records, and any other records connected with your home
- *Investment real estate:* Records connected with any other real estate you own
- *Receipts and warranties:* Receipts and warranties that don't fit into other categories
- *Taxes:* Copies of all returns and other related information
- *Personal:* Photocopies of important papers, list of safe deposit boxes, inventory of collections, membership cards in organizations, and any other personal papers
- *Estate file:* See description above

Organizing your records and keeping them up to date will save you a great deal of time and money, especially at tax time. Studies have shown that you can cut the costs of having your tax return prepared by 20% to 40% by having your tax records in better shape before you meet with your preparer.

FINANCIAL PLANNING: YOUR RETIREMENT INCOME

RETIREMENT PLANNING IS A FAR-reaching and important activity that involves every area of life, from housing to health to life-style preferences. Financial planning is a part of that process, perhaps the most important part. The amount of retirement income you have affects every other area of planning, including your housing, leisure-time activities, opportunities to visit your family, and your ability to secure the best health care and handle health emergencies.

It's never too early to begin planning for retirement, and it's never too late to begin formulating a retirement financial plan—even if you've already begun to draw a pension or Social Security. A healthy 65-year-old man has a life expectancy of almost 20 years, and a healthy 65-year-old woman has a life expectancy of almost 25 years. Realigning investments, making the most of assets, and even working to add to investment income can significantly improve the quality of your life.

ESTIMATING YOUR RETIREMENT INCOME AND EXPENSES

By organizing your financial records, calculating your net worth, and establishing a budget, you've already accomplished the important first steps in retirement financial planning. In addition, it is also important to realistically estimate your retirement income and expenses.

If you're close to retirement and have already made decisions about where you will live, what your housing expenses will be, and what kind of health care and insurance coverage you'll have, you can probably prepare a budget. If you haven't made these decisions, most experts agree that you can use a figure of 70% to 80% of your current expenses. You should use the higher percentage if your current income and expenses are low to moderate and the lower percentage if your current income is moderate to high.

To estimate your retirement income, you should calculate your:

- Annual Social Security benefits
- Annual pension benefits
- Annual income from current investments, including IRAs, Keogh plans, cash values of life insurance policies, annuities, and other funds earmarked for retirement

Subtracting the total of these three sources of income from your estimated annual expenses will give you an approximate idea of where you are financially. If your estimated expenses exceed your estimated income, you may have to:

- Increase your contributions to retirement plans and other investments
- Increase your return from investments
- Plan for a second career or part-time employment after retirement

Even if your estimated income meets or exceeds your estimated expenses, your job isn't over. At the very least, you should plan and follow an investment program that protects against inflation and builds a cushion to improve your life-style and for further protection against emergencies.

A number of excellent publications contain worksheets and charts that help calculate retirement income and expenses:

Workbook: *Think of Your Future: Preretirement Planning Workbook*
Cost: $24.95 (AARP member price $18.25) plus $1.75 postage
Contains: 303 pages in a three-ring binder. Prepared by AARP, and includes many worksheets and detailed information on setting and meeting financial goals, plus a list of resources. Very comprehensive
From: AARP Books/Scott, Foresman and Co.

1865 Miner Street
Des Plaines, IL 60016

Booklet: *Planning Your Retirement* (D12322)
Cost: Free
Contains: A 20-page overview of retirement planning, including financial planning
From: AARP Fulfillment
1909 K Street, NW
Washington, DC 20049

Resource: Ernst & Young/Kiplinger Guide to Retirement Security
Cost: $29.95
Contains: A package that includes a video and a guidebook with detailed worksheets for retirement planning
From: Changing Times
(800) 544-0155

Software: Retirement Solutions
Contains: A comprehensive computer program that guides users through a retirement plan based on a wide scope of objectives and contingencies

Workbook: *Looking Ahead to Your Financial Future*
Cost: $9.95
Contains: An excellent overview of financial planning, with easy to use retirement planning worksheets
From: PREP Project
Long Island University
Southhampton Campus
Southhampton, NY 11968

Book: *The Complete Retirement Planning Book* by Peter A. Dickinson
Cost: $10.95
Contains: A broad-based guide to retirement planning. The section on projecting retirement expenses and income includes particularly useful information on calculating the effects of inflation
From: E.P. Dutton

Workbook: Retirement Planning Workbook
Cost: Free
From: Oppenheimer Funds
  (800) 638-5660

Workbook: Retirement Planning Workbook
Cost: Free
From: T. Rowe Price
  (800) 638-5660

According to the U.S. Census Bureau, 87% of the income of Americans age 65 and over comes from:

- Social Security
- Employee pension plans
- Principle, interest, and dividends from investments

Of these three sources, it is income from investments that determines how comfortable a life-style people will enjoy in their retirement years. Although Social Security benefits repre-sents 44% of the total income of all people age 65 and over, these benefits make up only 22% of the total income of people age 65 and over with annual incomes of $20,000 or more. Investment income makes up 34% of the total income of those earning $20,000 or more.

Congress has recognized the importance of investment income in the retirement years and has in the last two decades passed legislation providing significant tax breaks to Americans who want to save money for their retirement over and above their Social Security taxes and pension contributions from their employers.

The establishment of investment opportunities, such as IRAs, Keogh plans, 401(K) salary reduction plans, and others, means that in order to prepare for a successful retirement you need to understand and protect your:

- Social Security benefits
- Employee pension benefits
- Other available retirement investment programs

YOUR SOCIAL SECURITY BENEFITS

Over 38 million Americans currently receive monthly Social Security checks. The most important points to keep in mind about Social Security are that your benefits come from the money you paid (or that your spouse paid) through your working years, and that you have the right to receive the maximum benefits to which you're entitled.

To obtain the maximum benefits to which you're entitled, you need to understand the benefit programs. The Social Security Administration has produced an extensive series of publications that help explain these basic benefits. Among them are:

Pamphlets:
- *An Introduction to Social Security*
- *Social Security . . . How It Works for You*
- *A Woman's Guide to Social Security*
- *What to Expect When You Visit a Social Security Office*
- *Retirement*
- *Disability*
- *Survivors*
- *How Your Social Security Check Is Affected by a Pension*
- *Thinking About Retiring*
- *If You Work After Your Retire*

• *Social Security Income for the Aged, Blind, and Disabled*

Cost: Free

From: Your local Social Security office (see telephone book)

or

Office of Public Inquiry
Social Security Administration
Department of Health and Human Services
6401 Security Blvd.
Baltimore, MD 21235
(800) 234-5772

Among the questions answered in these publications are:

1. *How do you qualify for Social Security benefits?*

Social Security benefits are paid from a government trust fund accumulated from contributions of working Americans and their employers. A percentage of wages, up to a specified maximum ($51,300 in 1990, for example) are deducted from each paycheck and then matched by the employer. Self-employed people pay into the system a percentage of their income, up to the same maximum level.

To qualify for benefits, you must have worked for a specified period of time in employment covered by Social Security. Social Security measures that eligibility in work credits, as measured by a specified minimum wage. In 1990, workers received one credit for:

• Each $520 earned, up to a total of four credits for the year

So, if you earned $2,080 or more in 1990, you received the maximum four credits for the year.

To obtain retirement benefits for you and your dependents, you have to accumulate 40 credits by working at least 10 years. Once you obtain 40 credits, you are fully insured for the rest of your life, even if you haven't worked for years before you begin to collect benefits.

To obtain disability benefits or insure eligibility for survivor benefits for your dependents, you must have acquired a minimum number of credits based on your age. Most workers must have earned at least 1 credit for every year since their 21st birthday.

2. *How are your benefits determined?*

Although work credits determine your eligibility, the actual amount that you (and those eligible to collect on your earnings) receive for any Social Security program is determined by your income during your working life. Maximum benefits are earned by those whose average income met or exceeded the annual maximum income subject to Social Security tax, while minimal benefits are paid to those who earned just enough to gain work credits. For example, for workers who retired at age 65 in 1989 and had steady incomes over the years, their retirement benefits would be:

• A worker who earned $10,000 in 1988 would have received a monthly benefit of $465 in 1989.

• A worker who earned $48,000 or more in 1988 would have a monthly benefit of $965.

3. *When can you collect your retirement benefits?*

For Americans who turn 62 before the year 2000, they can collect:

• Reduced benefits beginning at age 62

• Full benefits at age 65

• Increased benefits for each year worked between ages 65 and 69

Beginning in the year 2000, the minimum age for obtaining full benefits will gradually rise from 65 to 67. Eligible recipients can still begin to collect at age 62, but the benefits will be further reduced. Increased benefits will be paid for work credits earned for 5 years after the age for full benefits.

4. *How can your dependents collect on your retirement income?*

When you retire, your dependents can collect:

- Spouse: 50% of your benefit at age 65 or if caring for a child under 16 or disabled, or a reduced benefit at age 62
- Children: 50% if under age 18 or if older and disabled
- Divorced spouse: 50% of your benefit at age 65 or reduced benefit at age 62
- Grandchildren: 50% of your benefit if under 18, living in your home, and you provide over half of their support

If you die, your dependents can collect:

- Spouse: 100% of your benefit at age 65, reduced benefit at age 60, 75% of benefit if caring for a disabled child regardless of the spouse's age
- Children: 75% of benefit if under 18 or disabled
- Divorced spouse: Same as spouse
- Parents: Can receive benefits if over 62 and dependent upon you for over half their support

5. *What happens if you work while collecting Social Security?*

In 1990, people aged 65 to 69 could earn $9,360 from salary or self-employment without

a reduction in their Social Security benefits. Above $9,360 they lost $1 in benefits for each $3 of income. People age 70 and over can earn any amount without benefit reductions.

6. *Are Social Security benefits taxable?*

Up to 50% of your benefits may be taxed on your federal income tax return if your income exceeds a certain amount. In 1990, your benefits would begin to be taxed if your adjusted gross income exceeded $25,000 if you were single or $32,000 if you were married and filed jointly.

For more information:

> **Pamphlet:** • *Are My Social Security Benefits Taxable?* (D13539)
> **Cost:** Free
> **From:** AARP Fulfillment
> 1909 K Street, NW
> Washington, DC 20049

How to Check Your Social Security Benefits and Obtain a Benefits Estimate

The majority of Americans seldom or never check to see if their earnings and work credits have been properly recorded by the Social Security Administration, even though mistakes or omissions could cost them tens of thousands of dollars. As of 1988, the Social Security Administration was holding $82 billion in earnings that it hadn't been able to assign to individuals because of incomplete or inaccurate information. In most cases, the problem occurred when a person's name, Social Security number, or withholdings was incorrect on a W-2 form.

In 1988, the Social Security Administration developed a new form and procedure to allow everyone to not only check their earnings, but obtain an estimate of the benefits they will receive upon retirement or disability. Everyone with employment earnings covered by Social Security should obtain an earnings and benefit estimate statement at least every 3 years.

To obtain a statement:

> **Submit:** Form SSA-7004, *Request for Earnings and Benefit Estimate Statement*
> **Cost:** Free
> **From:** Call: (800) 234-5772
> Call or visit your local Social Security office
> **Write:** Office of Public Inquiry
> Social Security Administration
> Department of Health and Human Services
> 6401 Security Blvd.
> Baltimore, MD 21235
> **Write:** Consumer Information Center
> P.O. Box 100
> Pueblo, CO 81009

About 4 to 6 weeks later, you'll receive a statement that includes:

- The number of credits you've earned
- The number of credits, if any, you still need to earn to be eligible for disability, survivor, and retirement benefits
- A year by year listing of your earnings subject to Social Security tax
- A year by year listing of your Social Security tax payments
- Estimates of disability and survivor benefits for you and your family
- Estimates of your monthly retirement benefits at ages 62, 65, and 70

You should be aware that the statements may not reflect your credits and earnings for the previous 2 years—it takes the system a while to process the massive information submitted with tax returns each year. However, the records should be accurate for previous years. Check the listing of your tax payments and credits against your record of:

- Social Security withholding listed on all of the W-2 forms you received from your employer(s). Your employer was required to match the sum withheld from your salary, so the yearly Social Security tax payment listed on the statement should be double the amount withheld
- Social Security taxes you paid on self-employment income

You are responsible for insuring that your Social Security credits and payments are accurate. If you find any problems, contact your Social Security office immediately.

How to Apply for Social Security Benefits

It is your responsibility to apply for the Social Security benefits to which you are eligible. The Social Security Administration recommends that you apply 2 to 3 months before your retirement date. You should submit claims for survivor or disability benefits as soon as possible.

Applications can be made at your local Social Security office or over the telephone. If you're physically unable to get to a Social Security office, a representative will visit you. To apply for benefits, you will need:

- Your birth certificate
- Your Social Security number
- A W-2 form or income tax form from the previous year
- If applicable, proof of marriage, divorce, or disability

Don't delay applying if you lack one or more of these records. Your local Social Security office can suggest other acceptable records or help you locate the missing information.

When you apply for benefits, you may elect to receive your benefits in one of three ways:

- By mail to your home
- By mail to a relative or other representative
- Direct deposit into a bank account

How to Defend Your Rights to Full Benefits

If you are turned down for benefits or if you disagree with the amount of benefits you receive, you have the right to question those decisions. The procedure for appealing a decision or correcting a problem is:

- Within 60 days of receiving notice of a decision, you may ask for a reconsideration. Your local Social Security office will provide the proper form and tell you what written evidence you need. You submit the form and evidence to your local office, and they will notify you of the decision in writing.
- If you are still not satisfied, you may ask for a hearing before an administrative law judge. The hearing will be held in your area. Although you do not have to appear at the hearing, you may:
  – Appear in person
  – Have an attorney represent you
  – Bring witnesses to testify in your behalf
  After the hearing, you will be notified in writing of the decision.
- If you are still not satisfied, you may ask for a review by the Appeals Council in

Washington, DC. You may appear in person, or you can waive that right if the travel expense is too great. If the Appeals Council grants your request for a review, you will be notified of its decision in 6 months or more.

- If you still believe your case was not handled fairly, you may appeal the decision to the federal courts within 60 days of notification by the Appeals Council.

For more information about your right to question decisions:

Pamphlet: • *Your Right to Question Decisions Made on Your Social Security Claim*
From: Your local Social Security office
or
Office of Public Inquiry
Social Security Administration
Department of Health and Human Services
6401 Security Blvd.
Baltimore, MD 21235
(800) 234-5772

If you are retired, disabled, or have low income, you may be eligible for free legal assistance in appealing Social Security decisions. Contact your local area agency on aging (see pages 383–426).

If you are unable to obtain competent legal assistance on your own, you should look for a lawyer who specializes in solving Social Security problems by contacting:

Organization: National Organization of Social Security Claimants' Representatives
Cost: Free referral and brochure
Service: Provides referral to member attorneys who specialize in Social Security problems
For information: (800) 431-2804 (Ex. NY)
(914) 735-8812

Supplemental Social Security (SSI)

Supplemental Social Security (SSI) pays monthly income to people who are aged, blind, or disabled and who have little income and few assets. Although SSI is administered through Social Security offices, benefits are paid from the general revenues of the federal government, not from contributions to the Social Security system. Many recipients have insufficient credits to collect regular Social Security benefits or held jobs not covered by Social Security.

A recent federal study showed that less than half of all older Americans eligible for SSI payments apply for these benefits. For information, contact your local Social Security office for an application. The local office will provide assistance in completing the application and ob-taining the documentation. In many states, recipients approved for federal SSI benefits also receive additional benefits from the state. Most SSI recipients are also eligible for food stamps, and applications for food stamps are filled out in Social Security offices.

For more information about SSI:

Pamphlet: • *SSI*
Cost: Free
From: Your local Social Security office
or
Office of Public Inquiry
Social Security Administration
Department of Health and Human Services
6401 Security Blvd.
Baltimore, MD 21235
(800) 234-5772

YOUR COMPANY PENSION

About four of every five employed workers are covered by pension plans, and almost all of these people consider pension payments vital to their financial security after retirement. However, surveys have shown that pension plans are among the least understood of all employee benefits. To understand your pension plan, the following information is available:

Booklets: • *What You Should Know About the Pension Law*
• *Often-Asked Questions About Employee Retirement Benefits*
Cost: Free
From: Office of Public Affairs
Pension and Welfare Benefits Administration
U.S. Department of Labor
200 Constitution Avenue, NW
Washington, DC 20210

Booklet: • *Your Pension: Things You Should Know About Your Pension Plan*
Cost: Free
From: Pension Benefit Guaranty Corporation
2020 K Street, NW
Washington, DC 20006

Booklets: • Protecting Your Pension Money ($6.00)
• *Directory of Pension Assistance Resources* ($3.00)
From: Pension Rights Center
Pension Publications
918 16th St., NW, Suite 704
Washington, DC 20006

Booklet: A Guide to Understanding Your Pension Plan (D13533)
Cost: Free

From: AARP
1909 K. St., NW
Washington, DC 20049

Among the most important questions you might have about your pension are:

1. *When do I become eligible for my pension plan?*

Federal law requires that all employees age 21 and over must become participants in the plan after 2 years of employment. Workers may not be excluded from a plan or dropped from a plan because of age.

2. *How do I obtain the details of my pension plan?*

Every pension plan must be supervised by a Plan Administrator. Within 90 days after becoming a participant in the plan, you should receive from the Plan Administrator:

- Summary Plan Description, a booklet or similar document that is easy to understand and explains:
  - How the plan operates
  - When you're eligible to receive a pension
  - How to calculate your benefits
  - How to file a claim

The Plan administrator is also obligated to provide:

- Summary Annual Report, information on the financial activities of the pension plan during the year
- Survivor Coverage Data, which informs you of the plan's survivor coverage and how it affects you and your spouse

Finally, you, as an employee, have the right to request once each year an Individual Benefit Statement, which specifies the amount of benefits you've earned under the plan and whether you have a permanent right to them.

If you don't receive any of these documents, you should request them in writing or contact:

Agency: Division of Technical Assistance and Inquiries
Pension and Welfare Benefits Administration
U.S. Department of Labor
200 Constitution Avenue, NW
Washington, DC 20210
(202) 523-8776

3. *What types of pension plans are there?*

There are two basic types of pension plans, defined benefit and defined contribution. The Summary Plan Description will tell you what type you have. About 70% of all workers are covered by *defined benefit plans,* which promise a specified monthly benefit upon retirement computed on a formula based on years of service and annual income. The advantages of these plans are:

- They are financed from employer contributions
- The amount of the benefits is clearly stated
- Most are federally guaranteed to a maximum limit of $1,909 per month, and do not cover any promised severance pay, profit-sharing, or other lump-sum payments.

For additional information:

Booklet: *Your Guaranteed Pension*
Cost: Free
From: Insurance Operations Department
Coverage & Inquiries Branch

Pension Benefit Guarantee Corporation
2020 K Street, NW
Washington, DC 20006
(202) 778-8800

The disadvantages are:

- Benefits are very modest, normally averaging 1.5% of your annual salary for each year of service. That means a worker earning $20,000 after 10 years would receive $250 per month.
- An increasing number of companies are taking the excess investment income generated by these pension funds instead of using it to increase benefits.

Defined contribution plans do not guarantee a fixed monthly benefit. Under these plans, the employer is only obligated to make a specified contribution to an individual employee's pension account. For example, the contributions of many employers are determined by profit sharing or another formula based on company performance. In many cases, employees may also make an additional tax-deductible contribution to the account from their wages or salaries. The monthly benefit paid at retirement depends upon the return obtained from investing the money in the retirement account.

These plans are becoming increasingly popular because they free employers from the legal obligation to pay fixed benefits. The advantages of defined contribution plans are:

- Total annual contributions can be as high as 25% of one's salary, to a maximum of $30,000
- Contributions out of your salary are tax deductible up to $7,000 per year
- Employees benefit from all investment income, which means benefits can be much larger than fixed benefits from a defined benefit plan
- In some cases, employees can choose how their pension funds are invested
- At retirement, the amount in the pension fund can be taken as a lump sum, as well as converted to an annuity

The disadvantages are:

- These funds are not guaranteed
- An employee can suffer from poor returns on investment of contributions
- Profit-sharing contributions may drop or stop if the company has financial problems
- Employer contributions may be reduced or eliminated
- An employee can withdraw or borrow against pension contributions only in the case of a serious emergency

4. *What are vested pension rights?*

When your rights to a pension become permanent, or "vested," you will receive the defined benefit you have earned even if you leave your job. Beginning in 1989, federal law generally stipulates that an employee becomes fully vested after 5 years.

5. *What are your spouse's rights to pension benefits after you die?*

Under federal law, all plans must offer a married employee the right to elect a benefit schedule that provides for continued payments to a spouse after death, or provides that benefits will be paid if a vested employee dies before retirement age. In most cases, these rights extend to the divorced spouse, if reflected in the divorce agreement.

It is extremely important for married employees and their spouses to fully understand these rights.

Booklet: • *Protect Yourself: A Woman's Guide to Pension Rights* (D12258)
Cost: Free
From: AARP
1909 K Street, NW
Washington, DC 20049

Booklet: • *Facts About the Joint and Survivor Benefits of the Retirement Equity Act*
Cost: Free
From: Office of Public Affairs
Pension and Welfare Benefits Administration

U.S. Department of Labor
200 Constitution Avenue, NW
Washington, DC 20210

Handbook: *Your Pension Rights at Divorce: What Women Need to Know*
Contains: A comprehensive guide to a divorced spouse's rights to Social Security, private pensions, military and federal pensions, and other retirement programs. Includes questions to ask a lawyer.
Cost: Call Pension Rights Center
From: Pension Rights Center
Pension Publications
918 16th St., NW, Suite 704
Washington, DC 20006
(202) 296-3776

RETIREMENT INVESTMENT PROGRAMS

A defined contribution program set up by your employer to which you can add extra dollars is one important retirement investment program. Among other options are Individual Retirement Accounts (IRAs), Keogh plans, and SEP-IRA plans.

Individual Retirement Accounts

IRAs were designed to encourage people to save for retirement. The Internal Revenue Service (IRS) has authorized savings institutions, brokerage firms, mutual fund companies, and insurance companies to act as trustees or custodians for IRA accounts. Individuals can contact any of these to open an IRA account, then invest funds according to the plan they select.

The advantages of an IRA are:

• IRA accounts are easy to open and require no advance IRS approval

• For people whose contributions are deductible, they are the best tax shelter

• IRA funds can be invested in a wide variety of investments

The disadvantages of an IRA are:

• Withdrawals before age 59.5 are subject to a 10% penalty, as well as tax

• For people whose IRA contributions aren't tax deductible, employee contribution plans may offer more tax advantages

Any individual with earned income and spouses of individuals with earned income may open an IRA. Contributions to an IRA, up to the legal limit are fully tax deductible if:

• The individual is self-employed or employed by a firm that doesn't have a pension plan

- In 1988, if an individual employed by a firm with a pension plan has an adjusted gross income under $25,000 or a married couple has an adjusted gross income under $40,000

Contributions may be partially tax deductible if:

- An individual employed by a firm with a pension plan has an adjusted gross income between $25,000 and $35,000 or a married couple has an adjusted gross income of between $40,000 and $50,000

Contributions are not tax deductible if:

- An individual employed by a firm with a pension plan has an adjusted gross income over $35,000 or married couple has an adjusted gross income over $50,000

In all cases, however, all interest, dividends, and capital gains earned by funds invested in IRAs are exempt from taxation until the funds are withdrawn.

The contribution limits for any 1 year are:

- $2,000 for an individual with at least $2,000 in earnings
- $2,250 for an individual with at least $2,000 in earnings and a nonworking spouse
- $4,000 for a married couple, each of which had at least $2,000 in earnings

In the case of a married couple with one nonworker, the IRA contributions up to $2,250 may be distributed between the accounts of husband and wife in any manner, as long as no contribution exceeds $2,000.

The only exception to the $2,000 limit are lump-sum payments from corporate pension or profit-sharing plans that are "rolled over" into an IRA.

IRAs are discussed in detail in every general financial planning, investment, and retirement planning resource listed in this book. Every savings institution, brokerage firm, mutual fund, and insurance company has information about IRA accounts. Among the best information sources are:

Booklet: *IRA Owners Guide*
Cost: Free
From: Fidelity Investments
82 Devonshire Street
Boston, MA 02109
(800) 544-6666
(617) 523-1919
IRS Publication: No. 590: *Individual Retirement Arrangements*
Cost: Free
From: Any IRS office
or
Call (800) 424-3676

Keogh Plans and Simplified Employee Pension Plans (SEPs)

These are pension plans designed for self-employed people and employees of small companies. The advantage of establishing these plans is the ability to contribute substantial sums in addition to personal IRA contributions. Contributions to Keogh plans can be a maximum of 25% of income up to $30,000 per year, and contributions to SEP plans can be up to 15% of earned income to a maximum of $30,000 per year.

Both plans require that the employer make contributions for all employees. Of the two plans:

- Keoghs may allow larger contributions for self-employed individuals, sole proprietors, and employers age 50 and over who want to build the largest possible fund. However, Keogh plans require significant IRS paperwork.

- SEP plans are much easier to establish and operate for small businesses with employees, but generally permit smaller contributions for sole proprietors.

You should consult an accountant or attorney before making the decision about establishing a Keogh or SEP account.

Booklet: *The Pension Plan (Almost) Nobody Knows About*
Cost: $3.50
From: The Pension Rights Center
918 16th Street, NW, Suite 704
Washington, DC 20006
IRS Publications: • No. 590: *Individual Retirement Arrangements*
• *No. 535: Business Expenses*
• *No. 560: Self-Employed Retirement Plans*
Cost: Free
From: Any IRS office
or
Call (800) 424-3676

CHAPTER 3

BANKING SERVICES

OVER THE LAST DECADE, THE DEREGU-
lation of the banking industry has produced a
proliferation of financial services and products,
many of which are especially valuable and convenient to Americans age 50 and over. For example, you can now earn interest on the Social
Security check from the moment it's deposited
in your checking account or get cash from an
airport in the middle of the night in an emergency.

Unfortunately, the deregulation that
spawned these new services has also produced
a wide range of fees and charges, widely varying criteria for access to the products and services, and a significant increase in computer
errors and fraud. Even those of you who have
been using banking services for decades should
reeducate yourselves about shopping for financial services. If you don't, you could find
that continuing to use your bank on the corner
is costing you hundreds of dollars a year more
than it should.

SHOPPING FOR BANKING SERVICES

Deregulation of the financial industries has
blurred the distinctions between commercial
banks, savings and loan associations (S&Ls),
and credit unions to the point where you
should, in the words of financial columnist
Sylvia Porter, "view banks, S&Ls, and credit
unions as little more than financial supermarkets. If products or services in one become
shoddy, don't hesitate to look elsewhere."

Among the banking services offered by these
financial supermarkets are:

- Deposit services: Money can be depos-
  ited in your accounts
  - At walk-in or drive-up teller windows
  - Through 24-hour automatic teller ma-
    chines
  - Through bank-by-mail

- Through direct deposit of Social Security checks, paychecks, or other regular income
- Wire transfer from other institutions
- Payment services
  - Regular checking accounts
  - Interest-bearing checking accounts
  - Automatic bill-paying services
  - Certified checks
  - Cashiers checks
  - Travelers checks
  - Money orders
  - Debit cards
- Savings vehicles
  - Regular or passbook savings
  - Money market accounts
  - Certificates of deposit
  - U.S. Savings bonds
  - U.S. Treasury bonds
  - IRA and Keogh accounts
- Credit services
  - Overdraft checking
  - Unsecured loans
  - Secured loans
  - Automobile loans
  - Mortgage loans
  - Home equity loans
  - Bank credit cards
  - Education loans

- Trust services
  - Management of trusts
  - Management of estates

The common banking services that we'll discuss in this chapter are:

- Deposit services
- Payment services
- Safe deposit boxes and security vaults

For more information about selecting a financial institution:

> **Book:** *The Bank Book* by Edward Mrkvicka Jr.
> **Cost:** $8.95
> **Contains:** Guidelines for shopping for checking accounts and other banking services
> **From:** HarperCollins*Publishers*

> **Booklet:** *Financial Institutions: Important Consumer Information*
> **Cost:** $0.50
> **From:** Consumer Information Center
> P.O. Box 100
> Pueblo, CO 81009

WHAT TO LOOK FOR IN DEPOSIT AND PAYMENT SERVICES

In deposit services, you will want:

- Convenient locations
- Convenient hours, such as Saturday hours if you work
- No transaction fees for deposits and withdrawals made at automatic teller machines

- No fees for banking by mail
- No fees for direct depositing of Social Security and other checks

The most important payment service is a checking account. Most institutions offer three types of checking accounts:

- Regular checking account. You earn no interest on the balance and can write an unlimited number of checks per month. You may be charged a minimum monthly fee and/or a per check charge.
- NOW, or interest-bearing checking account. The main feature of NOW (for Negotiated Order of Withdrawal) accounts is that you earn interest on your account balance and avoid fees *if you maintain a specified minimum balance in your account.*
- Super NOW accounts. These pay higher interest than regular NOW accounts, but require a higher minimum balance.

The following questions should be asked when shopping for these services:

1. *Are there special programs for senior citizens?*

A 1988 survey revealed that 70% of commercial banks and 80% of S&Ls offered no-fee checking to older Americans. The minimum age for this special service ranged from 50 to 65, with 55 or 60 being the most common. Many institutions combine free checking with a package of other benefits that can include:

- Free travelers checks
- Special rates on certificates of deposit
- Low or no-fee MasterCard or Visa
- Overdraft checking privileges
- Special rates on loans
- Discounts on safe deposit box rentals

2. *Is there unlimited free checking, preferably with no minimum balance?*

When comparing banks with minimum-required balances, favor those that base any charge on your average balance over the entire month, rather than a bank that charges fees if your balance dips below the minimum for a day.

3. *Is interest paid on the entire checking account balance, not just the balance over the required minimum?*

4. *What are the fees for overdrafts, returned checks, stop payment orders, certified checks, and other special services?*

These fees can vary dramatically between institutions.

5. *How quickly are deposited funds made available?*

This point is extremely important to those on fixed incomes. All consumers now benefit from the federal Expedited Funds Availability Act, which mandates the following availability schedule for all deposits in checking, share draft, or NOW accounts:

- Available the next business day after the day of deposit for:
  - Cash
  - The first $100 of any deposit of checks
  - Government, cashier's, certified, or teller's checks
  - Checks written on another account at the same institution
  - Direct deposit of Social Security benefits
  - Other direct deposits and electronic credits

Available the third business day after the day of deposit for:

- The remainder, over $100, of checks written on local institutions

Available the seventh business day after day of deposit for:

- The remainder, over $100, of checks written on nonlocal institutions
- Deposits made at automated teller machines not belonging to your institution

The law allows the following exceptions:

- During the first 30 days of new accounts
- Redeposit of a check that had been returned unpaid
- Deposits of more than $5,000 in 1 day
- A pattern of overdrawing an account over a period of 6 months
- A strong reason to believe the deposited check will not be paid

HOW SAFE ARE YOUR DEPOSITS?

The recent crisis in the savings and loan industry evoked among many Americans the chilling fear that their hard earned savings could disappear. Fortunately, for most people these fears are groundless. Since confidence in our banking system is vital to the growth and stability of our economy, the federal government has developed an extensive deposit insurance system that provides quick reimbursement to depositors should an insured institution fail. Anyone who deposits money should understand the federal insurance system.

Deposit Insurance

Most banks, mutual savings banks, S&Ls, and some U.S. branches of foreign banks are members of the Federal Deposit Insurance Corporation (FDIC). The FDIC insures deposits through two separate funds: the Bank Insurance Fund (BIF) for banks and mutual savings banks and the Savings Association Fund (SAIF) for S&Ls. Both funds insure:

- All checking accounts, savings accounts, certificates of deposits, cashier's checks, bank checks, and travelers checks drawn on that bank up to a limit

of $100,000 for all accounts held by an individual in a bank. The $100,000 limit includes accounts in branches of an individual bank.

- An additional $100,000 limit for interests any individual has in one or more joint accounts, such as accounts held with a spouse, a child, or a business partnership.
- An additional $100,000 for funds held in IRA and Keogh accounts.

Experts caution every depositor to pay close attention to the details of the FDIC insurance plans. For example, everyone should understand that the $100,000 limit applies to the total of all accounts in all branches of a financial institution, not just one branch.

If you have significant sums on deposit, you should sit down with a representative of your bank regularly to make sure all of your deposits are insured. You can also obtain details about the FDIC coverage from:

Booklets:
- *Your Insured Deposit*
- *When a Bank Fails*
- *FDIC: Symbol of Confidence*
- *Annual Report of the FDIC*

Cost: Free
From: Corporate Communications Office
FDIC
550 17th Street, NW
Washington, DC 20429

Deposits in approximately 88% of credit unions are federally insured by the National Credit Union Share Insurance Fund (NCUSIF). The NCUSIF coverage limits are generally the same as those of the FDIC insurance funds. For detailed information, contact your credit union or:

Booklet: *Your Insured Funds*
Cost: Free
From: National Credit Union Administration
1776 G Street, NW
Washington, DC 20456
(202) 682-9600

A small number of S&Ls and credit unions are insured by state insurance funds, private funds, or have no insurance at all. While deposits (within the legal limits) in federally insured financial institutions are virtually risk-free, because they are backed by the U.S. government, this may not be the case with state insurance funds, private insurance funds, or self-insured institutions.

How to Determine the Financial Soundness of a Banking Service

The existence of the federal insurance system doesn't mean that you can ignore the financial soundness of an institution, particularly if you are establishing a significant banking arrangement. Financial failure of an institution can delay access to your funds for a short period of time. It can also mean loss of interest on savings accounts, changes in loan terms and payment schedules, and increases on fees, charges, and penalties.

The best way to check on the financial soundness of an institution is by obtaining a professional evaluation from one of the following sources:

Company: Veribanc
P.O. Box 2963
Woburn, MA 01888
(800) 442-2657 (EX MA)
(617) 243-0370
Service: Telephone rating service that ranks a bank or savings and loan on a three star scale (3, highest; 0, in serious trouble).
Cost: $10.00 for one institution, $2.00 for each additional institution (must be billed to credit card).

Report: *Call Report*
Cost: $2.40 (Do not send money—you will be billed)
Contains: Review of the financial condition of a bank (main banks only, not branches), emphasizing the strength of the bank's loans
From: FDIC
MISB Disclosure Group
Room F-518
550 17th Street, NW
Washington, DC 20429
(800) 424-5488
(202) 393-8400

Report: *Uniform Bank Performance Report*
Cost: $30.00
Service: A comprehensive financial report comparing banks within a certain state or county
From: Federal Financial Institutions Examination Council
U.B.P.R.
1776 6th Street, NW
Washington, DC 20006

USING A SAFE DEPOSIT BOX OR SECURITY VAULT

A safe deposit box is a valuable place to store important papers, jewelry, other valuables, and documents, such as an inventory of household goods. You should keep an inventory of the contents of your safe deposit box, its location, the location of the keys, and the list of names of people with access to your box in your estate file.

Sometimes, however, people fail to leave such information. To find out if a deceased family member had a safety deposit box:

> **Organization:** American Safe Deposit Association
> (317) 888-1118
> **Cost:** $75.00

> **Service:** Will attempt to locate safe deposit boxes in its member institutions

Safe deposit boxes are convenient. However, they may not be large enough if you have works of art, an extensive coin collection, or other bulky valuables. For larger storage, you should consider a security vault in a facility run by a private company. For more information:

> **Organization:** National Association of Private Security Vaults
> 3562 North Ocean Boulevard
> Fort Lauderdale, FL 33308
> (305) 565-7466
> **Cost:** Free
> **Service:** Information and referral to private vault companies

HOW TO FIND FORGOTTEN BANK ACCOUNTS AND OTHER UNCLAIMED FUNDS

As of early 1989, state governments in this country held more than $3 billion dollars never claimed by their rightful owners. Most of this impressive sum of money consisted of forgotten bank accounts, but you may also discover that you or a relative are entitled to unclaimed security deposits paid to landlords and utility companies, uncashed dividend checks, uncollected insurance proceeds, estates of deceased relatives, and several other sources.

There is no time limit for claiming any funds owed you, although the state government usually collects interest on the unclaimed money in return for the service of holding it. Many experts recommend checking with the appropriate office of the state government of any states in which you or deceased family members have resided. To locate the agency that holds unclaimed funds in any state, call the state government information number listed on pages 441–443.

DEALING WITH BANKING PROBLEMS AND DISPUTES

The proliferation of banking products and services, including the introduction of automatic teller machines and other types of electronic money transfers, has resulted in a significant increase in computer errors, fraud, and other problems, among them:

- Disputes over deposits, withdrawals, or payments
- Disputes over the speed of crediting deposits and payments
- Disputes over fees and service charges
- Disputes over interest credited on your savings or penalties for early withdrawal
- Disputes over interest and penalties charged on loans

To solve a dispute, your first recourse is to contact your bank or lender. However, if that doesn't work, you should take your complaint to the appropriate federal and state regulatory agencies, which are very effective in resolving consumer problems.

How to File a Complaint with Federal Agencies

All complaints against financial institutions should be filed in writing. Send a letter providing the details of the problem, the action you'd like taken, and copies of all documents. The appropriate agency to contact depends upon the type of financial institution involved.

Commercial Banks. If you have a complaint against a bank, you first must call the bank to determine if:

- The bank is *nationally chartered,* or if
- The bank is *state chartered* and *a member of the Federal Reserve System,* or if
- The bank is *state chartered, insured by FDIC,* but not a member of the Federal Reserve System

If the bank is *nationally chartered,* send your complaint to:

Comptroller of the Currency
Consumer Affairs Division
Washington, DC 20219
(202) 287-4265

If the bank is *state chartered* and *a member of the Federal Reserve System,* send your complaint to:

Board of Governors of the Federal Reserve System
Division of Consumer and Community Affairs
Washington, DC 20551
(202) 452-3946

Or to the nearest Federal Reserve Bank:

FEDERAL RESERVE BANK (FRB) ATLANTA
104 Marrietta Street, NW
Atlanta, GA 30303
(404) 521-8788

FRB BOSTON
600 Atlantic Avenue
Boston, MA 02210
(617) 973-3459

FRB CHICAGO
230 S. LaSalle Street
Chicago, IL 60604
(312) 322-5111

FRB CLEVELAND
1455 E. 6th St.
Cleveland, OH 49114
(216) 579-2047

FRB DALLAS
400 S. Akard Street
Station K
Dallas, TX 75202
(214) 651-6289

FRB KANSAS CITY
925 Grand Avenue

Kansas City, KS 64198
(816) 881-2402

FRB MINNEAPOLIS
250 Marquette Avenue
Minneapolis, MN 55401
(612) 340-2446

FRB NEW YORK
33 Liberty Street
New York, NY 10005
(212) 720-6134

FRB PHILADELPHIA
100 N. 6th St.
Philadelphia, PA 19106
(215) 574-6115

FRB RICHMOND
701 E. Byrd St.
Richmond, VA 23219
(801) 697-8000

FRB ST. LOUIS
411 Locust St.
St. Louis, MO 63102
(314) 444-8421

FRB SAN FRANCISCO
P.O. Box 7702
San Francisco, CA 94120
(415) 974-2163

If the bank is *state chartered, insured by FDIC*, but not a member of the Federal Reserve System, send your complaint to:

Federal Deposit Insurance Corporation
Office of Bank Consumer Affairs
Washington, DC 20429

(800) 424-5488 (Ex. DC)
(202) 898-3536

Savings and Loan Associations. Send your complaint to:

Office of Thrift Supervision
1700 G St., NW
Washington, DC 20552
(800) 842-6929 (Ex. DC)
(202) 906-6237

Credit Unions. Call your credit union and ask if it is *federally chartered*. If it is, send your complaint to:

National Credit Union Administration
Division of Consumer Affairs
1776 G St., NW
Washington, DC 20456
(202) 682-9600

Your State Banking Department

You should call your state banking department if you have questions about banking and rights. This information can be useful in organizing the complaint letter you send to federal agencies. Also, every state banking department will try to resolve problems with *state chartered* banks, S&Ls, and credit unions, and, in many cases, complaints against other financial institutions as well. For the number of your state banking department, look in your telephone directory under state government listings or call your state government information service (see listings pages 441–443).

PURCHASING AND USING CREDIT

MANY AMERICANS WERE RAISED TO BE wary of borrowing money. Today, however, credit offers many significant advantages.

- Credit allows you to take advantage of goods and services while you're paying for them.
- Credit is a valuable resource in an emergency, such as a sudden illness or accidental injury, or a major car repair.
- Credit offers convenience in purchasing goods and services. Credit cards eliminate the need to carry large amounts of cash while traveling, and they're a virtual necessity for renting an automobile.
- Federal law provides unique protection to consumers who purchase goods or services with credit cards. One such protection is a legal right to a full refund if merchandise or a service isn't delivered.

An excellent guide to credit that highlights these advantages is:

Booklet: *Managing Your Credit*
Cost: $1.25
Contains: Easy-to-understand explanations of consumer credit, credit protection laws, how to obtain and evaluate credit, shopping for credit, managing credit, and handling credit difficulties
From: Money Management Institute
Household International
2700 Sanders Road
Prospect Heights, IL 60070

YOUR CREDIT RIGHTS

Because credit can be such a valuable financial asset, the U.S. Congress has passed a series of landmark bills, which mandate that people be treated fairly and honestly by lenders. Everyone who borrows money or is considering borrowing money should be familiar with these rights. The best guide is:

Handbook: *Consumer Handbook to Credit Protection Laws*
Cost: Free
Contains: 44 pages of invaluable information on federal laws, as well as techniques for obtaining and managing credit
From: Publications Services—MS 138
Board of Governors of the Federal Reserve System
Washington, DC 20551

Unfortunately, the existence of these laws has not prevented widespread credit-related problems, especially in the areas of:

- Discrimination in granting credit
- Errors in credit bureau files
- Deceptive credit sales tactics
- Errors and deception in credit billing

How to Insure Your Equal Right to Credit

The Consumer Affairs Department of the American Association of Retired Persons (AARP) has found that women, especially those who become widowed and divorced, and senior citizens have proportionately greater problems obtaining credit than does the average American. As a result, a number of organizations have developed special publications outlining specific procedures for women and senior citizens to establish and protect their credit.

Three general publications of value to everyone who applies for credit are:

Fact Sheet: *Getting Credit*
Cost: Free

From: Consumer Credit Institute
American Financial Services Association
1101 14th Street, NW
Washington, DC 20005
(202) 289-0200

Booklet: *Establishing Good Credit*
Cost: $0.20 plus self-addressed stamped envelope
From: National Foundation for Consumer Credit
8701 Georgia Avenue, Suite 507
Silver Spring, MD 20910
(301) 589-5600

Publications that are especially written for women and older Americans are:

Pamphlet: • *Women's Credit Rights*
• *Credit Cards and Seniors*
Cost: $1.00 each
Contains: Discusses how a woman's credit rating can change with marital status, tells how to develop a personal credit history, and describes what to do if turned down for credit
From: Bankcard Holders of America
560 Herndon Pkwy, Suite 120
Herndon, VA 22070
(703) 481-1110

Pamphlets: • Equal Credit Opportunity and Women
• *Equal Credit Opportunity and Age*
Cost: Free
From: Office of Consumer Affairs
Federal Deposit Insurance Corporation
550 17th St., NW
Washington, DC 20429
(800) 424-5488 (Ex DC)
(202) 898-3536

Fact Sheet: *In Your Own Name—Women and Credit*
Cost: Free

From: Consumer Credit Institute
American Financial Services Association
1101 14th St., NW
Washington, DC 20005
(202) 289-0400

Booklets: • *Women and Credit Histories*
• *Credit and Older Americans*
Cost: Free
From: Public Reference
Federal Trade Commission
Washington, DC 20580
(202) 326-2222

Booklet: *Your Credit: A Complete Guide*
(D132286)
Cost: Free
From: AARP Fulfillment
1909 K St., NW
Washington, DC 20049

How to Correct Errors in Your Credit Bureau Files

Within 30 days of being turned down for credit, you can contact the credit bureau to get a free copy of your credit report. If you inspect the report in person, the credit bureau has to assign a person to explain the report to you. At any time, you have the right to obtain a copy of your credit report.

Pamphlet: *Understanding Credit Bureaus*
Cost: $1.00
From: Bankcard Holders of America
560 Herndon Pkwy, Suite 120
Herndon, VA 22070
(703) 481-1110

Booklet: *Building a Better Credit Record*
Cost: Free
Contains: Detailed explanation of credit bureaus and credit reports, including information on how to solve problems

From: Public Reference
Federal Trade Commission
Washington, DC 20580
(202) 326-2222

Fact Sheet: *What's in Your Credit Report*
Cost: Free
From: Consumer Credit Institute
American Financial Services Association
1101 14th Street, NW
Washington, DC 20005
(202) 289-0400

How to Detect Deceptive Credit Sales Practices

Almost all banks, S&Ls, credit unions, and major credit card companies must tell you, in plain language, the exact costs of the credit you're purchasing. Unfortunately, you cannot assume the same compliance when you're shopping for credit at local finance companies, retail stores, used car dealers, home improvement contractors, and many other types of firms. To defend yourself against deceptive practices, you should:

1. *Understand the Truth in Lending laws.*

The "Truth in Lending" Act requires lenders to compute the interest rate by a standard method, which is stated as the Annual Percentage Rate (APR) of the loan. If the loan is for a fixed amount with a fixed repayment period (as opposed to a credit line you can draw from any time), the payments must also be expressed as a dollar amount. The lender also has to explain in plain English any additional fees, penalties, and other terms of the loan. For more information, send for:

Pamphlet: *Buying and Borrowing: Cash in on the Facts*

Cost: Free
From: Federal Trade Commission
Office of Public Affairs
Room 421
Sixth St. and Pennsylvania Ave., NW
Washington, DC 20580
(202) 326-2180

2. *Find out if there have been complaints filed against the lender by contacting:*

- Your local Better Business Bureau (see listings, pages 452–459)
- Your state or local consumer affairs office (see listings, pages 443–452)

How to Detect and Solve Credit Billing Problems

Inspecting every bill carefully is important, because federal law gives you specific rights to dispute credit charges and withhold payment without penalty until the dispute is resolved. You can dispute for a number of reasons, including:

- A charge for goods or services you didn't purchase

- A charge that's not properly identified or that you don't understand completely
- Mathematical errors or failure to record payments or credits
- A charge for goods or services that weren't delivered on time or were unsatisfactory in some respect

If you dispute anything on your bill, federal law requires that you notify the lender within 60 days of receipt of your bill. On a separate piece of paper (not your bill), write:

- Your name and account number
- The dollar amount disputed
- A complete description of error, what you want corrected, and why
- Photocopies of sales receipts or other relevant documents

Send the letter by certified mail, return receipt requested. The lender must reply within 30 days, and your complaint must be investigated within 90 days. Until you receive a final answer, you do not have to pay the disputed charge or any finance charges connected with it.

SHOPPING FOR CREDIT

Many consumers don't realize that the costs and fees of credit vary widely. Companies charge for credit in two ways:

- Interest on the money lent
- Fees for making the loan and penalties for late payments

The factors involved when a lender calculates the charge for credit include:

- The cost of the money it lends you. For example, a bank that loans you money must either pay interest to a depositor or interest on a loan from a larger bank or the Federal Reserve Bank.
- The expenses of checking your credit, approving the loan, recording the transactions, billing, and recording payments.

- The risk involved in the loan. A company calculates the rate of default on each type of loan, and protects against that risk by charging higher interest rates to every borrower.

The least expensive types of credit are those secured by collateral, such as:

- Loans secured by savings accounts, stocks, bonds, or other financial assets (note: U.S. Savings bonds cannot be used as collateral for a loan)
- Home equity loans
- Automobile loans
- Loans against the cash value of life insurance policies
- Loans against money in pension funds
- Loans against other assets, such as jewelry, art work, or other valuables

The significant disadvantage of secured loans is that you lose the collateral if you default on the loan.

The more expensive loans are "unsecured loans," money lent on the basis of your income and credit history. Such loans include:

- Credit card purchases and cash advances
- Personal credit lines issued by banks and other financial institutions
- Overdraft privileges on your checking accounts
- Department store, gasoline company, and other retail charge cards

For more information on the types of credit and shopping for credit:

Pamphlets: • *The Forms of Credit We Use*
• *Credit and the Consumer*
Cost: $0.20 each, plus self-addressed stamped envelope
From: National Foundation for Consumer Credit
8701 Georgia Avenue, Suite 507
Silver Spring, MD 20910
(301) 589-5600

Credit Cards

Credit cards issued by banks, S&Ls, credit unions, and other institutions under the Mastercard or Visa name, along with the credit cards issued by American Express, Diners Club, Discovery, and Carte Blanche, are the most widely used credit instruments in the United States. However, the near-universal acceptance of these cards misleads many people into believing that one card is the same as another. The truth is that costs of a card and the services provided with the card vary tremendously from issuing company to issuing company, so much so that just changing from one Visa card to another could save a consumer as much as several hundred dollars per year.

The two major differences between cards are:

1. *Costs: Four important elements in evaluating the cost of a credit card are:*

- Annual fee: The yearly cost can range from no fee to as much as $100 for "premium" cards.
- Annual percentage rate: The interest rate charged on outstanding balances can range from as low as 12% to 22% or more.
- Grace period: Many credit card issuers give you a period of time from receipt

of your monthly bill to pay the entire outstanding balance without incurring interest charges, *if you have no previous balance on which you're already paying interest.* Other issuers begin to charge interest from the date of purchase.

- Other fees: Among the other charges you may see on your monthly statement are fees for cash advances, fees for other transactions, late fees, and fees for going over your credit limit. For example, fees for taking a cash advance of $500 can range from no charge to 4% of the amount, or $20.

2. *Features: Most credit cards offer "extra" features. The most features are offered by "premium" or "gold" cards that have more stringent credit requirements, higher credit limits, and higher annual fees.*

Three excellent resources for information about credit card selection and use are:

Organization: Bankcard Holders of America
560 Herndon Pkwy, Suite 120
Herndon, VA 22070
(703) 481-1110
Cost: $18.00 per year for membership
Services: The BHA is the only consumer organization that is exclusively dedicated to educating the public on their rights as credit consumers. Membership includes a bi-monthly newsletter with money-saving tips about credit cards and personal finance, insurance and travel discounts, free copies of all BHA publications (see below), and a toll-free hotline for members who are having credit card problems. Their publications include:
- *How to Choose a Credit Card*
- *All that Glitters Is Not Gold* (pros and cons of premium credit cards)

- *Ten Reasons to Shop with a Bank Card*
- *The Wide World of Plastic*

BHA also compiles and frequently updates the following lists ($1.50 per list):
No Annual Fee List (Banks nationwide that charge no annual fee for credit cards
Low Interest Rate List (Banks nationwide that charge lower than average interest rates)

Report: *Choosing a Credit Card*
Cost: $3.00 plus self-addressed stamped envelope
Contains: Excellent information on evaluating credit cards
From: Better Business Bureau of Greater New York
257 Park Avenue
New York, NY 10010

Kit: Credit Card Locator
Cost: $10.00
Contains: Lists more than 500 credit card issuers, with complete information about their terms. Also contains worksheets that allow comparison between the total cost of different cards
From: Consumer Credit Card Rating Service, Inc.
P.O. Box 5219
Ocean Park Station
Santa Monica, CA 90405
(213) 392-7720

Many credit card users are drawn to affinity credit cards, cards that are issued by a financial institution under an arrangement with a group or organization. An attractive option for consumers age 50 and older is:

Resource: Visa card available to members of the American Association of Retired Persons (AARP)

Requirements: Must be AARP member ($5.00 per year): Relatively low-cost card issued with special sensitivity to the credit problems of older Americans

For information: AARP Visa
P.O. Box 182151
Columbus, OH 43272
(800) 642-3310

TOO MUCH DEBT?

With the ready availability of credit, and the possibility of a substantial reduction of income due to unemployment, illness, or forced retirement, it's not unusual for people to find that they're having great difficulty making the payments on credit cards and other installment debt.

Your monthly payments on installment debt (except your mortgage payment) should not exceed 15% to 20% of your after-tax income. Other signs of trouble include using credit to pay for regular household expenses, such as food, clothing, rent, or utility bills; applying for new credit cards or credit lines to pay off old credit lines; and increasing the amount you owe each month.

If you feel your debt is getting out of control, or if an emergency prevents you from making installment debt payments, you should get professional help immediately. For help, contact:

Organization: National Foundation for Consumer Credit, Inc.
8701 Georgia Avenue, Suite 507
Silver Spring, MD 20910
(301) 589-5600

Services: Will provide referral to over 350 nonprofit Consumer Credit Counseling Services nationwide. Will provide free debt counseling services for families and individuals. Will also send the following pamphlets for $0.20 each plus a self-addressed stamped envelope:

- *Consumer Credit Counseling*
- *Getting a Hold on Credit*
- *Measuring and Using Your Credit Capacity*
- *The Emergency Problem (What to do about it)*
- *Fix Your Own Credit Problems*

If you are age 55 or over, contact:

Organization: Your local area agency on aging (see listing, pages 391–435)

Services: Many local and state governments fund programs which provide free credit counseling and legal services to older residents

Other valuable information is included in:

Pamphlets: • *Getting Out of Debt*
• *Managing Family Debt*
• *Re-Establishing Good Credit*
Cost: $1.00 each
From: Bankcard Holders of America
560 Herndon Pkwy, Suite 120
Herndon, VA 22070
(703) 481-1110

Pamphlet: *Solving Credit Problems*
Cost: Free
From: Public Reference
Federal Trade Commission
6th & Pennsylvania Avenue, NW
Washington, DC 20580
(202) 326-2222

DEALING WITH CREDIT FRAUD AND LOST
OR STOLEN CREDIT CARDS

Credit card fraud, including use of stolen credit cards, costs billions of dollars each year, and causes a great deal of anguish for the innocent people involved. That anguish, however, can be reduced by understanding that federal law limits a card holder's liability for unauthorized charges to $50 if the loss hasn't been reported, and no amount for any charges incurred after the card has been reported lost, stolen, or misused.

It is best, however, to take some simple steps to secure your credit cards and account numbers.

- Always keep an eye on your card when it's in the hands of a store clerk or other employee to insure that only one copy of a charge slip is processed
- Make sure that you receive all charge slip carbons or watch them destroyed
- Take a moment to insure that the card is in your possession before you leave the store

- Never, never, never give your credit card number to anyone or any company that calls you to sell a product or service
- Keep a complete list of all of your credit cards with account numbers in a safe place at home

If you find a card missing or suspect that it's being misused, you should immediately notify the company or companies involved. Toll-free telephone numbers for these companies are listed on your monthly statements.

For more information on credit card fraud:

Pamphlet: *Credit Card Fraud*
Cost: $1.00
From: Bankcard Holders of America
560 Herndon Pkwy, Suite 120
Herndon, VA 22070
(703) 481-1110

SAVINGS AND INVESTMENTS: AN OVERVIEW

Financial security in the second half of your life increasingly depends on how much you've been able to save and invest. Both Congress and private companies haved helped by establishing a variety of tax-deferred retirement plans. With the tremendous advantages of these plans, however, comes the burden of planning and monitoring the investments in those accounts. The level of income you will have in your retirement years depends partly on how well you make investment decisions.

That responsibility seems complicated to many people, especially as the number of savings and investment products continues to grow. Decades ago, investors had a limited number of options: savings accounts, stocks, bonds, and real estate. Today, a passing glance at the financial pages reveals such products as futures, options, warrants, CMOs, ADRs, Sallie Maes, and Freddie Macs. To the uninitiated, choosing the right product can appear as impossible as winning the lottery.

Fortunately, in this case, appearances are deceiving. The financial revolutions that pro-duced exotic and highly speculative investment products aimed at sophisticated investors also have produced an array of new convenient, inexpensive investment products and services that allow small investors to obtain the diversification, growth, and income previously available only to very wealthy individuals and institutions.

The result is that almost everyone who devotes some time and effort to the subject can responsibly make important investment decisions if he or she:

- Understands basic information about investment

- Understands the basic types of savings and investment products

- Chooses the right investment professionals

- Takes the right action to resolve problems and disputes involving investments

SAVINGS VERSUS INVESTMENT

Savings is money set aside for unexpected emergencies, health problems, and planned major purchases, such as a home, vacation home, a new car, or a special vacation. Experts recommend that you set aside a minimum of 3 to 6 months income for sudden emergencies. Because this savings is so important, you want to keep it in financial products that offer ready access to your money with virtually no risk that you'll lose any of the money you invest.

The goal of investment, on the other hand, is to produce both income and growth of the invested principle. Investing requires assuming more risk of losing some of the principle you invest in exchange for the chance of greater reward.

Exactly how much money you allocate to savings and to investments is a personal decision, one that's based partly on your personal circumstances and on your personal tolerance for risk.

THE RELATIONSHIP BETWEEN RISK AND INVESTMENT

Investments involve three basic types of risk:

- Risk of losing part or all of the principle invested
- Risk of having the purchasing power of your money eroded by inflation
- Risk of losing potential income by having money tied up in long-term investments paying low interest rates

Every investment carries one or more of the above risks. The most significant losses for Americans approaching or in retirement involve risk of losing principle. The majority of people who lose money on investments fail to keep in mind one extremely important investment maxim: the greater the prospective rewards, the greater the risk involved. As measured by the amount of fluctuation in the value of the original investment, investments fit into one of three basic risk categories:

- No or virtually no risk
  - Bank passbook and statement savings accounts
  - Checking, share draft, and NOW accounts
  - Certificates of deposit
  - Bank money market accounts
  - U.S. Treasury securities
  - U.S. Savings bonds
  - Money market mutual funds

- Low to moderate risk investments that offer the potential for long-term growth, as well as current income
  - Blue chip stocks
  - Municipal bonds
  - Corporate bonds
  - Blue chip foreign stocks
  - Life insurance annuities
  - Real estate
  - Government-backed mortgage obligations
  - Zero coupon bonds
  - Precious metals

- Speculative investments that offer the potential for dramatic growth but carry a very high risk of loss of the entire initial sum invested

- Commodities
- Options

- Index futures
- Speculative stocks

THE IMPORTANCE OF GROWTH AND DIVERSIFICATION

Those Americans age 50 and over shun speculation in favor of more conservative investments to protect their assets and insure income for retirement. That doesn't mean, however, that higher risk investments should be ignored.

Experts feel that growth is important for three reasons:

- Growth protects the purchasing power of your money against the ravages of inflation

- Growth allows you to improve your standard of living over a period of years, making it possible to afford a bigger house, to travel, to expand your recreation options, etc.

- Growth builds a larger nest egg to insure a more comfortable and more worry-free retirement

Likewise, most experts recommend spreading your money among several investments for the following reasons:

- There is no perfect investment that offers adequate growth, income, and safety. Achieving each of these goals requires different types of investments.

- Changing economic conditions require changing investment strategies.

- Putting all your eggs in one basket is unwise, because even the most stable corporation or financial institution could face unexpected financial problems in the future.

THE DANGERS OF INVESTMENT FRAUD

In 1990, investors were bilked out of an estimated $40 billion, according to the National Association of Securities Administrators Associations. Much of this money was lost to investment swindles and scams, such as selling shares in phony gold mines or dry oil wells. The rest results from dramatic losses in investments that were misrepresented or inappropriate for the investor's circumstances. Investors suffer these losses because:

1. They let greed overcome caution. For legitimate investments, the higher potential rewards carry a higher degree of risk. Swindlers commonly promise extraordinary rewards with little or no risk.

2. They don't understand the investment. Some investments require a great deal of specialized knowledge. However, most investments, appropriate for the majority of investors, are comprehensible, and legitimate investment representatives do try to insure that clients understand them.

3. They failed to investigate the individuals and companies involved.

4. They failed to carefully monitor their investments. If you can't get regular, useful financial information and statements, pull your money out.

Because investment fraud plays on basic human emotions, such as fear, insecurity, and greed, everyone with financial assets is potentially vulnerable. That's why we urge all of our readers to obtain and read carefully the following:

Booklets: • *What Every Investor Should Know*
• *Investigate Before You Invest*
Cost: Free
Contains: Important basic information for the protection of all investors
From: Securities and Exchange Commission
Public Reference Branch
Stop 2-6
450 Fifth Street, NW
Washington, DC 20549
(202) 272-5624

Booklets: • *Investor's Bill of Rights*
• *Investment Swindles: How They Work and How to Avoid Them*
Cost: Free
Contains: Vital information on evaluating investment opportunities and avoiding swindles. "Investment Swindles" includes 16 questions than can turn off a con man
From: National Futures Association
200 West Madison Street, Suite 1600
Chicago, IL 60606
(800) 621-3570
(800) 572-9400 (IL)

Book: *Investor Alert!*
Cost: $4.95 plus $1.00 postage

Contains: 192-page detailed description of the types of investment frauds and how to avoid them, prepared by the Council of Better Business Bureaus and the North American Securities Administrators Association
From: Council of Better Business Bureaus
4200 Wilson Blvd.
Arlington, VA 22203
(703) 276-0100

The shelves of libraries and bookstores are filled with books about investment. We recommend the following:

Booklet: *Your Savings and Investment Dollar*
Cost: $1.25
Contains: An excellent, easy to understand introduction to the subject of investment
From: Money Management Institute
Household International
2700 Sanders Road
Prospect Heights, IL 60070

Book: *Dun & Bradstreet Guide to $Your Investments$ 1991* by Nancy Dunnan
Cost: $12.95
Contains: A very valuable, comprehensive almanac on the subject of investing and investments
From: HarperPerennial
HarperCollins*Publishers*

Book: *J.K. Lasser's Personal Investment Annual* by Judith Hennington McGee and Jerrold Dickson
Cost: $17.95
Contains: Another excellent, comprehensive guide with extensive material on investment planning
From: J.K. Lasser Institute
Simon & Schuster Reference Division

BECOMING AN INFORMED INVESTOR

Every person who invests money should take the time to understand the basics of the stock market and other financial institutions. Without such economic literacy, you won't be able to make decisions involving your money or evaluate the advice of stockbrokers, financial planners, or money managers. Furthermore, you won't be able to monitor your investments intelligently to determine how effectively your money is working for you.

Among the resources you can consult to gain some basic knowledge are:

Brochure: *How to Invest: A Guide to Buying Stocks, Bonds, and Mutual Funds*
Cost: Free
Contains: 24-page simple guide to the basics of investing
From: Public Relations Department
Standard & Poor's
25 Broadway
New York, NY 10004

Book: *Stock Market Primer: The Classic Beginner's Guide to Wall Street* by Claude N. Rosenberg, Jr.
Cost: $18.95
Contains: Readable, informative guide to investment that begins with such basics as "What is a stock?" and "What is a bond?"
From: Warner Books

Booklet: *Investor's Kit*
Cost: $10.00
Contains: A number of booklets, including:
-*Glossary*
-*Understanding Stocks and Bonds*
-*Understanding Financial Statements*
-*Getting Help When You Invest*
From: New York Stock Exchange Publications
11 Wall Street

New York, NY 10005
(212) 656-2089

Organization: American Association of Individual Investors
625 North Michigan Avenue, Suite 1900
Chicago, IL 60611
(312) 280-0170
Cost: $48.00 per year membership
Services: National nonprofit organization with over 25 local chapters. Publishes very informative monthly magazine, a newsletter on computerized investing, prepares home-study courses in investing, provides techniques for selecting stocks, and publishes books and directories of great interest to individual investors

Magazine: *Changing Times*
Editors Park, MD 20782
(800) 544-0155
Cost: $2.50 per issue or $18.00 for 12 issues

Magazine: *Money* Magazine
P.O. Box 61792
Tampa, FL 33661
(800) 245-5999
Cost: $2.95 per issue, $33.95 per year

Magazine: Sylvia Porter's *Personal Finance* Magazine
P.O. Box 1928
Marion, OH 43305
Cost: $2.50 per issue, $8.97 for 10 issues per year

Magazine: *Financial World: The Magazine for Investors*
P.O. Box 10750
Des Moines, IA 50340
Cost: $44.95 per year

Newspaper: *The Wall Street Journal*
Subscriber Services
200 Burnett Rd
Chicopee, MA 01020
Cost: $129.00 per year

Newspaper: *Investor's Daily*
1941 Armacost Avenue
P.O. Box 25970
Los Angeles, CA 90025
Cost: $84.00 per year

Newspaper: *Barron's National Business and Financial Weekly*

Subscriber Services
200 Burnett Road
Chicopee, MA 01021
Cost: $2.00 per copy, $99.00 per year

Directory: *The Individual Investor's Guide to Investment Publications*
Cost: $21.50
Contains: Comprehensive guide to investment newsletters and other information
From: International Publishing Corporation
625 N. Michigan Avenue, Suite 1920
Chicago, IL 60611

CHAPTER 6

SAVINGS AND INVESTMENT OPTIONS

WE MENTIONED IN CHAPTER 5 THAT investment products can be divided into three categories:

- No-risk (or virtually no risk) products that provide current income but little growth
- Low- to moderate-risk products that offer the potential for growth along with current income

- Speculative products that offer the potential of dramatic growth but carry a high risk of loss of principle

In this chapter, we will present in detail the financial products that fall into each of the above categories, as well as mutual funds, an excellent method for making every type of investment.

NO- (OR VIRTUALLY NO) RISK INVESTMENTS

Until about 20 years ago, a passbook savings account was the only place the average American could put his or her savings. Today, there is a wide variety of safe products that offer higher income than passbook savings accounts. To evaluate these products, you first have to understand how basic interest income is calculated. When you see advertisements for many investments, you may see two interest rates quoted. These are:

- Annual interest rate
- Annual compounded yield

What's the difference? The first is simple interest, the rate used to compute what your money earns. For example, if you invest $1,000 at 8% simple interest annually, at the end of 1 year your investment would have earned $1,000 × 8% = $80.00. Your principle would then be $1,080.

Fortunately for all savers and investors, financial institutions long ago began computing and paying interest more frequently in order to compete for savings dollars. This is called compounding. For example, let's take that same $1,000 invested at 8%, but assume interest is paid at the end of every month.

Step 1: Divide 8% by 12 months to obtain a monthly rate of 0.67%

Step 2: Multiply $1,000 × 0.67% monthly interest = $6.67

Step 3: The total investment is now $1,006.67

Step 4: At the end of the second month, compute interest by multiplying $1,006.67 × 0.67% = $6.74. The principle is now $1,013.41

At the end of the year, the principle is $1,083 instead of $1,080. Compounding has increased the yield over the year from 8% to 8.3%.

If you're investing for the longer term, the important interest rate to consider is this annual compounded yield. However, the basic annual interest rate is more important when considering short-term investments of under a year.

For detailed information on evaluating interest rates:

Booklet: *The Arithmetic of Interest Rates*
Cost: Free
From: Public Information Department
Federal Reserve Bank of New York
33 Liberty Street
New York, NY 10045

Passbook or Statement Savings Accounts

The advantages of passbook or statement savings accounts are:

- Virtually no risk, if under the federal insurance $100,000 limit
- High liquidity, with unlimited withdrawals at any time
- Minimum initial investment as low as $50 and no minimum subsequent investment

The disadvantages of passbook savings accounts are:

- Low interest rates, normally 5.25% to 5.5%
- Interest is fully taxable
- Many institutions charge fees on small accounts
- No checks may be written on the account

NOW and Super NOW Accounts

NOW (Negotiable Order of Withdrawal) accounts and Super NOW accounts are the only types of investment that draw interest while allowing unlimited check-writing privileges. Most NOW accounts require that you maintain a minimum balance in order to earn interest and avoid fees. The interest rate on NOW and Super NOW accounts is comparable to, or slightly below, the interest paid on passbook savings accounts.

The advantages of NOW and Super NOW accounts are:

- Virtually risk-free, if balance is no more than the $100,000 federal insurance limit
- High liquidity, with unlimited check writing
- Interest is paid on the funds that would earn no interest in a regular checking account
- Many accounts charge no fees if a minimum balance is maintained

The disadvantages of NOW and Super NOW accounts are:

- Interest earned is fully taxable
- Fees can significantly reduce the yield on an account
- Additional fees and penalties for failing to keep a minimum balance can make a NOW account more expensive than a regular checking account
- Interest computation methods used by a bank can also reduce yield

The ideal NOW or Super NOW account:

- Has a low minimum balance
- Pays interest on the entire balance
- Charges no fees if the minimum balance is maintained
- Uses the average minimum balance over the entire month as the trigger for fees and penalties

For more information:

Booklet: *Introduction to NOW Accounts*
Cost: Free
From: AARP
1909 K Street, NW
Washington, DC 20049

Share-Draft Accounts

Share-draft accounts are checking accounts at credit unions. The advantages of these accounts are:

- Virtually risk-free, *if the credit union is insured by the NCUSIF,* up to the $100,000 limit
- They normally pay higher interest than NOW accounts at banks or S&Ls
- About three fourths of credit unions charge no fees for share-draft accounts
- High liquidity, with unlimited check-writing privileges

The disadvantages are:

- Interest earned is fully taxable
- Credit union office may be inconvenient to get to or may even be in another city, requiring you to bank by mail
- Other equally safe investments offer higher returns for funds over what you need to cover checks in any given month

For information on how to find a credit union in your area for which you may be eligible:

Contact: Credit Union National Organization
Public Relations Department
P.O. Box 431
Madison, WI 53701
(608) 231-4000

Certificates of Deposit

Time certificate of deposits, or CDs, are safe interest-bearing investments offered by virtually every bank and savings institution. As bank deposits, CDs issued by a federally insured institution are fully protected, if your total deposits with one bank do not exceed the $100,000 insurance limit.

By purchasing a CD you loan money to the bank at a specified interest rate for a specified period of time, ranging from 7 days to 5 years. The interest that you earn on a CD increases with the length of time and amount of money invested.

The advantages of CDs are:

- They are virtually risk-free, within insurance limits
- They can be purchased without paying a commission
- They generally pay significantly higher interest than passbook savings accounts, NOW accounts, or money market bank accounts
- Minimum investment can be as little as $100

The disadvantages of CDs are:

- Interest on CDs is fully taxable
- Most CDs are not liquid, because they carry severe penalties for early withdrawal

The benefits of buying CDs for IRA, Keogh, and other retirement accounts are:

- All interest earned is tax-free
- Many banks and savings institutions pay higher rates on CDs purchased for retirement accounts
- Almost all institutions allow penalty-free withdrawal of funds in CDs held in retirement accounts by individuals age 59.5 and older

Interest rates and terms of CDs can vary significantly from one institution to another. Buying CDs from the local bank where you have your checking account is convenient if you're investing small amounts of money. But that convenience could be expensive if you are buying CDs of $1,000 or more.

To maximize your earnings, you should:

- Buy short-term CDs if interest rates are low and longer-term CDs if interest rates are high.
- Pay close attention to how interest is calculated and paid. Choose a CD which features compounded interest rather than a CD for which simple interest is computed.
- Call several institutions to ask if they have special rates for older depositors—some institutions pay an extra percentage rate or additional interest on longer-term CDs as part of a senior citizen package.
- Consider out-of-town or out-of-state banks or savings institutions.

To find out which institutions are paying the highest rates:

Magazine: *Money* Magazine
Cost: $2.95 per issue
Contains: Lists the highest paying 6-month, 1-year, and 5-year CDs, with telephone number of bank and the Veribanc rating of the bank's financial stability. Also gives the nationwide average rates paid, a useful index for rating the offerings from your local banks. The only drawback is that the ratings are at least a month out of date

Newspaper: *Barron's National Business and Financial Weekly*

Cost: $2.00 per issue, $99.00 per year
Contains: Listing of five banks paying the highest yields on 6-month, 1-year, 2.5-year, and 5-year CDs. Listing includes method of compounding interest rate and effective yield over the life of the CD. Telephone numbers of the banks are not listed

Newsletter: *Income & Safety: The Consumer's Guide to High Yields*
3471 N. Federal Highway
Fort Lauderdale, FL 33306
Cost: Sample issue free

If you don't want to do your own shopping for the best rates, you should consider purchasing CDs through a brokerage firm. These firms shop as many as 200 institutions nationwide negotiating for the best rates. The advantages of purchasing CDs through a brokerage are:

- Rates paid tend to be significantly higher than the national average
- All CDs come from federally insured institutions, so deposits are risk-free up to $100,000
- Brokerage firms charge no commission because they receive a fee from the banks
- These CDs are more liquid than bank CDs, because the brokerage firm can resell them for you

The disadvantages of brokerage CDs are:

- Minimum investment varies from at least $1,000 to $10,000
- The highest yields may come from institutions that are less financially stable
- If interest rates rise, you may lose some of your principle if you sell the CD before its maturity date

For information about brokerage CDs, call your broker or see our listing of brokers on page 55.

Bank Money Market Accounts

Money market accounts are savings accounts that pay variable interest rates that rise and fall with other short-term interest rates, such as U.S. Treasury bills. The advantages of such accounts are:

- They are virtually risk-free, with deposits federally insured up to the $100,000 federal insurance limit
- They are very liquid, with no penalty for withdrawal of funds
- They offer limited check-writing privileges, normally three checks a month with a minimum of $250 per check
- They pay interest rates higher than NOW accounts or passbook savings accounts when interest rates are high

The disadvantages of bank money market accounts are:

- Minimum balances of $1,000 to $2,500 are normally required to earn interest
- They pay lower interest than money market mutual funds or Treasury bills
- Interest is fully taxable

Interest rates on money market accounts can vary as much as 2% or 3% from one bank to another. All of the publications listed above that rank the highest yields on CDs also list institutions offering the highest yield on money market accounts.

Money Market Mutual Funds

The development of the money market mutual fund in the early 1970s finally gave small investors a safe, easy method of earning interest on their savings well above the 5.25% or 5.5% paid by passbook savings accounts.

A money market mutual fund is a company that collects money from a great many individuals, then invests it in short-term money market instruments, such as U.S. government securities, very large (jumbo) CDs, and short-term loans to corporations or banks. The advantages of money market funds are:

- They can be purchased with no commission
- They pay interest rates comparable to short-term U.S. Treasury bills and higher rates than NOW accounts and bank money market funds
- They are very liquid, with most funds allowing unlimited checks (normally with a $100 minimum) to be written on the account
- Minimum investment required starts as low as $500, with the minimum for subsequent investments as low as $100
- They are low-risk, with almost all funds maintaining a steady $1.00 per share price, insuring no loss of principle
- Yields increase when interest rates rise, providing protection against inflation
- Some money market funds invest in tax-exempt securities, so that the interest that they pay is exempt from some or all income taxes

The disadvantages of money market mutual funds are:

- They are not federally insured, so they are not risk-free, as are bank deposits. However, no money market mutual fund has, to date, failed to meet its obligations to its investors
- Yield falls when interest rates fall
- Interest paid by funds that aren't tax-free are fully taxable
- Since most deposits are made by mail, they may not be as convenient as an account at a local bank

The risk factor is the primary concern of most investors. Although no money market fund has ever failed, investors can reduce risk by choosing:

- Money market funds that invest only in government securities backed by the U.S. government
- Money market funds whose principle is guaranteed by private insurance

Your will find a more detailed discussion on the organization of mutual funds and how to purchase them in this chapter, beginning on page 66. For more specific information on money market mutual funds:

Booklet: *Money Market Mutual Funds*
Cost: Free
Contains: 14-page explanation of money market mutual funds
From: Investment Company Institute
1600 M Street, NW
Washington, DC 20036
(202) 293-7700

Newsletter: *Income and Safety*
Cost: $49.00 per year, for 12 monthly issues
Contains: Rates money market funds for yield and safety

From: Institute for Econometric Research
3471 North Federal Highway
Fort Lauderdale, FL 33306
(800) 327-6720

Newsletter: *Donaghue'$ Moneyletter*
Cost: $49.00 for 6 months (12 issues);
$87.00 per year (24 issues)
Contains: Ratings of top-yielding money market funds, plus buy and sell recommendations, and model portfolios
From: Moneyletter
P.O. Box 540
Holliston, MA 01746

U.S. Treasury Securities

The U.S. government borrows money by issuing Treasury securities. These securities are backed by the U.S. government, and they are considered risk-free. Treasury securities are issued in three types, depending on the maturity:

Treasury Bills
    13-week maturity
    26-week maturity
    52-week maturity
Treasury Notes
    2-year maturity
    3-year maturity
    4-year maturity
    5-year maturity
    7-year maturity
    10-year maturity
Treasury Bonds
    30-year maturity

The advantages of Treasury securities are:

- They are virtually risk-free
- Interest paid on Treasury securities is exempt from state and local income tax
- Interest rates are higher than passbook savings, NOW accounts, and bank money market accounts
- Treasury securities are liquid, because they are traded in the financial marketplace
- Treasury securities can be purchased directly from the government with no commission charged
- Capital gains can accrue on Treasury securities if sold when interest rates go down

The disadvantages of Treasury securities are:

- Minimum investment is $10,000 for Treasury bills, $5,000 for Treasury notes, and $1,000 for Treasury bonds
- Interest rates are normally slightly lower than comparable CDs
- Capital losses can occur if Treasury securities are sold before maturity when interest rates rise
- Commissions are charged when Treasury securities are purchased or sold through banks, brokerage firms, or other institutions

The U.S. Treasury sells its securities through the banks of the Federal Reserve System. The majority of the securities are sold at auction: that is, banks, financial institutions, and bond dealers enter bids specifying the interest rates they will pay, and the securities are sold to those with the lowest bids.

However, individuals can also purchase Treasury securities directly on a noncompetitive basis by placing an order and agreeing to receive an interest rate computed from the average of competitive bids received.

The issue dates and minimum investment for Treasury securities are:

Treasury Bills
    13 weeks, issued
        every Monday, $10,000 minimum
    26 weeks, issued
        every Monday, $10,000 minimum
    52 weeks, issued
        every fourth
        Thursday, $10,000 minimum
Treasury Notes
    2 year, issued
        monthly, $5,000 minimum
    3, 4, 5, 7, 10 years,
        issued quarterly, $5,000 minimum
Treasury Bonds
    30 year,
        issued quarterly, $1,000 minimum

New Treasury securities can be purchased through commercial banks or brokerage houses for commissions that range from $10 to $35. But they can also be purchased directly from the U.S. Treasury or local Federal Reserve Banks and branch offices. You can order securities by mail, if postmarked no later than 1 day before the auction and in person, before 1:00 p.m. Eastern time on the day of the auction. Payment must be in the form of cash, cashier's check, certified personal check, or maturing U.S. Treasury securities. For applications and instructions, write or call:

Bureau of the Public Debt
Division of Customer Services
Washington, DC 20239
(202) 287-4113
(202) 287-4097 (For hearing impaired)
            or
Write or call your nearest Federal Reserve
    Banks or branches.

For more information on U.S. Treasury securities:

Book: *Buying Treasury Securities*
Cost: $4.50
From: Federal Reserve Bank of Richmond
P.O. Box 27471
Richmond, VA 23261

Pamphlets: • *Basic Information on Treasury Bills*
• *Basic Information on Treasury Notes and Bonds*
• *Buying Treasury Bills, Notes and Bonds Through the Treasury Direct System*
• *Estimating Return on Treasury Issues*
Cost: Free
From: Public Information Division
Federal Reserve Bank of New York
33 Liberty Street
New York, NY 10045

Pamphlets: • *Information About Marketable Treasury Securities*
• *Buying Treasury Securities*
• *Treasury Direct: Features*
• *Treasury Direct: Account Information*
• *Treasury Direct: Direct Deposit*
• *Treasury Direct: Registration Options*
• *Treasury Direct: Servicing Offices*
• *Treasury Direct: Reinvestment*
Cost: Free
From: Federal Reserve Bank of Philadelphia
Public Information Department
P.O. Box 66
Philadelphia, PA 19105

U.S. Savings Bonds

U.S. Savings bonds are securities designed for the small investor and backed by the U.S. government. There are two types of savings bonds currently issued, Series EE and Series HH.

Series EE Savings bonds are called accrual securities. That means, although interest accrues regularly, no interest is paid until the bond is redeemed, or cashed in. The advantages of Series EE Savings bonds are:

- They are virtually risk-free investments
- Minimum investment is as little as $25
- No commission is charged to buy them
- They pay a minimum of 6% interest, if held 5 years
- After 5 years, they pay an interest rate equal to 85% of the interest paid on 5-year Treasury notes
- Interest is exempt from state and local taxes
- No federal tax has to be paid on accruing interest until the bond is redeemed

The disadvantages of Series EE Savings bonds stem primarily from the fact that they were created as longer-term investments for individuals. To encourage long-term investment by individuals, the following regulations were implemented:

- They can't be redeemed until 6 months after purchase
- The interest rate paid after 6 months is based on a fixed scale beginning at 4.16%, and doesn't reach 6% until 5 years
- Savings bonds can't be sold or used for collateral for loans
- No individual can purchase more than $30,000 in savings bonds in any 1 year

Series HH Savings bonds cannot be purchased for cash. The only way you can buy them is by trading your Series EE bonds for them. The advantages of Series HH bonds are:

- They are virtually risk-free
- They are purchased without commission
- Interest paid is exempt from state and local taxes
- They are liquid and can be cashed in at any time
- You continue to defer paying federal taxes on the interest earned by the Series EE bonds until you cash in the Series HH bonds
- Series HH bonds pay interest in cash twice per year

The disadvantages of Series HH bonds are:

- Minimum investment is $500
- Interest paid is subject to federal income tax
- Bonds cannot be used as collateral for loans
- Purchases are subject to the overall limit of $30,000 per person per year

Because savings bond interest is tax-deferred, they are safe vehicles for extra funds you're saving for retirement after you've made your maximum allowable contributions to your IRA, Keogh, 401(K), or other tax-deferred retirement plans. They're also ideal as gifts to children, grandchildren, or for saving for some long-term major expense.

Savings bonds are sold at most banks and other financial institutions. Many employers offer automatic payroll deduction plans for the purchase of savings bonds. You can also order bonds by mail from:

Bureau of the Public Debt
200 Third Street
Parkersburg, VA 26106

For complete information about savings bonds:

Booklet: *The Savings Bonds Question and Answer Book*
Cost: $0.50
From: Consumer Information Center
P.O. Box 100
Pueblo, CO 81009

For current rate information on U.S. Savings bonds:

Call (800) USA-BONDS (Ex. DC)
(202) USA-8888 (DC only)

For information on rates paid on older Savings bonds, consult charts available from:

Office of Public Affairs
U.S. Savings Bonds Division
Department of the Treasury
Washington, DC 20226

Many people wonder what happens if a savings bond is lost, stolen, or damaged. The proper procedure is to obtain form PD1048 (lost or stolen) or form PD1934 (mutilated or partially destroyed) from your bank or from:

Bond Consultant Branch
Bureau of the Public Debt
200 Third Street
Parkersburg, VA 26106
(304) 420-6102

LOW- TO MODERATE-RISK INVESTMENTS

Common Stocks

When you buy a share of common stock, you become part owner of the company. In other words, you have equity in the company, so stocks are considered an equity investment. If the company grows and prospers, your shares grow in value. Historically, common stocks have been a very good investment. Between 1927 and 1987, stocks in the Standard and Poor 500 Index have annually returned 9.9%. That return represents nearly 7% annual growth after inflation is taken into account, making common stocks among the very best protections against rising prices.

The advantages of investing in common stocks are:

- Moderate to high potential for capital gains
- Stocks, especially those listed on the major exchanges, are very liquid

- Some stocks produce moderate current income in the form of dividends
- Tax on capital gains accrued from the increase in value of stocks is deferred until the shares are sold
- A loss from the sale of one stock can be deducted from the profit on the sale of another stock for tax purposes

The disadvantages of investing in common stocks are:

- Moderate to high risk of loss of some principal
- Dividends and capital gains from the sale of a stock are taxable
- Most stocks produce very low to low current income in the form of dividends
- Commissions must be paid to both buy and sell most stocks

There are a number of ways to purchase stocks. You can:

- Purchase mutual funds that invest in stocks
- Join or form an investment club
- Purchase stocks through a full-service broker
- Purchase stocks through a discount broker
- Purchase stocks through dividend reinvestment and cash purchase plans
- Purchase or sell stocks privately

1. *Purchase mutual funds that invest in stocks.*

We offer a thorough discussion of mutual funds later in this chapter, beginning on page 66.

2. *Join or form an investment club.*

An investment club is a group of 10 to 20 people who contribute from $10 to $50 per month into a common pool, which is then invested. The members meet to discuss investments, listen to guest speakers who are often stock brokers or executives of local firms, share research on individual stocks, then make investment decisions. About 600,000 people belong to about 30,000 investment clubs in the United States, with an average portfolio of about $55,000 per club. For more information:

Organization: National Association of Investors Corporation
Cost: $30.00 per year per club, plus $8.00 per member
Services: Membership in this nonprofit organization includes:
- Investors Manual for Investment Clubs
- Subscription to *Better Investing,* a monthly magazine

- *Free Investors Information Reports* on specific stocks
- $25,000 bond for protection against member dishonesty
- Meetings of 30 regional councils and Investor Fairs in 50 cities
- Low-cost accounting manuals and other investment forms and information services
- Discounts on investment books, newsletters, magazines, and services

For information: National Association of Investors Corporation
1515 East Eleven Mile Road
Royal Oak, MI 48067
(313) 543-0612

3. *Purchase stocks through a full-service broker.*

Full-service brokerage firms offer such services as:

- An individual broker who will monitor your portfolio, answer questions, make buy and sell recommendations, and execute your trades
- Detailed research reports on individual stocks
- Loans for the purchase of stocks and other securities
- Regular statements of your account activities
- Recording and holding your stock certificates
- Money market accounts for uninvested cash, such as dividends and proceeds of stock sales
- A library of investment research books and newsletters
- Seminars and lectures on investment products and strategies

The primary advantage of buying stocks through a full-service brokerage firm is the individual attention you will receive. (We discuss choosing investment professionals in Chapter 7.) Because of their high volume, the large national firms tend to cater more to small investors then do local and regional firms.

For more information about these full-service brokers, call:

A.G. Edwards & Co.	(314) 289-3000
Dean Witter Reynolds	(212) 392-2222
Kidder Peabody	(212) 510-3000
Merrill Lynch	(800) 637-7455
Paine Webber	(212) 713-2000
Prudential-Bache	(212) 214-1000
Shearson Lehman Hutton	(212) 298-2000

4. *Purchase stocks through discount brokerage firms.*

Discount brokerage firms will execute, buy, or sell orders for almost any type of security with the same efficiency as full-service brokers, but they are an option only for investors who make their own investment decision and take the time to monitor their portfolios. Some of the large discount firms offer money market accounts for idle cash, margin loans, IRA and other retirement accounts, and even some access to research reports.

Below are the toll-free telephone numbers of some independent discount brokers:

Charles Schwab and Co.	(800) 621-3700
	(CA) (800) 792-0988
Quick & Reilly	(800) 221-5220
	(NY) (800) 522-8712
Baker & Co.	(800) 321-1640
	(OH) (800) 362-2008
Pacific Brokerage	(800) 421-8395
	(CA) (800) 421-3214
StockCross	(800) 225-6196
	(MA) (800) 392-6104

T. Rowe Price Investment	(800) 322-5869
Vanguard Discount Brokerage	(800) 662-7447
Muriel Siebert & Co.	(800) 872-0711
W.T. Cabe & Co.	(800) 223-6555
Security Pacific	(800) 622-2040
Bull & Bear	(800) 262-5800
Wall Street Discount	(800) 221-4034
Waterhouse Securities	(800) 421-9563
Seaport Securities	(800) 221-9894
Wilmington Brokerage	(800) 345-7550
	(DE) (302) 651-1011

For a price comparison between discount brokers:

Booklet: *The Discount Brokerage Commission Survey: Stocks*
Cost: $19.95
Contains: Ranks 250 discount brokerage firms by commission charges. Includes addresses and telephone numbers
From: Mercer Financial Services, Inc.
80 Fifth Avenue, Suite 800
New York, NY 10011

For further information about using discount brokers:

Fact Sheet: *Better Business Bureau Advisory: Discount Brokers*
Cost: $2.00 plus self-addressed stamped envelope
From: Better Business Bureau of Metropolitan New York
257 Park Avenue South
New York, NY 10010
(212) 533-6200

5. *Purchase stocks through dividend reinvestment plans and cash purchase plans.*

Nearly 1,000 corporations offer stockholders the option of reinvesting their dividends in the purchase of additional shares. The advantages of these plans are:

- Most charge no commission or fees for the purchase of additional shares
- Many plans allow shareholders to make additional cash purchases of $12,000 to $120,000 per year without commissions
- A few plans offer a discount on the price of the stock

Dividend reinvestment and cash purchase plans make it possible for investors to make regular small purchases of stock without exorbitant commission charges. The advantages for investors with large sums to invest is substantial savings on commission. The primary disadvantage is lack of diversification provided by other regular investment plans, such as stock mutual funds.

You can obtain information on companies that offer dividend reinvestment plans from:

> **Book:** *Directory of Companies Offering Dividend Reinvestment Plans*
> **Cost:** $28.95
> **From:** Evergreen Enterprises
> P.O. Box 763
> Laurel, MD 20707

6. *Purchase or sell stocks privately.*

You can sell stocks to or purchase shares from another individual at no cost without using a broker. The procedure is:

- Seller obtains the actual stock certificates
- Seller signs the back of the certificates in the presence of a bank officer who will guarantee the signature
- Seller fills in the name, address, and Social Security number of the new owner on the back of the certificate
- Seller sends the certificates by registered mail to the transfer agent for the stock (gets address from the company)

- The transfer agent issues new certificates to the new owner

U.S. Government Mortgage-Backed Securities

Mortgage-backed certificates are backed by home mortgages and issued by the Government National Mortgage Association (GNMA, or Ginnie Mae). Ginnie Mae purchases home mortgages insured by the Federal Housing Authority and the Veterans Administrations, then sells them to individual investors and institutions. The monthly mortgage payments, which consist of both interest and principle, are passed through to the holders of GNMA certificates.

The advantages of GNMA certificates are:

- They are guaranteed by the U.S. government, making risk of default extremely low
- They pay interest rates 1% to 2% above U.S. Treasury securities
- They are traded on the secondary market, so they are liquid

The disadvantages of GNMA certificates are:

- Minimum purchase requirement is $25,000
- The interest paid is fully taxable
- The yield may change when interest rates fall and homeowners refinance at lower rates
- The monthly checks are not all the same
- When interest rates fall, the value of the certificates declines, producing a loss if they are sold on the secondary market

- Certificates must be purchased through brokerage firms, which charge a commission

Some of these disadvantages are eliminated by investing in mutual funds that invest in GNMA certificates, most of which charge no load, or sales fee.

High-Grade Corporate Bonds

Corporate bonds are loans from investors to corporations. Corporations issue two types:

- Secured, or senior bonds, which are backed by the value of real estate, equipment, or some other asset
- Unsecured, or junior bonds, which are backed only by the good faith of the corporation

The safest bonds, which are referred to as high-grade or investment-grade, are issued by financially stable, sound corporations. The financial industry depends primarily upon ratings of the safety of bonds issued by two firms, Standard & Poor's (S&P) and Moody's. Those ratings are:

	S & P	Moody's
Best quality	AAA	Aaa
High quality	AA	Aa
Upper medium	A	A
Medium	BBB	Baa
Speculative	BB	Ba
Low grade	B	B
Poor grade to default	CCC	Caa
Highly speculative default	CC	Ca
Lowest grade	C	C

Both services use + and − signs to indicate relative standings within each grade.

Bonds in the top three categories are considered high-grade bonds. Their advantages are:

- Risk of default is low
- They pay higher interest rates than U.S. Treasury securities
- Bonds of major corporations are traded on the New York Stock Exchange, thus offering liquidity
- Capital gains can be earned if bonds are sold when interest rates fall

The disadvantages of high-grade bonds are:

- Bond interest is fully taxable
- Interest is paid in cash, eliminating the benefits of compounding interest
- Capital losses can result if the bonds are sold before maturity at a time when interest rates have risen
- If interest rates fall, many bonds can be called, or redeemed before maturity by the corporation
- Bonds are purchased through brokerage firms, which charge commissions on the purchase
- Most experts recommend a portfolio of at least $100,000 to insure adequate diversity

Mutual funds that invest in high-grade corporate bonds are the best way to obtain diversity without a very high investment.

For more information on bonds:

Booklet: *How the Bond Market Works*
Cost: Free
From: Public Relations
Standard & Poor's Corporation
25 Broadway
New York, NY 10004

Municipal Bonds

Municipal bonds are issued by state and local governments to raise funds for a wide variety of purposes, from building roads to constructing a new sports stadium. Prior to the passage of the 1986 Tax Reform Act, interest paid on all municipal bonds was exempt from federal income tax, as well as state and local income tax if you lived in the jurisdiction that issued the bonds. The Tax Reform Act, however, created three basic classes of municipal bonds:

- General obligation bonds, which are issued for public purposes, such as building roads, schools, and government buildings. These remain fully tax exempt.
- Industrial development bonds, which are issued to finance plants or industrial parks leased to private companies. These are tax-exempt only for investors who are not subject to the federal alternative minimum tax.
- Taxable municipals, which are issued for what Congress considered nonessential activities, such as the construction of sports facilities. The interest from these bonds is taxable on federal returns, but is normally exempt from state and local taxes.

As with other bonds, the interest paid on the bond depends on the level of risk involved. Unlike other bonds, the interest rate also reflects the tax benefits involved—bonds that are exempt from federal, state, and local taxes pay lower interest than bonds exempt from just state and local taxes.

The higher your tax rate, the more benefit from earning federally tax exempt interest, as the table below demonstrates:

Tax-exempt yield (%)	Equivalent taxable yield for tax brackets		
	15%	28%	33%
5	5.88%	6.94%	7.46%
6	7.06%	8.33%	8.96%
7	8.24%	9.72%	10.42%
8	9.41%	11.11%	11.94%
9	10.59%	12.50%	13.43%

The benefit is even greater for bonds paying interest exempt from any state and local income taxes. For example, a couple earning $50,000 in New York City would have to find a taxable investment earning 11% to equal their net from a triple tax-exempt bond paying 7%.

Both Moody's and Standard & Poor's rate municipal bonds on the same scale they use for corporate bonds; that is, AAA or Aaa to C. Generally, the higher the bond is rated, the lower the interest rate.

One way to invest in municipal bonds is to purchase shares in a mutual fund that invests in these securities.

The second way to invest in municipal bonds is to purchase individual issues from a broker. Less sophisticated investors may profit from dealing with a reputable brokerage firm.

A very informative, easy to read guide to municipal bonds is:

Booklet: *An Investor's Guide to Tax Exempt Securities*
Cost: $0.45
From: Public Securities Association
40 Broad Street, 12th Floor
New York, NY 10004
(212) 809-7000

Zero Coupon Bonds

A zero coupon bond is a bond that pays no annual interest but is sold at a steep discount from the face value at which it can be redeemed at maturity. For example, a zero coupon bond that pays 12% interest and can be redeemed for $1,000 in 30 years sells for just $31 today.

The advantages of zero coupon bonds are:

- They lock in a fixed rate of interest for a specific period of time
- They are ideal for meeting a long-term financial goal, such as retirement, college expenses, or purchase of a vacation home
- Treasury-issued zeros are virtually risk-free
- Municipal zeros are exempt from federal taxation

The disadvantages of zero coupon bonds are:

- Although you don't receive interest annually, the IRS requires you to pay taxes annually on the bond's yearly increase in value
- Purchasers must pay a commission that can run from 1.5% to 5%
- Except for Treasury-issued products, zeros carry a higher risk than regular bonds of the same type—for example, if a corporation defaults on a 20-year bond after 10 years, the holders of zero coupon bonds would receive nothing, while holders of regular bonds would have received interest payments for 10 years
- Since most people buy zeros to hold to maturity, there is not a large secondary market, making them a relatively illiquid investment
- Since interest rates are fixed, zeros do not provide protection against inflation

Zero coupon bonds are most attractive as a worry-free investment for tax-deferred retirement accounts, such as IRAs, because investors don't have to worry about paying taxes annually on interest they don't receive. Tax-exempt municipal zero coupon bonds are also an option for saving for a special expense, such as purchase of a retirement home or contributing to a child's education. Zero coupon bonds are not appropriate investments for people who need current income.

For more information:

Booklet: *An Introduction to Zero Coupon Bonds*
Cost: Free
From: Thomson McKinnon Securities Inc.
Financial Square (16th Floor)
New York, NY 10005

Convertible Bonds

Convertible bonds are financial products that combine features of both common stocks and corporate bonds. Like bonds, convertibles pay a fixed interest rate for a set period of time. In addition, convertibles give the buyer the right to convert the bond into a fixed number of shares of the company's stock at a set price any time. That gives the buyer the chance to earn capital gains if the price of the stock rises.

The advantages of convertible bonds are:

- They offer higher income than common stock dividends
- They offer the potential for capital gains
- They generally fluctuate less in price than either common stock or corporate bonds
- They are actively traded and are very liquid

- Convertible bondholders have priority over stockholders should a company declare bankruptcy

The disadvantages of convertible bonds are:

- They pay lower interest than straight bonds
- They normally sell for a premium over the value of the common stock to which the bond can be converted
- Commissions must be paid to buy and sell convertibles
- Capital gains and interest are fully taxable
- Most convertibles have provisions allowing the company to force bondholders to cash them in when stock prices rise dramatically, limiting potential profits

Most financial experts consider convertible bonds a relatively conservative long-term investment, suitable for tax-deferred retirement accounts.

For more information:

Booklet: *Understanding Convertibles*
Cost: Free
From: New York Stock Exchange
11 Wall Street
New York, NY 10005

Annuities

In return for a certain premium, an insurance company contracts to pay you a set monthly amount from the time of your retirement until your death. This is an annuity. In the past decade, insurance companies have created a wide variety of new annuity products. These prod-ucts fall into one of two general types, each of which have a very different objective: deferred annuities and immediate annuities.

A deferred annuity is a form of retirement saving. Money is paid to an insurance company in one of three ways:

- A "single premium," or one lump-sum payment
- Installment payments over a specified period of time
- Variable payments over a period of years

The money, minus any sales charges and fees, is invested by the insurance company.

The advantages of deferred annuities are:

- All interest and capital gains earned are tax-deferred until they're withdrawn
- The risk of loss of principle with a financially stable insurance company is low
- Most contracts allow borrowing against the funds in the annuity
- In the event of your death, the funds in the annuity are passed directly to your beneficiary without going through probate

The disadvantages of deferred annuities are:

- Purchasing an annuity requires payment of sales charges and/or annual management fees
- Substantial penalties are normally charged for withdrawing funds, especially in the first 7 years
- The IRS requires payment of a 10% penalty on all funds withdrawn before age 59.5

An immediate annuity provides a certain monthly payment for every $1,000 invested. The initial sum invested in the annuity is a lump sum withdrawn from a deferred annuity, an IRA, another pension plan, or profits from the sale of a house or other substantial assets.

When you purchase an immediate annuity, you have to choose between four basic types of payments:

- Straight life provides a guaranteed monthly payment until your death. This option provides the highest monthly payments but leaves nothing for your heirs.

- Installment-refund annuities guarantee that you or your heirs will receive a sum at least equal to the amount of your initial investment. Once you've received monthly payments totaling your initial investment, your heirs receive nothing when you die.

- Period-certain annuities guarantee that you or your heirs will receive monthly payments for a certain period of time, normally from 5 to 20 years. The longer the guaranteed period, the lower the monthly payments.

- Joint and survivor annuities guarantee payments as long as you or your spouse live. An annuity that guarantees the same monthly payment for the life of your spouse after you die has the lowest monthly payment of any annuity.

The advantages of immediate annuities are:

- Guaranteed lifetime income, which eliminates the possibility of outliving one's savings

- Freedom from responsibility of managing one's money

- Except for straight-life annuities, your annuity passes to your beneficiaries or spouse without going through probate

The disadvantages of immediate annuities are:

- They offer no protection against inflation

- They generally pay a lower return than you could obtain by investing your own funds in secure investments, such as U.S. Treasury securities

- Income is taxable

- They are not liquid, because it is impossible to withdraw your principle

- There is a small risk of loss of principle if the insurance company goes bankrupt

For more information on annuities:

Booklet: *What You Should Know About Annuities*
Cost: Free
From: American Council of Life Insurance
1001 Pennsylvania Avenue, NW
Washington, DC 20004
(202) 624-2000

SPECULATIVE INVESTMENTS

Speculative investments offer the potential of very high return along with moderate to high risk. As such, they are appropriate only for so-phisticated investors with extra money—money that they do not and will not need to meet forseeable expenses and emergencies.

Real Estate Investment Trusts (REITs)

A real estate investment trust is a company that pools investors' money to purchase real estate or mortgages. Initially, a limited number of shares in a new REIT are offered directly to the public. After the initial offering, the shares are bought and sold either on a stock exchange or over the counter.

There are two basic types of REITs:

- Equity REITs invest directly in real estate. Some specialize in a specific kind of investment, such as multi-family housing, shopping centers, or commercial office buildings; others may invest in real estate only in a specific area of the country; still others may be more diverse. The income received by the company comes from rents collected and profits from real estate sold.
- Mortgage REITs purchase existing loans outstanding on housing or commercial real estate. The income received comes from repayment of the principle and interest on the mortgages.

The advantages of investing in REITs are:

- REITs offer the opportunity for moderate to high current income, especially because their incomes are not taxable
- Equity REITs offer the possibility of capital gains, making them hedges against inflation
- REIT shares are bought and sold, making them much more liquid than real estate
- Investing in REITs can require a small initial investment

The disadvantages of investing in REITs are:

- REIT shares carry a moderate to high risk of loss of principle
- Commissions must be paid to a brokerage firm to buy and sell REIT shares
- Income from REIT shares can fluctuate substantially as interest rates and the value of real estate rises and falls
- Dividends and capital gains are taxable as ordinary income. In some cases, however, part of the dividends may be considered return of capital invested and may not be taxable

Precious Metals

For years, precious metals, such as gold and silver, have provided protection against economic ravages, such as inflation, war, revolution, and currency collapse. Today, gold and silver are solid investments, but primarily in third-world countries with very unstable economies and political systems. However, many experts recommend that investors with large portfolios put a small percentage of their assets into precious metals as a hedge against rapid inflation, a serious depression, or other economic catastrophes.

The advantages of investing in gold and silver are:

- Protection against economic catastrophes
- Protection against very high inflation
- Gold and silver coins can be a rewarding hobby, as well as an investment
- The possibility of capital gains

The disadvantages of investing in gold and silver are:

- Gold and silver return no current income in the form of interest or dividends
- Buying precious metals involves paying commissions, as well as storage fees, insurance, and other expenses
- Prices fluctuate unpredictably, with a high risk of loss of principle
- Precious metals are not very liquid, meaning it may take time to find a buyer
- Scams and swindles involve investments in precious metals, including mining stocks, probably steal a larger portion of the estimated $40 billion in annual losses than any other kind of con game

For more information about purchasing precious metals:

Organization: Industry Council for Tangible Assets
(202) 783-3500
Cost: Free
Service: Provides information about dealers in precious metals

Booklet: *An Introduction to Investing in Gold*
Cost: Free
From: Gold Information Center
900 Third Avenue
New York, NY 10022
(212) 688-0474

Booklet: *How to Invest in Gold*
Cost: Free
From: The Gold Institute
1026 16th St., NW
Washington, DC 20036
(202) 783-0500

High Yield or "Junk" Bonds

The recent explosion in the number of corporate takeovers, mergers, and buyouts has been largely financed by the issuance of bonds that carry significantly higher risk but pay significantly higher yields (as much as 6% per year) than high-grade corporate bonds.

The risk involved in purchasing junk bonds makes them very speculative investments for individual investors. However, investors who can afford to assume high risk in exchange for high returns should consider purchasing the shares of professionally managed mutual funds that spread the risk by investing in a wide variety of junk bonds.

Futures

Originally designed to safeguard farmers against drastic swings in the prices of farm products, futures are contracts that lock in the current price at which a product would be bought or sold. In this way, the owner of a future is protected against unforeseeable rises or declines in the price of the product he or she wishes to buy or sell at some future date.

This practice of "hedging" through the buying and selling of future contracts has expanded to other types of products, such as:

- Precious metals (for example, a jeweler locks in the price of the gold needed for 6 months ahead so he or she can produce a catalog)
- Foreign currencies (for example, a firm that's just agreed to deliver a large order to a foreign customer a year from now may want to protect against a large drop in the value of that foreign currency)

- Financial futures (for example, a pension fund that must make fixed monthly payments might want to protect against a significant drop in interest rates)

What all hedgers have in common is that they actually have or will take possession of the products on which futures contracts are written, whether they be pork bellies, soy beans, bars of silver, foreign currencies, or U.S. Treasury bills. These hedgers, however, make up only a small portion of the people who buy and sell futures contracts. The majority of investors in futures contracts are "speculators" who are attempting to profit from their ability to predict the rise and fall in the prices of the products involved.

The advantages of futures trading are:

- A chance for very high capital gains
- Low initial margin requirements
- All profits are posted to the investor's account in cash at the end of each trading day
- Futures contracts are very liquid
- No interest must be paid on the difference between your margin payment and the total value of the futures contract

The disadvantages of futures trading are:

- Very high risk of loss of the initial investment or more
- Margin calls must be settled in cash at the end of each trading day
- Commissions must be paid to buy and sell futures contracts
- All profits are fully taxable

If you're interested in futures trading, you should first obtain the following publications:

Booklets: • *Basic Facts About Commodity Futures Trading*
• *Glossary of Trading Terms*
• *Spotter's Guide to Commodity Fraud*
• *Commodity Futures Trading Commission*
Cost: Free
From: Commodity Futures Trading Commission
2033 K Street, NW
Washington, DC 20581
(202) 254-8630

Booklets: • *Understanding Opportunities and Risks in Futures Trading*
• *Glossary of Futures Terms*
• *An Introduction to the National Futures Association*
Cost: Free
From: National Futures Association
200 W. Madison Street, Suite 1600
Chicago, IL 60606
(800) 621-3570 (Ex. IL)
(800) 572-9400 (IL)

Most of the commodity exchanges offer a variety of booklets and educational materials. The most elaborate is:

Kit: COMEX Educational Services Kit
Cost: Free
Contains: Numerous brochures and other materials on trading in precious metals
From: COMEX Marketing Department
Four World Trade Center
New York, NY 10048
(212) 938-2900

Information is also available from the following exchanges:

Exchange: Chicago Board of Trade
141 W. Jackson Blvd.
Chicago, IL 60604
(312) 435-3500

Exchange: Chicago Mercantile Exchange
30 S. Wacker Drive
Chicago, IL 60606
(312) 930-1000

Exchange: Chicago Rice and Cotton Exchange
141 W. Jackson Blvd.
Chicago, IL 60604
(312) 341-3078

Exchange: Kansas City Board of Trade
4800 Main Street, Suite 303
Kansas City, MO 64112
(816) 753-7500

Exchange: MidAmerica Commodity Exchange
141 W. Jackson Blvd.
Chicago, IL 60604
(312) 341-3000

Exchange: Minneapolis Grain Exchange
130 Grain Exchange
400 S. Fourth Street
Minneapolis, MN 55415
(612) 338-6212

Exchange: New York Futures Exchange
20 Broad Street, 10th Floor
New York, NY 10004
(212) 656-4949

Exchange: N.Y. Cotton Exchange
Four World Trade Center
New York, NY 10048
(212) 938-2650

Exchange: Coffee, Sugar, and Cocoa Exchange
Four World Trade Center
New York, NY 10048
(212) 938-2800

Exchange: N.Y. Mercantile Exchange
Four World Trade Center
New York, NY 10048
(212) 938-2222

Stock Options

A stock option is a financial product that is a cross between a common stock and a commodities future. In exchange for payment of a fee (a "premium"), you purchase the right to buy 100 shares of stock for a specified price (a "call") or sell 100 shares of stock for a specified price (a "put") for a specified period of time up to 9 months. For example, if you believe that the stock of a particular corporation, currently at $50 per share, is going to rise, you might purchase an option to buy 100 shares of the stock anytime in the next 9 months for a premium of $750. If the stock rises to $60 per share, you can exercise your option and make a profit of $250, or 33% on your original $750 (before commissions).

The advantages of stock options are:

- You can control a large amount of stock for a small investment
- Options are traded on the major exchanges and are very liquid
- If you sell a stock option on a stock you own, you receive income on the premium from the time of purchase

The disadvantages of stock options are:

- You have a high risk of losing your entire premium
- You earn no interest or dividends on your investment
- Income from option trading is fully taxable
- Your option declines in value as the expiration date approaches
- Trading in options requires very close attention to movement in the stock market
- Commissions to buy and sell options can significantly reduce profits

Warrants

A warrant is an option to purchase a specified number of shares of stock within a specified period of time. Unlike stock options, warrants are issued by the corporations themselves and have time limits that run from 5 years to perpetuity.

The advantages of warrants are:

- You control a large amount of stock with an investment of a relatively small amount of money
- The warrants of about 150 companies are actively traded, making them somewhat liquid
- Warrants offer excellent capital gains potential

The disadvantages of warrants are:

- Warrants pay no current income
- All of the initial investment may be lost if the warrant expires
- Warrant holders have no claim upon a company's assets in the event of bankruptcy or reorganization
- Income from sales of warrants or execution of stock purchase options are fully taxable
- Commissions must be paid to buy or sell warrants

MUTUAL FUNDS

"Just as there is no perfect person or painting or poem, so there is no perfect investment. But the one that comes closest for most people is the mutual fund."

Marshall Loeb
Managing Editor, Fortune Magazine

A mutual fund is a company that pools the money of a large number of investors to buy and sell stocks, bonds, bank certificates of deposit, or other securities under the supervision of professional management. Although mutual funds have existed for a century, the explosive growth of the industry has come only in the last 15 years. Between 1977 and 1987, total assets of American mutual funds soared from $51 billion to $716 billion.

Mutual funds have attracted significant investment dollars for the following reasons:

1. *Diversification.* Individual funds invest in as many as 1,000 different securities, limiting investment risk by reducing the danger of a steep decline in the price of one, two, even a dozen securities.

Large companies that offer a large number of funds with different investment objectives are called mutual fund families. These families offer investors the valuable service of transferring money from one fund to another with a telephone call, making it easy to diversify investment dollars between funds with different objectives.

2. *Professional management.* Today's investment markets are very complex and volatile, requiring the kind of professional management that only a handful of people with substantial assets can afford on their own.

3. *Liquidity.* You can redeem your shares easily at any time by writing a letter or, in many cases, making a telephone call. A sub-

stantial number of funds allow you to withdraw money by writing a check drawn against the value of your shares. Many large families of funds will automatically withdraw a specified sum of money from your bank account every month to purchase shares and will transfer money directly into your bank account from sale of shares. Most families of funds also allow you to transfer funds from one fund into another with a telephone call.

4. *Easy record keeping.* Mutual fund companies handle all details of security transactions, regularly distribute dividends and other profits, provide accurate year-end summaries for tax purposes, and provide toll-free telephone numbers to answer investors' questions or handle problems.

Some excellent introductions to mutual funds are:

Pamphlets: • *What Is a Mutual Fund?*
• *A Translation: Turning Invest-ment-ese into Investment Ease.*

Book: *The Mutual Fund Fact Book*
Cost: Free
From: Investment Company Institute
1600 M Street, NW
Washington, DC 20036
(202) 293-7700

Pamphlet: *What Is a Mutual Fund?*
Cost: Free
From: Fidelity Investments
82 Devonshire Street
Boston, MA 02109
(800) 544-6666

Resource List: *1990 Resource List*
Cost: Free
Contains: 4-page list of books, directories, newsletters, and other sources of information on mutual funds

From: Mutual Fund Education Alliance
1900 Erie, Suite 120
Kansas City, MO 64116
(816) 471-1454

The Costs of Investing in a Mutual Fund

Most mutual funds are called "open-end funds," because they place no limit on the amount of money they will accept. Almost all of these funds do have a minimum investment that they will accept. These minimums range from $10 to $10,000, but the most common range is $250 to $1,000.

Every dollar of your investment, however, doesn't go to work for you. Mutual fund companies are in business to make a profit. Therefore, they have to charge you for the services they provide. Basically, these charges fall into two general types:

1. *Sales charges.* Mutual funds can be purchased in two ways:

   • Through a stockbroker, financial planner, or other salesperson
   • Directly from the mutual fund company by telephone or mail

Funds that use salesmen to sell their products have to pay them a commission that comes out of your pocket. This commission is called a "load," and can be as much as 8.5% of your investment. Funds that sell directly to the public either charge no sales commission ("no load") or a commission between 1% and 3.5% ("low-load").

It is important to remember that a load is a charge for the advice and services involved in selling you your shares—none of it goes to the management of the mutual fund. Numerous studies have shown that paying a load in no way guarantees better performance. Lists of the top-performing mutual funds in every category include no-load, as well as load funds. Most experts agree that the sound advice of a qualified broker or financial planner is worth paying for, but only if you plan on retaining shares in the recommended funds for at least 1 to 3 years.

Investors who want to retain the flexibility of changing from one type of fund to another should avoid funds that charge loads. Some mutual fund companies have found two other ways to recoup the expense of advertising and marketing their products. One is annually charging shareholders a certain percentage of the assets of the fund, normally 0.5% to 1%, to cover marketing expenses. This charge, called a "12B 1 plan," is listed in the fund's prospectus.

Another method used by some funds is charging investors a fee to redeem their shares. This charge, called a "back load," can be as high as 6% of the total sales price.

2. *Management fees.* Every mutual fund charges shareholders an annual fee for managing their money. These fees vary between 0.5% and 3% of the assets of the fund. As with loads, studies have found no reliable correlation between the percentage of annual fee and the performance of the mutual fund.

How to Select a Mutual Fund

With over 2,000 mutual funds to choose from, the prospect of selecting the right fund for you may seem overwhelming. But shopping for a mutual fund will become much less overwhelming if you become familiar with the various categories used by the mutual fund industry to describe the different kinds of funds available.

- Aggressive growth funds: These funds, also called maximum capital gains funds, invest in common stocks with a high potential for rapid growth, especially small emerging companies.
  - Characteristics: high capital gains potential, low or no current income, high risk

- Growth funds: These funds invest in well-established companies thought to have long-term growth potential, instead of investing for current income.
  - Characteristics: moderate to high long-term capital gains potential, low current income, moderate to high risk

- Growth and Income funds: Also called equity income funds, these funds invest in companies that pay relatively high current dividends and also have long-term growth potential.
  - Characteristics: moderate long-term capital gains potential, low to moderate current income, moderate risk

- International funds: International equity funds can provide valuable diversification in a growth portfolio.
  - Characteristics: moderate to high capital gains potential, low current income, moderate to very high risk

- Sector funds: These funds invest only in companies in a specific industry, such as high-tech, capital goods, or biotechnology companies.
  - Characteristics: moderate to high capital gains potential, low current income, high to very high risk

- Precious metal funds: These funds specialize in the stocks of companies that produce gold, silver, or other precious metals.
  - Characteristics: moderate to high capital gains potential, low to moderate income, high to very high risk

- Balanced funds: These funds divide their investments roughly between stocks and bonds.
  - Characteristics: moderate capital gains potential, moderate current income, moderate risk
- Money market funds: These funds invest in very short-term financial instruments that carry so little risk that the per share value of the fund always remains fixed at $1.
  - Characteristics: no capital gains potential, moderate to high current income, very low risk
- U.S. government bond funds: These funds invest in U.S. Treasury bonds, and their rate of return is higher than that of money market funds. The interest paid by some U.S. government bond funds is exempt from state and local taxes in some states. Although Treasury bills are a totally safe investment, the per share value of the fund can rise and fall with interest rates. The volatility of a specific fund depends on the type of Treasury securities purchased by the fund: short-term bond funds pay the lowest interest and have the least volatility; intermediate bond funds pay higher interest and have more volatility; long-term bond funds pay the highest interest and have the most volatility.
  - Characteristics: low capital gains potential, moderate to high current income, low risk
- U.S. government mortgage-backed securities funds: These funds invest in packaged mortgages totally guaranteed by the U.S. government and issued by such agencies as the Government National Mortgage Association (Ginnie Mae) and the Federal National Mort-

gage Association (Freddie Mac). Because mortgages are long-term debt instruments, these funds have higher returns and more volatility than funds that invest in short- and intermediate-term U.S. Treasury bills.
  - Characteristics: low capital gains potential, moderate to high current income, low risk
- High-grade corporate bond funds: These funds invest in the bonds of very stable corporations with high credit ratings. They pay higher interest rates than funds that invest in bonds guaranteed by the U.S. government, and their per share price is more volatile.
  - Characteristics: low capital gains potential, high current income, low to moderate risk
- High-yield corporate bond funds: These funds invest primarily in what are called "junk bonds," bonds issued by less stable, creditworthy companies.
  - Characteristics: low capital gains potential, very high current income, moderate to high risk
- Tax-exempt bond funds: These funds invest solely in municipal bonds that pay interest exempt from federal income taxes. Some tax-exempt funds invest only in municipal bonds issued in one state, with the interest they pay exempt from state and local, as well as federal taxes. These funds range in risk from very safe tax-exempt money market funds to much more risky high-yield tax-exempt funds. In every category, these funds pay significantly lower interest rates than nontax-exempt funds.
  - Characteristics: low capital gains potential, moderate current income for investors in higher tax brackets, low risk

For more information on the types of mutual funds and the specific funds in each category:

Book: *Guide to Mutual Funds*
Cost: $2.00
Contains: 16-page explanation of mutual funds, plus a 130-page listing of mutual funds by investment objective. Issued annually. Listing includes:
- Name, address, and telephone number
- Year fund started
- Total assets of fund
- Minimum initial investment
- How shares are sold

From: Investment Company Institute
1600 M Street, NW
Washington, DC 20036
(202) 293-7700

Book: *Investor's Guide and Mutual Fund Directory*
Cost: $5.00 postpaid
Contains: 24-page explanation of mutual funds prepared by the Mutual Fund Education Alliance, an industry association for no-load and low-load funds. Also contains a 55-page listing by investment objective of over 400 no-load and low-load funds. Issued annually. Includes:
- Name, address, and telephone number
- Statement of investment objective
- Year fund started
- Total assets of fund
- Minimum purchase requirements
- Redemption procedures
- List of features, such as check writing, automatic reinvestment of dividends, telephone exchange, etc.

From: The Mutual Fund Education Alliance
1900 Erie, Suite 120
Kansas City, MO 64116
(816) 471-1454

Periodical: *Forbes* Magazine Annual Mutual Fund Issue
Issued: Every September
Cost: $3.95
Contains: The most valuable feature is a grading (A+ to F) of the performance of funds in up and down markets. Other information includes:
- Average annual return over 10 years
- Return for previous 12 months
- Total assets of fund
- Change in assets in last 12 months
- Maximum sales charge
- Annual expenses per $100 invested

Periodical: *Changing Times* Mutual Fund Issue
Issued: Every October
Cost: $2.50
Contains: Ranks funds by 1-year performance and lists 1-, 5-, and 10-year performance. Most valuable feature is a rating of the risk involved in each fund, on a scale of 1 to 9

Periodical: *Business Week* Mutual Fund Issue
Issued: Every February
Cost: $3.50
Contains: Ranks funds by 1-year performance, and lists performance over 5 and 10 years

Annual Directory: *Investor's Guide to No-Load Mutual Funds*
Cost: $19.95 (free with membership in the American Association of Individual Investors)
Contains: Useful information and advice on choosing a mutual fund, with detailed information on the performance of 300 no-load funds
From: American Association of Individual Investors
625 North Michigan Avenue

Chicago, IL 60611
(312) 280-0170

Annual Directory: *The Handbook for No-Load Fund Investors*
145 Palisades Av.
Dobbs Ferry, NY 10522
(914) 693-7420
Cost: $38.00
Contains: Very informative guide to choosing and monitoring no-load funds. Includes 1-, 5-, and 10-year performance records of 1,000 no-load funds

Annual Directory: *Donoghue's Mutual Fund Almanac*
Cost: $23.00
Contains: Includes 1-, 5-, and 10-year performance data for more than 1,800 mutual funds. Includes performance ratings
From: Donoghue Organization
P.O. Box 540
Holliston, MA 01746
(508) 429-5930

Annual Directory: *Wiesenberger's Investment Companies Annual*
Cost: $375.00
Contains: The "bible" of information on the performance of over 2,300 mutual funds. Too expensive to buy, but worth consulting at your library

From: Wiesenberger Investment Companies Service
210 South St
Boston, MA 02111
(617) 423-2020

How to Resolve a Problem with a Mutual Fund Company

All investment companies that manage mutual funds are regulated by the federal Securities and Exchange Commission (SEC). All brokers, financial planners, and others who act as representatives in the sales of mutual fund shares are also regulated by the SEC.

If you have a problem or complaint about any aspect of mutual fund investment that can't be resolved by the investment company and/or your broker, you can register your complaint with:

Office of Consumer Affairs
Securities and Exchange Commission
450 5th St., NW
(Mail Stop 2-6)
Washington, DC 20549
(202) 272-7440
(202) 272-7065 (TTY-Voice Telecommunications for the Deaf)
This office will refer you to the regional office nearest you.

CHAPTER 7

CHOOSING THE RIGHT INVESTMENT PROFESSIONALS

WHEN YOU INVEST MONEY, YOU should take the time to understand the basics of investing, to become familiar with investment products, and to monitor your investments. However, that doesn't mean that you might not profit from hiring professional advisors to help you make financial and investment decisions. Among the most important of those advisors are financial planners, stockbrokers, and investment managers.

FINANCIAL PLANNERS

A financial planner assists clients in developing financial strategies to achieve short-term or long-term investment goals, including retirement and estate planning. To date, most good financial planners have been trained as accountants, lawyers, bankers, insurance agents, or stock brokers. Some colleges now have formal programs in financial planning.

Unfortunately, there are no statutory educational or professional requirements, testing programs, or licensing procedures for financial planners, as there are for attorneys, physicians, real estate brokers, and insurance brokers. That means that anyone can use the title "financial planner," no matter how little training they may have had.

The result is, in some cases, fraud and abuse. Until the financial planning industry and state regulatory agencies can define and implement formal licensing procedures, consumers have to do their own investigation before hiring a financial planner.

The Role of a Financial Planner

A financial planner can help you in the following ways:

- Evaluate your financial status, including the quality of your investments, your retirement planning, your tax situation, and your estate planning

- Help you define your long- and short-term financial goals
- Identify areas in which you may need assistance, such as increasing the funds available for retirement, increasing the return on savings and investment, or adding insurance protection
- Prepare a detailed written financial plan that you fully understand
- Help you implement the plan choosing investments and, where necessary, obtaining the specialized service of lawyers, accountants, or other professionals
- Review and update your financial plan on a regular basis

How Financial Planners Are Paid

Financial planners are compensated in one of three ways:

- Commissions on recommended investments, such as insurance policies, mutual funds, and other securities. You should be very cautious in following the advice of a commissions-only planner—the primary purpose of some is to steer you into high-priced, high-commission investments.
- Fee plus commissions. These planners charge an initial fee to draw up a master plan, then add commissions if investments are made through them. Some of these planners deduct part of the commissions from the original fee. Again, some of these planners steer clients exclusively toward high-commission products.
- Fees-only. These planners are the most expensive, generally ranging from

$1,000 to $7,000 for the original plan. Some charge on an hourly basis to develop the plan and monitor investments.

Experts advise that your total annual cost for both commissions and fees should not exceed 1% to 2% of the total amount of you have to invest.

How to Find a Financial Planner

Although about 250,000 people in the United States use the title financial planner, only about one in five has sought to validate his or her professionalism by meeting the requirements for certification by and membership in one or more of five professional registries. These include:

Organization: Institute of Certified Financial Planners
2 Denver Highlands
10065 East Harvard Avenue
Denver, CO 80231
(800) 282-7526
(303) 751-7600
Designation: C.F.P. (Certified Financial Planner)
Requirements: Certified Financial Planners must have:
- Completed a 2-year, six-part program conducted by the College for Financial Planning. The six parts are:
  - Introduction to financial planning
  - Risk management
  - Investments
  - Tax planning and management
  - Retirement planning and employee benefits
  - Estate planning
- Pass extensive tests

- Meet ethical standards set and enforced by the International Board of Standards and Practices for Certified Financial Planners
- Take at least 30 hours of continuing education instruction each year to keep up to date

Publications:
- *First Steps to Financial Security: A Guide for Selecting a Certified Financial Planner*
- *Financial Planning: Past, Present, and Future* (Both free)

Referral services: Will provide free list of Certified Financial Planners in your area

Organization: American College
270 Bryn Mawr Avenue
Bryn Mawr, PA 19010
(215) 526-1000
Designation: Ch.F.C. (Chartered Financial Consultant)
Requirements: To obtain the designation, individuals must:
- Have 3 years experience as a planner
- Pass 10 2-hour examinations

Referral service: Will provide free list of Chartered Financial Consultants in your area

Organization: International Association for Financial Planning
2 Concourse Parkway
Atlanta, GA 30328
(404) 395-1605
Designation: R.F.P.P. (Registry of Financial Planning Practitioners)
Requirements: To obtain the designation, individuals must:
- Have financial planning as their major vocation
- Must have a degree related to planning
- Have at least 3 years experience
- Submit references from five clients

- Pass a 4-hour written exam
- Participate in continuing education

Referral: Publishes a Directory of Registry Financial Planners ($2.50). Will provide free referral to practitioners in your area
NOTE: This association has 24,000 members, but only 1,000 have earned the designation R.F.P.P.

Organization: International Association of Registered Financial Planners
4127 W. Cypress Street
Tampa, FL 33607
(813) 875-7352
Designation: R.F.P. (Registered Financial Planner)
Requirements: To earn the designation, individuals must:
- Have a college degree in economics, business, law, or another subject related to financial planning
- Have passed either a state exam to become an insurance agent or the National Association of Securities Dealers securities exam
- Have 4 years experience
- Participate in continuing education programs

Referral: Will send the names of three R.F.P.'s in your area upon receipt of a self-addressed stamped envelope

Organization: National Association of Personal Financial Advisors
1130 Lake Cook Road, Suite 105
Buffalo Grove, IL 60089
(800) 366-2732
(708) 537-7722
Designation: None
Requirements: Members must:
- Have education related to financial planning
- Must meet continuing education requirement
- Must charge clients fees only, not commissions

Publications: Brochure explaining fee-only planning and a disclosure form to fill out for a prospective planner (Free)

Referral: Will provide names, educational backgrounds, and years of experience for members in your area

In addition to referrals from the above organizations, you should also ask for referrals from your lawyer, accountant, credit counselor, or friends with similar financial situations. When you review the backgrounds of all the referrals, you may find that they present one or more of the following additional credentials:

- C.F.A. (Chartered Financial Analysts), signifying that the person has passed three very rigorous examinations covering a broad range of investment topics. Successful candidates spend an average of 450 hours studying for the exam, and they must meet rigid ethical standards

- C.L.U. (Chartered Life Underwriter), signifying that the person has completed course work, passed examinations, and acquired the experience necessary to earn this designation as a highly qualified insurance agent. This designation is granted by American College, which designates the Ch.F.C.

- M.S.F.S. (Master of Sciences in Financial Services), signifying considerable course work at the American College over and above that necessary to earn the Ch.F.C.

- J.D. (Juris Doctor), signifying an attorney

- C.P.A. (Certified Public Accountant), a highly trained accountant who has passed very rigorous examinations

- Registered Investment Advisor. Any person who provides advice on the purchase of specific securities must register with the Securities and Exchange Commission. Such registration filters out individuals with criminal records or past violations of securities regulations, but it doesn't indicate any experience or skill.

- Reg. Rep. (Registered Representative), signifying that the individual has passed extensive examinations that allow him or her to act as a broker of securities

For more information about selecting a financial planner:

Pamphlet: *What You Should Know About Financial Planners*

Cost: Free

From: New York State Department of Law Office of Public Information
120 Broadway
New York, NY 10271

Booklet: *Money Matters: How to Talk to and Select: Financial Planners, Lawyers, Tax Preparers, Real Estate Brokers* (D12380)

Cost: Free

From: AARP
1909 K Street, NW
Washington, DC 20049

Study: Financial Planning Abuse: A Growing Problem

Cost: Free

From: Consumer Federation of America
1424 16th Street, NW, Suite 604
Washington, DC 20036
(202) 389-6121

How to Resolve a Problem with Your Financial Planner

Although the financial planning industry is not fully regulated, there are a number of organizations and agencies that may have jurisdiction over your specific complaint. Among them are:

- The organization(s) that certify your financial planner. These organizations require that their members meet certain ethical and other standards, and all will attempt to mediate disputes.

- Your state's securities agency. In most states, financial planners who make specific investment recommendations must be registered as investment advisors. If your dispute involves specific investment recommendations, send your complaint to your state's securities agency. You can obtain the address and telephone number by looking in the telephone directory under your state government listing.

- Your state's consumer affairs agency (see listings, pages 443–452) and your local Better Business Bureau (see listings, pages 452–459) will attempt to mediate your dispute. If they feel that fraud or other illegal activity is involved, they will tell you how to proceed.

STOCK BROKERS

A stock broker helps you meet your investment objectives by:

- Assisting in the selection of securities
- Handling the purchase and sale of securities
- Monitoring your investments and assisting you in making the decision to sell

A stock broker makes his or her money from commissions on the purchase or sale of securities, and this commission is the same whether you lose or gain from the investment. Many investors find that the advice and service provided by a capable, reputable broker is well worth the cost of these commissions. Over the long run, a stock broker is only successful if his or her clients make money, increasing the number of their investments and recommending him or her to their friends.

How to Find and Work with a Stock Broker

It's not easy to find the right broker, but with a little time and effort you should be able to establish a good relationship with the right person. Here's our advice:

1. *Ask for recommendations for brokers with the knowledge and experience to help you meet your financial goals.*

   You might get recommendations from friends, co-workers, your lawyer, your accountant, your banker, your financial planner, or your tax preparer. But don't make a decision solely on the basis of recommendations.

2. *If recommendations don't produce enough names, write a letter to the branch manager of one or more brokerage offices.*

   If you simply walk into a brokerage office or call, you will probably be assigned to the "broker of the day," normally one of the newest and least experienced brokers at the firm. You'll get better results with a letter to the branch manager that outlines your objectives and the amount you have to invest, and then asks for a referral to the most appropriate broker in the firm.

3. *Call the brokerage firms who employ the brokers you're considering to ask if:*

- The firm is a member of one or more stock exchanges. The exchanges, such as the New York Stock Exchange, have financial requirements for members, scrutinize the conduct of member firms, and provide assistance in settling disputes.
- The firm is a member of the National Association of Securities Dealers (NASD). Every firm that sells securities must be a member of the NASD, which adopts and enforces securities laws and ethical standards.
- The firm is a member of the Securities Investor Protection Corporation (SICP). The SICP is a private nonprofit corporation that insures investors portfolios up to $500,000 in securities and $100,000 in uninvested cash in the event the brokerage firm becomes insolvent. (Note: The SICP does not insure against a loss of money invested.)
- The firm carries insurance above the SICP limit. Some brokerage firms carry additional insurance of up to $10 million per account.

While many excellent brokerage firms do not hold seats on a major exchange, you should be cautious about investing with brokers at firms that are not members of NASD and SICP.

4. *Arrange an interview with each broker.*

Ask the broker:

- How long he or she has been in business and how long he or she has been with the firm. Incompetent or dishonest brokers generally don't last a long time, especially with one firm.
- Discuss your investment objectives and ask about the kind of return you're likely to receive. Avoid brokers who promise unrealistic or extravagant results.
- Ask for a list of fees and commissions. Also ask about discounts—some full-service firms authorize brokers to give small discounts to any client that asks. Most give discounts based on the volume of securities transacted.
- Ask for several references from clients with investment objective similar to yours.

Also pay attention to the questions the broker asks you. Beware of a broker who doesn't take the time to get complete information about your income, net worth, financial obligations, tax situation, and investment goals.

5. *Check the references and verify the broker's background and experience through the National Association of Securities Dealers.*

Every broker must be registered with the Central Registration Depository administered by this brokerage industry organization. Every broker's file includes:

- The broker's employment history
- Record of any disciplinary proceedings against the broker by state regulators or the brokerage industry

- Information about nonbusiness-related criminal convictions

To obtain information about a broker:

Form: Information Request Form
Cost: Two background checks every 3 months are free; additional are $20.00 per request
To obtain form: NASD Public Disclosure Program
P.O. Box 9401

Gaithersburg, MD 20898
(301) 590-6500

For more information on selecting a broker:

Brochure: *Tips on Selecting a Stockbroker*
Cost: Free, with self-addressed stamped envelope
From: Council of Better Business Bureaus
4200 Wilson Blvd.
Arlington, VA 22203
(703) 276-0100

INVESTMENT MANAGERS AND ADVISERS

Many people with sizable amounts to invest—generally, a minimum of $50,000—choose to turn over the management of their portfolios to an investment manager or advisor. These managers may be individuals, large firms, the trust department of a bank, or a special unit of a brokerage firm. Normally, managers are granted the authority to buy and sell securities on behalf of the client. Their compensation is annual fees which range from 1% to 2% of the total assets of smaller accounts to 0.5% to 1% of the total assets of larger accounts. This fee is in addition to brokerage commissions and fees connected with buying and selling securities.

Referrals from lawyers, accountants, stockbrokers, financial planners, and other professionals are an excellent way to begin. If you have a large portfolio, you can obtain a list of managers from:

Investment Counsel Association of America
20 Exchange Place
New York, NY 10005
(212) 344-0999

For investors with over $100,000, another option is to hire a consultant or "talent scout,"

a professional whose job is to match your investment objectives with a competent, appropriate investment manager. Two associations that will provide referrals to talent scouts, who have met rigorous professional standards, are:

- Institute for Investment Management Consultants
P.O. Box 6123
Scottsdale, AZ 85261

- Investment Management Consultants Association
10200 E. Girard, Suite 340C
Denver, CO 80231
(303) 337-2424

When you meet with prospective managers, you should:

- Ask for detailed results of all money managed over at least 5 years, in order to judge overall performance in up and down markets
- Obtain complete fee information, as well as the details of brokerage arrangements used by the manager

- References to at least three customers with similar investment objectives and assets who have been clients for at least 2 years
- Ask how available the manager is for consultation and how frequently you meet for formal portfolio reviews
- Obtain sample portfolios appropriate for your investment objectives

After you've met with an investment manager, you should:

- Thoroughly check references
- Contact your state securities regulation agency to find out if the investment manager or firm has been the subject of investigation or disciplinary action
- Evaluate the manager's performance over the last 5 years against the average performance of the largest firms, as listed in:

Publication: *Investment Advisors Performance Survey*
Cost: $525.00 per year
Contains: Detailed performance information on 483 managers who control over $600 billion in assets
From: CDA Investments Technologies
1355 Picard Dr.
Rockville, MD 20850
(301) 975-9600

How to Resolve a Problem with Your Stock Broker Or Investment Manager

To resolve disputes, the securities industry has established the following set of procedures.

1. *Attempt to resolve complaints within the brokerage firm.*

Every securities firm is required to appoint a compliance officer who is charged with insuring that the firm operates within the legal and ethical guidelines established by the Securities and Exchange Commission, the National Association of Securities Dealers, state security regulation agency, stock exchanges, and other appropriate governing bodies.

2. *Forward the complaint to a regulatory body.*

A number of agencies and organizations share the responsibility of supervising the securities industry. If you cannot get satisfaction within your brokerage firm, you can forward your complaint to a regulatory body. These are described below.

National Association of Securities Dealers (NASD) has the power to censure, fine, suspend, or expel any registered broker or firm from the securities business. The NASD also regulates the over-the-counter stock market. Investor complaints should be sent to:

Consumer Arbitration Center
National Association of Securities Dealers
33 Whitehall St.
New York, NY 10004
(212) 858-4000

The Securities and Exchange Commission (SEC) is the chief federal regulatory body of the securities industry. Each regional office of the SEC has a Complaint Investigator who will investigate and attempt to informally mediate disputes. For the address of your regional office, contact the Securities and Exchange Commission (see page 71).

State Securities Agencies register and regulate the sale of securities within the state. The extent to which an agency can and will pursue consumer complaints varies from state to state.

To find out the procedure in your state, contact your state agency.

The Major Stock Exchanges will try to mediate a complaint against a member firm. You can send your complaint to:

> The New York Stock Exchange
> 11 Wall St.
> New York, NY 10005
> (212) 656-2000

> American Stock Exchange
> 86 Trinity Place
> New York, NY 10006
> (212) 306-1000

> Boston Stock Exchange
> One Boston Place
> Boston, MA 02108
> (617) 723-9500

> Chicago Board of Options Exchange
> 400 S. LaSalle St.
> Chicago, IL 60605
> (312) 786-5600

> Cincinnati Stock Exchange
> 205 Dixie Terminal Building
> Cincinnati, OH 45202
> (513) 621-1410

> Midwest Stock Exchange
> One Financial Plaza
> 440 S. LaSalle Street
> Chicago, IL 60605
> (312) 663-2222

> Pacific Stock Exchange
> 301 Pine Street
> San Francisco, CA 94104
> (415) 393-4000

> Philadelphia Stock Exchange
> 1900 Market Street
> Philadelphia, PA 19103
> (215) 496-5000

The Municipal Securities Rulemaking Board regulates the writing, selling, and trading of municipal bonds issued by state and local governments. You can submit complaints to:

> The Municipal Securities Rulemaking Board
> 1818 N Street, NW, Suite 800
> Washington, DC 20036

Complaints Involving the Trading of Futures falls under the federal jurisdiction of the Commodity Futures Trading Commission. The self-regulatory industry association is the National Futures Association. Both have procedures for mediating disputes.

> Commodity Futures Trading Commission
> Office of Proceedings
> 2033 K Street, NW
> Washington, DC 20581

> National Futures Association
> 200 W. Madison Street, Suite 1600
> Chicago, IL 60606
> (800) 621-3570 (Ex. IL)
> (312) 781-1410

Further assistance may be obtained from the specific exchanges on which futures and options are traded. You can send complaints to the Legal Department of the appropriate exchange (see listings, left column).

3. *Take your complaint to arbitration.*

If mediation does not resolve your complaint, the next step is to seek a binding legal decision. Almost all contracts between investors and brokerage firms mandate arbitration as the final resolution to all complaints and disputes.

Arbitration is a method of settling a dispute by presenting the facts of the case to an impartial person or persons who are knowledgeable in the areas of controversy. The advantages of arbitration are that the process is much faster and much less expensive than seeking a resolution through the courts. The cost of submitting a claim to arbitration starts at just $15 for amounts under $1,000, goes to $25 for $1,000 to $2,500 claims and $100 for $2,500 to $5,000 claim, then steadily climbs in increments to a maximum of $1,000 for claims of $500,000 or more. The disadvantage is that the Supreme Court has ruled that arbitration is final and binding. The decision of an arbitrator can be appealed to the courts only in very limited circumstances, such as provable fraud or conflict of interest on the part of the arbitrator.

Under the supervision of the SEC, the self-regulatory agencies of the securities industry and the exchanges have developed a Uniform Code of Arbitration Procedures under the supervision of the Securities Industries Conference on Arbitration. This code outlines two arbitration procedures:

- Simplified arbitration for small claims under $5,000
- Arbitration for claims over $5,000

These procedures are outlined in three free brochures:

Brochures: • *How to Proceed with Arbitration of a Small Claim*
• *Arbitration Procedures*
• *Code of Arbitration Procedures*
From: Office of Consumer Affairs
Securities and Exchange Commission
450 Fifth Street, NW, Room 2111
Mail Stop 2-6
Washington, DC 20549
(202) 272-7440
(202) 272-7065 (TTY Telecommunications for the Deaf)

INSURANCE

PEOPLE OVER 50 HAVE TO BE PARTICU-larly shrewd insurance consumers, for two reasons. First, because the cost of every type of insurance is partially based on risk, and costs of life, health, disability, and long-term care insurance rise steadily with age. The higher the cost, the larger the price spread between the best and the worst policies. Second, people age 50 and over are more likely to make major claims against these policies. Policies with inadequate coverage or major hidden exclusions can financially devastate the unwary consumer. In this chapter, we will provide complete information on purchasing life, automobile, homeowners, personal liability, and disability insurance. For information on health insurance, see Chapter 12.

GENERAL INFORMATION FOR INSURANCE CONSUMERS

The first step in obtaining the best coverage for the lowest price is to coordinate your entire insurance program, instead of just shopping for insurance piecemeal as you need it.

Buy Only the Insurance that You Really Need

Most people only need the following types of policies:

- Life insurance (if you have dependents)
- Health insurance
- Disability insurance
- Automobile insurance (if you own a car)
- Homeowners or renters insurance, including personal liability insurance
- Long-term care insurance

Almost all other types of insurance are extremely expensive for the limited coverage and benefits they provide. The National Insurance Consumer Organization lists a number of types of insurance you shouldn't buy, including:

- Flight insurance
- Cancer insurance
- Contact lens insurance
- Insurance that pays if you're mugged
- Credit insurance
- Mortgage insurance
- Rental car insurance
- Pet health insurance
- Health insurance that simply pays a per day amount if you're hospitalized
- Rain insurance, that pays if the weather's bad on your vacation

For more information about unnecessary insurance:

Pamphlet: *Consumer Alert: Coverages Not to Buy*
Cost: $1.00 plus self-addressed stamped envelope
From: National Insurance Consumers Organization
121 N. Payne Street
Alexandria, VA 22314
(703) 549-8050

Purchase Insurance Only from Financially Stable Companies

You will not get the insurance coverage you pay for if your insurance company declares bankruptcy before you file a claim. Financial experts recommend that you purchase insurance only from companies that have maintained a high level of financial stability over a long period of time.

One highly regarded opinion of the financial stability of insurance companies is provided by A.M. Best, a company that annually rates more than 1,500 insurance companies on a scale of A+ (Excellent) to C (inadequate assets to cover potential losses). Most insurance agencies and the reference departments of many large public libraries carry:

Directory: *Best's Insurance Reports*
From: A.M. Best
Ambest Road
Oldwick, NJ 08858
(201) 439-2200

Another rating service is:

Company: Weiss Research
Service: Provides a rating by telephone for $15, a written evaluation for $45, or a book with ratings of 1,963 companies for $189
Call: (800) 289-8100 (Ex. FL)
(407) 684-8100

The Insurance Forum Newsletter features unique information such as a list of companies that have been rated A+ or A by Best's for at least 10 years. For information on back issues and subscription costs:

Newsletter: *The Insurance Forum Newsletter*
P.O. Box 245
Elletsville, IN 47429

Investigate America's Best Kept Financial Secret—State Insurance Guaranty Funds

Americans holding insurance policies issued by bankrupt companies have lost tens of millions of dollars because they were unaware that some or all of the claims on these policies could have been paid by a state insurance guaranty fund. All 50 states have guaranty funds that cover homeowners, automobile, renters, property, and casualty insurance. 45 states (except Alaska, California, Colorado, Louisiana, New Jersey, and the District of Columbia) have funds that guarantee life and health insurance benefits.

The existance of these funds is so little-known because insurance brokers and agents in every state are prohibited by law from mentioning their existence when selling or advertising policies. State governments want to make sure that salesmen don't give consumers the mistaken impression that their claims will be paid fully and quickly in the event an insurance company becomes insolvent. The truth is that all states place limits on the types of policies and the amount of benefits that are guaranteed. Processing and paying claims on policies from bankrupt companies can take months, even years. Purchasing an insurance policy from a financially stable company is the best way to make sure that your claims are paid quickly.

However, every insurance consumer should find their present or prospective policies are guaranteed by:

- Asking the insurance agent or broker
- Calling the state insurance department (see your telephone directory under your state government listings or call your state government information service [see listings pages 441–443])

Spend Time Learning About Insurance

You can start becoming an educated insurance consumer by obtaining the following publications.

Booklet: *Insurance Checklist* (D1032)
Cost: Free

Contains: Information on reviewing coverage, comparing prices, and organizing insurance information
From: American Association of Retired Persons
1909 K Street, NW
Washington, DC 20049

Booklet: *Your Insurance Dollar*
Cost: $1.25
Contains: Informative, easy to follow 36-page general guide to the important types of insurance
From: Money Management Institute
Household International
2700 Sanders Road
Prospect Heights, IL 60070

Booklet: *Buyer's Guide to Insurance: What the Companies Won't Tell You*
Cost: $3.00 plus self-addressed stamped envelope
Contains: 16 pages of consumer information about major types of insurance
From: National Insurance Consumers Organization
121 N. Payne Street
Alexandria, VA 22314
(703) 549-8050

Book: *Policy Wise: The Practical Guide to Insurance Decisions for Older Consumers*
Cost: $5.95 (AARP member price $4.35) plus $1.75 postage
Contains: Complete guide to life, health, home, and auto insurance for older consumers, written by a consumer protection lawyer
From: AARP Books/Scott, Foresman and Co.
1865 Miner Street
Des Plains, IL 60016

An additional source of valuable consumer information is your state insurance department. These departments administer state insurance laws and handle consumer complaints. In addition, many have prepared consumer buying guides and specific cost comparisons between companies. Before you make a major insurance purchase, you should contact your state department. For the address and telephone number, consult your local telephone directory under your state government listings or call your state government information service (see listings, pages 441–443).

LIFE INSURANCE

Life insurance provides for your dependents in the event of your death. It is so important to so many Americans that Congress has exempted life insurance payments from income taxes (although it may be subject to estate taxes). But you may not need any life insurance at all if:

- You are single and have no dependents
- Your assets are sufficient to support your surviving spouse and other dependents
- You are retired, and the sum of Social Security, pension, and investment income are adequate to support your surviving spouse

Many people find that their need for life insurance is reduced when their children are grown, their mortgages are paid off, and they have established considerable equity in pensions and retirement accounts. Still, the majority of people age 50 and over need some life insurance to:

- Protect their surviving spouse and minor children
- Provide for the care of dependent older parents
- Provide for others who are fully or partially dependent on them, such as grandchildren, handicapped or disabled children, or other relatives

- Supplement retirement income that would be lost to a surviving spouse and dependents
- Pay funeral expenses and other death-related costs

Before you shop for life insurance, you should first determine exactly how much you need. You'll find a worksheet to help you in the booklet *Your Insurance Dollar* (see page 84), or in:

Pamphlet: *A Consumer's Guide to Life Insurance*
Cost: Free
From: The American Council of Life Insurance
Community and Consumer Relations
1001 Pennsylvania Avenue, NW
Washington, DC 20004
(202) 624-2000

You may be well-insured if you have any of the following:

- Group coverage provided as an employee benefit at work
- Group coverage provided with membership in a union, organization, or association
- Paid up coverage on any existing life insurance policies
- Any veterans insurance

The Types of Life Insurance

Term insurance provides protection only in exchange for payment of yearly premiums. It features:

- The lowest initial cost for the most coverage
- Premiums that steadily rise with age
- Protection that ends if payments aren't made
- No automatic renewal, which means the company can cancel coverage at the end of a term for medical or other reasons

In addition to term insurance, life insurance companies also offer a variety of other policies that offer not only protection, but also investment opportunities. These policies carry a much higher initial premium, but that premium may be permanently fixed instead of rising with age. Part of the premium payments are invested by the insurance company. Over the years, the policy builds a *cash value*. The advantages of cash-value policies are:

- Cash value increases are not taxable until the policy is cashed in
- The cash value goes to the policyholder when the policy is terminated
- Loans against the cash value can be taken at lower than market interest rates
- The cash value can be converted to a paid up life insurance, which remains in effect premium-free until death
- The cash value can be converted to an annuity or other type of regular monthly income

The primary disadvantages of cash-value policies are:

- Premiums are initially much higher than term insurance
- Cash value builds slowly during the first few years
- Low rates of return of some policies can wipe out the tax savings
- Rates of return are not guaranteed, but instead depend, to some extent, on the rise and fall of interest rates, the investment expertise of the insurance company, and generosity of the firm's board of directors

In recent years, the insurance industry has developed a bewildering variety of cash-value policies. The excellent guides to purchasing insurance listed above describe these types of policies in detail.

How to Find the Best Policy

There are many ways to find the best policy. Here are some of the steps we suggest.

1. *Obtain a "benchmark" quotation.*

One very important step recommended by the National Insurance Consumer Organization (NICO) is to find out the cost of policies from a company that has very competitive rates against which you can measure other policies you're considering. The company recommended by the NICO and other consumer organizations is:

Company: USAA Life
Description: Financially stable, highly rated company that sells low-cost term and universal life insurance by telephone only
Call: USAA Life
(800) 531-8000

2. *Obtain rates of "no-load" insurance policies.*

Salesmen generally receive a substantial commission based on the amount of the yearly premium. In recent years, some companies have begun selling universal life policies that pay the salesman a smaller flat fee rather than a commission. To obtain the name of a person who sells these no-commission ("no-load") policies:

> **Organization:** The Council of Life Insurance Consultants
> **Cost:** Free referrals
> **For information:** The Council of Life Insurance Consultants
> P.O. Box 803653
> Chicago, IL 60680
> (800) 533-0777

3. *Use a rate comparison service.*

A comparison service takes your personal information (age, health, amount of insurance required), then runs a computer check to discover the four or five least expensive policies among the companies that the service lists. These services are particularly valuable for people over 50, who have the most difficulty finding inexpensive insurance.

The major comparison services are:

> **Company:** Insurance Information, Inc.
> **Cost:** $50.00
> **Service:** This company compares the policies of several hundred companies, and it guarantees your fee will be refunded if its services don't save you at least $50.00. Unlike the other rating services, this company doesn't actually sell insurance
> **For information:** Insurance Information, Inc.
> 110 Breeds Hill Road, Suite #4
> Hyannis, MA 02601
> (800) 472-5800 (Ex. MA)
> (800) 225-5800 (MA)

> **Company:** SelectQuote Insurance Services
> **Cost:** Free
> **Services:** Monitors rates of about 200 companies rated A+ or A by Best and provides a list of the best policies. Much more complete selection for term insurance buyers than those seeking cash-value policies. Since the company sells insurance, it does not rate policies of companies that don't pay commissions, such as USAA Life
> **For information:** SelectQuote Insurance Services
> 140 Second Street
> San Francisco, CA 94105
> (800) 343-1985
> (415) 543-7338

> **Company:** InsuranceQuote Services
> **Cost:** Free
> **Services:** Monitors rates of about 200 companies rated A+ or A by Best, and selects the best for its rate comparisons. Since the company sells insurance, it does not rate policies of companies that don't pay commissions, such as USAA Life
> **For information:** InsuranceQuote Services
> 3200 N. Dobson Road, Building C
> Chandler, AZ 85224
> (800) 972-1104
> (602) 345-7241 (AZ)

4. *Consult an insurance agent.*

The ideal insurance agent is a trained professional who is as interested in serving you as he or she is in representing insurance companies. You should be able to trust your insurance agent to competently evaluate your entire financial position and seek out insurance products that best serve your needs, which means that consumers should take great care in choosing an insurance agent and should exercise caution before taking an agent's advice.

Some facts to keep in mind when looking for an insurance agent are:

- There are three types of insurance representatives:
  - An exclusive agent works for just one company (An independent agent represents more than one company)
  - A broker sells insurance, as well as other financial products
  - Independent agents may be able to choose from a wider variety of products, but their products may be more expensive because insurance companies pay higher commissions to independent agents than to their own agents. Brokers may be more impartial about your needs, but not as knowledgeable about insurance.

- Look for credentials indicating a highly trained agent. These include:
  - CLU (Chartered Life Underwriter) means that the agent has taken at least 2 years of courses and passed a set of rigorous exams.
  - CFP or ChFC (Certified Financial Planner or Chartered Financial Consultant) means that the agent has also met the rigorous education, experience, and test requirements to be a financial planner.

- Ask a prospective agent for the names of other financial professionals he or she uses as resources. A good agent should know when you need the services of an accountant, attorney, stockbroker, or financial planner, and should have relationships with these professionals. Beware of an agent who has no such relationships.

- All insurance agents must be licensed by the state. Before purchasing products from an agent, contact your state insurance agency and your local Better Business Bureau to find out if there is any record of complaints or disciplinary action against the agent or the company he or she represents.

For more information on the services an insurance agent can provide:

Pamphlets: • *Working with a Winner: Your Life Underwriter and You*
• *Shaping Your Financial Fitness*
Cost: Free
From: National Association of Life Underwriters
1922 F Street, NW
Washington, DC 20006
(202) 331-6000

Pamphlet: *CLU: Chartered Life Underwriter*
Referral: To CLUs in your area
From: American Society of CLU & ChFC
270 Bryn Mawr Avenue
Bryn Mawr, PA 19010
(215) 526-2500

5. *Evaluate the relative return on cash-value policies you're considering.*

To help you compare cash-value policies, the National Association of Insurance Commissioners has developed two indexes to help you compare policies:

- Interest-adjusted net payment cost index produces a number that represents the yearly cost of the insurance per each $1,000 of coverage over the first 10 years. The lower the number, the less expensive the policy.

- Surrender cost index measures the present cost of cash-value policies if you cancel them to take the cash in 10 years.

You should compare the numbers for the policies you're considering with your benchmark policy. You can also compare it with policies of other companies by going to the library to consult:

Monthly Report: *Best's Review*
Cost: Carried by many libraries
Contains: Annual data on the performance and costs of whole life and universal life policies
From: A.M. Best
Ambest Road
Oldwick, NJ 08858
(201) 439-2200

For a more complete evaluation, you can submit the policies you are considering to:

Organization: National Insurance Consumers Organization Rate of Return Service
Cost: $30.00 for first policy, $20.00 for additional policies
Services: The NICO prepares a computer analysis of each policy that shows the actual rate of return. It also produces a cost comparison between purchasing a cash-value policy and purchasing a term policy and investing the difference.
From: National Insurance Consumers Organization
121 N. Payne Street
Alexandria, VA 22314
(703) 549-8050

6. *Take advantage of your "free look" period.*

By law, you have 10 days to change your mind after purchasing a new life insurance policy. Use the period to do additional investigation. If you do change your mind, the insurance company must refund your premium payment without penalty.

7. *Don't buy credit insurance.*

Many lenders, including credit card companies and loan companies, offer credit insurance, a form of life insurance that pays off the loan in the event of your death. However, as we've seen before, buying insurance in large amounts is much less expensive than buying insurance in small amounts. If you need more insurance to pay off your debts, it is much less expensive to add an extra $50,000 in protection to your existing term policy than to pay for credit insurance in small amounts.

There is, however, an exception. Since credit insurance is available to any borrower, it may provide additional protection for individuals in poor health who aren't otherwise eligible for insurance.

8. *Beware of mail-order insurance.*

Most life insurance policies sold through unsolicited mail are very expensive, are riddled with clauses that may leave holes in your coverage, and are issued by companies not stable enough to win an A+ or A rating from Best's. Consumer experts recommend not buying mail-order insurance unless:

- It's less expensive than your benchmark rates
- You've compared the fine print of the policy line by line with other comprehensive policies
- You've checked Best's rating

For more information:

Booklet: *10 Do's Before You Buy Insurance by Mail*
Cost: Free
From: Direct Marketing Association
6 East 43rd Street
New York, NY 10017

For more information on purchasing life insurance:

Book: • *Taking the Bite Out of Insurance:*
• *How to Save Money on Life Insurance*

Cost: $11.95
Contains: Very detailed consumer information guide to every aspect of life insurance, written by James Hunt, former Vermont Commissioner of Banking and Insurance
From: National Insurance Consumer Organization
121 N. Payne Street
Alexandria, VA 22314
(703) 549-8050

Request: Lost Policy Questionnaire
Cost: Questionnaire is free, although fees may be assessed for difficult searches
Services: The council will search its database of current insurance policies and will, if necessary, query its member companies
From: American Council of Life Insurance
Policy Search Division
1001 Pennsylvania Avenue, NW
Washington, DC 20004
(202) 624-2000

How to Find Out if a Deceased Relative Had Life Insurance

Tragically, many people fail to maintain an up-to-date and complete vital-papers file (see Chapter 1) that includes information on all life insurance policies. Other people forget about old policies, which may have included paid-up insurance that's still in force. To locate a copy of any lost life insurance policies issued by a private company:

To find out about any GI insurance covering a serviceman who dies on active duty or who is a veteran, contact:

Agency: National Personnel Records Center
Cost: Free
For information: National Personnel Records Center
(314) 263-3901

AUTOMOBILE INSURANCE

Most people age 50 and over can expect to have their auto premiums reduced. The reason: lower accident rates means that many insurance companies give discounts ranging from 5% to 20% to older Americans who own cars.

What to Look for in a Policy

Most experts recommend that you:

- Carry at least $100,000 for injuries to one person, $300,000 for all injuries in one accident, $50,000 in property damages liability, and $25,000 for uninsured motorists

- Carry collision and comprehensive insurance only on cars that are less than 5 years old
- Carry the highest collision and comprehensive deductibles you can afford—at least $250 deductibles
- Avoid coverage duplicated by other policies and services you may already have, such as:
  - Medical payments insurance if your family is covered by group health care
  - Towing and emergency road service if you're a member of an auto club
  - Accidental death and dismemberment insurance, if you've got adequate life insurance coverage

– Rental car replacement coverage, if you can do without a car while yours is being fixed

For more basic information about auto insurance:

> **Booklet:** *Auto Insurance Basics*
> **Cost:** Free
> **From:** Insurance Information Institute
> 110 William Street
> New York, NY 10038
> (800) 221-4954 (Ex. NY)
> (212) 669-9200

> **Booklet:** *Information on Auto and Home Insurance*
> **Cost:** Free
> **Contains:** Information on what to look for in an auto policy and worksheets for comparing rates
> **From:** AARP
> 1909 K Street, NW
> Washington, DC 20049

How to Shop for Auto Insurance

1. *Obtain benchmark rates.*

The following companies, which sell insurance directly to consumers (instead of through agents), have very competitive rates in all locations. You should find these listed in your Yellow Pages. You should call all of them for quotations.

> GEICO
> State Farm
> Allstate
> Nationwide
> Colonial Penn
> USAA (For current and retired military officers only)
> AARP Auto Insurance (for AARP members only)

2. *Contact your auto club.*

Local affiliates of the American Automobile Association often offer very competitive insurance rates for members.

3. *Contact agent from company that issues your homeowners policy.*

Many insurance companies offer a combined discount if they write both automobile and homeowners insurance.

4. *Make sure company guarantees renewal of your policy.*

There is little you can do to prevent an automobile insurance company from dropping you if you pile up too many traffic tickets or are at fault in too many accidents. However, you should look for a company that won't drop you simply because of your age or because of an accident that was someone else's fault.

5. *Take a defensive driving course.*

In many states, the AARP offers an 8-hour defensive driving course to people 55 and over. People who complete the "55 Alive" course are eligible for discounts under the AARP's own automobile insurance and some other companies. For more information about defensive driving programs, contact your local area agency on aging (see pages 383–427) or write:

> 55 Alive
> Traffic Safety Department
> AARP
> 1909 K Street, NW
> Washington, DC 20049

6. *Investigate claim performance of insurance companies.*

Contact your state insurance department and ask about the complaint history of the insurance companies you are considering. Illinois, New York, and California annually publish lists of the companies recording the least and the most complaints from consumers.

7. *Check with your insurance company before you buy a new car.*

Automobile insurance rates for certain makes and models of automobiles are significantly higher than those of others similar in price, size, and features. The reason for this disparity is that insurance company records show certain models are stolen more frequently, are more likely to be in an accident, or are more likely to be badly damaged in an accident. Consequently, you should call your insurance company to find out the comparative insurance rates before you choose one model over another.

HOMEOWNERS AND RENTERS INSURANCE

Homeowners and renters insurance generally includes coverage for:

- Physical damage to your home, including the garage and other structures (except renters policies)
- Physical damage to or theft of personal belongings
- Expenses of living elsewhere while your home is being repaired
- Liability for injuries to others that occur on your property

Careful shopping cannot only save considerable money, but can also result in significantly better coverage.

The Basics of Homeowners Insurance

There are three standard forms of homeowners insurance:

- Basic (HO-1), which covers 11 perils, including fire and theft
- Broad (HO-2), which covers 18 perils, including damage caused by bursting pipes and damage caused by appliances

- Comprehensive (HO-5), which covers all risks except those specifically excluded, such as war, nuclear accidents, and floods

All homeowners policies specify a certain limit to the damages suffered to the home and other structures. Experts recommend a minimum insurance of 80% of the replacement value.

Policies specify two types of coverage for damage to the contents of a home or apartment:

- Actual cash value of the items lost or stolen, up to a certain limit. This means you get the depreciated value of all items
- Replacement value of the items lost or stolen, up to a certain limit

All regular policies severely limit the coverage for valuables, such as jewelry, art work, silver, gold, cash, furs, personal computers, and other frequently stolen items. Insuring these items over the minimal coverage requires purchasing riders to the policy at additional cost.

For more information:

Pamphlets: • *Insurance for the Home*
• *Tenants Insurance Basics*

Cost: Free
From: Insurance Information Institute
110 Williams Street
New York, NY 10038
(800) 221-4954 (Ex. NY)
(212) 669-9200

Booklet: *Information on Auto and Home
Insurance*
Cost: Free
Contains: Information on what to look for in
a homeowners policy and work-
sheets for comparing rates
From: AARP
1909 K Street, NW
Washington, DC 20049

Before You Shop for Homeowner's Insurance, Take a Household Inventory

A household inventory is a record of all of your personal belongings. It is vital for two reasons:

- Adding up the value of your possessions prevents you from being underinsured
- Meticulous records make for a full and fast payment of your claims

First, make a list of all your possessions. Convenient forms are normally available from insurance companies or:

Pamphlet: *Taking Inventory*
Cost: Free
From: Insurance Information Institute
110 Williams Street
New York, NY 10038
(800) 221-4954 (Ex. NY)
(212) 669-9200

Next, collect as many purchase receipts as possible, then record the purchase price and, where applicable, serial numbers of the items.

A valuable third step is to make a video tape of all your possessions in every room of your house. If you don't have a video camera, you can rent or borrow one.

The fourth step is to obtain a professional appraisal of valuable jewelry, art work, stamp collections, and other items you own. For information:

Organization: American Society of Appraisers
Services: Services and publications include:
- Free directory of members who are personal property appraisers
- Free pamphlet, *Information on the Appraisal Profession*
- *Directory of Professional Appraisal Services* ($5.00), which lists services in all fields
For information: American Society of Appraisers
P.O. Box 17265
Washington, DC 20041
(703) 478-2228

The last step is to place your written inventory and related receipts and items in your safe deposit box or other safe location away from your property.

How to Shop for Homeowner's Insurance

The following steps are among those you can take to obtain the best rate.

- Obtain benchmark rates by contacting any of the national companies offering insurance at competitive rates
- Obtain quotes from your automobile insurance company. Many companies give discounts to consumers who carry both auto and homeowners insurance with them

- Investigate discounts for retirees. AARP Homeowners Insurance and some other plans give discounts to retirees
- Ask about discounts for home security systems. Many states encourage insurance companies to give discounts to homeowners or tenants who install burglar alarms, smoke detectors, and other forms of home-protection devices
- Review your policy frequently. The value of your home and personal belongings can increase rapidly. You should review your coverage at least once per year

Special Flood Insurance

Even the more comprehensive homeowners policies normally exclude damage from floods. To protect homeowners in areas prone to flooding, the federal government has established its own National Flood Insurance Program. For information:

National Flood Insurance Program
9901-A George Palmer Highway
Lanham, MD 20706
(800) 638-6620
(301) 731-5300

Special Crime Insurance

Many residents and businesses in high-crime areas were unable to purchase theft insurance. So the federal government stepped in to provide such insurance, which is sold by insurance agents and brokers in eligible areas. For information:

Federal Crime Insurance Program
Federal Emergency Management Agency
P.O. Box 41033
Bethesda, MD 20815
(800) 638-8780
(301) 652-2637 (MD—call collect)

DISABILITY INSURANCE

Disability insurance provides protection in the event of illness or injury. About one in three Americans age 35 and over will be disabled for at least 3 months at some point in their working lives. People between the ages of 50 and 65 are three times more likely to become disabled than they are to die.

Disability insurance pays a specific monthly sum in the event that illness or injury prevents you from working. Among the major differences in disability policies are:

- Definition of disability. For example, you may suffer an injury serious enough to keep you from returning to your job as a construction worker, but not serious enough to prevent you from working as a store clerk. A good policy pays when you are unable to work at your regular profession, while a less comprehensive policy only pays if you aren't able to work at any type of job.
- Monthly payments. Most companies will not write policies for monthly payments greater than 60% of your regular monthly income.
- Waiting period. The longer the period of time between the onset of the disability and the beginning of payments, the less expensive the policy.

- Benefit period. The period of time during which you receive payments can range from a few months to a lifetime. The shorter the period, the less expensive the premium.
- Renewal provisions. The best policies are those that cannot be canceled by the company, although they are the most expensive.
- Partial payments. Many policies make partial payments if you return to work part-time or undergo rehabilitation.

> **Booklet:** *What You Should Know About Disability Insurance*
> **Cost:** Free
> **From:** Health Insurance Association of America
> 1001 Pennsylvania Avenue, NW
> Washington, DC 20004
> (800) 423-8000
> (202) 223-7780

You may already have disability insurance from:

- Social Security (if you're eligible)
- Workmen's compensation
- Veteran's administration (if your disability is connected to military service, or if you served in the military during a designated war period)

In 1990, the average monthly Social Security disability benefit for a single adult was about $555, while the average monthly benefit for a family was $975. The problems with relying on Social Security disability benefits are:

- Eligibility requirements are very stringent, requiring the recipient to have a serious health problem that produces total disability of more than a year or that will result in death
- Payments are made only in cases of such complete disability that the recipient is unable to work in any job in our economy
- Delays in receiving the first check may be 6 months or longer

Workmen's compensation payments vary from state to state, but the normal maximum payment is $300 to $500 per month. These payments are made only for work-related disabilities to workers covered under the programs.

In addition to government programs, about 20% of American workers are covered by group disability insurance programs provided by their employers. The quality and comprehensiveness of these programs varies widely, so you should obtain a copy of your policy and read it carefully.

HOW TO RESOLVE INSURANCE PROBLEMS AND COMPLAINTS

Among the common insurance problems or complaints are:

- Billing errors
- Disputes involving claims
- Disputes involving cancellation of policies

- Disputes involving terms of a policy
- Disputes involving rate increases

Insurance companies, brokers, and salespeople are regulated by each state insurance department. If you are unable to solve the problem with the company involved, send the complaint in writing to the appropriate state department (see pages 441–443).

You can also obtain information, advice, and referrals to appropriate agencies by contacting:

Organization: National Insurance
Consumer Hotline
(800) 942-4242

Services: Consumer assistance service operated by insurance industry associations

Organization: National Insurance
Consumer Organization
121 N. Payne St.
Alexandria, VA 22314
(703) 549-8050

TAXES AND TAX PREPARATION

EVERY FINANCIAL DECISION YOU MAKE has tax consequences. As with every other element of managing money, the more informed you are about taxes, the better decisions you'll make and the less you'll have to pay. Studies have shown that there are few people, rich or poor, who couldn't save money through better tax planning and return preparation.

There are a large number of resources you can turn to for tax information and assistance in preparing your return. Using these resources wisely will help you to take advantage of the significant tax breaks that the federal, state, and local governments provide to people who are planning for retirement or who have already retired.

To save money on your taxes you need to:

- Educate yourself about the federal tax laws and requirements
- Educate yourself about state laws and requirements
- Find the right tax preparation assistance
- Learn how to defend your rights to challenge the Internal Revenue Service

FEDERAL TAXES

The most important source of federal tax information is the Internal Revenue Service (IRS), which has, under the prodding of Congress, greatly increased its efforts to educate taxpayers in recent years. Among the information available from the IRS are:

- Federal tax publications
- The Tele-Tax toll-free information system
- Taxpayer education programs

Federal Tax Publications

Federal tax publications contain a wealth of detailed information about the tax system. They are free, and you can have them mailed to your home at no cost. Even if you don't prepare your own returns, these publications are an excellent reference source for information that can help you organize your records for your tax preparer and help you make important decisions with tax consequences.

The free tax publications that everyone 50 and over should request annually are:

Publication 17: *Your Federal Income Tax*
An extensive line-by-line explanation of the items on Form 1040, as well as Schedules A, B, D, E, R, SE, and Forms W-2, 2106, 2119, 2441, and 3903. Includes examples of typical situations and sample filled-in forms

Publication 501: *Exemptions and Standard Deduction*
Explains how and when you can take exemptions for yourself and dependents, as well as the higher standard deduction amounts for age and blindness

Publication 502: *Medical and Dental Expenses*
Explains how medical and dental expenses may be deducted, including many tips on deductions you may overlook

Publication 554: *Tax Information for Older Americans*
Focuses on tax information and deductions specially applicable to older Americans. Includes many examples and filled-in forms

Among the publications of most interest to many people age 50 and older are:

Publication 334: *Tax Guide for Small Business*
Explains how federal tax laws apply to small businesses. Divided into eight parts that range from general information on business organization and accounting to an explanation of tax credits available to businesses

Publication 448: *Federal Estate and Gift Taxes*
Explains in detail the federal estate taxes and the regulations on taxing gifts

Publication 504: *Tax Information for Divorced and Separated Individuals*
Explains tax rules on filing status, claiming dependents, and the tax treatment of alimony and property settlements

Publication 523: *Tax Information on Selling Your Home*
Explains how to calculate the gain in selling your home, and how you may defer taxes on that gain. Also covers the one-time exclusion for people 55 and older

Publication 524: *Credit for the Elderly Or for the Permanently and Totally Disabled*
Explains how to figure the credit for those 65 and older, as well as the credit for the disabled

Publication 526: *Charitable Contributions*
Explains how charitable contributions are claimed for tax purposes

Publication 530: *Tax Information for Owners of Homes, Condominiums, and Cooperative Apartments*
Explains in detail the deductions available for these types of property owners

Publication 544: *Sales and Other Dispositions of Assets*
Explains the tax consequences of selling any asset or transferring it to a

relative, such as art work, antiques, collectibles, etc.

Publication 545: *Interest Expense*
Explains what interest expenses can and cannot be deducted

Publication 550: *Investment Income and Expenses*
Explains the tax treatment of income from all types of investments

Publication 552: *Recordkeeping for Individuals and a List of Tax Publications*
Helps taxpayers decide what records to keep and how to organize their tax information

Publication 559: *Tax Information for Survivors, Executors, and Administrators*
Covers the many questions that result from the death of a spouse, relative, or other loved one

Publication 564: *Mutual Fund Distributions*
Explains how to report income from mutual funds

Publication 575: *Pension and Annuity Income*
Explains how to report income from pensions and annuities, as well as the rules for handling lump-sum distributions from profit-sharing or pension plans

Publication 590: *Individual Retirement Arrangements*
Explains the benefits of IRAs and the tax treatments of such investments

Publication 907: *Tax Information for Handicapped and Disabled Individuals*
Explains the tax rules for those who are handicapped or disabled, or those who have handicapped or disabled dependents

Publication 915: *Social Security Benefits and Equivalent Railroad Retirement Benefits*
Tax information for recipients of Social Security and railroad retirement benefits

Publication 929: *Tax Rules for Children and Dependents*
Explains the new laws affecting children and other dependents

The IRS also provides many other valuable free publications. You can obtain a complete listing of these, as well as any publication listed above from:

Toll-Free Number: (800) 424-3676
Service: You will receive forms or publications in 7 to 10 working days

Because so many Americans have access to a local library, the IRS also ships complete sets of publications and forms to more than 18,000 public libraries. All forms may be photocopied in libraries, and the photocopies are accepted by the IRS. Many of these libraries also stock audio and video cassettes containing educational materials produced by the IRS.

Tax and Refund Information and Assistance by Telephone

The IRS operates two different telephone information services:

- Tele-Tax provides recorded information on over 150 topics, as well as an automated system for obtaining information on the status of your tax refund

- Personalized tax information and preparation assistance is provided by trained IRS employees through a system of local and toll-free telephone numbers

The toll-free numbers for Tele-Tax are:

ALABAMA
(800) 554-4477

ALASKA
(800) 554-4477

ARIZONA
Phoenix 252-4909
Elsewhere (800) 554-4477

ARKANSAS
(800) 554-4477

CALIFORNIA
Counties of Amador, Calavaras,
Contra Costa, Marin,
and San Joaquin (800) 428-4032
Los Angeles 617-3177
Oakland 839-4245
Elsewhere (800) 544-4477

COLORADO
Denver 552-1118
Elsewhere (800) 554-4477

CONNECTICUT
(800) 554-4477

DELAWARE
(800) 554-4477

DISTRICT OF COLUMBIA
628-2929

FLORIDA
Jacksonville 353-9579
Elsewhere (800) 554-4477

GEORGIA
Atlanta 331-6572
Elsewhere (800) 554-4477

HAWAII
Oahu 541-1040
Elsewhere (800) 554-4477

IDAHO
(800) 554-4477

ILLINOIS
Chicago 829-6397
Springfield 789-0489
Elsewhere (800) 554-4477

INDIANA
Indianapolis 634-1550
Elsewhere (800) 554-4477

IOWA
(800) 554-4477

KANSAS
(800) 554-4477

KENTUCKY
(800) 554-4477

LOUISIANA
(800) 554-4477

MAINE
(800) 554-4477

MARYLAND
Baltimore 244-7306
Elsewhere (800) 554-4477

MASSACHUSETTS
Boston 523-8602
Elsewhere (800) 554-4477

MICHIGAN
Detroit 961-4284
Elsewhere (800) 554-4477

MINNESOTA
St. Paul 224-4288
Elsewhere (800) 554-4477

MISSISSIPPI
(800) 554-4477

MISSOURI
St. Louis 241-4700
Elsewhere (800) 554-4477

MONTANA
(800) 554-4477

NEBRASKA
Omaha 221-3324
Elsewhere (800) 554-4477

NEVADA
(800) 554-4477

NEW HAMPSHIRE
(800) 554-4477

NEW JERSEY
Newark 624-1223
Elsewhere (800) 554-4477

NEW MEXICO
(800) 554-4477

NEW YORK
Brooklyn 858-4461
Buffalo 856-9320
Manhattan 406-4080
Queens 858-4461
Staten Island 858-4461
Elsewhere (800) 554-4477

NORTH CAROLINA
(800) 554-4477

NORTH DAKOTA
(800) 554-4477

OHIO
Cincinnati 421-0329
Cleveland 522-3037
Elsewhere (800) 554-4477

OKLAHOMA
(800) 554-4477

OREGON
Portland 294-5363
Elsewhere (800) 554-4477

PENNSYLVANIA
Philadelphia 592-8946
Pittsburgh 281-3120
Elsewhere (800) 554-4477

RHODE ISLAND
(800) 554-4477

SOUTH CAROLINA
(800) 554-4477

SOUTH DAKOTA
(800) 554-4477

TENNESSEE
Nashville 242-1541
Elsewhere (800) 554-4477

TEXAS
Dallas 767-1792
Houston 850-8801
Elsewhere (800) 554-4477

UTAH
(800) 554-4477

VERMONT
(800) 554-4477

VIRGINIA
Richmond 771-2369
Elsewhere (800) 554-4477

WASHINGTON
Seattle 343-7221
Elsewhere (800) 554-4477

WEST VIRGINIA
(800) 554-4477

WISCONSIN
Milwaukee 291-1783
Elsewhere (800) 554-4477

WYOMING
(800) 554-4477

The Tele-Tax service provides information on many tax-related subjects, listed by the number you press (if you have touch-tone service) or ask the operator for (if have rotary/pulse service).

Tax Information for Aliens and U.S. Citizens

Living Abroad

701 Resident and nonresident alien
702 Dual-status aliens
703 Alien tax clearance
704 Foreign earned income credit—general
705 Foreign earned income credit—who qualifies?
706 Foreign earned income exclusion
707 Foreign tax credit

Topics in Spanish

751 Who must file?
752 Which form to use?
753 Filing status—married, single, separated
754 Filing status—head of household, widow
755 Earned income credit
756 Highlights of tax changes
757 Forms and publications—how to order
758 Alien tax clearance
759 Refunds—how long should they take
760 IRS help available
761 Social Security and tier 1 RR retirement
762 Social Security Benefit Statement SSA-1099

IRS agents will answer all kinds of tax information and preparation questions, a service provided nationwide through a combination of toll-free local and (800) numbers.

ALABAMA
(800) 424-1040

ALASKA
Anchorage 561-7484
Elsewhere (800) 424-1040

ARIZONA
Phoenix 257-1233
Elsewhere (800) 424-1040

ARKANSAS
(800) 424-1040

CALIFORNIA
Call the number listed in the White Pages of the telephone directory under "U.S. Government, Internal Revenue Service, Federal Tax Assistance"

COLORADO
Denver 825-7041
Elsewhere (800) 424-1040

CONNECTICUT
(800) 424-1040

DELAWARE
(800) 424-1040

DISTRICT OF COLUMBIA
(800) 488-3100

FLORIDA
Jacksonville 354-1760
Elsewhere (800) 424-1040

GEORGIA
Atlanta 522-0050
Elsewhere (800) 424-1040

HAWAII
Oahu 541-1040
Elsewhere (800) 424-1040

IDAHO
(800) 424-1040

ILLINOIS
Chicago 435-1040
Elsewhere (800) 424-1040

INDIANA
Indianapolis 269-5477
Elsewhere (800) 424-1040

IOWA
Des Moines 283-0523
Elsewhere (800) 424-1040

KANSAS
(800) 424-1040

KENTUCKY
(800) 424-1040

LOUISIANA
(800) 424-1040

MAINE
(800) 424-1040

MARYLAND
Baltimore 962-2590
Montgomery County 488-3100
Prince George's County 488-3100
Elsewhere (800) 424-1040

MASSACHUSETTS
Boston 523-1040
Elsewhere (800) 424-1040

MICHIGAN
Detroit 237-0800
Elsewhere (800) 424-1040

MINNESOTA
Minneapolis 291-1422
St. Paul 291-1422
Elsewhere (800) 424-1040

MISSISSIPPI
(800) 424-1040

MISSOURI
St. Louis 342-1040
Elsewhere (800) 424-1040

MONTANA
(800) 424-1040

NEBRASKA
Omaha 422-1500
Elsewhere (800) 424-1040

NEVADA
(800) 424-1040

NEW HAMPSHIRE
(800) 424-1040

NEW JERSEY
Newark 622-0600
Elsewhere (800) 424-1040

NEW MEXICO
(800) 424-1040

NEW YORK
Bronx 732-0100
Brooklyn 596-3770
Buffalo 855-3955
Manhattan 732-0100
Nassau 222-1131
Queens 596-3770
Staten Island 596-3770
Suffolk 724-5000
Westchester County 997-1510
Elsewhere (800) 424-1040

NORTH CAROLINA
(800) 424-1040

NORTH DAKOTA
(800) 424-1040

OHIO
Cincinnati 621-6281
Cleveland 522-3000
Elsewhere (800) 424-1040

OKLAHOMA
(800) 424-1040

OREGON
Eugene 485-8286
Portland 221-3960
Salem 581-8721
Elsewhere (800) 424-1040

PENNSYLVANIA
Philadelphia 574-9900
Pittsburgh 281-0112
Elsewhere (800) 424-1040

RHODE ISLAND
(800) 424-1040

SOUTH CAROLINA
(800) 424-1040

SOUTH DAKOTA
(800) 424-1040

TENNESSEE
Nashville 259-4601
Elsewhere (800) 424-1040

TEXAS
Dallas 742-2440
El Paso 532-6116
Ft. Worth 263-9229
Houston 965-0440
Elsewhere (800) 424-1040

UTAH
(800) 424-1040

VERMONT
(800) 424-1040

VIRGINIA
Bailey's Crossroads 557-9230
Richmond 649-2361
Elsewhere (800) 424-1040

WASHINGTON
Seattle 442-1040
Elsewhere (800) 424-1040

WEST VIRGINIA
(800) 424-1040

WISCONSIN
Milwaukee 271-3780
Elsewhere (800) 424-1040

WYOMING
(800) 424-1040

Taxpayer Education Programs

Every IRS office has a Taxpayer Education Co-ordinator who supervises the following programs:

- *Community Outreach Tax Assistance.* The IRS conducts group meetings and information seminars for groups of people with similar interests and problems, such as retirees, farmers, small business owners, and investors.
- *Small Business Workshops.* These are full day, free seminars on all elements of taxation affecting small business and the self-employed.
- *Volunteer training.* The IRS conducts a large number of training programs for adults who are interested in helping others with their tax returns through a number of outreach programs (see below). The training received by these volunteers helps them a great deal in their own tax planning and preparation.
- *Films.* The IRS has a number of audio and video cassettes on how to fill out Forms 1040EZ, 1040A, 1040, and Schedules A and B, including tax tips. These materials are in many libraries and are also available on loan from the IRS to local organizations. Among the most relevant are:
  The New Tax Law and You
  The IRS Tax Guide to Retirement
  How to Fill Out Your Tax Return

Other Sources of Federal Tax Information

The following two publications provide an excellent overview that will help you in tax planning:

Booklet: *Retirement Income Tax Guide*
Cost: Free
Contains: Complete information on preparing your federal return, updated and re-issued on January 1 of each year by the Tax-Aide Program Department of AARP
From: AARP
401 Watson Plaza Drive
Los Angeles, CA 90712

Booklet: *Federal Income Tax Guide for Older Americans*
Cost: Free
Contains: An informative annual publication produced by the staff of the Select Committee on Aging of the U.S. House of Representatives
From: Select Committee on Aging
U.S. House of Representatives
712 House Office Building, Annex #1
Washington, DC 20515

You will find in libraries and bookstores a number of excellent tax preparation guides. Their advantages are:

- They combine into one volume information from dozens of IRS publications, making them much easier to use
- They expand on, interpret, and explain the official IRS positions, this helps to make better decisions about your tax problems

The best of these tax guides are:

Book: *Guide to Income Tax Preparation by Consumer Reports Books*
Cost: $10.95
Contains: An easy to read 554-page guide. A major advantage is a 16-page "tax organizer" that helps get your records in shape
From: Consumer Reports Books

Book: *J.K. Lasser's Your Income Tax*
Cost: $10.95
Contains: 501 pages of very detailed information that includes a very detailed index
From: J.K. Lasser Institute (Prentice Hall Reference)

Book: *The Arthur Young Tax Guide*
Cost: $10.95
Contains: 656 pages, includes the entire text of IRS publication 17, with extensive comment
From: Ballantine Books

Book: *H&R Block Income Tax Workbook*
Cost: $9.95
Contains: 512-page guide prepared by the largest tax preparation firm
From: Macmillan

STATE AND LOCAL TAXES

If you're an average taxpayer, taxes levied by state and local govenments total about half of your federal income tax payments every year. Saving money on your taxes requires paying as close attention to these taxes as to those collected by the IRS

The three types of taxes that make up the major share of your nonfederal taxes are:

- Income taxes
- Property taxes
- Sales taxes

Forty-three states and a number of cities have income taxes. Fortunately, many of these governments provide income tax exemptions, deductions, and credits for older residents that are far more generous than those allowed on federal returns.

Property taxes, taxes levied on the assessed value of homes and multi-unit dwellings, affect every homeowner and renter in every state. However, many states and most local governments provide exemptions, credits, and refunds for older and low-income taxpayers.

Unfortunately, there's little that most taxpayers can do to significantly reduce the amount they pay in sales taxes in 47 states. A few states exempt certain items from sales tax (such as prescription drugs) for residents age 65 or older.

To help you save money on your state taxes, we've compiled information from the tax agencies of every state. For each state, we have listed the state tax information and assistance offices.

Every state tax office will send publications with detailed information about their tax programs and benefits. For information about local property and other tax benfits, you can contact:

- The Tax Assessor's Office of your local government
- Your local area agency on aging (see pages 383–427)

ALABAMA
Alabama Department of Revenue
Taxpayers Assistance Program
Suite 200, Folsom Administrative Building
64 N. Union Street
Montgomery, AL 36130
(205) 261-3362

ALASKA
Alaska Department of Revenue
P.O. Box 5
Juneau, AK 99811
(907) 465-2300

ARIZONA
Taxpayer Information and Assistance
Arizona Department of Revenue
P.O. Box 29086
Phoenix, AZ 85038
(800) 352-4090 (AZ only)
(602) 255-3381
(602) 542-4021 (TTD for the deaf)

ARKANSAS
Department of Finance and Administration
1509 W. 7th Street, Room 401
P.O. Box 1272
Little Rock, AR 72201
(501) 371-2242

CALIFORNIA
State Board of Equalization
1020 N. Street
Sacramento, CA 95814
(916) 445-3956

COLORADO
Department of Revenue
140 West 6th Avenue
Denver, CO 80204
(800) 332-2087
(303) 534-1209

CONNECTICUT
Taxpayer Services Division
Department of Revenue Services
92 Farmington Avenue
Hartford, CT 06105

DELAWARE
Taxpayer Assistance Section
Division of Revenue
9th & French Streets
Wilmington, DE 19801
(800) 292-7826
(302) 571-3310

DISTRICT OF COLUMBIA
Department of Finance and Revenue
300 Indiana Avenue, NW

Washington, DC 20001
(202) 727-6460

FLORIDA
Taxpayer Assistance Section
Fletcher Building
Tallahassee, FL 32399
(800) 872-9909
(904) 468-6800

GEORGIA
Department of Revenue
Taxpayer Assistance
322 Plaza Level, W. Tower
Floyd Building
Atlanta, GA 30334

HAWAII
State of Hawaii
Department of Taxation
P.O. Box 259
Honolulu, HI 96809
(808) 548-7650

IDAHO
Idaho State Tax Commission
700 West State Street
P.O. Box 56
Boise, ID 83756
(208) 334-7660

ILLINOIS
Department of Revenue
101 West Jefferson
Springfield, IL 62708
(217) 785-2602

INDIANA
Indiana Department of Revenue
100 North Senate Avenue, Room 209
Indianapolis, IN 46204
(800) 382-4646 (IN only)
(317) 232-2240

IOWA
Iowa Department of Revenue and Finance
Hoover State Office Building

East 13th & Walnut
Des Moines, IA 50319
(515) 281-3135

KANSAS
Department of Revenue
2nd Floor, State Office Building
10th & Harrison
Topeka, KS 66612
(913) 296-3041

KENTUCKY
Taxpayer Service Center
Revenue Cabinet
Frankfort, KY 40620
(502) 564-4580

LOUISIANA
Department of Revenue and Taxation
330 N. Ardenwood
P.O. Box 201
Baton Rouge, LA 70821
(504) 925-7537 (General Information)
(504) 925-7532 (Forms)
(504) 925-4611 (Income Tax)

MAINE
Bureau of Taxation
Income Tax Section
State Office Building
Augusta, ME 04333
(800) 452-1983 (Assistance, January-
    April, ME only)
(800) 338-5811 (Forms, year round,
    ME only)
(207) 289-3695

MARYLAND
State Comptroller
P.O. Box 466
Annapolis, MD 21404
(301) 974-3801

MASSACHUSETTS
Massachusetts Department of Revenue
100 Cambridge Street

Boston, MA 02204
(800) 392-6089

MICHIGAN
Department of Treasury
430 W. Allegan Street
Lansing, MI 48922
(800) 877-6424 (Taxpayer Assistance, MI
   only)
(800) 367-6263 (Forms)
(517) 373-2910
(517) 373-9419 (TDD for the deaf)

MINNESOTA
Department of Revenue
Cenntennial Office Building
St. Paul, MN 55145
(612) 296-3401

MISSISSIPPI
Mississippi State Tax Commission
P.O. Box 1033
Jackson, MS 39205
(601) 359-1321

MISSOURI
Department of Revenue
P.O. Box 629
Jefferson City, MO 65105
(314) 751-4450

MONTANA
Montana Department of Revenue
Mitchell Building
Helena, MT 59620
(800) 332-6103 (January-April, MT only)
(406) 444-2460

NEBRASKA
Nebraska Department of Revenue
Nebraska State Office Building
301 Centennial Mall South
Lincoln, NE 68509
(800) 742-7474 (NE only)
(402) 471-5729

NEVADA
Department of Taxation
Capital Mall Complex
Carson City, NV 89710
(702) 885-4892

NEW HAMPSHIRE
Department of Revenue Administration
61 South Spring Street
Concord, NH 03301
(603) 271-2191

NEW JERSEY
Taxpayer Services
New Jersey Division of Taxation
50 Barrack Street, CN-269
Trenton, NJ 08646
(800) 323-4400 (NJ only)
(609) 292-6400

NEW MEXICO
New Mexico Taxation and Revenue Depart-
   ment
P.O. Box 630
Santa Fe, NM 87509
(505) 827-0700

NEW YORK
Department of Taxation and Finance
Campus Tax and Finance Building 9
Albany, NY 12227
(518) 457-7358

NORTH CAROLINA
Department of Revenue
Revenue Building
Raleigh, NC 27640
(919) 733-7210

NORTH DAKOTA
North Dakota Tax Department
State Capitol
Bismark, ND 58505
(800) 472-2110 (ND only)
(701) 224-2770

OHIO
Department of Taxation
State Office Tower
P.O. Box 530
Columbus, OH 43266
(800) 282-1780 (OH only)
(614) 846-6712

OKLAHOMA
State Tax Commission
2501 Lincoln Blvd.
Oklahoma City, OK 73194
(405) 521-3115

OREGON
Information and Taxpayer Assistance
Department of Revenue
Revenue Building
955 Center Street NE
Salem, OR 97310
(503) 371-2244

PENNSYLVANIA
Department of Revenue
4th & Walnut Street
Strawberry Square, 11th Floor
Harrisburg, PA 17128
(717) 783-3680

RHODE ISLAND
Department of Administration
Division of Taxation
289 Promenade Street
Providence, RI 02908
(401) 277-2905

SOUTH CAROLINA
South Carolina Tax Commission
P.O. Box 125
Columbia, SC 29214
(803) 737-5000

SOUTH DAKOTA
Department of Revenue
Richard F. Kneip Building

700 Governors Drive
Pierre, SD 57501
(605) 773-3311

TENNESSEE
Department of Revenue
Andrew Jackson State Office Building
500 Deaderick Street
Nashville, TN 37242
(615) 741-2461

TEXAS
State Property Tax Board
P.O. Box 15900
Austin, TX 78761
(800) 252-9121

UTAH
State Tax Commission
Heber Wells Office Building
160 East 300 South
Salt Lake City, UT 84134
(801) 530-4848

VERMONT
Vermont State Tax Department
P.O. Box 694
109 State Street
Montpelier, VT 05602
(802) 828-2865 (Taxpayer Assistance, VT
    only)
(802) 828-2515 (Forms, VT only)

VIRGINIA
Department of Taxation
P.O. Box 6-L
Richmond, VA 23282
(804) 257-8005

WASHINGTON
Taxpayer Information and Education Sec-
    tion
Department of Revenue

Olympia, WA 98504
(800) 233-6349

WEST VIRGINIA
West Virginia State Tax Department
Taxpayer Services Division
P.O. Box 3784
Charleston, WV 25337
(800) 642-9016 (WV only)
(304) 348-3333

WISCONSIN
State of Wisconsin
Department of Revenue
P.O. Box 8933
Madison, WI 53708
(608) 266-6466

WYOMING
Department of Revenue and Taxation
Herschler Building
122 West 25th Street
Cheyenne, WY 82002
(307) 777-7961

For more information about state and local taxes:

Fact Sheets: *Relocation Tax Guide (D13400)*
Cost: Free
Contains: 50 state guide to state and local taxes
From: AARP Fulfillment
1909 K Street, NW
Washington, DC 20049

PREPARING YOUR RETURNS

You may need some assistance in preparing your tax return, either free help or the assistance of a professional preparer.

The AARP Tax-Aide Program

An invaluable resource for all taxpayers age 60 and over who don't have complicated returns is:

Program: AARP Tax-Aide Program
Cost: Free
Service: Each year, the AARP, in cooperation with the Internal Revenue Service, trains over 25,000 volunteers who assist older taxpayers at 9,000 locations nationwide
For information: Call:
  Your local senior center
  Your local area agency on aging
  (see page 383–427)

Your IRS toll-free number (see above)
or write:
Tax-Aide Program
AARP
1909 K Street, NW
Washington, DC 20049

If there is no Tax-Aide location in your area, there may be volunteers trained by the IRS:

Program: Tax Counseling for the Elderly
Cost: Free
Service: Volunteer tax preparation similar to the Tax-Aide
For information: Call your IRS toll-free number

Program: Volunteer Income Tax Assistance
Cost: Free

Service: Volunteer tax preparation for low-income, non-English speaking and handicapped people, as well as older taxpayers

For information: Call your local IRS toll-free number

Program: Student Tax Clinics
Cost: Free
Service: Law school and graduate accounting school students gain experience by assisting taxpayers in preparing their returns, under the supervision of the IRS. These clinics normally can provide more sophisticated help than that provided by other volunteer programs
For information: Call your local IRS toll-free number

Tax Preparation Programs for Personnel Computers

An option for people with computers is using one of the excellent tax-preparation software programs available. Among the best are:

Program: *Tax Preparer*
Contains: Requires 192K RAM
Includes preparation of Forms 1040 and 1040-ES, Schedules A, B, C, D, E, F, R, and SE, and standard forms

Program: J.K. Lasser's Your Income Tax
Contains: Requires 256K RAM
Includes a copy of the J.K. Lasser tax manual and preparation of Forms 1040, 1040A, and 1040EZ, Schedules A, B, C, D, E, F, R, and SE, and standard forms

Program: *Ask DAN About Your Taxes*
Contains: Requires 512K RAM
Includes preparation of Forms 1040 and 1040-ES, Schedules A, B, C, D, E, F, R, and SE, and standard forms

Program: *PC/TaxCut*
Contains: Requires 312K RAM
Includes preparation of Forms 1040 and 1040-ES, Schedules A, B, C, D, E, F, R, and SE, and standard forms

Program: *TurboTax*
Contains: Requires 256K RAM
Includes preparation of Forms 1040 and 1040-ES, Schedules A, B, C, D, E, F, R, and SE, and standard forms Separate programs are available for the following states:
Alabama
Arizona
California
Colorado
Georgia
Illinois
Indiana
Kansas
Louisiana
Maryland
Massachusetts
Michigan
Minnesota
Missouri
New Jersey
New Mexico
New York
North Carolina
Ohio
Oklahoma
Oregon
Pennsylvania
South Carolina
Utah
Virginia
Wisconsin

Professional Tax Preparers

There are no professional requirements or standards for tax preparers. According to the IRS, anyone who furnishes a taxpayer with sufficient information and advice to complete a return is a tax preparer. Although the IRS monitors tax preparers and, if evidence of fraud is uncovered, prosecutes them, anyone can set up practice.

The best way to avoid problems is to educate yourself on the basic types of services available.

National Tax Services. By far the largest of these is H&R Block, which annually opens offices in thousands of storefronts across the country. Tax preparers hired by Block are required to attend a 75-hour training course in tax preparation, and other national services have similar requirements. The advantages of these services are:

- They are inexpensive, with the average fee ranging from $30 to $100
- Block and some other companies guarantee their work, paying the penalties assessed due to their mistakes
- A representative will accompany a customer to an audit in order to explain how the return was computed

The disadvantages of these services:

- The preparers are not qualified to handle complicated returns
- While they can appear before the IRS to explain mathematical calculations, they cannot represent you before the IRS
- While the service may promise to pay penalties and interest, you are responsible for additional taxes levied by the IRS should the preparer make a mistake
- They provide no tax planning advice

Local Tax Services. Locally owned and operated tax preparation services spring up every tax season in many localities. Their advantages are:

- They are very inexpensive
- Some preparers have extensive knowledge of state and local taxes
- Some guarantee to pay penalties and interest due to their errors

The disadvantages of dealing with a local service are:

- Many preparers have little or no training
- Some are "fly-by-night" operators who disappear after April 15, leaving you unable to answer IRS inquiries about your return
- Some may fail to actually file your returns, leaving you open to severe penalties
- Most are not qualified to handle complicated returns
- These preparers cannot represent you before the IRS
- They do not provide tax planning information

Most experts recommend that you take advantage of the free tax preparation advice offered by the IRS or free programs, such as Tax-Aide, before you turn to a local preparer.

Enrolled Agents. An Enrolled Agent has demonstrated special competence in the field of taxation and is authorized to represent taxpayers before all administrative levels of the IRS. To become an Enrolled Agent, a person has to have either passed a comprehensive 2-day examination given by the U.S. Treasury Department or have at least 5 years service as an employee of the IRS.

The advantages of having an Enrolled Agent prepare your returns are:

- Their fees tend to be lower than those of certified public accountants (CPAs) and tax attorneys
- They are full-time tax specialists
- They must keep up with changes in tax laws through continuing education, or they lose their IRS certification
- They can represent you through all stages of audit and appeal process with the IRS
- They offer tax planning advice

The disadvantages of turning to an Enrolled Agent are:

- They are not as qualified to help you with overall financial planning as a CPA
- Unlike a tax attorney, they cannot represent you in federal courts

For more information about Enrolled Agents and referral to one or more in your area:

Organization: National Association of Enrolled Agents
Cost of referral: Free
From: National Association of Enrolled Agents
6000 Executive Boulevard, Suite 205
Rockville, MD 20852
(800) 424-4339 (24-hour service)

Public Accountants. Public accountants normally have academic degrees in accounting and, in many states, are licensed by the state. About 40% of the members of the National Society of Public Accountants have met the requirements to become Enrolled Agents, and these accountants are most likely to provide competent tax preparation and counseling.

Certified Public Accountants. Certified Public Accountants (CPAs) must have degrees in accounting, must have passed rigorous national exams, are licensed by individual states, and must meet continuing education requirements. The advantages of hiring CPAs are that:

- They are highly trained and regulated by states and industry associations
- They are the most qualified professionals, providing year-round financial advice and tax planning
- They are allowed to represent you before the IRS

The disadvantages of hiring CPAs are:

- Their fees range from $100 an hour upward
- Not all CPAs are tax experts
- Some CPAs only handle business returns, not individual returns

To find a CPA in your area,

Organization: American Institute of CPAs
1211 Avenue of the Americas
New York, NY 10036
(212) 575-6200

Tax Attorneys. Tax attorneys specialize in tax law, but seldom prepare individual returns. Rather, they provide legal advice in complicated matters involving taxes, investments, and estate planning. Their fees can range from $100 to $400 an hour. Tax attorneys are the only professionals allowed to represent you in criminal cases or other tax appeals that reach the courts.

DEFENDING YOUR RIGHTS TO CHALLENGE THE IRS

Everybody makes mistakes, including both taxpayers and the employees of the IRS. If the IRS believes that you've made mistakes, they will contact you in one of two ways:

- Sending a notice asking for information or assessing additional taxes and penalties
- Notifying you of a tax audit

What to Do if You Receive a Notice

Among the most common reasons for a notice are:

- Mathematical errors on your return
- Your failure to record income, such as interest income, reported to the IRS
- Assessment of penalties and interest for insufficient withholding or estimated tax payments

If you agree with the notice, all you have to do is sign enclosed form and send in a check for the requested amount. If you disagree, you should:

- Call the telephone number printed on the notice and explain why you dispute the notice. For example, your bank may have made an error reporting the interest or the IRS might have lost or misapplied an estimated tax payment. Normally, the IRS will drop the request for payment after you furnish written proof, such as a statement of error from your bank or a canceled check.
- If you still disagree after furnishing evidence, call the IRS and ask to speak to a Problems Resolution Officer. These officers are trained to cut through red tape to mediate such problems.
- If you still aren't satisfied and the problem involves a substantial sum, you should hire a tax attorney. If the problem is a small sum, you can bring the matter to the attention of your congressman.

The Audit

Slightly more than 1% of all tax returns were audited by the IRS in 1987. The chances of being audited generally increased with income and with the complexity of the return.

The IRS conducts three different kinds of audits:

- A correspondence audit merely requires you to furnish records to back up your return
- An office audit requires you to bring all of your documentations for part or all of your return to an IRS office
- A field audit involves an IRS auditor coming to your home or business to conduct the audit

You have the right to schedule the audit for a date that is convenient to you and that gives you adequate time to organize your records. You also have the right to be represented by an Enrolled Agent, CPA, or tax attorney.

You can send the representative to the audit in your place, or you can bring him or her with you. You can also bring a witness, such as the commercial preparer who completed your return.

When the audit is completed, you may be asked to pay extra taxes or penalties. If you don't agree, you may appeal the decision. If your appeal is turned down, you have the option to take your case to U.S. Tax Court.

For more information:

Publication 556: *Examination of Returns, Appeal Rights, and Claims for Refunds*
Cost: Free
Call: (800) 424-3676

GIVING TO CHARITY WISELY

IN 1987, ACCORDING TO THE AMERICAN Association of Fund Raising Counsel Trust for Philanthropy, contributions to charities in this country reached a record high of $94 billion, over 80% of which was given by individuals.

Unfortunately, part of that money did not go to the needy, but to the greedy and the wasteful. Among the many appeals for funds from legitimate and very valuable charities are some solicitations from:

- Some individuals and organizations whose appeals are totally fraudulent

- Some organizations which spend so much money on salaries and fund raising that as little as a few cents of every dollar contributed actually goes to the intended cause

The solution to the problem of fraud and misrepresentation is not to stop giving, but to give wisely. Following are the many resources, publications, and services that can make sure you'll enjoy the kind of satisfaction that comes from knowing your money is working hard to make America a better place in which to live.

PLANNING YOUR CHARITABLE GIVING

How much should you give? On the average, Americans annually contribute about 2% of their income to charity, or an average of about $500 per year per family. Only you can determine how much is appropriate in your circumstances. However, in budgeting for charity, keep in mind that some or all of your contributions may be tax-deductible.

For detailed information on planning your charitable contributions:

Booklet: *Tips on Charitable Giving*
Cost: Free, with self-addressed stamped envelope

From: Philanthropic Advisory Service
Council of Better Business Bureaus,
Department 023
Washington, DC 20042

Newsletter: *Insight*
Cost: $20.00 per year for 4 issues (checks payable to PAS/CBBB)
Contains: Information on philanthropy
From: Philanthropic Advisory Service
Council of Better Business Bureaus,
Department 023
Washington, DC 20042

DEDUCTING YOUR CONTRIBUTIONS

One of the benefits of contributing to worthwhile causes is that these contributions can be tax-deductible. Some points to remember are:

1. Charitable contributions of up to 50% of adjusted gross income are deductible, but *only if deductions are itemized on the tax return. Taxpayers who take the standard deduction cannot make additional deductions for charitable contributions.*

2. *In addition to the money you contribute to charity, you can also deduct a sum equal to the "fair market value" of goods and property you donate to an eligible charity.*

3. *The value of time or services donated to a charity are not deductible, but out-of-pocket expenses related to those services, such as transportation expenses, are deductible.*

4. *Just because an organization is "tax exempt" (exempt from paying federal taxes) doesn't mean that contributions to it are "tax-deductible."*

For more information on tax deductions for charitable contributions:

> **Booklet:** *Tips on Tax Deductions for Charitable Contributions*
> **Cost:** $1.00 plus self-addressed stamped envelope (checks payable to PAAS/CBBB)
> **Contains:** Information on the types of nonprofit organizations, their tax status, and general information on tax deductions

> **From:** Philanthropic Advisory Service
> Council of Better Business Bureaus,
> Department 023
> Washington, DC 20042

> **Booklet:** *How Much Really Is Tax Deductible?*
> **Cost:** Free
> **From:** Independent Sector
> 1828 L Street, NW
> Washington, DC 20036
> (202) 223-8100
> **IRS Publications:** • 448: *Federal Estate and Gift Taxes*
> • *526: Charitable Deductions*
> • *529: Miscellaneous Deductions*
> • *561: Determining the Value of Donated Property*
> • *585: Voluntary Tax Methods to Help Finance Political Campaigns*
> **Cost:** Free
> **From:** Your local IRS office (look in telephone book) or Call 1-800-424-3676

To find out if contributions to a specific organization are tax deductible, ask the organization for a copy of its "Letter of Determination," a formal notification received from the IRS when tax-exempt status is approved. You can also consult:

> **IRS Publication:** 78: *Cumulative List of Organizations*
> **Cost:** Free
> **Contains:** Annual listing of thousands of organizations to which contributions are deductible
> **From:** Your local IRS office
> or Call 1-800-424-3676

CHOOSING THE RIGHT CHARITY

The Philanthropic Advisory Service of the Council of Better Business Bureaus has developed a set of "Standards for Charitable Solicitations." In general, these standards require:

- Public accountability should be fulfilled through the issuance of detailed annual reports and financial statements
- Use of funds must be reasonable. The Bureau defines "reasonable" as a minimum of 50% of an organization's revenues are devoted to programs and activities related to the organization's purpose, leaving 50% or less for administrative and fund-raising costs. A more ideal ratio for an efficient charity is two thirds to programs and activities, one third to administrative and fund-raising costs
- Solicitations and informational materials should be truthful and clearly descriptive, both in whole and in part
- Fund raising should be adequately controlled, honest, and conducted without excessive pressure
- The organizations should have an adequate and active governing structure that includes independent board members

For complete information about these standards:

Booklet: *Standards for Charitable Solicitations*
Cost: Free, with self-addressed stamped envelope
From: Philanthropic Advisory Service
Council of Better Business Bureaus, Department 023
Washington, DC 20042

The Philanthropic Advisory Service constantly evaluates how closely national charitable organizations adhere to these standards. If you are interested in these evaluations:

Newsletter: *Give But Give Wisely*
Cost: $1.00 per issue, $10.00 per year for 6 issues

Contains: Lists of organizations that meet the standards, organizations that are under evaluation, and organizations that have not cooperated with the Better Business Bureaus
From: Philanthropic Advisory Service
Council of Better Business Bureaus, Department 023
Washington, DC 20042

Reports: PAS reports on individual charities
Cost: 3 or less are free, with self-addressed stamped envelope
From: Philanthropic Advisory Service
Council of Better Business Bureaus, Department 023
Washington, DC 20042

The National Charities Information Bureau also evaluates charities on the basis of adherence to standards similar to those of the Philanthropic Advisory Service:

Booklet: *Wise Giving Guide*
Cost: Free
Contains: The NCIB standards, plus lists of organizations that meet standards, organizations that fail to meet standards, and organizations that have not provided adequate information
From: National Charities Information Bureau
19 Union Square West
New York, NY 10003

Report: NCIB reports on individual charities
Cost: Up to 3 are free
From: National Charities Information Bureau
19 Union Square West
New York, NY 10003

Information about local charities can often be obtained from your local Better Business Bureau (see listing, pages 452–459).

PROTECTING YOURSELF AGAINST FRAUD AND IMPROPER SOLICITATIONS

Always be careful when approached to make a charitable contribution. Some wise procedures to follow include:

- Always write a check instead of giving cash
- Always make the check payable to the charity, not to the individual collecting the money
- Ask for the complete name and complete address of the organization. Many unethical groups take names that sound very much like the names of reputable charities. If you're solicited by telephone, insist on the full name and telephone number of the person calling you. Then hang up, and call back
- Never give in when a telephone solicitor says that your contribution has to be given to a "runner" who will come to your house to pick it up. Any legitimate charity can wait a day for your contribution to be mailed. Groups that aren't legitimate don't want your contribution to be mailed, because that makes them vulnerable to tough federal prosecution on mail fraud charges
- Do not be fooled by requests for contributions that are deliberately designed to look like bills. Such solicitations are illegal
- You are under no legal obligation to pay for or to return unsolicited merchandise sent to you, such as greeting cards, calendars, etc.

Some additional information that will help you give wisely:

Booklets: *Tips on Solicitations by Police and Firefighter Organizations *TB8* Tips on Handling Unwanted Direct Mail from Charitable Organizations*
Cost: $1.00 each, with self-addressed stamped envelope
From: Philanthropic Advisory Service Council of Better Business Bureaus, Department 023 Washington, DC 20042

Your Health

If I'd known I was going to live to be 100, I'd have taken better care of myself.

Jazz great Eubie Blake, on his 100th birthday

One of the most dramatic statistical stories in America today is that the average life expectancy has risen almost 5 years since 1970. People turning 65 today can expect, on the average, to live well into their 80s. This longevity has rewritten our long-standing definitions of "middle age" and "old age." The latter is now reserved for people in their 80s and older.

Much of this increase in longevity has come from treatment techniques developed through research. Yet more dramatic than the treatments themselves has been a growing body of evidence that health problems and aging do not go hand in hand. Many of the health conditions, problems, and diseases that disabled and killed older Americans are now partly or largely preventable. People who take the time to become better educated about health and the aging process, who follow sensible health prevention practices, and who are knowledgeable health-care consumers, have dramatically better chances of living healthy, unrestricted lives into their 80s and beyond.

This section focuses on hundreds of important health facts and resources. You'll learn:

- How to stay healthy through sensible prevention
- How to purchase and use prescription drugs
- How to reduce the costs of health care and services
- How to select the right physician and other health professionals
- How to find information and treatment for every major health problem and disease
- How to manage the difficult task of caring for a chronically ill person at home
- How to find rehabilitation facilities and other help for temporarily or permanently handicapping or disabling conditions

CHAPTER 11

HEALTHY LIVING: AN OVERVIEW

As IMPORTANT AS HEALTH IS TO ALL of us, it's surprising that many people pay more attention to maintaining their homes or cars than they do to maintaining their bodies. Fortunately, it is never to late to begin a preventative maintenance program. Changing your health habits, even late in life, can dramatically reduce the chances of contracting many serious illnesses. That's why it's important for you to learn about good health strategies, assess your own health risks and problems, and begin a program of sensible prevention.

EDUCATING YOURSELF ABOUT HEALTH

With the cost of medical care reaching 10% of our entire gross national product, the federal government and nonprofit organizations have stepped up their health education efforts. As a result, most of us can acquire a library of health information materials easily and inexpensively. Among the best are:

Booklet: *Strategies for Good Health* (D12261)
Cost: Free
Contains: A 28-page overview of good health habits for older Americans
From: AARP Fulfillment
1909 K Street, NW
Washington, DC 20049

Book: *Age Pages*
Cost: $3.50
Contains: A 100-page collection of 35 fact sheets offering practical health promotion information. These *Age Pages* were prepared by the National Institute on Aging and the U.S. Public Health Service
From: Consumer Information Center
P.O. Box 100
Pueblo, CO 81009

Organization: National Health Information Clearinghouse
Services: Operates toll-free hotline to answer health questions and directs

callers to the appropriate resources. Issues a number of publications, including:

- *Healthy People: The Surgeon General's Report on Health Promotion and Disease Prevention* ($1.00)
- *Behavior Patterns and Health* ($2.00)
- *Health Information Resources in the Federal Government* ($2.00)

For information: National Health Information Center
P.O. Box 1133
Washington, DC 20013
(800) 336-4797 (Ex. MD)
(301) 565-4167

Resource Guide: *Staying Healthy: A Bibliography of Health Promotion Materials*
Cost: $2.25
Contains: A 72-page guide to current information in all areas of health promotion and disease prevention
From: Superintendent of Documents
U.S. Government Printing Office
Washington, DC 20402
(202) 783-3238

Booklets: • *Health Resources for Older Women* ($1.75)

- *The Healthy Heart Handbook for Women* ($1.25)

From: Superintendent of Documents
U.S. Government Printing Office
Washington, DC 20402
(202) 783-3238

Booklets: • *Answers About Aging*
- *Age Words: A Glossary on Health and Aging*
- *What Is Your Aging I.Q.?*
- *To Understand the Aging Process*
Cost: Free
From: NIA Information Center
2209 Distribution Circle
Silver Spring, MD 20910
(301) 495-3455

Book: *The American Medical Association Straight-Talk, No Nonsense Guide to Health and Well-Being After 50*
Cost: $8.95
Contains: A comprehensive guide to physical and emotional health aimed at readers age 45 and older
From: Random House

Booklet: *Staying Healthy As You Get Older*
Cost: Free
From: American Society for Internal Medicine
1101 Vermont Ave., NW
Washington, DC 20008
(202) 289-1700

HOW'S *YOUR* HEALTH?

After you've acquired some general knowledge about health and the normal aging process, you should evaluate yourself and your life-style. If you have specific health complaints or problems, or if you haven't had a physical examination recently, you should have a physician conduct such a physical (see Chapter 13 for information on selecting a physician). In addition, self-assessment guides can give you an idea of your general level of risk for heart disease, high blood pressure, cancer, diabetes, and other common conditions. Two easy to use self-assessment guides are:

Test: *Healthstyle: A Self-Test*
Cost: Free

Contains: A 2-page, 24 question form that scores health risks on a scale of 1-10 and gives suggestions for improvement

From: National Health Information Center
P.O. Box 1133
Washington, DC 20013
(800) 336-4797 (Ex. MD)
(301) 565-4167

Test: *Hope Health Appraisal*
Cost: $3.95
Contains: Twelve self-scoring health tests, along with prevention techniques
From: International Health Awareness Center
157 South Kalamazoo Mall, Suite 482
Kalamazoo, MI 49007
(616) 343-0770

MAINTAINING GOOD HEALTH

The material above and your own health appraisal should alert you to a number of important steps everyone can take to maintain good health and reduce the chances of serious illness and disease:

- Stop smoking and other use of tobacco products
- Control blood pressure
- Eat right
- Maintain proper weight
- Exercise regularly
- Use prescription and over-the-counter medications properly
- Reduce the risks of accidents

Stop Smoking Now

The Surgeon General of the United States has said that "cigarette smoking is clearly identified as the chief preventable cause of death in our society." All the negative effects of smoking can be summed up in one statistic calculated by the National Center for Health Statistics: the life of a 25-year-old smoker will be, on the average, 8.3 years shorter than the life of a nonsmoker. Smokers are three times more likely to die of cancer than nonsmokers, and they have more than double the risk of heart attack, stroke, and other serious disease. The best programs and publications that will alert you to the health risks of tobacco and help you stop smoking include:

Organization: The American Cancer Society
Services: Many of the Cancer Society's 3,100 local units sponsor "Fresh Start" Stop Smoking Clinics, each of which is led by a trained professional. The organization also issues many free publications, including:
- *Quitter's Guide: 7 Day Plan to Help You Quit Smoking*
- *How to Quit Cigarettes*
- *If You Smoke, Take This Risk Test*
- *Fifty Most Often Asked Questions About Smoking*
- *Facts on Lung Cancer*
- *Facts on Oral Cancer*
- *Quit Smoking—The Lives You Save Could Be Those*

For information: Contact your local American Cancer Society office (see White Pages)

or

American Cancer Society
1599 Clifton Road NE
Atlanta, GA 30329

(800) 227-2345 (Ex. GA)
(404) 320-3333

Organization: American Lung Association
Services: Hundreds of local ALA affiliates sponsor 7-week "Freedom from Smoking Clinics" run by trained volunteers and professionals. Among the organization's publications are:
- *Freedom from Smoking in 20 Days*
- *A Lifetime of Freedom from Smoking*
- *Help a Friend Stop Smoking*
- *Stop Smoking/Stay Trim*

For information: Contact your local American Lung Association office (see White Pages)

or

American Lung Association
1740 Broadway
New York, NY 10019

Organization: National Cancer Institute
Office of Cancer Communications
Building 31, Room 10A-24
9000 Rockville Pike
Bethesda, MD 20892
(800) 422-6237 (Ex. MD)
(800) 492-6600 (MD)
Services: Toll-free hotline provides information on quitting smoking and referral to programs. Publications include:
- *Clearing the Air: A Guide to Quitting Smoking*
- *Why Do You Smoke?*
- *You've Kicked the Habit for Good*

Organization: Office on Smoking and Health
Technical Information Center
Park Building, Room 1-10
5600 Fishers Lane
Rockville, MD 20857
(301) 443-1575
Services: Coordinates smoking education, prevention, and research efforts for the Department of Health and Human Services. Publications include:
- *State and Local Programs on Smoking and Health (A directory of stop smoking programs across the country)*
- *No More Butts, A Guide to Quitting Smoking*
- *Self-Test For Smokers*
- *Smoking, Tobacco and Health*

Organization: American Heart Association
Services: Many local affiliates conduct stop-smoking programs and clinics
For information: Contact your local American Heart Association (see White Pages)

or

American Heart Association
7320 Greenville Avenue
Dallas, TX 75231
(800) 527-6941 (Ex. TX)
(214) 750-5300

Control High Blood Pressure

The Joint National Committee on Detection, Evaluation and Treatment of High Blood Pressure uses readings of 160/90 (read as "160 over 90") as the upper limit of normal adult blood pressure. A staggering 58 million adult Americans have readings that exceed this limit, including 57% of people age 55 to 64 and 64% of people age 65 and older. High blood pressure increases the risk of both heart attacks and strokes.

You are more likely to have high blood pressure if you are over 50, if you are African-American, if you have a family history of high blood pressure, or if you are a woman. However, anyone can develop high blood pressure. However, most hypertension sufferers can reduce their blood pressure to normal levels if they:

- Maintain proper weight
- Reduce intake of sodium
- Exercise
- Don't smoke
- Avoid caffeine
- Decrease consumption of fats and increase fiber

In the event that these kinds of changes don't control your high blood pressure, physicians can treat the condition with medication. For more information:

Organization: High Blood Pressure Information Center
4733 Bethesda Ave.
Bethesda, MD 20814
(301) 951-3260
Services: Coordinates education, research, and health-promotion efforts. Free publications include:
- *High Blood Pressure and What You Can Do About It*
- *High Blood Pressure: Things You and Your Family Should Know*
- *Questions About Weight, Salt and High Blood Pressure*

Booklet: *A Primer on High Blood Pressure*
Cost: Free
From: Office of Public Affairs
Public Health Service
Food and Drug Administration
5600 Fishers Lane
Rockville, MD 20857

Age Page: *High Blood Pressure: A Common But Controllable Disorder*
Cost: Free
From: NIA Information Center
2209 Distribution Circle
Silver Spring, MD 20910
(301) 495-3455

Booklet: *High Blood Pressure*
Cost: Free

From: American Heart Association
7320 Greenville Avenue
Dallas, TX 75231
(800) 527-6941 (Ex. TX)
(214) 750-5300

Booklet: *About Your High Blood Pressure Medicines*
Cost: Free
From: U.S. Pharmacopeial Convention
12601 Twinbrook Parkway
Rockville, MD 20852
(800) 227-8772 (Ex. MD)
(301) 881-0666

Eating Right

Good nutrition and good health go hand in hand. Eating right provides energy for your everyday activities and plays a key role in maintaining a positive mental attitude. In addition, a balanced diet is a proven factor in reducing the risk of many kinds of illness, including heart disease, high blood pressure, stroke, cancer, diabetes, digestive disorders, osteoporosis, and sleep disorders. Evidence is accumulating that poor nutrition is the cause of many health problems in older people that had been previously attributed to aging.

The U.S. Department of Agriculture has developed the following guidelines that suggest you should:

Eat a Balanced Diet. Even though you probably find yourself cutting down on the amount of food you eat as you grow older, you have to be very careful not to cut down on the variety of foods you eat. Every meal should include selections from the four basic food groups:

- Milk group, which includes cheese and yogurt
- Meat group, which includes eggs, fish, legumes, nuts, and seeds

- Vegetable and fruit group
- Bread and cereal group

Avoid Too Much Fat.   It is especially important to avoid saturated fats which contain cholesterol. Research has shown that diets high in fat, even cholesterol-free fat, contribute to higher risks of cancer and digestive diseases. Since the the incidence of these conditions also increases with age, limiting fat consumption is particularly important for people age 50 and over.

Research has shown that blood cholesterol readings of 200 milligrams or higher are associated with an increased risk of heart attacks and strokes, and that danger also increases with age. The Harvard Medical School has estimated that every 1% reduction in blood cholesterol results in a 2% reduction in your risk of having a heart attack. The best way to prevent or reduce high blood cholesterol readings is by reducing fat in the diet.

Increase Your Consumption of Carbohydrates and Dietary Fiber.   The healthiest diet is one in which most of the calories are provided by potatoes, breads, cereals, pasta, rice, and other complex carbohydrates. An added benefit of eating foods made from whole grains is that they contain significant amounts of dietary fiber, the indigestible portion of plant foods (grains, vegetables, nuts, seeds, fruits). High-fiber diets tend to prevent constipation and reduce the risks of serious colon conditions, such as diverticulosis, which affects an estimated 50% of people age 60 and over. High-fiber diets are also helpful with weight-loss programs and may reduce the risks of cancer and heart disease.

Drink Enough Fluids.   Water is the single most important substance that human beings consume. However, as many as a third of people age 65 and over consume so little fluid that they are risking their health. The U.S. Department of Agriculture recommends every adult consume two quarts of liquid per day.

Reduce Your Intake of Sodium.   Excess salt intake is associated not only with an increased risk of high blood pressure, but also with swelling of parts of the body and severe headaches.

Meet Your Body's Vitamin and Mineral Requirements.   A study conducted by the National Institute on Aging revealed that approximately 33% of Americans age 65 and over had diets that were consistently deficient in one or more important vitamins or minerals.

The federal government has established the following dietary guidelines for men and women age 51 and over:

	Men	Women
Protein (g)	56	44
Vitamins		
Vitamin A ([AQ4]xx)	1000	800
Vitamin D (xx)	5	5
Vitamin E (xx)	10	8
Vitamin K (xx)	100	100
Vitamin C (mg)	60	60
Thiamin (mg)	1.2	1.0
Riboflavin	1.4	1.2
Niacin (mg)	16	13
Vitamin B_6 (mg)	2.2	2.0
Folacin (xx)	400	400
Vitamin B_{12}	3.0	3.0
Minerals		
Calcium (mg)	800	800
Phosphorus (mg)	800	800
Magnesium (mg)	350	300
Iron (mg)	10	10
Zinc (mg)	15	15
Iodine (xx)	150	150

Translating these guidelines into a practical, everyday nutritional program that you can live with requires further education. Begin by reviewing your diet in detail with your physician. This is especially important if you are taking prescription medications or are being treated for a chronic disease or condition.

For information on nutrition, contact:

Organization: American Dietetic Association
216 W. Jackson Blvd.
Chicago, IL 60606
(312) 899-0040
Services: Answers nutrition questions, provides referrals to dietitians, and provides educational materials

You should also assemble a nutrition library from these excellent resources:

Booklets:
- *Dietary Guidelines for Americans* ($0.50)
- *Diet, Nutrition, and Cancer Prevention: The Good News* (Free)
- *Eating to Lower Your High Blood Cholesterol* ($2.00)
- *Consumer's Guide to Food Labels* (Free)
- *Food Additives* (Free)
- *Fruit: Something Good That's Not Illegal, Immoral Or Fattening* (Free)
- *The Nutritional Gender Gap at the Dinner Table* (Free)
- *Nutritive Values of Foods* ($2.75)
- *Some Facts and Myths About Vitamins* (Free)
- *Diet and the Elderly* (Free)
- *A Word About Low Sodium Diets* (Free)
- *Making Food Dollars Count* ($0.50)
- *A Primer on Dietary Minerals* (Free)

- *The Safe Food*
- *Your Kitchen Guide* (Free)
- *Safe Food to Go* (Free)
- *Thrifty Meals for Two* ($2.50)
- *Diet, Exercise, and Other Keys to a Healthy Heart* (Free)
From: Consumer Information Center
P.O. Box 100
Pueblo, CO 81002

Booklet: *Eating for Your Health* (D12164)
Cost: Free
From: AARP Fulfillment
1909 K Street, NW
Washington, DC 20049

Booklets:
- *Facts About Cholesterol*
- *Eating to Lower Your High Blood Cholesterol*
- *So You Have High Blood Cholesterol*
Cost: Free
From: National Cholesterol Education Program
4733 Bethesda Ave.
Bethesda, MD 20814
(301) 951-3260

Booklet: Easy Eating for Well-Seasoned Adults (Free)
From: National Clearinghouse for Primary Care Information
8201 Greensboro Drive, Suite 600
McLean, VA 22102
(703) 821-8955

Booklet: *Be Your Best: Nutrition After 50*
Cost: Free
From: American Institute for Cancer Research
1759 R Street, NW
Washington, DC 20009
(800) 843-8114
(202) 328-7744

Booklet: *Diet, Nutrition and Cancer: A Guide to Food Choices*
Cost: Free
National Cancer Institute
Call: (800) 422-6237

Age Pages: • *Nutrition, A Lifelong Concern*
• *Be Sensible About Salt*
• *Dietary Supplements: More Is Not Always Better*
Cost: Free
From: NIA Information Center
2209 Distribution Circle
Silver Spring, MD 20910
(301) 495-3455

Information: *Dietary Guidelines and Your Health*
Cost: $4.50
Contains: A packet of seven booklets from the U.S. Department of Agriculture containing important information on nutrition and health
From: Superintendent of Documents
U.S. Government Printing Office
Washington, DC 20402
(202) 783-3238

Organization: Food and Nutrition Information Center
National Agricultural Library Building
Beltsville, MD 20705
(301) 344-3719
Service: Answers questions about the federal dietary guidelines and any other nutrition-related information, including questions on vitamins and other dietary supplements

Organization: Center for Science in the Public Interest
1501 16th Street, NE
Washington, DC 20036
(202) 332-9110
Services: Nonprofit organization that produces many programs and publications stressing good nutrition and proper diet, including:

• *Saturated Fat Attack* ($5.00)
• *Guess What's Coming to Dinner* ($3.50)
• *Shopping Smart* ($3.50)
• *The Complete Eater's Digest and Nutrition Scorecard* ($11.95)
• *Eater's Choice: The Food Lover's Guide to Lower Cholesterol* ($12.95)
• *The Over 50 Cookbook: Eating Well When You Just Can't Eat the Way You Used To* ($14.95)
• *Nutrition Action Healthletter* ($19.95 per year for 12 issues)

Lose Weight

Medical research tells us that there is no proven link between a few extra pounds and increased risk of serious disease. Obesity, however, is a factor in heart disease, high blood pressure, diabetes, and many other conditions.

Gerontology Research Center Table

	Normal weight range for men and women (age range)		
	40–49	50–59	60–69
4'10"	99–127	107–135	115–142
4'11"	103–131	111–139	119–147
5'0"	106–135	114–143	123–152
5'1"	110–140	118–148	127–157
5'2"	113–144	122–153	131–163
5'3"	117–149	126–158	135–168
5'4"	121–154	130–163	140–173
5'5"	125–159	134–168	144–179
5'6"	129–164	138–174	148–184
5'7"	133–169	143–179	153–190
5'8"	137–174	147–184	158–196
5'9"	141–179	151–190	162–201
5'10"	145–184	156–195	167–207
5'11"	149–190	160–201	172–213
6'0"	153–195	165–207	177–219
6'1"	157–200	169–213	182–225
6'2"	162–206	174–219	187–232
6'3"	166–212	179–225	192–238
6'4"	171–218	184–231	197–244

The most important question to ask is, "what should I weigh?" For older Americans, the best answer is a table compiled from research by the Gerontology Research Center of the National Institute on Aging. This table, which lists the normal weight range by age and height for both sexes, reflects the fact that some weight gain with age is normal and harmless.

If your weight is below the range listed above, you shouldn't be concerned, provided that you haven't experienced recent dramatic weight loss and provided that you've had a physical examination in the last year. It's more likely, however, that your weight exceeds the upper limit of the range listed above.

If so, you need to lose weight. The recommended approach to dieting is a fundamental change to a healthier life-style centered around a balanced diet and exercise. People over age 40 should also see their physician before starting a weight-loss program, especially one involving exercise. Medical supervision and a slow, steady approach to losing weight is the right approach.

Unfortunately, dieting over a long period of time isn't easy. That's why weight loss is a thriving area for health fraud and quackery. Fad diets, especially quick weight loss plans, can pose significant health risks for people age 50 and over. Before you embark on a diet plan, you should read:

> **Booklets:** • *Diet Books Sell Well, But . . .* (No. 84-1093)
> • *How to Take Weight Off Without Getting Ripped Off* (No. 85-1116)
> • *About Body Wraps, Pills and Other Magic Wands for Losing Weight*
> **Cost:** Free
> **From:** Food and Drug Administration Office of Consumer Affairs Public Inquiries 5600 Fishers Lane

> Rockville, MD 20857
> (301) 443-3170

Many dieters find self-help groups a valuable source of information and support. Among the leading groups are:

> **Organization:** Overeaters Anonymous
> P.O. Box 92870
> Los Angeles, CA 90009
> (213) 542-8363
> **Services:** Self-help group modeled on Alcoholics Anonymous. Makes referrals to 7,000 local chapters

> **Organization:** T.O.P.S. (Take Off Pounds Sensibly)
> P.O. Box 07360
> 4575 South Fifth Street
> Milwaukee, WI 53207
> (414) 482-4620
> **Services:** 12,000 local self-help groups meet weekly to help people attain and maintain their goal weights

Exercise Regularly

Every year, more and more research shows that regular physical activity can help the human body maintain, repair, and improve itself to an amazing degree, even for people with illnesses and disabilities. The following benefits of exercise can be enjoyed by people of any age, including those in their 80s and beyond:

- Reduces the risks of heart attacks and stroke
- Lowers blood pressure
- Increases stamina
- Strengthens muscles and slows loss of muscle tissue
- Extends the life of nerve cells
- Reduces the chances of getting diabetes and reduces the severity of the illness

- Significantly reduces bone loss
- Slows deterioration of the joints, especially for people with arthritis
- Controls body weight more easily
- Reduces the effects of stress
- Produces a more positive mental attitude
- Improves sleep
- Slows the effects of aging on the skin
- Makes the body's use of vitamins more efficient
- Improves flexibility

This doesn't mean, of course, that you should head out the front door to jog 3 miles. If it has been a while since you've exercised, if you are taking medication regularly, or if you have a medical condition, illness, or disability, you should see your doctor before starting any type of exercise program.

A complete exercise program will contain two basic types of activities:

- Those designed to increase flexibility and strength, such as calisthenics, stretching, and lifting light weights
- Those designed to improve your cardiovascular system, such as walking, swimming, and jogging

The best way to improve your flexibility and strength is by joining a structured exercise program or class. You can probably find a class designed specifically for your age group and physical condition by contacting any number of sources, including:

- Your local senior center see White Pages or call your local area agency on aging (see listings, pages 383–427)
- Your local Y (see White Pages)

- Your local parks and recreation department (see telephone directory under your city government listing)
- Your local adult or continuing education program (see telephone directory under your local school system listing)

Another increasingly popular option is exercising along with a video. This option allows you to exercise at your convenience and in the privacy of your home. There are a number of exercise videos targeted to people of all ages. One guide that can help you choose an appropriate tape is:

Booklet: *Complete Guide to Exercise Videos*
Cost: Free
Contains: Objective descriptions of videos and magazine ratings of videos aimed at everyone from beginners to older Americans by a reputable mail-order video dealer
From: College Video Specialties
5390 Main Street NE
Minneapolis, MN 55421

Improving your cardiovascular fitness requires increasing the workload of your heart and lungs over a period of time. By that, experts mean that you engage in a strenuous activity that increases your heart rate to a "target range" that depends on your age, such as:

Age	Target pulse rate
40	125–150
50	120–145
55	115–140
60	112–135
65	108–130
70	104–125

To increase your endurance, you need to develop it to the point where you can sustain an increased heart rate for at least 20 minutes at a time, at least three times per week.

By far, the most popular form of cardiovascular activity for people age 50 and over is walking. If you've been very sedentary, you can begin to build endurance by such simple steps as parking at the far end of the lot when you go to the store. When you feel stronger, you can begin taking walks for distances that you've measured in your car. In bad weather, you can drive to a local mall to do your walking—in fact, many malls have organized walking clubs that provide companionship along with exercise. Swimming, another form of cardiovascular exercise, is especially appropriate for people with arthritis or other joint problems. Many local YMCAs, adult education programs, and parks and recreation departments sponsor special swimming programs for older people.

There are, of course, many other exercise options that are explained in detail in the following excellent resources:

Age Page: *Don't Take It Easy—Exercise!*
Cost: Free
From: NIA Information Center
2209 Distribution Circle
Silver Spring, MD 20910
(301) 495-3455

Booklet: *Pep Up Your Life: A Fitness Book for Seniors* (D549)
Cost: Free
From: AARP Fulfillment
1909 K Street, NW
Washington, DC 20049

Booklets: • *Exercise and Weight Control* ($0.50)
• *Fitness Fundamentals* ($1.00)
• *Everybody's Walking for Fitness* ($0.50)
• *Getting Fit Your Way* ($3.00)
From: Consumer Information Center
P.O. Box 100
Pueblo, CO 81002

Organization: National Association for Human Development
1620 Eye Street, NW
Washington, DC 20006
(202) 331-1737
Services: Publishes material on health and physical fitness for older adults, including:
• Active People Over 60
• Health and Fitness Program Manual

Booklet: *'E' Is for Exercise*
Cost: Free
From: Your local chapter of the American Heart Association (see White Pages)
or
American Heart Association
7320 Greenville Avenue
Dallas, TX 75231
(800) 527-6941 (Ex. TX)
(214) 750-5300

Booklets: • *Adult Physical Fitness* ($4.50)
• *Aqua Dynamics* ($3.75)
• *Introduction to Running: One Step at a Time* ($1.00)
• *Promoting Health, Preventing Disease: Objectives for the Nation* ($5.00)
• *Introduction to Physical Fitness* ($2.75)
• *Walking for Exercise and Pleasure* ($1.00)
From: Superintendent of Documents
U.S. Government Printing Office
Washington, DC 20402
(202) 783-3238

Booklets: • *The Fitness Challenge in the Later Years*
• *Walking for Exercise and Pleasure*
• *Staying With It: A Guide to Lifetime Adherence to a Physical Fitness Program*
• *Presidential Sports Awards*
Cost: Free

From: President's Council on Physical Fitness and Sports
450 Fifth Street, NW, Suite 7103
Washington, DC 20001
(202) 272-3430

Booklets: • *Exercise and Your Heart*
• *NHLBI Facts About Exercise: How to Get Started*
• *NHLBI Facts About Exercise: Sample Exercise Programs*
• *NHLBI Facts About Exercise: What Is Fact and What Is Fiction?*
Cost: Free
From: National Heart, Lung and Blood Institute
National Institutes of Health
Building 31, Room 4A-21
9000 Rockville Pike
Bethesda, MD 20892
(301) 496-4236

Booklet: *Exercises for Health*
Cost: $1.00
From: American Physical Therapy Association
1111 North Fairfax Street
Alexandria, VA 22314
(703) 684-2782

Resource list: Healthfinder: Exercise for Older Americans
Cost: $1.00
From: National Health Information Center
P.O. Box 1133
Washington, DC 20013
(800) 336-4797

Booklet: *Exercises for People with Arthritis*
Cost: Free
From: Arthritis Information Clearinghouse
P.O. Box 9782
Arlington, VA 22209
(703) 588-8250

Organization: Aerobics and Fitness Foundation
Services: Toll-free hotline answers questions about fitness and aerobics and provides information. Publications (send self-addressed stamped envelope) include:
• *Low Impact, No Stress Aerobics* (Free)
• *What to Look for in a Good Instructor and Health Club* (Free)
• Fact sheets on: ($0.50 each)
  – Shin splints
  – Fiber
  – Do's and don'ts of aerobics
For information: Aerobics and Fitness Foundation
15250 Ventura #310
Sherman Oaks, CA 91403
(800) 233-4886

Organization: Women's Sports Foundation
342 Madison Avenue, #728
New York, NY 10173
(800) 227-3988 (Ex. NY)
(212) 972-9170
Services: Provides information on health and fitness through toll-free number

Use Prescription and Over-the-Counter Medications Safely

According to the U.S. Food and Drug Administration, drug interactions, drug and food interactions, misuse, and other problems involving prescription and nonprescription medications kill an estimated 130,000 people each year, the substantial majority of which are age 50 and over. In addition, hundreds of thousands of patients suffer serious medical complications from drug interactions, some of which mimic the symptoms of serious illnesses, such as Alzheimer's disease. Finally, about half of all people who receive prescriptions fail to take them properly, which can be medically harmful.

Communicating with Your Physician.
You should discuss:

- All of the prescription and over-the-counter medications you're currently taking
- Any past reactions or side effects to drugs you've experienced
- Any allergies you have
- Specific instructions for taking the medication(s) prescribed
- A complete list of the potential side effects of the medication
- Instructions on what to do if a reaction occurs

Understanding Your Prescription. According to the American Society of Hospital Pharmacists, the following information should appear on a prescription:

1. The patient's name and address
2. The superscription "Rx" as a heading for the prescribed medication
3. The name and strength of the drug
4. Quantity of the drug
5. Directions for use, which normally follows the notation "sig." The most commonly used abbreviations, all of which derive from Latin, are:
   qd—every day
   BID—twice a day
   TID—three times a day
   QID—four times a day
   q_____h—every _____ hours
   ac—before meals
   pc—after meals
   prn—when needed
6. Refill information
7. Date

8. The prescriber's name, address, and registry number
9. The prescriber's signature

If this information isn't legible or complete, have your doctor rewrite the prescription.

Choosing a Pharmacist. Pharmacists often have more time to answer questions than physicians, and they may be more sensitive to possible interactions or side effects. Also, many large drugstores and chains keep a record of all your medications on a computer database that will automatically alert the pharmacist to a potential problem when a new medication is entered.

For information on choosing a pharmacist and asking the right questions of your physician:

Booklet: *Healthy Questions: How to Choose and Talk to Physicians, Dentists, Vision Care Specialists, and Pharmacists* (D12094)
Cost: Free
From: AARP Fulfillment
1909 K Street, NW
Washington, DC 20049

Finally, you should take the time to educate yourself about the proper use of medication. Among the resources you can obtain are:

Booklets: • *Food and Drug Interactions*
• *Some Things You Should Know About Prescription Drugs*
Cost: Free ($1.00 handling if ordering both)
From: Consumer Information Center
P.O. Box 100
Pueblo, CO 81009

Booklet: *Using Your Medications Wisely* (D317)
Cost: Free

From: AARP Fulfillment
1909 K St., NW
Washington, DC 20049

Booklets: • *Doctors, Patients Don't Communicate*
• *Does Your Medicine Chest Need First Aid?*
• *A Guide to the Proper Use of Tranquilizers*
• *Why People Don't Take Medicines Properly*
• *OTC Drug Labels: "Must Reading"*
Cost: Free
From: Food and Drug Administration
Office of Consumer Affairs
Public Inquiries
5600 Fishers Lane
Rockville, MD 21207
(301) 443-3170

Age Page: *Safe Use of Medicines by Older People*
Cost: Free
From: NIA Information Center
2209 Distribution Circle
Silver Spring, MD 20910
(301) 495-3455

Booklet: *Medicines and You*
Cost: Free
Contains: 62-page description of how your age, your genetic make up, and your diet can affect the way medicines work in your body
From: National Institute of General Medical Sciences NIH
Building 31, Room 4A-52
9000 Rockville Pike
Bethesda, MD 20892
(301) 496-7301

Booklet: *About Your Medicines*
Cost: Free
From: U.S. Pharmacopeial Convention
12601 Twinbrook Parkway

Rockville, MD 20852
(800) 227-8772 (Ex. MD)
(301) 881-0666

Booklet: *Self-Medication Awareness Test*
Cost: Free
From: American Pharmarcutical Association
2215 Constitution Ave., NW
Washington, DC 20077
(202) 628-4410

Book: *50+: The Graedon's People's Pharmacy for Older Adults* by Joe and Teresa Graedon
Cost: $13.95
Contains: A comprehensive, readable 460-page guide to safe and sensible use of medications by older people
From: Bantam Books

Organization: Council on Family Health
420 Lexington Avenue
New York, NY 10017
(212) 210-8836
Service: An organization sponsored by manufacturers of medicines that issues a variety of publications on safe use of medicines, personal health, and health emergencies

Organization: AARP Pharmacy Service
Box 19209
Alexandria, VA 22320
Services: The largest nonprofit mail-order pharmacy in the world, offering savings on prescription medicine, nonprescription medicines, vitamins, and health products to AARP members. Most prescriptions are accompanied by a "Medication Information Leaflet" that describes the drug and alerts users to potential side effects. Also publishes:
• *The AARP Pharmacy Prescription Drug Handbook* ($9.95): Provides easy to understand descriptions of

more than 1,000 drugs commonly prescribed for people 50 and over. Contains 40-page full color pill identification chart

Reduce the Risk of Accidents

Accidents are the third leading cause of death (after cancer and heart attacks) in the United States. National Safety Council statistics show that accidental injuries, especially from falls and burns, become more frequent and more serious as people grow older. Although people age 65 and over make up about 11% of the U.S. population, they account for approximately 23% of all accidental deaths. Nearly one million people age 65 and over suffer disabling injuries in accidents every year.

The leading cause of accidental death among older adults is automobile accidents. One factor is failure to wear a seat belt, an omission which ranks along with cigarette smoking and high blood pressure as one of the major health risks. A second factor is failure to compensate for the effects of aging and inattention while driving. For example, both night vision and peripheral vision deteriorate with age. To compensate, an older driver should try to plan as many trips as possible during daylight hours, obey speed limits, pay increased attention to traffic signs, increase the distance between his or her car and the car ahead, and be especially cautious at intersections.

However, many drivers find it hard to change habits by themselves. That is why the AARP, in connection with automobile clubs, developed:

Program: 55 Alive/Mature Driving
Services: The AARP has trained over 3,000 volunteers to conduct 8-hour driver improvement programs for people age 55 and over. Many automobile insurance companies give discounts to people who have completed this program, which is held in many localities nationwide
For information: Traffic Safety AARP
1909 K Street, NW
Washington, DC 20049

Second in number to automobile accidents are injuries suffered in and around the home. A majority of these accidents could be prevented by a safety inspection of the home. For example, thousands of older people are seriously injured in falls each year because carpeting hasn't been tacked down, stair railings or steps are loose, stair treads are ripped, or kitchen floors are too slippery. To significantly lower the risk of household accidents, be especially alert to these kinds of easy-to-fix problems.

Booklet: *Home Safety Kit*
Cost: Free
Contains: Enables older adults and their families to conduct safety audits in the home
From: AARP Fulfillment
1909 K Street, NW
Washington, DC 20049

Age Page: *Accidents and the Elderly*
Cost: Free
From: NIA Information Center
2209 Distribution Circle
Silver Spring, MD 20910
(301) 495-3455

Organization: National Safety Council
444 North Michigan Avenue
Chicago, IL 60611
(800) 621-7619
(312) 527-4800
Services: Offers educational material and advice on accident prevention and other safety guidelines through a toll-free number

A third source of accidental injury is consumer products, including electric appliances, heating systems, stoves, furniture, and power equipment. To reduce your risk of injury, be sure to keep all such consumer products in good working order.

Organization: Consumer Product Safety Commission

Services: Operates a toll-free number for consumer product complaints and information. Publishes a large number of free fact sheets on consumer product safety, including:
- *Home Safety Checklist for Senior Consumers*
- *Safer Products, Safer People*
- *The Home Electrical System*
- *CPSC Guide to Electrical Safety*
- *Hazard Hunt*
- *Wake Up! Smoke Detectors*
- *What You Should Know About Home Fire Safety*
- *Extension Cords and Wall Outlets*
- *Space Heaters*
- *Television Fire and Shock Hazards*

Call: To file a complaint or ask about specific products (800) 638-2772

Write: For fact sheets and publication lists: Consumer Product Safety Commission
5401 Westband Ave.
Bethesda, MD 20207

Poisoning is another leading cause of accidental injury or death. By your phone, you should keep the telephone number of:

Organization: Your local poison control center

Services: A nationwide network of more than 100 poison control centers has been established under the guidance of the federal government. These centers have telephone lines manned 24 hours a day to answer questions and provide information in emergencies

For information: The number should be listed in the front of your telephone directory. If not, look under "Poison Control"

THE COST OF HEALTH CARE

Hᴇᴀʟᴛʜ ᴄᴀʀᴇ ᴄᴏsᴛs ʜᴀᴠᴇ sᴏᴀʀᴇᴅ ɪɴ recent decades, reaching 10% of our entire gross national product. Your health care costs will, on the average, rise as you grow older. Without proper health insurance and attention to reducing health care expenses, you may not be able to meet the bills for routine care, let alone cope with the expenses of serious or chronic illness or injury.

Your health insurance needs are determined by your age. Except for those who are permanently disabled or have very low incomes, Americans under age 65 are responsible for meeting all of their medical expenses, either through private health insurance or out of their own pockets. All Americans age 65 and over are eligible for the federal Medicare program, which provides coverage for some basic medical, hospital, and surgical services. However, many important health expenses aren't covered by Medicare, especially for people with long-term or catastrophic illnesses.

In this chapter, we will show you how to meet the costs of medical services, hospitalization, prescription drugs, and other health services.

HEALTH INSURANCE FOR PEOPLE UNDER AGE 65

Health insurance in the United States is a major industry. We suggest you take the time to learn about the various kinds of coverage in order to become a better consumer.

The Average Policy

The typical policy can include the following:

1. *Basic hospitalization insurance*

This provides payment for hospital room charges, nursing services, medications and supplies, operating room fees, and tests and procedures.

2. *Basic medical/surgical insurance*

This provides coverage for physician's fees for treatment performed in the hospital or in a doctor's office.

3. Major medical insurance

Major medical insurance provides coverage for the costs of major surgery or serious illness above the coverage provided by basic insurance. Major medical insurance normally covers total costs up to $1 million or more.

4. Prescription coverage

Prescription coverage pays part or all of the costs of medication prescribed by a physician.

The actual amount of total medical expenses paid by an insurance plan varies widely. Among the differences are:

1. Deductibles

Many plans require the policyholder to pay a certain amount per year or per illness before insurance coverage begins. This deductible can range from nothing to $1,000 or more.

2. Co-insurance

Many plans require that the insured pay a certain percentage of all expenses, commonly 20%. Some plans require co-insurance payment only up to a certain dollar figure, such as $2,500.

3. Usual and customary charges

This phrase refers to a "standard" payment the insurance company agrees to pay for every kind of illness, procedure, or test. For example, if the usual and customary charge for setting a broken limb is $75 and your doctor charges $100, you're responsible for the full difference.

4. Exclusions

All plans exclude certain types of expenses from reimbursal. For example, many plans won't pay for routine physical exams, part or all of mental health expenses, alternative treat-ments, such as acupuncture, or a variety of other exclusions.

5. Preexisting conditions

Many plans will not cover any medical expenses incurred while treating disease or conditions developed before the plan took effect until a waiting period has passed. This waiting period could be 2 years or more.

6. Dependent coverage

Some plans cover dependents fully, while others have significant limitations or exclusions.

For more information:

Organization: Health Insurance Association of America
Publications Division
1001 Pennsylvania Ave. NW
Washington, DC 20004
(800) 423-8000 (Ex. DC)
(202) 223-7780
Services: Answers consumer questions about health insurance and provides a number of publications through a toll-free telephone number

Booklet: *Your Insurance Dollar*
Cost: $1.00
From: Money Management Institute
2700 Sanders Road
Prospect Heights, IL 60070

Book: *Policy Wise: The Practical Guide to Insurance Decisions for the Older Consumer*
Cost: $5.95 (AARP member price $4.35) plus $1.75 postage
From: AARP Books/Scott Foresman and Co.
1865 Miner Street
Des Plaines, IL 60016

If You Become Unemployed Or Retire Early

The Federal Consolidated Omnibus Budget Reconciliation Act of 1985 (COBRA) requires most employers with health insurance plans to continue coverage of retired and unemployed former employees and their dependents for a minimum of 18 months. The employer may charge the former employee, but that charge cannot exceed the normal group rate plus a 2% service charge. Dependents may be entitled to coverage after the death of or divorce from a former employee. To find out more:

> **Booklet:** *Consumer Notes: Group Health Insurance Continuation*
> **Cost:** Free
> **From:** Health Insurance Association of America
> (800) 423-8000
> (202) 223-7780

> **Booklet:** *Group Health Insurance Continuation*
> **Cost:** Free (with self-addressed, stamped envelope)
> **From:** Older Women's League
> 730 Eleventh St., NW, Suite 300
> Washington, DC 20001
> (202) 783-6686

If you feel that you have been unfairly denied the right to continue your health insurance coverage, you should contact:

> **Resource:** Department of Labor
> Division of Technical Assistance
> Room North 5658
> 200 Constitution Avenue, NW
> Washington, DC 20210
> (202) 523-8784

Shopping for Health Insurance

It will generally cost you more to buy an individual health insurance policy than it will to belong to a group policy. If you are not covered by health insurance at work or if you're looking for a less expensive alternative to your current plan, your first step should be to search for medical insurance offered by a group to which you do or could belong. Examples are unions, guilds, consumer organizations, athletic leagues, and voluntary organizations.

If you don't belong to any such group or do not wish to join one, you can contact one group open to anyone who wishes to obtain health insurance:

> **Organization:** Co-op America
> **Services:** A nonprofit consumer organization that focuses on promoting socially responsible buying and investing. Members are eligible for group health and life insurance through Consumers United Insurance Company. Information on the insurance program will be sent to new members
> **Cost:** $15.00 for Co-op America membership
> **For information:** Co-op America
> 210 M Street, NW
> Washington, DC 20063
> (202) 872-5307

A third alternative for the self-employed or small business owners is group insurance offered through local Chambers of Commerce. Normally, you must be a member of a Chamber to be eligible for the insurance. For information, contact your local Chamber of Commerce.

A fourth alternative is your local Blue Cross/Blue Shield company. Blue Cross/Blue Shield is a nationwide association of individual nonprofit companies that offer medical, hospital, and major medical insurance. Many local

Blue Cross/Blue Shield companies offer health insurance policies to individuals. These policies are generally convenient for consumers, because many doctors and almost all hospitals will bill Blue Cross/Blue Shield directly, saving you the inconvenience of filing claim forms yourself. However, the cost and quality of Blue Cross/Blue Shield compared with insurance offered by for-profit companies varies widely from state to state. To obtain information about Blue Cross/Blue Shield in your area:

> **For information:** Call Blue Cross/Blue Shield (see White Pages)
> or
> Blue Cross/Blue Shields Associations
> 676 North St. Clair Street
> Chicago, IL 60611
> (312) 440-6000

Finally, you should obtain policy information and price quotations from for-profit insurance companies by contacting an independent insurance agent. For information on finding a good insurance agent, see pages 87–88.

Before You Purchase a Health Insurance Policy . . .

You should take the time to check on your insurance company's financial stability and record of service to policyholders. For complete information on how to do this, see Chapter 8, pages 82–96.

Note: Most states have enacted laws that give consumers the right to receive a full refund if they cancel an insurance policy within 10 to 15 days. Take advantage of this "free look" period if you haven't had time to check out the company before enrolling.

HMOs: An Alternative to Conventional Health Insurance

Health Maintenance Organizations (HMOs) provide complete medical care in return for a fixed monthly fee. HMOs are as much as 25% less expensive than conventional health insurance, primarily because members pay no deductibles or co-insurance payments for any type of medical care. Because health care costs for HMO members are fixed, they are especially attractive to retirees and other people with fixed incomes who have to carefully budget for all expenses. While some HMOs are limited to employees of corporations with which they have signed contracts, others are open to individuals.

One disadvantage of HMOs is that members are limited to receiving health care and services from physicians, clinics, and hospitals designated by the HMO. In some cases, this can mean longer waits for appointments, crowded offices, and less individual attention than that provided by independent physicians. When shopping for an HMO, you should evaluate the physicians who will be providing your primary care by using the information on selecting physicians and health professionals in the next chapter, pages 155–163.

Another disadvantage is that a significant number of HMOs have gone out of business or have been merged with other companies because of financial and administrative problems. Bankruptcy of an HMO leaves members without insurance and with no way to recoup the insurance premiums they have paid. Mergers of HMOs can mean changing physicians and longer trips for medical and hospital care. Evaluating the financial health of an HMO is difficult. Your best protection is joining an HMO that has been in business for several years and that has contracts with major hospitals.

To locate HMOs in your area, you should look in the Yellow Pages under "Health Maintenance Organizations" or contact the national trade association of HMOs:

Organization: Group Health Association of America
1129 20th Street, NW, Suite 600
Washington, DC 20036
(202) 778-3200

The AARP will consult a directory to see if there is an HMO near you if you write:

Organization: Health Advocacy Services
AARP
1909 K Street, NW
Washington, DC 20049

For more detailed information on evaluating HMOs, you should send for:

Booklets: • *More Health for Your Dollar: An Older Person's Guide to HMOs* (D1195)

• *Choosing an HMO: An Evaluation Checklist* (D12444)
Cost: Free
From: AARP Fulfillment
1909 K Street, NW
Washington, DC 20049

Of special interest to people age 65 and over are HMOs which have signed contracts with the federal government to provide services to Medicare recipients. For more information on how these contracts work:

Pamphlet: *Medicare and Prepayment Plans*
Cost: Free
From: U.S. Department of Health and Human Services
Health Care Financing Administration
East High Rise Building
6325 Security Blvd.
Baltimore, MD 21207
(800) 888-1988
(301) 966-3000

HEALTH INSURANCE FOR PEOPLE OVER AGE 65

For people age 65 and older, a complete health insurance program means combining Medicare with private insurance that covers the gaps in the federal program.

Medicare

Medicare is a federal health insurance program for people age 65 and older, as well as certain disabled people under age 65. You are automatically entitled to Medicare coverage if you are receiving or are entitled to receive:

- Social Security benefits
- Railroad retirement benefits
- Federal government pensions

If you're not sure about your eligibility for Social Security, you can refer to Chapter 2 for information.

Medicare has two parts, Part A and Part B. Part A is free. Part B is optional, and carries a monthly charge ($31 per month in 1990). This monthly charge is deducted from your Social Security check if you are receiving benefits or billed to you if you are not yet retired.

If you are receiving a Social Security check when you turn 65, you are automatically enrolled in Part A. If you are not yet retired, you have to apply at your local Social Security office (see White Pages under U.S. Government listing) for Part A *at least 3 months before your 65th birthday.* Retired or not, you must apply at your local Social Security office for Part B benefits *at least 3 months before your 65th birthday.* Applying by these deadlines is extremely important. If you miss the deadline, you can't sign up again until January 1 through March 31 of the next year, and your benefits won't start until the following July 1. Your premiums for Part B coverage will also be higher than if you signed up 3 months before your 65th birthday.

It is also important for you to understand what Parts A and B cover:

- Part A: Hospitalization Insurance
- Coverage includes:
  - Up to 90 days per year for a semiprivate room and board, nursing and miscellaneous hospital services, and supplies
  - 100 days of skilled nursing care in an acute care institution
  - Medically necessary skilled nursing care at home
  - Hospice care for the terminally ill
  - Blood transfusions

Under Part A, the patient is responsible for paying significant deductibles and co-insurance payments. For example, in 1989, patients paid deductibles of $560 for each hospital stay. Medicare paid the remaining hospital charges for the first 60 days of hospitalization. For days 61-90, patients paid a co-insurance charge of $150 per day. Medicare also paid all the costs of the first 20 days of skilled nursing home care, but charged a co-insurance payment of $80 per day for days 21-100. Skilled nursing care at home, hospice care, and blood transfusions also involved co-payments.

- Part B: Medical Insurance
- Coverage includes:
  - Physician and surgeon services in or out of hospitals, except for routine physical exams

- Medical services and supplies received on an outpatient basis, such as x-rays, lab tests, ambulance service, wheelchairs, etc.
- Physical therapy and speech therapy, if done under a doctor's supervision

Medicare pays 80% of the "approved" charge for each product or service, after you pay an annual $75 deductible, 100% of approved charges after the $75 deductible, and 20% co-insurance payments have reached $1,370.

The most important fact to understand about Part B coverage is that all reimbursements are based upon Medicare's "approved" fee for that product or service. For example, Medicare's approved fee for a certain procedure may be $50. If you've satisfied your annual deductible, Medicare will pay 80% of this fee, or $40. However, your doctor may actually charge $75 for the procedure, leaving you with a bill for $35. Any medical expenses you pay over the "approved" fee do not count toward your annual deductible or the yearly $1,370 out of pocket expense limit.

Among the other expenses not covered at all by Parts A or B are:

- Private duty nursing
- Skilled nursing home care beyond 100 days per year
- Custodial care in a nursing home or at home
- Routine physical exams and immunizations
- Prescription drugs
- Dental care
- Eyeglasses or hearing aids
- Care received outside of the United States

For more information about Medicare:

Booklets: • *Your Medicare Handbook Medicare*
• *How To Fill Out a Medicare Claim Form*
• *Your Medicare Recordkeeper*
Cost: Free
From: Your local Social Security office (see telephone directory under 'U.S. Government')

or

Health Care Financing Administration (800) 888-1998

Booklet: *Medicare: What It Covers, What It Doesn't* (D13133)
Cost: Free
From: AARP Fulfillment
1909 K St., NW
Washington, DC 20049

Challenging the Medicare System

The Health Advocacy Services Department of AARP strongly recommends that you challenge any Medicare reimbursement decision with which you disagree, even for relatively small amounts of money. The reason for this advice is a study that showed more than half of all such appeals resulted in increased reimbursements and less money out of Medicare recipients' pockets. For more information on challenging Medicare:

Booklet: *Knowing Your Rights: Medicare's Prospective Payment System* (D12330)
Cost: Free
From: AARP Fulfillment
1909 K St., NW
Washington, DC 20049

Program: Medicare/Medicaid Assistance Program

Services: The AARP has trained volunteers to help Medicare recipients with claims and appeals in more than 32 states. The AARP will also answer written questions about Medicare
For information: Health Advocacy Services
AARP
1909 K Street, NW
Washington, DC 20049

Book: *Your Real Medicare Handbook*
Cost: $8.00
Contains: Detailed, easy-to-understand explanation of Medicare programs, forms, and appeal procedures
From: Center for Public Representation
121 S. Pinckney Street
Madison, WI 53703
(608) 251-4008

Organization: Legal Counsel for the Elderly
Services: A national support center to improve the quality of legal services to older Americans. Publications include:
• *Self-Help Handbook: Medicare* ($6.95 plus $2.00 postage)
• Medicare series, four practical guides that help resolve Medicare problems:
• *Eligibility Book* ($5.95 plus $1.00 postage)
• *General Problems Book* ($5.95 plus $1.00 postage)
• *Hospital, Hospice, and Nursing Home Care Book* ($5.95 plus $1.00 postage)
• *Doctor Services* ($5.95 plus $1.00 postage)
All four $19.95 plus $2.50 postage
From: LCE, Inc.
P.O. Box 19269-K
Washington, DC 20036

Organization: Your state Medicare insurance carrier

Services: The federal government hires private insurance companies in each state to process Medicare claims. By law, each carrier must have a toll-free telephone number to answer questions and take complaints. For the number of the carrier in your state:

> White Pages under "Medicare Claims Information"
> Your local Social Security office (see telephone directory under "U.S. Government")
> Your local area agency on aging (see pages 383–427)
> Medicare hotline: (800) 888-1998

Programs: Medicare Advocacy Services: Many states and localities have funded programs that provide legal assistance to older people, including Medicare advocacy
For information: Your local area agency on aging (see pages 383–427.)

You should be wary of Medicare consultants. Because Medicare is so complex, a large number of small businesses offer to process Medicare claims and pursue appeals in return for a fee. Many of these companies offer a legitimate service that relieve consumers of the responsibility of filing claim forms for a modest fee ($8 for a simple claim form, on the average). However, this field has also attracted a significant number of con artists who make elaborate promises and charge exorbitant fees.

To avoid fraud:

- Beware of people who promise you very large settlements to claims rejected by Medicare

- Before you pay, check out the company by calling:

– Your local Better Business Bureau (see pages 452–459)
– Your state or local consumer protection agency (see pages 443–452)

How to Purchase Private "Medigap" Insurance

In the last decade, many companies have eliminated or reduced health care coverage for retirees. Therefore, a majority of Americans 65 and over need to purchase "Medigap" policies that fill some or all of the "gaps" in Medicare coverage.

This need has produced hundreds of different policies, many of which are offered to consumers through television advertising, direct mail, and even telephone solicitation. However, the quality and costs of these policies vary widely. The worst of these policies is a waste of money because they virtually duplicate Medicare coverage; the best provide nearly complete coverage against catastrophic illness.

The first step in purchasing a Medigap policy is to obtain a benchmark quotation from an insurance program that has been highly rated by consumer advocates. That program is:

Program: AARP Group Health Insurance Program
Services: Medicare supplement plan for AARP members
For information: AARP Group Health Insurance program
P.O. Box 7000
Allentown, PA 18175
(800) 523-5800 (Ex. PA)
(800) 492-2024

The second step is to take advantage of publications and information resources that will help you compare and evaluate individual policies. Because Medicare itself is complicated, this process can be more difficult than purchasing other forms of insurance, such as life or automobile insurance. Among these resources are:

Organization: Health Care Financing Administration
Services: Operates toll-free hotline to answer questions about Medicare. Will send the following free booklet:
Guide to Health Insurance for People with Medicare
Contact: Department of Health and Human Services
Health Care Financing Administration
6325 Security Blvd.
Baltimore, MD 21207
(800) 888-1998
(301) 966-3000

Booklets: • *Health Care Finances: A Guide for Adult Children and Their Parents*
• *The Consumer's Guide to Medicare Supplement Insurance*
Cost: Free
From: Health Insurance Association of America

1001 Pennsylvania Avenue, NW
Washington, DC 20004
(800) 423-8000
(202) 223-7780

Fact Sheets: Factsheets on Medicare and Health Care
Cost: Free
From: National Consumers League
Suite 516
815 15th St., NW
Washington, DC 20005
(202) 639-8140

Organization: Your state insurance department services: Many state insurance departments have publications explaining Medicare and supplementary health insurance programs. This department may also provide information on the level of complaints registered against specific insurance companies
For information: See your telephone directory under your state government listings or call your state government information service (see listings, pages 441–443)

HEALTH PROGRAMS FOR LOW INCOME AMERICANS

There are two government programs that provide special medical care for low income Americans. The most important is Medicaid, a joint federal/state program that pays most of the out-of-pocket Medicare expenses and offers additional medical services (e.g., dental care and eye care) for people who meet the income and asset requirements. Generally, people who are eligible for Supplemental Social Security (SSI) are eligible for Medicaid. However, eligibility criteria and benefits vary from state to state.

Medicaid normally removes the need for any other kind of supplemental health insurance. It also may cover long-term custodial care, eliminating the need for long-term care insurance (see pages 152–153). For information on Medicaid, contact your local area agency on aging (see listings, pages 383–427) or your state welfare agency (obtain number by calling your state government information services [see listings, pages 441–443]).

A second program is the Hill Burton Hospital Free Care Program. Under this program, the U.S. Public Health Administration has arranged for over 5,000 hospitals and clinics nationwide to provide free health care services to low-in-

come individuals meeting program requirements. The actual services provided and eligibility requirements are different for every institution in the program. Information and referrals
are available through a toll-free hotline:

> **Program:** Hill-Burton Hospital Free Care
> Program
> BHMORD-JRSA
> 5600 Fishers Lane

Rockville, MD 20857
(800) 638-0742 (Ex. MD, AK, HI)
(800) 492-0359 (MD)
(AK & HI residents must write)

> **Book:** *Managing Your Health Care Fi-*
> *nances*
> **Cost:** $7.95
> **From:** United Seniors Health Cooperative
> 1334 G St., NW
> Washington, DC 20005

HEALTH CARE FOR VETERANS

The U.S Department of Veterans Affairs (VA)
maintains a nationwide network of hospitals and
clinics that provide health care services and
hospital services to eligible veterans. Eligible
veterans include those who suffered service-
connected disabilities, service-connected illness, veterans of certain wars, and veterans
who meet certain income requirements. For information about veterans benefits:

> **Booklet:** *Federal Benefits for Veterans and*
> *Dependents*

> **Cost:** $2.25
> **From:** Consumer Information Center
> P.O. Box 100
> Pueblo, CO 81009

This publication lists all VA regional offices
and medical facilities. To provide information
about VA programs and facilities, the VA maintains toll-free numbers in all parts of the country. To get the number in your area, see your
White Pages under "U.S. Government."

PAYING FOR PRESCRIPTION DRUGS

Medicare doesn't cover the cost of prescription
drugs and other necessary health supplies. As
a result, the annual costs of medications can be
extremely high, especially for those people who
have to take medication on a long-term basis.

Saving Money on Your Drugs

There are many ways to spend less on prescription drugs. We suggest you take the time to do
the following:

1. *Comparison shop*

Prices vary widely from pharmacy to pharmacy for the exact same medication. In addition, many pharmacies give senior citizen discounts to people above a certain age, such as 62
or 65. Consumer surveys have shown as much
as a 30% difference between pharmacies.

2. *Ask your physician and pharmacists about*
   generic drugs

A company that develops a brand new drug
is protected by a patent that gives the company

exclusive rights to sell the drugs for 17 years under a brand name. After the patent expires, other companies can legally begin to manufacture and sell the same medications as "generic," or nonbrand name drugs.

Generic drugs are considerably less expensive than their brand name equivalents. And, by federal law, generic drugs must be identical to the brand name drugs in:

- Active ingredients
- Strength
- Dosage form (for example, tablet, liquid)
- Route of administration (for example, mouth, injection)
- Amount of drug released into the bloodstream

Recently, investigations by the Food and Drug Administration have revealed that some manufacturers have submitted false test results or bribed administrators in order to get approval to manufacture generic drugs. The same investigations have also revealed that the vast majority of generic drugs are safe and effective. You should rely on the advice of your physicians and pharmacists, as well as educating yourself about generic drugs by obtaining:

Booklets: • *Myths and Facts of Generic Drugs*
• *Some Things You Should Know About Prescription Drugs*
Cost: Free ($1.00 handling if ordering both)
From: Consumer Information Center
P.O. Box 100
Pueblo, CO 81009

Booklet: *A Consumer Guide to Generic Drugs*
Cost: Free
Contains: This 24-page reference contains:
• An explanation of the Food and

Drug Administration testing program that assures that generic drugs provide the exact same quality, purity, and effectiveness as equivalent brand name drugs
• A complete listing of all prescription tablets and capsules for which generic versions are available
• Comparative prices for brand name and generic drugs
From: Generic Pharmaceutical Industry Association
200 Madison Avenue, Suite 2404
New York, NY 10016
(212) 683-1881

3. *Shop by mail*

If you receive a prescription for a painkiller or antibiotic, you need it filled quickly. However, if you take one or more medications on a long-term basis, you can save a considerable amount of money by buying in quantity from a mail-order pharmacy.

Organization: AARP Pharmacy Service
Cost: Services available to AARP members ($5.00 per year) Sells a wide variety of discount vitamins, over-the-counter medications, and health supplies, as well as prescription drugs
For information: AARP Pharmacy
P.O. Box 19229
Alexandria, VA 22320

Organization: America's Pharmacy
P.O. Box 10490
Des Moines, IA 50306

4. *Investigate state programs*

Investigate state programs that subsidize the costs of prescription drugs. Many states have established programs that help older Americans meet the cost of prescription medications. For information, contact your local area agency on aging (see listings, pages 383–427)

LONG-TERM CARE INSURANCE

About 40% of Americans will sometime in the future require nursing home care, and this care can impoverish them and place an intolerable financial burden on their families. The need for this care increases dramatically with age, and so too does the importance of purchasing insurance that helps meet the very heavy costs of nursing home stays. About 90% of those who purchase long-term care policies today are age 60 or older.

The best time to purchase a policy is between ages 50 and 59, for two reasons. First, premiums increase dramatically at age 60 and over. Second, people with a serious disease or illness normally can't purchase long-term care policies, and the risk of developing such a condition increases with age.

How to Shop for the Best Policies

Over 100 different companies currently offer long-term care insurance. These policies are relatively complicated insurance products. Among the most important features are:

- The per-day benefit paid, which ranges from $25 to $150 per day. You should purchase a policy which pays the average cost of nursing homes in your area.

- Coverage limits. Policies provide benefits for periods of time from 2 to 6 years, or an equivalent lifetime dollar limit.

- Waiting period. The length of time you're in a hospital before collecting benefits can range from none to 100 days. The longer the waiting period, the less expensive the policy.

- Inflation protection. A policy that covers the average per-day costs of nursing home care today may pay less than a quarter of the costs 20 years from now.

- Financial soundness of the insurance company. You've wasted your premiums if your insurance company has gone bankrupt when it's time to file a claim. For information on how to check on the financial health of insurance companies, see Chapter 8, pages 82–96.

- Prior hospitalizations. Many patients go from home care to nursing home care without having a medical crisis that requires hospitalization. A policy that requires hospitalization before entering a nursing home may be worthless to many people.

- Exclusions. Buried in the fine print of many policies are clauses denying benefits to people suffering from Alzheimer's disease and other dementia. Since dementia is a common reason people need custodial care, some experts recommend obtaining a statement from an insurance company specifically stating Alzheimer's disease is covered.

- Home care. Many policies pay partial benefits for custodial care in the patient's own home.

Although these guidelines serve as an introduction, they are no substitute for the solid research into the subject necessary before you commit to a policy. Among the resources you'll want to consult are:

Manual: *Long-Term Care: A Dollars and Sense Guide*
Cost: $6.95
Contains: 58-page manual on purchasing long-term care insurance

From: United States Health Cooperative
1334 G Street, NW, Suite 500
Washington, DC 20005
(202) 393-6222

Booklet: *The Consumer's Guide to Long Term Care Insurance*
Cost: Free
From: Health Insurance Association of America
1001 Pennsylvania Avenue, NW
Washington, DC 20004
(800) 423-8000
(202) 223-7780

Booklet: *Before You Buy: A Guide to Long-Term Care Insurance* (D12893)
Cost: Free

From: AARP Fulfillment
1909 K St., NW
Washington, DC 20049

Booklet: *An Educated Buyer's Guide to Long-Term Care Insurance*
Cost: Free
From: Blue Cross of Western Pennsylvania
Consumer Programs
Fifth Avenue Place
Pittsburgh, PA 15222

Many state insurance departments also have publications on purchasing long-term care insurance. See your telephone directory under your state government listings or call your state government information service (see listings pages 441–443).

CHAPTER 13

FINDING THE BEST MEDICAL
AND DENTAL CARE

IF YOU ARE AGE 50 OR OVER, THE DECI-
sions you make about choosing health services
and products are perhaps the most important
and expensive decisions you make as a consumer. People who take an active role in their
health decisions and who educate themselves
about health services and products end up with
the best care at the lowest price.

The way to begin your self-education is to
obtain some of the following excellent general
guides:

Booklet: *Healthy Questions: How to Talk
to and Select Physicians, Pharmacists, Dentists and Vision Care Specialists* (D12094)
Cost: Free
From: AARP
1909 K Street, NW
Washington, DC 20049

Booklet: *Buying Quality Health Care*
Cost: Free
From: Center for Health Affairs
Project Hope
Two Wisconsin Circle, Suite 500

Chevy Chase, MD 20815
(301) 656-7401

Organization: People's Medical Society
462 Walnut St.
Allentown, PA 18102
(215) 770-1670
Services: America's largest consumer health
organization. Educates consumers
about health care costs and choices.
Publications include:
• Newsletter (monthly, $15.00 per
year)
• *150 Ways to Lower Your Medical
Costs* (83-page book, $7.95)

Booklet: *Being a Wise Health Care Consumer*
Contains: 32-page, information-packed
guide to choosing health products
and services
Cost: $4.00
From: American Institute for Preventive
Medicine
19111 West 10 Mile Road, Suite 101
Southfield, MI 48075
(800) 345-2476

The information in these publications, along with the rest of the information and resources in this chapter, will help you select the right doctors, obtain the best medical care in an emergency, make the most informed decisions when facing surgery, make the most informed decisions when you face a hospital stay, avoid health fraud, obtain the best dental care, and resolve health-related problems and disputes.

FINDING THE RIGHT DOCTORS

Getting the best medical care begins with the process of selecting the right physicians, including:

- A primary care physician
- Specialists
- Physicians to treat emergencies

Your Primary Care Physician

Your primary care physician is the doctor you turn to for such basic services as routine examinations, immunizations, screening for diseases and conditions, treatment of minor injuries and common complaints, and diagnosis of any health problem. This doctor, over time, becomes familiar with your medical history, family situation, mental health, living environment, and special stresses caused by occupational and other situations. Your primary care physician refers you to specialists, if needed, and coordinates your care during hospitalization or treatment by more than one specialist. In the past, most primary care physicians were known as "general practitioners," or nonspecialists. Today, most are either internists (physicians who treat adults), family practitioners, or geriatrician, who concentrate on providing primary care to older patients.

Most primary care doctors are medical doctors (M.D.), who have completed training at a medical school and have a minimum of 1 year of postgraduate training at a hospital. Virtually all physicians today continue with a minimum 3 to 6 years of additional training in a medical specialty. All physicians must hold a license in each state in which they practice, and licensing procedures include passing rigorous examinations.

How do you find the best primary care physician for you?

Collect Names of Prospective Area Doctors. You can do this by consulting with:

- Friends and relatives, particularly those with similar medical histories or conditions
- Your local medical society or local hospital referral service (see Yellow Pages under "Physicians and Surgeons Information Bureaus")
- Yellow Pages under "Physicians"— most Yellow Pages list physicians by speciality, as well as alphabetically
- Your local senior center or area agency on aging (see pages 383–427)

Organization: American Academy of Family Physicians
8880 Ward Parkway
Kansas City, MO 64114
(816) 333-9700

Organization: American Society for Internal Medicine

1101 Vermont Ave., NW
Washington, DC 20005
(202) 289-1700

To locate a geriatrician, contact:

Organization: American Geriatrics Society
770 Lexington Ave., Suite 400
New York, NY 10021
(212) 308-1414

Organization: American Osteopathic Association
142 E. Ontario St.
Chicago, IL 60611
(312) 280-5800

Organization: Prologue
Consumer Health Services, Inc.
5720 Flatiron Parkway
Boulder, CO 80301
(303) 442-1111
Service: A free consumer-oriented physician and dentist referral service that operates in Denver, District of Columbia, Houston, Dallas/Ft. Worth, Chicago, Milwaukee, Kansas City, and Philadelphia
For referral: (800) DOCTORS

Publications: • *20 Questions to Ask When Selecting a New Doctor*
• *20 Questions to Ask When Selecting a New Dentist*
Cost: Free

Evaluate the Physicians on Your List.

Once you obtain the names of one or more physicians, you should evaluate each one with great care. The factors you'll want to consider can be broken down into three basic areas of consideration. The first two, professional and practical considerations, consist of questions you can ask over the telephone. The third, personal considerations, are difficult to evaluate without making an appointment to see the physician.

The important professional considerations are:

- Does the physician have a large number of patients in your age group? Ideally, you want a primary care physician with a great deal of knowledge and experience with the many particular physical, mental, emotional, sexual, and social aspects of those in your age group.

- Does the doctor have special expertise in any significant medical problem or conditions you may have? For example, certain family physicians may have special interests in weight control, sports injuries, or arthritis, even though they don't have an official speciality in that area.

- How long has the physician been practicing? Experience is a factor for primary care physicians.

- Is the doctor board-certified? While many competent doctors aren't, board certification means that a physician has met another set of rigid standardizations and, depending on the specialty, may have to participate in continuing education and recertification programs.

- Does the physician have admitting privileges at a good local hospital? Generally, the highest quality hospitals have the most reputable local physicians on their staffs.

Among the important practical considerations are:

- Does the doctor accept your insurance? If you're on Medicare, does the physician accept assignment?

- How convenient is the office location?

- How convenient are the office hours?

- Are the on-call physicians affiliated with your doctor qualified, accessible, and easy to deal with?

- Are patients informed of fees for routine visits and procedures before any procedure or test is performed? Does the physician accept credit cards? Will the office make special payment arrangements in case of unusually high bills?

- Does the physician make house calls in emergencies? Will he or she meet you at the emergency room, if necessary?

- Does the office have x-ray equipment, blood testing laboratory, treadmill for stress tests, and other equipment for common testing and diagnostic procedures? Besides saving you valuable time and effort, testing done in the doctor's office is less expensive than that done in a hospital.

Finally, after you've assured yourself that a physician is professionally competent and that his or her practice suits your requirements, perhaps the most important consideration that remains is the doctor's personality and style of practice. Your primary care physician should be someone you can trust, confide in, and feel comfortable with, no matter how personal or even embarrassing the situation.

You can begin to weigh these personal considerations in your initial visit. However, as with other relationships, time will be required before you can make a decision about how compatible you'll be.

- What is the doctor's communication style? A physician should be courteous and unhurried, and should give you un-divided attention. He should talk to you in language you understand and answer your questions willingly and fully. He should take seriously any fears and concerns you have.

- Does the physician explain the reasons for tests, procedures, or injections that he or she orders? Does he or she report test results promptly and explain what they mean?

- Does the doctor explain what to expect in the hours and days ahead? Does he or she give you symptoms or signs that indicate you should call or come back to the office? Does he or she explain the side effects of prescription medications?

- Is the physician cost-conscious? Does he or she prescribe generic drugs whenever he or she can? Does he or she suggest alternatives to expensive tests and procedures?

Verify Physician Credentials. A small minority of doctors have either falsified their credentials or are not licensed physicians at all. If you want to make absolutely certain that your doctor has been honest with you, you can obtain complete information about the credentials of any physician by calling:

> **Organization:** American Medical Association
> 535 N. Dearborn St.
> Chicago, IL 60610
> (312) 645-5000

Finding the Right Specialist

In medical terms, specialists provide secondary rather than primary care (even though primary care is a speciality in itself). That means that you would normally be referred to a specialist for treatment of a condition or disease diagnosed by your primary care physician.

Most doctors who specialize have passed additional examinations and met other requirements to be certified by one of 23 national boards that set rigorous standards for medical specialities; for example, the American Board of Surgery, the American Board of Internal Medicine, etc. The following is a descriptive list of the major specialties:

- Allergists treat allergies
- Anesthesiologists administer anesthetics used in surgery and other procedures
- Cardiologists treat heart conditions and diseases
- Dermatologists treat skin diseases and conditions
- Emergency medicine physicians specialize in treating accidental injuries and other acute conditions
- Endocrinologists treat hormonal and metabolic disorders
- Gastroenterologists treat disorders of the digestive system
- Gynecologists treat disorders of the female reproductive system
- Hematologists specialize in blood diseases
- Internists specialize in treating adults
- Nephrologists treat kidney diseases
- Neurologists specialize in the brain and central nervous system
- Pathologists specialize in evaluating condition of tissues, organs, and body fluids
- Pediatricians specialize in treating children and adolescents

- Obstetricians specialize in pregnancy and delivering babies
- Oncologists treat cancers
- Ophthalmologists treat eye problems and diseases
- Orthopedists specialize in problems with bones
- Otolaryngologists treat ear, nose, and throat conditions
- Physiatrists specialize in rehabilitation of muscle and skeletal conditions
- Plastic surgeons specialize in reconstructive and cosmetic surgery
- Psychiatrists treat mental and emotional problems
- Radiologists use x-rays and radiation to diagnose and treat diseases and other problems
- Surgeons perform operations
- Urologists treat urinary problems and diseases

There are some situations in which you would look for a specialist directly; for example, most women see a gynecologist at least once a year, pregnant women need an obstetrician, or you may want an ophthalmologist to conduct eye exams and prescribe corrective lens. However, even in these instances, you will receive overall better health care if your primary care physician and any specialists communicate with each other.

If you do have to find a specialist on your own, you can obtain referrals from:

- Your local medical society or other referral service (see Yellow Pages under "Physicians and Surgeons Information Bureaus")
- Yellow Pages under "Physicians" (most have listings by specialty)

- Information clearinghouses and special-interest organizations dealing with a specific disease or condition. For example, if you're looking for a specialist in the treatment of diabetes, we list several referral sources in Chapter 14 of this book under "Diabetes"

- A local medical school or high-quality teaching hospital—most staff physicians treat private patients

Once you have names of specialists, you should evaluate them for professional, practical, and personal considerations as carefully as you evaluated your primary care physician. If your condition is long-term or serious, it is even more important that your specialist be accessible, willing to answer questions fully, patient with your fears and concerns, and conscious of your financial situation. Indeed, your trust and confidence in the specialist may play a critical role in your recovery.

FACING SURGERY

In emergency situations, such as acute appendicitis or injuries from an accident, patients and their families seldom have time to reflect on the decision whether or not to have surgery or to obtain a second opinion. However, when a doctor advises nonemergency surgery, every patient should seek a second opinion. Because all surgery is expensive and carries risk, many private insurance companies require second opinions before they will pay for an operation. Almost all medical insurance programs, including Medicare and Medicaid, will pay for second opinions. Although you can obtain a referral from the physician who is recommending the surgery, that referral might be to another physician who shares your doctor's opinion. Therefore, it's better to obtain a referral from other sources, including:

Hotline: National Second Opinion Hotline
Services: Provides referrals to physicians for second opinions
Call: (800) 638-6833 (Ex. MD)
(800) 492-6603 (MD)

For more information on making decisions about surgery:

Booklet: *Thinking of Having Surgery*
Cost: Free
From: Surgery
HHS
Washington, DC 20201

Organization: American College of Surgeons
Office of Public Information
55 East Erie Street
Chicago, IL 60611
(312) 664-4050
Services: Provides a series of free brochures, including:
- *When You Need an Operation Series* (4 booklets)
Brochures on frequently performed operations, including:
- *About Hernia Repair*
- *About Cataract Surgery in Adults*
- *About Low-Back Pain*
- *About Prostatectomy*
- *About Hysterectomy*

FACING HOSPITALIZATION

About one in every 10 Americans is hospitalized during the average year, and that percentage rises with age. Hospital stays are not pleasant, and it's difficult for patients facing admission to think about anything other than their medical conditions. However, it's possible to minimize the unpleasantness and risks of hospital stays if you:

- Make sure the hospital admission is necessary. Obtain a second opinion not only if you're facing surgery, but in all nonemergency situations in which your doctor recommends hospitalization. Legitimate medical alternatives may exist that allow you to be treated on an outpatient basis or that will reduce the time you spend in the hospital.

- Choose the hospital carefully. Although evaluating a hospital is difficult, one invaluable resource that can help is:

Book: *Consumer's Guide to Hospitals*
Contains: Valuable information on judging the qualities of 6,000 hospitals nationwide, guidelines for getting good care, and tips for keeping the costs down
Cost: $10.00
From: Consumer's Checkbook
806 15th Street, NW, Suite 925
Washington, DC 20005

- Learn how to cut the costs of hospitalization. Costs for identical procedures can vary as much as 50%, even among hospitals in a small community. Asking prices ahead of time is always wise.

- Make sure you and your loved ones get the best possible care and are treated with respect and dignity by sending for:

Booklet: *Patient's Bill of Rights*
Cost: Free
From: American Hospital Association
840 North Lake Shore Drive
Chicago, IL 60611
(800) 242-2626
(312) 280-6000

- Investigate hospices, an alternative source of care for the terminally ill. A hospice is a special residence facility devoted solely to caring for terminally ill patients. The goal of most hospices is to provide a comfortable, dignified, "home atmosphere," while providing care by a team that includes physicians, nurses, social workers, physical therapists, and counselors trained in working with the terminally ill and their families. Because hospices are less expensive and more attractive than hospitals, demand has been growing rapidly. This demand has been fueled by the relatively recent decision by Medicare to pay for hospice care. With so many new hospices being built, there is a range of quality of facilities and the care provided. Where alternatives are available, you should take time to inspect them.

One important resource for information and referrals is:

Organization: National Hospice Organization
1901 North Fort Myer Drive
Arlington, VA 22209
(703) 243-5900
Services: Provides information about hospices, publishes a national directory of hospices, and will provide a list of facilities in your area

Booklet: *A Consumer's Guide to Hospice Care*

Cost: $4.00
From: Foundation for Hospice and Home
Care
519 C St., NE
Washington, DC 20002
(202) 547-7424

Booklet: *Hospices: A Time for Peace*
Cost: Free
From: National Council of Senior Citizens
925 15th Street, NW
Washington, DC 20005
(202) 347-8800

AVOIDING HEALTH CARE FRAUD

Health care fraud is one of the most common and the most dangerous form of consumer fraud, and by far the most frequent victims are Americans age 50 and over. The perpetrators of health care fraud not only take an estimated $10 billion per year from Americans, but cause untold deaths and unnecessary suffering because victims avoid legitimate treatments or endure additional harmful health consequences of the fraud itself.

Health fraud falls into three main categories:

- False claims about drugs or cosmetics
- Unsubstantiated food fads and diets or unjustified food supplements
- Ineffective medical treatments and devices

The targets for medical con men are primarily people who suffer from chronic diseases or conditions. Among the most common target areas are:

- Arthritis
- Cancer
- Weight loss
- Baldness
- Aging
- Fitness
- Alcoholism and drug abuse
- Hemorrhoids
- High blood pressure

For more information about the types of health care fraud and descriptions of typical scams:

Reprints: • *Critiquing Quack Ads* (No. 85-4196)
- *Open Season on Quacks*
- *Fraudulent Flab Remover* (No. 83-4166)
- *Hocus-Pocus as Applied to Arthritis* (No. 85-1080)
- *The Big Quack Attack: Medical Devices* (No. 84-4022)
- *FDA Warns Weight Loss Wraps and Suits Are Frauds* (No. T84-88)
Cost: Free
From: U.S. Department of Health and Human Services
Public Health Services
U.S. Food and Drug Administration
Office of Public Affairs
5600 Fishers Lane
Rockville, MD 20857

Organization: National Council Against Health Fraud
2800 Main Street
Kansas City, MO 64108
(800) 821-6671
Services: Operates toll-free hotline that answers questions and concerns about health fraud and quackery

Booklet: *Quackery: The Billion Dollar "Miracle" Business*
Cost: Free
From: S. James

Consumer Information Center
P.O. Box 100
Pueblo, CO 81009

Booklet: *Quackery and the Elderly*
Cost: Free with self-addressed stamped envelope
From: Council of Better Business Bureaus
4200 Wilson Blvd.
Arlington, VA 22203
(703) 276-0100

If you're considering using any health product, service, or treatment that has not been
recommended or prescribed by your physician,
you should check with one or more of the following:

- Your physician, pharmacist, or other
health care professional.

- Food and Drug Administration
Office of Consumer Affairs
5600 Fishers Lane, Room 14-71
Rockville, MD 20857
(301) 443-3170

- Your local Better Business Bureau (see
White Pages or listings on pages 452–
459).

- Your state or local Consumer Affairs
office (see pages 443–452).

- Your local Postmaster or Postal Inspec-
tor, if you received the sales material in
question in the mail. You can also file a
complaint or receive information by
writing:

Consumer Advocate
U.S. Postal Service
475 L'Enfant Plaza West, SW
Washington, DC 20260
(202) 268-2284

FINDING THE RIGHT DENTIST

Because modern preventative techniques have
been developed only over the last two decades,
few Americans over age 50 will be free from
lost teeth, gum disease, tooth discoloration, ill-
fitted dentures, and other serious dental problems. Finding the right dental care is more important for older Americans than for other
adults.

The Dentist

Dental care can be a significant expense, especially for the majority of Americans who don't
have dental insurance. The problem can be particularly difficult for people who are retired,
since Medicare (with the exception of accidental injury and some types of oral surgery)

doesn't pay for dental care. The only advantage
consumers have is that there is a great deal of
competition among dentists today, so it's possible to shop for a dentist who provides a high
level of service at reasonable prices.

Most people need the services of general
practitioners, who make up 80% of all dentists.
Although any licensed dentist can perform any
type of dental procedure, specialized work is
usually performed by the following specialists:

- Oral and maxillofacial surgeons perform
oral surgery and treat injuries, diseases,
and defects of the jaw, mouth, and face.
They also do extractions and perform
oral implant surgery.

- Periodontists specialize in diseases of
the gums.

- Endodontists specialize in root canals and other treatments of the tooth pulp.
- Prosthodontists design and fit dentures, bridges, and other tooth replacements.

Everyone should select a general practitioner for routine dental care. Among the sources of information are:

- Your family doctor
- Local dental society or dental referral service (see Yellow Pages under "Dentists")
- Relatives and friends

State dental associations sponsor a number of free and low cost services for older people. To locate programs in your state, contact:

- Your area agency on aging (see listings, pages 383–427)

American Dental Association
211 East Chicago Ave.
Chicago, IL 60611
(312) 440-2860

Some special circumstances may influence your choice of a dentist. For example, people age 65 and older with significant dental problems, as well as other health problems may want to find a professional who specializes in geriatric dentistry. For referral, contact:

Referral: American Society for Geriatric Dentistry
211 East Chicago Ave., Suite 1616

Chicago, IL 60611
(312) 440-2660
Cost: Free referral

People who are handicapped or confined to the house may need a dentist who makes house calls. To find such a dentist, contact your local dental society or dentist referral service (See Yellow Pages under "Dentists") or contact:

Organization: National Foundation of Dentistry for the Handicapped
1726 Champa, Suite 422
Denver, CO 80202
(303) 573-0264

When you contact the office of a prospective dentist, you should ask:

- What are the fees for routine check-up, cleaning, and other common procedures?
- Does the dentist employ a dental hygienist (treatment by a hygienist is generally less expensive)?
- Does the dentist accept your dental insurance?
- Does the dentist take a complete medical history that includes any medical conditions that may affect your treatment, such as allergies, diabetes, heart conditions, and bleeding problems?
- Does the dentist have arrangements to provide emergency care?
- Does the dentist emphasize prevention and give advice on home care?
- Does the dentist provide written estimates for complex procedures?

CHAPTER 14

A GUIDE TO COMMON HEALTH PROBLEMS OF LATER LIFE

No MATTER HOW HEALTHY YOU ARE or how good your medical care is, you—and those close to you—will need medical care for both minor health problems (common cold, allergies, injuries) and serious health problems in your lifetime. While you can't prevent them, your actions can play a key role in either the successful treatment of these problems, or in the case of chronic conditions or disease, coping with their effects. In the following pages, you'll find, in alphabetical order, a comprehensive listing of the major health problems and conditions likely to affect Americans as they grow older. For each, you will find:

- A profile of the disease or condition, including symptoms for early detection

- A listing of the important sources of information about the disease or condition

- Complete information on finding the best treatment

- Information on prevention, if applicable

- Information on living with the disease or condition, including community services and support groups, when applicable

If you don't find the disease or condition you are looking for in this chapter, you can find information about treatment and support groups from:

Organization: National Health Information Center
P.O. Box 1133
Washington, DC 20013
(800) 336-4797 (Ex MD)
(301) 565-4167
Organization: National Self-Help Clearinghouse
23 West 42nd St.
New York, NY 10036
(212) 642-2944

ALCOHOL USE AND ABUSE

Alcohol abuse may well touch more American lives than any other health problem. According to a Louis Harris survey, two thirds of all adults know someone who drinks too much, and for a third of all adults, that person is a close friend or relative. An estimated one in 10 adults actually has a serious drinking problem.

As people grow older, alcohol use can become as much of a problem as alcohol abuse, for two reasons. First, consumption of alcohol may have negative effects on people who suffer from a wide variety of diseases, from diabetes to osteoporosis. Second, the combination of alcohol and many prescription and over-the-counter medications can cause reactions ranging from unpleasant to life-threatening.

The result is that as many as 25% of all hospital admissions for people age 50 to 64, and 50% of all hospital admissions for people age 65 and older, involve alcohol use or abuse. Alcohol abuse by a spouse or other relative is also a significant factor in wife abuse, elderly abuse, and stress-related conditions.

Although alcohol problems are so prevalent, they are often undetected. The problems include:

- Denial of the problem by the drinker is almost universal
- Many older Americans spend a great deal of time alone
- Many of the signs of alcoholism or a drug-alcohol interaction are attributed to other diseases or the aging process itself, such as:
  – Forgetfulness
  – Trembling or other motor coordination problems
  – Depression or irritability
  – Weight loss
  – Slurred speech
  – Difficulty sleeping
- Tolerance for alcohol decreases with age, so a level of consumption that falls into the category of "moderate" for a 35-year-old may be "excessive" consumption for a 65-year-old

For these reasons, detecting or preventing an alcohol problem depends upon self-education about the dangers of alcohol and the signs of alcohol abuse.

General Sources of Information

Organization: National Council on Alcoholism
12 West 21st Street, Suite 700
New York, NY 10010
(800) 622-2255
(212) 206-6770

Services: This voluntary organization coordinates over 200 local chapters that makes referrals to treatment centers and works to inform the public about the problems of alcoholism. Referral hotline operates 24 hours per day, 7 days a week. Among its many publications are:
- *Alcoholics Are Sick People Who Can Be Helped* ($0.50)
- *Danger Signals for Women Drinkers* ($0.25)
- *Facts on Alcoholism and Alcohol-Related Problems* ($0.10)
- *Alcoholism and Alcohol-Related Problems Among Women* ($0.10)
- *How to Know an Alcoholic* ($0.60)
- *Older People and Alcoholism* ($0.75)

- *The Plight of the Older Alcoholic* ($0.40)
- *What Are the Signs of Alcoholism? NCA's Self Test* ($0.25)
- *Phases of Alcohol Addiction in Males* ($0.40)
- *New Primer on Alcoholism* ($5.00)
- *500 Drugs the Alcoholic Should Avoid* ($3.00)
  (Postage and handling)

Organization: National Clearinghouse for Alcohol Information
P.O. Box 2345
Rockville, MD 20852
(301) 468-2600
Services: Answers questions about alcohol abuse and provides a wide variety of free publications, including:

Age Page: • *Aging and Alcohol Abuse* (MS301)
- *Alcohol and the Body: Update* (MS251)
- *Alcohol and the Elderly: Update* (MS306)
- *Alcohol and Safety: Update* (MS311)
- *Facing Up to Alcoholism* (RP0092)
- *Alcohol and the Elderly* (RP0477)
- *Publications Catalog* (EN8400)
- *Retirement and Alcohol Problems* (RP0540)
- *Someone Close Drinks Too Much* (RP0104)
- *The Fact Is: It's Dangerous to Drink Alcohol While Taking Certain Medications*

Booklet: *Liquor May Be Quicker But . . .*
Cost: Free
Contains: A reprint from FDA Consumer that discusses the problems of alcohol and drug interactions

From: Food and Drug Administration
HFE-88 5600
Fishers Lane
Rockville, MD 20857

Treatment for Alcoholism

There are many different kinds of treatment programs for people with alcohol problems. These include private clinics, nonprofit clinics, inpatient and outpatient hospital programs, and a wide variety of counseling services. Referrals to treatment programs may be obtained from your family physician, your clergyman, or your employer (many corporations have established assistance programs for employees with drinking problems). Other sources of referral are:

Organization: Your local Alcoholism Council
Service: Provides detailed information on local treatment programs and support groups
For information: See your White Pages under "Alcoholism"
or
Call: (800) 622-2255

Another excellent source of information on alcoholism and referral to local alcoholism treatment programs is your state department of alcohol services. See your telephone directory under your state government listings or call your state government information service (see listings pages 449–451).

Support Groups for Alcoholics

Completion of a treatment program is only the first step in alleviating a problem with alcohol. For most recovering alcoholics, participation in a self-help program is vital in fighting the desire to drink again.

Organization: Alcoholics Anonymous (AA)
Services: In its own words, AA is 'a fellowship of men and women who share their experience, strength and hope with each other that they may solve their common problem and help others to recover from alcoholism. The core of the program is recovering alcoholics meeting together in one of America's 34,000 AA groups to help each other refrain from drinking. There's no charge for joining AA or attending meetings, although a voluntary collection is taken after each meeting to cover costs. AA publishes a wide variety of materials, which explain its very successful program and contain the moving stories of AA members, including:

* *Living Sober* ($1.20)
* *This Is A.A.* ($0.15)
* *44 Questions—Most Common Questions About A.A.* ($0.20)
* *Is A.A. for You?* ($0.10)
* *A.A. for Women* ($0.20)
* *Time to Start Living—For Older Alcoholics* (in large print: $0.40)
* *The A.A. Member—Medications and Other Drugs* ($0.15)
* *Letter to a Woman Alcoholic* ($0.15)
* *Is There an Alcoholic in Your Life?* ($0.15)

For information: Call your local AA group (see White Pages)

or

Alcoholics Anonymous
P.O. Box 459
New York, NY 10163
(212) 686-1100

Organization: The Calix Society
7601 Wayzata Blvd.
Minneapolis, MN 55426
(612) 546-0544
Services: The Calix Society is "an association of Catholic alcoholics who are maintaining their sobriety through affiliation with and participation in the Fellowship of Alcoholics Anonymous." The society has about 60 local groups

Organization: Women for Sobriety
Quakertown, PA 18951
(215) 536-8026
Services: A self-help program solely for women alcoholics that has hundreds of local "New Life" groups throughout the United States

Support Groups for Family Members of People with Alcohol Problems

Alcohol abuse can have devastating consequences for the family members and friends of the person with a drinking problem. The problems can range from stress-related conditions to physical abuse. Fortunately, there are a wide variety of resources to help these family members:

Booklets:
* *The Alcoholic Spouse* ($0.50)
* *Alcoholics Are Sick People Who Can Be Helped* ($0.25)
* *Do's and Don'ts for Wives of Alcoholics* ($0.50)
* *Intervention* ($1.00)

Cost: Price above plus $1.25 postage and handling
From: National Council on Alcoholism
Publications Manager
12 W. 21st Street, Suite 700
New York, NY 10010
(800) 622-2255
(212) 206-6770

Organization: Al-Anon Family Groups
Services: Al-Anon is an association of over 26,000 local self-help groups that offer support and assistance to people

whose lives are affected by a problem drinker. Al-Anon publishes many informative books and booklets, including:

Books:
- *Al-Anon Faces Alcoholism* ($6.00)
- *The Dilemma of the Alcoholic Marriage* ($4.50)
- *One Day at a Time in Al-Anon* (large print $7.50)
- *Al-Anon Family Groups* ($5.00)

Booklets:
- *Al-Anon, You and the Alcoholic* ($0.25)
- *A Guide for the Family of the Alcoholic* ($0.25)
- *Alcoholism: The Family Disease* ($0.50)
- *Alcoholism: A Merry-Go-Round Named Denial* ($0.50)
- *Freedom from Despair* ($0.10)
- *So You Love an Alcoholic* ($0.15)
- *What Do You Do About an Alcoholic's Drinking?* ($0.20)
- *Understanding Ourselves and Alcoholism* ($0.15)
- *Al-Anon Is for Men* ($0.15)
- *"What's Next?" Asks the Husband of an Alcoholic* ($0.30)
- *Does She Drink Too Much?* ($0.40)
- *Al-Anon Is for Adult Children of Alcoholics* ($0.25)

Cost: No postage and handling on prepaid orders. Make checks payable to "AFG, Inc."

For information: Call your local Al-Anon group (see White Pages)

or

Al-Anon Family Group Headquarters
P.O. Box 862, Midtown Station
New York, NY 10018
(800) 356-9996
(212) 245-3151

Organization: National Association of Children of Alcoholics
31582 Coast Hwy., Suite B
South Laguna, CA 92677
(714) 499-3889

Services: Sponsors self-help groups for adult children of alcoholics across the country

ALZHEIMER'S DISEASE

Alzheimer's disease is a degenerative, irreversible brain disorder that gradually destroys brain cells and shrinks the brain. The result is a progression from short-term memory loss to mental confusion to dementia, the loss of ability to perceive, think, and remember. In the last decade, Alzheimer's has become perhaps the most feared of all diseases that strike Americans as they grow older. A 1989 study by the Harvard Medical School produced the startling information that four million Americans may suffer from Alzheimer's disease, which was double the previous estimate. This study showed that 45% of all people age 85 and over suffer from dementia. Because the fastest growing age group in America is people age 85 and over, Alzheimer's disease will place an increasingly large burden on the medical and social support systems of this country, unless a cure is found.

The key fact in an early diagnosis of Alzheimer's disease is that significant memory loss and confusion are not normal characteristics of aging. An older person experiencing more than minor forgetfulness should consult a physician.

There are many causes of memory problems besides Alzheimer's, including depression, side effects of medication, thyroid problems, vascular disease, alcoholism, and vitamin deficiencies. Approximately 70 conditions can cause dementia. Some of these are reversible and others can be stabilized.

While recent research has linked Alzheimer's disease to a deficiency of certain brain chemicals, there is no single definitive clinical test for Alzheimer's disease. As a result, diagnosis results partly from an assessment of the patient's condition and partly from eliminating other probable causes.

General Sources of Information

Organization: Alzheimer's Disease and Related Disorders Association
70 E. Lake Street
Chicago, IL 60601
(800) 621-0379 (Ex. IL)
(800) 572-6037 (IL)
Services: The ADRDA acts as a clearinghouse for information on all aspects of Alzheimer's Disease. The association provides:
- A toll-free hotline to answer questions
- Referrals to local support groups, medical specialists, adult day-care programs, and other resources
- Referrals to local ADRDA chapters that have numerous support and education programs
- An information packet on Alzheimer's disease and a quarterly newsletter

Organization: Brookdale Center on Aging, Alzheimer's Respite Hotline
Service: Provides information packets for family caregivers
For information: Alzheimer's Respite Hotline
(800) 648-2673

Pamphlets: • *Q & A: Alzheimer's Disease*
• *Progress Report on Alzheimer's Disease: Vol.III*
Cost: Free
From: NIA Information Center
2209 Distribution Circle
Silver Spring, MD 20910

Booklet: *The Dementias: Hope Through Research*

Cost: Free
From: National Institute of Neurological and Communicative Disorders and Stroke
Public Information Office
Building 31, Room 8A06
Bethesda, MD 20892
(301) 496-5751

Guide: *Tracer Bullet 87-2: Alzheimer's Disease*
Cost: Free
From: Science Reference Section
Science and Technology Division
Library of Congress
10 First Street, SE
Washington, DC 20540

Treating Alzheimer's Disease

Despite intensive research, there is currently no effective treatment for Alzheimer's disease. In the words of the U.S. Office of Technical Assessment: "The focus of most medical management is family education—training caregivers to adapt to the patient, simplify the individual's living space, and referring relatives to family support services."

The need for education and support of loved ones is critical, because of the increasingly intensive care the patient will need over the years. A recent study showed that the average Alzheimer's patient lived 8.7 years after the onset of the disease, with some patients living up to 25 years. This means that the average patient needs constant supervision for a number of years.

This supervision is so demanding that Alzheimer's often claims what experts call a "second victim," the spouse or family member who becomes the primary caregiver for the patient. This caregiver often suffers from severe exhaustion and stress. The financial consequences of caring for the patient can also be devastating for the caregiver.

The seriousness of the consequences and

the length of the course of the disease mean that primary caregivers and other loved ones need more education about Alzheimer's and more support than do the loved ones of those who suffer from any other disease.

Among the best comprehensive guides to caring for a person with Alzheimer's disease are:

Book: *Understanding Alzheimer's Disease: What It Is, How to Treat It, How to Cope with It* edited by Miriam K. Aronson
Cost: $15.95
Contains: Produced under the auspices of the Alzheimer's Disease and Related Disorder's Association, this book provides a comprehensive guide to the devastating disease through contributions by 26 leading specialists. The book has four parts:
1. Diagnosis, possible causes, and treatment strategies
2. Coping with Alzheimer's disease, with emphasis on needs of family and friends
3. Legal and financial aspects of the disease, including legal planning and how to receive government benefits
4. Future directions of research
From: Charles Scribner's Sons

Book: *Confronting Alzheimer's Disease* by the American Association of Homes for the Aging
Cost: $19.95 (softcover)
Contains: The book covers all aspects of the disease and caregiving, with special attention to the concerns of loved ones of patients who are in nursing homes
From: National Health Publishing
99 Painters Mil Road
Owings Mills, MD 21117
(800) 446-2221

Book: *Losing a Million Minds: Confronting the Tragedy of Alzheimer's Disease and Other Dementias*
Cost: $24.00 for 543-page book (S/N 052-003-01059-3) $2.50 for 79-page summary (S/N 052-003-01061-5)
Contains: Comprehensive assessment of the problems caused by Alzheimer's and the present care systems for victims, prepared by the U.S. Office of Technical Assessment
From: Superintendent of Documents
U.S. Government Printing Office
Washington, DC 20402
(202) 783-3238

Book: *The 36 Hour Day: A Family Guide to Caring for Persons with Alzheimer's Disease, Related Dementing Illness, and Memory Loss* by Nancy Mace and Peter Rabins, M.D.
Cost: $5.95
Contains: A sympathetic and practical book for caregivers
From: Warner Books

ARTHRITIS

"Arthritis" means inflammation of one or more joints in the body. This term covers over 100 different medical conditions, which differ widely in severity, symptoms, and treatment. Collectively, the conditions we call arthritis at least occasionally hamper the daily activities of about half of all older Americans.

The three most common conditions that fall under the category "arthritis" are:

- Osteoarthritis—a degenerative condition caused by wear and tear on the inside surfaces of joints. X-rays show that virtually every person over age 60 shows some evidence of osteoarthritis. In the vast majority of cases, however, the disease is mild, causing no symptoms or mild joint pain and stiffness. The people who suffer more serious pain and some disability usually have problems with their knees, hips, and spine.

- Rheumatoid arthritis—a more serious, potentially crippling condition caused by inflammation of the membrane surrounding the joints. It most commonly appears between ages 40 and 50, and afflicts three times as many women as men.
- Gout (or gouty arthritis)—joint pain caused by an excess of uric acid in the body. Gout afflicts many more men than women, but it is normally treatable with medication.

General Sources of Information

Organization: The Arthritis Foundation
1314 Spring Street, NW
Atlanta, GA 30309
(800) 422-1492 (Ex. GA)
(404) 872-7100
Services: Large voluntary nonprofit organization:
- Works to find the causes and cures for arthritis
- Supervises 75 local chapters that provide services to arthritis patients and referrals to qualified physicians
- Issues numerous publications, including:
  - *Arthritis: The Basic Facts*
  - *Rheumatoid Arthritis: Patient Handbook*
  - *Osteoarthritis: Patient Handbook*

- *Surgery*
- *Self-Help Manual for Arthritis Patients*
- *Living with Arthritis*
- *A Serious Look at the Facts*
- *Quackery and Unproven Remedies*
- *About Gout*
- *Aspirin for Arthritis*
- *Diet and Arthritis*
- *Understanding Inflammation*
- *Arthritis in Women*

Agency: National Arthritis and Musculoskeletal and Skin Diseases Information Clearinghouse (NIAMS)
Box AMS
Bethesda, MD 20892
(301) 468-3235
Services: Supports research into arthritis and publishes bibliographies, catalogs, guides, and reports, including the following free publications:
- *Publication Order Form*
- *Directory of Information Resources*
- *Bibliographies:*
  - *Activities of Daily Living*
  - *Drug Information for Patients*
  - *Gout: Patient Education Materials*
  - *Joint Replacement Education Materials*
- *Arthritis, Rheumatic Disease, and Related Diseases*
- *Medicine for the Layman: Arthritis*

Booklets:
- *For Treating Arthritis, Start with Aspirin* (537)
- *Arthritis* (543V)
Cost: Free
From: S. James
Consumer Information Center
P.O. Box 100
Pueblo, CO 81009

Age Page: Arthritis Advice
Cost: Free
From: National Institute on Aging
Building 31, Room 5C35
Bethesda, MD 20892

Treatment for Arthritis

The first place to seek treatment for arthritis is your family physician. Most conditions are mild and are treatable under the supervision and direction of a family doctor.

Specialists in arthritis are called rheumatologists. You can obtain a referral to a specialist from your local physician, by calling your local medical society, from your local chapter of the Arthritis Foundation, or by contacting:

Organization: The Arthritis Foundation
(800) 422-1492
(404) 872-7100

Another source of treatment is one of the multipurpose arthritis centers that receives support from the National Institute of Health. You can obtain information from:

Organization: National Arthritis, Musculo-skeletal and Skin Disease Information Clearinghouse
(301) 468-3235

Most symptoms of arthritis are treated with a wide variety of medications. Although these drugs allow many patients to lead much more comfortable lives, they can also have serious side effects and can interact with other prescription medication. One especially good chapter on the subject of medication and arthritis is in:

Book: *50+: The Graedon's People's Pharmacy for Older Adults* by Joe and Teresa Graedon

Cost: $13.95
From: Bantam Books

Exercise can also alleviate the symptoms and retard the progression of arthritis. The Arthritis Foundation has developed a number of exercise programs, in connection with such organizations as the YMCA and AARP. For information, contact:

- Your local YMCA
- Your local chapter of the Arthritis Foundation (see your local White Pages)
- The Arthritis Foundation (see telephone numbers above)

You may also want to send for:

Bibliography: *Exercise and Arthritis*
Cost: $4.00
Contains: Extensive listings of books, articles, and other resource material on exercise and arthritis
From: The National Arthritis and Musculo-skeletal and Skin Diseases Clearinghouse
Box AMS
Bethesda, MD 20892

Unfortunately, none of the above treatment methods are cures. That's why arthritis sufferers are so vulnerable to health care fraud, spending five times more money on fraudulent or unproven treatments, medications, or devices than this country spends on research to cure arthritis. Every person who suffers from arthritis should read our material on Health Care Fraud (see Chapter 13).

Coping with Arthritis

Arthritis can make difficult most of the everyday movements most Americans take for granted, from turning a doorknob to opening a jar to getting out of a chair. Fortunately, American designers and manufacturers produce a wide variety of products designed to allow arthritis sufferers to lead normal lives in their own homes. Some sources of special interest to arthritis sufferers are:

Catalog: *The Rehab Shoppe: Products for the Physically Challenged*
Cost: Free
From: Cleo, Inc.
3957 Mayfield Road
Cleveland, OH 44121
(800) 321-0595 (Ex. OH)
(216) 382-9700

Catalog: *Medical Self Care Catalog*
11 Chapel Street
P.O. Box 1099
Augusta, ME 04330
Cost: Free

Catalog: *Ways and Means*
28001 Citrin Drive
Romulus, MI 48174
Cost: Free

Catalog: *Comfortably Yours*
52 West Hunter Avenue
Maywood, NJ 07607
Cost: Free

Book: *The Gadget Book*
Cost: $10.95 (AARP member price $x.xx)
Contains: A description of hundreds of special products to make life easier for people with some limitation or handicap
From: AARP Books/Scott, Foresman and Co.
1865 Miner Street
Des Plaines, IL 60056

Book: *The Illustrated Directory of Handicapped Products*
Cost: $12.95 plus shipping
Contains: Descriptions, pictures, and prices of products from more than 1,000 manufacturers
From: Trio Publications
497 Cameron Way
Buffalo Grove, IL 60089

ASTHMA AND ALLERGIES

Asthma and allergies are both caused by certain specific genetically inherited characteristics of the body's immune system. In the case of allergy, the body's immune system is unusually sensitive to the presence of some substance. The immune system overreacts, producing antibodies that can cause symptoms ranging in severity from sneezing or itching to, in rare cases, death.

Asthma, which is generally a more serious and debilitating condition, results from a special sensitivity of the respiratory tract. In an asthma attack, the tissues of the bronchial tubes or lungs swell, making breathing difficult. Attacks can range from mild to life-threatening. While asthma most often develops in childhood, it can occur anytime in life. Most asthma is allergy-related, although some are believed to be produced by other unknown causes.

A majority of people with asthma and allergies have had the conditions since early in life. However, a significant number of older Americans find themselves developing allergies, primarily for two reasons:

• Environmental changes, such as a change of residence or from the introduction of pollutants into their homes

- Chemical changes in the body, such as the hormonal changes involved in menopause

Unfortunately, even lifelong allergy and asthma sufferers misunderstand the symptoms, receive inadequate treatment, or simply live with the discomfort and inconvenience.

General Sources of Information

Hotline: The Asthma Hotline
(800) 222-5864 (Ex. CO)
(303) 355-5864
Services: A trained nurse from the National Jewish Hospital National Asthma Center will answer questions about asthma and provide referrals to specialists all over the country

Organization: National Institute of Allergy and Infectious Disease (NIAID)
Building 31, Room 7A-32
Bethesda, MD 20892
(301) 496-5717
Services: Coordinates research and education efforts on asthma and allergies. Provides information and issues free publications, including:
- *Allergies: Questions and Answers*
- *Asthma*
- *Drug Allergy*
- *Dust Allergy*
- *Insect Allergy*
- *Mold Allergy*
- *Poison Ivy Allergy*
- *Pollen Allergy*
- *Understanding the Immune System*

Booklet: *Allergies: Medicine for the Layman*
Cost: Free

From: Office of Clinical Center Communications
Warren G. Magnuson Clinical Center
Building 10, Room 5C-305
Bethesda, MD 20892
(301) 496-2563

Organization: Asthma and Allergy Foundation of America
1717 Massachusetts Ave., NW
Washington, DC 20005
(202) 265-0265
Services: National nonprofit organization that supports research and education programs. Will answer questions, provide referrals to local chapters, and send a list of low-cost publications

Organization: American Allergy Association
Box 7273
Menlo Park, CA 94026
(415) 322-1663
Services: Provides information and self-help for people with food and chemical allergies

Organization: American Lung Association
Services: Through local chapters, provides information, referrals and support services to people with asthma. Publications include:
- *About Asthma*
- *Asthma Facts*
- *Controlling Asthma*
For information: Your local American Lung Association Chapter (see White Pages)
or
American Lung Association
1740 Broadway
New York, NY 10019
(212) 315-8700

Treatment for Asthma and Allergies

The first source of treatment is your primary care physician, who can treat most allergies and mild asthma. For more serious problems, your physician may refer you to a specialist known as an allergist. An additional source of referral for people with asthma is:

Organization: Asthma Care Association of
America
P.O. Box 568
Ossining, NY 10362
(914) 762-2110

An alternative source of treatment for people with allergies is a relatively new medical speciality called "clinical ecology." These physicians believe that many allergies are caused by intolerance to certain chemicals either in food or in the environment. For more information and referral:

Organization: American Academy of Environmental Medicine
P.O. Box 16106
Denver, CO 80216
(303) 622-9755

BURNS

Over two million Americans suffer serious burns every year. People age 65 and over are significantly more likely to be victims than any other adults, for two reasons. First, accidental fires are more likely to begin in their homes because of carelessness or inadequate home maintenance. Second, mobility problems make it more difficult for some older people to escape when a fire occurs.

Burn victims must undergo extensive physical therapy and rehabilitation, an extremely painful process that causes great stress on them and their families. During rehabilitation,

an important source of information and support is:

Organization: Phoenix Society
11 Rust Hill Road
Levittown, PA 19056
(215) 946-4788
Services: Recovered burn victims work with severely burned people and their families during and after hospitalization. Provides information and referrals through almost 100 local chapters

CANCER

Cancer is a general term for more than 100 different diseases, all of which are characterized by the growth and spread of abnormal cells in the body. Cancer is a much-feared and very much misunderstood disease. Indeed, many Americans don't realize that in recent years, there have been extraordinary advances in treating many forms of cancer, saving thousands of lives every year.

According to the American Cancer Society, about one in four Americans will develop one form of cancer in their lifetime, and about one million new cases occur every year. However, almost half of those who develop cancer will be alive and free from signs of the disease 5 years after the initial diagnosis, a higher survival rate than for heart attack victims.

An important key to early diagnosis is

learning the more common early warning signs of cancer:

- Change in bowel or bladder habits
- A sore that does not heal
- Unusual bleeding or discharge
- Thickening or lump in the breast or elsewhere
- Indigestion or difficulty in swallowing
- Obvious change in wart or mole
- Nagging cough or hoarseness

Other possible signs include unusual tiredness, persistent headaches, weight loss, or excessive bruising.

All of these symptoms can be caused by many other conditions besides cancer. However, since early detection of cancer is critical, you should schedule a complete medical examination by your physician immediately.

General Sources of Information

Fact Sheet: Age Page: Cancer Facts for People Over 50
Cost: Free
From: National Institute on Aging
Building 31, Room 5C35
Bethesda, MD 20892

Organization: Cancer Information Service
Office of Cancer Communications
Building 31, Room 10A24
Bethesda, MD 20892
(800) 422-6237 (Ex. AK, HI, and DC and suburbs)
(800) 638-6070 (AK)
(202) 636-5700 (DC and suburbs)
(808) 524-1234 (HI—call collect if long distance)
Services: Sponsored by the National Cancer Institute, this service answers questions, provides referrals, and issues many publications, including:

- *Cancer Prevention*
- *Diet, Nutrition, and Cancer Prevention: A Guide to Food Choices*
- *Everything Doesn't Cause Cancer*
- *What You Need to Know About Cancer*
- *Radiation Therapy and You: A Guide to Self-Help During Treatment*
- *Chemotherapy and You: A Guide to Self-Help During Treatment*
- *Taking Time: Support for People with Cancer and Those Who Care About Them*
- *Eating Hints: Recipes and Tips for Better Nutrition During Cancer Treatment*
- *What You Need to Know About . . .*
  - *Adult Leukemia*
  - *Cancer of the Bladder*
  - *Cancer of the Brain and Spinal Column*
  - *Cancer of the Colon and Rectum*
  - *Cancer of the Esophagus*
  - *Cancer of the Kidney*
  - *Cancer of the Larynx*
  - *Cancer of the Lung*
  - *Cancer of the Mouth*
  - *Cancer of the Ovary*
  - *Cancer of the Pancreas*
  - *Cancer of the Prostate*
  - *Cancer of the Skin*
  - *Cancer of the Stomach*
  - *Cancer of the Testes*
  - *Cancer of the Uterus*
  - *Cancer of the Bones*
  - *Hodgkin's Disease*
  - *Melanoma*
  - *Multiple Myeloma*
  - *Non-Hodgkin's Lymphoma*
  Research reports (variety of subjects)

Organization: American Cancer Society
Services: The major voluntary organization that sponsors research, education, and services to cancer patients and

their families through over 100 local chapters. Publications include 10- to 20-page fact sheets on most types of cancer

For information: Your local American Cancer Society chapter (see White Pages)
or
American Cancer Society
1599 Clifford Road, NE
Atlanta, GA 30329
(800) 227-2345
(404) 320-3333

Hotline: AMC Cancer Information Line
(800) 525-3777 (Ex. CO, AK, and HI)
(303) 233-6501 (AK and HI call collect if long distance)
Service: Professional cancer counselors answer questions, send written materials, and provide advice and reassurance to cancer sufferers and their families. Will review general treatment procedures and help callers determine a course of action

Booklets: • *Diet, Nutrition and Cancers of the Colon and Rectum*
• *The Cancer Process*
• *Dietary Fiber to Lower Cancer Risk*
• *Dietary Guidelines to Lower Cancer Risk*
• *All About Fats and Cancer Risk*
• *Menus and Recipes to Lower Cancer Risk*
• *Facts You Should Know About Outdoor Cooking*
Cost: Free
From: American Institute for Cancer Research
500 N. Washington St.
Falls Church, VA 22046
(703) 237-0159

Organization: National Technical Information Service
Service: Publishes reports, bibliographies, and research summaries on cancer research, including:

• Cancergrams: abstracts of recently published articles
• Directory of Cancer Research Information Resources: updated constantly
For information: You can receive a list of publications and prices from:
National Technical Information Service
5285 Port Royal Road
Springfield, VA 22161
(703) 487-4600

Organization: Association for Brain Tumor Research
2910 W. Montrose Ave.
Chicago, IL 60618
(312) 286-5571
Services: Organizes self-help groups for patients with brain tumors and their families. Provides referrals and publishes booklets, pamphlets, and bibliographies

Booklet: *Brain Tumors: Hope Through Research*
Cost: Free
From: National Institute on Aging
Building 31, Room 5C35
Bethesda, MD 20892

Organization: Leukemia Society of America
733 Third Ave.
New York, NY 10017
(212) 573-8484
Services: Provides educational materials and support for leukemia patients and their families

A Special Note to Women About Breast Cancer

Breast cancer is the most common type of cancer in women, with about 125,000 new cases and about 40,000 deaths annually, and the risk of breast cancer increases significantly when a woman reaches age 50. An estimated 24,000 of those deaths could have been prevented through early detection. Early detection requires women to take responsibility for that detection by:

- Conducting a breast self-examination once a month
- Having a mammogram, a breast scan with low-level radiation, every 1 to 2 years after age 40 and annually after age 50

Booklets: • *Breast Exams: What You Should Know*
• *Why Women Don't Get Mammograms (and Why They Should)*
Cost: Free ($1.00 postage and handling if ordering two booklets)
From: Consumer Information Center
P.O. Box 100
Pueblo, CO 81009

Booklet: *Breast Cancer: We're Making Progress Every Day*
Cost: Free
Call: (800)-422-6237 (Ex. AK, HI, and DC and suburbs) (800-638-6070 (AK)
(202) 636-5700 (DC and suburbs)
(808) 524-1234 (HI—call collect if long distance)

Booklets: *Special Touch: A Personal Plan of Action for Breast Health Finding a Lump in Your Breast Mammography: Saving More Lives*
Cost: Free
From: Your local chapter of the American Cancer Society (see White Pages)
or
American Cancer Society
1599 Clifford Road, NE
Atlanta, GA 30329
(800) 227-2345
(404) 320-3333

Organization: American College of Radiology
1981 Preston White Drive
Reston, VA 22091
(800) 227-5463 (Ex. VA)
(703) 648-8900
Services: Developing an accreditation program for mammography centers. Will provide referrals to mammography centers and free publications, including:
• *Mammography: A Patient's Guide to Breast X-Ray Examination*
• *Radiology: A Patient's Guide to Diagnostic Imaging*

Information: High Priority Shower Card
Cost: Free
Contains: Laminated card to hang in the shower with instructions for breast self-examination
From: AMC Cancer Research Center
Shower Card
Box 1987
Denver, CO 80201
(800) 525-3777 (Ex. CO)
(303) 233-6501

Treatment for Cancer

Treatment should begin as soon as possible after detection. But choosing the right physician and hospital to treat you is a very important decision, for two reasons:

- Because cancer is the subject of so much research and so many research breakthroughs, you should be treated by a physician who has access to the latest information and techniques
- You want to choose a physician who has extensive experience with your type of cancer, because experience means ear-

lier detection of problems and side effects

One method to find a qualified specialist in your area is to ask your physician about:

Computer Service: PDQ (Physicians Data Query)

Service: A computer service for physicians that maintains a directory of specialists in all types of cancers. PDQ also contains detailed information on the preferred current treatments for all types of cancers and summaries of the important experimental treatment programs

For information: Most hospitals and some physicians can access PDQ from their computers. For further information, a doctor can contact:
National Cancer Institute
Department of Health and Human Services
9000 Rockville Pike
Building 31, Room 10A24
Bethesda, MD 20205
(301) 496-5583

You can get referrals to treatment centers directly by calling:

Hotline: Cancer Information Line
(800) 422-6237 (Ex. AK, HI, and DC and suburbs)
(800) 638-6070 (AK)
(202) 636-5700 (DC and suburbs)
(808) 524-1234 (HI—call collect if long distance)

Service: Information services sponsored by the National Cancer Institute

When you call, you can ask about the three types of cancer treatment programs sponsored by the National Cancer Institute (NCI). These are:

- Comprehensive cancer centers. These centers meet major NCI criteria for diagnosis and treatment of cancer, they participate in clinical studies, and they conduct research. There are 21 comprehensive cancer centers across the country.
- Clinical cancer centers. These centers meet NCI criteria for diagnosis and treatment, but they do not conduct research.
- Clinical community oncology program centers. These centers are designed to bring the latest treatment techniques to areas of the country without major cancer centers.

Finally, you can obtain information on treatment centers by calling:

Organization: Your local chapter of the American Cancer Society (see White Pages)
or
American Cancer Society
(800) 227-2345
(404) 320-3333

Once you've found a specialist or treatment center, you'll be examined further, then given a treatment program that will include one or more of the following general treatments:

- Radiation
- Chemotherapy
- Surgery

Self-Help and Support Groups for Cancer Patients and Their Families

The diagnosis of cancer almost invariably brings with it fear and depression. Patients and their families can profit greatly from the support of others during the course of their illness. Fortunately, there are many self-help and support groups, including:

Programs: • I Can Cope
 • Cansurmount
 • Reach to Recover (for mastectomy patients)
 • Association of Laryngectomies
Description: The above are four of the many programs sponsored by the American Cancer Society and its local chapters
For information: Your local American Cancer Society chapter (see White Pages)
or
American Cancer Society
1599 Clifford Road, NE
Atlanta, GA 30329
(800) 227-2345
(404) 320-3333
or
Your hospital's social service office
or
Your local area agency on aging (see pages 383–427)

Organization: National Coalition for Cancer Survivorship
323 Eighth Street, SW
Albuquerque, NM 87102
(505) 764-9956
Services: Assists over 50 affiliated self-help groups and develops publications and programs to help cancer patients and survivors

Organization: Y-Me Breast Cancer Support Program
18229 Harwood Avenue
Homewood, IL 60430
(800) 221-2141 (Ex. IL)
(312) 799-8338
Services: Information and support services for breast cancer patients and their families. Operates toll-free information number

Organization: Make Today Count
101-1/2 S. Union Street
Alexandria, VA 22314
(703) 548-9674
Services: Coordinates over 300 chapters that provide support for people with life-threatening illnesses

THE COMMON COLD AND INFLUENZA

The common cold generally poses few health risks to people who are in generally good health—unless they fail to take care of themselves. That care is primarily self-care with over-the-counter medications. The Food and Drug Administration estimates that Americans could save $11 billion per year treating themselves for routine colds without going to see a physician. *Caution:* Anyone with any serious or chronic health problem should consult their physician in the case of any symptoms of illness, no matter how minor.

Influenza is a much more serious matter, especially for people with health problems and those age 65 and older. Influenza or the "flu" is an acute respiratory infection caused by a virus. Flu and pneumonia, the most common complications of the flu, are the sixth leading cause of death in the United States. That's why almost all health experts recommend that older Americans, especially those with health problems, receive a flu shot in the fall. These inoculations are prepared each year under the supervision of the U.S. Centers for Disease Control, and they provide protection against the strains of flu that they believe will be most prevalent the upcoming winter.

Because of the health risks of the flu, most

communities offer free flu shots to older residents. To find out when they will be given in your area, call your local senior center or your local area agency on aging (see pages 383–427).

If you are age 65 or older, or if you have a chronic health problem, you should send for the following information:

Booklets: • *A Doctor's Advice on Self Care*
• *The Common Cold: Relief, but No Cure*

Cost: Free ($1.00 if ordering both)
From: Consumer Information Center
P.O. Box 100
Pueblo, CO 81009

Booklet: *Flu*
Cost: Free
From: NIAID/NIH
Building 31, Room 7A-32
Bethesda, MD 20892

DIABETES

Diabetes is a condition in which the body cannot convert foods properly into the energy needed for daily activity. The result is that the level of glucose in the blood rises to dangerous levels, causing such symptoms as frequent urination, weight loss, thirst, fatigue, blurred vision, itching, and skin infections. Left untreated, diabetes can cause kidney damage, vision problems, and circulation problems.

About 10 million Americans suffer from diabetes. About 10% of these people produce no insulin at all, and thus have to take insulin every day. These "insulin-dependent" diabetics most commonly develop the disease in childhood.

The most common form of diabetes is "noninsulin-dependent" or "adult onset" diabetes. This condition usually develops after age 40, and about 80% of those who develop the condition are overweight. An estimated five million Americans, the majority of them age 50 and over, suffer from undetected noninsulin-dependent diabetes, one reason that diabetes is the seventh leading cause of death in the United States This lack of detection is particularly tragic because this form of diabetes can normally be controlled through weight loss, exercise, and following a balanced diet.

General Sources of Information

Organization: National Diabetes Information Clearinghouse
Box NDIC
Bethesda, MD 20892
(301) 468-2162
Services: This federal information service answers questions, provides referrals to other federal agencies and non-profit organizations, and publishes the following booklets free of charge:
• *Age Page: Dealing with Diabetes*
• *Facts About Insulin-Dependent Diabetes*
• *Noninsulin-Dependent Diabetes*
• *The Diabetes Dictionary*
• *Dental Tips for Diabetics*
• *Diabetic Retinopathy*
• *Foot Care for the Diabetic Patient*
• *Periodontal Disease & Diabetes*
• *Self Blood Glucose Monitoring* Bibliographies; $2.00 each
  – *Diabetes and Aging*
  – *Diet and Nutrition for People with Diabetes*
  – *Cookbooks for People with Diabetes*

- *Sports and Exercise for People with Diabetes*
- *Foot Care and Diabetes*
- *Materials and Aids for the Visually Impaired Diabetic*

Organization: The American Diabetes Association
National Service Center
1660 Duke Street
P.O. Box 25757
Alexandria, VA 22313
(800) 232-3472
(703) 549-1500

Services: National voluntary organization that funds major research and supervises over 700 local affiliates and chapters that provide a wide variety of services and support for diabetics and their families. Publishes a wide variety of booklets and other sources of information on all aspects of diabetes, including the following material:
- Publications list
- *What You Need to Know About Diabetes*
- *Diabetes and You: Adults* ($1.20)
- *Diabetes and You: Seniors* ($1.20)
- *Buyers Guide to Diabetes Products* ($2.50)

- *Diabetes in the Family* ($11.45)
- *Diabetes: Reach for Health and Freedom* ($11.45)

Treatment for Diabetes

Since the majority of adult diabetics can control their condition through diet and exercise, diabetes is considered a self-help disease. In the majority of cases, diabetes can be diagnosed by a family physician or internist, who is qualified to supervise a patient's self-care and monitor progress.

Patients who develop complications should consult a specialist, called a diabetologist. You can find a specialist by contacting your local chapter of the American Diabetes Association (see White Pages).

The largest and most widely known diabetes research and treatment center is:

The Joslin Diabetes Center
One Joslin Place
Boston, MA 02215
(617) 732-2440

DIGESTIVE DISORDERS

Our digestive system is a complex group of organs that convert the food we eat into the nutrients our body needs and removes the waste products of digestion. Because of the complexity of the process and the number of organs involved, digestive problems are very common, especially as we grow older. An estimated half of all adult Americans suffer from some kind of digestive problem, and one in nine has a chronic digestive disease. Digestive disorders account for more hospital admissions than any other type of disorder.

The body organs involved in digestion include:

- Esophagus
- Stomach
- Liver
- Pancreas
- Gallbladder
- Small intestine
- Colon

Although digestive problems tend to increase with age, there are few if any problems directly related to the normal aging process. Rather, many digestive problems tend to develop over a period of time due to improper diet, bad eating habits, lack of exercise, stress, excessive consumption of alcohol and caffeine, smoking, and use of over-the-counter and prescription medications. Still other digestive problems result from infections or unknown causes.

Some important warning signs of digestive problems are:

- Severe or recurring stomach pains
- Blood in vomit or recurring vomiting
- Sudden change in bowel habits or consistency of stools lasting a few days or more
- Blood in stools or coal-black stools
- Jaundice (yellowing of the skin and whites of the eyes) or darkening of the urine
- Pain or difficulty in swallowing food
- Continuing loss of appetite or unplanned weight loss
- Diarrhea that wakes you up at night

Some conditions, such as heartburn, indigestion, or gas, may cause occasional discomfort but lead to no serious problems. Other conditions, such as liver disease, ulcers, inflammatory bowel disease, gallstones, and colitis, can be more serious and require extended medical treatment. That's why anyone suffering from any of the above symptoms should see their doctor.

General Sources of Information

Since so many digestive conditions or diseases can be prevented or improved by modifying our life-styles, it's extremely important that we all educate ourselves about digestive diseases and prevention. Among the sources of information are:

Organization: National Digestive Diseases Clearinghouse
Box NDDIC
Bethesda, MD 20892
(301) 468-6344

Services: Answers questions from the public, provides referrals to physicians and treatment centers, and provides many free publications, including:
- *Digestive Health and Disease: A Glossary*
- *Facts and Fallacies About Digestive Diseases*
- *Your Digestive System and How It Works*
- *Diagnostic Tests for Digestive Diseases*
- *Bleeding in the Digestive Tract*
- *Gas in the Digestive Tract*
- *What Is Constipation?*
- *Resources on Dietary Fiber*
- *Heartburn*
- *Inflammatory Bowel Disease*
- *Irritable Bowel Syndrome*
- *Ulcerative Colitis*
- *Diarrhea: Infectious and Other Causes*
- *What Is Hiatal Hernia?*
- *Lactose Intolerance*
- *What Is Dyspepsia?*
- *Smoking and Your Digestive System*
- *Hemorrhoids*
- *About Stomach Ulcers*
- *Cirrhosis of the Liver*
- *Diverticulosis and Diverticulitis*
- *Peptic Ulcer*
- *What Is Pancreatis?*
- *Gallstones*

Age Pages: *Digestive Do's and Don'ts Constipation*
Cost: Free

From: National Institute on Aging
Building 31, Room 5C35
Bethesda, MD 20892

Among the most common and serious types of digestive diseases are liver and gallbladder diseases. Liver diseases, such as cirrhosis and hepatitis, are the third leading cause of disease-related deaths in the United States. Tragically, there are no known cures for most serious liver diseases. However, the most serious ones are potentially preventable. The best source of information on liver disease, gallbladder disease, and prevention is:

Organization: American Liver Foundation
998 Pompton Avenue
Cedar Grove, NJ 07009
(800) 223-0179
(201) 857-2626

Services: Supports research and education for liver and gallbladder diseases. Issues many publications, including fact sheets on 19 less common conditions and the following pamphlets:
- *Your Liver Lets You Live*
- *I'm Your Liver*
- *Myths of Alcohol and the Liver*
- *Diet and Your Liver*
- *Cirrhosis—Many Causes*
- *Gallstones and Gallbladder Disorders*
- *Facts on Liver Transplantation*
- *Biliary Atresia*
- *Hemochromatosis: Not So Rare*
- *Viral Hepatitis: Everybody's Problem*

Cost: Pamphlets are $0.25 each, with $2.00 fee for postage and handling. Set of all 19 fact sheets is $3.00

Treatment for Digestive Diseases and Disorders

Many digestive diseases and disorders can be treated by your primary care physician. However, in the case of chronic or serious problems, care is provided by gastroenterologists, specialists in digestive disorders. You can obtain a referral from your doctor, or by contacting:

Organization: American Digestive Disease Society
7720 Wisconsin Avenue
Bethesda, MD 20814

Services: This society is a nonprofit organization which helps people understand and deal with digestive problems. Among the society's services are:
- *Living Healthy*, a periodical sent to members that focuses on living with specific digestive problems
- GUTLINE, a national telephone call-in service which allows the public to talk to medical specialists
- FOODPHONE, a national telephone service which allows the public to talk to experts in nutrition Referral service to direct patients to medical specialists
- Dietary plans for people suffering from a number of conditions, including inflammatory bowel disease, gallstones, and excessive gas A series of free "Person to Person" brochures on specific conditions, including
  Colon Cancer
  Irritable Bowel
  Diverticulosis
  Peptic Ulcer
  Inflammatory Bowel Disease
  Acid Reflux and Hiatal Hernia

For GUTLINE: Call (301) 652-9293 Tuesdays only, 7:30 to 9:00 p.m. EST

For FOODLINE: Call (301) 652-9293 Wednesdays only, 7:30 to 9:00 p.m. EST

Support Groups for People with Serious Digestive Diseases and Disorders

Common types of digestive disorders involve diseases of the colon, ileitis and colitis. Information on support groups and other services is available from:

> **Organization:** National Foundation for Ileitis & Colitis
> 444 Park Avenue South, 11th Floor
> New York, NY 10016
> (212) 685-3440
> **Services:** Support and education for patients and their families. Has over 50 local chapters

Special support and information for sufferers of hemochromatosis, a hereditary condition in which the body retains too much iron, are available from:

> **Organization:** Iron Overload Disease Association
> 224 Datura Street, Suite 911

West Palm Beach, FL 33401
(407) 840-8512

Some patients with colon cancer or other serious disorders have undergone an ostomy, a procedure that involves removing part or all of the colon and diverting the body's waste products for collection in a bag worn outside of the body. This type of surgery is often traumatic, and many patients need moral and practical support to return to a normal life. One important resource is:

> **Organization:** United Ostomy Association
> 36 Executive Park, Suite 120
> Irvine, CA 92714
> (714) 660-8624
> **Services:** Provides materials and support to over 600 local chapters

DRUG ABUSE AND ADDICTION

According to the National Institute on Drug Abuse, 60% of hospital admissions for drug overdoses and 70% of drug-related deaths resulted from misuse of prescription medications, primarily sedatives and tranquilizers. Many of the more serious emergencies involve people who combine prescription drugs with abuse of alcohol.

A small but growing number of people age 50 and over do use or abuse such illegal drugs as cocaine and marijuana. However, "hidden" addictions to prescription drugs or to drug-alcohol combinations is by far the most common problem among mature Americans. Yet, both the person involved and family members often ignore or deny problems. Sometimes, forgetfulness, excessive sleeping, and other symptoms are dismissed as signs of depression or aging.

In these cases, family members often have to intervene. One place to start is to contact the physician who is prescribing the medication and who may not be aware that it is being combined

with alcohol. A second source of information is the many alcohol abuse information sources and self-help groups (see Alcoholism in this chapter). Finally, other sources of information, referral, and help are:

> **Organization:** National Institute on Drug Abuse
> Information Office
> 5600 Fishers Lane, Room 10A46
> Rockville, MD 20857
> (800) 662-4357
> (301) 443-6500
> **Services:** Provides information on drug abuse and treatment programs, as well as referrels to programs.

> **Organization:** Hazelton Foundation
> P.O. Box 176
> Center City, MN 55021
> (800) 328-9000 (Ex. MN)
> (800) 262-5010 (MN)
> **Services:** Operates one of the largest and

best known treatment programs for chemical dependency. Publishes over 1,500 books, pamphlets, and other resource materials. Operates toll-free hotline for information and referrals for chemical dependency

Organization: Narcotics Anonymous
Services: National self-help group for drug abusers modeled on Alcoholics Anonymous. Has over 12,000 local groups, and operates hotlines in most major cities
For information: Local Narcotics Anonymous (see White Pages)
or
Narcotics Anonymous
P.O. Box 9999
Van Nuys, CA 91409
(818) 780-3951

Hotline: National Cocaine Hotline
(800) 262-2463
Service: Offers information, counseling, and referrals for people with cocaine addictions

Organization: Drugs Anonymous
P.O. Box 473 Ansonia Station
New York, NY 10023
(212) 874-0700
Services: Nationwide self-help program modeled on Alcoholics Anonymous that emphasizes help for people addicted to pills

Organization: Your state alcohol and drug abuse agency
For information: See your telephone directory under your state government listings or call your state government information service, pages 441–443.

EPILEPSY

Epilepsy isn't a disease, but rather a group of symptoms caused by a number of different conditions. These symptoms involve a sudden excess of electrical activity in the brain, producing small- or large-scale seizures. The condition normally appears before age 20, but can arise at any age. About two million Americans, about 1% of the population, are epileptics.

With medication, the vast majority of epileptics can lead normal lives. Sources of information include:

Organization: Epilepsy Foundation of America
4351 Garden City Drive, Suite 406
Landover, MD 20785
(301) 459-3700
Services: Most important source of information and referral to medical special-

ists, support groups, rehabilitation programs, and other services

Booklet: *Epilepsy: Medicine for the Layman*
Cost: Free
From: Office of Clinical Communications
Warren G. Magnuson Clinical Center
National Institutes of Health
Building 10, Room 5C-305
Bethesda, MD 20892
(301) 496-2563

Booklet: *Epilepsy: Hope Through Research*
Cost: Free
From: National Institute of Neurological and Communicative Disorders and Stroke
National Institutes of Health
Building 31, Room 8A-06
9000 Rockville Pike
Bethesda, MD 20892
(301) 496-5751

FOOT PROBLEMS

Americans age 50 and over often suffer from foot problems and injuries, many of which stem from other conditions such as arthritis, osteoporosis, or diabetes. For information:

> **Organization:** American Podiatric Medical Association
> 9312 Old Georgetown Rd.
> Bethesda, MD 20814
> (301) 571-9200

Services: Provides referral to podiatrists, doctors who specialize in the diagnosis and treatment of foot injuries, problems, and diseases. Will provide free publications, including:
- Your Podiatrist Talks About Foot Care and Aging
- Arthritis and Your Feet
- Your Podiatrist Talks About Diabetes

HEARING LOSS

Hearing loss is one of the most common medical conditions in this country, afflicting an estimated 20 million Americans. Amazingly, only 3.5 million of these people have sought treatment for their problem. Since people are more likely to have hearing problems when they get older, failure to recognize or admit to a problem needlessly impairs the quality of life of many of you who are age 50 and over. Most people with hearing problems can be helped by surgery, medication, special training, a hearing aid, or alternate listening devices.

Among the signs of a hearing impairment are:

- Words are difficult to understand

- Certain sounds, such as the dripping of a faucet or the high notes of an instrument, can't be heard

- Another person's speech sounds slurred or mumbled

- Television programs, movies, concerts, or parties are less enjoyable because much goes unheard

While not a substitute for a comprehensive test conducted by a doctor, one quick and easy way to find out if you or a loved one may be experiencing some hearing loss is to take a simple hearing test over the phone.

> **Resource:** Dial-A-Hearing Screening Test
> **Cost:** Free
> **Service:** By calling a toll-free number, you receive a local number you can call to get a simple hearing screening test. A recorded message will play a series of tones at different pitches. If you can't hear some or all of the tones, you should seek help. The national toll-free number also makes referrals to local hearing specialists
> **Call:** (800) 222-3277 (Ex. PA)
> (800) 345-3277 (PA)

> **Resource:** Johns Hopkins Hospital Hearing and Speech Clinic
> **Cost:** Free, except for cost of telephone call
> **Service:** Recorded message plays a simple hearing test 24 hours a day
> **Call:** (301) 955-3434

General Sources of Information

> **Resource:** Hearing Helpline
> The Better Hearing Institute
> 5021-B Backlick Road

Annandale, VA 22003
(800) 327-9355 (Ex. VA)
(800) 424-8576 (VA)
Cost: Free
Services: The Better Hearing Institute, a nonprofit educational organization, operates a toll-free hotline that:
- Answers questions about symptoms, hearing loss, hearing aids, surgery, and finances
- Makes referrals to medical specialists and self-help groups
- Sends free publications, including:
  - *You Should Hear What You're Missing*
  - *We Overcame Hearing Loss*
  - *Overcome Hearing Loss Now*
  - *Questions & Answers About the Better Hearing Institute*

Organization: National Institute on Deafness and Other Communication Disorders
Information Office
9000 Rockville Pike
Bethesda, MD 20892
(301) 496-5751
Services: Distributes information on deafness, hearing loss, and other communication disorders affecting older people. Evaluates treatments and hearing devices, and funds research programs. Will answer questions, make referrals, and provide a list of publications.

Booklet: *Have You Heard? Hearing Loss and Aging* (D12219)
Cost: Free
Contains: Detailed information on how to detect hearing loss, the causes of loss, and how to obtain treatment
From: AARP
1909 K Street, NW
Washington, DC 20049

Fact Sheet: *Age Page: Hearing Loss and the Elderly*
Cost: Free
From: National Institute on Aging
Building 31, Room 5C35
Bethesda, MD 20892

Booklet: *Facts About Hearing*
Cost: Free
Contains: Information on symptoms of and types of hearing loss, as well as how to obtain treatment
From: National Hearing Aid Society
20361 Middlebelt Road
Livonia, MI 48152
(800) 521-5247 (Ex. MI, AK, HI)
(313) 478-2610

Booklet: *I Think I Have a Hearing Problem! What Should I Do?*
Cost: $2.50
From: Self-Help for Hard of Hearing People (SHHH)
7800 Wisconsin Avenue
Bethesda, MD 20814
(301) 657-2249 (VOICE)
(301) 657-2249 (TDD)

Treatment for a Hearing Problem

First, you should make an appointment with your family physician, who can detect and treat simple hearing problems. If the problem is more complicated, your family physician may refer you to a specialist, an otologist or otolaryngologist. If your family physician is unable to make a referral, you can contact:

Resource: American Academy of Otolaryngology
1101 Vermont Avenue, NW, Suite 302
Washington, DC 20005
(202) 289-4607

Hotline: Hearing Hotline
(800) 327-9355 (Ex. VA)
(800) 424-8576 (VA)

These specialists may be able to correct the hearing problem through medication or surgery. If a medical solution isn't possible, these specialists may refer a patient to an audiologist, a specially trained medical technician who uses sophisticated techniques to measure hearing ability and determine if hearing aids or other amplification devices can help. For more information:

Organization: National Association for Hearing and Speech Action
10801 Rockville Pike
Rockville, MD 20852
(800) 638-8255 (Voice/TDD) (Ex. MD)
(301) 897-8682 (Voice/TDD) (MD)
Cost: Free
Services: Operates a toll-free number to:
- Answer hearing and speech questions
- Make referrals to certified audiologists and other professionals
- Send free brochures, including:
  - *Hearing Impairment and the Audiologist*
  - *Hearing Aids and Hearing Help*
  - *Communication Disorders and Aging*
  - *Does Your Health Insurance Benefits Cover Speech, Language, and Hearing Help?*

Treatment for Other Hearing Related Problems

One common symptom of ear problems, as well as some other conditions, is sudden attacks of dizziness and other balance problems. One resource is:

Organization: Dizziness and Balance Disorders Association
Resource Center
1015 Northwest 22nd Ave., Room 300
Portland, OR 97210
(503) 229-7348
Services: Provides information on dizziness, hearing loss, and balance disorders, and makes referrals to local resources and services

Another common condition that is found most often in people age 55 and older is Tinnitus, a constant ringing or buzzing in the ear or head. One resource is:

Organization: American Tinnitus Association
P.O. Box 5
Portland, OR 97207
(503) 248-9985
Services: Sponsors self-help groups nationwide, makes referrels to specialists, and provides a number of free information pamphlets

How to Purchase a Hearing Aid

Many hearing problems can be significantly improved by use of a hearing aid. However, purchasers should take great care in selecting a dispenser and purchasing a hearing aid, because this is an area that has seen a significant amount of consumer fraud. As a result, the Food and Drug Administration (FDA) requires that every person purchasing a hearing aid must obtain a written statement from a licensed physician stating that a medical evaluation has been performed in the last 6 months. Adult patients age 18 or older can sign a waiver for this requirement, but the hearing aid dispenser must actively encourage them to obtain a medical evaluation. To obtain information about the FDA regulations or to complain about a problem with a hearing aid dispenser:

Organization: Food and Drug Administration
Bureau of Medical Devices
Division of Compliance Operations (HFK-116)
8757 Georgia Avenue
Silver Spring, MD 20910
Cost: Free
Service: The FDA will investigate consumer complaints. The agency will also send the fact sheet:
- *It's Not Only a Good Idea—It's the Law*

The best way to avoid problems is to educate yourself about hearing aids and take care in selecting a hearing aid dispenser. Among the best resources are:

Service: Hearing Aid Hotline
Cost: Free
Provides: Will answer questions about hearing loss and will send a consumer information kit that includes:
- Information about hearing, hearing loss, and hearing aids
- A list of qualified hearing instrument specialists in the caller's area
From: National Hearing Aid Society
20361 Middlebelt
Livonia, MI 48152
(800) 521-5247 (Ex. MI, AK, and HI)
(313) 478-2610

Booklet: *Tuning in on Hearing Aids*
Cost: Free
From: Department of Health and Human Services
Public Health Services
Food and Drug Administration
5600 Fishers Lane
Rockville, MD 20857

Report: *Product Report: Hearing Aids* (D13766)
Cost: Free
From: AARP Fulfillment
1909 K St., NW
Washington, DC 20041

Booklet: *Facts About Hearing and Hearing Aids*
Cost: Free
From: FDA/Hearing Aids
8757 Georgia Avenue
Silver Spring, MD 20910

Booklet: *Facts About Hearing Aids*
Cost: Free with self-addressed stamped envelope
From: Council of Better Business Bureaus
4200 Wilson Blvd.
Arlington, VA 22203
(203) 276-0600

Booklet: *How to Buy a Hearing Aid*
Cost: Free
From: National Association for Hearing and Speech Action
10801 Rockville Pike
Rockville, MD 20852
(800) 638-8255 (Ex. MD)
(301) 897-8682
Resource: Hearing Aid Performance Measurement Program
Cost: Free
Services: The Veterans Administration annually tests a number of hearing aid models submitted by manufacturers and reports on those tests. The VA will supply information on brands tested and those found to be of high quality
Contact: Director of Information Services
Veterans Administration
810 Vermont Avenue, NW
Washington, DC 20420

Booklets: • *A Consumer's Guide for Purchasing a Hearing Aid* ($1.25)

- *ABC's of Hearing Aids* ($2.00)
- *How to File a Complaint Regarding a Hearing Aid* ($3.00)
- *Troubleshooting Your Hearing Aid* ($1.25)

Cost: $1.00 postage for orders of $5.00, $2.00 for orders of $5.00 to $10.00, $3.00 for orders $10.00 to $20.00

From: SHHH Publications
7800 Wisconsin Avenue
Bethesda, MD 20814

If You Can't Afford a Hearing Aid

Many of the hearing hotlines listed above will provide information about financial assistance. One national nonprofit resource is:

Resource: HEAR NOW
4001 South Magnolia Way, Suite 100
Denver, CO 80237
(800) 648-4327 (Ex. CO)
(300) 758-4919 (Voice/TDD)

Service: HEAR NOW has established a fund that provides grants and/or low-interest loans to cover the cost of hearing aids or other technical devices. Funds are allocated through a national lottery held annually

Coping with Hearing Loss

Coping with an impairment of hearing is a long-term process for both the person affected and their friends and relatives. Their are a number of resources that can help, including:

Organization: Self-Help for Hard of Hearing People (SHHH)
7800 Wisconsin Avenue
Bethesda, MD 20814
(301) 657-2248 (Voice)
(301) 657-2249 (TTY)

Cost: $12.00 per year membership dues

Services: SHHH is the major national self-help, educational, and resource organization for people who have hearing impairments and their families. Among their services are:
- A journal about hearing loss published six times per year
- Organizing over 200 local support groups
- Referral and advisory service
- Information and resource center
- Many detailed publications on all aspects of coping with hearing loss and communicating

Organization: Alexander Graham Bell Association for the Deaf
3417 Volta Place, NW
Washington, DC 20007
(202) 337-5220 (Voice/TDD)

Cost: Membership $35.00 per year, $20.00 per year for age 65 and older

Services: Publishes a wide variety of journals, newsletters, and brochures. Provides information and referral services. Organizes local self-help groups

Organization: National Information Center on Deafness

Service: Provides information on deafness and hearing loss in later life

Contact: Gallaudet College
800 Florida Avenue, NE
Washington, DC 20002
(202) 651-5000 (Voice)
(202) 651-5976 (TDD)

Booklet: *Hearing Loss: Hope Through Research*

Cost: Free

From: Office of Scientific and Health Reports
National Institute of Neurological and Communicative Disorders
Building 31, Room 8A06
Bethesda, MD 20892

Assistive Listening Devices

In addition to hearing aids, a wide variety of other technological devices can assist hearing impaired and deaf people in their everyday lives. Among these devices are:

- TDD (Telecommunication Device for the Deaf), which allows deaf and hearing impaired people to communicate over the telephone
- TV decoder, which allows deaf people to see captioning on certain television programs
- Telephone amplifiers, which filter out background noises and amplify voices
- Signaling devices, which flash lights or give off vibrations when the door bell or telephone rings

For information, contact:

Organization: National Technical Institute for the Deaf
One Lomb Memorial Drive
P.O. Box 9887
Rochester, NY 14623
(716) 475-6824 (Voice/TDD)
Service: Compiles information on technological devices for deaf and hearing impaired persons

Organization: Telecommunications for the Deaf, Inc.
814 Thayer Avenue
Silver Spring, MD 20910
(301) 589-3006
Service: Installs TDDs and TV decoders and acts as a consumer advocate

Hotline: Tele-Consumer Hotline
1910 K Street, NW
Washington, DC 20006
(800) 332-1124 (Voice/TDD)

Service: Maintains a directory of over 300 services that relay messages from TDD users to hearing people and hearing people to TDD users

Organization: AT&T Special Needs Center
Service: AT&T offers a variety of special equipment, services, and discounts to the hearing impaired and the deaf
Contact: (800) 233-1222

Catalog: Radio Shack Special Needs Catalog
Department 957SN
300 One Tandy Center
Fort Worth, TX 76102
Cost: Free
Contains: Catalog of special equipment sold by Radio Shack, some of which is of interest to hearing impaired and deaf people

Catalog: Communication Aids for Children and Adults
Cost: Free
Contains: Communication devices for hearing impaired and deaf adults, as well as those with speech problems
From: Crestwood Company
P.O. Box 04606
Milwaukee, WI 53204

Hearing Dogs

Just as seeing eye dogs have been trained to work with the blind, hearing dogs are trained to alert deaf owners to ringing phones and doorbells, children crying, smoke alarms going off, and other important sounds. For information:

Organization: Hearing Dog, Inc.
5901 E. 89th Avenue
Henderson, CO 80640
(303) 287-3277 (Voice/TDD)

Booklet: *Hearing Guide Dog Program*
Cost: $1.25 plus $1.00 postage and handling
From: SHHH Publications
7800 Wisconsin Avenue
Bethesda, MD 20814

Support and Self-Help Groups for the Deaf

Among the important resources for deaf adults are:

Organization: The National Association of the Deaf
814 Thayer Avenue
Silver Spring, MD 20910
(301) 587-1788
Cost: Membership $25.00 per year
Services: Largest advocacy, research, and information service for deaf Americans. Sponsors a wide variety of programs, activities, and publications

Organization: Deafpride, Inc.
1350 Potomac Ave., SE
Washington, DC 20003
(202) 675-6700
Service: Nonprofit advocacy organization for the deaf

Organization: National Center for Law and the Deaf
Gallaudet College
800 Florida Avenue, NE
Washington, DC 20002
(202) 651-5454
Service: Provides a variety of legal services and programs for the deaf

Organization: National Fraternal Society of the Deaf
1300 Northwest Highway
Mt. Prospect, IL 60056
(312) 392-9282 (Voice)
(312) 392-1409 (TDD)
Service: Sponsors insurance program and other activities

HEART AND CARDIOVASCULAR DISEASES

Heart disease has been the number one cause of death in the United States since 1910. The U.S. Public Health Service calculates that heart disease has caused half of all deaths in this country since 1949. Heart disease costs Americans almost $100 billion annually. The irony of these statistics is that heart disease is, to a great extent, preventable. In fact, increased awareness of the importance of proper diet and exercise in maintaining a healthy heart has contributed to a recent decline in heart attack deaths.

Over three quarters of all heart attacks are caused by diseased coronary arteries, which supply blood to the heart. Over the course of years, deposits of fat and minerals can build up in these arteries, making them hard (instead of elastic) and narrowing them so that blood flow is restricted. This hardening of the arteries, which is known as atherosclerosis, vastly increases the chance that a clot can block or restrict the flow of blood to the heart. When the flow of blood is cut off, the section of heart muscle depending on that blood can die, and thus interrupt the rhythm of the heart—in other words, a heart attack occurs.

The severity of the heart attack depends on, among many factors, the artery blocked, the length of blockage time, the amount of heart muscle affected, and the general health of the victim.

The symptoms of a heart attack vary, but the usual warning signs are:

- Uncomfortable pressure, fullness, squeezing, or pain in the center of the chest lasting for 2 minutes or more
- Pain spreading to the shoulders, neck, jaw, arms, or back
- Dizziness, fainting, sweating, nausea, and/or shortness of breath

Tens of thousands of lives could be saved every year if victims sought medical help immediately. Unfortunately, it's very common for heart attack victims to deny they're having an attack, either because the idea is frightening or they're afraid of being embarrassed if it turns out to be a false alarm. That's why doctors instruct spouses, relatives, and friends to ignore denials and call for medical help if they suspect a heart attack.

General Sources of Information

Organization: American Heart Association
Services: Supports research and education programs to prevent and treat heart disease. Coordinates many local groups that conduct education activities and organizes support programs for heart attack victims and their families. Publications include:
- *Fact Sheet on Heart Attack, Stroke, and Risk Factors*
- *Heart Attack and Stroke: Signals and Action*
- *About High Blood Pressure*
- *Smoking and Heart Disease*
- *The American Heart Association Diet*
- *About Your Heart and Diet*
- *About Your Heart and Smoking*
- *Heart Attack*
- *After a Heart Attack*
- *Nutrition Labeling*
- *Cholesterol and Your Heart*
- *E Is for Exercise*

For information: Your local American Heart Association office (see White Pages)

or

American Heart Association
7320 Greenville Avenue
Dallas, TX 75231
(214) 750-5300

Booklets: *Heart Attacks* ($1.00)
The Healthy Heart Handbook for Women ($1.25)
So You Have High Blood Cholesterol ($1.00)
From: R. Woods
Consumer Information Center
P.O. Box 100
Pueblo, CO 81009
Reprint: *The Fight Against Heart Disease* (No. 86-1126)
Cost: Free
From: Office of Public Affairs
Public Health Services
Food and Drug Administration
5600 Fishers Lane
Rockville, MD 20857

Publications: • *Arteriosclerosis Diabetes and Cardiovascular Disease*
- *Exercise and Your Heart*
- *A Handbook of Heart Terms*
- *How Doctors Diagnose Heart Disease*
- *Heart Attacks*
Cost: Free
From: National Heart, Lung and Blood Institute
Building 31, Room 4A21
Bethesda, MD 20892
(301) 496-4236

Treatment for Heart and Cardiovascular Diseases

The medical specialists who treat heart disease are cardiologists. If you can't obtain a referral to a cardiologist from your primary care physician, you can contact your local chapter of the American Heart Association.

Heart disease is the subject of a tremendous volume of research that has developed many new treatment techniques. Many of the leading authorities on these new techniques are the staff of the 23 government-sponsored cardiovascular disease research centers. You can obtain information about these centers from:

> **Organization:** National Heart, Lung and Blood Institute
> Building 31, Room 4A21
> Bethesda, MD 20892
> (301) 496-4236

Support Groups for Heart and Cardiovascular Disease Patients

Recovering from heart disease often requires changes in life-style that are hard to accomplish without the support of not only loved ones, but others who have gone or are going through the same process. Among the many excellent sources of support and information are:

> **Organization:** The Mended Hearts
> **Services:** Over 150 local support groups for

heart patients and their families, sponsored by the American Heart Association

> **For information:** Your local American Heart Association office (see White Pages)
>
> or
>
> American Heart Association
> 7320 Greenville Avenue
> Dallas, TX 75231
> (214) 750-5300

> **Organization:** Heartline
> **Services:** Publishes HEARTLINE, a monthly newsletter for heart patients and their families, plus a number of pamphlets, including:
> - *Non-Drug Treatment of Hypertension* ($3.25)
> - *Anatomy of a Heart Attack* ($2.50)
> - *Stress Management* ($3.25)
> - *Culinary Hearts Kitchen Course* ($5.25)
> - *How Do Angina Medicines Work?* ($2.50)
> - *Common Cardiac Drugs* ($5.25)
> **Cost:** Subscription to HEARTLINE is $15.00 per year
> **For information:** HEARTLINE
> The Cleveland Clinic Foundation
> 9500 Euclid Avenue
> Cleveland, OH 44106

HUNTINGTON'S DISEASE

Huntington's disease is an inherited condition that causes progressive degeneration of the central nervous system. It not only leads to loss of muscle control, but can cause mental deterioration that is often mistaken for mental illness or drunkenness.

Early mental and physical symptoms are

muscle spasms and tics, memory loss, slurred speech, depression, listlessness, and walking difficulties. There is no definitive diagnostic method. The key to early detection is knowledge of family history, since Huntington's disease is an inherited disorder.

Although there is no cure, medication,

physical therapy, and psychological counseling can slow the progression of the disease and help both patients and their families cope. The most important resources are:

Organization: Huntington's Disease Society of America
140 West 22nd Street, 6th Floor
New York, NY 10011
(800) 345-4372
(212) 242-1968
Services: Information, referrals, and services to patients and their families. Operates toll-free hotline

Organization: National Institute of Neurological and Communicative Disorders and Stroke
National Institutes of Health
Building 31, Room 8A-06
Bethesda, MD 20892
(301) 496-5751
Services: Information, research, and referrals for patients, families, and physicians. Publishes free booklet:
* *Huntington's Disease: Hope Through Research*

HYPOTHERMIA

Hypothermia is a condition marked by an abnormally low body temperature, usually 96°F or less. According to the National Institute on Aging (NIA), accidental hypothermia kills approximately 25,000 Americans annually, almost all of them older Americans. The NIA estimates 2.5 million older Americans are in particular danger from hypothermia because of:

* Prescription medications, such as sedatives, antidepressants, tranquilizers, and cardiovascular drugs, that adversely affect the body's ability to generate heat
* Conditions or diseases that limit activity, such as severe arthritis, Parkinson's disease, strokes, and heart disease
* Alcohol consumption
* Poor nutrition

* Poorly insulated homes and inadequate winter clothing

Hypothermia can even be dangerous at mild temperatures of 50° to 65°. Symptoms include stiff muscles, poor coordination, slowed breathing and heart rate, pale and cold skin, and mental confusion or apathy. Hypothermia requires immediate medical treatment.

For more information:

Brochure: *Accidental Hypothermia: A Winter Hazard for Older People*
Cost: Free
From: NIA Information Center
2209 Distribution Circle
Silver Spring, MD 20910
(301) 495-3455

Booklet: *Hypothermia/Heat Stress*
Cost: Free
From: Consumer Information Center
P.O. Box 100
Pueblo, CO 81009

KIDNEY AND URINARY TRACT DISORDERS

The functions of the kidneys, which are critical to life, include:

- Removing waste products from the body
- Chemically balancing body fluids
- Releasing hormones that regulate blood pressure
- Synthesizing vitamins that produce growth
- Controlling the production of red blood cells

Kidney problems range from minor urinary tract infections to diseases that stop their function, a problem which is fatal without artificial cleansing of the blood (dialysis) or kidney transplants. During the course of a year, about 12 million Americans suffer from kidney or urinary tract disease.

Since serious kidney disease is life-threatening, early detection of the problem is important. The six warning signs are:

- Burning or difficulty during urination
- More frequent urination, particularly at night
- Passage of blood-appearing urine
- Puffiness around the eyes and swelling of hands and feet
- Pain in the small of the back just below the ribs that is not aggravated by movement
- High blood pressure

The most common kidney condition, and an extremely painful one, is the crystallization of minerals in the urine into kidney stones. About 4% of Americans develop kidney stones at some point in their lives.

General Sources of Information

Organization: National Kidney and Urologic Diseases Clearinghouse
Box NKUDIC
Bethesda, MD 20892
(301) 468-6345

Services: Coordinates research, compiles a computerized database of resource material, answers questions from the public and makes referrals, and distributes free publications, including:
- *When Your Kidneys Fail: A Handbook for Patients and Their Families*
- *Understanding Urinary Tract Infections*
- *Prevention and Treatment of Kidney Stones*

Organization: National Kidney Foundation
30 East 33rd Street
New York, NY 10016
(800) 622-9010 (Ex. NY)
(212) 889-2210

Services: A nonprofit organization that supports research, patient services, a nationwide organ donor program, professional education, and public information through a toll-free telephone number. Supports 54 local chapters. Free publications include:
- *What Everyone Should Know*
- *About Kidneys and Kidney Disease*
- *About Kidney Stones*
- *Dialysis*
- *Diabetes and Kidney Disease*
- *High Blood Pressure and Your Kidneys*

- *The Organ Donor Program Transplantation*
- *Urinary Tract Obstructions*
- *Warning Signs of Kidney Disease*
- *Living with High Blood Pressure*

Treatment for Kidney and Urinary Tract Disorders

Other than simple urinary tract infections, kidney diseases and conditions should be treated by a nephrologist, a specialist in kidney disease, or a urologist, a specialist in urinary tract diseases. In the case of serious kidney disease, patients may need regular dialysis or even a kidney transplant. Both procedures are expensive and traumatic for patients and family alike. One source of information and financial support is:

Organization: American Kidney Fund
315 Wisconsin Avenue, Suite 203E
Bethesda, MD 20814
(800) 638-8299 (Ex. MD)
(800) 492-8361 (MD)
Services: Provides information on kidney

disease and organ transplants through a toll-free hotline. Grants financial assistance to needy kidney patients. Free publications include:
- *Facts About Kidney Diseases and Their Treatment*
- *Facts About Kidney Stones*
- *Give a Kidney*
- *Dialysis Patient*
- *High Blood Pressure and Its Effects on the Kidneys*

Support for Kidney Patients

An organization that provides significant help and support to kidney patients and their families is:

Organization: American Association of Kidney Patients
One Davis Blvd.
Tampa, FL 33606
(813) 251-0725
Services: Self-help group for kidney patients and their families with 26 local chapters. Provides information and educational materials

LUPUS

Lupus is a serious disorder marked by a defect in the body's immune system that leads to the creation of antibodies that attack normal tissue and organs. The symptoms of the disease depend upon the parts of the body attacked, but among the most common are arthritis-like symptoms—joint pain, fatigue, and muscle weakness. The most serious cases are those in which the kidneys and other organs are the targets of attack. The disease can arise at any age, but most commonly appears in young women.

The name "lupus" means "wolf-like" and refers to a characteristic "butterfly rash" that appears over the cheekbones and gives a wolfish appearance. However, in many cases, the rash is absent or doesn't appear until later in the course of the disease. In addition to arthritis-like complaints, other symptoms include chronic loss of appetite, low-grade unexplained fever, puffiness of the joints, and frequent infections or illnesses. Because these symptoms are common to many conditions, lupus is difficult to diagnose. Once a diagnosis is made and the condition is treated, more than 75% of lupus patients live a normal life span.

For information and referral:

Organization: Lupus Foundation of America
1717 Massachusetts Avenue, NW
Washington, DC 20036
(800) 558-0121
(202) 328-4550
Services: Organizes support groups, provides information and referrals to medical specialists through a toll-free number

Organization: American Lupus Society
23751 Madison Street
Torrance, CA 95050
(213) 373-1335
Services: Support groups in information for lupus patients and their families

Organization: Arthritis Foundation
Services: Publishes a booklet on lupus and provides information on treatment and services to patients and their families.
For information: Your local Arthritis Foundation Chapter (see White Pages)
or
Arthritis Foundation
1314 Spring Street, NW
Atlanta, GA 30309
(800) 422-1492
(404) 872-7100

LUNG DISEASES

Over nine million Americans, most of them age 50 and over, suffer from breathing difficulties produced by chronic pulmonary disease or chronic lung disease. Among the common diseases that restrict the amount of oxygen that circulates in the bloodstream are emphysema, the destruction of air sacs in the lungs, and chronic bronchitis, an inflammation of the tubes leading into the lungs. Most chronic pulmonary diseases aren't detected until serious and irreparable damage has been done.

Virtually all the conditions that fall into this category are caused either by cigarette smoking or breathing tiny dust particles, such as asbestos, quartz dust, or coal dust. Nonsmokers who do not face occupational hazards on the job have almost no risk of developing chronic pulmonary disease, so these conditions are preventable.

Among the sources of information and referrals for lung disease patients and their families are:

Organization: American Lung Association
Services: Major source of information, referral, and patient support through over 140 local chapters. Free publications include:
- *About Lungs and Lung Disease*
- *As You Live . . . You Breathe*
- *Chronic Bronchitis Facts*
- *Lung Hazards in the Workplace*
- *Shortness of Breath Facts*
- *Emphysema Facts*
- *Facts in Brief About Lung Disease*
- *Chronic Cough Facts*
- *Dust Diseases Facts*
For information: Your local chapter of the American Lung Association (see White Pages)
or
American Lung Association
1740 Broadway
New York, NY 10019
(212) 315-8700

Hotline: National Asthma Center — Lungline
(800) 222-5864 (Ex. CO)
(303) 398-1477
Services: Answers questions about chronic lung diseases, as well as asthma

Organization: National Heart, Lung, and Blood Institute
National Institutes of Health
Building 31, Room 4A-21
Bethesda, MD 20892
(301) 496-4236
Services: Sponsors extensive research, pro-

vides information and referrals, and issues publications, including:
- *Chronic Obstructive Pulmonary Disease*
- *The Lungs: Medicine for the Layman*

Organization: Emphysema Anonymous
P.O. Box 3224
Seminole, FL 34642
(813) 391-9977
Services: Self-help and information for people with emphysema and their families

LYME DISEASE

Lyme disease, or lyme arthritis, is caused by a germ which enters the body through the bite of a deer tick, a tiny insect the size of the period at the end of this sentence. This condition, which is named for Old Lyme, Connecticut, the city in which it was first diagnosed, has been spreading rapidly through many areas of the country, and has become a major health hazard. Lyme disease poses a special danger for older Americans, who may avoid seeking treatment because the symptoms are similar to those of arthritis.

The best way to prevent Lyme disease is to recognize the ticks that carry the disease and the environment in which they are found. For information:

Booklet: *Questions About Lyme Disease?*
Cost: Free with self-addressed stamped envelope
From: LYME-AID, Inc.
1456 Second Avenue, Suite 121
New York, NY 10021

Organization: Lyme Borreliosis Foundation
P.O. Box 462
Tolland, CT 06084
(203) 871-2900
Services: Information, referrals, and self-help for victims of Lyme disease

MULTIPLE SCLEROSIS

Multiple sclerosis (MS) is a disease that destroys the myelin, the substance that coats the nerve fibers and allows nerve impulses to be transmitted properly. The disease, which normally strikes between ages 20 and 40, is characterized by dramatic flare-ups followed by long periods of remission. Many MS sufferers live near-normal lives, whereas in 10% to 20% of victims the disease is progressively crippling.

Although early diagnosis of MS may be difficult, that diagnosis is invariably made before a patient is 40 or 45. After diagnosis, treatment should be conducted under the supervision of a medical center that specializes in MS. For information:

Organization: National Multiple Sclerosis Society
205 East 42nd Street
New York, NY 10017
(800) 624-8236 (Leave message to receive free information packet)
(800) 227-3166 (For other information)
(212) 986-3240
Services: Through its 140 chapters, the Society is the major source of information and self-help to patients and their families. Provides referral to MS treatment centers and, where necessary, physical therapy and rehabilitation centers

Booklet: *Multiple Sclerosis: Hope Through Research*
Cost: Free
From: National Institute of Neurological and Communicative Disorders and Stroke
National Institutes of Health
Building 31, Room 8A-06
Bethesda, MD 20892

NEUROMUSCULAR DISORDERS

Almost 50 different diseases afflict the muscles of the body and the nerves that control these muscles, including:

- Muscular dystrophy, a group of diseases that cause a wasting away of muscles
- Amyotrophic lateral sclerosis (Lou Gehrig's Disease), in which certain nerves that control muscle activity are destroyed, causing muscles to atrophy
- Myastenia gravis, a disease in which the body's immune system attacks the muscles, causing weakness and fatigue
- Ataxia, conditions characterized by a loss or lack of control over voluntary muscles

Any symptoms of muscle weakness, trembling, fatigue, or other unusual signs should lead to an appointment with a family physician. If that physician suspects a neuromuscular disorder, he or she can make a referral to one of over 240 clinics that are part of a network coordinated by the Muscular Dystrophy Association (MDA). If referred by a physician through the MDA, patients are not billed for costs above those paid for by health insurance and other medical assistance programs. For information:

Organization: Muscular Dystrophy Association
810 Seventh Avenue
New York, NY 10019
(212) 586-0808
Services: Makes referrals to network of treatment centers, supports research, and provides a wide variety of information to patients and their families. Free publications include:
- *ALS*
- *Muscular Dystrophy Fact Sheet*
- *Myasthenia Gravis*
- *101 Questions and Answers About Muscular Dystrophy*
- *Plasmapheresis*
- *Spinal Muscular Atrophy*

Organization: The ALS Association
15300 Ventura Blvd., Suite 315
Sherman Oaks, CA 91403
(818) 990-2151
Services: Funds research and provides information and support to ALS victims and their families

Organization: Myasthenia Gravis Foundation
53 West Jackson Blvd., Suite 909
Chicago, IL 60604
(312) 427-6252

Services: Information, support, and referrals to patients and their families. Helps provide reduced-cost medication and clinic services

Organization: National Ataxia Foundation
600 Twelve Oaks Center
15500 Wayzata Blvd.
Wayzata, MN 55391
(612) 473-7666

Services: Information and referral for ataxia patients

Booklets: • *ALS: Lou Gehrig's Disease: Hope Through Research*
• *Myasthenia Gravis: Hope Through Research*

Cost: Free

From: National Institute of Neurological and Communicative Disorders and Stroke
National Institutes of Health
Building 31, Room 8A-06
Bethesda, MD 20892

OSTEOPOROSIS

Every woman is at risk for osteoporosis, a condition in which the bones become progressively thinner and more brittle. This condition afflicts about eight times as many women as men, including one in four women over age 60. Osteoporosis is a major cause of fractures of the hip, spine, wrist, legs, and other bones. Among those most at risk are: fair-skinned women; women who are thin or small-framed; women with a family history of osteoporosis; and women who have had their ovaries removed before the normal age of menopause.

Osteoporosis usually begins without any noticeable symptoms. The condition can progress for years without causing pain, until it is brought to light by a major fracture or other significant medical problem. Until recently, the major problem in early detection of the condition was that simple x-rays don't show bone loss until over 30% of the bone is gone. Today, however, medical science has developed sophisticated tests that subject bones to radiation, then measure the amount of radiation absorbed to obtain a calculation of bone density.

Although this early detection of bone loss can be important, most experts don't recommend that every woman undergo this routine screening process. The exposure to radiation may be unnecessary for women who aren't at high risk for the disease. The Food and Drug Administration recommends that all women consult with their family physicians before making the decision to go to an osteoporosis detection center.

General Sources of Information

Booklet: *Osteoporosis Testing*
Cost: Free
From: Food and Drug Administration
Office of Consumer Affairs, HFE-88
5600 Fishers Lane
Rockville, MD 20857

Fact Sheet: *Osteoporosis: The Bone Thinner*
Cost: Free

From: NIA Information Center
2209 Distribution Circle
Silver Spring, MD 20910

Booklets: *Osteoporosis, Calcium and Estrogen* (Free) *Osteoporosis: Cause, Treatment, Prevention* ($0.50)
From: Consumer Information Center
P.O. Box 100
Pueblo, CO 81009

Report: *Osteoporosis*
Cost: Free
From: National Institutes of Health
Office of Medical Applications
Research Building 1, Room 216
Bethesda, MD 20892

Booklet: *Osteoporosis*
Cost: Free
From: American College of Orthopedic Surgeons
222 South Prospect Avenue
Park Ridge, IL 60068
(708) 823-7186

Bibliography: *Osteoporosis: Patient Education Materials*
Cost: $2.00
From: National Arthritis and Musculoskeletal and Skin Diseases Information Clearinghouse
Box AMS
Bethesda, MD 20892

Treatment for Osteoporosis

Osteoporosis is treated by orthopedists, who specialize in diseases and conditions of the bones. You can obtain a referral to a specialist from your primary care physician or by contacting:

Organization: American Academy of Orthopaedic Surgeons
222 South Prospect Ave.
Park Ridge, IL 60068
(312) 823-7186
Services: Will help individuals locate a board-certified orthopaedist and will provide information about the prevention and treatment of osteoporosis

Organization: National Osteoporosis Foundation
1625 Eye Street, NW, Suite 1011
Washington, DC 20006
(202) 223-2226
Service: Provides public information, supports research, and makes referrals to medical specialists.
Publications include:
• *Osteoporosis: A Woman's Guide*

PAGET'S DISEASE

Paget's disease is a progressive condition in which bone breaks down and is reformed at an abnormally rapid pace. The results can be more fragile bones susceptible to bowing, fractures, pain, and arthritis in the joints. About three million Americans over age 40 have Paget's disease, which occurs most frequently between ages 50 and 70. Paget's disease often produces no symptoms, and it is accidentally diagnosed in x-rays taken for another purpose. The symptoms that can occur are pain and a sensation of heat through the skin over the painful bone area.

Many patients with Paget's disease require no treatment at all. For patients with severe pain and other symptoms, recently developed drug treatments have effectively relieved symptoms and slowed the process of the disease. For more information:

Organization: Paget's Disease Foundation
165 Cadman Plaza East
Brooklyn, NY 11201
(718) 596-1043

Services: Provides information, answers questions, and makes referrals to physicians who specialize in treating Paget's disease

Booklet: *Understanding Paget's Disease*
Cost: Free
From: National Institute of Arthritis and Musculoskeletal and Skin Diseases
National Institutes of Health
Building 31, Room 9A-04
Bethesda, MD 20892
(301) 496-3583

CHRONIC PAIN

Eighty-six million Americans suffer from severe pain at some point during a year, and 21 million people had more than 100 days of pain in the last 365 days. Despite the havoc chronic pain causes to the lives of many adults, health professionals have, in the past, ignored or minimized its importance. Needless suffering and inadequate medical treatment have resulted. In recent years, however, chronic pain has received increased attention by the medical community and by special support groups for sufferers.

The most common type of recurring pain is the headache, which in 1988 crippled more people than all motorcycle, car, and industrial accidents combined. Other common causes are lower back pain, arthritis, sciatica, and cancer. Finally, a significant number of Americans suffer from recurrent pain for which doctors have been unable to trace to an organic source.

General Sources of Information

Organization: National Chronic Pain Outreach Association
4922 Hampden Lane

Bethesda, MD 20814
(301) 652-4948
Services: The NCPOA is a nonprofit organization that sponsors local support groups for people with chronic pain and their families. These local groups hold regular meetings, hear guest speakers, maintain listings of resources, and operate telephone networks to provide emotional support. Membership costs $15.00 per year, and includes (nonmember prices):
- *Lifeline Newsletter*
- *NCPOA Chapter Roster*
- *Recommended Reading List* ($0.50)
- *Flare-Up Coping Tips* ($0.50)
- *Choosing a Pain Clinic or Specialist* ($1.00)
- *The Mind-Body Dilemma* ($1.00)
- *Pain Management Strategies* ($0.50)
- *Arthritis and Bradykinins* ($0.50)
- *Neuropathy Pain* ($0.50)

Organization: American Chronic Pain Association
257 Old Haymaker Road
Monroeville, PA 15146

(916) 632-0922
(412) 856-9676

Services: The American Chronic Pain Association is a nonprofit self-help organization with about 150 local groups that provides mutual support for chronic pain sufferers. All members receive the 115-page ACPA Members ManualCost of manual: $10.00 plus $2.50 postage and handling

Organization: National Headache Foundation
5252 N. Western Avenue
Chicago, IL 60625
(800) 843-2256 (Ex. IL and AK)
(800) 523-8858 (IL)
(312) 878-7715

Services: This organization serves to educate the public about headaches, support research, and serves as an information source for patients, physicians, and family members. The foundation operates a toll-free information hotline. Among the organization's publications are:
- *The Headache Chart* ($1.00)
- *The Headache Handbook* ($0.50)
- *Diet for the Headache Patient* (Free)
- *Fact Sheet on Migraine Headaches* (Free)
- *Fact Sheet on Cluster Headaches* (Free)
- *Fact Sheet on Muscle Contraction* (Free)
- *The Relaxation Tape* ($9.00)

Organization: National Committee on the Treatment of Intractable Pain
P.O. Box 9553, Friendship Station
Washington, DC 20016
(202) 965-6717

Services: Collects information about effective methods of pain control and makes this information available to health professionals and the public. Will send a list of materials

Pamphlets: • *Chronic Pain: Hope Through Research*
• *Headache: Hope Through Research*
Cost: Free
From: National Institute of Neurological and Communicative Disorders and Stroke
Building 31, Room 8A06
Bethesda, MD 20892

Booklet: *Pain Control*
Cost: Free
From: American Cancer Society
1599 Clifton Road
Atlanta, GA 30329
(800) 227-2345 (Ex. GA)
(404) 320-3333

Treatment for Pain

The approaches to the treatment of pain include:

- Medication
- Relaxation therapy
- Acupuncture
- Biofeedback
- Exercise
- Physical therapy, including electric stimulation, whirlpool baths, paraffin baths, massage, and heat
- Psychotherapy
- Surgery
- Nutrition and diet

Today, most experts believe that the best approach to dealing with pain is by going to a pain clinic, where treatment is offered by a team of specialists. To locate a pain clinic, contact:

- Your physician
- Your local medical society (see White Pages of your telephone directory)
- The National Chronic Pain Outreach Association at (301) 652-4948

Headache sufferers can often gain relief at special headache clinics. To locate a headache clinic near you, contact:

- Your physician
- The National Headache Foundation at (800) 843-2256 (Ex. IL and AK), (800) 523-8858 (IL), (312) 878-7715

PARKINSON'S DISEASE

Parkinson's disease is a progressive neurological condition that afflicts an estimated 1.5 million Americans. The chances of getting this disease increase with age—the largest number of sufferers experienced their first symptoms between ages 60 and 70. To date, no cure for Parkinson's exists.

The first symptoms of Parkinson's disease are usually a growing difficulty in getting out of a chair or in changing other positions, diminished blinking, a woodeness of facial expression, muscle stiffness, and a shaking tremor of the hands. One side of the body is normally affected before the other. The more advanced effects of the disease are stooped posture, loss of facial expression, difficulty walking and talking, impaired balance, and impairment of handwriting.

Parkinson's disease is thought to result from a deficiency of dopamine (a brain chemical that facilities the transmission of nerve impulses) and, perhaps, from other chemicals as well. The disease is not communicable and there is thus far no conclusive evidence that it is hereditary.

General Sources of Information

Organization: Parkinson's Disease Foundation
William Black Medical Research Building

640 West 168th Street
New York, NY 10032
(212) 923-4700
Services: Sponsors research and promotes education about Parkinson's Disease. Issues publications, including:
- *Newsletter,* a free newsletter with information for patients and caregivers
- *Exercises for the Parkinson's Patient with Hints for Daily Living* (Free)
- *The Parkinson's Patient at Home* (Free)
- *Parkinson's Disease: Progress, Promise, and Hope!* (Free)

Organization: Parkinson's Educational Program
1800 Park Newport, No. 302
Newport Beach, CA 92660
(800) 344-7872 (Ex. CA)
(714) 250-2975
Services: Coordinates over 400 local support groups and provides information to patients and to physicians and health professionals

Organization: National Parkinson Foundation, Inc.
1501 NW Ninth Avenue
Miami, FL 33136

(800) 327-4545 (Ex. FL)
(800) 433-7022 (FL)
(305) 547-6666

Services: Provides public information, referrals to physicians, and educational materials such as:
- *The Parkinson's Patient: What You and Your Family Should Know*
- *The Parkinson Handbook*
- *Starting a Support Group*
- *Together We Can Make Parkinson's a Thing of the Past*
- *Parkinson Report* (newsletter)

Treatment for Parkinson's Disease

Parkinson's disease is primarily treated by administering .MD4/L-dopa, a substance that the body converts to dopamine. While drug therapy isn't a cure and doesn't stop the slow progression of the disease, it has significantly increased the ability of patients to function. The earlier the diagnosis is made and treatment begins, the better.

Medication, however, isn't the only treatment. In the words of the Parkinson's Disease Foundation, "it is evident that exercise and physical therapy are vitally important if patients are to maintain mobility." Because depression is frequently a problem for Parkinson's patients, support encouragement from other Parkinson's patients and family members is crucial to maintaining the will to fight the disease.

Referrals to Parkinson's specialists, as well as information about exercise programs, are available from:

Organization: United Parkinson Foundation
360 West Superior Street
Chicago, IL 60610
(312) 664-2344

Services: A membership organization for patients, their families, and health professionals. Supports research, makes referrals, and distributes exercise information, including:
- *One Step at a Time* (An exercise manual)

Organization: American Parkinson Disease Association
116 John Street
New York, NY 10038
(800) 223-2732 (Ex. NY)
(212) 732-9550

Services: Voluntary organization that promotes research, supervises over 200 local support groups, and operates 31 local centers where Parkinson's patients can obtain free examinations, information, and referral to specialists. Also issues publications, including:
- *A Manual for Patients with Parkinson's Disease*
- *Home Exercises for Patients with Parkinson's.MDRV/ Diseases*
- *Speech Problems and Swallowing Problems in Parkinson's Disease*
- *Aids, Equipment and Suggestions to Help the Patient with Parkinson's Disease in the Activities of Daily Living*

Support for Parkinson's Patients and Their Families

The problems faced by Parkinson's disease patients and their families are similar to those faced by families afflicted with many other handicaps, disabilities, and chronic debilitating conditions. For more information, see our chapters on caregiving (pages 274–287) and assistance for the handicapped (pages 297–308).

POLIO: PROBLEMS OF LATE EFFECTS

Polio, the most feared disease of children three decades ago, has been virtually eliminated by vaccines. However, approximately 25% of the survivors of polio may experience late effects of the disease in their later years. Symptoms of the late effects of polio include unaccustomed fatigue, weakness in muscles, pain in muscles or joints, and sleep, breathing, and swallowing problems. If you or a family member has had polio and is experiencing such symptoms, contact your physician or:

Organization: International Polio Network
4502 Maryland Avenue
St. Louis, MO 63108
(314) 361-0475
Cost: $8.00 per year for polio sufferers, $15.00 for health professionals
Services: Publishes *Polio Network News,* a quarterly newsletter for polio survivors
Publishes *Post-Polio Directory* of 250 support groups, 60 clinics, and 100 health professionals
Organizes conferences and workshops

Book: *Handbook on the Late Effects of Poliomyelitis for Physicians and Survivors*
Cost: $6.95 postpaid

PROSTATE DISORDERS

The prostate is a small male organ about the size of a walnut that surrounds the urethra, the tube through which urine passes out of the body. During sexual activity, the prostate secretes fluid which helps transport sperm. At about age 50, the prostate begins to grow. In many older men, this growth advances to the point where it restricts flow through the urethea, causing the urge to urinate frequently, difficulty starting the flow of urine, and dribbling after urination. When this occurs, surgical techniques may be necessary to remove part of the prostate or the entire organ. In addition, not all prostate problems are benign. Prostate cancer is relatively common. Fortunately, malignant prostate tumors grow very slowly, and surgery is normally successful in eradicating the disease.

Both types of prostate problems are more treatable with early detection. Most problems can be solved without harming sexual functions.

Age Page: *Prostate Problems*
Cost: Free
From: NIA Information Center
2209 Distribution Circle
Silver Spring, MD 20910
(301) 495-3455

RARE DISEASES AND DISORDERS

A rare disease or disorder is one that, by common medical definition, afflicts 5,000 or fewer Americans. An astounding 20 million Americans suffer from such disorders. These people often have a great deal of difficulty finding information on their diseases, locating medical specialists and treatment centers, and finding support services. In addition, pharmaceutical companies are often reluctant to manufacture medications for these conditions, because the market is so small, even if the medications produce major breakthroughs. These medications that can't find a manufacturer are called "orphan drugs." Recently, however, resources have been developed for people afflicted with rare diseases and disorders, including:

Organization: National Information Center for Orphan Drugs and Rare Diseases
P.O. Box 1133
Washington, DC 20013
(800) 456-3505
Services: Gathers information on rare diseases and orphan drugs, and pro-

vides that information to health professionals and patients via a toll-free hotline

Organization: National Organization for Rare Disorders
P.O. Box 8923
New Fairfield, CT 06812
(800) 447-6673
(203) 746-6518
Services: Nonprofit organization with a membership made up of national health organizations, researchers, physicians, and individuals. Collects information on rare disorders and provides that information and referrals to patients. Operates computer database of information on rare disorders that's accessible from personal computers

SCLERODERMA

Scleroderma is a disorder of the connective tissue of the body. The skin becomes thick and tight due to the replacement of normal elastic tissue with dense fibrous tissue, limiting movement of hands, feet, joints, etc. Early symptoms include itching, skin ulceration, and pain. In severe cases, internal organs can be damaged. The disease progresses over many years, so patients over age 50 normally need specialized medical care and support. Information on this condition and referrals to local

support groups and physicians are available from:

Organization: Scleroderma Society
1725 York Avenue
New York, NY 10128
(212) 427-7040

Organization: United Scleroderma Foundation
P.O. Box 350
Watsonville, CA 95077
(800) 722-4673

SEXUAL DYSFUNCTION AND SEXUALLY TRANSMITTED DISEASES

The Starr-Weiner report, a scientific survey of Americans age 60 to 91, blasted the myth that people's sex drives go into retirement when they do. The report found that 80% of older Americans were sexually active, with a sexual frequency among couples of slightly more than

once a week. Although both men's and women's sexual response time slows, and patterns of lovemaking change with age, sex is as important a part of the lives of older Americans as it was in earlier years.

The recognition that older Americans are

and should be sexually active has two important implications:

- Impotence and other sexual dysfunctions should be and can be treated
- Older Americans have to continue to practice safe sex and be aware of the problems of sexually transmitted diseases

Sexual Dysfunction

Male impotence is not an inevitable consequence of aging or of disease. In many cases, impotence can be solved through correcting physical problems, changing medication, therapy, or penile implants. Similarly, lack of desire or fear of sexual activity by women, especially after such operations as hysterectomies or mastectomies, can also be eliminated through counseling.

People with sexual fears or problems should first consult their primary care physician. Often, changes in medication or a discussion of irrational fears (such as fear of sexual activity after a heart attack or stroke) may solve the problem. The next step is referral to a urologist (for male impotence) or a gynecologist for a complete physical examination.

In many cases, counseling or therapy from a certified sexual dysfunction clinic or sex therapist is necessary. For referral to a certified therapist or center:

Organization: American Association of Sex Educators, Counselors, and Therapists
435 N. Michigan Ave.
Chicago, IL 60611
(312) 644-0828

A source of publications and consumer pamphlets dealing with sex and sexual dysfunction is:

Organization: Sex Information and Education Council of the United States
32 Washington Place
New York, NY 10003
(212) 819-9770

An important self-help organization is:

Organization: Impotents Anonymous
119 South Ruth Street
Maryville, TN 37801
(615) 983-6064
Services: A self-help organization with over 100 chapters nationwide. Each chapter has a urologist specializing in impotence as a medical advisor. The national office will make referrals to urologists and others specializing in impotence. The organization also organizes chapters of I-Anon, a self-help group for spouses and loved ones. Send a self-addressed stamped envelope

Organization: Recovery of Male Potency
(800) 835-6833 (Ex. MI)
(313) 966-3219
Service: Provides an information packet and referrel to local self-help groups

AIDS and Other Sexually Transmitted Diseases

The National Center for Health Statistics estimates that there are 11 million new cases of sexually transmitted diseases each year. Those cases included 4.6 million cases of chlamydia,

1.8 million cases of gonorrhea, 1 million cases of venereal warts, 500,000 cases of herpes, 20,000 cases of syphillis, and 20,000 cases of AIDS.

Growing older is no protection from sexually transmitted diseases, including the deadly AIDS virus. The only protection is safe-sex techniques, including use of condoms and careful selection of sex partners. In addition, everyone should take the time to educate themselves about sexually transmitted diseases and seek treatment at the first sign of any symptoms. Among the information sources are:

Booklets: • *Sexually Transmitted Diseases*
• *Genital Herpes*
Cost: Free
From: NIAID/NIH
Building 31, Room 7A-32
Bethesda, MD 20892
(301) 496-5717

Hotline: VD Hotline
(800) 227-8922

Services: Provides information on a confidential basis about sexually transmitted diseases and makes referrals to clinics and medical specialists

Hotline: National AIDS Hotline
(800) 458-5231 (Recording, general information)
(800) 447-2437 (Live operator)
(202) 646-8182 (DC)
(202) 245-6867 (AK and HI—call collect)
Services: Answers questions, will provide literature, and makes referrals to treatment centers
Brochures: • *AIDS, Sex and You*
• *AIDS and Your Job—Are There Risks?*
• *Facts about AIDS and Drug Abuse*
• *Gay and Bisexual Men and AIDS*
• *If Your Test for Antibodies to the AIDS Virus Is Positive...*
Cost: Free
From: AIDS
1515 Wilson Blvd., Suite 700
Rosslyn, VA 22209

SKIN DISORDERS AND COSMETIC SURGERY

Few of us wouldn't want to retain from youth our smooth, soft skin and full, thick head of hair. Unfortunately, our appearance ages along with the rest of us, and there are no medical miracles that can prevent us from looking older. However, medical research has made discoveries that can slow down the process and help prevent the most serious of skin problems and diseases.

Sun—The Enemy of Our Skin

There is a widespread belief that being tan makes a person look healthy; however, in real-

ity, exposure to the sun causes the most severe signs of aging skin and skin problems. These include:

- Dark patches or "age spots"
- Thickened, leathery-looking skin
- Lines and wrinkles around the eyes, upper lip, and the neck and hands
- Skin cancer

Skin cancer, or malignant melanoma, afflicts 300,000 Americans a year. The risk of skin cancer is directly related to exposure to the sun. Although most skin cancers are easily treatable, they can be dangerous if neglected. For more information:

Booklets: • *Melanoma/Skin Cancer*
• *The Sun and Your Skin*
• *Skin Care Under the Sun*
• *Lifelong Healthy Skin*
Cost: Free with self-addressed stamped envelope
From: Patient Information Pamphlets
American Academy of Dermatology
1567 Maple Ave.
Evanston, IL 60201
(708) 869-3954

Organization: Skin Cancer Foundation
245 Fifth Avenue, Suite 2402
New York, NY 10016
(212) 725-5176
Services: Provides a variety of materials on preventing skin cancer and sponsors skin cancer screening clinics

Booklet: *Cancer of the Skin*
Cost: Free
From: National Cancer Institute
Office of Cancer Communications
Building 31, Room 10-A18
Bethesda, MD 20892
(800) 638-6694

Booklet: *Facts on Skin Cancer*
Cost: Free
From: Your local chapter of the American Cancer Society (see White Pages) or American Cancer Society
1599 Clifton Road, NE
Atlanta, GA 30329
(800) 227-2345
(404) 320-3333

Other Skin-Related Disorders

Common skin problems, such as rashes or athlete's foot, can be diagnosed and treated by your primary care physician. However, many people with more serious problems or conditions, or people who want to take advantage of the latest research into preventative skin care, should consult a dermatologist, a physician who specializes in the care of the skin. Among the new techniques used by dermatologists include the prescription drug Retin-A, which has demonstrated some effectiveness in treating wrinkles and other age-related skin problems. However, for every valuable treatment or medication there are dozens that are either useless or that actually contribute to skin problems. Scams based on anti-aging claims constitute a multibillion dollar a year business. Before you waste your money, consult your physician or a dermatologist for advice on skin care and the following problems:

• Moles
• Warts
• Varicose veins and spider veins
• Reactions to cosmetics and other substances applied to skin
• Psoriasis
• Athlete's foot

To find a dermatologist:

• Ask your primary care physician
• Obtain recommendations from friends
• Look in the Yellow Pages (under "Physicians")

For more information on skin problems:

Organization: American Academy of Dermatology
Patient Information Pamphlets
1567 Maple Ave.
Evanston, IL 60201
(708) 869-3954
Services: Issues publications on skin problems, including:
- *Your Skin . . . Your Dermatologist . . . And You*
- *Common Sense About Moles*
- *A Dermatologist Talks About Warts*
- *Facts About Black Skin*
- *Facts About Dermatologic Surgery*
- *Spider Vein, Varicose Vein Therapy*
- *Psoriasis*
- *Vitiligo*
- *Reactions to Cosmetics*
- *Athlete's Foot*
- *Hand Eczema*
- *Urticaria/Hives*
Cost: Free with self-addressed stamped envelope

Organization: National Psoriasis Foundation
6443 S.W. Beaverton Highway, Suite 210
Portland, OR 97221
(503) 297-1545

Treating Hair Loss

Many men become obsessed with hair loss as they grow older. Unfortunately, most hair loss is genetically programmed and therefore not preventable—despite the claims of hucksters who rake in over $1 billion every year for useless products and treatments. There are some medications and treatments that can slow hair loss for some men and surgical techniques that can replace hair on the scalp. To avoid fraud, only consider treatments and procedures recommended by a dermatologist or other physician.

Booklet: *Hair Loss*
Cost: Free with self-addressed stamped envelope
From: Patient Information Pamphlets
American Academy of Dermatology
1567 Maple Ave.
Evanston, IL 60201
(708) 869-3954

Cosmetic Surgery

Cosmetic surgery done solely to improve a patient's physical appearance is a $2 billion business. Like any other surgical procedure, cosmetic surgery carries with it the risk of complications. Cosmetic surgery is also expensive, and these expenses are normally not covered by health insurance. Because of physical and emotional factors, not every person is a candidate for every kind of cosmetic procedure.

The most important step to take if you're considering cosmetic surgery is to find the right physician. A significant number of physicians who offer cosmetic surgery procedures are not board-certified plastic surgeons or surgeons who are board-certified in dermatology or otolaryngology (ear, nose, and throat). If you are unable to obtain a referral from your primary care physician, you can contact two organizations that will provide information about procedures and referrals to board-certified plastic surgeons through the following toll-free numbers:

Organization: American Academy of Facial, Plastic and Reconstructive Surgery
1101 Vermont Avenue, NW, Suite 104
Washington, DC 20005

(800) 332-3223
(202) 842-4500

Organization: American Society of Plastic and Reconstructive Surgery
444 E. Algonquin Rd.
Arlington Heights, IL 60005
(800) 635-0635 (Ex. IL)
(708) 228-9900

SLEEPING DISORDERS

Our need for sleep diminishes as we get older. At the same time, our patterns of sleep change, too. For example, many people find themselves waking more easily, while others may need a nap in the afternoon, then a reduced period of sleep at night. Occasional insomnia, or inability to sleep, is extremely common.

However, many other factors besides normal aging can affect our sleep, including medications, illnesses, depression, and hormonal changes. These factors can produce sleep disorders such as:

- Severe insomnia, the inability to sleep for more than several nights in a row
- Apnea, a condition in which a person awakens because he or she stops breathing during sleep
- Narcolepsy, a condition that causes a person to suddenly fall asleep at inappropriate times

An estimated one in five older adults may need medical treatment or sleep therapy for sleep disorders.

Treatment for Sleep Disorders

The first step in solving a sleep problem is to schedule a visit with your family physician.

Some very simple steps, such as changing a medication, changing eating habits, cutting out alcohol, and eliminating use of over-the-counter sleep medications can solve the problem. If not, referrals to specialists may be in order. One source of help is a psychologist or psychiatrist, if the root of the problem is depression or some other emotional problem. A second alternative is a special sleep-disorder clinic. To obtain a referral:

Organization: American Sleep Disorders Association
604 Second Street, SW
Rochester, MN 55902
(507) 287-6006

Organization: American Narcolepsy Association
P.O. Box 1187
San Carlos, CA 94070
(415) 591-7979

For general suggestions on improving your sleep:

Booklet: *A to Zzzzzz Guide to Better Sleep*
Cost: Free
From: The Better Sleep Council
333 Commerce Street
Alexandria, VA 22314
(703) 683-8371

Facts About Snoring

The likelihood that you snore increases with your age. Studies have shown that about 60% of men and 40% of women age 60 and over regularly snore.

Causes of mild to moderate snoring include eating heavily or drinking before bed, poor muscle tone, and a blockage of the nose. Most snorers can benefit from:

- Avoiding a heavy meal and alcohol within 3 hours of sleep
- Exercising regularly
- Losing weight

- Sleeping on two pillows or elevating the head off the mattress

For more serious problems, you should consult your family physician, who may refer you to a specialist. For more information:

Booklet: *Snoring: Not Funny, Not Hopeless*
Cost: Free, with self-addressed stamped envelope
From: American Academy of Otolaryngology—Head and Neck Surgery
1101 Vermont Avenue, NW, Suite 302
Washington, DC 20005
(202) 289-4607

STROKE

A stroke occurs when the blood supply to a part of the brain is interrupted, either because an artery becomes blocked or because an artery bursts, leaking blood into the brain. The result of a stroke is the death of some brain cells. The after-effects can range from very severe to very minor, depending upon the length of the interruption and the function and number of the brain cells affected.

The likelihood of suffering a stroke increases with age, especially after age 65. Although stroke is the third leading cause of death in the United States, most victims survive. In 1985, according to the American Heart Association, about 500,000 people suffered strokes and of these, 152,000 died. Approximately two million stroke victims are alive today.

The leading causes of strokes are:

- High blood pressure
- Artherosclerosis
- Heart disease
- Diabetes

- Obesity
- Smoking
- Blow to the head
- Brain tumor

The incidence of strokes, including fatal strokes, has been declining over the last decade, largely due to increasing control of high blood pressure and more attention to the dangers of cholesterol in the diet. For more information on hypertension, see our section on High Blood Pressure, pages 128–129. For more information on atherosclerosis and heart disease, see our section on Heart Disease, pages 193–195.

About half of all strokes are preceded by "mini-strokes," which physicians call "transient ischemic attacks" (TIAs). According to the American Heart Association, the warnings signs of stroke include:

- Sudden weakness or numbness of face, arm, and leg on one side of the body

- Loss of speech or trouble talking or understanding speech
- Dimness or loss of vision, particularly in only one eye
- Unexplained dizziness, unsteadiness, or sudden falls

Anyone experiencing these symptoms should seek medical help immediately.

The result of a stroke may be impairment of any activity controlled by the brain, such as:

- Difficulty speaking or understanding speech
- Partial paralysis
- Inability to control facial muscles
- Inability to see or hear
- Loss of memory

The effects of a stroke may be very slight or very severe, and they may be either permanent or temporary. The degree of recovery from the stroke depends upon the combination of the following factors:

- The type and amount of brain damage
- The general health of the patient
- The patient's personality and emotional state
- The support received by the patient from family and friends
- The quality of the care received

The first two factors fall into the area of prevention: treatment of high blood pressure, treatment of heart disease, proper nutrition, dieting, controlling diabetes, moderate use of alcohol, and avoiding tobacco products.

The last three factors are interrelated. For example, a patient's willingness to battle his or her condition during long rehabilitation often depends on the level of support received from loved ones. Similarly, the quality of care can affect the morale of both the patient and family.

General Sources of Information

Booklets: *Heart Attack and Stroke: Signals and Action Strokes: A Guide for the Family*
From: Your local American Heart Association chapter (see White Pages)
or
American Heart Association
7320 Greenville Avenue
Dallas, TX 75231
(214) 750-5300

Booklets: • *Understanding Stroke* ($0.35)
• *Handy, Helpful Hints for Independent Living After Stroke* ($1.10)
• *Organizing a Stroke Club* ($1.10)
From: National Easter Seal Society
70 E. Lake St.
Chicago, IL 60601
(312) 726-6200

Booklets: • *Stroke — Hope Through Research*
• *Aphasia — Hope Through Research*
• *What You Should Know About Stroke and Stroke Prevention*
• *NINCDS Research Program on Stroke*
• *Catalog of Publications*
Cost: Free
From: National Institute of Neurological and Communicative Disorders and Stroke
National Institute of Health Building
31, Room 8A06
Bethesda, MD 20205
(301) 496-5751

Organization: National Stroke Association
300 East Hampden Avenue, Suite 240
Englewood, CO 80110
(303) 762-9922

Services: Provides education and support to stroke victims and their families. Produces many publications, including:

- *The Road Ahead: A Stroke Recovery Guide* (153-page book, $14.-50)
- *Stroke — What It Is, What Causes It* ($1.00)
- *Living at Home After a Stroke* ($2.00)
- *Stroke: Questions and Answers* ($3.00)
- *Stroke Prevention: Reducing Your Risk* ($2.00)
- *Home Exercises for Stroke Patients* ($2.00)
- *Understanding Speech and Language Problems After a Stroke* ($2.00)
- *Be Stroke Smart Packet* (Series of 24 articles, $12.00)

Booklet: *Stroke*
Cost: Free
From: Consumer Information Center
P.O. Box 100
Pueblo, CO 81009

Finding the Right Rehabilitation Services

When a stroke victim arrives at a hospital, neurologists (physicians specializing in the brain and central nervous system) and other specialists concentrate on treating and stabilizing the patient. However, this emergency medical treatment is only the first step in what can be a long process of recovery.

This process of recovery is called rehabilitation. Depending on the damage caused by the stroke, rehabilitation can include:

- Physical therapy
- Speech therapy
- Occupational therapy
- Respiratory therapy
- Fitting of prosthetics/orthotics
- Recreation therapy
- Teaching independent living skills
- Psychological counseling
- Family counseling

Most hospitals offer rehabilitation services. A significant number have special programs specifically designed for the needs of stroke victims and their families. A list of some of these special programs may be obtained from:

Resource Guide: *Patient Education Materials on Stroke*
Cost: $2.00
Contains: A 41-page listing of stroke rehabilitation facilities, as well as a resource guide
From: American Physical Therapy Association
Information Services
1111 N. Fairfax Street
Alexandria, VA 22314
(800) 999-2782 (Ex. 513)
(703) 684-2782

Other sources of information and referrals are:

Organization: National Easter Seal Society
Services: Coordinates state and local societies that provide information and services to people with disabilities from any cause, including stroke
For information: Your local Easter Seal Society (see White Pages)
or
National Easter Seal Society
70 E. Lake St.
Chicago, IL 60601
(312) 726-6200

Organization: American Academy of Physical Medicine and Rehabilitation
122 S. Michigan Ave., Suite 1300
Chicago, IL 60603
(312) 922-9366
Services: Will refer individuals to board-certified rehabilitation specialists

Organization: American Academy of Physical Medicine and Rehabilitation
122 South Michigan Avenue
Chicago, IL 60603
(312) 922-9366
Services: Provides referrals to board-certified physicians specializing in rehabilitation

Information on occupational therapy and referral to accredited occupational therapy programs is available from:

Organization: American Occupational Therapy Association
P.O. Box 1725
1383 Piccard Drive
Rockville, MD 20850
(301) 948-9626

Information on speech problems and referrals to therapists can be obtained from:

Organization: National Association for Hearing and Speech Action
10801 Rockville Pike
Rockville, MD 20852
(800) 638-8255 (Ex. MD, AK, and HI)
(301) 897-8682

Self-Help and Support Groups for Stroke Patients and Family Members

Depression, both for the patient and family members, is a common poststroke problem. This depression often stems from the overwhelming number of problems that can occur during rehabilitation, including the difficulties of caring for a stroke victim in the home during rehabilitation. That's why many stroke victims and their families seek the moral and practical support offered by local self-help organizations. Among the major programs are:

Program: Stroke Clubs
Services: Over 300 local groups sponsored by the American Heart Association
For information: Your local chapter of the American Heart Association (see White Pages)
or
American Heart Association
7320 Greenville Avenue
Dallas, TX 75231
(214) 750-5300

Organization: National Stroke Association
300 East Hampden Avenue, Suite 240
Englewood, CO 80110
(303) 762-9922
Services: Provides assistance in developing local stroke clubs and stroke support groups. Provides referrals to local groups

Organization: Courage Stroke International
c/o Courage Center
3915 Golden Valley Road
Golden Valley, MN 55422
(800) 553-6321 (Ex. MN)
(612) 588-0811
Services: Promotes development of and provides support to over 700 local organizations

Newsletter: *Stroke Clubs, International Newsletter*
805 12th Street
Galveston, TX 77550
(409) 762-1022
Cost: Free
Contains: Provides a forum for stroke patients to support each other and share their experiences

Stroke victims and their families will also find important and valuable information in our chapters on caregiving and on assisting the handicapped.

URINARY INCONTINENCE

Urinary incontinence, the loss of urinary control, affects an estimated 12 million Americans, including one in eight of those over age 65. Although the majority of the people involved are women, men can be incontinent, too. Although it is common, many people involved are severely embarrassed and shamed by their problem, so they withdraw from social activities that involve leaving the home. Many family members of older people who become incontinent assume that there is no alternative except a move to a nursing home.

The truth is, however, that a majority of people who suffer from incontinence can be significantly helped or cured. Many more people can become active again through incontinence aids. Every person who suffers even occasional incontinence should seek help immediately. For more information:

Age Page: *Urinary Incontinence*
Cost: Free
From: NIA Information Center
2209 Distribution Circle
Silver Spring, MD 20910
(301) 495-3455

Organization: Simon Foundation
P.O. Box 815
Wilmette, IL 60091
(800) 237-4666
(312) 864-3913
Services: Nonprofit organization provides information about urinary incontinence, incontinence aids, and referral to treatment centers and specialists through a toll-free hotline

Organization: Help for Incontinent People
P.O. Box 544
Union, SC 29379
(803) 585-8789
Services: Organizes self-help groups, publishes newsletter and resource guide

Organization: Continence Restored, Inc.
785 Park Avenue
New York, NY 10021
(212) 879-3131
Service: Establishes a network of support groups to provide information to patients and their families

VISION DISORDERS, EYE CARE, AND BLINDNESS

Vision is the most important sense for most Americans, and regular eye examinations become increasingly important as we grow older. Over 100 million Americans need corrective lens to see properly, 11 million have vision problems that can't be completely corrected by lens, and about two million don't have sufficient vision to read ordinary newsprint.

Most people's eyes last them a lifetime.

However, some changes in vision are related to the normal aging process, including:

- Increased difficulty changing focus from near to far objects and vice versa
- Need for more light to see
- Increased sensitivity to headlight glare and bright sunlight

- Diminishing of peripheral vision
- Ability to distinguish colors quickly may diminish
- Night vision may deteriorate

Most people compensate for these changes automatically, although it's important to be aware of them when driving an automobile.

Other age-related changes require attention from an eye care professional:

- Presbyopia, a blurring of near vision that often requires prescribing bifocal lens
- Spots or "floaters," specks of material or patterns

Still other problems are more serious and require extended care, including:

- Glaucoma, a disease in which fluid pressure builds in the eyeball. Glaucoma is incurable, but the progression of the disease can be arrested through medication and other treatment. Early detection is extremely important, because damage done to the eye before treatment is not reversible. Excessive fluid pressure in the eye is detectable through a simple test.
- Cataracts are a clouding of the lenses of the eye, making it progressively harder to see. About two thirds of all people between ages 65 and 74 show signs of cataracts. However, more than nine of 10 patients can have their vision restored by surgical removal of the lens and replacement with an artificial lens, contact lens, or glasses.
- Age-related macular degeneration is a condition which affects the macula, a small portion of the retina, the light-sensing tissue that lines the inside of the eye. Changes in the macula, which normally occur after age 65, make it difficult for people to read, drive, or see sharply straight ahead. However, this condition seldom causes total blindness, and most patients can either see almost normally or can move independently through the use of special low-vision devices.
- Diabetic retinopathy is a visual impairment that is caused by diabetes. The small blood vessels in the retina begin to leak fluid into the tissues of the retina.

General Sources of Information

Among the sources of information on vision and aging are:

Brochures: *Your Vision: The Second 50 Years*
Driving Tips for Older Adults
Contact Lens After 40
Living with Low Vision
Cost: Free with self-addressed stamped envelope
From: Communications Center
American Optometric Association
243 N. Lindberg Blvd.
St. Louis, MO 63141
(314) 991-4100

Organization: National Eye Institute
National Institutes of Health
Building 31, Room 6A-32
Bethesda, MD 20205
(301) 496-5248
Services: Supports research into vision problems, provides referrals, and issues publications, including:
- *Know Your Eyes*
- *Glaucoma*

- *Diabetic Retinopathy*
- *Cataracts*
- *Age-Related Macular Degeneration*
- *Refractive Errors*
- *Optic Nerve Diseases*
- *Corneal Diseases*
- *Color Deficiency*
- *Retinitis Pigmentosa*
- *Keeping an Eye on Glaucoma*
- *IOLs — New Lens for Old Eyes*
- *Vitreous Floaters*
- *Ocular Histophasommosis Syndrome*

Organization: National Center for Vision and Aging
111 East 59th Street
New York, NY 10022
(800) 334-5497
(212) 355-2200

Services: Promotes an understanding of the vision problems of older Americans. Operates toll-free hotline to answer questions and provides referrals to older people, their families, and vision professionals. Publications include:
A Better View of You (Free)
Low Vision Catalog ($10.00)

Brochures: • *Cataract: Clouding the Lens of Sight*
- *Diabetic Retinopathy*
- *Dry Eye: Understanding Your Condition*
- *Facts and Myths: Misconceptions About Eye Care Floaters and Flashes: Should You Be Concerned*
- *Glaucoma: It Can Take Your Sight Away*
- *Headache: Are Your Eyes at Fault*
- *Home Eye*

Test: For Children and Adults Laser Surgery of the Eye Low Vision: Help Can Make a Difference Macular Degener-

ation Medical Eye Examination: By Your Ophthalmologist Seeing Well: As You Grow Older

Cost: Free with self-addressed stamped envelope

From: American Academy of Ophthalmology
655 Beach Street
San Francisco, CA 94109
(415) 561-8500

How Often Should You Have an Eye Examination?

Experts differ about how often routine eye examinations should be conducted. The cautious approach is an annual eye examination after age 50. If you have any vision or symptoms whatsoever, you should arrange for an examination immediately.

Three kinds of health professionals are involved in eye care:

- *Ophthalmologists* are physicians who specialize in treatment of the eye. Ophthalmologists diagnose eye disease, prescribe corrective lens and medications, and perform eye surgery.

- *Optometrists* are not medical doctors, but rather graduates of a school of optometry. They are trained to diagnose refractive errors, prescribe corrective lens, and to diagnose many kinds of eye diseases. Optometrists cannot prescribe medication nor perform surgery. They normally refer patients with eye diseases to ophthalmologists for complete diagnosis and treatment.

- *Opticians* are trained professionals who grind, dispense, and fit corrective lens. Opticians do not examine eyes for refractive errors or disease.

Most medical insurance plans do not pay for routine eye examinations. There are, however, alternatives available. If you are age 65 or older, you can take advantage of:

Resource: National Eye Care Project

Services: Under the sponsorship of the American Academy of Ophthalmology, volunteer eye-care specialists provide necessary care to U.S. citizens age 65 and older in all 50 states. The name of a specialist can be obtained by calling a toll-free national Helpline, or by contacting your local area agency on aging. The volunteers accept Medicare fees or the amount covered by private insurance as full payment. If patients are covered by neither, the service is free

Contact: Helpline
(800) 222-3937 8 a.m. to 5 p.m.
(415) 561-8500
Pacific time, weekdays

Free testing for glaucoma is among the many services provided by:

Organization: National Society to Prevent Blindness

Services: Prevent Blindness is the oldest voluntary organization in its field. The organization has developed a special program known as LifeSight to make people aware of what they can do to preserve their sight during the aging process. Through its 27 affiliates, Prevent Blindness offers free glaucoma testing in many parts of the country, conducts educational programs, and distributes publications, among them:
  - *Family Home Eye Test,* which contains tests for glaucoma and age-related macular degeneration, as well as near and far vision
  - *Growing Older with Good Vision*
  - *Four Most Common Vision Problems Among Older People*

  - *Living with Low Vision*
  - *Healthy Habits that Promote Good Vision*
  - *Budgeting for Proper Eye Care*
  - *Preventing Injuries Through Good Vision*
  - *Age-Related Macular Degeneration*
  - *Cataract*
  - *Checklist for Your Eye Doctor Appointment*
  - *Diabetic Retinopathy*
  - *Family Eye Check Reminder*
  - *Glaucoma*
  - *Glaucoma Patient Guide*
  - *Signs of Possible Eye Trouble in Adults*
  - *Sunglasses*
  - *Television and Your Eyes*
  - *Your Eyes for a Lifetime of Sight*

Contact: For information about glaucoma testing and for copies of the above publications, call your state affiliate of Prevent Blindness (see White Pages)
or
Prevent Blindness
500 East Remington Road
Schaumburg, IL 60173
(800) 221-3004
(708) 843-2020

Free or low-cost eye examinations are also offered by local health departments (see your White Pages) or at local health fairs (watch for announcements in newspapers).

Low Vision

Low vision is a term that has been used since the 1960s to describe a loss of vision that cannot be corrected by medical or surgical procedures. If a person's ability to perform basic day-to-day tasks at home or at work are affected by an inability to see, that person has low vision. Between 1.7 and 2 million people have such a disability. Of these, only about 400,000 are totally blind. Although many of the remaining people meet the federal definition of legally blind, they retain some useful sight.

If you have low vision, the quality of your life can be improved by a wide variety of visual services and aids that are now available. These services, aids, and support programs are available through a number of national organizations.

The first step to take if you have some visual impairment is to find one of the 250 U.S. clinics that specialize in providing low-vision services. You can obtain a referral to the nearest clinic and other important information from:

Organization: American Council of the Blind
1010 Vermont Avenue, NW, Suite 1100
Washington, DC 20005
(800) 424-8666
(202) 393-3666

Services: Provides toll-free information service that answers questions about blindness and visual impairment, as well as providing referrals to low-vision clinics, other medical specialists, and local community services and support groups. Publications include:
- *Catalogue of Products for Blind & Visually Impaired Persons* (Free)
- *Useful Publications for Older Persons with Diminishing Or Impaired Vision* (Free)
- *Low Vision Aids and Large Print Materials* (Free)
- *Aging and Blindness— Making the Most of Impaired Vision* (Free) — *Resource Handbooks and Self-Help Guides*

Among the other sources of information are:

Resource Guide: *Low Vision*
Cost: Free

From: National Eye Institute
National Institutes of Health
Building 31, Room 6A-29
Bethesda, MD 20892
(301) 496-5248

Organization: Vision Foundation
2 Mt. Auburn Street
Auburn, MA 01172
(617) 926-4232
(800) 852-3029 (MA)

Services: An information network for blind and visually impaired people. Publishes (in large print) a wide variety of guides to every type of service, aid, or resource, including:
- *Publications List* (Free)
- *Vision Resource List* ($2.00)
- *Coping With Sight Loss: The Vision Resource Book* (200 pages, covering every topic from financial benefits to low-vision aids, $12.00)

Organization: American Foundation for the Blind
15 W. 16th Street
New York, NY 10011
(800) 232-5463 (Ex. NY)
(212) 620-2020

Services: Information and referral service for the blind and visually impaired. Publishes recorded, braille, and large print material, and manufactures special aids and appliances. Publications include:
- *Low Vision Questions and Answers: Definitions, Aids, Services* (Free)
- *Making Life More Liveable—Simple Adaptations for the Home* ($5.00)
- *Products for People with Vision Problems* (Free)
- *Aging and Vision* (Free)
  Provides toll-free service that provides information on the latest

technological devices for people with low vision, as well as referrals to local government and nonprofit services for the visually handicapped

Publications: • *First Steps* ($2.00)
• *Getting Around Your Home* ($2.00)
• *Community Handbook: Where and How to Find Services ($4.00)*
From: Vacations and Community Services for the Blind
817 Broadway, 11th Floor
New York, NY 10003
(212) 477-3800

Book: *Caring for the Visually Impaired Older Person* ($7.00)
From: Minneapolis Society for the Blind
1936 Lyndale Avenue, South
Minneapolis, MN 55403

Organization: National Association for the Visually Handicapped
22 W. 21st St.
New York, NY 10010
(212) 889-3141
Services: Publishes a number of information guides and catalogs of aids for the visually impaired

Organization: Council of Citizens with Low Vision
1400 N. Drake Rd., #218
Kalamazoo, MI 49007
(616) 381-9566
Services: Coordinates numerous local support groups and provides information and referral to people with low vision

Organization: RP Foundation Fighting Blindness
1401 Mt. Royal Avenue, 4th Floor
Baltimore, MD 21217

(800) 638-2300 (Ex. MD)
(301) 225-9400
Services: Supports research and provides information and referral to people with diseases of the retina, such as retinitis pigmentosa, macular degeneration, and diabetes retinitis. Coordinates over 60 local information and referral services for people with diseases of the retina. Has toll-free information and referral service

Organization: Association for the Education and Rehabilitation of the Blind and the Visually Handicapped
206 N. Washington, Suite 320
Alexandria, VA 22314
(703) 548-1884
Services: Development of rehabilitation programs and information and referral for blind and visually handicapped people

Organization: Blinded Veterans Association
477 H Street, NW
Washington, DC 20001
(202) 371-8880
Services: Information, referral, and advocacy for blind and visually impaired veterans

Devices and Aids for People with Low Vision and the Blind

A number of companies publish catalogs of devices and aids, including:

Catalog: Sense-Sations
Associated Services for the Blind
919 Walnut Street
Philadelphia, PA 19107
(800) 876-5456 (Ex. PA)
(215) 627-3304

Catalog: The Magnification Center
3620 E. Thomas Road, Suite D-124
Phoenix, AZ 85018
(602) 956-6637

Catalog: Vis-Aids, Inc.
102-09 Jamaica Avenue
P.O. Box 26
Richmond Hill, NY 11418
(800) 346-9579 (Ex. NY)
(718) 847-4734

Catalog: Independent Living Aids
1500 New Horizons Blvd.
Amityville, NY 11701
(800) 262-7827 (Ex. KY)
(800) 645-7171 (KY)

Reading Materials for People with Low Vision and the Blind

Enjoyment of printed material, including newspapers, magazines, and books, is extremely important to people whose access to other forms of recreation is limited by low vision or blindness. Fortunately, there are a variety of services that can provide this material in a usable form, including:

- Large print
- Records
- Cassettes
- Braille

Among the resources are:

Organization: National Library Service for the Blind and Physically Handicapped
1291 Taylor Street, NW
Washington, DC 20542
(800) 424-8567
(202) 287-5100

Services: Manages a network that provides materials to visually impaired, blind, and handicapped people by mail through their local libraries. Material can be ordered through a toll-free number

Organization: Recording for the Blind
Services: Provides free audiocassettes of books for people who can't read printed material To register:
(609) 452-0606 To borrow cassettes (once registered):
(800) 221-4729

Organization: Talking Books Program
(800) 424-9100
(202) 287-5700
Services: Lends a wide range of recorded and braille books through a network of local libraries

Among the sources of large print material are:

Publisher: Doubleday Large Print Home Library
501 Franklin Avenue
Garden City, NY 11530
(800) 343-4000

Publisher: New York Times Large Print Weekly
P.O. Box 2570
Boulder, CO 80302
(800) 631-2500

Publisher: G.K. Hall Large Print Books
70 Lincoln Street
Boston, MA 02111
(800) 343-2806 (Ex. MA, AL, and HI)
(617) 423-3990

Publisher: Isis Large Print Books
ABC-CLIO
2040 A.P.S.
Box 4397
Santa Barbara, CA 93140

(800) 422-2546 (Ex. CA)
(800) 824-2103 (CA)

Among the sources of writing aids, educational aids, and tools are:

> **Company:** American Printing House for the
> Blind
> 1839 Frankfort Avenue
> P.O. Box 6085
> Louisville, KY 40206
> (502) 895-2405

Brailling products are available from:

> **Organization:** Perkins School for the Blind
> 175 N. Beacon Street
> Watertown, MA 02172
> (617) 924-3490

Especially for the Blind

Most organizations listed above serve both the blind and those with low vision. One organization specifically for the blind is:

> **Organization:** National Federation for the
> Blind
> 1800 Johnson Street
> Baltimore, MD 21230
> (800) 638-7518
> (301) 659-9314
> **Services:** Acts as advocate for the blind.
> Serves the blind through 51 state chapters. Among its most important service is:
> Job Opportunities for the Blind Program, which matches blind people with job openings
> Operates toll-free number for information and job referrals

WOMEN'S HEALTH CONCERNS

Women face two special health concerns as they grow older that we have not yet discussed. The first is the difficult emotional adjustments necessary when women become widows. Although men face adjustments at the death of a spouse, there are more than nine times as many widows as widowers in America.

The second special concern is menopause. The average age of menopause in this country is 50, although the normal age range is from 45 to 55. Menopause is a mid-point in a gradual process called the climeractic, a 10- or 15-year period in which the woman's body produces decreasing amounts of the hormones estrogen and progesterone. This reduction causes menstrual periods to stop, but the reduction continues past menopause.

For most women, menopause takes place smoothly. About 80% of women experience no or mild symptoms. Another 20% have symptoms severe enough to seek medical attention. All women should take the time to understand both the normal process of menopause and the range of symptoms that can occur.

One excellent source of public education materials on a number of women's health topics is:

> **Organization:** American College of Obstetricians and Gynecologists
> 600 Maryland Ave., SW, Suite 300 East
> Washington, DC 20024
> (202) 638-5577
> **Services:** Provides referrel to board certified specialists and publishes a number of free pamphlets including:
> • The Menopause Years
> • Estrogen Use
> • Preventing Osteoporosis

Premenopausal Problems

Women who are still menstruating may continue to have the physical pain and emotional swings characteristic of premenstrual syndrome (PMS), a condition that the medical community has only recently and belatedly recognized as a legitimate medical problem. Treatments are available for many of the problems caused by PMS. For information:

> **Organization:** PMS Action
> P.O. Box 16292
> Irving, CA 92713
> (800) 272-4767 (Ex. CA)
> (800) 332-4767 (CA)
> **Services:** Toll-free hotline offers a newsletter, information, and referrals to physicians

Surgical Menopause

About 25% of women age 50 and over have had a hysterectomy, the surgical removal of the uterus. About 35 million American women have undergone the procedure, which is performed on over 500,000 women annually. When just the uterus is removed and one or both ovaries remain, menstrual periods stop but menopause may proceed normally. When both ovaries are removed, complete menopause takes place abruptly, with often intense side effects.

Many medical experts believe a significant number of those hysterectomies are unnecessary. Almost everyone recommends obtaining a second opinion and information on alternative treatments for conditions other than those that are life-threatening, such as cancer or unstoppable bleeding. For more information:

> **Organization:** HERS (Hysterectomy Educational Resources and Services)
> 422 Bryn Mawr Avenue
> Bryn Cynwyd, PA 19004
> (215) 667-7757
> **Services:** Among the services HERS provides:
> - Referral for second opinions
> - Copies of over 1,000 medical and scientific journal articles (fee)
> - Information on alternatives to a hysterectomy
> - Counseling for women who have had the operation
> - A newsletter covering topics of interest to those who are contemplating or have had a hysterectomy ($20.00 for 4 issues)
> - Back issues of the newsletter
> - Annual conferences

Natural Menopause

The most common physical symptoms of menopause are hot flashes and vaginal dryness and irritation. It may also bring mood swings, depression, irritability, sleeplessness, joint pain, fatigue, excess sweating, headaches, and breathlessness. These symptoms may be due in part to the change in hormonal levels, but they may also be caused by other factors, such as nutrition, general health, exercise habits, medications, and general attitude toward life.

It is difficult for a woman to make the decision herself about whether or not she needs medical assistance. The best advice is to find a physician, normally a gynecologist, who is knowledgeable about menopause and its effects. In some cases, a physician may recommend hormonal replacement therapy (HRT), which involves taking estrogen and other substances. While HRT does alleviate the physical symptoms of menopause, it also has possible side effects.

For more information:

Booklets: • *The Menopause Time of Life*
• *Answers About Aging: The Aging Woman*
Cost: Free
From: NIA Information Center
2209 Distribution Circle
Silver Spring, MD 20910
(301) 495-3455

Organization: National Women's Health Network

1325 G St., NW
Washington, DC 20005
(202) 347-1140
Services: A clearinghouse of information on all areas of health care for women. Answers questions and publishes a newsletter

Resource Guide: Health Resources for Older Women
Cost: $1.75
From: Consumer Information Center
P.O. Box 100
Pueblo, CO 81009

CHAPTER 15

MENTAL HEALTH

ALL OF US KNOW THAT THE QUALITY of our lives depends at least as much on our state of mind as the state of our body. Indeed, our emotional health and our physical health are interrelated in complex ways. For example, stress, anxiety, and depression may trigger or complicate physical conditions. On the other hand, some emotional problems, such as depression, can be caused by biochemical changes in the body.

Research sponsored by the National Institute of Mental Health has revealed that a majority of American adults experience more than mild emotional problems at some point in their lives. At any given time, an estimated 35 million Americans suffer from some form of mental illness, a figure higher than the total of all people who suffer from heart disease, cancer, and lung disease combined. A disproportionately large number of these problems come after age 50. The primary reason is that older Americans are more likely to encounter situations and conditions that can trigger emotional problems, such as bereavement, retirement, or serious physical illness.

Fortunately, the overwhelming majority of these problems are treatable, and those who seek treatment live happier, more productive lives than those who don't get the help they need. Unfortunately, most older Americans are much less likely to seek help when they are depressed or unusually anxious when they suffer from a physical problem. This reluctance often stems from:

- The fear that seeking help with emotional problems means that a person is "crazy"
- The lethargy and pessimism that is part of many emotional problems
- A lack of knowledge about how and where to seek help

Older people who need but don't receive mental health care can begin a spiral of rapid physical and emotional deterioration that cannot only take years off their life, but take the joy out of the years they have left. Failure to obtain treatment contributes to suicide rates among

Americans age 50 and over that are higher than for any other age group.

Of course, some forms of mental illness are both severe and difficult to treat. Many of the 2% of the American population who suffer from severe mental illness don't get the advantage of the best care and support services available. And many family members of these seriously ill people cope with their problems without realizing the resources available to them.

In this chapter, we will discuss the factors that promote mental health, describe the major types of mental health problems, and list the resources that allow patients and their families to solve or cope with them.

KEEPING MENTALLY FIT

Despite the claims of many self-help books, no one is happy, emotionally stable, or completely rational all the time. Our range of normal emotions includes fear, anxiety, guilt, anger, sadness, depression, and feelings of inadequacy. All of us are also occasionally forgetful, occasionally act irrationally or irresponsibly, or occasionally drift off into a daydream or fantasy. It is only when emotions, irrational actions, or fantasies dominate our lives or interfere with our work, social, or family lives, that professional help is needed.

The need to seek professional help for a mental health problem does not result from a "failure of will" or "lack of self control." No one is immune to mental illness, just as no one is immune to all physical illness.

However, there are two ways in which you can reduce the likelihood and severity of mental health problems. The first way is to make practical life-style changes that have been shown to reduce the incidence of some forms of mental illness. The second is understanding and preparing yourself for some of the common problems associated with mental health problems.

Changing the Way You Live

Reduce Stress. Stress brings about chemical changes in the body that prepares our heart, muscles, nervous system, and other organs to meet a challenge. These changes are natural and, in appropriate circumstances, necessary. Problems arise, however, when stress dominates our lives. The results can be physical problems, such as ulcers or headaches, and mental problems, such as depression, anxiety, and irritability.

Exercise Regularly. Exercise results in the release of body chemicals that reduce tension and promote relaxation. Exercise also reduces the likelihood of heart disease, high blood pressure, and other physical illnesses that can trigger mental health problems.

Learn to Relax. Relaxation techniques, such as meditation and yoga, have been shown to reduce stress and promote mental health.

Maintain an Active Social Life. In terms of mental health, contact with other people is often the best medicine. Older people who make use of the social opportunities provided by senior centers have significantly fewer serious mental health problems than older people who are isolated.

Eat a Balanced Diet. Dietary problems, such as vitamin deficiencies, inadequate calorie intake, and high sugar consumption, can trigger mental health problems.

Understanding and Anticipating Potential Problems

It is important to take the time to understand and prepare yourself for some of the events and circumstances in life that often trigger mental health problems, such as retirement, aging, divorce, and the death of a spouse. We discuss these events and circumstances in detail in later sections of this book. However, some valuable information about the relationship of some of these events and circumstances to mental health is available:

Publications:
- *Plain Talk About Aging*
- *Plain Talk About Handling Stress*
- *Plain Talk About the Art of Relaxation*
- *Plain Talk About Biofeedback*
- *Plain Talk About Feelings of Guilt*
- *Plain Talk About Physical Fitness and Mental Health*
- *Plain Talk About Mutual Help Groups*

Cost: Free

From: National Institute of Mental Health
Public Inquiries Branch
Room 15C-05
Office of Scientific Information
5600 Fishers Lane
Rockville, MD 20857
(301) 443-4513

WHEN TO SEEK HELP

The American Mental Health Fund has identified a number of signs that a person might benefit from professional mental health treatment. It is important to emphasize that none of these signs are normal consequences of aging:

- Marked personality change over time
- Confused thinking; strange or grandiose ideas
- Prolonged severe depression, apathy, or extreme highs and lows
- Excessive anxieties, fears, or suspiciousness; blaming others
- Withdrawal from society; friendlessness; abnormal self-centeredness
- Denial of obvious problems; strong resistance to help
- Thinking or talking about suicide
- Numerous, unexplained physical ailments; marked changes in eating or sleeping patterns

- Anger or hostility out of proportion to the situation
- Delusions, hallucinations, hearing voices
- Abuse of alcohol or drugs
- Growing inability to cope with problems and daily activities, such as job or personal needs

More information about recognizing mental health problems is contained in the following important publications:

Booklets:
- *A Consumer's Guide to Mental Health Services* (Free)
- *You Are Not Alone: Facts About Mental Health & Mental Illness* ($1.00)

From: Consumer Information Center
P.O. Box 100
Pueblo, CO 81009

Booklet: *What You Don't Know About Mental Illness Could Fill a Booklet*

Cost: Free
From: The American Mental Health Fund
3299 Woodburn Rd.
Annandale, VA 22003
(800) 433-5959
(703) 573-2200

The most common specific diseases and conditions that can produce some of these signs are discussed below.

Depression

Depression is so widespread that it's often called the "common cold" of mental health problems. All of us experience periods of depression, and most of us pull through them with the help of our friends and loved ones. However, an estimated 5% of the American population suffer from major depressions that require professional treatment.

Depression can have many different causes and symptoms. The form that is often most obvious is triggered by an event, such as death of a spouse, loss of a job, or a serious illness. Depression can also result from a chemical imbalance in the body or can be a side effect of certain diseases and medications. Recently, researchers have discovered a significant number of people whose depression is triggered by the reduced amount of sunlight in winter time.

Although major depression is common, it is also one of the most treatable of mental heath problems. An estimated 90% of people suffering from major depression can be helped by some combination of counseling, therapy, and medication.

For more information on depression:

Booklets: • *Using Drugs to Lift the Dark Veil of Depression*
• *Depressive Disorders: Treatments Bring New Hope*

• *Helpful Facts About Depressive Disorders*

Fact Sheet: Depression in the Elderly
Cost: Free
From: National Institute of Mental Health
Public Inquiries Branch
Parklawn Building, Room 15C-05
5600 Fishers Lane
Rockville, MD 20857
(301) 443-4513

Organization: National Depressive and Manic-Depressive Association
Merchandise Mart
P.O. Box 3395
Chicago, IL 60654
(312) 939-2442
Services: Provides information, referrals, and support to patients and their families

Organization: National Foundation for Depressive Illness
20 Charles Street
New York, NY 10014
(800) 248-4344 (Ex. NY)
(212) 924-9171
Services: Provides information and referrals for patients and their families

Manic-Depressive Illness

Over one million Americans suffer from manic-depression, a condition marked by abrupt mood swings from deep depression to a state of euphoria marked by grandiose thinking, hyperactivity, and other forms of manic behavior. The period of time spent in each state can range from days to months. Some manic-depressives are almost constantly depressed or manic, while others may go years, even decades, between attacks.

Unfortunately, manic-depression often goes undiagnosed. The tragedy for the victims is that most could lead nearly normal lives with drug therapy.

For more information and referral to specialists, contact the National Depressive and Manic-Depressive Association listed above.

Anxiety Disorders

From time to time, all of us face situations that make us nervous or afraid. About 15 million Americans experience nervousness, anxiety, or fear that's not related to a specific situation or that is unreasonably prolonged or severe. Some of these people suffer from a "free-floating anxiety," or a general state of nervousness. Two of the most common and serious forms of this type of anxiety disorder are:

- Posttraumatic anxiety. This condition commonly develops after a traumatic personal experience, such as being involved in a serious accident, witnessing a violent death, or being the victim of a crime. Effective treatments include counseling along with short-term use of anti-anxiety drugs.

- Panic disorder. In this condition, patients are struck without warning by the physical symptoms of severe fright, such as shortness of breath, dizziness, sweating, and palpitations. Many victims believe that they're having heart attacks and seek hospital treatment. Most sufferers are helped by drug therapy.

Millions of other Americans suffer from unreasonable fears connected with a specific object, experience, or situation that are known as:

- Phobias. These powerful but unreasonable fears range from common claustro-

phobia and fear of flying to the extremely disabling agoraphobia (fear of open spaces and crowds) which makes many victims virtual prisoners in their homes. Many people with phobias are too embarrassed to seek professional help. That is a shame, because 90% can defeat their fears through therapy.

For more information about anxiety disorders and phobias:

Booklet: *Phobias and Panic*
Cost: Free
From: National Institute of Mental Health
Public Inquiries Branch
Parklawn Building, Room 15C-05
5600 Fishers Lane
Rockville, MD 20857
(301) 443-4513

Organization: Phobia Society of America
133 Rollins Avenue, Suite 4-B
Rockville, MD 20852
(301) 231-9350
Services: Organizes local chapters for patients and their families and makes referrals to certified phobia therapists

Organization: Freedom From Fear
308 Seaview Ave.
Staten Island, NY 10305
(718) 351-1717
Services: Will provide referral to qualified specialists in your area and will send an information packet that includes the booklets:
• Panic Disorder
• Choosing a Psychiatrist

Organizations: Agoraphobics in Motion
605 West Eleven Mile Road
Royal Oak, MI 48067
(313) 547-0400
Services: Self-help groups for people who suffer from agoraphobia and anxiety

Obsessive-Compulsive Disorders

Among the most common obsessive-compulsive behaviors are frequent hand-washing, bathing, hair-pulling, or housecleaning. Many sufferers find their conditions embarrassing and are extremely reluctant to seek treatment. One way to overcome this reluctance is for family members to obtain information about the condition from:

> **Organization:** Obsessive-Compulsive Disorders Foundation
> P.O. Box 9573
> New Haven, CT 06538
> (203) 772-0565
> **Services:** Provides educational materials and support for patients and their families

Schizophrenia

About 2% of American adults suffer from severe mental illness that is marked by psychosis, an impairment of thinking that produces severely abnormal interpretations of reality. About half of these people suffer from some form of schizophrenia, a disease marked by social withdrawal and disorganized, often bizarre behavior.

In recent years, advances in drug therapy have allowed many severely mentally ill people, including schizophrenics, to lead more normal lives. However, medical research has made little progress in preventing or curing schizophrenia and other forms of severe mental illness, and the percentage of adults suffering from such illnesses has been steady for decades.

For more information:

> **Publication:** *Schizophrenia: Questions and Answers*
> **Cost:** Free
> **From:** National Institute of Mental Health
> Public Inquiries Branch
> Parklawn Building, Room 15C-05
> 5600 Fishers Lane
> Rockville, MD 20857
> (301) 443-4513

TREATMENT FOR MENTAL HEALTH PROBLEMS

Mental health treatment is provided by a number of different professionals, and finding the right help can seem confusing. Many people who could benefit from counseling are also reluctant to seek help for financial reasons. The information below will allow you to distinguish between the various mental health professionals and make use of resources that will direct you to the best and least expensive help available.

What to Do in a Mental Health Emergency

A mental health emergency is a situation in which a person becomes violent, goes completely out of control, or threatens or attempts suicide. In dangerous situations, in which a person is an immediate danger to others or himself or herself, the police are the best source of help. In emergencies in which violence is not involved, you can seek help for the patient from:

- A hospital emergency room. Most hospitals have mental health professionals either on the premises or on call to handle emergency situations.

- Your local crisis hotline or suicide prevention hotline. Thinking or talking about suicide is a strong sign that a person is suffering from serious depression and needs medical help immediately. A crisis or suicide prevention hotline can provide immediate counseling and referral to the best help. The number of your local hotline should be listed in the front of your local telephone directory. If you can't find it, call your local telephone information. Another source of information and referral is:

Organization: American Association of Suicidology
2459 S. Ash
Denver, CO 80222
(303) 692-0985
Services: Promotes study of suicide and provides support for suicide prevention programs and hotlines, as well as support groups for survivors of suicide. Publications include:
- *Suicide Prevention and Crisis Intervention Agencies in the United States—A Directory* ($10.00)
- *Directory of Survivors of Suicide Support Groups* ($5.00)
- *Before It's Too Late: What to Do When Someone You Know Attempts Suicide* (Free)
- *Suicide—It Doesn't Have to Happen* (Free)

How to Find Help In Nonemergency Situations

The first person to contact is your family physician. A number of mental problems are caused by diseases, medications, diet, or other conditions that a family doctor can treat. If the family physician can't treat the problem, you may need the help of one of a number of different mental health professionals, including the following.

Psychiatrists. Psychiatrists are medical doctors who specialize in mental disorders. Psychiatrists are the only mental health professionals who can prescribe drugs and medical therapies. Generally, Medicare will pay for mental health treatment only when performed by a psychiatrist or under the supervision of a psychiatrist. Almost all private medical insurance pays for treatment for psychiatric treatment.

Clinical Psychologists. Clinical pschologists work with individuals, groups, and families to resolve problems, but they cannot prescribe drugs or perform medical examinations. Most states require psychologists to have completed a doctoral degree and have passed a state examination in order to be licensed. Most private medical insurance will pay part or all of the cost of therapy provided by a licensed psychologist.

Psychotherapists. Psychotherapist is a generic term for mental health professionals who treat patients. This title is used by some clinical psychiatrists, psychiatric social workers, marriage and family counselors, mental health counselors, and, unfortunately, by some people with little serious academic training. As a result, the qualifications of others who call themselves psychotherapists vary widely, so prospective patients have to look beyond the title to the specific training of the therapist they are considering. Therapy conducted by many psychotherapists is not covered by medical insurance, so all patients should check with their insurance companies before the first session.

Psychiatric Nurses. Psychiatric nurses are professional nurses who have advanced academic training, such as masters degrees or more, in their specialty. They conduct therapy and staff mental health hospitals and programs, often under the supervision of other professionals. Services may be covered by medical insurance.

Psychiatric Social Workers. Psychiatric social workers have completed masters programs in social work, as well as specialized training in diagnosing and counseling people with mental problems. Many have met the requirements of the Academy of Certified Social Workers (ACSW). Their services may be covered by medical insurance.

Mental Health Counselors. Mental health counselors provide professional counseling services involving psychotherapy, human development, learning therapy, and group dynamics to individuals, couples, and families. Clinical mental health counselors must have a masters degree and several years training before being certified by the National Academy of Certified Clinical Mental Health Counselors. Their services may be covered by health insurance.

Case Managers. Case managers are individuals who assist severely and chronically mentally ill individuals and their families in obtaining needed medical care and social services.

It's very difficult for any person having mental problems or a family member to know exactly what kind of care is needed. The choices include not only the type(s) of professional needed, but also the type of care, such as inpatient, outpatient, partial hospitalization, group therapy, or at-home aftercare.

A family physician may be able to provide the appropriate referrals. If not, there are a number of other sources of information, referral, and support, including:

Organization: Local Community Mental Health Centers
Services: Several hundred community mental health centers provide a variety of diagnostic, referral, treatment, and support services for mental health problems. Many services and programs involve no or low fees for eligible residents
For information: See your Yellow Pages under "Mental Health Services"
or

National Council of Community Mental Health Centers
12300 Twinbrook Parkway, Suite 320
Rockville, MD 20852
(301) 984-6200

Organization: National Institute of Mental Health
(301) 443-4513
Services: Provides a list of outpatient clinics, psychiatric hospitals, partial care organizations, and mental health professionals in your area

Organization: American Association for Geriatric Psychiatry
P.O. Box 376-A
Greenbelt, MD 20770
(301) 220-0952
Services: Provides referral to specialists in the mental health needs of older persons. Issues pamphlets for the general public

Organization: National Mental Health Association
1021 Prince Street
Alexandria, VA 22314
(703) 684-7722
Services: Supports research and education programs about mental health. Organizes local chapters in most states that provide a wealth of information about mental health problems, resources, and support services. The state associations are also excellent sources of referral to mental health professionals

Organization: Your local area agency on aging
Services: Maintains information on mental heath programs aimed specifically at older Americans
For information: See listing, pages 383–427

Organization: Your State Mental Health Department
Services: Coordinates mental health programs and provides information and referrals
For information: Call your state government information number (see listings, pages 441–443)

Organization: American Psychiatric Association
1400 K Street, NW
Washington, DC 20005
(202) 682-6239
Services: Provides information and referral to psychiatrists

Organization: American Psychological Association
1200 17th Street, NW
Washington, DC 20036
(202) 955-7600
Services: Provides information and referrals to clinical psychologists

Organization: National Association of Social Workers
7981 Eastern Avenue

Silver Spring, MD 20910
(301) 565-0333
Services: Provides information and referral to psychiatric social workers

Organization: American Mental Health Counselors Association
5999 Stevenson Avenue
Alexandria, VA 22304
(800) 354-2008 (Ex. VA)
(703) 823-9800
Services: Provides referral to mental health counselors

Organization: American Association for Marriage and Family Therapy
1717 K Street, NW
Washington, DC 20006
(202) 429-1825
Services: Provides referral to accredited marriage and family counselors

Organization: American Nurses' Association
2420 Pershing Road
Kansas City, MO 64108
(816) 474-5720
Services: Provides information about psychiatric nurses

SELF-HELP AND SUPPORT GROUPS

Emotional and practical support are critical to recovery, both for patients and their families. Among the many excellent organizations are:

Organization: National Alliance for the Mentally Ill
2101 Wilson Blvd., Suite 302
Arlington, VA 22201
(703) 524-7600
Services: Over 700 local chapters provide emotional and educational support for the seriously mentally ill and their families

Organization: National Mental Health Consumers' Association
311 South Juniper Street, Suite 902
Philadelphia, PA 19107
(215) 735-2465
Services: Acts as an advocate for consumers of mental health services. Has over 500 local groups

Organization: National Alliance of Mental Patients
P.O. Box 618

Sioux Falls, SD 57101
(605) 334-4067

Services: Forms self-help groups and conducts other activities to improve the quality of life for current and former mental patients

Organization: Emotions Anonymous
P.O. Box 4245
St. Paul, MN 55104
(612) 647-9712

Services: Emotions Anonymous, patterned on Alcoholics Anonymous, is a fellowship of people who come together to help each other overcome emotional problems and difficulties, including anger, depression, anxiety, phobias, and grief. This organization has over 1,500 local groups

Organization: Recovery, Inc.
802 N. Dearborn Street
Chicago, IL 60610
(312) 337-5661

Services: Recovery, Inc. has over 900 local organizations that bring people together in a self-help method of controlling mental problems

Organization: National Self-Help Clearinghouse
33 West 42nd St.
New York, NY 10036
(212) 642-2944

Services: Will provide referral to appropriate self-help groups

The Important Decisions, Transitions, and Difficulties of Everyday Life

The need to make decisions and deal with difficulties and problems does not, unfortunately, disappear as we grow older. Although life experience is a significant advantage, illness, financial need, bereavement, and other problems can make it more, rather than less, difficult to cope with tasks that range from buying a major appliance to deciding whether or not to move. In this section, we present a wide range of resources that will help you make decisions and deal with difficulties in such areas as:

- Your legal rights
- Your consumer rights
- Your job and your job rights
- Your housing needs
- Crime
- Caregiving for a spouse or relative
- Divorce
- Death of a spouse
- Living with a handicap or disability

CHAPTER 16

YOUR LEGAL RIGHTS

THE MORE COMPLICATED OUR LIVES become, the more we need to know how to secure our legal rights. Legal issues come into play when you:

- Buy, sell, or refinance a house
- Prepare a will and plan an estate
- Assume responsibility for an aging parent or relative
- Obtain a divorce and enforce related court orders
- Seek maximum Social Security and pension benefits
- Seek maximum Medicare and Medicaid benefits
- Enforce consumer rights
- Encounter age or sex discrimination in employment
- Become involved in landlord-tenant disputes
- Have tax problems
- Develop consumer credit problems

Most conflicts can be resolved without resorting to legal action. However, we all find ourselves in situations that can't be resolved without a lawyer. That's why, in this chapter, we provide information and resources that will help you:

- Fully understand all of your legal rights
- Seek free legal assistance
- Purchase the best legal help at the right cost
- Explore alternatives to litigation
- Resolve disputes involving attorneys

Finally, we'll also discuss information and resources that will help you avoid and, if necessary, resolve consumer problems—the most common legal-related problems faced by Americans age 50 and over.

YOUR LEGAL RIGHTS AS AN OLDER AMERICAN

Older Americans enjoy all the legal rights and protections of our legal system. However, everyone age 50 and over should be aware of special problems and protections that can commonly affect their lives, such as protections against discrimination, Social Security and Medicare rights, special protections for tenants, and many others. Among the excellent sources of information about your legal rights are:

Organization: Legal Counsel for the Elderly
P.O. Box 96474
Washington, DC 20090
Services: This arm of AARP publishes a number of useful publications, including:
- *Your Legal Rights Calendar*: An annual wall calendar that contains information on legal rights and resources ($5.95)
  Medicare Series: Solutions to Medicare problems, including:
  - *Eligibility: General Problems* ($4.95)
  - *Hospital, Hospice and Nursing Home Care* ($4.95)
  - *Doctor Services* ($5.95)
- Self-Help Handbooks: Common sense guides to
  - *Social Security Disability* ($3.95)
  - *Social Security Retirement* ($3.95)

Publication: *Tomorrow's Choices: Preparing Now for Future Legal, Financial and Health Care Decisions* (D13479)
Cost: Free
From: AARP Fulfillment
1909 K Street, NW
Washington, DC 20049

Book: *Your Legal Rights Later in Life* by John Regan
Cost: $13.95 (AARP member price $10.35) plus $1.75 postage
Contains: A comprehensive 272-page guide to your legal rights
From: AARP Books/Scott, Foresman and Co.
1865 Miner Street
Des Plaines, IL 60016

Booklet: *Your Rights Over Age 50*
Cost: $3.00
Contains: An overview of basic rights prepared by the American Bar Association. When ordering, also ask for a list of other ABA publications
From: American Bar Association
Information Services
750 N. Lake Shore Drive
Chicago, IL 60611
(312) 988-5158

Publication: *The Rights of Older Persons*
Cost: $9.45
Contains: A comprehensive guide prepared by the American Civil Liberties Union
From: Southern Illinois University Press
P.O. Box 3697
Carbondale, IL 62902

Publications: *Consumer Resource Fact Sheets*
Cost: $0.50 for fact sheet on an individual state
Contains: A list of booklets and other information—available from the state bar association, consumer protection office, and other resources—that provide information on legal rights and purchasing legal services in that state
From: National Resource Center for Consumers of Legal Services

1444 Eye St., NW
Washington, DC 20005
(202) 842-3503

Organization: National Senior Citizen Law Center

2025 M Street, NW, Suite 400
Washington, DC 20036
(202) 887-5280
Services: Provides information on legal rights of older Americans in a number of areas

FREE LEGAL SERVICES

In 1987, Congress amended the Older Americans Act to require every state to mandate that each Area Agency on Aging set aside a minimum percentage of its funding to provide free legal assistance to older people. For information on free legal services, contact your local area agency on aging (see listings, pages 383–427).

A number of state and local governments, often in cooperation with bar associations and law schools, have developed additional programs to provide legal assistance to older Americans. For a listing of these programs in your state:

Organization: American Bar Association Commission on Legal Problems of the Elderly

1800 M Street, NW
Washington, DC 20036
(202) 331-2297

Additional sources of legal assistance may be found in:

Directory: Directory of Legal Services for Older Adults
From: Institute on Law and the Rights of Older Adults
Brookdale Center on Aging
425 East 25th St.
New York, NY 10010
(212) 481-4426

PURCHASING LEGAL SERVICES

Organizations offering free legal assistance tend to be very busy, which is one reason why many people who qualify for these services opt for hiring an attorney on their own. Your options are to:

- Join a legal services plan
- Use a legal clinic
- Hire a private attorney

Legal Service Plans

One low-cost effective option for handling routine legal problems is joining a legal services plan. In exchange for a membership fee, these plans offer free legal consultation, some free legal services, and a fixed hourly rate for services not covered by the plan. These plans save members money in two ways:

- Members can use lawyers to review contracts, solve consumer problems, and perform other simple services that they would otherwise not purchase, saving money and preventing problems.
- Members save a significant amount of money on the average hourly rate for services purchased.

The primary disadvantage of legal services is the limited choice of attorneys. The list of attorneys in your area might not include the top specialists in certain areas, such as medical malpractice, age discrimination, or criminal law. Many legal service plans are organized by companies, unions, and other organizations. A number, however, are available to the general public. For a list of these plans and other information:

> **Organization:** National Resource Center for Consumers of Legal Services
> 1444 Eye St., NW
> Washington, DC 20005
> (202) 842-3503

Legal Clinics

A second option is legal clinics, discount law offices that advertise heavily on television and in Yellow Page listings. These clinics often offer substantial savings and quicker service for routine matters, such as simple wills, real estate closings, uncontested divorces, simple personal liability cases, etc. See your Yellow Pages for the listings of these legal services.

Private Attorneys

A third option is hiring an attorney on your own. Among the sources of referral are:

- Friends and family members
- Local senior organizations, such as a local chapter of AARP

- An attorney referral service operated by a local bar association or other group (see Yellow Pages under "AttorneyReferral Service")

> **Directory:** *Martindale-Hubbell Law Directory*
> **Contains:** A reference book available at most large public libraries that lists the qualifications of attorneys in your community, an evaluation of those attorneys by judges and fellow lawyers, and a description of their specialties

For more information on selecting a lawyer:

> **Booklet:** *The American Lawyer: How to Choose and Use One*
> **Cost:** $3.00
> **From:** American Bar Association
> Information Services
> 750 N. Lake Shore Drive
> Chicago, IL 60611
> (312) 988-5158

> **Publication:** *Money Matters: How to Talk to and Selec Lawyers, Financial Planners, Tax Preparers and Real Estate Brokers* (D12380)
> **Cost:** Free
> **From:** AARP Fulfillment
> 1909 K Street, NW
> Washington, DC 20049

If You Need a Foreign Lawyer

People who need a foreign lawyer for settling a relative's estate or other reasons can obtain referrals from:

> **Organization:** Overseas Citizens Services
> U.S. Department of State
> Room 4800
> Washington, DC 20520
> (202) 647-3666

ALTERNATIVES TO LITIGATION

One easy and inexpensive alternative to hiring an attorney for smaller disputes is Small Claims Court, a part of almost every state or local judicial system in the country. These courts resolve disputes up to a certain dollar limit, normally $3,000 to $5,000. The procedure is simple: to file a claim, you fill out a form and make a small payment, normally $25 to $50. The party you are making the claim against is legally notified, and a date is set for a hearing in front of a small claims judge. Although you are allowed to hire an attorney for the hearing, you can represent yourself and you can bring witnesses. Shortly after the hearing, you're informed of the judge's decision.

For information, contact your local Small Claims Court (see White Pages under your local or state government listing).

A second alternative is arbitration or mediation. This procedure requires both parties to agree on an arbitrator, an independent third party who is often hired through an impartial arbitration service. The arbiter reviews the evidence from both sides and holds a hearing. Shortly afterward, the arbiter issues a decision.

The advantages of arbitration are that it is much faster and much less expensive than a law suit. The disadvantage is that the results are binding, meaning you cannot appeal the decision to the court system.

For information about arbitration:

Pamphlet: *Neighborhood Dispute Resolution: Helping Seniors—Seniors Helping*
Cost: Free
From: AARP Fulfillment
1909 K Street, NW
Washington, DC 20049

Organization: American Arbitration Association
140 W. 51st Street
New York, NY 10020
(212) 484-4000

You can also find local mediators by looking in the Yellow Pages under "Mediation Services."

COMPLAINTS AGAINST AN ATTORNEY

All local and state bar associations have established procedures for resolving fee disputes and other attorney-client problems. For more information, contact your local or state bar association (see White Pages).

YOUR CONSUMER RIGHTS

Fraud, shoddy merchandise, poor service, and other consumer problems cost Americans over $100 billion every year. Since Americans age 50 and over control half of all discretionary income, you are more likely to shoulder some of this loss than are people in any other age group.

A chorus of complaints from victimized consumers has produced a response by both government and private industry. This response has two basic parts:

- Consumer information programs that help educate consumers on how to get the most for their money and choose products and services that are the most reliable and most suitable for their needs
- Consumer protection legislation and industry standards that, among other benefits, create public and private bodies that help resolve consumer complaints

Consumer Information Programs

Earlier in this book, we discussed how to be a smart consumer in many important areas of life, such as financial services, credit, and health care. Among the sources of reliable, detailed information on other types of products and services are:

Organization: Council of Better Business Bureaus
4200 Wilson Blvd.
Arlington, VA 22203
(703) 276-0100
Services: Publishes more than 80 different "Tips On . . ."booklets that contain important information for buyers. Send self-addressed stamped envelope for a list of publications. Most booklets are $1.00

Organization: Federal Trade Commission Public Reference Branch
Washington, DC 20580
(202) 326-2222
Services: The FTC has a number of free consumer brochures on a wide variety of subjects. Send for a free publication list

Another excellent source of information is consumer brochures published by trade and industry associations. As examples, below are materials available from trade associations in two common areas of consumer concern: consumer electronics and jewelry:

Organization: Consumer Affairs
Electronic Industries Association
2001 Eye St., NW
Washington, DC 20006
(202) 457-4977
Services: Provides very informative consumer publications, such as:
- *Consumers Should Know: How to Buy a Personal Computer* (6" × 9" envelope, $0.65 postage)
- *Consumers Should Know: How to Buy a Telephone*
- *Consumers Should Know: All About Compact Discs and Players*
- *Consumers Should Know: Something About Interference*
- *Consumers Should Know: All About Stereo Television*
- *Consumers Should Know: How to Buy, Use, and Care for VCRs, Camcorders, and Tape*
- *Consumers Should Know: About the Care and Service of Audio and Video Products*
- *Consumers Should Know: Something About Home Automation*
- *Consumers Should Know: All About Auto Electronics Products* ($0.45 postage)
- *Video Products Safety—A Guide for Consumers*
- *Audio Products Safety—A Guide for Consumers*
- *Television Safety—A Guide for Consumers*
- *Audio Headset Safety—A Guide for Consumers*
- *Facts About Television Receivers and Cable Systems*

- *Office of Consumer Affairs Consumer Publication List*

Cost: Free with self-addressed business envelope with $0.25 postage (except where indicated above)

Organization: American Gem Society
5901 West Third Street
Los Angeles, CA 90036
(213) 936-4367

Services: Will send a free Consumer Kit that includes information on purchasing gold, diamonds, and other jewelry, as well as material on investing in gems and obtaining accurate appraisals from an accredited gem laboratory. Will also send a list of accredited jewelers, who meet the society's strict standards of training and ethics

Similar detailed information is available from trade associations in nearly every field. You can obtain the addresses of trade associations from:

Publication: *Encyclopedia of Associations*
From: The reference section of your local library

A very complete bibliography of consumer information is:

Bibliography: Consumer Protection Bibliography
Cost: Free
From: Federal Trade Commission
Public Reference Branch
Washington, DC 20580
(202) 326-2222

A guide to companies, as well as trade associations, that can answer questions and provide information is:

Publication: *AT&T Toll-Free 800*

Directory: Consumer's Edition
Cost: $9.95
Contains: Over 80,000 toll-free numbers for consumers
From: (800) 426-8686

Other sources of buying information are the guides in the Household Finance Money Management Institute series:

Publications: • *Your Home Furnishings and Equipment Dollar*
• *Your Food Dollar*
• *Your Automobile Dollar*
• *Your Housing Dollar*
• *Your Travel Dollar*
Cost: $1.25 each
From: Money Management Institute
Household International
2700 Sanders Road
Prospect Heights, IL 60070

One excellent source of information on brand comparisons is:

Publication: *Consumer Reports*
Subscription Department
Box 53009
Boulder, CO 80321
Cost: $18.00 per year for 11 issues plus annual *Consumer Buyers Guide*
Contains: Detailed product comparisons prepared by the impartial, nonprofit Consumers Union

Protect Yourself Before and After Your Purchase

Making an informed decision is only part of the task of protecting your rights. Among other important pre- and postpurchase steps are:

- Read all warranties and contracts carefully. Always make sure that all promises from salesmen are in writing, especially guaranteed return and exchange policies and guaranteed delivery dates.

- Carefully examine the product or results of the service to make sure you got what you paid for.

- Read all instructions on use of the product and securing your warranty rights.

- Keep all sales receipts, instruction books, warranties, and other correspondence in a separate file.

Special Information About Service Contracts

Nearly all dealers who sell electronic products, appliances, automobiles, and a variety of other products also sell service contracts that extend the warranties on their products for lengths of time ranging from 6 months to several years. According to the National Association of Retail Dealers of America, about one in every seven consumers purchased service contracts totaling $1 billion in 1987.

Most consumer experts, however, consider service contracts to be a poor buy in most circumstances. The primary reason is that the profit to the dealer in selling service contracts is 40% or more. That means that the dealer or service company expects to provide no more than $60 in service to a customer who pays $100 for a service contract.

Experts do point out that service contracts may be a good value for consumers who use their equipment or appliances far more than normal—for example, a very large family which does several loads of wash per day. A service contract may also be worthwhile if you live in an area where it's difficult to get service without a contract.

If you are considering the purchase of a service, you should send for:

Pamphlet: *Facts for Consumers: Service Contracts*
Cost: Free
From: Federal Trade Commission
Public Reference Branch
Washington, DC 20580
(202) 326-2222

Booklet: *Consumers Should Know: Service Contracts/Service*
Cost: Free, with self-addressed stamped envelope
From: Electronic Industries Association
2001 Eye St., NW
Washington, DC 20006
(202) 457-4977

Purchasing Goods Through Mail Order, Telephone Solicitations, and Direct Sales

You should use extra caution when purchasing goods and services through direct solicitation by phone, mail, or door-to-door sales. This is especially true today, because the ease and convenience of shopping from the home has led to a proliferation of direct sales companies and solicitations.

In order to have the advantages of shopping at home without the unpleasantness, you should take special care to become an informed consumer. Special information on shopping at home is available from two trade associations:

Organization: Direct Marketing Association
6 East 43rd Street
New York, NY 10017
Services: Industry association for direct mail and telephone sales firm. Provides a number of consumer publications, including:

- *Guidelines for Telephone Shopping* (Free)
- *The World in Your Mailbox* (Free)
- *Shopping at Home* (Free)
- *How Did They Get My Name?* (Free)
- *Great Catalogue Guide*—a guide to over 750 mail order catalogues ($2.00)

Send self-addressed stamped envelope

Organization: Direct Selling Association
1776 K Street, NW, Suite 600
Washington, DC 20006
(202) 293-5760
Services: Association establishes and enforces code of ethics for companies. Free publications:
Shop Smartly: Tips for Buying Direct
Smart Shopping: Why People Buy Direct
Who's Who in Direct Selling—a list of member companies

The U.S. Postal Service has the responsibility of investigating and prosecuting mail fraud. For information:

Pamphlet: *Mail Order Rights Consumer Card*
Cost: Free
From: The Consumer Advocate
U.S. Postal Service
Washington, DC 20260
(202) 268-2284

How to Solve Consumer Problems

No matter how carefully you shop, problems are likely to occur. The vast majority of these problems can be favorably resolved if you know what to do and whom to contact. Your first step should be to obtain:

Book: *Consumer's Resource Handbook*
Cost: Free
Contains: This publication of the Office of the President for Consumer Affairs and the U.S. Office of Consumer Affairs belongs in every American household. This 100-page book contains detailed information on how to be a smart consumer and how to complain. It also includes over 1,000 government and private resources consumers can turn to if problems occur
From: Consumer Information Center
P.O. Box 100
Pueblo, CO 81009

Booklet: *How to Write a Wrong: Complain Effectively and Get Results* (D1126)
Cost: Free
From: AARP Fulfillment
1909 K St., NW
Washington, DC 20049

These publications will be useful as you follow the steps below:

- Contact the manager or other supervisor of the store or business with which you had the problem
- If that doesn't work, write a letter to the headquarters of the company. The contacts for many large companies are listed in the *Consumer Resource Handbook.* You can obtain the addresses of other companies in one of the following reference books in your public library:
  - *Standard & Poor's Register of Corporations, Directors and Executives.*
  - *Standard Directory of Advertisers*

- *Thomas Register of American Manufacturers*
- *Trade Names Directory*

- If your problem is still unresolved, you can turn to your state or local consumer protection office (see listings, pages 443–452), your local Better Business Bureau (see listings pages 452–459), and Federal Trade Commission Correspondence Branch Washington, DC 20580. These agencies may intervene on your behalf with the store, company, or manufacturer from which you purchased the product or service. They may also refer you to other resources, including:
Other federal, state, and local agencies. For example, the Federal Reserve Board will mediate disputes with banks Occupational and professional licensing boards. For example, the licensing board for physicians will investigate complaints against doctors

- Third-party or trade association mediation services. One such service used by many companies is:

Program: Better Business Bureau National Consumer Arbitration Program
Services: This service mediates disputes submitted by consumers and companies
For information: Better Business Bureau National Consumer Arbitration Program
Council of Better Business Bureaus
4200 Wilson Blvd.
Arlington, VA 22203
(703) 276-0100

A number of trade associations also have formal dispute mediation services. Some examples are:

Resource: Major Appliance Consumer Action Panel
20 North Wacker Drive
Chicago, IL 60606
(800) 621-0477 (Ex. IL)
(312) 984-5858
Services: Mediates disputes involving major appliances

Resource: Home Owners Warranty Program
P.O. Box 152087
Irving, TX 75015
(800) 433-7657
Services: Resolves problems in homes built by builders who are members of the program

Resource: Electronic Industries Association
Office of Consumer Affairs
2001 Eye Street, NW
Washington, DC 20006
Service: This office will attempt to resolve disputes involving the following electronic products:

Televisions	Hand calculators
Radios	VCRs
Hi-fi's	Compact discs/players
Stereos	Personal computers
Audio components	Personal telephones
Video systems	Car audio products
Tape recorders	

- If you are still not satisfied, you may want to consider taking legal action. For information about legal action, see the section of this chapter on "Your Legal Rights as an Older American," pages 242–244.

Special Resources for Resolving Disputes with Automobile Dealers and Manufacturers

Disputes over automobile warranties and product reliability are perhaps the most common of all consumer complaints. Many of them can be resolved on the local level. The proper procedure to resolve a problem or complaint is:

- Start with the management of the dealership—the sales manager, customer relations manager, or dealership owner
- If the problem is still unresolved, contact the district or national customer relations office of the manufacturer. For a listing of these offices, send for:

Publication: *Automotive Customer Relations Directory*
Cost: $4.00
From: NADA
8400 Westpark Drive
McLean, VA 22102

- If the problem is still unresolved, you can turn to one of the impartial third-party dispute resolution programs that have been set up by the automotive industry and consumer groups. These programs are:

Program: AUTOLINE
Services: This program is administered by the Council of Better Business Bureaus for disputes involving the following manufacturers:
General Motors
Nissan
Volkswagen
Audi
Honda
Peugeot
Porsche
Saab—Scania
AMC—Jeep—Renault
For information: Call the toll-free information (800-555-1212) to ask for the AUTOLINE toll-free number for your state or contact:
AUTOLINE
Counsel of Better Business Bureaus
4200 Wilson Blvd.
Arlington, VA 22203
(703) 276-0100

Program: AUTOCAP
8400 Westpark Drive
McLean, VA 22102
(703) 821-7144
Services: AUTOCAP (Automotive Consumer Action Program) is sponsored by state and local automobile dealers in accordance with regulations established by the National Association of Automobile Dealers. AUTOCAP will attempt to mediate any disputes between customers and member dealers.

Program: Chrysler Customer Arbitration Board
26311 Lawrence Ave.
Centerline, MI 48288
(800) 992-1997
Services: Dispute arbitration program for Chrysler owners

Program: Ford Consumer Appeals Board
P.O. Box 1805
Dearborn, MI 48121
(800) 241-8450 (Ex. MI)
(313) 337-6950
Services: Dispute resolution for Ford, Lincoln, and Mercury owners

Program: Toyota
(800) 331-4331

Services: Toyota offers arbitration through the American
Automobile Association Complaint Arbitration Services

Before you go to arbitration, you might want to bolster your case by finding out if other owners have had the same problem. You can obtain a form for registering your own complaint and find out whether your car has been recalled by the manufacturer by calling:

Organization: National Highway Traffic Safety Administration
Auto Safety Hotline
(800) 424-9393 (Ex. DC)
(212) 366-0123

For $20 to $25, you can obtain a complete list of all consumer complaints, manufacturer service bulletins, and current investigations of your year, make and model by writing:

Organization: DOT/NHTSA
Technical Reference Division
NAD-52, Room 5110
400 Seventh St., NW
Washington, DC 20590

For more information on pursuing your rights through arbitration:

Publication: *The Center for Auto Safety Consumer Guide to Better Business Bureau Arbitration*
Cost: $15.00
From: BBB Arbitration Guide
Center for Auto Safety Publications
2001 S Street, NW
Washington, DC 20009
(202) 328-7700

● If you're not satisfied after the above procedures, your problem may fall under an increasing number of "lemon" laws passed by states. For information and assistance:

Organization: Your state consumer protection office (see listings, pages 443–452)

Publication: *The Lemon Book: The A to Z Handbook for Car Owners*
Center for Auto Safety
2001 S Street, NW
Washington, DC 20009
(202) 328-7700
Cost: $7.95 plus $1.00 postage
Contains: A wealth of information for new and used car owners written by Ralph Nader and the Center for Auto Safety

CHAPTER 17

EMPLOYMENT RIGHTS AND OPPORTUNITIES

A MAJORITY OF AMERICANS AGE 50 AND over are employed, either full or part time. An increasing percentage of retired Americans are seeking work, a trend encouraged by a more generous limit on employment earnings for people who want to retain full Social Security payments. Such work not only provides valuable income, but social contacts and strong feelings of achievement as well. Many more retired Americans enjoy these social contacts and strong feelings of achievement by working as volunteers in a wide variety of community service organizations.

In this chapter, we provide information and resources concerning:

- Your job rights and how to fight discrimination in the job you have
- Finding a new job or second career
- Starting your own business
- Finding the right volunteer opportunity

YOUR EMPLOYMENT RIGHTS: FIGHTING DISCRIMINATION

No one is guaranteed a job. However, federal and state laws do protect job seekers and job holders against several different kinds of discrimination. If you are working or planning to work in the future, you should understand your rights and the procedures for protecting those rights.

Age Discrimination

The attitude toward older workers is beginning to undergo significant change. With fewer young people entering the work force, older workers are increasingly needed to fill jobs in our thriving economy. Studies have also revealed that older workers, on the average, have better skills, demonstrate a more positive attitude, and are more reliable than those in any other age group. As a result, an increasing number of corporations are actively recruiting older workers.

Unfortunately, in many other companies, older workers continue to face discrimination both in seeking employment and while on the job. The two primary reasons are that older workers command higher salaries and have higher health care costs, factors that influence companies that concentrate on increasing short-term profit.

Fortunately, people age 40 and over are protected by the Federal Age Discrimination in Employment Act. This act applies to private employers of 20 or more people, labor unions with 25 or more members, and all federal, state, and local governments. This law prevents:

- Discrimination in hiring
- Discrimination in advancement and training
- Discrimination in compensation
- Discriminatory demotions
- Discriminatory layoffs
- Discriminatory terminations
- Age harassment
- Discrimination in employee benefits
- Mandatory retirements (in most cases)

Every working person age 40 and over should be aware of his or her job rights. Among the valuable publications are:

> **Publication:** *The Age Discrimination in Employment Act Guarantees You Certain Rights: Here's How* (D12386)
> **Cost:** Free

> **From:** AARP Fulfillment
> 1909 K Street, NW
> Washington, DC 20049

> **Publications:** • *Age Discrimination Is Against the Law*
> • *Laws Enforced by the EEOC*
> **Cost:** Free
> **From:** Equal Employment Opportunity Commission
> 1801 L St., NW
> Washington, DC 20507
> (800) 872-3362

The Age Discrimination in Employment Act sets forth very specific procedures that you must follow if you believe you've been discriminated against. First, you must decide whether to file a complaint or a charge. A complaint can be filed anonymously. However, the Equal Employment Opportunity Commission (EEOC) gives complaints very low priority. Also filing a complaint does not preserve your right to file a private lawsuit against your employer.

If you file a charge of discrimination, you agree that your employer will be told who filed the charge. The law prohibits discrimination or retaliation against those who file charges. The most important fact to know about filing charges is:

- *You must file a charge of discrimination with the EEOC within 180 days from the time that the discrimination occurs*

In states that have age discrimination laws, that time period is extended to 300 days, but experts caution that filing within 180 is always safer. If you don't file a charge within the time frame, you lose your right to file a lawsuit against your employer.

To file a charge, contact:

Organization: Equal Employment Opportunity Commission
Services: The EEOC will send you free publications and provide complete information about filing a charge. EEOC field offices will conduct an investigation and a hearing into your charges
For information: (800) 872-3362

Many U.S. states also have enacted age discrimination laws. For information, contact your local area agency on aging (see listings, pages 383–427) or your state department of labor (see your telephone directory under your state government listings or call your state government information service see listings, pages 441–443).

If you chose to file a private suit, you may be eligible for free or low-cost legal services. See Chapter 16 on obtaining legal services.

Sexual Discrimination or Harassment

Federal laws prohibit any form of discrimination based on sex, including different pay scales for men and women. Federal and state laws also prohibit sexual harassment on the job. For more information:

Publication: *A Working Woman's Guide to Her Job Rights*
Cost: Free
From: U.S. Department of Labor
Office of the Secretary
Women's Bureau
Washington, DC 20210
(202) 523-6652

Organization: National Commission on Working Women
1325 G St., NW
Washington, DC 20005
(202) 737-5764

Services: Works to improve working conditions for women and answers questions about equal pay, employee benefits, age discrimination, and other issues

If you feel that you have been the victim of sexual discrimination or harassment, you can file a complaint or charge with the EEOC. The procedures are identical to those followed in age discrimination cases. You can also obtain information and assistance from the Woman's Bureau of the U.S. Department of Labor (see address above).

Racial Discrimination

The Federal Civil Rights Act of 1964 prohibited racial discrimination in employment. If you feel you have suffered from such discrimination, you can file a complaint or charge with the EEOC. The procedures are identical to those followed in age discrimination cases.

Discrimination Based on a Handicap or Disability

A 1989 federal law prohibited job discrimination based on a person's handicap or disability. If you feel you have suffered from such discrimination, you can file a complaint or charge with the EEOC. The procedures are identical to those followed in age discrimination cases.

For Additional Help Fighting Discrimination

Anyone who suffers from discrimination based on age, sex, race, or physical condition can file a complaint with:

Organization: U.S. Commission on Civil Rights

1121 Vermont Avenue, NW
Washington, DC 20425
(202) 376-8312
(800) 552-6843

Services: Collects information on and enforces federal civil rights laws. Issues many publications, including:

- *Last Hired, First Fired: Layoffs and Civil Rights*
- *Civil Rights Directory*
- *A Guide to Federal Laws Prohibiting Sex Discrimination*
- *Getting Uncle Sam to Enforce Your Civil Rights*

FINDING A JOB AND CHANGING CAREERS

Looking for work can be a frightening prospect, especially for people who are either returning to the work force after a long period of time or who want to change careers. Some comforting news is that at any given time, about 40 million Americans are looking for a new job. A second, and more comforting piece of information is that almost all these people find jobs. The reason is that the U.S. economy has been creating new employment opportunities at a rate greater than any other world economy. The U.S. Department of Labor has projected a 25% increase in the number of new jobs between 1985 and 1995, a figure double the 13% increase in the U.S. population. Although we read so much about the influence of technology in creating jobs, only one of every 25 new jobs involves "high tech" fields. The end result is that if you want a job, you're likely to find one.

That doesn't mean, of course, you'll find an opening that provides the income and satisfaction you're looking for. Finding the right job requires an organized approach to finding and evaluating a job. Among the resources that can help you are:

Publication: *Working Options: How to Plan Your Job Search and Your Work Life* (D12403)
Cost: Free
Contains: An excellent 28-page guide to employment for people age 50 and over

From: AARP Fulfillment
1909 K Street, NW
Washington, DC 20049

Publications: • *Matching Yourself with the World of Work* ($1.00)
- *Merchandising Your Job Talents* ($2.75)
- *Resumes, Application Forms, Cover Letters, and Interviews* ($1.00)

Contains: Very valuable guides prepared by the U.S. Department of Labor
From: Consumer Information Center
P.O. Box 100
Pueblo, CO 81009

Organization: AARP Worker Equity Initiative
1909 K Street, NW
Washington, DC 20049
Services: This division of AARP conducts "Think of Your Future," employment planning workshops for those wishing to enter or re-enter the job market, provides information on work options, makes referrals to special programs, and provides information on age discrimination

Publication: *Women in Their Dynamic Years* (D12344)
Cost: Free
Contains: A collection of articles about work opportunities and life-style is-

sues for middle-aged and older women

From: AARP Fulfillment
1909 K Street, NW
Washington, DC 20049

Organization: Catalyst
250 Park Avenue South
New York, NY 10003
(212) 777-8900
Services: Compiles and publishes the National Directory of Career Resource Centers, a listing of 178 centers that provides career and educational counseling. Catalyst also has detailed briefs on 40 occupations

Organization: Your local office of your state employment service
Services: Federal law requires every state to devote a portion of its funds under the Older Americans Act to employ at least one specialist in every employment service office to help older residents find jobs. These offices provide a wide variety of information and job placement services, including coordination of job programs aimed specifically at older Americans
For information: See your White Pages under your state government listing or call your state government information service (see listings, pages 441–443)

Organization: National Association of Older Worker Employment Services National Council on Aging
600 Maryland Avenue, NW, West Wing 100
Washington, DC 20024
Services: This unit of the National Council on Aging provides information on all aspects of employment, as well as referral to public and private older worker employment services

Organization: Displaced Homemakers
1411 K St., NW, Suite 930
Washington, DC 20005
(202) 628-6767
Services: Provides a wide variety of information and support services to women re-entering the labor market after divorce or death of a spouse

Organization: Operation Able
180 N. Wabash
Chicago, IL 60601
(312) 782-3335
Services: Provides job training and placement for older workers

Organization: Senior Career Planning & Placement Service
257 Park Ave. South
New York, NY 10010
(212) 529-6660
Services: Places retired executives in full and part time positions across the country.

Program: Senior Community Service Employment Program
AARP
1909 K Street, NW
Washington, DC 20049
Services: Provides job placement for low-income people age 55 and older, allowing them to gain work experience

Program: Senior Environmental Employment Program
AARP
1909 K Street, NW
Washington, DC 20049
Services: Provides work opportunities with the Environmental Protection Agency for older adults

Program: Senior Aides
National Council of Senior Citizens
925 15th Street, NW

Washington, DC 20005
(212) 347-8800
Service: Provides job opportunities in the government and private sector for workers age 55 and older

Program: Job Training Partnership Act
U.S. Department of Labor
Washington, DC 20036
Services: This program of the U.S. Department of Labor provides special vocational testing, training, and placement of eligible older workers

Organization: National Association of Temporary Services
119 South Saint Asaph Street
Alexandria, VA 22314
(703) 549-6287
Services: Industry organization for the temporary help industry, which provides every conceivable type of placement for workers who want part-time or occasional work. Publishes free brochure for older workers and a directory of member firms

Organization: Association of Part-Time Professionals
7655 Old Springhouse Road
McLean, VA 22102
(703) 734-7975
Services: Provides information and assistance to professionals seeking part-time work

Organization: Federal Job Information Centers
Services: The U.S. Office of Personnel Management has a number of centers across the country that provide information on job opportunities with the federal government
For information: Your nearest federal information center (see listings, pages 439–441)
or
Office of Personnel Management
1900 E Street, NW
Washington, DC 20415
(202) 632-9594

STARTING YOUR OWN BUSINESS

Many older people who want to change careers or return to the work force decide to start their own businesses. The most important source of information and financial assistance is:

Organization: Small Business Administration
Services: The SBA provides to small businesses:
An extensive catalog of business development publications
SCORE, which provides free counseling by retired executives
Small business loan guarantees
Special loan programs for minority and women business owners

For recorded information: SBA Answer Desk
(800) 368-5855 (Ex. DC)
(202) 653-7561
For free catalog: SBA
P.O. Box 15434
Fort Worth, TX 76119
For information: contact your nearest SBA office:

BOSTON
(617) 565-5590

NEW YORK
(212) 264-7772

PHILADELPHIA
(215) 962-3816

ATLANTA
(404) 347-2441

CHICAGO
(312) 353-0359

DALLAS
(214) 767-7643

KANSAS CITY
(816) 374-6757

DENVER
(303) 534-7518

SAN FRANCISCO
(415) 556-7487

SEATTLE
(206) 442-5676

Another excellent source of assistance is:

Organization: Your state business development assistance office
Services: Provides information, referral, and
assistance to small business owners
For information: See your White Pages
under your state government listings
or
Your state government information
office (see listings, pages 441–443)

One source of capital is:

Organization: National Association of
Small Business Investment Companies
1156 15th Street, NW, Suite 1101
Washington, DC 20005
(202) 833-8230
Services: Small business investment companies are venture capital firms licensed
by the Small Business Administration.
They help finance businesses through

equity participation and loans. A list
of members and eligibility requirements is available for $5.00

Special sources of assistance for women
are:

Organization: National Association of
Women Business Owners
600 South Federal
Chicago, IL 60605
(312) 922-0465

Organization: American Women's Economic Development Corporation
60 East 42nd Street, Suite 405
New York, NY 10165
(800) 222-2933 (Ex. NY)
(800) 442-2933 (NY)
(212) 692-9100

Organization: Office of Women's Business
Ownership
Small Business Administration
1414 L Street, NW, Room 414
Washington, DC 20416
(202) 653-8000

Special help for minority businessmen is
available from:

Organization: Minority Business Development Agency
U.S. Department of Commerce
14th and Constitution, NW
Washington, DC 20230
(202) 377-2414

Organization: Office of Minority Small
Business
Small Business Administration
1441 L Street, NW, Room 602
Washington, DC 20416
(202) 653-6407

If you're interested in purchasing a franchise:

Organization: International Franchise Association
1350 New York Avenue, NW, Suite 900
Washington, DC 20005
(202) 628-8000

Services: Provides information about selecting and purchasing a franchise, including:
* *Answers to the 21 Most Commonly Asked Questions About Franchising* ($1.00)
* *What You Need to Know When You Buy a Franchise* ($6.95)

Publication: *Franchise Opportunities Handbook*

Cost: $12.95

Contains: A guide to purchasing a franchise, prepared by the U.S. Department of Commerce

From: (202) 783-3238

Publication: *Franchise and Business Opportunities*

Cost: Free

Contains: A guide to avoiding fraud when purchasing a franchise

From: Federal Trade Commission
Office of Consumer and Business Education
600 E Street, NW
Washington, DC 20580

VOLUNTEERISM

Tens of millions of older Americans volunteer their time to community-service organizations. Among the benefits are:

* A strong sense of personal satisfaction
* Experience that can help in obtaining employment
* Social contact with a wide variety of people
* A contribution to the improvement of the quality of life in your community

Among the resources for people interested in volunteering are:

Organization: AARP Volunteer Talent Bank

Services: This division of AARP acts as a clearinghouse for people age 55 and over who are interested in becoming volunteers. Applicants fill out registration forms listing their interests, then are paired with openings in their area. For information, send for the following free publications:
* *AARP Volunteer Talent Bank*
* *Volunteer Now!*
* *AARP Health Care Volunteers*
* *Becoming A School Partner*

From: AARP Fulfillment
1909 K Street, NW
Washington, DC 20049

Organization: Your local Volunteer Bureau

Services: Most cities have Volunteer Bureaus that act as a central clearinghouse to match people who want to volunteer with the most appropriate organizations and agencies that need their help

For information: See your telephone directory or contact:
Volunteer
1111 19th St., Suite 500
Arlington, VA 22209
(703) 276-0542

Organization: ACTION
Washington, DC 20525
Services: The Federal Domestic Volunteer agency operates three programs that involve over 500,000 volunteers age 60 and older. These are:
- Foster Grandparent Program, in which older adults work with children
- Senior Companion Program, in which volunteers assist other older Americans
- RSVP (Retired Senior Volunteer Program), which places volunteers in a wide variety of community-service programs

Organization: Peace Corps
Washington, DC 20526
(800) 424-8580
Services: Thousands of older Americans have served in over 65 countries in the last two decades. There is no upper age limit for Peace Corps volunteers

Organization: SCORE
1129 20th Street, NW
Washington, DC 20036
(800) 368-5855
Services: The Service Corp of Retired Executives has over 730 chapters that offer counseling to small businesses by volunteer businessmen and professionals

Organization: CASA (Court Appointed Special Volunteers)
909 NE 43rd Street, Suite 202
Seattle, WA 98102
(206) 547-1059
Services: CASA volunteers help attorneys and social workers investigate the plight of the more than 270,000 children abandoned or neglected by their families each year. CASA volunteers are appointed by courts and advise

judges on what actions are in the best interests of the child

Organization: International Executive Service Corps
P.O. Box 10005
Stamford, CT 06904
(203) 967-6000
Services: This organization recruits retired businessmen and executives to work as volunteers in more than 35 countries around the world

Organization: National Association of Partners in Education
601 Wythe Street, Suite 200
Alexandria, VA 22314
(703) 836-4880
Services: Organizes programs that involve older Americans working as volunteers in schools

Program: Family Friends
National Council on Aging
600 Maryland Avenue, SW, West Wing 100
Washington, DC 20001
Services: Matches volunteers age 55 and over with disabled children age 12 and under

Organization: American Red Cross
Services: Older Americans serve as volunteers in over 2,800 local Red Cross chapters
For information: Call the Office of Volunteer Personnel at your local American Red Cross chapter (see White Pages)

Organization: Your local area agency on aging
Services: Many area agencies have formal programs for matching older residents with volunteer openings. Many also use volunteers in their own programs.

For information: Your local area agency on aging (see listings, pages 383–427)

Organization: Your local senior center
Services: Almost all local senior centers use volunteers in their own programs, and many act as clearinghouses for other volunteer programs
For information: See White Pages
or
Your area agency on aging (see listings, pages 391–435)

CHAPTER 18

HOUSING CHOICES

WHERE WE LIVE IS ONE OF THE MOST important factors in the quality of all of our lives. As our lives change—as we marry, have children, change jobs—we have to reevaluate our housing wants and needs. Many Americans find that their housing needs change more drastically when they get older than at other times in life. At the same time, housing decisions can get more complicated for reasons that include financial limitations, death of a spouse, illness or physical limitations, and strong emotional ties to a residence. Fortunately, there are a large number of resources available to help in the decision-making process.

The first step is to assemble some basic information about housing choices, including:

Publications: *Your Home, Your Choice Housing Options for Older Americans* (D12143)
Cost: Free
From: AARP Fulfillment
1909 K Street, NW
Washington, DC 20049

Publication: *Planning Your Retirement Housing*
Cost: $8.95 plus $1.75 postage and handling
Contains: This book is a comprehensive look at all housing options for older Americans
From: AARP Books/Scott, Foresman and Co.
1865 Miner Street
Des Plaines, IL 60016

Publications: • *Housing for Older Adults: Options and Answers* ($10.00)
• *Housing and Living Arrangements for the Elderly: A Selected Bibliography* ($6.00)
• *Housing Choices of Older Americans* ($7.00)
From: National Council on Aging
600 Maryland Avenue, SW, West Wing 100
Washington, DC 20024
(800) 424-9046

Publication: *The Older American's Guide to Housing and Living Arrangements*

Cost: $9.95 plus $2.15 postage
From: Consumer's Union
Mount Vernon, NY 10553

This information will help you make the most basic housing decision: to stay in your present home or find a new residence.

STAYING IN YOUR OWN HOME

Although the word "retirement" often calls up the image of a move to Florida, Arizona, or other such havens, the majority of older people choose to stay in their own homes. There are a number of options that may make it possible for you to stay in your home. You could:

- Find ways to cut the expense of owning a home or staying in an apartment
- Increase income or meet unexpected expenses by tapping the equity in your home
- Make your home environment safer to reduce risks of accidental injury or disease
- Adapt the home to make it more comfortable and appropriate for your needs
- Protect yourself and your home against crime

How to Reduce Your Housing Costs

Among the ways to save on your housing costs are:

Reduce Utility Costs. Utility costs, especially heating expenses, can be burdensome for all homeowners. Studies have shown that some retired people on fixed incomes spend as much as 20% of their incomes on utility bills. This problem has led to a number of programs to help older Americans deal with these problems. Some of the programs are supported by state or local funding, while others are instituted by local utility companies. These programs include:

- Subsidies to help meet the costs of heating and other utilities
- Free or low-cost home weatherization programs to cut heating and cooling bills
- Free or low-cost home energy audits
- Budgeting programs to spread heating expenses over the entire year
- Procedures for sending notices to relatives or friends if utility bills go unpaid

For information on these programs, contact:

- Your local area agency on aging (see pages 383–427)
- Your local utility company (see your utility bill or your telephone directory)
- Your state public utility commission (see your telephone directory under your state government listings or call your state government information service, pages 441–443).

An excellent source of free information about saving energy is:

Organization: Conservation and Renewable Energy Inquiry and Referral Service

P.O. Box 8900
Silver Spring, MD 20907
(800) 523-2929 (Ex. AK and HI)
(800) 233-3071 (AK and HI)
Services: This service, funded by the U.S. Department of Energy, has a wide variety of publications and information services for homeowners

Reduce Or Eliminate Property Taxes.

Most state and local governments have enacted legislation that provides one or more types of property tax relief to both homeowners and renters. For information, review the information on state taxes in Chapter 9.

Share Your Residence with Another Person.

Sharing your home with one or more persons can provide invaluable financial assistance, as well as welcome companionship. There are three ways to find someone to share your home or apartment. You can:

- Find a relative or friend as a housesharer. This is the easiest and often the most comfortable arrangement
- Find a person on your own. This requires placing advertisements and interviewing prospective housemates
- Take advantage of a shared housing matching service. Many communities have established services that match homeowners with prospective homesharers through carefully developed screening procedures.

Information on shared housing is available from:

Publication: *Is Homesharing for You? A Self-Help Guide for Homeowners and Renters* ($2.75)

Contains: A complete discussion of the subject, including questionnaires for homeowners and homesharers, as as well as guidelines for interviewing
From: Shared Housing Resource Center
6344 Green Street
Philadelphia, PA 19144
(215) 848-1220

Publication: *Living with Tenants: How to Happily Share Your House with Renters for Profit and Security*
Cost: $7.00
From: The Housing Connection
P.O. Box 5536
Arlington, VA 22205

Publication: *Shared Living: Individual Planning Guide*
Cost: $2.00
From: Boston Community Development, Inc.
178 Tremont Street
Boston, MA 12111

Organization: Shared Housing Resource Center
6344 Green Street
Philadelphia, PA 19144
(215) 848-1220
Services: Serves as a clearinghouse for information on shared housing and assists in the development of group shared residences and shared housing matching services. Will provide referrals to local organizations

Save Money on Home Maintenance and Repairs.

Both the cost of and the effort involved in maintaining a home can be burdensome to many older homeowners and renters. That is the reason many state and local communities have established special programs to provide no-cost or low-cost handyman and other home repair services to eligible homeowners and renters. For information, contact your local area agency on aging (see listings, pages 383–427).

Take Advantage of the Equity in Your Home

Approximately 80% of homeowners age 65 and over own their residences free and clear of any mortgage. The Special Committee on Aging of the U.S. Senate has estimated that the cumulative home equity of these homeowners totals more than $600 billion. The Committee further found that tapping this equity to provide current income, pay for needed home repairs, pay for health-related modifications, such as ramps and elevators, or to pay for needed health care and health insurance would improve the quality of life for millions of older Americans.

There are two ways in which this equity can be tapped.

Home Equity Loans. A home equity loan is a loan granted by a financial institution in exchange for a second mortgage on the home or property. The advantages of a home equity loan are:

- Obtaining a loan is generally quick and much easier than obtaining a first mortgage
- The funds are received in a lump sum, or established as a credit line to be drawn upon as needed
- Payment term can range from 2 to 20 years
- The interest rate is generally lower than any other consumer loan
- Interest on a home equity loan is often tax-deductible

The disadvantages of home equity loans are:

- Loan rates, terms, and costs vary widely from lender to lender, making shopping for the best terms very confusing and time-consuming
- If loans are not repaid, the borrower can lose his or her home

Experts recommend home equity loans only for people who need large amounts of money for important major expenses, such as medical care, major home repairs, or major home improvements. Home equity loans should only be taken out by people with sufficient income to meet repayment schedules.

Before shopping for a home equity loan, read Chapter 4, Purchasing and Using Credit, pages 30–37. Other specific resources are:

Publication: *Letting Your Home Equity Work for You*
Cost: Free with self-addressed stamped envelope
From: Mortgage Bankers Association of America
1125 15th Street, NW
Washington, DC 20005
(202) 861-1929

Publication: *Borrowing Against Your Home: The Risks, Pitfalls, and Advantages of Home Equity Loans* (D12987)
Cost: Free
From: AARP Fulfillment
1909 K Street, NW
Washington, DC 20049

Home Equity Conversions. Home equity conversions are a method of converting the equity in your home into a regular monthly income rather than a lump-sum loan. They are more like annuities than loans, because the size of your monthly payments depends on your age and life expectancy. The advantages of home equity conversions are:

- Homeowners receive a regular monthly income for a specific period of time, commonly their life
- No repayments are due until the homeowner dies or sells the home
- Interest on the loans is generally lower than other forms of consumer loans

The disadvantages of home equity conversions are:

- Unless the value of the home rises dramatically, there is little equity for unexpected large expenses
- Monthly payments are generally fixed, providing no protection against inflation
- Most loans require the home to be sold when the homeowner dies, preventing the home from being willed to a spouse or other heirs

The availability of home equity conversion loans increased dramatically in 1989, when the Federal Housing Administration began insuring reverse mortgages. For information:

Organization: Federal Housing Administration
(800) 245-2691
Services: Through this toll-free telephone number, the FHA will provide the names of local lenders participating in the FHA-insured reverse mortgage program and will send material

Another source of referral to lenders is:

Organization: National Center for Home Equity Conversion
348 West Main Street
Marshall, MN 56258

Services: Will provide a complete list of public and private lenders upon receipt of a self-addressed, stamped envelope. Also publishes a complete guide to equity conversion that shows the consequences of each type of reverse mortgages ($35.00)

Anyone entering into such an arrangement is urged to consult an attorney or other financial expert. A very useful and impartial source of information is:

Publication: *Home-Made Money: A Consumers Guide to Home Equity Conversion* (D12894)
Cost: Free
From: AARP Fulfillment
1909 K Street, NW
Washington, DC 20049

Adapt Your Home for Comfort and Safety

Elsewhere in the book we discuss a wide variety of resources that can help a disabled or seriously ill person remain in his or her home. However, there are a great many things all older people can and should do to insure that their homes will be safe and comfortable now and in the years to come, even if they don't have significant illnesses or handicaps. These steps fall into two general areas: making the interior environment safer, and adapting the interior for ease of living.

Improve the Quality of the Indoor Environment in Your Home. Many health problems can be caused or exacerbated by indoor air pollution. One excellent guide to maintaining indoor air quality is:

Publication: *The Inside Story: A Guide to Indoor Air Quality*
Cost: Free
From: Office of Air and Radiation
Environmental Protection Agency
Washington, DC 20460

Adapt Your Home to Your Needs. The quality of all of our lives is better when our homes fit our needs, and this is especially true as we grow older. There are a number of resources for people interested in both major and minor adaptations. Some valuable sources of information are:

Publication: *The Do-Able Renewable Home* (D12470)
Cost: Free
Contains: Valuable guide to adapting a home for any special limitation or need. Includes comprehensive list of resources
From: AARP Fulfillment
1909 K Street, NW
Washington, DC 20049

Book: *Adaptable Housing*
Cost: $3.00
Contains: An architect's guide to adaptable housing, developed for the U.S. Department of Housing and Urban Development
From: HUD Information Clearinghouse
(800) 245-2691

Book: *Design for Aging*
Cost: $40.00, plus $3.00 shipping
Contains: An architect's guide published by the American Institute of Architects. Written primarily for designing institutions or apartments, but contains many ideas of use in designing a home
From: AIA Order Department
Nine Jay Gould Court

P.O. Box 740
Waldorf, MD 20601

Protect Yourself and Your Home Against Crime

Crime is one of the major fears and problems of all Americans, regardless of age group. About one of every four American households is touched by crime during the course of the average year.

Publications: *AARP How-to Crime Prevention Series*
Cost: Free
Contains: A series of 7 pamphlets:
- *Conduct a Security Survey* (D396)
- *Protect You and Your Car* (D393)
- *Protect Your Home* (D395)
- *Protect Your Neighborhood* (D397)
- *Spot a Con Artist* (D394)
- *Protect Your Rural Homestead* (D12244)
- *Report Suspicious Activities* (D12779)
From: AARP Fulfillment
1909 K Street, NW
Washington, DC 20049

Publications:
- *How to Crimeproof Your Home*
- *How to Be Streetwise—and Safe*
- *How to Protect Yourself Against Sexual Assault*
- *Senior Citizens Against Crime*
- *How to Prevent Rural Crime*
- *How Not to Get Conned*
- *Arson—How Not to Get Burned*
- *How to Protect Your Neighborhood*
- *How to Protect Children*
Cost: Free
From: Crime Prevention Coalition
P.O. Box 6600
Rockville, MD 20850

Each year, more than five million homes are burglarized. Homes without electronic alarm systems are about six times as likely to suffer an illegal entry than homes with security systems. Many alarm systems automatically warn of fire, as well as an attempted entry. For these reasons, most insurance companies give discounts, as much as 15%, on homeowner policies insuring houses with electronic systems installed.

Home security systems range from inexpensive detectors that sound a siren or bell if disturbed to professionally installed sensors that automatically dial a central monitoring office or the police department. If you're considering the purchase of a system:

Pamphlet: *Plain Talk About Home Burglar Alarm Systems*
Cost: $1.00 plus self-addressed stamped envelope
Contains: Basic information compiled by the National Crime Prevention Institute
From: University of Louisville Shelby Campus
Louisville, KY 40292

Booklet: *Bless This House: A Home Security Audit*
Cost: Free
From: Corporate Affairs
Aetna Life and Casualty
151 Farmington Avenue
Hartford, CT 06156

Pamphlet: *Considerations When Looking for a Home Burglar Alarm System*
Cost: $2.00 postpaid
From: National Burglar and Fire Alarm Association
1120 19th Street, NW
Washington, DC 20036

Book: *The Complete Guide to Home and Auto Burglar Alarms*
Cost: $12.95 plus $1.00 shipping
From: Baker Publishing
16245 Armstead Street
Grenada Hills, CA 91344

For Renters: Understanding and Protecting Your Rights

Many renters, young and old alike, feel increasingly vulnerable to sudden eviction, large rent increases, or other actions by landlords. Older Americans often have the protection of federal laws and special laws enacted by state and local governments. Two valuable publications are:

Publication: *Rental Housing*
Cost: Free
From: AARP Fulfillment
1909 K St., NW
Washington, DC 20049

Publication: *Wise Rental Practices*
Cost: Free
From: U.S. Department of Housing and Urban Development
Washington, DC 20410

Specific assistance and information on local laws and legal assistance with landlord-tenant disputes is available from your local area agency on aging (see listings, pages 383–427). You can also make a formal complaint about discrimination based on age, race, religion, sex, national origin, family status or handicaps by calling:

Organization: Fair Housing and Equal Opportunity Hotline
(800) 424-8590 (Ex. DC)
(202) 426-3500

CHOOSING ANOTHER RESIDENCE

People decide to choose another residence for a number of reasons, including a desire to move to a warmer climate, find less expensive or more manageable housing, or seek the companionship of family or friends. Changing residences can involve four basic steps:

- Selling one's home
- Selecting a new residence
- Purchasing a new residence
- Arranging the move

How to Sell Your Home

The majority of homeowners enlist the services of a real estate broker to sell their homes. In exchange for a commission that is normally 6% of the purchase price, the broker assists the homeowner by helping to establish a price, advises on home repairs and improvements that will help sell the home, places advertisements in local papers, places "For Sale" signs on the property, screens prospective buyers, shows the home, and acts as a go-between in negotiating the sale. In many areas, the listing brokers have formal arrangements to share commissions with other brokers in the area, which is known as "multiple listing." Such listings vastly increase the number of potential buyers.

Since licenses to sell real estate are relatively easy to obtain, there are a lot of inexperienced people in the field who are often less likely to sell your home quickly and at the right price. The best way to find a broker is through recommendations from friends and acquaintances. You should look for a broker who has worked in your community for a number of years, and you should check his or her record with your local Better Business Bureau. Before you make a final decision, you should ask about a discount on commissions, which is becoming more common as competition in the real estate business increases.

For more information on selecting and working with a broker:

Organization: National Association of Realtors
430 North Michigan Avenue
Chicago, IL 60611
(312) 670-3780

Deciding What You Need

There are a number of options available to people who want to change residences. The most common one is to purchase a smaller home or condominium. However, there are other options, including:

Accessory Apartments. An accessory apartment, or separate apartment, is created out of one or more rooms in a single-family house owned by a family member, neighbor, or other person. The creation of an accessory apartment requires the approval of zoning boards in many areas, but an increasing number of communities have policies to grant zoning approval when older family members will occupy the apartment. For information:

Publication: *Legal Issues in Accessory Apartments*
Cost: Free
From: AARP Fulfillment
1909 K Street, NW
Washington, DC 20049

Publication: *Accessory Apartments: Using Surplus Space in Single Family Houses*
Cost: $10.00

From: American Planning Association
1776 Massachusetts Ave., NW
Washington, DC 20036
(202) 872-0611

ECHO Housing Units. ECHO stands for "Elder Cottage Housing Opportunity." These units are small, self-contained, portable cottages that can be placed on the property of an existing house. ECHO units are specifically designed for older residents, are inexpensive, and are increasingly acceptable to local zoning boards. For information:

Publication: *ECHO Housing: Zoning Issues and Other Considerations*
Cost: Free
From: AARP Fulfillment
1909 K Street, NW
Washington, DC 20049

Congregate Housing Developments. Developments such as these offer individual apartments or dwelling units, but provide heavy housecleaning, group meals, and social and recreational activities. Many are partially subsidized by local communities. For information, contact your area agency on aging.

Continuing Care Retirement Communities. These communities offer a range of accommodations from individual apartments to skilled nursing home care. Individuals normally sign a lifetime contract when entering the community, which provides a specific range of services in exchange for a one-time payment and monthly fees. For information:

Publication: *The Continuing Care Retirement Community: A Guidebook for Consumers*
Cost: $2.00
From: American Association of Homes for the Aging
1129 20th St., NW

Washington, DC 20036
(202) 296-5960
Publication: *National Continuing Care Directory*
Cost: $13.95 plus $1.75 postage
From: AARP Books/Scott, Foresman and Company
1865 Miner Street
Des Plains, IL 60026

Publication: *A Consumer Guide to Life-Care Communities*
Cost: $4.00
From: National Consumers League
815 15th Street, NW
Washington, DC 20005
(202) 639-8140

Financing a New Home Or Condominium

Many older Americans are able to pay cash for a new, smaller residence out of the proceeds of the sale of their previous residence. Those who seek financing are often bewildered by the vast new array of mortgages that have appeared on the market in the last decade. Even people who have purchased several homes need to re-educate themselves about home financing if they haven't shopped for a mortgage in the last few years. Among the excellent sources of information are:

Booklets:
- *How to Shop for a Mortgage*
- *What Happens After You Apply for a Mortgage*
- *How to Save Half on Interest Costs*
- *A Consumer's Glossary of Mortgage Terms*
- *Your Mortgage Deductions Under the New Tax Code*
- *How to Own Your Home in 12–19 Years*

- *Self Test—How Much House Can You Afford*
- *Closing the Loan: A Consumer's Guide to Settlement Costs*
- *Refinancing Your Mortgage*
- *Letting Your Equity Work For You: A Consumer's Guide to Second Mortgages*

Cost: Free, with self-addressed stamped envelope
From: Communications Department
Mortgage Bankers Association of America
1125 Fifteenth Street, NW
Washington, DC 2005

Booklets:
- *A Consumer's Guide to Mortgage Lock-Ins*
- *A Consumer's Guide to Mortgage Closings*
- *Consumer Handbook on Adjustable Rate Mortgages*
- *A Consumer's Guide to Mortgage Refinancing*

Cost: Free
From: Publication Services
Board of Governors of the Federal Reserve System
Room M-P-503, Stop 138
20th and C Streets, NW
Washington, DC 20551

Publication: *The Mortgage Money Guide*
Cost: $1.00
From: Consumer Information Center
P.O. Box 100
Pueblo, CO 81009

Solving Mortgage Loan Problems

You should first try to resolve any problem involving a current or pending mortgage loan with the lending institution involved. If that fails, another resource is:

Resource: Mortgage Bankers Association of America
Service: A consumer with a complaint against a mortgage lender should send a letter stating:
1. The name of the company
2. The company representative(s) who are involved in the problem
3. Complete description of the problem, with documentation

If the company is a member of the association, the complaint is forwarded to the head of the company. The Mortgage Bankers Association estimates 85% to 90% of problems are resolved

If the company is not a member of the association, the consumer is referred to the appropriate state regulatory office.
Contact: Mortgage Bankers Association of America
1125 Fifteenth Street, NW
Washington, DC 20005
(202) 861-1929

Moving Your Belongings

Moving can be a very traumatic and expensive experience. You can save yourself a lot of time and trouble by carefully selecting the mover and understanding your rights. Some valuable resources are:

Publication: *When You Move: Your Rights and Responsibilities*
Cost: Free

From: Interstate Commerce Commission
Office of Compliance and Consumer
Assistance
12th Street and Constitution Avenue
Washington, DC 20423
(202) 275-7148

Publication: *The Moving Book*
Cost: Free
Contains: A helpful guide to moving pre-
pared by AT&T
From: (800) 225-5288

CHAPTER 19

CAREGIVING

Assuming responsibility for some or all of the care for a seriously or chronically ill or disabled spouse, parent, or other loved one at home is one of the most difficult and demanding tasks in our society. As America ages, it is also becoming one of the most common. In 1990, a survey by the American Association of Retired Persons (AARP) revealed that seven million households were caring for an aging relative. The average age of the caregiver was 46; the average age of the person being cared for was 77.

For almost every caregiver, the decision to assume responsibility is a difficult one. In some cases, the necessity becomes suddenly apparent after a stroke, accident, heart attack, or other medical emergency. In many other cases, the realization that a spouse, parent, or sibling needs assistance comes slowly over time.

No matter how great the need, it is common for both caregivers and those cared for to experience some resentment of the new relationship. In too many relationships, that resentment increases as the responsibilities of the caregiver grow. The AARP study and others have shown that the demands of caring for an older person can, in many cases, negatively affect every aspect of a caregiver's life, from health to employment to the relationship with a spouse.

Fortunately, problems faced by caregivers have received increasing attention from public agencies and private organizations in recent years. Many special programs, services, and resources to train and support caregivers have been developed. Those who take advantage of the information and support available are much more likely to manage the problems of caregiving in a way that allows them to enjoy the immense satisfaction of improving the quality of life of a loved one.

LEARNING ABOUT CAREGIVING

Although the task of caring for an older person is very different from raising a child, both are responsibilities that require a wide range of knowledge and skills. Almost all new parents seek to acquire the necessary knowledge and skills by reading books, consulting a pediatrician frequently, and sharing problems and solutions with other new parents. Tragically, however, a majority of caregivers of the elderly take on their new responsibility without seeking any information, services, or support.

The first step in making caregiving manageable is to obtain some of the excellent publications on caregiving and make contact with relevant resource organizations. These include:

Book: *Caregiving: Helping an Aging Loved One*
Cost: $13.95 (AARP member price $9.95) plus $1.75 shipping
Contains: A 318-page guide to all facets of caregiving
From: AARP Books/Scott, Foresman and Co.
400 S. Edward Street
Mt. Prospect, IL 60056

Book: *Information for Caregivers of the Elderly: Resource Manual*
Cost: $10.00 plus $2.00 postage
From: Center on Aging Studies
University of Missouri—Kansas City
7220 Holmes
Kansas City, MO 64108

Publications: *Resources for Caregivers Kit*
Cost: Free
Contains: A number of booklets, including:
- *The Right Place at the Right Time* (D12843)
- *A Checklist of Concerns/Resources for Caregivers* (D12898)
- *A Handbook About Care in the Home* (D955)

- *Miles Away and Still Caring* (D12748)
- *Coping and Caring: Living with Alzheimer's Disease* (D12441)
- *Domestic Mistreatment of the Elderly* (D12810)
- *A Path for Caregivers* (D12957)

From: AARP
Program Resources Department/BS
1909 K Street, NW
Washington, DC 20049

Resource: Senior Helpline
F-274 HFAC
Brigham Young University
Provo, UT 84602
(800) 328-7576 (EX UT)
(801) 378-7576
Services: Toll-free number that provides access to over 100 taped messages providing information of interest to older Americans. A list of topics covered is available free by mail.

Resource: National Council on the Aging
West Wing 100
600 Maryland Ave., SW
Washington, DC 20024
(800) 424-9046 (Ex DC)
(202) 497-1200
Services: Will provide information and referral to other resources and agencies to help provide care for an older American

Organization: NCOA Family Caregivers of the Aging
600 Maryland Avenue, SW
Washington, DC 20024
(202) 479-1200
Services: This organization, a program of the National Council on the Aging, offers practical help to caregivers and serves as a resource for referrals to adult day-care centers, senior cen-

ters, support groups, and other programs. Publications include:

- *Caregiving,* a newsletter published 10 times per year and sent to all members
- *Family Home Caring Guides,* a series of eight guides to Community Resources, Understanding Medicare, Long Term Care—Medicaid, Long Distance Caregiving, Partners for Health, Avoiding Home Accidents, Options for Housing, and Legal and Financial Planning ($4.00 for set)
- *Ideabook on Caregiver Support Groups,* which includes a directory of over 300 groups ($5.00)
- *Guides for Caregiver Support Groups* ($2.00)
- *Caregiver Tips,* a series of brochures ($3.00 per set)

Add 10% of order, minimum $2.00 for postage and handling

Cost: $25.00 per year membership

Manual: *Caregiving: A Handbook for Caregivers*
Cost: $20.00
Contains: A three-ring binder of publications dealing with
common problems faced by caregivers
From: NSC Education and Family Support Services
Good Samaritan Hospital and Medical Center
1015 NW 22nd Avenue
Portland, OR 97210
(503) 229-7348

Newsletter: *Parent Care*
Contains: A national newsletter of resources for assisting family caregivers. Also available are *Parent Care Special Reports* on a variety of subjects
Cost: Information and sample copy are free

From: Parent Care
University of Kansas Gerontology Center
316 Strong Hall
Lawrence, Kansas 66045

Publication: *Long Term Care: A Dollar and Sense Guide*
From: United Seniors Health Cooperative
1334 G Street, NW, Suite 500
Washington, DC 20005
(202) 393-6222

Guide: *Where to Turn for Help for Older Persons: A Guide for Action on Behalf of an Older Person*
Cost: $1.75
Contains: Questions and answers about information and resources for all areas of life, prepared by the Administration on Aging
From: Superintendent of Documents
U.S. Government Printing Office
Washington, DC 20402

Book: *Mainstay: A Companion Guide for Spouse of the Chronically Ill*
Cost: $17.95
Contains: A comprehensive book about the effects of caring for a chronically ill spouse that also covers the practical aspects of caregiving
From: Little, Brown and Co.
205 Lexington Avenue
New York, NY 10016

Book: *Women Take Care: The Consequences of Caregiving in Today's Society*
Cost: $9.95 paperback
Contains: Written by the co-founders of the Older Women's League, this book describes the task of caregiving, spells out the options available to families in all areas, and contains a 23-page list of resources

From: Older Women's League
730 Eleventh Street, NW
Washington, DC 20001
(202) 783-6686

Book: *Help for Families of the Aging*
Cost: $39.95
Contains: A manual for conducting an eight-week seminar on caring for aging relatives that includes an 80-page workbook for caregivers
From: Support Source

420-4 Rutgers Avenue
Swarthmore, PA 19081

Organization: Children of Aging Parents
2761 Trenton Road
Levittown, PA 19506
(215) 945-6900
Services: Self-help group for children caring for parents. Publishes newsletter, provides referrals to local organizations, publishes many valuable books and brochures, and assists in starting local support groups

CAREGIVING RESOURCES IN YOUR COMMUNITY

Once you begin to understand about caregiving, the next step is to gather information about the specific resources available in your community.

Previously in this book, we covered in detail how to locate information and resources in several areas that are of critical importance to caregivers. These include:

- Providing advice on day-to-day financial matters
- Managing savings and investments
- Purchasing insurance
- Understanding and taking advantage of Social Security benefits
- Understanding and taking advantage of pension benefits
- Finding the best health care
- Understanding Medicare and Medicaid
- Purchasing the best private health insurance
- Locating information and resources for specific diseases and conditions
- Finding the right help for mental health problems

In almost every community in the United States, there are organizations that provide an array of other services that can greatly relieve the burden on caregivers. These services can be divided into three types:

- Home health care services
- Respite services
- Other services

Home Health Care Services

Caring for a chronically ill or disabled person at home is the least expensive and most comfortable alternative. Among the available home health care services are:

- Medical care and supervision
- Nursing care and supervision
- Social work services
- Physical therapy
- Occupational therapy
- Inhalation therapy
- Speech therapy

- Medical technician services
- Equipment and supply services
- Nutritional guidance
- Pharmaceutical services
- Health aide services

In many communities, some of these services may be provided through public agencies or nonprofit organizations. Information about these services is available from your local area agency on aging or the other community resources mentioned above. In most cases, however, these free services are limited to a period of recuperation after the return home from hospitalization for illness or surgery. Once these services are exhausted, most people have to turn to private home care agencies.

Private home care agencies provide services ranging from skilled nursing care to homemaking services. For information:

Organization: Foundation for Hospice and Home Care
519 C Street, NE
Washington, DC 20002
(202) 547-7424
Services: Will provide referrel to accredited and approved homemaker and home health aide services. Publishes consumer guides, including:
• All About Homecare
• Family Caregiver's Guide

Organization: National League of Nursing
350 Hudson Street
New York, NY 10014
(800) 669-1656 (Ex. NY)
(212) 989-9393
Services: Operates national Home Care Hotline to answer questions about home care resources and provide referrals to accredited agencies. Also takes reports of abuses or complaints

Organization: Visiting Nurse Associations of America
1391 N. Speca Blvd.
P.O. Box 4637
Denver, CO 80204
(800) 426-2547
Services: Will provide referrals to local associations that provide home nursing and other assistance

The best source of referral to a home health care service is recommendations from friends or family. Another excellent source is the discharge planning office of a local hospital. Most of these offices have extensive experience with local home health care providers and can provide information and referrals to those who have proved reputable. A third source of information is the Yellow Pages under "Home Health Care Agencies."

There are three types of organizations you'll find listed under home health care:

- Home care agencies that employ and are responsible for the home health care workers
- Registries of nurses that act simply as referral groups
- Employment agencies that handle home health care workers

Home health care agencies may be the preferable choice for long-term continuing care. Among the qualifications you will look for are:

- Is the organization licensed? (All home care agencies must be licensed in 12 states and some must be licensed in 25 additional states)
- Is the organization accredited?
- Is the organization a member of the National Association for Home Care?
- Is the organization certified by Medicare and Blue Cross/Blue Shield?

- Are employees of the organization bonded in case of theft or misconduct?

Even if all these criteria are met, you should check the record of the organization by contacting:

Organization: Joint Commission on Accreditation of Health Care Organizations
Services: Will provide information about accreditation of home health care organizations
For information: (708) 916-5741

For more detailed information on home health care, you can consult:

Book: *Home Heath Care: A Complete Guide for Patients and Their Families* by Jo-Ann Friedman
Cost: $14.95
Contains: A comprehensive 600-page guide to all aspects of home health care, including a resource listing and index
From: Fawcett Books

Book: *The Home Health Care Solution* by Janet Zhun Nassif
Cost: $9.95
Contains: Another comprehensive and easy-to-read guide to home health care
From: HarperCollins*Publishers*

Booklet: *A Handbook About Care in the Home* (D955)
Cost: Free
From: AARP Fulfillment
1909 K Street, NW
Washington, DC 20049

Booklet: *A Consumer's Guide to Home Health Care*
Cost: $5.00
From: National Consumer's League

815 15th Street, NW, Suite 516
Washington, DC 20005
(202) 639-8140

Relief for the Home Care Giver

As we have pointed out previously in this book, Medicare does not pay for custodial care of ill or disabled people in the home. In many cases, the cost of purchasing such care is prohibitive. Even if the caregiver does not work outside the home, he or she needs relief from the constant responsibility of caring for another person.

One increasingly available alternative is adult day-care centers. These generally low-cost programs provide transportation to and from the center, as well as custodial care, recreation, meals, and other activities during the day. Many adult day-care programs are housed in senior centers. If your nearest senior center doesn't have such a program, you can find a center by calling your local area agency on aging or:

Organization: National Institute on Adult Day Care
National Council on Aging
600 Maryland Avenue SW
Washington, DC 20024
(800) 424-9046
(202) 479-1200

A second option is a volunteer program that sends a trained person to the home to continue care while the caregiver gets a rest. Many of these programs are sponsored by local United Ways, Red Cross chapters, or local churches. One formal national program is:

Program: Respite
Sponsor: National Council of Catholic Women
Description: Respite is a national program in which volunteers are trained to

provide a break, or "respite" for family members who are caring for an elderly person suffering from Alzheimer's Disease or other condition requiring constant supervision. In early 1989, the program had trained over 4,000 volunteers in over 80 dioceses

Program materials: 64-page training manual for those interested in starting a Respite program.

Cost: $8.00 plus $1.50 postage
Video on RESPITE program can be borrowed.

Cost: $8.00 handling charge.

For local information: Contact your local diocesan Council of Catholic Women

For program materials and other information: National Council of Catholic Women
U.S. Catholic Conference
3211 Fourth St., NE
Washington, DC 20017
(202) 659-6000

A third alternative is a respite program that involves a short stay in a nursing home or other caregiving facility while the caregiver takes a vacation. To locate such a program, contact your local area agency on aging, local senior center, or call local nursing homes.

Other Services

Among the other valuable services offered in many communities are:

- Homemaker services
- Chore and errand services, including minor home repairs, snow shoveling and lawn mowing, grocery shopping, and picking up medications
- Home-delivered meals and free foodstuffs
- Congregate meal programs that often include transportation to and from the meal site
- Telephone reassurance, which involves a phone call to the person once or twice a day
- Emergency response systems that allow a person to immediately summon help after a fall or other accident
- Transportation and escort services for medical visits, shopping, and recreation

In every part of the country, the coordinating agencies for the majority of these services are your local agency on aging and your local senior center.

Other organizations that are a source of significant information and referrals are:

Organizations: United Way Information and Referral Services

Services: Provides information on many types of community services to the elderly and disabled

For information: See your White Pages under "United Way" or Yellow Pages under "Information Services" or see listings, pages (434–439)

Organization: American Red Cross

Services: The more than 3,000 local chapters of the Red Cross provide a variety of services, some of which may be of value to caregivers

For information: See your White Pages under "American Red Cross"

Organization: Family Service America
11700 W. Lake Park Drive
Milwaukee, WI 53224
(414) 359-2111

Services: Family Services America is a network of more than 290 local agencies that provide a variety of services to families, including those strained by caregiving. Provides referral to local agencies

Organization: Catholic Charities
Services: Local Catholic Charities provide a variety of human and social services to both Catholics and non-Catholics
For information: See White Pages under "Catholic Charities"
                      or
National Conference of Catholic Charities

1319 F St., NW
Washington, DC 20009
(202) 639-8400

Organization: Your local church
Services: Many local churches and local denomination headquarters provide chore and shopping services, telephone reassurance, home-delivered-meals, transportation and escort services, and other assistance
For information: Contact your church pastor or the local headquarters of your denomination (see telephone directory) or your local council of churches (see telephone directory).

ALTERNATIVES TO HOME CARE

Eventually, most caregivers have to face the decision about finding an alternative to care in the home. Board and care homes and nursing homes are the two primary alternatives for people who need assistance with personal care.

Board and Care Homes

Board and care homes provide rooms on a rental basis along with meals, laundry services, and varying levels of personal care and supervision. These residences, which are also called rest homes or adult care homes, do not offer medical services but may have medical personnel on call.

Nationally, almost one million older adults live in board and care homes. The quality of the care ranges from excellent and caring to atrocious.

Nursing Homes

Nursing homes are residences that offer several levels of care:

- Skilled nursing facilities provide round-the-clock nursing supervision and related services. Medicare will only pay for care in a skilled nursing facility under limited circumstances.

- Intermediate care facilities provide personal care assistance and a more limited amount of nursing and medical care.

- Multilevel facilities provide both types of care under one roof.

Entering residents or their families normally can't choose the level of care. Rather, that determination is made by medical personnel. But both residents and their families can and should take great care in selecting the nursing home.

Evaluating a nursing home is complex. Fortunately, there are excellent resources available that make it easier to make an informed decision and to solve problems once a person is in residence. All of these resources are of great value in selecting a board and care home as well. Among them are:

Organization: State Nursing Home Licensure Offices

Services: These offices issue certifications for institutions that qualify for Medicare and Medicaid. They also inspect board and care homes and nursing homes to insure that they meet state regulations. Will supply copies of state regulations and certify that homes meet standards

For information: Call your state nursing home licensure office (see telephone directory under your state government listings or call your state government information service see listings, pages 441–443).

Organization: American Association of Homes for the Aging
1129 20th Street, NW, Suite 400
Washington, DC 20036
(202) 296-5960

Services: National association of nonprofit nursing homes and other organizations providing care for older persons. Through one of 37 state organizations, will provide a listing of facilities near you. Issues many publications, including:
- *Choosing a Nursing Home* (Free with self-addressed stamped envelope)
- *The Nursing Home and You: Partners in Caring for a Relative with Alzheimer's Disease* ($5.00)
- *The Nursing Home, Alzheimer's and You* (Free with self-addressed stamped envelope)
- *AAHA Directory of Members* (includes state associations and aging organizations, $6.00 to retirees, $12.00 to other individuals)

Organization: National Citizen's Coalition for Nursing Home Reform
1424 16th St. NW

Washington, DC 20005
(202) 797-0657

Services: Leading consumer organization devoted to the rights of nursing home residents. Publishes a monthly journal and other information about nursing home operations and reform. Provides information and referral to local organizations that assist people in choosing a nursing home and insuring quality care

Publication: *Health Care Financing Administration Nursing Home Survey*

Contains: HCFA evaluated 15,600 nursing homes to determine the quality of care, then issued reports listing deficiencies in each home, indicating which difficiencies were one-time or long-term, and reporting any enforcement action taken by government agencies. These reports were published in 93 volumes priced from $10 to $30. The appropriate volumes are available for inspection at:
- AARP Area Offices
- Your local Area Agency on Aging (see listings, pages 383–427)
- Your state nursing home ombudsman (call your state government information office, pages 441–443)

If you wish to purchase the volume covering nursing homes in your area, contact:

Superintendent of Documents
U.S. Government Printing Office
Washington, DC 20402
(202) 783-3238

Organization: Concerned Relatives of Nursing Home Patients
3130 Mayfield Road
Cleveland Heights, OH 44118
(216) 321-0403

Services: Provides information on nursing home placement and financial assistance, and channels complaints to the appropriate governmental agencies

Booklet: • *A Family's Guide to Selecting, Financing and Asserting Rights in a Nursing Home*
Cost: $8.00
Contains: Excellent guide to choosing a home and asserting rights
From: Center for Public Representation
520 University Avenue
Madison, WI 53703

Organization: American Health Care Association
1201 L St., NW
Washington, DC 20005
(202) 842-4444
Services: Federation of state associations of licensed nursing homes. Provides referral to state organizations and publishes a consumer's guide to selecting a nursing home

Organization: State Nursing Home Ombudsman
Services: The federal Older Americans Act mandated that all states establish a Nursing Home Ombudsman to act as an advocate for nursing home residents. This Ombudsman function is a part of the state agency on aging. In addition to acting as an advocate, many state agencies on aging have publications and referral services to help older residents and their families select long-term care facilities. Everyone should contact their state agency on aging before making a final decision on a facility
For information: Your state agency on aging (see listings, pages 383–427)

Publication: *Directory of Nursing Homes: A State-by-State Listing of Facilities*-Cost: $195.00, but available in many libraries
Contains: 1,280-page guide to nursing homes that includes information on accreditation, licensing, facilities, services, costs, and other information
From: Oryx Press
2214 North Central at Encanto
Phoenix, AZ 85004

Booklet: *Tips on Choosing a Long Term Care Facility*
Cost: $0.25 plus self-addressed stamped envelope
From: Council of Better Business Bureaus
4200 Wilson Blvd.
Arlington, VA 22203

Publication: *Nursing Home Care*
Cost: Free
From: U.S. Department of Health and Human Services
Health Care Financing Administration
Division of Long Term Care
Baltimore, MD 21207

Booklet: *A Checklist for Choosing a Nursing Home*
Cost: Free
From: Aetna Insurance Corporate Affairs
151 Farmington Avenue
Hartford, CT 06156
(203) 273-0123

Publications: • *Nursing Home Evaluation* ($1.00)
• *The Challenge of Choosing a Nursing Home* ($1.00)
• *Nursing Homes and How to Apply* ($0.50)

Send self-addressed stamped envelope
From: Children of Aging Parents
2761 Trenton Road
Levittown, PA 19056
(215) 945-6900

Booklet: *Nursing Home Life: A Guide for Residents and Families* (D13063)
Cost: Free
From: AARP Fulfillment
1909 K Street, NW
Washington, DC 20049

PREPARING FOR INCAPACITY

All caregivers and those they care for have to prepare for the fact that the caregiver might have to take the responsibility for making financial, medical, and other decisions. Planning is crucial, because incapacity may come suddenly, and along with it the need to use financial assets or make life and death medical decisions. Making such plans is vital for everyone in a caregiving or potential caregiving situation, especially for married couples with modest assets that would have to be used in an emergency.

Making Decisions for Others

There are several different ways in which a caregiver can assume part or all of the decision-making responsibility for another person.

Authorization gives a caregiver the right to act in one specific matter, such as access to a safe deposit box, signature rights on a checking account, or authorization to be notified if utility bills or mortgage payments are not taken care of on time. Generally, giving such authorization is simple and doesn't require the assistance of an attorney.

Power of attorney is the granting of the rights of one person to act as agent for another for one or more specific purposes, such as managing investments. Legally, however, a power of attorney requires that the person granting the power have the capacity to understand the decisions being made by the agent. So a power of attorney is invalidated should a person become incapacitated.

A *durable power of attorney* survives the incapacity of the person granting the power. Durable powers of attorney are legal in all 50 states. The advantage of a durable power of attorney is that an individual makes his or her own choice of who will make such decisions. In the absence of such a document, a court hearing is necessary to appoint a guardian or conservator. Because of their complexity, durable powers of attorney should be drawn up by an attorney. *Guardianship* or *conservatorship* refers to the appointment by a court of law of one person or persons to assume decision-making responsibility for another. Generally, *guardianship* is used to refer to the power to make decisions about personal and health care matters, while *conservatorship* refers to financial decision-making. The disadvantages are that the person who becomes incapacitated has no choice in the appointment and that the process can be expensive. The primary advantage is that the guardian is legally responsible to the court in the event of improper behavior.

A *living will* is a legal document that allows a person to make decisions about the level of medical care that will be provided in the event of terminal illness. Through a living will, a person can direct that no extraordinary measures be taken in the event of a terminal condition. Living wills are now legal in 36 states. In most states, residents can obtain a living will form that can be signed in the presence of witnesses without the assistance of an attorney. Because it is impossible to prepare for every medical eventuality, most experts recommend that a living will be combined with a durable power of attorney to insure compliance with the wishes of the patient.

It's vital for everyone to learn about these alternatives. Among the resources are:

Publication: *Taking Charge of the End of Your Life*
Cost: $7.00
From: Older Women's League
730 Eleventh Street, NW, Suite 300
Washington, DC 20001
(202) 783-6686

Book: *Decision-Making, Incapacity and the Elderly*
Cost: $34.95 plus $2.00 postage
Contains: A comprehensive guide to the subject, written for attorneys, as well as individuals
From: Legal Counsel for the Elderly
P.O. Box 19269-K
Washington, DC 20036

Booklet: *Tommorrow's Choices: Preparing Now for Future Legal, Financial and Health Care Decisions* (D13479)
Cost: Free
From: AARP Fulfillment
1909 K Street, NW
Washington, DC 20049

Publications: • *The Physician and the Hopelessly Ill Patient: Legal, Medical and Ethical Guidelines* ($5.00)
• *What You Should Know About Durable Power of Attorney* (Free)
From: Society for the Right to Die
250 West 57th Street
New York, NY 10107
(212) 246-6973

Organization: Concern for the Dying
Services: Provides information on living wills, forms for states in which living wills are legal, and assistance to people signing living wills and their families
For information: Concern for the Dying
250 West 57th Street
New York, NY 10107
(212) 246-6962

Booklet: *Health Care Powers of Attorney* (D13895)
Cost: Free
Contains: Sample legal forms and information prepared by AARP with the assistance of the American Bar Association
From: AARP Fulfillment
1909 K St., NW
Washington, DC 20049
Form: Values History Form
Institute of Public Law
1117 Stanford N.E.
Albuquerque, NM 87131
Cost: $3.00
Contains: A unique document prepared by the Institute of Public Law of the University of New Mexico. Part I includes space for listing the location of such important documents as powers of attorney and a living will. Part II consists of a series of questions that allow the individual to express his or her fundimental attitudes toward living, dying, suffering and death. These answers could be critically important if a living will is challenged in court.

After you are familiar with the alternatives, you should consult an attorney to insure that problems will be kept to a minimum. Although legal services can be expensive, there are a number of programs that provide free or low-cost legal services to older residents. For complete information, see pages 243–244.

If the Responsibility of Making Decisions Is Overwhelming . . .

Many caregivers don't feel that they have the time or the in-depth knowledge to assess the needs of the older person they are caring for and to make the best decisions based on those needs. These people can benefit from two special services provided by many public and private social service agencies:

- Professional assessment of the needs of an older or disabled person
- Professional case management, the assumption of responsibility for managing the overall care of an older or disabled person

The local area agencies on aging, your state agency on aging, or one of the other resources above can probably provide you with information about case management. An additional source of assistance and information in many states is:

Organization: Adult Protective Services Agency
Services: Most states have established this type of agency to assess the needs of an older person, particularly a person who lives alone. This agency may refer the older person to a case manager or may provide additional services, such as a temporary residence for recuperation after a hospital stay
For information: See your White Pages under your state government listing
or
Contact your state agency on aging (see listings, pages 383–427)

or
Call your state government information service (see listings, pages 441–443)

Because case managers who work for nonprofit organizations are often overwhelmed, an increasing number of people are hiring private geriatric care managers to supervise the care of a loved one. You can obtain a directory of private geriatric care managers from:

Organization: Aging Network Services
4400 East-West Highway
Bethesda, MD 20814
(301) 657-4329

Organization: National Association of Private Geriatric Care Managers
1315 Talbott Tower
Dayton, OH 45402
(513) 222-2621

You can also obtain a list of case managers from:

Publication: *List of Case Managers in Your State*
Cost: $1.00 plus self-addressed stamped envelope
From: Children of Aging Parents
2761 Trenton Road
Levittown, PA 19056
(215) 945-6900

An excellent source of information is:

Booklet: *Care Management: Arranging for Long Term Care* (D13803)
Cost: Free
From: AARP Fulfillment
1909 K St., NW
Washington, DC 20049

SUPPORT GROUPS FOR CAREGIVERS

Most caregivers find that caregiver support groups make all the difference in the world in managing their emotions and solving many practical problems. One source of information is:

Directory: *Care Sharing: A Directory of Geriatric Case Managers and Caregiver Support Groups*

Cost: $15.00

From: Children of Aging Parents
2761 Trenton Road
Levittown, PA 19056
(215) 945-6900

CHAPTER 20

THE MAJOR CRISES OF FAMILY LIFE

MARRIAGE AND FAMILY LIFE ARE THE foundations upon which many older Americans build their lives. This is why a crisis that rocks that foundation can be so catastrophic—emotionally, financially, even physically. However, domestic violence, divorce, and death of a spouse are so common that there are a large number of resources that provide vital information and support for people coping with these crises.

DOMESTIC VIOLENCE

Violence in the home is one of the most common and most tragic problems in America. It is also perhaps the least commonly reported crime. The result is that tens of millions of victims of violence continue to suffer unnecessarily. It is the moral and legal duty of everyone—victims, family members, neighbors, friends, and witnesses—to report abuse when it occurs.

Spouse Abuse

Surveys have shown that between 20% and 50% of American couples have suffered violence regularly in their marriages. Domestic vi-

olence occurs in relationships between people of all ages, including those in the normal retirement years. Although the vast majority of victims of this violence are women, the percentage of men who are victims increases with age.

The most tragic aspect of domestic violence is that the abused and battered spouse commonly fails to seek help out of feelings of fear, guilt, and shame. These feelings tend to be stronger in older Americans who were raised believing in male authority in marriage, and that marriages should be held together at all costs. The result is a pattern of violence that can continue for decades.

The most important step in breaking the pattern of domestic violence is to realize that spouse abuse is a crime. Absolutely no one deserves to be beaten. Every victim is entitled to protection. That protection can be provided by the following sources.

- The police: The majority of American police departments now treat spouse abuse as a serious crime. Every victim, and every witness to spouse abuse (family members, neighbors, etc.), has the right and the duty to call in law enforcement authorities. Such intervention is necessary, because very few batterers seek help on their own.

- Battered women's shelters: Most larger communities across the United States have shelters where battered women can seek refuge, financial and emotional support, and counseling.

- The courts: Battered spouses have the right to seek a court order of protection which makes it a crime for abusing spouses to enter their homes, workplaces, or to approach them in public.

Among the resources for information and assistance are:

Organization: Local battered women's shelter
For information: See White Pages under "Battered Women"
or
Call your local information and referral service (see listings, pages 434–443)
or
Your local police department

Publication: *Plain Talk About Wife Abuse* (Pub. No. 83-1265)
Cost: Free
From: Department of Health and Human Services
Public Health Service

Alcohol, Drug Abuse and Mental Health Administration
5600 Fishers Lane
Rockville, MD 20857

Organization: National Coalition Against Domestic Violence
P.O. Box 15127
Washington, DC 20003
(800) 333-7233
(202) 293-8860
Services: Clearinghouse for information and referral for victims of domestic violence. Can provide information on local services and shelters

Organization: Batterers Anonymous
1269 North E Street
San Bernardino, CA 92405
(714) 355-1100
Services: Self-help group for men who batter women, modeled on Alcoholics Anonymous

Elder Abuse

Abuse of older people by family members, domestic workers, institutional staff members, and others has become a major national problem. Studies have shown that as many as 10% of all elderly people suffer regular abuse.

The tragedy of this abuse is that the victims are often too weak, too ill, too confused, and too frightened to do anything. The only preventative measure is for everyone to be alert to signs of abuse of friends, family members, or neighbors—no matter what their economic or home circumstances. For more information:

Publications: *Domestic Mistreatment of the Elderly: Towards Prevention (D12810)*
Domestic Mistreatment of the Elderly: Some Do's and Don'ts (D12885)

Cost: Free
From: AARP Fulfillment
1909 K Street, NW
Washington, DC 20049

Cases of suspected abuse of older people can be reported to your state or local office of protective services. These agencies are charged with investigating possible abuse and intervening to provide alternative housing and other protective measures. To locate the protective services agency in your area, call your local area agency on aging (see listings, pages 383–427).

Child Abuse

Physical and sexual abuse of children is the third, and perhaps most terrible, common form of violence that can occur within families and other care situations. The consequences of such abuse can be so catastrophic to the victimized children that it is the responsibility of everyone—parent, grandparent, aunt or uncle, neighbor, teacher, or simply observer—to be alert to the signs of abuse and to take the proper course of action.

Most states and localities have established hotlines that people can call to report suspected cases of child abuse or mistreatment. These hotlines guarantee anonymity to the callers. To obtain the number for your area, check the White Pages, call your local police department, or call the national hotline below:

Hotline: ChildHelp National Child Abuse Hotline
(800) 422-4453
Services: Provides information and referral, including free publication, *Child Abuse and You*

For information about child abuse:

Organization: National Center on Child Abuse and Neglect
P.O. Box 1182
Washington, DC 20013
(202) 245-0586
Services: This office of the federal Department of Health and Human Services provides information, statistics, and referrals to local agencies

Organization: National Committee for the Prevention of Child Abuse
332 S. Michigan Avenue, Suite 950
Chicago, IL 60604
(312) 663-3520
Services: National clearinghouse for information and services to abused children and abusing parents. Publishes dozens of valuable booklets and books, and provides a free catalog of these publications

Booklet: *Take Time Out to Be a Better Parent and Prevent Child Abuse*
Cost: Free
From: The National Exchange Club Foundation for the Prevention of Child Abuse
3050 Central Avenue
Toledo, OH 43606

If You, or a Relative or Friend, Become a Victim

Becoming a victim of any type of crime is a traumatic experience, even if significant injury or loss is not involved. Fortunately, there has been an explosion in the number of resources that can help victims emotionally, practically, and financially since 1975. The most important resource is:

Organization: Victim Service Program
Services: There are over 5,000 victim service programs nationwide that pro-

vide a wide variety of services to crime victims and their families

For information: Call your local police department

or

See the White Pages

or

National Organization for Victim Assistance
717 D Street, NW
Washington, DC 20004
(202) 393-6682

DIVORCE

The U.S. Census Bureau has estimated that more than half of all marriages involving people now in their forties will eventually end in divorce. Divorce can produce two basic types of problems: the first are the legal and financial problems caused by the divorce process, as well as the process of setting up two independent households; the second is dealing with the emotional problems that inevitably come with the end of a marriage.

Legal and Financial Resources

Couples in the process of divorce have two basic options for working out a divorce settlement and obtaining the court decree.

- Each party can hire an attorney to do the negotiating and file for divorce. This option is effective, but often expensive, especially for women without employment income. Chapter 16 contains information on obtaining free or low-cost legal services.

- The couple obtains the services of an impartial mediator to reach a settlement. Using a mediator is much faster and much less expensive than hiring attorneys, if both people involved submit the disputes in good faith. For information about mediation:

Organization: The Academy of Family Mediators
P.O. Box 10501
Eugene, OR 97440
(503) 345-1205
Services: Provides referral to mediators who meet its strict standards

Organization: American Arbitration Association
140 West 51st Street
New York, NY 10020
(212) 484-4000
Services: Provides services described in free brochure, *Family Mediation Rules*

Coping with the emotional impact of divorce can be easier with the help of a good therapist. We have included detailed information on finding help in Chapter 15 (Mental Health). Another source of referral is:

Organization: American Association for Marriage and Family Therapy
1717 K Street, NW, Suite 407
Washington, DC 20006
(202) 429-1825
Services: Will provide referrals to member therapists who specialize in the problems connected with divorce (send self-addressed stamped envelope)

Support groups can also play a crucial role in coping. These groups include:

Organization: Displaced Homemakers
Network
1411 K St., NW
Suite 930
Washington, DC 20005
(202) 628-6767
Services: A coalition of local groups that
provides a wide range of information
and services for women who are on
their own

Organization: Older Women's League
730 Eleventh St., NW
Washington, DC 20001
(202) 783-6686
Services: Through local chapters, provides
information, support groups, and services

Organization: Women's Legal Defense
Fund
2000 P Street, NW, Suite 400
Washington, DC 20036
(202) 887-0364
Services: Provides information and publications on women's legal problems, including those associated with divorce

Publication: *Divorce After 50: Challenges
and Choices* (D12909)
Cost: Free
From: AARP
1909 K Street, NW
Washington, DC 20049

Organization: Parents Without Partners
8807 Colesville Rd.
Silver Spring, MD 20916
(301) 588-9354
Services: A self-help group for single parents
of both sexes

Organization: North American Conference
of Separated and Divorced Catholics
1100 S. Goodman Street
Rochester, NY 14620
(716) 271-1320
Services: A self-help group open to people
of all religions that has over 3,000
local groups

Organization: National Organization for
Men
381 Park Avenue South
New York, NY 10016
(212) 686-6253
Services: Newsletter, local support groups,
and information for men going
through divorces

One of the most difficult problems associated with divorce is the plight of grandparents who are denied visitation rights with their
grandchildren. One group that provides information and support is:

Organization: Grandparents'   Children's
Rights
5728 Bayonne Avenue
Haslett, MI 48840
(517) 339-8663

DEATH OF A SPOUSE

Census Bureau statistics also show that nine
out of 10 women will be widowed during their
lifetime. The death of a spouse can be an extremely traumatic event. Many of the support
groups that help divorced women also have information of interest to widows and widowers.

There are, however, a number of special resources to deal with these special problems.

Coping with the death of a spouse is eased
by proper preparation. The first step in that
preparation is estate planning, including the
preparation of a will.

Estate Planning

All experts strongly urge everyone to have an up-to-date will, especially people age 50 and over. Yet two thirds of all Americans still die without having completed a will, an oversight that often creates serious problems and conflicts for their heirs.

One reason many people fail to make a will is that they believe it is complicated and expensive. However, free or low-cost help in completing a will is available in many parts of the country. For information, contact your local area agency on aging. For more information on obtaining legal services, see Chapter 16.

Among the other important resources you can consult are:

> **Book:** *The Essential Guide to Wills, Estates, Trusts and Death Taxes*
> **Cost:** $12.95 (AARP member price $9.95) plus $1.75 postage
> **Contains:** A 261-page guide to all areas of this important subject

> **Book:** *Legal Rights Late in Life*
> **Cost:** $13.95 (AARP member price $10.35) plus $1.75 postage
> **Contains:** Very useful information on wills, probate, and planning for incapacity
> **Both From:** AARP Books/Scott, Foresman and Co.
> 1865 Miner Street
> Des Plaines, IL 60016

Funeral Planning

After the death of a spouse, the first task that must be faced is planning a funeral and burial. As with every other aspect of the last stages of life, funeral planning is best begun well in advance. At the very least, older persons and their families should acquaint themselves with the general subject and prepare for the decision-making process.

The first important step in funeral planning is to understand that in response to many complaints about deceptive funeral practices, the Federal Trade Commission instituted a funeral industry trade regulation in 1984. Among other things, that regulation requires that:

- All funeral providers must give detailed price information over the telephone, allowing comparison shopping
- All funeral providers must give you a detailed written price list
- All funeral providers may not falsely state that embalming is required by law and must disclose in writing that you have the right to choose alternatives, such as direct burial or cremation
- All funeral providers must disclose in writing any charges for arranging purchases, such as flowers, newspaper obituaries, etc.
- All funeral providers may not tell you that state or local law requires purchase of a casket for cremation
- All funeral providers must disclose in writing that you have the right to choose only the funeral goods and services you want
- All funeral providers must give you an itemized statement of all charges after you make your selection of products and services

For further information or to register complaints:

> **Publication:** *Consumer Guide to the FTC Funeral Rule*
> **Cost:** Free
> **From:** Federal Trade Commission
> Bureau of Consumer Protection
> Washington, DC 20580

Most states also have a licensing board that regulates the funeral industry, issues state regulations, and handles complaints. To locate the board in your state, see the White Pages under your state government listing, call your state information service office (see listings, pages 441–443), or contact:

Organization: Conference of Funeral Service Examining Boards
520 E. Van Trees Street
P.O. Box 497
Washington, IN 47501
(812) 254-7887

Among the other important sources of information about funeral planning are:

Book: *It's Your Choice*
Cost: $4.95 (AARP member price $3.00) plus $1.75 postage
Contains: A complete manual of funeral planning
From: AARP Books/Scott, Foreman and Co.
1865 Miner Street
Des Plaines, IL 60016
Brochure: *Prepaying Your Funeral: Some Questions to Ask*
Cost: Free
From: AARP Fulfillment
1909 K Street, NW
Washington, DC 20049

Organization: National Funeral Directors Association
Services: This association has two important consumer services. First, it issues a wide variety of free publications, including:
- *Anatomical Gifts*
- *Cremation*
- *Death Away from Home*
- *Easing the Burden*
- *Embalming*

- *Funerals Are for the Living*
- *Funeral Costs*
- *Funeral Etiquette*
- *Grief*
- *Helping Groups*
- *In Service of Others*
- *Living When Your Spouse Has Died*
- *Living with Dying*
- *Suicide*
- *The Traditional Funeral*
- *A Way to Remember*
- *What Are My Options?*
- *What Can I Do to Help?*
- *When Death Occurs*
- *When Your Parent Dies*
- *Will I Ever Stop Hurting?*

The second service is the Funeral Service Consumer Arbitration Board, which mediates disputes between individuals and funeral providers
For publications: NFDA Learning Resources Center
1121 West Oklahoma Avenue
Milwaukee, WI 53227
(414) 541-2500
For arbitration: Funeral Service Consumer Arbitration Program
P.O. Box 27641
Milwaukee, WI 53227
(800) 662-7666

Organization: Cremation Association of North America
111 East Wacker Drive
Chicago, IL 60601
(312) 644-6610
Services: Provides the following publications ($0.50 along with self-addressed stamped envelope)
- *Cremation Explained*
- *Choices to Make Now for the Future*
- *Cremation Is Not the End*
- *So You've Chosen Cremation*
- *Cremation Memorials*

Organization: Continental Association of Funeral and Memorial Societies
2001 S. Street, NW, Suite 530
Washington, DC 20009
(202) 745-0634

Services: Disseminates information about alternatives for funeral planning. Provides information and referral to "memorial societies," nonprofit groups that arrange for low-cost funeral services to members

Organization: The U.S. Department of Veterans Affairs

Services: All veterans of military service are entitled to a burial plot in a federal cemetery, a marker for the grave, and an American flag for the casket. The families of all deceased veterans are also eligible for a small burial allowance

For information: National Cemetary System
Department of Veterans Affairs
810 Vermont Ave., NW
Washington, DC 20420
(202) 233-5012

How to Arrange for Organ and Tissue Donations

A growing number of people believe that the best memorial is a donation of usable organs, tissues, and bodies for transplant and medical research. For information and organ donor cards:

Organization: The Living Bank
P.O. Box 7625
Houston, TX 77005
(800) 528-2971 (Ex. TX)
(713) 528-2971

Support for the Surviving Spouse

Among the resources for widowed persons are:

Organization: Widowed Persons Service
AARP
1909 K Street, NW
Washington, DC 20049

Services: Social outreach and support service for widows and widowers organized by AARP

Publication: *On Being Alone: A Guide for Widowed Persons* (D150)
Cost: Free
From: AARP
1909 K Street, NW
Washington, DC 20049

Publication: *Final Details: A Guide for Survivors When Death Occurs*
Cost: Free
Contains: Four-page fact sheet for each of the 50 states, prepared by AARP
From: AARP
1909 K Street, NW
Washington, DC 20049

Publications: • *Survival Handbook for Widows* ($6.95, AARP member price, $4.95 plus $1.75 postage)
• *Alone—Not Lonely; Independent Living for Women Over Fifty* ($6.95, AARP member price $4.95 plus $1.75 postage)
From: AARP Books/Scott Foresman and Co.
1865 Miner Street
Des Plaines, IL 60016

Publication: *What Do You Do Now?*
Cost: $1.30
From: Life Insurance Marketing and Research Association

P.O. Box 208
Hartford, CT 06141

Organization: The Theos Foundation
Penn Hills Mall
Suite 410

Pittsburgh, PA 15235
(412) 243-4299

Services: Referral to local sources of financial and emotional counseling for widows and widowers

CHAPTER 21

COPING WITH A HANDICAP OR DISABILITY

AT ANY GIVEN TIME, APPROXIMATELY 37 million Americans have some physical or emotional problem that limits their ability to lead a normal life. Approximately 13.5 million Americans, 7% of the population, have a severely limiting handicap or disability. A wide range of conditions, diseases, and injuries can be the cause of these limitations, such as arthritis, stroke, heart disease, paralysis, amputation, multiple sclerosis, Parkinson's disease, brain tumors or disease, burns, fractures, major surgery, hearing loss, blindness, and chronic pain. Since incidence of many of these conditions and diseases increases dramatically with age, more older people must cope with a disability or handicap than those in any other age group.

When many people hear the words "handicapped" or "disabled," they tend to think of people in wheelchairs, amputees, or the blind. In truth, however, a handicap or disability is any condition that makes it difficult to perform any normal everyday activity, from walking up stairs to turning a doorknob. People who don't understand this broader definition may never think of turning to resources that can greatly improve the quality of their lives. For example, special adaptive living products, including clothing, makes it possible for many people to continue living independently who would otherwise need assistance from others in a group residence. Similarly, special travel tours and services open new vistas for people who have avoided traveling for a wide variety of reasons ranging from difficulty reading airport signs to problems packing and handling luggage.

Previously in this book, we have discussed two very important aspects of dealing with a handicap or disability:

- Finding and paying for the very best medical care

- Taking advantage of all the information, resources, and support programs dealing with the specific medical disorders

There are, however, many other general resources that can provide information, services, financial assistance, products, and emotional support to people with handicaps or disabilities, no matter what the cause.

GENERAL SOURCES OF INFORMATION

Many sources of information and support are available from the federal government, state and local governments, and the private sector. Among the federal resources are:

Booklet: *Pocket Guide to Federal Help for Individuals with Disabilities*
Cost: $1.00
Contains: A 26-page guide to federal assistance programs for people with disabilities
From: Consumer Information Center
P.O. Box 100
Pueblo, CO 81009

Organization: Clearinghouse on the Handicapped
Switzer Building, Room 3132
330 C Street, SW
Washington, DC 20202
(202) 732-1244
Services: Central referral and information source for all types of handicaps. Provides information on federal benefits, funding, and legislation, as well as making referrals to federal, state, local, and nonprofit agencies and organizations

Organization: National Rehabilitation Information Center
8455 Colesville Road, Suite 935
Silver Spring, MD 20910
(800) 346-2742 (Ex. MD)
(301) 588-9284
Services: Provides information on disability-related research, resources, and products for independent living. Produces fact sheets, resource guides, a quarterly newsletter, and technical publications

Organization: U.S. Department of Veterans Affairs

Services: Provides a wide variety of programs to individuals with disabilities and handicaps that are related to military service
For information: Your local VA office (see White Pages under "U.S. Government, Veterans Department")
or
U.S. Department of Veterans Affairs
810 Vermont Ave., NW
Washington, DC 20420
(202) 233-2567

All states have coordinated programs of vocational rehabilitation and independent living to help individuals with disabilities become employable, independent, and integrated into the community. The federal government provides significant funding for these programs, but each state determines the specific way funds are allocated, the specific services provided, and the specific eligibility requirements. For information, contact your state vocational rehabilitation office (see your telephone directory under your state government listings or call your state government information office, see listings on pages 441–443).

Local governments provide a wide variety of other programs for older Americans with handicaps or disabilities. For information on these programs, contact your local Area Agency on Aging or your local Senior Center.

Among the many private sources of information, referral, and services for people with all kinds of handicaps and disabilities are:

Directory: *Directory of Organizations Interested in People with Disabilities*
Cost: Free
Contains: A listing of services, addresses, and telephone numbers of 100 organizations

From: Disabled American Veterans
807 Maine Ave., SW
Washington, DC 20024
(202) 554-3501

Resource: ABLEDATA

Services: A computerized database which references more than 15,000 products for people with disabilities. Information can be obtained by a toll-free call

For information: Adaptive Equipment Center
Newington Children's Hospital
181 East Cedar Street
Newington, CT 06111
(800) 344-5404

Organization: Information Center for Individuals with Disabilities
Ft. Point 19
27-43 Wormwood St.
Boston, MA 02210
(617) 727-5540
(800) 462-5015 (MA)

Services: Provides information on programs and resources sponsored by governments on all levels, as well as private groups. Provides detailed information on important aspects of daily living with a handicap, such as travel, recreation, and personal care

Organization: Accent on Information
Box 700
Bloomington, IL 61702
(309) 378-2961

Services: Accent is an extraordinarily valuable information source for people with all kinds of disabilities and handicaps. Accent has three types of services:

- Accent on Information is a computer retrieval service that accesses a database consisting of independent living aids, assistive devices, and how-to information on dressing, clothing, eating, arts and crafts,

and many other areas of life. A nominal fee is charged for each computer search

Accent on Living Magazine ($6.00 per year) is a quarterly publication containing up-to-date information and articles for the disabled

Accent Special Publications:

- *Ideas for Making Your Home Accessible* ($6.50 plus $0.95 shipping)
- *Recreation and Sports* ($4.95 plus $0.95 shipping)
- *Wheelchairs and Accessories* ($7.50 plus $0.95 shipping)
- *Going Places in Your Own Vehicle* ($6.50 plus $0.95 shipping)
- *Traveling Like Everybody Else* ($11.95 plus $0.95 shipping)
- *Aging with a Disability* ($26.95 plus $1.35 shipping)
- *Earning a Living* ($9.50 plus $0.95 shipping)
- *Sexual Adjustment: A Guide for the Spinal Cord Injured* ($4.95 plus $0.95 shipping)
- *Accent Buyer's Guide* ($10.00 plus $0.95 shipping)

Organization: National Easter Seal Society

Services: Nonprofit organization that provides information, referrals, and support to people with disabilities from any cause. Supports over 200 rehabilitation facilities through its local chapters. Issues numerous publications

For information: Your local Easter Seal Society (see White Pages)
or
National Easter Seal Society
70 E. Lake St.
Chicago, IL 60601
(312) 726-6200

Organization: National Association of the Physically Handicapped

76 Elm Street
London, OH 43140
(614) 852-1664

Services: Self-help organization for the physically handicapped with local chapters throughout the United States. Activities range from social to employment to lobbying for new legislation

Organization: Learning How
P.O. Box 35481
Charlotte, NC 28235
(704) 376-4735

Services: 140 local chapters provide self-help and mutual support for physical handicapped adults

Organization: United Together
3111 Haworth Hall
Lawrence, KS 66045
(913) 864-4950

Services: Acts as advocacy, information, and referral service for those with physical and mental disabilities

Organization: National Shut-In Society
P.O. Box 986, Village Station
New York, NY 10014
(212) 222-7699

Services: Offers a national network by which chronically ill and housebound people communicate with each other by letter and tape

Organization: Catholics United for Spiritual Action
176 West 8th Street
Bayonne, NJ 07002
(201) 437-0412

Services: National organization, open to people of all faiths, that organizes communication between the handicapped and chronically ill

Organization: Gazette International Networking Institute

4502 Maryland Avenue
St. Louis, MO 63108
(314) 361-0475

Services: Provides information and publications for people with many physical disabilities. Publishes *Rehabilitation Gazette* and organizes independent living conferences

Organization: American Physical Therapy Association
1111 North Fairfax Street
Alexandria, VA 22314
(703) 684-2782

Services: Provides referrals to physical therapists. Publishes numerous bibliographies and resource guides for people with a wide variety of physical handicaps and disabilities

Organization: Disabled American Veterans (DAV)
807 Maine Avenue, SW
Washington, DC 20024
(202) 554-3501

Services: Trained professionals in 68 local offices assist disabled veterans in filing for benefits and programs. The DAV also acts as an advocate for the disabled, and provides support and services

The special resources for people with spinal cord injuries and others who use wheelchairs are:

Book: *Spinal Network: The Total Resource for the Wheelchair Community*
Cost: $24.95
Contains: This comprehensive resource guide has been called "a Whole Earth catalog for a disabled person." The book contains not only resource lists, but personal profiles, cartoons, illustrations, and articles about every area of life from sports to sex and romance

From: Spinal Network
P.O. Box 4162
Boulder, CO 80306
(800) 338-5412 (Ex. CO)
(303) 449-5412

Organization: National Spinal Cord Injury
Association
600 W. Cummings Park
Woburn, MA 01801
(617) 935-2722
Services: Major source of information, referral, and services to people with spinal cord injuries or diseases. Sponsors
research and acts as advocate for
people who use wheelchairs for mobility. Publishes national resource directory

Organization: American Paralysis Association
500 Morris Ave.
Springfield, NJ 07081
(800) 225-0292 (Ex. NJ)
(201) 379-2690
Services: Supports research into central nervous system injuries and disorders.
Publishes a newsletter, fact sheets,
and research summaries. Provides
support and services through local
chapters

Organization: Spinal Cord Society
2410 Lakeview Dr.
Fergus Falls, MN 56537
(218) 739-5252
Services: Provides information and referral
to patients and their families through
a toll-free hotline

Organization: Paralyzed American Veterans
801 18th Street, NW
Washington, DC 20006
(202) 872-1300
Services: Through local chapters, provides
self-help and support for paralyzed

veterans and their families. Especially
active in sports and recreation programs for wheelchair users

An organization that focuses on the problems of amputees is:

Organization: National Amputation Foundation
12-45 150th Street
Whitestone, NY 11357
(718) 767-0596
Services: National nonprofit organization
that provides information and services to all amputees. Maintains a
center for the manufacture and repair
of prosthetic devices. Arranges visits
to new amputees from amputees who
have adjusted to their handicap. Issues numerous publications, including:
• *Handbook for Lower Extremity
Amputees* ($6.00)
• *Single Handed for Arm Amputees*
($4.00)
• *A Manual for Below-Knee Amputees* ($3.00)
• *A Manual for Above-Knee Am-
putees* ($3.00)
• *Things to Know About Amputa-
tion and Artificial Limbs* ($1.00)
• *What to Expect When You Lose a
Limb* ($3.00)
• *On the Road to Recovery* ($1.00)
• *List of Major Handicapped Sports
Organizations and Resources*
(Free)

Resources for people who use ventilators
are:

Organization: International Ventilator
Users Network
4502 Maryland Avenue
St. Louis, MO 63108
(314) 361-0475
Dues: $5.00 per year for ventilator

users, $15.00 for health professionals
Services: Publishes a biannual newsletter and sponsors conferences

Publication: *Rehabilitation Gazette: International Journal of Independent Living by Individuals with Disabilities*
Cost: $15 per year for individuals, $20 for institutions
Contains: Wide variety of articles and resources for every aspect of living independently while using ventilators

From: Rehabilitation Gazette
4502 Maryland Avenue
St. Louis, MO 63108
(314) 361-0475

Suppliers: List of equipment manufacturers and distributors of ventilators and accessories
Cost: Free with self-addressed stamped envelope
From: IPN
4502 Maryland Avenue
St. Louis, MO 63108
(314) 361-0475

COMPUTER ASSISTANCE FOR THE DISABLED

Computers can be of enormous value to disabled or handicapped people. The value of a computer ranges from making communication possible for people who are paralyzed to opening up communication lines with people all over the country for people who spend a great deal of their time at home.

Important sources of information are:

Organization: Apple Computer Office of Special Education
20525 Mariani Avenue
Cupertino, CA 95014
(408) 996-1010
Services: Maintains a database describing thousands of adaptive devices, software programs, disability organizations, publications, and networks. Will send computer resource guide "Connections"

Organization: IBM National Support Center for Persons with Disabilities
P.O. Box 2150
Atlanta, GA 30055
(800) 426-2133

Services: Maintains information on how computers can help people with disabilities at home, in the work place, and in education. Operates a discount purchase program for the disabled. Makes referrals to other organizations

Organization: Technical Aids and Assistance for the Disabled Center
16630 Beverly
Tinley Park, IL 60477
Services: Assists people with severe disabilities to gain access to computer technology. Operates computer bulletin board, lends equipment, and provides information and counseling

Organization: Center for Computer Assistance to the Disabled
2501 Avenue J, Suite 100
Arlington, TX 76006
Services: Provides information and publishes free newsletter

Publication: Computer Disability News
National Easter Seal Society
70 E. Lake St.

Chicago, IL 60601
(312) 726-6202
Cost: $15.00 per year for 4 issues
Contains: Information on new software and hardware, lists of resources, interviews, book reviews, and other articles of interest to people with disabilities and their families

Newspaper: *Closing the Gap*
P.O. Box 68
Henderson, MN 56044
Cost: $6 per year for 12 issues
Contains: Wide variety of articles help people with disabilities who use computers

EMPLOYMENT OPPORTUNITIES

Holding a job provides not only income, but a feeling of self-worth and satisfaction. Many people with physical and mental disabilities can and do hold jobs. Most of the general resources listed above provide information on vocational rehabilitation and job placement.

One primary source of specific help for handicapped job seekers is the more than 2,000 local state Employment Service offices. Each of these offices is mandated by law to employ a specially trained person to work with disabled people and, when necessary, to refer them to other agencies to get all the help they need. To locate the office nearest you, look in the White Pages under your state government listings.

Another source of information is:

Organization: Job Accommodation Network
West Virginia University
809 Allen Hall
P.O. Box 6122
Morgantown, WV 26506
(800) 526-7234 (Ex. WV)
(800) 526-4698
Services: National information network for handicapped job seekers and employers who want to hire the disabled

Other important resources are:

Organization: President's Commission on the Employment of People with Disabilities
1111 20th Street, NW, Room 636
Washington, DC 20210
(202) 653-5044
Services: Publishes a newsletter, *Disability USA,* and provides other information about the employment of the handicapped

Organization: Human Resources Center
I.U. Willets Road
Albertson, NY 11507
(516) 747-5400
Services: A nonprofit organization that was a pioneer in the education and rehabilitation of people with disabilities. Conducts many information and training programs, as well as organizing and Industry-Labor Council of over 100 major corporations and unions that work to develop job opportunities for the disabled

One major employer that makes a special effort to open doors for the disabled is the federal government. For the location of the nearest Federal Job Center, call the nearest Federal Information Center (see listings, pages 439–441). State and local governments also have their own civil service systems. For information on state and local government jobs, consult the specialist at your local state employment service office.

A private resource is:

Organization: Goodwill Industries
Services: Provides vocational rehabilitation, vocational evaluation and assessment, adjustment services, skills training, and job placement
For information: Your local Goodwill Industries (see White Pages)
or
Goodwill Industries of America
9200 Wisconsin Avenue

Bethesda, MD 20814
(301) 530-6500

Handicapped individuals interested in going into business for themselves may qualify for loans and other assistance from the Small Business Administration (SBA). For information, contact your local SBA Office (see listings, pages 258–259), or write:

Small Business Administration
Director, Office of Business Loans
1441 L Street, NW
Washington, DC 20416

SPORTS AND RECREATION

Sports and recreation are as important in the lives of people with disabilities and impairments as they are in the lives of other Americans. Many recreation and sports programs are conducted through and by the general resources listed above, as well by senior centers and local area agencies on aging. Also, many of the sports, recreation, and hobbyist groups listed in Section Four of this book also have programs of interest to disabled persons. Finally, some local parks and recreation departments offer special programs and trips.

A large number of other organizations conduct special programs and competitions:

Organization: Special Recreation Digest
362 Koser Avenue
Iowa City, IA 52240
Cost: $39.95 per year for 4 issues
Contains: Exhaustive coverage of resources, information, funding, and all other aspects of special recreation. Subscribers have access to a comprehensive library and database of information. The organization also publishes:

Special Recreation Compendium of 1,500 Resources for the Disabled ($49.95), a comprehensive 500-page directory of national and international programs

Organization: National Therapeutic Recreation Society
3101 Park Center Drive, 12th Floor
Alexandria, VA 22302
(703) 820-4940
Services: Provides information and referrals to recreational facilities, programs, and resources, as well as referrals to local recreational therapists

Organization: National Handicapped Sports and Recreation Association
1145 19th Street, NW
Washington, DC 20036
(301) 652-7505
Services: Through local chapters, sponsors and promotes physical fitness, sports, and indoor recreation programs for people with physical limitations

Organization: American Alliance for
Health, Physical Education, Recreation and Dance Programs for the
Handicapped
1900 Association Drive
Reston, VA 22091
(703) 476-3400
Services: Coordinates many leisure, recreation, and physical fitness programs
for people with special needs

Directory: Sports Organizations and Resources
Contains: A free directory of sports organizations and sources of special sports
equipment for the disabled, including
modifications for bicycles, boats, skis,
and other kinds of equipment
From: National Amputation Foundation
12-45 150th Street
Whitestone, NY 11357
(718) 767-0596

Organization: Office of Special Constituencies
National Endowment for the Arts
110 Pennsylvania Avenue, NW
Washington, DC 20506
Services: Acts as advocates and provides
funding for arts programs aimed at
special constituencies, including the
handicapped. Provides resource lists
of programs and organizations

Organization: Access to Recreation, Inc.
2509 E. Thousand Oaks Blvd., Suite
430
Thousand Oaks, CA 91362
(800) 634-4351 (Ex. CA)
(805) 498-7535
Services: Acts as a clearinghouse on recreational equipment adapted for use by
those with physical limitations. Publishes mail-order catalog

TRAVEL

People with every kind of handicap or disability
want to lead as normal a life as possible. Part
of a normal life is the ability to travel—for business, for family reunions or emergencies, and
for recreation. Today, new designs of buildings
and vehicles, as well as new regulations requiring attention to the special needs of disabled
people, have opened the door more widely to
travel. Unfortunately, few travel agents are
well-versed in travel for the handicapped. As a
result, disabled people and their families have
to educate themselves through the following
resources.

The first step in making travel easier is to
consult general publications, including:

Book: *Access to the World: A Travel Guide
for the Handicapped* by Louise
Weiss

Cost: $8.95
Contains: A treasure trove of vital informa-
tion that belongs on every bookshelf
From: Facts-on-File, Inc.

Books: *Travel for the Disabled: A Hand-
book of Travel Resources and 500
Worldwide Access Guides Directory
of Travel Agencies for the Disabled
Wheelchair Vagabonds*
Cost: $14.95 per book plus $2.00 shipping
and handling
From: The Disability Bookshop
P.O. Box 129
Vancouver, WA 98666

Book: *The Physically Disabled Traveler's
Guide*
Cost: $11.95

Contains: 167-page guide to travel agencies, specialized tours, associations, access guides, and camps
From: Resource Directories
3103 Executive Parkway, Suite 212
Toledo, OH 43606
(419) 536-5353

Book: *International Directory of Access Guides*
Cost: $5.00
Contains: A directory of access guides for the handicapped to many travel systems, cities, attractions, parks, hotels, and other places in the United States, Canada, and 21 other countries
From: Rehabilitation International Access Guide Directory
1123 Broadway, Suite 704
New York, NY 10010

Publication: *Travel Information Packet*
Cost: $5.00
Contains: Lists of tour operators, agencies, books and access guides for physically limited travelers
From: LTD Travel
116 Harbor Seal Court
San Mateo, CA 94404

Booklet: *A List of Guidebooks for Handicapped Travelers*
Cost: Free
From: President's Committee on Employment of the Handicapped
1111 20th Street, NW, Room 636
Washington, DC 20210

Organization: Travel Information Service
Moss Rehabilitation Hospital
12th Street and Tabor Road
Philadelphia, PA 19141
(215) 329-5715
Service: For a modest fee, this nonprofit service will furnish information to the disabled about hotels, motels, cruise ships, airlines, historical sites, resorts,

and other locations in the United States and around the world

Newsletter: *LTD Travel Newsletter*
116 Harbor Seal Court
San Mateo, CA 94404
Cost: $15.00 per year for 4 issues
Contains: Tips, information, services, and personal experiences of disabled travelers

Newsletter: *The Itinerary*
P.O. Box 1084
Bayonne, NJ 07002
Cost: $9.00 per year for 6 issues
Contains: Covers destinations and tours for disabled travelers

Organization: Braille Institute Press
Braille Institute
741 N. Vermont Avenue
Los Angeles, CA 90029
(213) 663-1111
Services: Publishes guidebooks in braille for blind travelers

Travel Agencies and Tour Operators

A number of travel agencies and tour operators specialize in arranging travel for people with all kinds of disabilities or handicaps. An organization of such agencies and operators that will provide information is:

Organization: Society for the Advancement of Travel for the Handicapped (SATH)
26 Court Street
Brooklyn, NY 11242
(718) 858-5483
Services: Provides referral to travel agencies and tour operators, as well as information about accessibility and facilities. Send self-addressed stamped envelope

Another excellent source of information is:

Organization: Mobility International
P.O. Box 3551
Eugene, OR 97403
(503) 343-1284

Services: Offers a wide range of international exchange programs and other travel and education programs for the disabled. Publishes quarterly newsletter and has other membership benefits

HOME HEALTH CARE AND INDEPENDENT LIVING PRODUCTS

In the last few decades, rehabilitation engineers have produced a vast array of new products for use by people with physical disabilities and limitations. We have listed above a number of resources that will identify such products, particularly ABLEDATA and the catalog issued by Access. Many disabled people and their families who don't have a specific idea of their needs find it useful to leaf through catalogs of these products to see the variety available and order directly. Among the major catalog companies are:

Fred Sammons, Inc.
145 Tower Drive
Burr Ridge, IL 60521
(800) 323-5547

J.A. Preston Corp
60 Page Road

Clifton, NJ 07012
(800) 631-7277 (Ex. NJ)
(201) 777-2700

Abbey Medical Catalogue
933 E. Sandhill Avenue
Carson, CA 90746
(800) 421-5126 (Ex. CA)
(800) 262-1294 (CA)

Cleo Living Aids
3957 Mayfield Road
Cleveland, OH 44121
(800) 321-0595 (Ex. OH)
(800) 222-2536 (OH)

Prentke Romich Co.
RD 2, Box 191
Shreve, OH 44676
(216) 567-2001

Living a Rich, Rewarding Life

In the first three sections of this book, we have discussed every aspect of personal finance, health, and the common problems and crises of everyday life. But adequate income, good health, and the ability to handle problems do not, in and of themselves, make for a rich, happy, productive life. Rather, the quality of all of our lives tends to depend on how we use our financial resources, physical abilities, and the hours available to us.

In this section of the book, we will discuss activities and resources that enrich our hours, days, months, and years. This section includes educational programs of all types, participating in sports, spectator sports, travel, hobbies, and other leisure-time activities. These activities are, more than anything else, what makes our lives rich, full, and rewarding.

EDUCATIONAL OPPORTUNITIES

MORE THAN 10 MILLION ADULTS AGE 50 and older, many of whom have been out of the classroom for decades, are turning to education for self-fulfillment, for career advancement or preparation for a new career, or simply for entertainment and recreation. The range of educational opportunities for adults includes programs that allow you to:

- Learn to read and obtain a high school degree
- Advance in your career or start a new career
- Pursue a college degree
- Explore new interests and hobbies
- Combine education with travel in the United States and abroad

Two excellent general resources for adults interested in education of all types are:

Organization: Institute of Lifetime Learning

Services: This division of AARP promotes opportunities for older persons to continue to learn, prepare for new careers, and become involved in new technologies. Serves as a resource center for specific questions. Publishes the following free publications:
- *Learning Opportunities for Older Persons*
- *College Centers for Older Learners*

For information: Institute of Lifetime Learning
AARP 1909 K Street, NW
Washington, DC 20049
For publications: AARP Fulfillment
1909 K Street, NW
Washington, DC 20049

Book: *New Horizons: The Education and Career Planning Guide for Adults*
Cost: $8.95 plus $1.75 postage
From: Peterson's Guides
P.O. Box 2123
Princeton, NJ 08543

LITERACY AND HIGH SCHOOL DEGREE PROGRAMS

Many older Americans had to drop out of school in their teens to help their families economically. As a result, according to the National Center for Education Statistics, 36% of Americans age 55 and over do not have a high school diploma, and one in five older Americans is functionally illiterate. Fortunately, there are a number of excellent programs available to people, who are near or in their retirement years, which can open the world of reading and lead to the proud achievement of a high school diploma.

Learning How to Read

It's never to late to learn how to read. Many communities have formal literacy programs staffed by older volunteers who understand the difficulties faced by older students. If you have a friend or family member who can't read, you can find a literacy program for them by calling:

- Your local senior center
- Your local area agency on aging (pages 383–427)
- Your local community information and referral service (pages 434–439)
- Your local Adult or Continuing Education department (see telephone directory under your local government listing)

People interested in volunteering to help others learn to read should send for:

> **Brochure:** *Making America Literate: How You Can Help* (D12755)
> **Cost:** Free
> **From:** AARP Fulfillment
> 1909 K Street, NW
> Washington, DC 20049

The High School Equivalency Diploma

Most colleges and universities routinely require a high school diploma for admission. But today, almost all such institutions stand ready to admit the tens of millions of older adults who didn't finish high school in their teens. These institutions accept adults who have obtained the legal equivalent of a high school diploma.

By far the most common way to obtain a high school equivalency diploma is by achieving a satisfactory score on the nationally administered General Educational Development (GED) test. The GED consists of five separate tests: mathematics, English grammar and usage, social studies, science, and reading comprehension. Classes to prepare people for taking the GED tests are conducted in most locales during the regular school year. Upon attainment of a satisfactory score (which varies from state to state), the testee is issued the legal equivalent of a high school diploma by the state department of education.

For general information on obtaining a high school equivalency degree:

> **Booklet:** *Wish You Had Finished High School? You Can Do It Now!* (D13048)
> **Cost:** Free
> **From:** AARP Fulfillment
> 1909 K St., NW
> Washington, DC 20049

For information about requirements for a high school equivalency diploma and GED preparation classes, contact the Adult Education or Continuing Education Department of your local school system (see telephone directory under your local government listing) or contact your state education department (see telephone directory under your state government listing or call your state government information service, see pages 441–443).

To help prepare for the GED exam:

> **Book:** *Passing the GED*
> **Cost:** $8.95
> **Contains:** 722 pages of instruction and sample tests
> **From:** Scott, Foresman Lifelong Learning
> Order Department
> 1900 East Lake Avenue
> Glenview, IL 60025

There are two other significant programs that help adults achieve high school diplomas:

> **Program:** Competency-Based High School Diploma
> **Description:** Adults are given credit for their life skills and given an individualized course of study. They earn a regular diploma from a local high school
> **For information:** Contact your local adult or continuing education department (see telephone directory under local government listing)

> or
> Your state department of education (see listing above)
> or
> Director
> APL Project
> Education Annex S 21
> The University of Texas
> Austin, TX 78712

> **Program:** New York State External High School Diploma
> **Open to:** Residents of:
>
> | | |
> |---|---|
> | New York | Michigan |
> | Connecticut | Montana |
> | Maryland | Rhode Island |
> | Massachusetts | Virginia |
>
> **Description:** High school diploma program that includes formal counseling
> **For information:** Assistant Commissioner for Occupational and Continuing Education
> New York State Education Department
> Albany, NY 12234
> (send self-addressed stamped envelope)

ADVANCING YOUR CAREER

Many older Americans, especially those returning to work or looking for part-time work after retirement, can benefit from courses that update existing skills or obtain training in new ones. For example, people interested in office work have turned to courses to learn word processing or data processing skills that are much in demand in the workplace.

Four sources of such instruction are:

- Trade and technical schools
- Business and specialized schools
- Adult education programs
- Home study programs

Trade and Technical Schools

The best trade and technical schools have modern equipment, knowledgeable instructors, a good placement department to find jobs for graduates, and participation in tuition assistance programs. Unfortunately, there are also a significant number of trade and technical schools that offer poor or useless training. The first step in finding a school is to contact:

> **Organization:** National Association of Trade and Technical Schools
> 2251 Wisconsin Avenue, NW, Suite 200
> Washington, DC 20007
> (202) 333-1021
> **Services:** Is recognized by the U.S. Department of Education as the accrediting agency for private trade and technical schools. Publishes *Handbook of Trade and Technical Careers and Training* (Free) and a directory of accredited schools ($1.50)

The next step is to verify the reputation of the school by calling:

- Your local Better Business Bureau
- Your local consumer affairs office
- Your state department of education

The quality of training provided is more difficult to ascertain. The best advice is to ask the admissions office of the school to provide the names of several local companies that have recently hired graduates. Then call the Personnel Office of the companies to ask if in fact graduates have been hired and what opinion the company has of the training provided by the school.

Business and Specialized Schools

Business and specialized schools offer courses in a specific occupation, such as business administration, accounting, travel agent, or restaurant management. To locate such a school:

> **Organization:** Association of Independent Colleges and Schools
> 1 Dupont Circle, NW

Washington, DC 20036
(202) 659-2460
> **Services:** Recognized as the accrediting agency for business and specialized schools. Issues annual free *Directory of Educational Institutions*

Adult Education Courses

Most of the nation's school systems offer a wide variety of courses for adults. These courses, held primarily in the evening, cover a wide range of subjects from hobbies (for example, gardening, chess, stamp collecting) to practical subjects (for example, auto mechanics, carpentry, interior decorating) to personal finance (for example, investing, how to buy a home) to business-related subjects (for example, computers, accounting, typing). Most of these courses are noncredit, but many are useful in pursuing second careers. Most adult or continuing education programs offer discounts to adults over age 60 or 65.

For information about classes in your community, contact:

- The Adult/Continuing Education Office of your local school system
- Your local senior center

Home Study Programs

A list of primarily technical and vocational home study courses is:

> **Directory:** *Directory of Accredited Home Study Schools*
> **Cost:** Free
> **From:** National Home Study Council
> 1601 18th Street, NW
> Washington, DC 20009
> (202) 234-5100

THE COLLEGE DEGREE

Many older adults finally have the time to begin or finish work toward either an Associate (2-year) or Bachelors (4-year) college degree. Completing degree requirements can bring a profound sense of self-fulfillment, as well as practical benefits in pursuing a career or avocation.

Pursuing a degree is also much easier for adults today than it was decades ago. One reason is the new profusion of ways for adults to receive a significant amount of college course credit for the knowledge and experience they've acquired over the years. The second reason is that a wide variety of financial assistance programs and tuition discounts are available to them.

How to Select a College or University

People seeking a degree program have a choice of attending two types of institutions.

Community Colleges. Community colleges provide 2-year programs corresponding to the first 2 years of instruction at a 4-year college or university. These schools normally don't have dormitories, so their programs and schedules are geared for adults, including those who want a part-time course of study. Tuition and other charges at the more than 1,200 community colleges in the United States are normally lower than the fees at 4-year schools, and many offer tuition discounts for older students.

Four-Year Colleges and Universities. These offer programs leading to bachelors or graduate degrees. Most offer dormitories for students, as well as nonresident programs. Many have part-time programs with evening and weekend classes.

You can obtain the names of the 3,000 accredited colleges and universities in *The Education Directory,* which is available in the reference section of most libraries. Other directories are:

> **Books:** • *Peterson's Guide to Two Year Colleges* ($11.95)
> • *Peterson's Guide to Four Year Colleges* ($14.95)
> • *Who Offers Part-Time Degree Programs?* ($7.95)
> **Cost:** Price above plus:
> $1.75 for orders under $10.00
> $2.75 for orders between $10.00 and $20.00
> $3.75 for orders between $20.00 and $40.00
> **From:** Peterson's Guides
> P.O. Box 2123
> Princeton, NJ 08543

> **Book:** *Community, Junior and Technical College Directory*
> **Cost:** $35.00
> **From:** Publishers Services
> 80 S. Early Street
> Alexandria, VA 22304

The Admissions Department at every school will send you, upon request, college catalogs and other valuable information that will help you evaluate the school's programs.

Getting College Credit for Your Life Experiences

Many people acquire an impressive amount of knowledge throughout their life from work, travel, hobbies, volunteer work, and military service. Many are surprised to learn that this life experience can often be translated into college credit, sometimes shaving as much as a year or more from the academic work needed to acquire a degree.

One method of acquiring credit is through the College Level Examination Program (CLEP). There are two types of CLEP tests: a test of general knowledge in five areas, English composition, math, social sciences, natural sciences, and humanities; and specific subject matter tests in business, education, and other subjects. CLEP tests are administered at nearly 1,000 locations nationwide during the third week of each month. CLEP scores are accepted by most community colleges and many 4-year colleges and universities. For information:

Booklet: *Moving Ahead with CLEP*
Cost: Free
Contains: General information and a registration form
From: Educational Testing Service
Box 56-0
Departmental Examinations
Princeton, NJ 08541

A program that compliments CLEP is the DANTES (Defense Activity for Non-Traditional Education Support) program. This program was originally designed to allow people to obtain college credit for knowledge received during military service. It has been expanded to allow the general public to take tests in a wide variety of subjects ranging from business to auto mechanics. For information about the tests and a list of institutions that administer them:

Organization: DANTES Program Office
P-166 Educational Testing Service
Princeton, NJ 08541

Another testing program similar to the CLEP tests is the Proficiency Examination Program of the American College Testing Program (ACT PEP). These tests are less widely accepted than the CLEP tests, so you should check with specific colleges you're considering before you register. For information:

Program: ACT Proficiency Examination Program
P.O. Box 168
Iowa City, IA 52243

A fourth method of obtaining college credit is by passing examinations prepared by the faculty members of the college departments in which you hope to study. For example, you may be allowed to take an exam in lieu of a freshman level English, history, or business administration course. For information, you should talk to the Admissions Office of the colleges or universities to which you are applying.

A final method is to find an institution that will conduct a special assessment of your "experiential learning," or what you've learned in life. For further information and a list of colleges that give such credit:

Organization: Council for Adult and Experiential Learning
10840 Little Patuxent Parkway
Columbia, MD 21044
(301) 997-3535

College Admissions Examinations

Colleges and universities granting 4-year degrees normally require candidates for admission to take one of two major college entrance examinations: the Scholastic Aptitude Tests (SATs) or the American College Testing assessments (ACTs). For information:

Program: The College Board Admissions Testing Program
P.O. Box 592
Princeton, NJ 08541

Program: ACT Registration
Box 414
Iowa City, IA 52234

Many institutions do, however, have special admission requirements for adult students that include waiving the requirement for preadmission testing upon request. You should specifically ask about this exemption before completing your examination.

Financial Aid for Degree Programs As Well As Trade, Technical, Business Programs

Many people who return to school as adults think scholarships and other financial aid are primarily for younger students. In truth, older adults who demonstrate certain levels of financial need are equally eligible for a wide variety of scholarships, grants, and loan programs.

There are seven primary sources of information about financial aid programs:

1. The Financial Aid Office of the institution is the first and best place to begin. This office normally has information and application forms for many sources of assistance. Members of the staff will help students prepare a realistic budget for the school year and will help them fill out the necessary forms and applications.

2. The U.S. government offers five major federal financial aid programs. For information:

    Booklets: • *The Student*
    • Five Federal Financial Aid Programs
    • Federal Financial Aid for Men and Women Resuming Their Education and Training
    Cost: Free

From: Federal Student Aid Program
P.O. Box 84
Washington, DC 20044
(800) 333-4636

3. Each state government has an office that implements some federal aid programs, as well as programs developed by that state. For information, see the telephone directory under your state government listing or call your state government information number, pages 441–443.

4. Tuition discounts for older students. For a list of colleges and universities that offer tuition discounts in a specific state:

    Directory: Tuition Listing for (State)
    Cost: Free
    From: AARP Fulfillment
    D 12401
    P.O. Box 2400
    Long Beach, CA 90801

5. Grants and scholarships offered by businesses, professional organizations, and other organizations and associations. Many companies provide tuition assistance for employees. For information, contact your company personnel office. In addition, many clubs and organizations offer scholarships and other grants to members or family of members. In addition to contacting organizations to which you belong, you may find additional listings by contacting:

    • Your local library's reference section
    • The financial aid offices of colleges and universities

    In addition, many congressional offices have listings of scholarships and grant programs.

6. The Veterans Administration and other organizations have programs to assist veterans of military service. For a listing of such programs:

Brochure: *Need a Lift?*
Cost: $1.00
Contains: A comprehensive listing of educational opportunities, loans, scholarships, and other assistance to veterans
From: The American Legion Education Program
Indianapolis, IN 46206

7. State and local social service agencies have a variety of programs for low-income, handicapped, and other individuals. For information, contact:

- Your local area agency on aging, pages 383–427
- Your state education office
- Your state vocational rehabilitation office

Home Study Courses for College Credit

A directory of over 70 colleges offering credit courses has been compiled by the National University Continuing Education Association:

Directory: *The Independent Study Catalog*
Cost: $8.95 plus $1.75 postage
From: Peterson's Book Order Department
P.O. Box 2123
Princeton, NJ 08543

Another source of home instruction is televised courses broadcast over public television stations. For information:

Program: Annenberg CPB Project
1111 16th Street, NW
Washington, DC 20036

COURSE WORK FOR SELF-FULFILLMENT AND FUN

A growing number of colleges and universities have instituted special learning programs aimed at older Americans. These programs generally:

- Require no testing or other academic qualifications
- Feature both academic and practical programs (such as cooking and exercise classes)
- Have no testing or grading
- Include access to college libraries and use of other facilities
- Emphasize social contact with peers of the same age group
- Charge very low to moderate fees

The Institute of Lifetime Learning, the continuing education service of the American Association of Retired Persons (AARP) serves as the clearinghouse for information about these college centers. For general information:

Booklet: *College Centers for Older Learners* (D12489)
Cost: Free
Contains: General information about college center programs and a list of institutions with such programs
From: AARP
1909 K Street, NW
Washington, DC 20049

The Institute of Lifetime Learning of the AARP developed a series of minicourses for use by groups of older people. For information:

Program: Minicourse Order Form (D 168)
AARP Fulfillment
P.O. Box 2400
Long Beach, CA 90801

Many other colleges and universities have special discounts and other noncredit programs for older adults. For information, contact the admissions office of your local institutions. You may also be able to get information from your local senior center or your local area agency on aging.

LEARN WHILE TRAVELING

Thousands of programs combining education and travel are offered by Elderhostel, Interhostel, and other programs discussed elsewhere in this book (see pages 320–348). Information about these and many other opportunities are listed in:

Book: *Learning Vacations*
Cost: $9.95 plus $1.75 postage
From: Peterson's Book Order Department
166 Bunn Drive
Princeton, NJ 09540

TRAVEL

AMERICANS AGE 50 AND OLDER SPEND more money on travel than any other age group—and everyone in the travel industry knows that. The competition for your travel dollars is intense, and the result is a plethora of discounts that can shave 25% to 50% off the costs of some trips, giving you more money for additional travel or recreation.

Of course, even the least expensive trip is no bargain if you don't have a good time. There is a lot more to planning a trip than finding the most economical arrangements. You want to travel and stay in comfort, travel at a suitable place, and visit destinations that fit with your interests and energies.

In this chapter, we will provide information and resources for every aspect of travel, including:

- The basics of travel preparation
- A guide to travel information
- A step-by-step guide to all travel arrangements
- The basics of traveling to foreign countries
- Other valuable information for travelers

TRAVEL PREPARATION: AN OVERVIEW

Before you decide on specific trips, you should take the following steps:

- Join a seniors organization
- Establish a relationship with the right travel agent

- Learn how to recognize and avoid travel fraud

Join a Seniors Organization

In the introduction to this book, we recommended joining the American Association of

Retired Persons (AARP), one of America's best bargains for people age 50 and over at $5 per year or $12 for a 3-year membership. AARP membership is perhaps more valuable for travel than for any other benefit. AARP members, and the members of several other senior organizations, are eligible for many travel discounts at age 50 that nonmembers cannot get until age 60 or 65. The nominal membership fees for these organizations will pay for themselves many times over. Several national senior organizations have travel services that include discounts, as well as arranging special tours:

Organization: AARP
1909 K Street, NW
Washington, DC 20049
(202) 872-4700

Organization: National Council of Senior Citizens
925 15th Street, NW
Washington, DC 20005
(202) 347-8800

Organization: Mature Outlook
6001 N. Clark St.
Chicago, IL 60660
(800) 336-6330

Organization: Catholic Golden Age
400 Lackawanna Avenue
Scranton, PA 18503
(217) 342-3294

Organization: National Alliance of Senior Citizens
2525 Wilson Blvd.
Arlington, VA 22201
(703) 528-4380

Organization: Gray Panthers
311 S. Juniper St.
Philadelphia, PA 19107
(215) 545-6555

Choosing the Right Travel Agent

Many travelers can and do make their own travel arrangements, especially for simple trips. However, purchasing travel arrangements from airfare to tours is increasingly complex, to the point where a computer system is almost a necessity for comparison shopping. Finding a competent, knowledgeable, and reliable travel agent is a key step in arranging the best trips.

What should you look for in a travel agent? The important qualities include:

- Experienced staff that has traveled extensively to destinations and on the type of tours in which you're most interested and has served many clients with similar interests.

- An extensive file of brochures, guidebooks, directories, and travel videos. Good travel agents encourage clients to browse in their offices and to borrow material to take home. Increasingly, previewing prospective trips by video can narrow down your travel choices.

- An up-to-date computer system, and the willingness to use all the resources of that system. Too many travel agents pursue the first arrangements that pop up on the computer screen.

- The inclination to get to know clients and search out special opportunities to meet their needs. An agent should be willing to meet with you in person, extensively explore your likes, dislikes, and needs, then maintain a file of that information to use in booking future trips.

- Have established relationships with consolidators, charter operators, and other sources of discount transportation and preferred hotel rates.

- Willingness to handle complaints. All travelers eventually run into problems. Your agent should aggressively pursue your complaints, including seeking refunds.
- Convenience. Your travel agent should accept credit cards, deliver tickets, and be accessible during business hours.
- Active membership in the American Society of Travel Agents. To become an active member, an agency must be in good standing with all the major travel industry organizations and must subscribe to the Society's standards of ethical conduct and ethics. For more information:

Organization: American Society of Travel Agents
Services: Establishes standards of conduct for travel agencies and agents. Resolves disputes involving member agencies through its Consumer Affairs Department. Issues free publications, including:
– You and Your Travel Agent
– Questions Most Frequently Asked About ASTA
– Traveling Safely
– Travel Tips
– Packing Tips
– Car Rental
– Cruise Safety
– Holiday Travel
– Hotels: An Insider's Guide
– Overseas Travel
– The U.S. Welcomes Handicapped Visitors (Send self-addressed stamped envelope)
For information: ASTA
P.O. Box 23992
Washington, DC 20026
(703) 739-2782

- Acquisition of two additional indications of professionalism. Some dedicated travel agents have taken the time to prepare for and successfully complete two rigorous examinations:
  – Travel Career Development Diploma, awarded by the Institute of Certified Travel Agents
  – Proficiency Examination, administered by the American Society of Travel Agents

Recognizing and Avoiding Travel Fraud

In recent years, travel fraud has become a multibillion dollar business in America. Among the many common scams are:

- Postcards that announce *You have been selected to receive a free trip*
- Mail or telephone offers of a *free* or low-cost vacation if you send in a *membership fee*

Whatever the approach, the salesperson will attempt to convince you that you're getting a "great deal," will use high pressure and time pressure tactics, will attempt to get you to use a credit card over the phone, or will tell you that you have to send money by messenger or overnight mail to reserve the trip. To avoid these frauds, you should first educate yourself about travel fraud:

Brochure: *Telemarketing Travel Fraud*
Cost: Free
From: Public Reference
Federal Trade Commission
Washington, DC 20580

The second step is to make arrangements through reputable travel agents, travel companies, travel services, and other well-established organizations. If you have any doubts about an organization, you should contact your local Better Business Bureau or your state or local Consumer Protection Office.

FINDING FREE TRAVEL INFORMATION

Every state, most cities and resort areas, and almost all foreign countries have established tourist bureaus or visitor and convention bureaus that:

- Distribute free booklets, brochures, pamphlets, and fact sheets that provide copious information on tourist attractions, accommodations, and tourist facilities and services.
- Provide, often through toll-free numbers, the answers to specific questions, from where you can get a fishing license to the availability of special medical treatment.
- In many cases, offer discount coupon books, discount tours, or discount travel booking services for all travelers.
- Provide information on senior citizen discounts, tours, and special services.

You should make it a point to contact the state tourist bureaus or national tourist bureaus of all of your possible destinations as far ahead of time as possible. You will find a complete listing of U.S. and international tourist bureaus in the Appendix (pages 467–480).

CHOOSING THE BEST TRAVEL ARRANGEMENTS

Although a good travel agent can provide valuable advice, the final choice of where to go, how to travel, and where to stay is up to you. The more informed you are about travel arrangements, the more likely you are to choose the right trips at the right price. In the following pages, we'll provide information and resources that will allow you to make informed choices in purchasing packaged tours, air travel, rail travel, bus travel, hotel accommodations, and other arrangements.

How to Select a Tour

A tour is a travel package that normally includes transportation, accommodations, and transport to and from the airport(s). Sightseeing, attraction admissions, meals, and other services may also be included. The package is put together by a tour operator, who sells the tours to the public through travel agencies, airlines, nonprofit organizations, or directly through advertisements. Tours are generally one of two types:

- Escorted tours normally include a tour guide, who shepherds the travelers during the trip
- Independent tours provide airfare and accommodations, but no escorts during the stay

The advantages of taking a tour are:

- They are normally less expensive than traveling on your own, because tour operators purchase the parts of the package at wholesale rates

- They save the time and effort of individual vacation planning
- The package price allows you to budget accurately in advance
- Tours and tour guides can make travel more relaxing for less experienced travelers
- Tours provide the companionship of others, many of whom often share similar interests

The disadvantages of taking a tour are:

- They lock you into a fixed itinerary that's expensive to modify if you're unhappy with the accommodations
- Tours can be tedious if you don't like the tour guide or some of your tour companions
- Your vacation can be canceled at the last minute or aborted if the tour operator runs into financial difficulties or for a variety of other reasons. You could also lose part or all of your deposit under such circumstances

One method to protect yourself against the problem of default by a tour operator is to purchase a package only from a company that is a member of the National Tour Association (NTC) or the U.S. Tour Operators Association. Both groups have stringent financial and ethical standards for members, as well as reserve funds to provide refunds in the rare case that a member company has financial problems. For more information on purchasing tours from members of these groups:

Publication: *How to Select a Package Tour*
Cost: Free

From: U.S. Tour Operators Association
211 East 51st Street, Suite 12B
New York, NY 10022
(212) 944-5727

Publication: *Travel Together*
Cost: Free
From: National Tour Association
546 East Main Street
P.O. Box 3071
Lexington, KY 40596

To find a tour you'll enjoy, you may want to make arrangements through a travel organization that specializes in travel for people age 50 and over. These organizations include:

AARP Travel Service
5855 Green Valley Circle
Culver City, CA 90230
(800) 227-7737

Saga Holidays
120 Bolyston Street
Boston, MA 02116
(800) 343-0273 (Ex. MA)
(800) 462-3322 (MA)

Grand Circle Travel
347 Congress Street
Boston, MA 02210
(800) 248-3737 (Ex. MA)
(800) 535-8333 (MA)

National Alliance of Senior Citizens
        Travel Club
2525 Wilson Blvd.
Arlington, VA
(703) 528-4380

Mature Outlook
6001 N. Clark Street
Chicago, IL 60660
(800) 336-6330

September Days Club
2751 Buford Highway NE

Atlanta, GA 30324
(800) 241-5050 (Ex. GA)
(404) 325-4000

National Council of Senior Citizens
925 15th Street, NW
Washington, DC 20005
(202) 347-8800

Breeze Tours
2750 Stickney Point Road
Sarasota, FL 33581
(800) 237-5630 (Ex. FL)
(800) 282-5630 (FL)

Senior Escorted Tours
223 N. Main Street
Cape May Court House, NJ 08210
(800) 257-8910

Every year, tens of thousands of travelers take advantage of the following travel programs designed especially for older Americans:

Organization: Interhostel
University of New Hampshire
6 Garrison Avenue
Durham, NH 03824
(603) 862-1147

Services: Interhostel is an international study-travel program for adults age 50 and older. The program, sponsored by the University of New Hampshire, consists of two-week trips to over a dozen locations annually. Each tour is hosted by an overseas college or university, which arranges lectures, seminars, sightseeing, field trips, and interactions with local citizens

Organization: Elderhostel
80 Boylston Street, Suite 400
Boston, MA 02116
(617) 426-8056

Services: Elderhostel offers more than 1,200 one-week courses for people age 60 and older at colleges and universities in the United States and throughout the world. Participants generally sleep in dormitories and eat in college dining halls. Courses include every imaginable topic from gourmet cooking to world religion to the history of the lumberjack. The free catalog alone is fascinating reading

Program: Close Up Foundation
1235 Jefferson Davis Highway
Arlington, VA 22202
(800) 232-2000

Services: Offers week-long visits to Washington, DC, which include discussions, lectures, and other educational opportunities for mature citizens

Most tours charge steep *supplements* for single travelers. One way around these additional charges is an agency that pairs single travelers, a great many of whom are age 50 and over:

Travel Partners Club
P.O. Box 2368
Crystal River, FL 32629

Singleworld
444 Madison Avenue
New York, NY 10022
(800) 223-6490

Saga Holiday Club
120 Boylston Street
Boston, MA 02116
(800) 343-0273 (Ex. MA)
(800) 462-3322 (MA)

Travel Companion Exchange
P.O. Box 833
Amityville, NY 11701
(516) 454-0880

Traveling by Air in the United States

Traveling by air is by far the fastest way to get to a distant destination. Unfortunately, the fare structures of many airlines are extremely complex. Flight delays, cancellations, lost baggage, and other hassles can also turn a simple trip into an ordeal. However, an informed, careful traveler will generally fly as cheaply and comfortably as possible.

Among the steps you can take to save money on air fares is to:

Comparison Shop. Ideally, your travel agent will take all of your travel decisions, then use the agency's computer to search out the absolute lowest fares. However, because a travel agency's commission on air travel reservations is only 5% of the air fare, your agent may recommend flights to you based on a quick computer search instead of spending extra time digging for further savings. That is why you may save money by doing some comparison shopping of your own before you book the flights recommended by your travel agent.

Make a list of all airlines that fly to your destination. You can obtain that information from a travel agent, by calling the reservation service of any airline, or from the *Official Airline Guide* (OAG), a monthly publication listing all flights to and from every U.S. destination, including fairs. The OAG is carried by many libraries and is available on many computer services, such as Compuserve and Genie. The OAG also publishes:

> **Directory:** *OAG Pocket Flight Guide*
> **Cost:** $5.00 for monthly issue at some airline newsstands
> $59.00 subscription for 12 issues per year plus *Frequent Flyer* magazine

> **Contains:** The schedules of major airlines by destination for the United States, Canada, Mexico, and the Caribbean
> **From:** Official Airline Guide
> (800) 323-3537 (Ex. IL)
> (800) 942-1888 (IL)

Once you obtain the names of the airlines, you can call each one by using toll-free numbers listed in your Yellow Pages under "Air Line Companies" or available from toll-free information, (800) 555-1212. When you call, provide the reservations agent with all of the travel decisions (for example, choice of airport, departure dates, etc.) that you have previously determined.

Senior Citizen Discounts. Always ask about senior citizen discounts. Increased attention to older travelers has given rise to an increased number of discount programs. The value of these programs varies widely, depending on the type of program, the type of frequency of travel, and the restrictions involved. Also, airlines begin, change, or end programs on very short notice.

The basic types of programs include:

1. Flight coupons or passes. Some airlines sell qualified seniors a book of coupons, each one of which is good for a one-way flight, or a pass that allows travel throughout the system for a year. These programs carry significant restrictions on days of travel, times of travel, and destinations. The U.S. airlines offering these passes are:

Airline	Minimum Age	Toll-free Number
Delta	62	(800) 221-1212
Eastern	62	(800) 327-8376
Pan Am	62	(800) 221-1111
Piedmont	65	(800) 251-5720
TWA	65	(800) 422-3205

2. Straight discounts. The most common senior discount is a straight discount on the airfare. For example, one airline might offer a 15% discount off any fare to travelers who can prove they are age 62 and over. Another might offer a 10% discount on most fares to members of AARP, effectively lowering the age requirement to 50. Many straight discount programs don't apply to all fares or all flights. Some allow purchase of a ticket for a companion at the same price. The airlines offering straight discounts are:

Airline	Minimum Age	Toll-free Number
Alaska	60	(800) 426-0333
American	*	(800) 433-7300
Braniff	65	(800) 272-6433
Continental	62	(800) 525-0280
Hawaiian	65	(800) 367-5320
Northwest	62	(800) 225-2525
PSA	65	(800) 722-7287
Southwest	65	(800 531-5601
United	62	(800) 241-6522
USAir	65	(800) 428-4322

* Discount to members of AARP only.

3. Airline clubs for seniors. Seven U.S. airlines have special clubs for senior travelers. In return for a membership fee (normally $25), members get a discount of 10% on all fares with no restrictions on travel. Club members also get bonus miles on frequent-flier plans, discount membership in airport clubs, hotel rental car discounts, and notice of discount tours and packages. Most clubs allow a younger spouse to get the same benefits for an additional fee of $75 or $100. At press time, the U.S. airlines with clubs for seniors were:

Airline	Minimum Age	Toll-free Number
American	60	(800) 433-7300
Continental	65	(800) 525-0280

Airline	Minimum Age	Toll-free Number
Eastern	65	(800) 327-8376
Midwest Express	65	(800) 452-2022
Northwest	55	(800) 225-2525
TWA	62	(800) 422-3205
United	60	(800) 241-6522

Deciding whether or not to take advantage of a senior discount program is simple. Ask the airline, travel agent, or travel reservation service to compare the lowest generally available fare to the lowest available senior citizen discount fare. If the lowest fare involves joining an airline club for senior citizens, don't let the membership fee deter you from joining the club. Even if the savings doesn't cover the small membership fee, the other benefits make joining the smart decision.

Personal Emergency Travel. Ask for special fares if you are traveling for a personal emergency. Airfares for flights booked at the last minute can be three or four times the lowest excursion fare. Flying full fare can cause financial hardship for people who have to make last-minute travel arrangements because of the serious illness or death of a family member. That's why most major airlines will allow people traveling because of the death of an immediate family member to pay the couch excursion fare instead of the full fare. Most major airlines will generally provide the same benefit to people traveling because of the serious illness of an immediate family member.

Frequent-Flyer Programs. Ask about frequent-flyer benefits. All of the major U.S. airlines have programs that provide rewards, in the form of upgrades to first class or free travel, for passengers who accumulate a certain number of miles flying on that airline. All of the programs have arrangements with hotel chains and car rental companies that allow passengers to get mileage credit for hotel stays and auto rentals, as well as use awards for free hotel stays and auto rentals. All programs also have reciprocal arrangements with several international airlines, allowing substantial mileage credits for overseas trips.

Membership in the frequent-flier programs is free. You can request a membership application or even sign up over the phone when making your reservation. Applications are also available on all flights. Even occasional travelers should take the time to sign up. With lodging and car rental credits, mileage can add up more quickly than most people realize.

By following all of the above steps, you should find the lowest fare for the most convenient flights. However, that doesn't mean that you will enjoy your trip. In recent years, a surge in the number of passengers, air traffic control problems, and deregulation of the airline industry has resulted in additional flight delays, flight cancellations, lost luggage, overbooking, and other problems. Everyone who travels should be aware of their rights as passengers and the proper procedures to follow in the event of problems. For information:

Book: *How to Fly: The Consumer Federal of America Airline Survival Guide*
Cost: $7.95
From: CFA Airline Guide
1424 16th Street, NW, Suite 604
Washington, DC 20036
(202) 387-6121

Booklet: *Fly—Rights*
Cost: Free
Contains: A 32-page guide for airline travelers
From: Consumer Affairs
U.S. Department of Transportation
Washington, DC 20590
(202) 366-2220

Booklet: *Facts and Advice for Airline Passengers*

Cost: $2.00
From: Aviation Consumer Action Project
P.O. Box 19029
Washington, DC 20036

Organization: Airline Passengers of America
Services: Publishes newsletter with information on air travel, operates baggage retrieval assistance program, and provides flight insurance. Also operates FLIGHTTALK, a 24 hour a day service that provides information on travel delays, flight schedules, and passenger rights at every airport across the country.
Cost: $24.00 per year
From: Airline Passengers of America
4224 King Street
Alexandria, VA 22302
(703) 824-0505

If you need assistance or want to register a complaint, the Department of Transportation urges consumers to call or write:

Organization: Office of Community and Consumer Affairs
U.S. Department of Transportation
400 7th Street, SW Room 10405
Washington, DC 20590

Hotline: (202) 366-2220

If you have a complaint related to safety:

Organization: Community and Consumer Liaison Division
APA-400 Federal Aviation Administration
800 Independence Avenue, SW
Washington, DC 20591
(800) 322-7873

Traveling by Air to Other Countries

The procedures for trip planning, purchasing tickets, and obtaining the lowest fare for flights to other countries are in most ways the same as finding the lowest domestic airfare. The differences, including additional ways to purchase discount air travel, are discussed below.

Senior discounts are much less common on foreign air carriers than on U.S. airlines. Senior discounts are more available for flights within a foreign country than they are on flights from and to the United States. If you are booking your own international flights directly with an airline, the senior discount program of a U.S. airline with international flights may save you money over a foreign carrier. But because fares vary so widely, you have to comparison shop for your specific itinerary.

The foreign airlines with senior discount programs are:

Air Canada	(800) 422-6232 (NY Ex.)
	(212) 869-1900
British Airways	(800) 247-9297
Canadian Airlines	
International	(800) 426-7000
Finnair	(800) 223-5700
KLM Dutch Airlines	(800) 777-5553
Mexicana	(800) 531-7921
SAS Scandinavian	
Airlines	(800) 221-2350 (NY Ex.)
	(718) 657-7700
TAP Air Portugal	(800) 221-7370

Air transportation that is part of tour packages is often the least expensive way to travel. In addition to the many tours operated by companies mentioned in other parts of this book, almost all foreign-owned airlines offer a wide variety of tours. You can receive elaborate brochures and other information by calling the toll-free numbers for foreign carriers listed in your Yellow Pages under "Air Line Companies" or available from toll-free information, (800) 555-1212.

Discount air fares may be available on charter flights. The difference between a charter and discount tickets on scheduled airlines is that when you buy a ticket, you enter into a contractual arrangement with a tour operator who has subcontracted with an airline to do the actual flying. This means that you may have a more difficult time obtaining a refund in the event of problems, and that your trip may be seriously delayed, canceled, or rerouted in the event of mechanical difficulties or problems selling out the entire flight.

The safest way to purchase a charter flight is through a travel agent who has had extensive dealings with a reliable charter operator. For additional protection, you should arrange through the travel agent trip-interruption insurance that provides for a refund if the tour operator goes bankrupt.

Traveling by Rail

Traveling by rail can be a leisurely, economical, and convenient way to tour the United States or foreign countries. A bonus for older Americans is that many rail systems offer substantial fare discounts and/or system passes that can save additional dollars.

Amtrak, which operates intercity rail service in the United States, provides a 25% discount off normal one-way and round-trip fares to passengers age 65 and older. These discounts are not available during major holidays and other peak travel periods. However, the senior citizen discount is often not the lowest fare. Amtrak also offers many round-trip excursion fares and special fares for couples and families. Some of these fares are restricted to certain travel periods or days, while others are available even during holidays. Whenever you call Amtrak, always ask for both the senior citizen discount and the lowest available excursion or special fares.

For information:

> **Organization:** Amtrak
> (800) 872-7245

Almost all commuter rail lines in the United States offer substantial discounts to older travelers. The age at which these discounts take effect varies from 60 to 65, and some lines impose restrictions on travel hours.

For information about commuter rail discounts and schedules, contact the state or local tourism bureau, consult the Yellow Pages under "Railroads," or write:

> **Organization:** American Public Transit Association
> 1201 New York Avenue, NW
> Washington, DC 20005

Rail Canada gives all people age 65 and older a discount of one third off all one-way and round-trip fares, with no restrictions or blackout periods. However, as with Amtrak, special excursion fares may be a better bargain at certain times of the year.

For information:

> **Organization:** Canada Tourism Office
> 1251 Avenue of the Americas
> New York, NY 10020
> (212) 757-4917

A wide variety of rail passes and discounts are available on European rail systems. Among them are:

> **Program:** Eurailpass
> **Service:** The Eurailpass offers unlimited rail travel in all of Western Europe (except Great Britain) during a certain period of time. For travelers who are planning to cover at least 1,500 miles

in more than one country, Eurailpass represent at least a 50% discount over regular fares. Eurailpasses must be purchased before leaving the United States

For information: TRAINS
P.O. Box M
Staten Island, NY 10305
(212) 254-2525

Program: BritRail
Service: A BritRail pass allows unlimited travel in England, Scotland, and Wales for a specified period of time. Senior citizens age 65 and over can purchase a first class BritRail pass for the cost of a second class pass. These passes must be purchased before leaving the United States
For information: BritRail
40 W. 57 St.
New York, NY 10019
(212) 583-1616

Organization: French National Railroads
Service: France Vacances provides unlimited travel within France for a specified period of time. The French National Railroads also offers a 50% discount to women age 60 and over and men age 62 and over
For information: French National Railroads
610 Fifth Avenue
New York, NY 10020
(212) 582-2110

Organization: GermanRail
Service: GermanRail Tourist Card offers unlimited rail travel for a specified period of time, plus other travel benefits
For information: GermanRail
747 Third Avenue
New York, NY 10017
(212) 308-3300

Organization: Italian Railroads
Service: Italian Tourist Tickets provide un-

limited travel for a specified period of time

For information: Italian National Railroads
630 Fifth Avenue
New York, NY 10111
(212) 245-4822

The national railroad systems of the following countries also provide unlimited travel rail passes and/or senior citizen discounts. Complete information can be obtained from each country's tourist bureau in the United States (see listings, pages 471–480).

Austria
Belgium
Denmark
Finland
Greece
Ireland
Netherlands
Portugal
Romania
Spain
Sweden
Switzerland
Yugoslavia

Traveling by Bus

Bus travel is not only economical, but allows more chances to see the countryside than train or air travel.

In the United States, Trailways recently merged with Greyhound to form one major national intercity bus company. This new company offers:

Program: Greyhound Golden Savers Club
Service: Provides 15% discount off all fares to those age 65 or over

For information: Call your local Greyhound terminal (see White Pages)

Greyhound also offers a variety of special promotional and excursion fares that you should always compare to the Golden Savers Club fares.

Gray Line Sightseeing operates bus sightseeing tours in many parts of the country. Gray Line offers a 15% discount to members of AARP. For information:

Organization: Gray Line Sightseeing
For information: Call your local Gray Line office (see White Pages)
or
(800) 892-8687

Traveling by Ship

Cruising is an extremely popular form of travel among older vacationers. However, choosing the right ship for the right trip at the right price can be difficult. Among the steps you can take to ensure an enjoyable cruise at the best price are:

- Do some research about cruising and cruise ships. Consult:

Book: *Berlitz Complete Handbook to Cruising*
Cost: $13.95
Contains: A 16-chapter guide to every aspect of cruising that contains extensive data and ratings of 148 cruise ships. The material in this book is prepared by the International Cruise Passengers Association, a consumer group for cruise passengers
From: Your local bookstore
or
(800) 428-7267

Organization: International Cruise Passengers Association
Box 886, F.D.R. Station
New York, NY 10150
(212) 486-8482

Services: Publishes *Cruise Digest Reports,* a magazine that contains news, reviews, and feature articles on all aspects of cruising. The ICPA also acts as an advocate for cruise safety and high standards of service

Cost: $20.00 per year, which includes 6 issues of *Cruise Digest Reports*

Directory: OHRG Cruise Directory
500 Plaza Drive
Secaucus, NJ 07096

Contains: Includes detailed information on every major cruise ship, including passenger capacity, facilities, accommodations, services, tipping policy, dress requirements, and a wealth of other data. Available at many public libraries and travel agents

Organization: World Ocean & Cruise Line Society
P.O. Box 92
Stamford, CT 06904

Services: Issues monthly newsletter, offers discounts, and books cruises

- Book cruises through a reliable, experienced travel agent. About 95% of all cruises are booked through travel agencies or organizations. One excellent way to insure that a cruise will meet your expectations is to book a cruise through one of the travel companies that specializes in tours for older Americans (see listings, pages 324–325). Another is to find a travel agent who has booked trips for people with similar travel interests and habits to you and who has actually cruised on the ships recommended.

- Ask about senior citizen discounts. An increasing number of cruise lines offer discounts for passengers age 60 and older. Always ask about these discounts when booking a cruise.

- Save money by booking very early or at the last minute. Because cruise ship operators are anxious to guarantee that cabins will be filled, they generally offer substantial discounts for travelers who book 6 months or more in advance. Check with your travel agent for the amount of these discounts, as well as any cancellation penalties and procedures. Some agencies that specialize in cruise discounts are:

Cruises of Distinction	(800) 634-3445
South Florida Cruises	(800) 327-7447
Stand-Buys	(800) 255-0200
Cruise Line Inc.	(800) 777-0707

Even greater discounts (50% to 80%) can be obtained from cruise ship operators who find themselves with empty cabins a few days before sailing time. Among the organizations that act as agents for cruise lines in selling these last minute accommodations are:

Spur of the Moment Cruises
10780 Jefferson Blvd.
Culver City, CA 90230
(213) 839-2418

Last Minute Cruise Club
870 9th Street
San Pedro, CA 90731
(213) 519-1717

South Florida Cruises
2005 Cypress Road, Suite D-207
Fort Lauderdale, FL 33309
(800) 327-7447 (Ex. FL)
(305) 493-7447

The number of freighters that carry passengers has dwindled in recent years. However, there are still cabins available for trips that people seeking relaxation and solitude find appealing. Among the sources of information are:

Freighter Travel Association
40-21 Bell Blvd.
Bayside, NY

Freighter World Cruises
180 S. Lake Avenue, Suite 335
Pasadena, CA 91101

Freighter Travel Club
P.O. Box 12693
Salem, OR 97309

Traveling by Auto in the United States

More people travel to their vacation destinations by automobile than by any other form of transportation. If you are traveling in your own car, the most important precaution you can take is protecting yourself against emergencies by joining AAA or another automobile club.

Automobile clubs, which have a combined membership of 40 million people in the United States, offer one of two types of emergency service:

- Full-service clubs offer toll-free numbers and dispatch help from affiliated service stations that provide the service (up to a defined limit) as part of your membership fee
- Limited-service clubs require you to find a service station and pay for the service. You are then reimbursed up to the club limit for that service

People who seldom travel by car and have a good relationship with a local service station may find limited service clubs the best option. Most other people should choose full-service clubs.

Both full-service and limited-service clubs also provide a selection of other services in exchange for a yearly membership fee. Those services include:

- Free maps and trip-routing service
- Emergency cash when stranded away from home
- Emergency check cashing at participating stations
- Free arrest bond for motor vehicle violations
- Accidental death and dismemberment insurance
- Travel discounts and booking services
- Lodging and car rental discounts
- Car buying services
- Lost key protection
- Stolen car rewards

The best way to select an automobile club is to call or write for complete information, comparing benefits you'll use to the annual cost of membership.

The full-service automobile clubs are:

Organization: American Automobile Association
Services: About 70% of all auto club members belong to Triple A. AAA has a very large number of participating stations. While road service is offered nationwide, specific benefits and membership fees vary from club to club. Many clubs do offer discounts to senior citizens
For information: Call your local AAA club

Organization: AARP Motoring Plan
Services: This plan, open only to people age 50 and older (and their spouses) who are members of AARP. The plan is administered by the Amoco Motor Club, one of the largest full-service clubs
For information: AARP Motoring Plan
P.O. Box 9041
Des Moines, IA 50369
(800) 334-3300

Organization: Allstate Motor Club
Services: This club offers a discount for retirees
For information: Allstate Motor Club
1500 W. Shure Drive
Arlington Heights, IL 60004
(800) 323-6282

Organization: Amoco Motor Club
For information: Amoco Motor Club
P.O. Box 9014
Des Moines, IA 50306
(800) 334-3300

Organization: Cross Country Motor Club
For information: Cross Country Motor Club
270 Mystic Avenue
Boston, MA 02155
(800) 225-1575

Organization: Mobil Auto Club
For information: Mobil Auto Club
200 N. Martingale Road
Schaumburg, IL 60173
(800) 621-5581

Organization: Montgomery Ward Auto Club
For information: Montgomery Ward Auto Club
200 N. Martingale Road
Schaumburg, IL 60173
(800) 621-5151

Organization: Safe Driver Motor Club
For information: Safe Driver Motor Club
P.O. Box 2800
Torrance, CA 90509
(800) 272-6669

The limited-service clubs are:

Organization: Chevron Travel Club
P.O. Box P
Concord, CA 94524
(800) 222-0585

Organization: Exxon Travel Club
P.O. Box 3633
Houston, TX 77253
(800) 680-5723

Organization: Shell Motorist Club
P.O. Box 2463
Houston, TX 77001
(800) 621-8663

Organization: Texaco Star Club
P.O. Box 224669
Dallas, TX 75222
(800) 348-2022

Many travelers combine air travel with automobile rentals at their destinations. But comparative shopping for automobile rentals can be very complicated. The reason is not only that "list" rates vary widely, but many extra charges can sharply increase the bill when you drop off the car. Obtaining the lowest rate requires some careful comparison shopping. The best procedures include those cited below.

Call the four major national car rental companies. These companies have a vast network of locations, including almost all airport terminals. They also have sophisticated nationwide arrangements for emergency road service and, if necessary, car replacement

All of these companies offer discounts to members of senior organizations, such as

AARP, members of automobile clubs, such as AAA, and members of a variety of other organizations. These discounts can make their rates competitive with other discount car rental firms.

For information:

Avis	(800) 331-1212
Budget	(800) 527-0700
Hertz	(800) 654-3131 (Ex. OK)
	(800) 522-3711 (OK)
National	(800) CAR-RENT

Check with one or more of the other national car rental companies that have locations at or near most major airports. These companies generally quote rates below the regular rates of the major national companies. However, fuel charges and other fees can make them more expensive.

These companies include:

Agency Rent-A-Car	(800) 321-1972 (Ex. OH)
	(800) 362-0654 (OH)
Alamo Rent-A-Car	(800) 327-9633
American International Rent-A-Car	(800) 527-0202
Dollar Rent-A-Car	(800) 421-6868
General Rent-A-Car	(800) 327-7607
Payless Car Rental	(800) 237-2804
Snappy Car Rentals	(800) 669-4800
Thrifty Rent-A-Car	(800) 367-2277

If you're staying in a location for a while, you may also be able to save money by renting an automobile from local care dealerships, such as a local Ford or General Motors dealer. You can find these dealers by looking in the local Yellow Pages under "Automobile Renting and Leasing."

Ask for car rental information when you book air travel or hotel accommodations. Many airlines and hotels have arranged substantial car rental discounts for customers who book the rentals through them.

Traveling by Auto in Other Countries

You can legally drive in the following countries if you have a valid U.S. state-issued drivers license:

Australia

Canada

Ireland

New Zealand

United Kingdom

Belgium

Luxembourg

France

Israel

Mexico

Norway

Finland

Sweden

Denmark

Switzerland

Caribbean (most countries)

In other countries, however, you need to obtain:

Document: International Driving Permit
Cost: $5.00 plus two passport-sized photographs and a valid U.S. license
From: Any AAA office and certain other motor clubs

Most countries in the western hemisphere accept the International Driving Permit. However, Brazil and Uruguay will only accept another document, which is also valid in other Central and South American countries:

Document: Inter-American Driving Permit
Cost: $5.00 plus two passport-sized photographs and a valid U.S. license
From: Any AAA office and certain other motor clubs

All major national U.S. automobile rental companies have locations throughout Canada, Mexico, Europe, the Caribbean, and in many other countries. For information, call the reservation numbers listed above. When obtaining rate quotations, make sure that insurance is included, since your personal automobile insurance policy does not normally cover driving outside of the United States. You can also obtain rental information and quotations from:

Auto Europe	(800) 223-5555
Europe by Car	(800) 223-1516
Eurorent	(800) 521-2235 (Ex. MI)
Rent-A-Car	(800) 482-2854

Finally, you should also check with airlines about Fly/Drive programs that can save considerable money.

In addition to the questions of driver's license mentioned above, there are three major considerations in renting an automobile abroad that don't apply in the United States:

- Many rental vehicles in Europe have stick shifts, rather than automatic transmissions

- Gasoline cost in other countries can be double or triple the U.S. cost

- Older drivers who want to rent a car overseas may find that rental companies will not rent to drivers above a certain age in certain countries. For example, in Ireland, Budget and National Car Rental have age limits of 75, while

Dollar Car Rental stops renting at age 69. Two other major car rental firms, Hertz and Avis, have no age limit in Ireland, but do apply age limits in other countries. Always ask about an age limit when making an overseas car rental reservation. If the first company you try has a limit, chances are another company will rent you an automobile.

How to Find the Best Hotel Accommodations and Other Lodging

Deciding how to get to a destination is only part of travel planning. An equally important consideration is where you are going to stay. Among the major options for travelers are:

- Hotels and motels
- Bed and Breakfasts
- Hostels and YMCAs
- Home exchanges
- Villa, condo, or house rentals
- Camping

Hotels and Motels. The rates you'll find quoted in the brochure for a hotel or motel are referred to in the industry as the "rack rate," or "list price." Few knowledgeable travelers, however, wind up paying rack rates for lodging. There are an enormous number of ways to reduce the cost of staying in almost all hotels and motels. Before you call the toll-free reservation numbers of a hotel or motel chain see Yellow Pages or call toll-free information, (800) 555-1212, you should know about the following.

- Senior citizen discounts. A majority of hotel and motel chains in the United States offer discounts to older guests. The most common minimum age at which the discounts start is 60, but almost all chains grant the same discount to members of AARP and other senior organizations open to people age 50 and over. These discounts average 10% to 15%, and they sometimes are restricted to certain days or times of the year.

- A smaller number of hotel and motel chains have special clubs or programs that offer discounts of up to 50% on reservations made in advance. The chains offering these programs include:

Days Inn	(800) 247-5152
Hampton Inns	(800) 426-7866
Hilton Hotels	(214) 239-0511
Holiday Inns	(800) 465-4329
Howard Johnson	(800) 634-3464
Marriott	(800) 228-9290
Omni International	(800) 228-3323
Radisson Hotels	(800) 228-9822
Sheraton	(800) 325-3535
Travelodge	(800) 255-3050

In addition to lodging discounts, some chains offer discounts on restaurant meals and gift shop purchases.

- Weekend, off season, or other special promotional packages. Most hotels, motels, and resorts offer a variety of discount packages that may be lower than the senior citizen discount rates.
- Preferred or "corporate" rates. These rates, which range from 10% to 40% below "rack" rates, are available through:
  - Large travel agencies and other agencies who use hotel booking services
  - Members of a hotel chain's special club or frequent stay program
  - Members of certain clubs and organizations
  - Members of discount travel clubs

The availability of hotel accommodations at preferred rates is an important consideration when choosing a travel agency. If your agency doesn't have such a service, other sources of preferred rates are (Note: membership fees may be required):

American Automobile Association	Your local AAA office or (703) 222-4700
American Express Membership Travel	(800) 872-6357
International Airline Passengers Association	(800) 527-5888

- Half price or second night free programs. A number of travel clubs offer either 50% discounts off the rack rates at participating hotels or have made arrangements for members to stay two nights for the price of one. There are normally restrictions on both types of programs imposed by individual hotels. Among the clubs offering such programs are:

Amoco Motor Club	(800) 334-3300
Amoco Traveler	(800) 247-1055 (Ex. IL)
	(312) 465-7062
Concierge Card	(800) 346-1022
Encore	(800) 638-0930
Entertainment Publications	(313) 637-8400
Hotel Express	(703) 934-6017
Montgomery Ward Travel	(800) 621-5505 (Ex. IL)
	(312) 490-7485
OAG Travel Club	(800) 358-5858
Privilege Card	(800) 359-0066
Quest	(800) 325-2400
Sears Discount Travel	(800) 331-0257 (Ex. IL)
	(800) 826-4398 (IL)

- Consider budget hotel chains that provide a room with two beds for two people for under $50. Most of these chains provide comfortable rooms, color television sets, and in-room telephones at all locations. In addition, most give a 10% discount to senior citizens and many extend that discount to members of AARP or other senior organizations. For reservations and information:

Budgetel Inns	(800) 428-3438
Comfort Inns	(800) 228-5150
Downtowner/Passport Inns	(800) 238-6161
Drury Inns	(800) 325-8300
Econo Lodges	(800) 446-6900
Exel Inns	(800) 356-8013
Family Inns	(800) 251-9752
Friendship Inns	(800) 453-4511
Hampton Inn	(800) 426-7866
Ha'Penny Inns	(800) 854-6111
Imperial Inn	(800) 368-4400
Knights Inn	(614) 866-1569
La Quinta	(800) 531-5900
Motel 6	(505) 891-6161
National 9 Inn	(800) 524-9999
Red Carpet Inn	(800) 251-1962
Red Roof Inns	(800) 843-7663
Regal 8 Inn	(800) 851-8888
Rodeway Inns	(800) 228-2000
Scottish Inns	(800) 251-1962
Shoney's Inn	(800) 222-2222
Sixpence Inn	(714) 250-1922
Super 8 Motels	(800) 843-1991
Susse Chalet	(800) 258-1980
Vagabond Inns	(800) 522-1555

Hotels and motels are not your only accommodation options.

Bed and Breakfast Establishments (B&Bs).

B&Bs are normally private homes that offer comfortable lodging in a private room and a continental breakfast at rates that can be much lower than local hotels. Information about B&Bs can be obtained from state and local tourist bureaus (see listings, pages 467–471) or from directories issued by the following organizations:

American Bed & Breakfast Association
16 Village Green, Suite 203
Crofton, MD 21114
(301) 261-0180

National Bed & Breakfast Association
P.O. Box 332
Norwalk, CT 06852
(203) 847-6196

Bed & Breakfast Home Directory
P.O. Box 491
Cupertino, CA 95014

Bed & Breakfast League
P.O. Box 9490
Washington, DC 20016
(202) 363-7767

Accommodations in Hostels, College Dormitories, and YMCAs.

Hostels are low-cost, clean, safe accommodations for travelers who don't mind sleeping in dormitory-style rooms and sharing a kitchen, recreation, and bathroom facilities. There are more than 250 hostels in the United States and more than 5,000 worldwide. In this country, about 10% of all guests in hostels are age 55 and over. Average cost of nightly accommodations ranges from $5 to $13. For information:

Organization: American Youth Hostels
P.O. Box 37613
Washington, DC 20013
(202) 783-6161

Cost: $20.00 per year membership for ages 18–54, $10.00 for age 55 and over

Services: Membership allows stays at all United States andworld hostels. Members receive a directory of American hostels. Members can purchase:

- *International Handbook,* Vol. 1, a guide to European hostels ($8.95)
- *International Handbook,* Vol. 2, a guide to hostels in other areas of the world ($8.95)

Members receive a twice yearly magazine and can purchase Eurail passes through AYH. AYH also organizes a large number of tours, some of which are specifically for people age 50 and over

Directory: Directory of Campus Accommodations
Cost: $9.95
Contains: Listings for 650 universities worldwide that rent dormitory space during the summer months
From: Campus Travel Service
Box 5007
Laguna Beach, CA 92652
(714) 497-3044

Directory: *Y's Way to Visit North America and Worldwide*
Cost: $0.45 plus self-addressed stamped envelope
Contains: A listing of accommodations in 103 YMCAs worldwide
From: Y's Way International
356 West 34th Street
New York, NY 10001
(212) 760-5856

Home Exchange. The obvious advantage of exchanging homes with residents of another country is the substantial savings on hotel accommodations. Many people also find staying in a home more comfortable and relaxing than staying in a hotel or hostel. An added bonus is closer contact with the people and culture of the country.

Among the agencies that arrange home exchanges are:

Worldwide Home Exchange
6103 Biltmore Avenue
Baltimore, MD 21215

Global Home Exchange & Travel Service
P.O. Box 2015

S. Burlington, VT 05401
(802) 985-3825

Home Exchange International
185 Park Row
P.O. Box 878
New York, NY 10038
(212) 349-5340

International Home Exchange Service
P.O. Box 3975
San Francisco, CA 94119
(415) 382-0300

Inter Service Home Exchange
Box 87
Glen Echo, MD 20812
(301) 229-7567

Vacation Exchange Club
12006 111th Avenue
Youngstown, AZ 85363
(602) 972-2186

Visiting Friends, Inc.
P.O. Box 231
Lake Jackson, TX 77566
(409) 297-7367

The Travelers' Directory
1501 Wylie Drive
Modesto, CA 95355
(209) 524-9399

A special program for older Americans is:

Senior Travel Exchange Program
P.O. Box H
Santa Maria, CA 93456

Villa, Condominium, Or House Rentals.
A vacation rental of a villa, condominium, house, or cottage can provide more space than a hotel or resort at a price that is more economical, especially for parties of four people or more. Most travel agencies have contacts with specialized agencies and brokers that arrange

vacation rentals all over the world. If your travel agent does not have such contacts, you can contact these agencies directly, including:

Condo Club	(Ex. NJ)	(800) 272-6636
		(201) 842-5161
Four Star Living		(212) 355-2755
Rent A Home		
International		(206) 545-6963
Rent A Vacation		
Everywhere		(716) 454-6440
Villas International		(800) 221-2260
		(Ex. NY)
		(212) 929-7585

You can often arrange rentals with local companies that manage rental units. For referrals, contact:

Organization: Association of Vacation
Home Rental Managers
Box 341
Walnut Creek, CA 94596
(415) 947-3876

A number of publications list rentals all over the world, including:

Publication: *World-Wide Home Rental Guide*
Cost: $9.00 per year for 4 issues
From: World-Wide Home Rental Guide
130 Lincoln Avenue, Suite 842
Sante Fe, NM 87501
(505) 988-5188

Camping. America has over 20,000 campgrounds on both public and private lands that accommodate recreational vehicles and tent campers. Many of these campgrounds offer discounts to older Americans. For information and trip planning assistance:

Book: *National Park Camping Guide* (S/N 024-005-01028-9)
Cost: $3.50

Contains: Detailed information on 440 developed campsites in our country's 354 national parks. The Golden Eagle Passport, free to everyone age 62 and over, provides free admission to national parks and 50% discount on camping fees
From: Superintendent of Documents
U.S. Government Printing Office
Washington, DC 20402
(202) 783-3238

Organization: U.S. Forest Service
Services: Forest Service supervises more than 6,000 campgrounds in 156 forests. Information on camping in a national forest is available from the forest supervisor of each individual forest. For a list of forest supervisors, request order no. FS-65
For information: Forest Service
U.S. Department of Agriculture
Office of Information
P.O. Box 2417
Washington, DC 20013

Organization: Bureau of Land Management
Services: Supervises over 300 million acres in the western United States. Will provide camping information
For information: Bureau of Land Management
Public Affairs Office
1800 C Street, NW
Washington, DC 20240

Organization: U.S. Fish & Wildlife Service
Services: Supervises 448 national wildlife refuges, some of which allow camping. Publishes free *National Wildlife Refuges—A Visitor's Guide*
For information: U.S. Fish & Wildlife Service
Publications Department
4401 N. Fairfax, Room 130
Arlington, VA 22201

Organization: State Parks
Services: Every state operates a system of state parks, many of which have camping facilities. Admission to many of these systems is free to older Americans
For information: Call or write the state office of tourism (see pages 467–471)

Organization: Kampgrounds of America (KOA)
Services: Largest private campground chain, with over 650 locations nationwide. KOA Value Card ($4.00) provides a 10% discount at all locations. Directory is free at all locations or $3.00 by mail
For information: KOA
P.O. Box 30162
Billings, MT 5914
(406) 248-7444

Organization: Leisure Systems, Inc.
Services: Operates Safari Campgrounds and Yogi Bear Jellystone Campgrounds. Gives 15% discounts to those 65 and over, with their own identification card. ID cards may be obtained at any campground or send $2.00 and photostat of driver's license or other proof of age
For information: Leisure Systems, Inc.
14 S. Third Avenue
Sturgeon Bay, WI 54235
(800) 558-2954

Organization: American Automobile Association (AAA)
Services: Publishes regional AAA Campbook for every area of the country that includes listing of sites, costs, and services. Free to AAA members
For information: Call local AAA office (see White Pages)

Organization: Go Camping America!
Services: Information service sponsored by the Recreational Vehicle Industry Association. Publishes free *Recreation Vehicle Reference Lists*, which include:
  RV Public Shows
  RV Rental Sources
  Campground Information
  State Campground Associations
  Camping Clubs
  Publications for Campers and RV Owners
  RV Accessibility for the Handicapped
Also publishes free:
  Go Camping America brochure
  Catalog of Publications About the RV Life-Style
For information: Go Camping America!
P.O. Box 2669
Reston, VA 22090
(703) 620-6003

Directory: *Rand McNally RV Park & Campground Directory*
Cost: $13.95 plus $2.25 postage
From: Simon & Schuster
200 Old Tappan Road
Old Tappan, NJ 07675

Directory: *Trailer Life RV Campground & Services Directory*
Cost: $10.95 plus $2.25 postage
From: TL Enterprises
29901 Agoura Road
Agoura, CA 91301

Many campers and RV owners enjoy benefits of membership in organizations, including:

Organization: Good Sam RV Owners Club
c/o Susan Bray
22901 Agoura Road
Agoura, CA 91301
(818) 991-4980

Organization: National Campers and Hikers Association
c/o Fran Opela

4804 Transit Road
Depew, NY 104043
(716) 668-6242

Organization: The National RV Owners
Club

International Family Recreation Association
P.O. Drawer 17148
Pensacola, FL 32522
(904) 477-2123

TRAVELING ABROAD

The best way to enjoy any trip abroad, whether it's for business, pleasure, or study, is to prepare ahead of time. The more you learn about passports, visas, customs, and other travel basics, the less likely you are to have difficulties while on your trip.

Two excellent general guides are:

Booklets: *Your Trip Abroad* ($1.00)
Travel Tips for Senior Citizens ($1.00)
From: Consumer Information Center
P.O. Box 100
Pueblo, CO 81009

How to Obtain a Passport

A valid U.S. passport is required for entry to most foreign countries and for readmittance to the United States. People applying for their first passport must apply in person, while people who have been issued a passport within the last 12 years and who have their old passports may apply by mail. You may apply for passports at many federal and state courts and at many post offices. The application may take 1 or more months to process. For information about obtaining a passport, the location of the passport application site nearest you, and information about obtaining a passport quickly in an emergency, contact one of the passport offices below:

Boston Passport Agency
10 Causeway Street
Boston, MA 02222
(617) 565-6990 (Public Inquiries)

Chicago Passport Agency
Suite 380, Klucyzynski Federal Building
230 South Dearborn Street
Chicago, IL 60604
(312) 353-5426 (Recording)
(312) 353-7155 (Public Inquiries)

Honolulu Passport Agency
Room C-106, New Federal Building
300 Ala Moana Blvd.
P.O. Box 50185
Honolulu, HI 96850
(808) 541-1919 (Recording)
(808) 541-1918 (Public Inquiries)

Houston Passport Agency
One Allen Center
500 Dallas Street
Houston, TX 77002
(713) 653-3153 (Public Inquiries)

Los Angeles Passport Agency
Room 13100, 11000 Wilshire Blvd.
Los Angeles, CA 90024
(213) 209-7070 (Recording)
(213) 209-7075 (Public Inquiries)

Miami Passport Agency
16th Floor, Federal Office Building
51 Southwest First Avenue
Miami, FL 33130

(305) 536-5395 (Recording)
(305) 536-4681 (Public Inquiries)

New Orleans Passport Agency
Postal Services Building
Room T-12005
701 Loyola Avenue
New Orleans, LA 70013
(504) 589-6728 (Recording)
(504) 589-6161 (Public Inquiries)

New York Passport Agency
Room 270, Rockefeller Center
630 Fifth Avenue
New York, NY 10111
(212) 541-7700 (Recording)
(212) 541-7710 (Public Inquiries)

Philadelphia Passport Agency
Room 4426, Federal Building
600 Arch Street
Philadelphia, PA 19106
(215) 597-7482 (Recording)
(215) 597-7480 (Public Inquiries)

San Francisco Passport Agency
Suite 200, 525 Market Street
San Francisco, CA 94105
(415) 974-7972 (Recording)
(415) 974-9941 (Public Inquiries)

Seattle Passport Agency
Room 992, Federal Office Building
915 Second Avenue
Seattle, WA 98174
(206) 442-7941 (Recording)
(206) 442-7945 (Public Inquiries)

Stamford Passport Agency
One Landmark Square
Stamford, CT 06901
(203) 325-4401 (Recording)
(203) 325-3538 (Public Inquiries)

How to Obtain Visas

To enter many countries, you need a visa, a stamp or endorsement placed in your passport that permits you to visit a specific country for a specific period of time. In most cases, visas must be obtained before you leave the United States. For information about visa requirements:

Publication: *Foreign Visa Requirements*
Cost: $0.50
Contains: A list of foreign countries that require visas and addresses where visas may be obtained
From: Consumer Information Center
P.O. Box 100
Pueblo, CO 81009

Immunizations and Other Health Matters

Information on vaccination and certificate requirements, U.S. Public Health Service recommendations, and other medical information for travelers is available in:

Publication: *Health Information for International Travel*
Cost: $4.75

Booklet: *PHS-731 International Certificates of Vaccination* as Approved by the World Health Organization
Cost: $2.00
From: Superintendent of Documents
U.S. Government Printing Office
Washington, DC 20402

Many travelers fear becoming ill or otherwise needing medical treatment while they are abroad. Among the resources that can ease that fear are:

Organization: International Association for Medical Assistance to Travelers (IAMAT)

Cost: Membership free, but donations are welcomed

Services: Members receive a directory of IAMAT centers and IAMAT approved English-speaking physicians in over 450 cities in 120 countries. IAMAT physicians are available 24 hours a day, and they all agree to charge standard fees. IAMAT also has several valuable publications, including:

- *World Climate Chart,* which includes average temperatures, recommended clothing, and recommendations about food and sanitary conditions
- *World Immunization Chart*
- *How to Adapt to Altitude*
- *How to Avoid Travelers Diarrhea*
- *Personal Health in Warm Countries*
- *How to Protect Yourself Against Malaria*

For information: IAMAT
417 Center Street
Lewiston, NY 14092
(716) 754-4883

Organization: Intermedic, Inc.

Cost: $6.00 per year for one person, $10.00 for family

Services: Provides directory of approved physicians in over 90 countries who have agreed upon fixed charges. Provides information and answers questions about immunizations, health risks, and other health- related problems

For information: Intermedic, Inc.
777 Third Avenue
New York, NY 10017
(212) 486-8900

Program: Global Assist

Cost: Free to American Express members

Services: Provides referrals to physicians and assistance in obtaining prescriptions and other medical supplies all over the world

For information: (800) 554-2639 (U.S.)
(202) 783-7474 (Call collect from overseas)

Another final problem that can be encountered while traveling is that some health insurance programs, including Medicare, do not pay for treatment received out of the country. You should check with your insurance company before you leave. If you are not covered, you should consider purchasing travel health insurance, which is often packaged with insurance that covers trip cancellation, emergency evacuation, and loss of luggage and personal items. This coverage is sometimes provided as a benefit by certain credit card and travelers check companies.

Among the companies that provide emergency health insurance:

Access America	(800) 284-8300 (NY Ex.)
	(212) 490-5345
ARM Carefree	(800) 645-2424 (NY Ex.)
	(516) 294-0220
Travel Assistance	(800) 821-2828 (DC Ex.)
International	(202) 347-6615
Health Care	(800) 237-6615 (VA Ex.)
Abroad	(703) 281-9500
International SOS	(800) 523-8930 (TX Ex.)
Assistance	(214) 404-9980
Travel Guard	(800) 826-1300 (WI Ex.)
International	(715) 345-0505
WorldCare Travel	(800) 521-4822 (DC Ex.)
Assistance	(202) 293-2623

Student Identification

Any American of any age who is a registered student can take advantage of student discounts abroad by obtaining a Student Identity Card.

For information:

Council on International Educational Exchange
205 East 42nd Street
New York, NY 10017

Travel Information from the U.S. Government

The U.S. government has some low-cost publications that can acquaint you with the countries you're visiting. Among them are:

Publication: *Background Notes*
Contains: Current information on the people, culture, geography, history, government, economy, and political conditions of 170 countries. Order by country name ($2.00 per country)

Publications: *Tips for Travelers*
Cost: $1.00 each
Contains: Advice for travelers prepared by the State Department for certain countries or regions. The titles are: *Tips for Travelers to . . .*
– *the Caribbean*
– *to Cuba*
– *to Eastern Europe and Yugoslavia*
– *to Mexico*
– *to the Middle East and North Africa*
– *to the People's Republic of China*
– *to South Asia*
– *to Sub-Saharan Africa*
– *to the USSR*
From: Superintendent of Documents
U.S. Government Printing Office
Washington, DC 20402

Traveling Safely

Political unrest and terrorism are concerns in today's world, although the vast majority of travelers have no experience with them. For general information:

Booklet: *A Safe Trip Abroad*
Cost: $1.00
From: Superintendent of Documents
U.S. Government Printing Office
Washington, DC 20402

For specific information about current problems in the country you wish to visit:

Organization: Department of State Citizen Emergency Center
Service: Provides information about travel advisories and other travel cautions
Call: (202) 647-5225

A quarterly publication that focuses on security while traveling is:

Publication: *Travel Wise*
Cost: Free
From: American Express Travelers Cheques
Department 220
220 Vesey Street
New York, NY 10285

Paying for Goods and Services While You're Traveling Abroad

Even travelers embarking on a package tour have to plan for the additional expenses of meals, tips, souvenirs and other purchases, taxis, and a myriad of incidental expenses. One important step in planning is to understand the rate of exchange between U.S. dollars and the currency of the country or countries you're visiting.

Foreign exchange rates are printed daily in most major U.S. newspapers. You can also contact:

Organization: Ruesch International
Services: Provides recorded message that

gives the current exchange rates for major foreign currencies. Will send the following free publications:

- *Foreign Currency Guide,* containing currency conversion tables and tipping customs
- *6 Foreign Exchange Tips for the Traveler*

For information: Ruesch International
1140 19th Street, NW
Washington, DC 20036
(800) 424-2923 (Ex. DC)
(202) 887-0990
(202) 887-0980 (Recorded Message)

Organization: Deak Perera
Services: Buys and sells foreign currencies, issues free foreign currency travelers checks, and provides information on foreign currency exchange rates through a recorded number
For information: Deak Perera
1800 K Street, NW
Washington, DC 20006
(800) 368-5683
(202) 872-8470
(202) 872-1630 (Recorded Message)

The three basic ways to pay for goods and services in foreign countries are:

- Currency. Experts recommend that you exchange U.S. dollars for a small amount of foreign currency before departure or at the airport upon arrival, to pay for taxis, tips, etc. However, carrying larger amounts of cash is dangerous.

- Travelers checks. Travelers checks are a safe and convenient way to carry money. The cost of purchasing travelers checks is normally 1% of the total face value of the checks. However, free travelers checks are available from:

AAA members can get free American Express travelers checks from any AAA office

Deak Perera (listed above) issues free travelers checks in foreign currencies

Many banks provide free travelers checks as part of their special packages for older depositors

- Credit cards. Credit cards are now widely accepted in most foreign countries. Using credit cards eliminates the charges for converting U.S. dollars into foreign currencies and provides a detailed record of expenditures. In an increasing number of foreign countries, Americans can use their credit cards to get cash from automatic teller machines. For information:

American Express	(800) 227-4669
Mastercard	(800) 223-3320
Visa	(800) 227-6811

Calling the United States from Another Country

Calling home from abroad can be very expensive and complicated. However, new services from two national long distance companies can slash the expense. They are:

Program: AT&T USA Direct
Service: Customers call an international toll-free number that connects them with an operator in the United States, who in turn places the credit card or collect call
For information: (800) 874-4000

Program: MCI Call USA
Service: Same as AT&T service above
For information: (800) 444-4444

Help from American Consuls

U.S. consular officers, located in embassies and consulates around the world, are available to provide advice for travelers with serious legal, medical, or financial problems. They also provide other services, such as assistance with lost passports, information on absentee voting, making available U.S. tax forms, and notarizing documents. They can also provide assistance and the necessary documents when a U.S. citizen dies or gives birth abroad.

Consular officials do not, however, perform travel services or mediate disputes with hotels, tour companies, or other foreign nationals. The U.S. government also does not:

- Pay for legal services
- Pay for medical care
- Provide money in financial emergencies
- Pay for medically necessary evacuation home
- Pay for transportation home of the body of a U.S. citizen

These expenses, which can be considerable, are often covered by travelers insurance policies.

For information on locating U.S. consular officers:

Publication: *Key Officers of Foreign Service Posts*
Cost: $1.75
From: Superintendent of Documents
U.S. Government Printing Office
Washington, DC 20402

Customs Regulations

Shopping is one of the pleasures of traveling to other countries. However, every item pur-chased abroad is potentially subject to customs regulations. Many travelers have had unpleasant surprises when purchases were subject to heavy duty or even confiscated on their return to the states. Shoppers can also have pleasant surprises. A large number of popular purchases from over 140 developing countries can be brought back into the U.S. duty-free under the "GSP" program.

For information on customs regulations:

Pamphlets: *Know Before You Go: Customs Hints for Returning Residents*
GSP and the Traveler
U.S. Customs International Mail Imports
Trademark Information for Travelers
Cost: Free
From: U.S. Custom Service
P.O. Box 7407
Washington, DC 20044

The U.S. Department of Agriculture has special regulations that may cause you problems if you bring food, plant, and animal products into this country. For information:

Pamphlet: *Travelers Tips on Bringing Food, Plant and Animal Products into the U.S.*
Cost: Free
From: Animal and Plant Health Inspection Service
U.S. Department of Agriculture
732 Federal Building
6505 Belcrest Road
Hyattsville, MD 20782

The U.S. government also has restrictions on the import of wildlife and wildlife products, especially related to endangered species. For information:

Pamphlet: *Buyer Beware!*
Cost: Free

From: Publications Unit
U.S. Fish and Wildlife Service

Department of the Interior
Washington, DC 20240

OTHER VALUABLE RESOURCES FOR TRAVELERS

Emergency Help When You're Traveling

Traveling can be frightening, especially when an emergency occurs, such as sudden illness or theft of money, tickets, and valuables. One source of help in many cities is:

Organization: Travelers Aid International
Services: Provides emergency assistance for travelers, including:

Information and referral
Counseling
Food and shelter
Financial assistance
Protective travel services
For information: Local Travelers Aid Society (see White Pages)

or

Travelers Aid
1001 Connecticut Avenue, NW, Suite 504
Washington, DC 20036
(202) 659-9468

CHAPTER 24

SPORTS

PARTICIPATING IN SPORTS

The last decade has witnessed an explosion in participation rates by Americans 50 and over in a wide variety of sports and outdoor activities. Part of this increase has developed from a huge growth in the number of special recreation programs and competitions for older athletes sponsored by organizations from local parks and recreation departments to the national Senior Olympics movement. The other part has resulted from increased participation by older Americans in a wide variety of activities and sports open to people of any age group. In this chapter, we cover the gamut of resources for everyone who wants to participate in most major sports.

Senior Games/Senior Olympics

The Senior Games are rapidly growing competitions for athletes age 50 and over. Competitions are held in many states in a wide variety of sports, including archery, basketball, badminton, bowling, cycling, golf, tennis, racquetball, swimming, track and field, shuffleboard, aerobic dancing, bocci ball, basketball shooting, table tennis, croquet, horseshoes, fly casting, and softball. Many senior games are part of the Senior Olympics, a series of competitions in 34 sports that culminates in a national U.S. Senior Olympics competition. Senior athletic competitions emphasize the social and recreational aspects of sports as much as the actual competition. Senior game athletes have ranged in age up to 101.

For information about forming a senior games competition:

Organization: Senior Games Development Council
200 Castlewood Drive
North Palm Beach, FL 33408
(303) 842-3600

Information on the Senior Olympics is available from:

Organization: U.S. National Senior Olympics
14323 S. Outer Forty Road, Suite N300
Chesterfield, MO 63017
(314) 878-4900

If you're interested in participating, contact your local area agency on aging, your local senior center, your local Parks and Recreation Department (see White Pages under your local government listing), or the Appendix (pages 427–433), for a complete state-by-state listing of local area senior game centers.

Archery

Archery is a sport in which people from a wide variety of age groups can compete. Avid archers may want to join:

Organization: National Archery Association
1750 E. Boulder Street
Colorado Springs, CO 80909
(719) 578-4576
Services: Members receive *U.S. Archer* magazine bimonthly and the *NAA Newsletter* four times per year. Members are also eligible to participate in sanctioned tournaments, many of which have Senior divisions for male and female archers age 50 and over. Membership dues are $15.00 per year

Badminton

Badminton is more than a popular backyard game. Competitions, many with divisions for players age 40 and older, are sponsored by clubs all over the country. For information:

Organization: U.S. Badminton Association
501 West Sixth Street
Papillion, NE 68046
(402) 592-7309

Bicycling

Bicycling is one of the best and most enjoyable forms of aerobic exercise, with one of every six adults cycling regularly. Many of these have so much fun that they move on to two other levels of involvement: competing in bicycle races and touring by bicycle.

Bicycle races are sponsored by almost 1,000 local cycling clubs across the country. For information:

Organization: U.S. Cycling Federation
1750 E. Boulder Street
Colorado Springs, CO 80909
(303) 578-4581
Services: Coordinates activities of local cycling clubs. Competitions usually include divisions for abilities ranging from beginner to advanced, and competitors are divided into 5-year age categories beginning at age 30 (for example, 30–34, 35–39, 40–45, etc.). Members receive a monthly magazine and license to participate in races.
Cost: $32.00 per year

Additional information about bicycle competitions and events can usually be obtained at local bicycle shops (see Yellow Pages under "Bicycle Dealers").

More than 200 organizations and tour companies sponsor U.S. and international bicycle tours. Many tours accommodate beginning riders by providing transportation over difficult sections. Tours range from camping tours to those that include overnight stays at luxury hotels. Guides to these tours include:

Publication: *The Tourfinder*
Cost: Free
Contains: Information on nearly 200 tour operators
From: League of American Wheelmen
6707 Whitestone Road, Suite 209
Baltimore, MD 21207
(301) 944-3399

Organization: American Youth Hostels
P.O. Box 37613
Washington, DC 20013
(202) 783-6161
Services: Sponsors special bicycle tours for people age 50 and over. Riders stay overnight at hostels in this country and abroad

Other sponsors of inexpensive tours are the conservation organizations listed under "Hiking" in this section (see pages 355–357).

Billiards

Many billiard parlors offer discounts to older players, as well as senior tournaments. For more information about the sport of billiards contact:

Organization: Billiard Congress of America
1901 Broadway, Suite 110
Iowa City, IA 52240
(319) 351-2112
Cost: $3.00 per year
Services: Player members receive a copy of the *Official Rule Book* and are eligible to participate in sanctioned tournaments

Boating

Americans own over 14 million pleasure boats, with almost one out of every five adults listing boating as a favorite activity. Many boat-owning families take their vacations on the water. In fact, boats with sleeping, kitchen, and toilet facilities qualify as "second homes" under IRS regulations, allowing full deduction of interest expenses (see Chapter 9, Taxes and Tax Preparation, pages 97–117, for complete information).

If you are interested in buying a boat, the National Marine Manufacturer's Association recommends that your first step should be attending one or more major boat shows. You'll be able to see thousands of different boats, engines, and other marine equipment. You can comparison shop for prices, talk with dealers and factory representatives, and explore special boat-show pricing and financing options. For a list of boat shows:

Directory: *International Boat Shows*
Cost: $2.00
Contains: A comprehensive listing of boat shows in the United States and abroad
From: National Marine Manufacturers Association
401 N. Michigan Avenue
Chicago, IL 60611
(312) 836-4747

Included in the costs of purchasing a boat are:

- Cost of boat
- Cost of engine (or sails)
- Cost of trailer
- Cost of options
- Delivery charges
- Make-ready charges
- State taxes

Most dealers require a down payment of 20% to 25%, and most offer financing packages. However, shopping for a boat loan can save as much money or more as shopping for any other type of loan. You should definitely get prices from a number of lenders, including your bank (see Chapter 4, Purchasing and Using Credit, pages 30–37).

Your yearly cost for operating a boat will include:

- Maintenance and repair
- Dockage or moorage
- Winter storage
- Loan payments
- Insurance
- Fuel (or new sails)

Federal law states that all boats with an engine or other propulsion machinery must be registered with the state in which the boat is principally used (the U.S. Coast Guard registers boats for New Hampshire and Alaska). In addition, many states require that yachts (sailboats without engines) also be registered. In addition, the federal government and many states have additional regulations concerning required equipment and operating procedures.

For information about federal regulations:

> **Brochure:** *Federal Requirements for Recreational Boats*
> **Cost:** Free
> **From:** U.S. Department of Transportation
> U.S. Coast Guard
> 2100 Second Street, SW
> Washington, DC 20593

Registering a boat is only part of boat ownership. Equally important is boat safety. Over 6,000 people die every year in boating accidents and many more are seriously injured. Boating courses are not only a must for novice owners, but a good idea as refreshers for the more experienced.

Many boating groups and organizations promote courses at local boat shows. The Coast Guard Auxiliary conducts many classes and in-

formation programs (see listings above). Another source of classes is:

> **Organization:** Boat/U.S.
> 880 S. Pickett Street
> Alexandria, VA 22304
> (800) 336-2628 (Ex. VA)
> (800) 245-2628 (VA)
> (703) 823-9550
> **Services:** Conducts boat-handling classes at more than 500 locations in the United States, including local lakes. Distributes boating safety materials, including free packet of six brochures, "6 Pack for Boating"

Many sailing classes are offered at the local level. Call a local yacht club, your local parks and recreation department, or look in the Yellow Pages under "Boating Instruction." Another excellent source of information is:

> **Organization:** National Sailing Industry Association
> 401 N. Michigan Dr.
> Chicago, IL 60611
> (312) 836-4747
> **Service:** Operates toll-free hotline that provides referral to more than 450 sailing schools certified by the American Sailing Association
> **Call:** (800) 447-4700

The U.S. government has prepared a basic self-instruction course:

> **Publication:** *Skipper's Course* (S/N 050-012-00225-8)
> **Cost:** $6.50
> **From:** U.S. Government Printing Office
> Superintendent of Documents
> Washington, DC 20402
> (202) 783-3238

Many boaters enjoy joining organizations, including:

Organization: American Canoe Association
P.O. Box 1190
Newington, VA 22122
(703) 550-7523

Organization: American Power Boat Association
17640 East Nine Mile Road
East Detroit, MI 48021
(313) 773-9700

Organization: U.S. Yacht Racing Union
Box 209
Newport, RI 02840
(401) 849-5200

Bocce

Bocce, or lawn bowling, is a popular sport in many areas of the country. For information:

Organization: U.S. Bocce Federation
1065 South Sheridan Blvd.
Denver, CO 80226
(303) 934-7211

Bowling

More than six million Americans age 55 and older go bowling at least once during the course of a year, and over two million bowlers participate weekly in senior bowling leagues. the fastest growing of all types of leagues. Senior membership in the American Bowling Congress increased 40% between 1987 and 1989, making bowling the fastest growing of all sports for older Americans.

With this phenomenal growth rate, it is not surprising that many bowling lanes offer discounts and other incentives to individual senior bowlers and those who want to form leagues.

For more information, ask at your local lanes or contact:

Organization: American Bowling Congress
5301 South 76th Street
Greendale, WI 53129
(414) 421-6400
Services: Coordinate amateur bowling in the United States. Sanctions tournaments and provides other information and assistance to bowlers. Publishes free brochure, *Local, State, National Programs for Senior Bowlers*

Program: Seniors on a Roll
National Bowling Council
1919 Pennsylvania Avenue, NW, Suite 504
Washington, DC 20006
(202) 659-9070
Services: Provides information on senior bowling programs and competitions

Croquet

Croquet has become one of the fastest growing adult participation sports in the United States. The number of participants has increased 5,000% since 1977, and the number of new croquet clubs is growing by an average of one per week. For information about the sport and location of the clubs:

Organization: United States Croquet Association
500 Avenue of Champions
Palm Beach Gardens, FL 33418
(407) 627-3999
Cost: Information/referral is free
Services: Sanctions tournaments, issues publications, and serves as a clearinghouse for information on croquet clubs, resorts, retirement community programs, and all other aspects of the sport

Fishing

Nearly one of every three adults fishes at least once during the course of the year. Fishing is a source of relaxation and pleasure that's inexpensive and accessible to the vast majority of Americans.

For older Americans, the cost of fishing is further reduced because almost all states and local governments provide free or discount fishing licenses to senior citizen residents. The age requirements for these discounts generally range from 60 to 65. Some states and local governments also provide free or discount licenses to older Americans who are visiting in the state. Most states also provide publications, maps, and other information of interest to outdoor sportsmen. For information, contact the appropriate state tourism bureau (see listings, pages 467–471).

Many fishermen increase their enjoyment of the sport by joining a fishing organization. These include:

> **Organization:** U.S. Bass Fishing Association
> 435 E. Main St.
> Mesa, AZ 85203
> (602) 834-5045

> **Organization:** Sport Fishing Institute
> 1010 Massachusetts Avenue, NW,
> Suite 110
> Washington, DC 20001
> (202) 898-0770

> **Organization:** International Game Fish Association
> 3000 East Las Olas Blvd.
> Ft. Lauderdale, FL 33316
> (305) 467-0161

> **Organization:** Bass, Inc.
> P.O. Box 17900
> Montgomery, AL 36141
> (205) 272-9530

Many fishermen also enjoy competing in fishing competitions. Information can be obtained from many local bait and tackle shops (see Yellow Pages under "Fishing Tackle-Retail"). Information is also included in the major fishing publications, including:

> **Publication:** *Field and Stream*
> 2 Park Avenue
> New York, NY 10016
> **Cost:** $15.94 per year for 12 issues

> **Publication:** *Rod & Reel*
> P.O. Box 42000
> Bergenfield, NJ 07621
> **Cost:**

Golf

The enormous success of the PGA Senior Golf Tour for professionals age 50 and over has refocused attention on the fact that golf is not only one of the most popular sports for older Americans, but also one that can be played competitively over an entire life span. The golf industry aggressively seeks older Americans as customers, offering special programs and discounts.

Most public golf courses in the United States give discounts to older golfers. In your home area, see the Yellow Pages under "Golf Courses—Public" for telephone numbers. Information about special tournaments, lessons, and other golf-related activities can usually be obtained from:

- Your local parks and recreation department
- Your local senior center
- Local golf driving ranges and pro shops

One national program that provides free golf at a wide variety of courses plus other benefits is:

Organization: National Senior Sports Association

Services: Membership organization for people age 50+. Members receive a special discount on "The Golf Card," which entitles them to play twice for free at more than 1,200 courses in the United States and abroad. Golf card members also receive subscription to the *Golf Traveler* magazine and directory of courses. NSSA members also are eligible for special tournaments and golf vacations in the United States and abroad

For information: National Senior Sports Association
10560 Main Street, Suite 205
Fairfax, VA 22030
(703) 549-6711

Many states and local areas have special publications and programs for visiting golfers. If you're planning to travel, contact the appropriate state tourism bureau ahead of time for information. Many hotels and resorts also have special arrangements and discounts for golfing guests. The tourist bureaus of many foreign governments have information on golf courses and competitions.

The governing body of U.S. golf is:

Organization: U.S. Golf Association (USGA)
P.O. Box 708
Far Hills, NJ 07931
(201) 234-2300

Services: Establishes rules of golf, rules of competition, administers the handicapping system, and governs the sport. Publishes rule book. Golfers may join as associate members

Among the golf associations for senior golfers are:

Organization: American Seniors Golf Association
P.O. Box 6645
Clearwater, FL 33518

Organization: North Carolina Senior Golf Association
P.O. Box 488
Wilson, NC 27894

Organization: Retired Military Seniors
P.O. Box 7293
Laguna Niguel, CA 92677

Organization: Society of Seniors
5523 Lincoln Street
Bethesda, MD 20817

Handball

For information about handball competitions, clubs, and rules:

Organization: U.S. Handball Association
930 North Benton Avenue
Tucson, AZ 85711
(602) 795-0434

Hiking

The number of adults who hike has doubled since 1969. For one out of every eight adults, hiking in America's millions of acres of beautiful wilderness is a frequent activity. Not only is following wilderness trails relaxing and enjoyable, but it is also a valuable form of aerobic exercise that helps keep participants healthy and fit.

Everyone interested in hiking can join:

Organization: American Hiking Society
1015 31st Street, NW

Washington, DC 20007
(703) 385-3252
Cost: $18.00 per year individual, $25.00 per year for a family
Services: Publishes the *American Hiker,* a monthly newsletter that contains invaluable information on hiking organizations, trail guides, equipment, and issues affecting the wilderness. Acts as advocate for protecting wilderness areas. Provides a listing of 53 local hiking and trail clubs that sponsor outings and issue publications. Publishes free brochure: *Hiking Safety*

Many hikers like to combine their hikes with public service. The American Hiking Society publishes quarterly a directory of organizations and government agencies that use volunteers to help maintain trails and perform other public services:

Directory: *Helping Out in the Outdoors*
Cost: $3.00 for 1 issue, $12.00 for yearly subscription
From: The American Hiking Society
1015 31st Street, NW
Washington, DC 20007
(703) 385-3252

Another organization that specializes in outdoor activities for women over 40 is:

Organization: Outdoor Vacations for Women over 40
P.O. Box 200
Groton, MA 01450
(617) 448-3331
Services: Organizes hiking, biking, camping, boating, and skiing vacations for women over age 40

Other organizations of interest to hikers are:

Organization: The Nature Conservancy
1815 North Lynn Street
Arlington, VA 22209
(703) 841-5300
Cost: $15.00 per year, $25.00 per family
Services: This organization of nearly one half million finds endangered national lands and communities, organizes their acquisition as nature preserves, and manages many preserves with staff and volunteers. The organization protects over 3.3 million acres, and manages nearly 1,000 preserves. Members receive a bimonthly magazine, a directory of preserves open to visitors, and the chance to participate in volunteer projects and nature tours

Organization: The Wilderness Society
1400 Eye Street, NW
Washington, DC 20005
(202) 842-3400
Cost: $30.00 per year
Services: An organization with over 200,000 members that acts as an advocate for protecting the American wilderness. Members receive the quarterly *Wilderness* magazine, book discounts, and information about threats to the environment

Organization: The Sierra Club
730 Polk St.
San Francisco, CA 94109
(415) 776-2211
Services: America's oldest grass roots conservation and environmental action association. Members receive Sierra magazine, discounts on books and other publications, and membership in local chapters. The 57 local chapters and other regional groups sponsor meetings and other activities. National Outing Program sponsors over 250 hiking, bicycling, or boating trips annually

Cost: $33.00 per year individual, $41.00 joint membership

Organization: Izaak Walton League of America
1401 Wilson Blvd., Level B
Arlington, VA 22209
(703) 528-1818

For hikers interested in obtaining maps, the U.S. government has prepared the free brochure:

Brochure: *Types of Maps Published by the U.S. Government*
From: U.S. Geological Survey
National Cartographic Information Center
1507 National Center
Reston, VA 22092

Horseback Riding

Many private stables offer discount lessons and rentals to older Americans, either on their own or through local senior centers or parks and recreation departments. For information, see Yellow Pages under "Riding Academies" or contact your local senior center or parks and recreation department.

For information about riding, horse ownership, and competitions:

Organization: American Horse Council
1700 K Street, NW, Number 300
Washington, DC 20006
(202) 296-4031

Horseshoes

An estimated 30,000,000 Americans pitch horseshoes at least once a year, and the sport has reached headlines because it's a favorite leisure activity of President George Bush. A new spurt of serious popularity has occurred because of the development of indoor horseshoe pitching pits. For more information:

Organization: The National Horseshoe Pitchers Association
Box 278
Munroe Falls, OH 44262
(216) 688-6522
Services: Establishes rules, publishes a monthly news digest, organizes tournaments and travel, and provides referral to over 60 local chapters

Hunting

About one in every 10 adults hunts at least once a year. Many states give a discount on hunting licenses to older hunters. For information about hunting seasons, licenses, and opportunities in each state, contact:

- The state tourism bureau
- The state fish and game commission

Hunting safety is a major concern of everyone in the sport, including older hunters. For information about hunting safety programs:

Organization: National Rifle Association
1600 Rhode Island Avenue, NW
Washington, DC 20036
(202) 828-6000

Organization: North American Hunting Club
P.O. Box 35557
Minneapolis, MN 55435
(612) 941-7654

Of special interest to bow hunters are:

Organization: Fred Bean Sports Club
R.R. 4
4600 S.W. 41st Blvd.
Gainsville, FL 32601
(904) 376-2327

Organization: National Crossbow Hunters
Association
118 Main Street
Wadsworth, OH 44281

Paddle Tennis

For information on the sport of paddle tennis and competitions:

Organization: U.S. Paddle Tennis Association
189 Seeley Street
Brooklyn, NY 11218

Racquetball

Racquetball has become the most popular indoor racquet game, played annually by 6% of American adults. For information about tournaments, contact local racquetball courts (see Yellow Pages under "Racquetball Courts") or:

Organization: American Amateur Racquetball Association
815 North Weber
Colorado Springs, CO 80903
(303) 635-5396

Running

Over the last two decades, running has become an increasingly popular pastime for older Americans. As a consequence, there has been an explosion in the number of competitions for "masters," runners age 40 and over. These competitions, most of which are open to runners of all experience and ability, include long-distance running, cross-country running, and track events.

The governing body for many of these competition is:

Organization: The Athletics Congress (TAC)
Services: Replaced the American Athletic Union as the governing body of amateur sports in 1979. Membership is open to anyone, and members may participate in hundreds of events sponsored by TAC's 56 local associations
For information: The Athletics Congress
200 S. Capitol Avenue
Indianapolis, IN 46225
(317) 638-9155

For a list of masters long-distance running events:

Organization: TAC Masters Long Distance
Running Committee
Carol Langenbach
4261 S. 184th Street
Seattle, WA 98188
(206) 433-8868

For a list of masters track and field competitions:

Organization: TAC Masters Track and Field
Committee
Al Sheehan
P.O. Box 2372
Van Nuys, CA 91404
(818) 785-1895

An excellent publication for all masters runners is:

Publication: *National Masters News*
    P.O. Box 5185
    Pasadena, CA 91107
Cost: $18.75 for 12 issues per year

More information about running may be obtained from:

Organization: Road Runners Club of America
    629 S. Washington Street
    Alexandria, VA 22314
    (703) 836-0558

Runners interested in entering marathons can find information on upcoming events listed in:

Publication: *Runner's World*
    33 East Minor Street
    Emmaus, PA 18049

Shooting

Organizations of interest to people who enjoy shooting are:

Organization: Amateur Trapshooting Association
    601 West National Road
    Vandalia, OH 45377
    (513) 898-4638

Organization: National Skeet Shooting Association
    P.O. Box 680007
    San Antonio, TX 78268
    (512) 688-3371

Organization: National Shooting Sports Foundation
    555 Danbury Road
    Wilton, CT 06897
    (203) 762-1320

Skiing—Cross Country

Cross-country skiing is a rapidly growing sport, which is a wonderful aerobic exercise, as well as mentally invigorating. Instructions in cross-country skiing are offered by almost all cross-country ski areas throughout the country. To find cross-country areas near you:

Directory: *Destinations*
Cost: $2.00
Contains: National directory of cross-country ski areas
From: Cross Country Ski Areas of America
    259 Bolton Road
    Winchester, NH 03470
    (603) 239-4341

Almost all of these areas offer discounts to senior skiers.

You don't have to go to a private cross-country ski area to enjoy the sport. Many national and state parks have cross-country skiing trails. Americans age 62 and over can obtain free admission to all national parks, as well as free admission to many state parks. For more information, see pages 434–443.

If you're interested in competing in cross-country ski races that are separated by ages up to 75 and over:

Organization: World Masters Cross Country Skiing Association
    P.O. Box 718
    Hayward, WI 54843
    (715) 634-4891

Skiing—Downhill

Because the number of young people is dwindling rapidly, the downhill-skiing industry has launched an aggressive campaign to introduce this exciting sport to more older Americans.

Almost every ski area in the country offers free or inexpensive lessons to beginners, as well as free or discount lift tickets. For information about ski resorts, contact the appropriate state tourism bureau (see listings, pages 467–471).

In addition to discounts, many local ski areas sponsor special clubs for seniors that include other benefits, such as free parking, discount meals and lodging, social events, discounts on equipment, and other benefits. Among the national ski organizations are:

Organization: The Over-The-Hill Gang
13791 E. Rice Place
Aurora, CA 80015
(303) 699-6404
Services: Open to people age 50 and older. Organizes ski trips and other outdoor activities. Local groups have special skiing arrangements with local ski areas that include discounts, free services, and social events

Organization: 70+ Ski Club
c/o Lloyd Lambert
104 East Side Drive
Ballston Lake, NY 12019
(518) 399-5458
Cost: $5.00 lifetime membership
Services: Open to downhill skiers age 70 and older. Members receive a newsletter, a long list of ski areas at which they can ski free or for a discount, and opportunities to join special trips to the major ski areas of the world. Members include former President Jerry Ford

Organization: U.S. Ski Association
P.O. Box 100
Provo, UT 84060
(801) 649-9090

If you're interested in competing, you can contact "National Standard Race" (NASTAR), a national program that organizes races for men and women of all abilities up to age 70+ You can register at most ski areas or:

Organization: NASTAR
P.O. Box 4580
Aspen, CO 81612
(303) 925-7864

Softball

Organized senior softball is one of the newest and fastest growing senior sports, with over 3,000 leagues in play. To find a league contact your local department of parks and recreation (see White Pages under your city government listing) or contact:

Organization: Senior Softball-USA
Bob Mitchell, President
9 Fleet Court
Sacramento, CA 95831
(916) 393-8566

Organization: NASCS (National Association of Senior Citizen Softball)
Ken Maas, President
P.O. Box 1085
Mt. Clemens, MI 48046
(313) 791-9520

Squash Racquets

For information about the sport and competitions:

Organization: U.S. Squash Racquets Association
211 Ford Road
Bala-Cynwyd, PA 19004
(215) 667-4006

Swimming

Swimming is among the best exercises for Americans of all ages. It is particularly valuable for people with arthritis or other conditions that make walking, running, or cycling difficult.

Older Americans can find places to swim in almost every community. Most municipal pools and beaches, most YMCAs and YWCAs, and most other nonprofit organizations provide free or discount swimming passes to senior citizens, with the qualifying age ranging from 55 to 65. For information, call your local parks and recreation department, the adult education department of your local school system, your local senior center, or your local YMCA or YWCA.

Another resource for avid swimmers is the U.S. Masters Swimming Program, organized program of swimming for adults age 19 and over. There are over 450 local Masters Swim Clubs throughout the United States. The facilities available to members range from just swimming pools to exercise equipment and other health club amenities. Masters Swimming Clubs also sponsor competitions divided into 5-year age groups that range up to "90 and over." Membership is just $9 per year, and includes subscription to a national newsletter. For information:

> **Organization:** U.S. Masters Swimming
> 2 Peters Avenue
> Rutland, MA 01543
> (508) 886-6631

Table Tennis

Tens of millions of Americans play table tennis (ping pong) in their basements and rec rooms. Organized competitions often include divisions for older age groups. For information:

> **Organization:** U.S. Table Tennis Association
> 1750 East Boulder Street
> Colorado Springs, CO 80909
> (303) 578-4583

Tennis

Few sports are more popular with Americans age 50 and over than tennis. And few sports organizations have made as much effort to develop information and programs for senior tennis players than the U.S. Tennis Association (USTA). The USTA has formed the USTA Senior Tennis Council to coordinate senior tennis and disseminate information. The USTA publishes:

> **Directory:** *USTA Senior Tennis Directory*
> **Cost:** $5.00 plus $1.50 postage
> **Contains:** A comprehensive guide for players age 50 and over that includes descriptions and addresses for more than 200 programs all over the country
> **From:** USTA Publications Department
> 707 Alexander Road
> Princeton, NJ 08540
> (609) 452-2580

For answers to specific questions:

> **Organization:** USTA Senior Tennis Council
> 1212 Avenue of the Americas
> New York, NY 10036
> (212) 302-3322

Many cities, towns, and counties provide free or discount season passes to local tennis facilities to older Americans. For information, contact your local parks and recreation department or call your local senior center.

Walking

In our discussion of physical fitness and exercise, we pointed out that walking has become the favorite aerobic activity of older Americans. Those interested in doing more than strolling around the block might want to contact two organizations that sponsor walking tours and clubs:

Organization: The Walkers Club of America
445 E. 86th Street
New York, NY 10128

Organization: The Walkways Center
1400 16th Street, NW
Washington, DC 20036
(202) 234-5299

Racewalking has also become an increasingly popular athletic activity. For more information about masters competitions for those age 40 and older:

Organization: The Athletics Congress
200 S. Capitol Avenue
Indianapolis, IN 46225
(317) 638-9155

Walking is also a featured event in many senior games and senior olympics (see above).

SPECTATOR SPORTS

Seven of every 10 adult Americans classify themselves as sports fans, and part of the fun of being a fan is attending a sports event in person. In this chapter, we include the telephone numbers of the major American sports teams and events. If you're planning to attend a sports event while you're traveling, plan ahead—many are sold out by the day of the competition. When you contact a team or event, always ask about senior citizen discounts—while they are less common in sports than in other areas of recreation, they do exist. You should also ask about discounts and other benefits if you are purchasing tickets for a group of 10 or more people. Finally, ask about arrangements for people in wheelchairs or with other disabilities—most teams and events have special parking and seating areas.

MAJOR LEAGUE BASEBALL

Over 21 million people attend major league baseball games during the course of a year, and millions more watch the players in spring training during Florida or Arizona vacations. To obtain information:

Spring Training Sites

AMERICAN LEAGUE

BALTIMORE ORIOLES
Miami, FL
(407) 588-3309

BOSTON RED SOX
Winter Haven, FL
(813) 293-3900

CALIFORNIA ANGELS
Mesa, AZ
(714) 937-6700

CHICAGO WHITE SOX
Sarasota, FL
(813) 953-3388

CLEVELAND INDIANS
Tucson, AZ
(602) 791-4266

DETROIT TIGERS
Lakeland, FL
(813) 682-1401

KANSAS CITY ROYALS
Orlando, FL
(800) 826-1939 (Ex. FL)
(800) 525-8233

MILWAUKEE BREWERS
Chandler, AZ
(602) 821-2200

MINNESOTA TWINS
Orlando, FL
(407) 849-6346

NEW YORK YANKEES
Fort Lauderdale, FL
(305) 776-1921

OAKLAND ATHLETICS
Phoenix, AZ
(800) 366-3269

SEATTLE MARINERS
Tempe, AZ
(602) 438-8900

TEXAS RANGERS
Port Charlotte, FL
(813) 625-9500

TORONTO BLUE JAYS
Dunedin, FL
(813) 733-9302

NATIONAL LEAGUE

ATLANTA BRAVES
West Palm Beach, FL
(407) 683-6100

CHICAGO CUBS
Mesa, AZ
(602) 964-4467

CINCINNATI REDS
Plant City, FL
(813) 752-7337

HOUSTON ASTROS
Kissimmee, FL
(407) 839-3900

LOS ANGELES DODGERS
Vero Beach, FL
(407) 569-4900

MONTREAL EXPOS
West Palm Beach, FL
(407) 689-9121

NEW YORK METS
Port St. Lucie, FL
(407) 879-7378

PHILADELPHIA PHILLIES
Clearwater, FL
(813) 442-8496

PITTSBURGH PIRATES
Bradenton, FL
(813) 748-4610

ST. LOUIS CARDINALS
St. Petersburg, FL
(813) 822-3384

SAN DIEGO PADRES
Yuma, AZ
(602) 782-2567

SAN FRANCISCO GIANTS
Scottsdale, AZ
(602) 994-5123

Regular Season

AMERICAN LEAGUE

BALTIMORE ORIOLES
(301) 243-9800

BOSTON RED SOX
(617) 267-9440

CALIFORNIA ANGELS
(714) 937-6700

CHICAGO WHITE SOX
(312) 924-1000

CLEVELAND INDIANS
(216) 961-1200

DETROIT TIGERS
(313) 962-4000

KANSAS CITY ROYALS
(816) 921-2200

MILWAUKEE BREWERS
(414) 933-1818

MINNESOTA TWINS
(612) 375-7444

NEW YORK YANKEES
(212) 293-6000

OAKLAND ATHLETICS
(415) 638-4900

SEATTLE MARINERS
(206) 628-3555

TEXAS RANGERS
(817) 273-5222

TORONTO BLUE JAYS
(416) 595-0077

NATIONAL LEAGUE

ATLANTA BRAVES
(404) 577-9100

CHICAGO CUBS
(312) 281-5050

CINCINNATI REDS
(513) 421-7337

HOUSTON ASTROS
(713) 799-9500

LOS ANGELES DODGERS
(213) 224-1530

MONTREAL EXPOS
(514) 253-3434

NEW YORK METS
(718) 507-6387

PHILADELPHIA PHILLIES
(215) 463-1000

PITTSBURGH PIRATES
(412) 323-5000

ST. LOUIS CARDINALS
(314) 421-3060

SAN DIEGO PADRES
(619) 283-7294

SAN FRANCISCO GIANTS
(415) 468-3700

Professional Football

The National Football League (NFL) tops all sports in the size of its television-viewing audience. The NFL teams are:

ATLANTA FALCONS
(404) 261-5400

BUFFALO BILLS
(716) 648-1800

CHICAGO BEARS
(312) 295-6600

CINCINNATI BENGALS
(513) 621-3550

CLEVELAND BROWNS
(216) 695-5555

DALLAS COWBOYS
(214) 556-9900

DENVER BRONCOS
(303) 433-7466

DETROIT LIONS
(313) 335-4131

GREEN BAY PACKERS
(414) 494-2351

HOUSTON OILERS
(713) 797-9111

INDIANAPOLIS COLTS
(317) 297-7000

KANSAS CITY CHIEFS
(816) 924-9300

LOS ANGELES RAIDERS
(213) 322-3451

LOS ANGELES RAMS
(714) 535-7267

MIAMI DOLPHINS
(305) 620-5000

MINNESOTA VIKINGS
(612) 828-6500

NEW ENGLAND PATRIOTS
(617) 543-7911

NEW ORLEANS SAINTS
(504) 733-0255

NEW YORK GIANTS
(201) 935-8111

NEW YORK JETS
(212) 421-6600

PHILADELPHIA EAGLES
(215) 463-2500

PHOENIX CARDINALS
(602) 967-1402

PITTSBURGH STEELERS
(412) 323-1200

SAN DIEGO CHARGERS
(619) 280-2111

SAN FRANCISCO 49ERS
(408) 562-4949

SEATTLE SEAHAWKS
(206) 827-9777

TAMPA BAY BUCCANEERS
(813) 870-2700

WASHINGTON REDSKINS
(703) 471-9100

College Bowl Games

BLUEBONNET BOWL
3300 Main, Third Floor
Houston, TX 77002
(713) 520-0816

COTTON BOWL
Box 47420
Dallas, TX 75247
(214) 638-2695

FIESTA BOWL
5144 East Camelback Road
Phoenix, AZ 85018
(602) 947-2998

GATOR BOWL
1801 Art Museum Drive
Jacksonville, FL 32207

HULA BOWL
1000 Lower Campus Road
Honolulu, HI 96822

ORANGE BOWL
P.O. Box 350748
Miami, FL 33135

ROSE BOWL
391 South Orange Grove Road
Pasadena, CA 91184

SUGAR BOWL
Louisiana Superdome
1500 Sugar Bowl Drive
New Orleans, LA 70112

Professional Basketball

Seven million Americans witness the thrills of
NBA basketball during the average season. For
ticket information:

ATLANTA HAWKS
(404) 681-3600

BOSTON CELTICS
(617) 523-6050

CHARLOTTE HORNETS
(704) 376-6430

CHICAGO BULLS
(312) 853-3636

CLEVELAND CAVALIERS
(216) 659-9100

DALLAS MAVERICKS
(214) 988-0117

DENVER NUGGETS
(303) 893-6700

DETROIT PISTONS
(313) 377-0100

GOLDEN STATE WARRIORS
(415) 638-6300

HOUSTON ROCKETS
(713) 627-0600

INDIANA PACERS
(317) 263-2100

LOS ANGELES CLIPPERS
(213) 748-8000

LOS ANGELES LAKERS
(213) 674-6000

MIAMI HEAT
(305) 577-4328

MILWAUKEE BUCKS
(414) 272-0500

MINNESOTA TIMBERWOLVES
(612) 544-3865

NEW JERSEY NETS
(201) 935-8888

NEW YORK KNICKERBOCKERS
(212) 563-8054

ORLANDO MAGIC
(305) 422-7433

PHILADELPHIA 76ERS
(215) 339-7600

PHOENIX SUNS
(602) 266-5753

PORTLAND TRAIL BLAZERS
(503) 234-9291

SACRAMENTO KINGS
(916) 928-6900

SAN ANTONIO SPURS
(512) 224-4611

SEATTLE SUPERSONICS
(206) 281-5850

UTAH JAZZ
(801) 355-3865

WASHINGTON BULLETS
(301) 773-2255

Professional Hockey

Professional hockey is a sport that must be seen in person to be truly appreciated. For ticket information:

BOSTON BRUINS
(617) 227-3206

BUFFALO SABRES
(716) 856-7300

CALGARY FLAMES
(403) 261-0475

CHICAGO BLACK HAWKS
(312) 733-5300

DETROIT RED WINGS
(313) 567-6000

EDMONTON OILERS
(403) 474-8561

HARTFORD WHALERS
(203) 728-3366

LOS ANGELES KINGS
(213) 419-3100

MINNESOTA NORTH STARS
(612) 853-9333

MONTREAL CANADIANS
(514) 932-2582

NEW JERSEY DEVILS
(201) 935-6050

NEW YORK ISLANDERS
(516) 794-4100

NEW YORK RANGERS
(212) 563-8000

PHILADELPHIA FLYERS
(215) 465-4500

PITTSBURGH PENGUINS
(412) 642-1800

QUEBEC NORDIQUES
(418) 529-8441

ST. LOUIS BLUES
(314) 781-5300

TORONTO MAPLE LEAFS
(416) 977-1641

VANCOUVER CANUCKS
(604) 254-5141

WASHINGTON CAPITOLS
(301) 967-5880

WINNIPEG JETS
(204) 772-9491

Professional Golf

Among the most popular spectator sports for adults are tournaments on the three professional golf tours:

- Men's PGA Tour
- Men's Senior PGA Tour
- Ladies PGA Tour

For a schedule of men's PGA and Senior PGA tour events:

PGA Tour
Sawgrass
Ponte Verdra Beach, FL 32082
(904) 285-3700

For a schedule of Ladies PGA tour events:

Ladies Professional Golf Association
4675 Sweetwater Blvd.
Sugar Land, TX 77479
(713) 980-5742

For information on the major U.S. golf tournaments:

THE MASTERS
Augusta National Golf Club
P.O. Box 2086
Augusta, GA 30913
(404) 738-7761

THE U.S. OPEN
U.S. Open Tournament Office
524 Post Street
San Francisco, CA 94102
(415) 587-0240

THE PGA CHAMPIONSHIP
PGA National Golf Club
1000 Avenue of Champions
Palm Beach Garden, FL 33410
(305) 694-1987

Professional Bowling

For a listing of events on the men's professional bowlers tour:

Professional Bowlers Association of America
1720 Merriman Road
Akron, OH 44313
(216) 836-5568

For a list of ladies professional bowling tour tournaments:

Ladies Pro Bowlers Tour
7171 Cherryvale Blvd.
Rockford, IL 61112
(815) 332-5756

Major Sports Events

Below are the addresses and telephone numbers you can contact for information on the other major annual events in the world of sports:

TENNIS GRAND SLAM EVENTS

United States Open
USTA
1212 Avenue of the Americas
New York, NY 10036
(212) 302-3322

Wimbledon/The Championships
All England Lawn Tennis & Croquet Club
Church Road, Wimbledon
SW19 5AE England
44-1-946-2244

Australian Open
P.O. Box 6002
Melbourne 3004
Victoria, Australia
61-3-267-3969

French Open
French Tennis Federation

Stade Roland Garros
2 Avenue Gordon Bennett
75016 Paris, France
4-743-9681

INDIANAPOLIS 500

Indianapolis Motor Speedway
4790 West 16th Street
Indianapolis, IN 46222
(317) 242-2501

NCAA BASKETBALL CHAMPIONSHIPS

NCAA
Nall Avenue at 63rd Street
P.O. Box 1906
Mission, KS 66201
(913) 384-3220

U.S. FIGURE SKATING CHAMPIONSHIPS

U.S. Figure Skating Association
20 First Street
Colorado Springs, CO 80906
(303) 635-5200

TRIPLE CROWN OF THOROUGHBRED
    HORSE RACING

Kentucky Derby
Churchill Downs
P.O. Box 8427
Louisville, KY 40208

Preakness
Pimlico Racecourse
Baltimore, MD 21215

Belmont Stakes
Belmont Park
P.O. Box 90
Jamaica, NY 11417

MARATHON RACES

Boston Marathon
17 Main Street
Hopkinton, MA 02574

New York City Marathon
NY Road Runners Club
9 East 89th Street
New York, NY 10128

U.S. GYMNASTICS CHAMPIONSHIPS

U.S. Gymnastics Federation
201 S. Capitol
Indianapolis, IN 46225
(317) 237-5050

OLYMPIC GAMES

U.S. Olympic Committee
1750 East Boulder Street
Colorado Springs, CO 80909
(719) 632-5551

CHAPTER 25

ARTS AND CRAFTS AND HOBBIES

ONE OF THE PLEASURES OF LIFE IS AN absorbing hobby to pursue in our leisure hours. Added to the intellectual stimulation of a hobby are two additional benefits:

- The opportunity to meet other people with similar interests

- The chance, in some cases, to produce additional income from, the hobby

Both the social contact and the additional income can be important, especially in the retirement years. In this chapter, we'll explore these opportunities as we list the resources for a wide variety of hobbies.

ARTS AND CRAFTS

Many people enjoy working with their hands to produce paintings, pottery, or other fine handicrafts, not only for their own pleasure but also for gifts to family and friends. There are a large number of programs that help older people interested in crafts to:

- Develop and improve skills
- Provide free or low-cost materials and supplies
- Provide an outlet for sales of the finished work

The sources of arts and craft classes and instruction are:

- Your local senior center
- Your local area agency on aging
- Your local adult education program
- Your local parks and recreation department
- Local craft supply stores

In most states, the central coordinating body for many special arts and crafts programs directed specifically to older residents is:

Organization: Your state arts council
For information: Call the number below:

ALABAMA
(205) 261-4076

ALASKA
(907) 279-1558

ARIZONA
(602) 255-5882

ARKANSAS
(501) 371-2539

CALIFORNIA
(916) 445-1530

COLORADO
(303) 866-2617

CONNECTICUT
(203) 566-4770

DELAWARE
(302) 571-3540

DISTRICT OF COLUMBIA
(202) 724-5613

FLORIDA
(904) 487-1083

GEORGIA
(404) 656-7520

HAWAII
(808) 548-4145

IDAHO
(208) 334-2119

ILLINOIS
(217) 793-6750

INDIANA
(317) 232-1268

IOWA
(515) 281-4451

KENTUCKY
(502) 564-8076

LOUISIANA
(504) 925-3930

MAINE
(207) 289-2724

MASSACHUSETTS
(617) 727-3668

MICHIGAN
800) 572-1160

MINNESOTA
(800) 652-9747

MISSOURI
(314) 444-6845

MONTANA
(406) 444-6430

NEBRASKA
(402) 554-2122

NEVADA
(702) 789-0225

NEW HAMPSHIRE
(603) 271-2789

NEW JERSEY
(609) 292-6130

NEW YORK
(212) 587-4967

NORTH CAROLINA
(919) 733-2821

NORTH DAKOTA
(701) 237-8962

PENNSYLVANIA
(717) 787-6883

RHODE ISLAND
(401) 277-3880

SOUTH CAROLINA
(803) 758-3442

SOUTH DAKOTA
(605) 339-6646

TENNESSEE
(615) 741-1701

TEXAS
(800) 252-9415

UTAH
(801) 533-5895

VERMONT
(802) 828-3291

VIRGINIA
(804) 225-3132

WASHINGTON
(206) 753-3860

WISCONSIN
(608) 266-0190

Two other sources of publications, bibliographies, and resource lists are:

Organization: The American Craft Council
40 W. 53rd Street
New York, NY 10019
(212) 956-3535
Services: Provides information and publications on all aspects of contemporary crafts, including *Craft Horizons,* a magazine

Organization: National Endowment for the Arts Program Information Office
Washington, DC 20506
(202) 682-5400

Services: Makes grants to craft producers and craft organizations and provides information on existing programs

Most people who are involved in crafts eventually find themselves with a significant surplus of finished goods. The U.S. government has found that there is a significant untapped market for handicrafts that can produce important income for its producers.

The three ways to sell craft products are to:

- Sell the work directly to the public from the home, from a shop, at a flea market or street fair, or at a yard sale
- Sell the work to a retail outlet or give the work to a shop that sells on consignment
- Join with other craft people to sell their combined works at special sales or through their own retail outlet. These cooperative efforts are often organized at senior centers or craft classes.

There are many valuable resources for people who want to sell crafts. Among them are:

Organization: The Elder Craftsmen
135 East 65th Street
New York, NY 10021
(212) 861-5260
Services: This nonprofit organization works to educate, encourage, and advise older people in the making and selling of fine handicrafts. The organization operates a retail outlet in New York City and issues several publications, including:
- *Office Sales and Planning Guide for Senior Craft Programs,* a 64-page handbook ($5.00)
- *Opportunities for Crafts for Older Adults: A Partial Listing of Nationwide Shops and Cooperatives* ($1.25)

- *The Elder Craftsmen Shop Guideline for Consigning Craftspeople* (Free)
- *Setting Up Shop the Elder Craftsmen Way* (Free)
- *Checklist for Successful Crafts* (Free)

Send self-addressed stamped envelope for free publications

Organization: Agricultural Cooperative Service
Services: This service of the U.S. Department of Agriculture has a number of publications of interest to people who want to organize a crafts cooperative, including:
- *Cooperative Approach to Crafts for Senior*
- *Citizens* ($1.25)
- *Craft Resources* ($1.00)

For information: U.S. Department of Agriculture
Cooperative Extension Service
Washington, DC 20250
(202) 447-3029

Publication: *The Quality Crafts Market*
521 Fifth Avenue, Suite 1700
New York, NY 10017
Cost: $24.00 per year for 12 issues
Contains: Articles on all phases of the crafts business

A special source of information for native American craftsmen is:

Organization: Indian Arts and Crafts Board
U.S. Department of the Interior
Washington, DC 20240

GENEALOGY—TRACING YOUR ROOTS

A 1987 Gallup poll revealed that seven million American adults, most of them age 50 and over, considered genealogy one of their favorite hobbies, and another 20 million adults were interested in tracing their family roots. If you're one of these people, you may not realize the considerable resources available to you in constructing a family tree for the enjoyment of yourself and your children.

One place to begin is to track down birth, death and marriage records of your parents, grandparents, and other ancestors whose names you know. If you know where they lived, you might be able to obtain birth, death, marriage, and divorce certificates from the appropriate state office of vital statistics (see listings, pages 459–466).

In many cases, however, state records are incomplete, especially those that date back

more than half a century. You can turn next to the extensive records of:

Organization: The National Archives
Services: The National Archives has on microfilm all census records up to 1910 (census records are sealed for 80 years to protect privacy). The archives also has immigration and passenger ship arrival information from major ports for much of this country's history, as well as extensive military records. For complete information on taking advantage of these records, send for:
Genealogical Research in the National Archives ($17.00)
From: National Archives Trust Fund Board
Box 129

The National Archives and Records
Administration
Washington, DC 20408

An equally rich source of information is:

Organization: Family History Library
Services: This immense research facility of
the Church of Latter Day Saints has
information on over two billion people and is connected to more than
1,250 local family research centers in
the United States and 43 countries.
These records are open to the general
public. The library will conduct
searches for a fee, and will also sell
computer software to allow you to
access their records from your home
computer. Publications include:
A Guide to the Research Genealogical Library
TB24($0.75)
Research Outline: United States
($0.25)
For information: The Church of Jesus Christ
of the Latter Day Saints Genealogical
Library
50 E. North Temple Street
Salt Lake City, UT 84150
(801) 240-2331
(801) 240-2584 (Computer Software
Information)

Two other major genealogical collections
are:

Organization: New England Historic
Genealogical Society

101 Newberry Street
Boston, MA 02116
(617) 536-5740

Organization: National Society of the
Daughters of the American Revolution Library
Memorial Continental Hall
1776 D Street, NW
Washington, DC 20006
(202) 628-1776

If you're interested in books on genealogy,
you will want to send for:

Publication: *Current Genealogy Catalog*
Cost: $5.00
From: Goodspeed's Book Shop
7 Beacon Street
Boston, MA 02108

If tracing your family history is very complicated, you might want to hire a professional
genealogist to conduct the search. For recommendations to certified, ethical professionals:

Organization: Board for Certification of
Genealogists
P.O. Box 19165
Washington, DC 20036
Service: Will send roster of persons certified
for $3.00

Publication: List of accredited genealogists
Cost: Free
From: The Church of Jesus Christ of the Lat-
ter Day Saints Genealogical Library
50 E. North Temple Street
Salt Lake City, UT 84150

GAMES

Many older Americans are avid players of cards
and board games, such as checkers and chess.

If you're one of them, you can find special programs and competitions by contacting your

local senior center or your local parks and recreation department.

If you are serious about contract bridge, you can contact:

Organization: American Contract Bridge League
Public Relations
P.O. Box 161192
Memphis, TN 38186
(901) 332-5586, ext. 301
Cost: $15.00 per year
Services: Members, whose average age is 57, receive a monthly magazine, discounts on travel, health insurance, referral to more than 600 accredited teachers and 4,200 bridge clubs, and the opportunity to participate in tournaments at levels ranging from novice to expert

Chess players will want to join:

Organization: U.S. Chess Federation
186 Route 9W
New Windsor, NY 12550
(914) 562-8350
Costs: Membership $30.00 per year, $20.00 to those age 65 and older. Membership benefits include:
Chess Life magazine
Access to rated chess play
Postal chess
Chess by computer modem
Discounts on chess books and equipment
Mastercard and Visa cards
Group insurance program
Through the Federation and the 50 state chess federations, members can participate in many tournaments, including special tournaments for players age 50 and older. The U.S. Senior Open for players age 50 and over is held annually

COMPUTING

The number of home computers has quadrupled over the past 5 years. An organization of special interest to older adults is:

Organization: SeniorNet
University of San Francisco
School of Education
San Francisco, CA 94117
(415) 666-6505
Services: SeniorNet is a nationwide network of computer-using people age 55 and older. This network can be accessed through computers located at sites in

35 states, or by anyone with a personal computer and modem at home. membership is $10.00 per year. Benefits include a newsletter, discounts on networking computer time, discount publications, and a guide to using the network. On-line services include electronic mail, bulletin board, health information, news databases, and special interest groups. Also publishes:
Computers for Kids Over Sixty
($8.50 plus $1.00 postage and handling)

GARDENING

Gardening is the number one hobby in the United States. Nearly 70% of Americans age 50 and over consider themselves gardeners. One way to increase your satisfaction from growing things is to join a garden club. Some senior centers organize garden clubs specifically for older residents. To find other garden clubs in your community, contact a local nursery, or write:

> **Organization:** National Council of State Garden Clubs
> 4401 Magnolia Avenue
> St. Louis, MO 63110
> (314) 776-7574

> **Organization:** Men's Garden Clubs of America
> 5560 Merle Hay Road
> Johnstown, IA 50131
> (515) 278-0295

The gardening industry has established an organization that provides a wealth of gardening information to the general public. Contact:

> **Organization:** Gardens for All
> The National Gardening Association
> 180 Flynn Avenue
> Burlington, VT 05401
> (802) 863-1308

Another excellent source of free publications and advice is your local county extension service (see White Pages under your county government listing) or write:

> Extension Service
> U.S. Department of Agriculture
> Washington, DC 20250

Excellent guides to gardening materials and supplies are:

> **Catalog:** *Gardening by Mail 2: A Source Book*
> **Cost:** $18.50 ($19.50 in California)
> **Contains:** A directory of mail order resources for everything connected with gardening
> **From:** Tusker Press
> P.O. Box 1338
> Sebastopol, CA 95473

> **Book:** *The Gardener's Book of Sources* by William Bryant Logan
> **Cost:** $12.95
> **Contains:** Over 1,000 resources for gardeners
> **From:** Penguin Books

COLLECTING

Many Americans take great pleasure in collecting things. The type of collections range from the widespread hobbies of stamp and coin collecting to less common avocations, such as collecting credit cards or old stock certificates. Almost all collectors pursue their hobbies for the sheer fun of it. However, over the course of time, many of these collections appreciate so much in value that they become substantial financial assets.

If You Don't Know What Your Collection Is Worth . . . .

Many people who collect for the fun of it don't have a clear idea of what their collection is worth. Neither do most people who come into possession of someone else's collection. In both cases, it's worth the time to assess the value of the collection.

Among the sources of information are:

- Published price lists. Later in this chapter we list several publications that list prices for many different kinds of collectibles. Before using these price lists, you should know that:

  The price listed is often the retail price, while the price you may be offered by a dealer for the same item, may be as low as half the retail price

  Prices for collectibles depend greatly on the exact condition of each individual item

  The prices listed can be a year or more out of date, because of the time it takes to write, print, and distribute the books

- Dealers. Most dealers purchase, as well as sell collectibles. Some appraise collections for free, while others charge a fee. Keep in mind that the price a dealer will pay for an entire collection is normally lower than the sum total individual collectors may pay for individual pieces in the collection. Selling individual pieces, however, requires much more time and expense.

- Hobbyist organizations. Many organizations have appraisal services available to members.

- Publications and newsletters. Almost all collectors' publications and newsletters contain large numbers of buy and sell ads. The prices quoted in these ads can provide an idea of the current value of many items.

- Auction houses. The major auction houses have departments that will appraise especially valuable items or collections.

- Shows and conventions. Most collectors' shows and conventions are packed with dealers. Surveying the items offered for sale can give you an idea of current prices.

- Professional appraisers. Collectors' organizations and publications often have information about appraisers who specialize in specific collectibles. To obtain a written appraisal of a valuable collection, you might want to hire a professional appraisor by contacting:

Organization: American Society of Appraisors
P.O. Box 17265
Washington, DC 20041
(703) 478-2228
Services: Services and publications include:
  - Free directory of members who are personal property appraisors
  - Free pamphlet, *Information on the Appraisal Profession*
  - *Directory of Professional Appraisal Services* ($5.00), which lists services in all fields

For More Information About Collecting

We've assembled a listing of books, price lists, publications, and organizations of interest to collectors, including:

GENERAL RESOURCES

Book: *National Avocational Organizations*
Contains: Listing of hobby and collectible groups, indexed by type
From: Reference collections of many large libraries

Book: *Cash for Your Undiscovered Treasures*
Cost: $19.95 plus $3.00 shipping and handling

Contains: Names and addresses of 1,500 dealers and collectors who buy through the mail
From: Treasure Hunt Publications
P.O. Box 699
Clearmont, CA 91711

Booklet: *How to Turn Your Household "Junk" into a Small Fortune*
Cost: $5.00
Contains: Advice on selling collectibles, plus names of collectors and dealers
From: Venture Publishing
253 W. 72nd Street, Suite 211A
New York, NY 10023

Organization: Collector Books
P.O. Box 3009
Paducah, KY 42002
(800) 626-5420 (Ex. KY)
Services: Publishes and distributes books on almost every conceivable form of collectible from glass to Disney memorabilia
Cost: Catalog free

Book: *Kovels' Antiques & Collectibles Price List*
Cost: $10.95
From: Crown Publishers

Book: *Kovels' Guide to Selling Your Antiques & Collectibles by Ralph and Terry Kovel*
Cost: $9.95
From: Crown Publishers

Book: *Shroeder's Antiques Price Guide* by Sharon and Bob Huxford
Cost: $11.95
From: Collector Books
P.O. Box 3009
Paducah, KY 42001

Book: *Warman's Americana & Collectibles* by Harry L. Rinker
Cost: $13.95 plus $2.00 postage and handling
Contains: Lists collectibles alphabetically, including prices, references, and clubs
From: Warman Publishing
P.O. Box 1112
Willow Grove, PA 19090

Periodical: *Antique Trader Weekly*
P.O. Box 1050
Dubuque, IA 52001
Cost: $24.00 per year
Contains: Classified ads for antiques and collectibles

Periodical: *Antique Week*
P.O.Box 90
Knightstown, IN 46148
Cost: $22.45 per year for 52 issues plus yearly antique shop guide

Periodical: *Collectors' Showcase*
1018 Rosecrans Street
San Diego, CA 92106
Cost: $24.95 for 12 issues
Contains: Classified ads for antiques and collectibles

Periodical: *Antiques and Collecting Hobbies*
1006 S. Michigan Avenue
Chicago, IL 60605
Cost: $19.95 for 12 issues
Contains: Classified ads for antiques and collectibles

Periodical: *Maine Antique Digest*
P.O. Box 645
Waldoboro, ME 04572
Cost: $17.95 for 10 issues
Contains: Classified ads for antiques and collectibles

AUTOGRAPHS

Organization: Universal Autograph Collectors Club
P.O. Box 6181
Washington, DC 20044
Cost: $18.00 per year

CAMERAS

Periodical: *The Shutterbug*
P.O. Box F
Titusville, FL 32781
(305) 269-3211
Cost: $19.95 for 12 issues

COINS

Booklet: *A Consumer's Guide to Coin Investment*
Cost: Free
Contains: A valuable 40-page guide to collecting coins prepared by Blanchard and Co. in cooperation with the U.S. Consumer Information Center and the U.S. Postal Service
From: Blanchard & Co.
2400 Jefferson Highway
Jefferson, LA 70121

Organization: Coin and Bullion Dealer Accreditation Program
25 E Street, NW, 8th Floor
Washington, DC 20001
Services: Establishes and enforces a strict code of ethics for member dealers. Will send free directory of accreditated dealers

Organization: American Numismatic Association
818 N. Cascade Avenue
Colorado Springs, CO 80903
(719) 632-2646
Services: Membership organization for coin collectors. Issues magazine and publi-

cations, provides appraisal services, and provides referral to local groups

Organization: American Numismatic Society
Broadway at 155th Street
New York, NY 10032
(212) 234-3130
Services: Membership organization for coin collectors that provides a variety of services

COLLECTIBLE SECURITIES

Periodical: *Friends of Financial History*
Cost: $25.00 per year for 4 issues
From: R.M. Smythe & Co.
Broadway
New York, NY 10004
(212) 943-1880

DOLLS

Pamphlet: *Doll Identification Chart*
Cost: Free with self-addressed stamped envelope
Appraisal: Theriault's
Cost: $6.00
From: Theriault's
P.O. Box 151
Annapolis, MD 21404

BASEBALL CARDS

Periodical: *Sports Collector Digest*
Cost: $29.95 per year

Periodical: *Baseball Card News*
Cost: $17.50 per year
From: Krause Publications
700 E. State Street
Iola, WI 54990

COMIC BOOKS

Price Guide: *The Official Overstreet Comic Book Price Guide*

Cost: $12.95
From: The House of Collectibles

Periodical: *Comics Buyer's Guide*
Cost: $27.95 per year
From: Krause Publications
700 E. State Street
Iola, WI 54990

DEPRESSION GLASS

Association: National Depression Glass Association, Inc.
P.O. Box 11123
Springfield, MO 65808
Cost: $10.00 annual dues

Periodical: *The Daze*
P.O. Box 57
Otisville, MI 48463
Cost: $15.00 per year

PAPERWEIGHTS

Organization: Paperweight Collectors Association
P.O. Box 468
New Hyde Park, NY 11040
Cost: $10.00 per year

Book: *Collectors' Paperweights Price Guide and Catalogue*
Cost: $15.00
From: Paperweight Press
Chestnut Street
Santa Cruz, CA 95060

PHONOGRAPH RECORDS

Publication: *Goldmine*
700 E. State Street
Iola, WI 54990
Cost: $35.00 per year for 26 issues
Contains: Ads from dealers and collectors

PLAYBOY MAGAZINES

Book: *The Playboy Collectors Guide & Price List*
Cost: $10.95 plus $2.00 shipping
From: Budget Enterprises
P.O. Box 592
Snowden Station
Montreal, Quebec H3X 3T7

POLITICAL MEMORABILIA

Association: The American Political Items Collectors
P.O. Box 340339
San Antonio, TX 78234
Cost: $20.00 annual dues
Appraisals: Free, with photo, description, and self-addressed stamped envelope

POSTCARDS

Periodical: *Postcard Collectors*
Cost: $14.95 per year
From: Krause Publications
700 E. State Street
Iola, WI 54990

PRINTS

Organization: International Fine Print Dealers Association
485 Madison Avenue
New York, NY 10033
Service: Provides referral to member dealers

SHEET MUSIC

Organization: The National Sheet Music Society
1597 Fair Park Avenue
Los Angeles, CA 90041
Cost: $15.00 per year

Services: Publishes newsletter with many sales ads

SPOONS

Organization: American Spoon Collectors
4922 State Line
Westwood Hills, KS 66205

SPORTS MEMORABILIA

Book: *An Illustrated Guide to Non-Paper Sports Collectibles* by Ted Hake and Rager Steckler
Cost: $18.00
From: Hake's Americana and Collectibles Press
Box 1444
York, PA 17405

Periodical: *Sports Collector Digest*
Cost: $29.95 per year
From: Krause Publications
700 E. State Street
Iola, WI 54990

STAMPS

Organization: American Philatelic Society
Cost: $21.00 per year
Services: The largest U.S. stamp collectors organization offers a plethora of benefits, including:
Subscription to monthly magazine, *The American Philatelist'*
Low-cost stamp collection insurance
Buy at home stamp sales service
Discount stamp-collecting publications
Authentication service for members
Free estate advisory service to help heirs of a deceased member
For information: American Philatelic Society
P.O. Box 8000
State College, PA 16803
(814) 237-3803

Organization: American Stamp Dealers' Association
Services: Establishes and enforces strict code of ethics for stamp dealers. Provides free directory of members. Publishes a number of free pamphlets, including *Selling a Stamp Collection*. Operates the Philatelic Users Group, an organization that provides collectors with discounts on purchases, discount publications, and free admission to stamp shows ($7.50 per year dues)
For information: American Stamp Dealers Association
3 School Street
Glen Cove, NY 11542
(800) 645-3826
(516) 775-3600

Organization: Philatelic Foundation
Service: For a fee, will authenticate stamps
For information: Philatelic Foundation
21 E. 40th St.
New York, NY 10016
(212) 889-6483

Publication: *Scott's Stamp Monthly*
Cost: $18.00 per year for 12 issues
From: Scott's Stamp Monthly
P.O. Box 828
Sidney, OH 45365

Publication: *Linn's Stamp News*
Cost: $25.00 per year for 52 issues
From: Linn's Stamp News
P.O. Box 29
Sydney, OH 45365

TOYS

Dealer: Hake's Americana and Collectibles
Service: Publishes mail order auction catalogs, generally 4 times per year

Cost: $3.00 per catalog, $10.00 for 4 catalogs

For information: Ted Hake
Hake's Americana and Collectibles
P.O. Box 1444
York, PA 17405

Periodical: *Toy Shop*
Cost: $15.95 per year
From: Krause Publications
700 E. State Street
Iola, WI 54990

Book: *Modern American Toys, 1930-1980*
by Linda Baker
Cost: $19.95 plus $1.00 postage and handling
From: Collector Books
P.O. Box 3009
Paducah, KY 42001

WATCHES

Book: *The Official Price Guide to Watches*
by Cooksey Shugart and Tom Engle
Cost: $14.95
From: (800) 638-6460

WINE

Auction House: Christie's
200 W. Superior Street
Chicago, IL 60610

Publication: *The Wine Spectator*
Cost: $11.95 per year for 9 issues
From: The Wine Spectator
P.O. Box 1960
Marion, OH 43305
(800) 443-0100

APPENDIX A

SENIOR CENTERS AND AGENCIES ON AGING

STATE AND LOCAL AREA AGENCIES ON AGING

The Federal Older Americans Act mandated a wide variety of programs and services for older Americans. Every state government and most local governments have also enacted legislation providing many forms of assistance for older people. State agencies on aging (and, in most states, a network of local area agencies on aging) coordinate all these programs and services, act as central information and referral services, and provide case management and other assistance to older people and their families. Many of these agencies publish extensive resource guides and other information. As we have noted repeatedly throughout this book, these agencies are essential points of contact for all older Americans and their families.

The state and local area agencies on aging are (*Note:* in states with no local listings, the state agency serves as a central coordination point for all information and services):

ALABAMA
Commission on Aging
136 Catoma Street

Montgomery, AL 36130
(205) 261-5743

NORTHWEST COUNCIL OF LOCAL GOVERN-
MENTS
Area Agencies on Aging
P.O. Box L
438 S.W. Hamilton Street
Russellville, AL 35653
(205) 332-9173

WEST ALABAMA PLANNING AND DEVELOP-
MENT COMMISSION
7601 Robert Cardinal Airport Road
Tuscaloose, AL 35406
(205) 345-5545

MIDDLE ALABAMA AGENCY ON AGING
P.O. Box 1270
Columbiana, AL 35051

JEFFERSON COUNTY OFFICE OF SENIOR CITIZEN
ACTIVITIES
2601 Highland Avenue South

Birmingham, AL 35205
(205) 251-2992

EAST ALABAMA REGIONAL PLANNING AND DE-
VELOPMENT COMMISSION
P.O. Box 2186
1130 Quintard Avenue
Anniston, AL 36202
(205) 237-6741

SOUTH CENTRAL ALABAMA DEVELOPMENT
COMMISSION
P.O. Box 20028
Montgomery, AL 36120
(205) 281-2196

ALABAMA TOMBIGEE REGIONAL COMMISSION
P.O. Box 269
Camden, AL 36726
(205) 682-4234

SOUTHEAST ALABAMA REGIONAL PLANNING
AND DEVELOPMENT COMMISSION
P.O. Box Drawer 1886
Dothan, AL 36302
(205) 793-0446

AREA AGENCY ON AGING—SOUTH ALABAMA
REGIONAL PLANNING COMMISSION
150 N. Royal Street
P.O. Box 1665
Mobile, AL 36602
(205) 433-6541

CENTRAL ALABAMA AGING CONSORTIUM
818 S. Perry Street, Suite 1
Montgomery, AL 36104
(205) 265-8320

LEE COUNTY AREA COUNCIL OF GOVERN-
MENTS
P.O. Box 2186
Opelika, AL 36801

NORTH CENTRAL ALABAMA REGIONAL COUN-
CIL OF GOVERNMENTS
402 Lee Street, NE

P.O. Box C
Decatur, AL 35602
(205) 355-4515

TOP OF ALABAMA REGIONAL COUNCIL OF
GOVERNMENTS
115 Washington Street, SE
Huntsville, AL 35801
(205) 533-3330

ALASKA
Older Alaskans Commission
Department of Administration
Pouch C-Mail Station 0209
Juneau, AK 99811
(907) 465-3250

ARIZONA
Aging and Adult Administration
Department of Economic Security
1400 West Washington Street
Phoenix, AZ 85007
(602) 542-4446

REGION 1 AREA AGENCY ON AGING
1366 East Thomas Road, Suite 108
Phoenix, AZ 85014
(602) 264-2255

PIMA COUNCIL ON AGING
2919 E. Broadway
Tucson, AZ 85716
(602) 795-5800

NORTHERN ARIZONA COUNCIL OF GOVERN-
MENTS
119 East Aspen
P.O. Box 57
Flagstaff, AZ 86002
(602) 774-1895

DISTRICT IV COUNCIL OF GOVERNMENTS
Area Agency on Aging
1100 South Maple Avenue
Yuma, AZ 85364
(602) 782-1886

PINAL/GILA COUNCIL FOR SENIOR CITIZENS
Area Agency on Aging
408 N. Sacaton
Casa Grande, AZ 85222

SOUTHEASTERN ARIZONA GOVERNMENTS OR-
GANIZATION
SEAGO Area Agency on Aging
118 Arizona Street
Bisbee, AZ 85603
(602) 432-5301

NAVAJO NATIONAL AREA AGENCY ON AGING
Division of Health Improvements
Aging Department
P.O. Drawer 1390
Window Rock, AZ 86515
(602) 871-4941

INTER TRIBAL COUNCIL OF ARIZONA, INC.
4205 N. 7th Avenue
Phoenix, AZ 85013
(602) 248-0071

ARKANSAS
Division of Aging and Adult Services
Department of Social and Rehabilitative Ser-
vices
Donaghey Building, Suite 1417
7th and Main Streets
Little Rock, AR 72201
(501) 682-2441

NORTHWEST ARKANSAS AREA AGENCY ON
AGING
910 Highway 65 North
Northvale Shopping Center
P.O. Box 1795
Harrison, AR 72601
(501) 741-1144
(800) 432-9721

WHITE RIVER AREA AGENCY ON AGING
3998 Harrison Street
Batesville, AR 72503
(501) 793-4431

EAST ARKANSAS AREA AGENCY ON AGING
311 South Main
P.O. Box 5035
Jonesboro, AR 72403
(501) 972-5980
(800) 382-3265

SOUTHEAST ARKANSAS AREA AGENCY ON
AGING
115 E. 5th Street, Suite 301
Pine Bluff, AR 71611
(501) 534-3268
(800) 272-2025

CENTRAL ARKANSAS AREA AGENCY ON AGING
P.O. Box 5988
706 West 4th Street
North Little Rock, AR 72119
(501) 758-2294
(800) 482-6359

WEST CENTRAL ARKANSAS AREA AGENCY ON
AGING
624 Malvern Avenue
Hot Springs, AR 71901
(501) 321-2811
(800) 272-2138

SOUTHWEST ARKANSAS AREA AGENCY ON
AGING
811 Calhoun Drive
P.O. Box 1863
Magnolia, AR 71753
(501) 234-7410

WESTERN ARKANSAS AREA AGENCY ON AGING
P.O. Box 1724
115 N. 10th Street
Fort Smith, AR 72902
(501) 783-4500

CALIFORNIA
Department of Aging
1600 K Street
Sacramento, CA 95814
(916) 322-5290

AREA I AGENCY ON AGING
3300 Glenwood Street
Eureka, CA 95501
(707) 442-3763

AREA AGENCY ON AGING
P.O. Box 1400
228 Butte Street
Yreka, CA 96097
(916) 842-1687

PSA 3 AREA AGENCY ON AGING
California State University
2nd & Normal Streets
Chico, CA 95929
(916) 895-5961

AREA 4 AGENCY ON AGING
2862 Arden Way, Suite 101
Sacramento, CA 95825
(916) 447-7063

MARIN COUNTY AREA AGENCY ON AGING
Civic Center, Room 257
San Rafael, CA 94903
(415) 499-7396

SAN FRANCISCO CITY AND COUNTY COMMIS-
SION ON AGING
25 Van Ness Street, Suite 650
San Franscisco, CA 94102
(415) 671-4233

CONTRA COSTA COUNTY OFFICE ON AGING
2425 Bisso Lane, Suite 110
Concord, CA 94520
(415) 671-4233

SAN MATEO AREA AGENCY ON AGING
617 Hamilton Avenue
Redwood City, CA 94063
(415) 363-4511

ALAMEDA COUNTY DEPARTMENT ON AGING
1234 E. 14th Street, Suite 207
San Leandro, CA 94578
(415) 874-7233

COUNCIL ON AGING OF SANTA CLARA
COUNTY
2131 The Alameda
San Jose, CA 95126
(408) 296-8290

SAN JOAQUIN COUNTY AREA AGENCY ON
AGING
124 N. El Dorado Street
Stockton, CA 95202
(209) 944-2448

CENTRAL SIERRA AREA AGENCY ON AGING
56 North Washington Street
Sonora, CA 95370
(209) 532-6272

SENIORS COUNCIL OF SANTA CRUZ AND SAN
BENITO COUNTIES
234 Santa Cruz Avenue
Aptos, CA 95003
08) 688-0400

FRESNO-MADERA AREA AGENCY ON AGING
2220 Tulare Street
Fresno, CA 93721
(209) 455-3278

KINGS-TULARE AREA AGENCY ON AGING
1920 West Princeton Drive
Suite A and B
Visalia, CA 93277
(209) 733-1079

INYO-MONO AREA AGENCY ON AGING
P.O. Box 1799
Bishop, CA 93514
(714) 873-4248

CENTRAL COAST COMMISSION FOR SENIOR
CITIZENS
122C West El Camino
Santa Maria, CA 93454
(805) 925-9554

VENTURA COUNTY AREA AGENCY ON AGING
505 Poli Street, 3rd Floor

Ventura, CA 93001
(805) 654-3600

LOS ANGELES COUNTY DEPARTMENT OF SEN-
IOR CITIZEN AFFAIRS
1102 Crenshaw Blvd.
Los Angeles, CA 90019
(213) 857-6403

OFFICE OF AGING
686 E. Mill Street
San Bernardino, CA 92415
(714) 387-2423

COUNTY OF RIVERSIDE OFFICE ON AGING
2023 Chicago Avenue
Riverside, CA 92507

COUNTY OF ORANGE AREA AGENCY ON
AGING
1300 S. Grand Avenue, Building B
Santa Ana, CA 92705
(714) 834-6017

SAN DIEGO COUNTY AREA AGENCY ON AGING
9395 Hazard Way
San Diego, CA 92123
(619) 495-5885

IMPERIAL COUNTY AREA AGENCY ON AGING
1331 S. Clark Road
El Centro, CA 92243
(619) 352-8521

LOS ANGELES CITY DEPARTMENT OF AGING
600 South Spring Street, No. 900
Los Angeles, CA 90014
(213) 485-4685

MENDOCINO-LAKE AREA AGENCY ON AGING
413A N. Lake Street
Ukiah, CA 95482
(707) 462-1954

SONOMA COUNTY AREA AGENCY ON AGING
940 Hopper Avenue

Santa Rosa, CA 95403
(707) 527-3138

SOLANO/NAPA AREA AGENCY ON AGING
1814 Capitol Street
Vallejo, CA 94590
(707) 644-6612

EL DORADO COUNTY AREA AGENCY ON
AGING
937 Spring Street
Placerville, CA 95667
(916) 626-2149

STANISLAUS COUNTY AREA AGENCY ON
AGING
1020 15th Street
Modesto, CA 95354
(209) 526-6700

MERCED COUNTY AREA AGENCY ON AGING
2150 M Street, Suite 3
Merced, CA 95340
(209) 385-7550

KERN COUNTY OFFICE ON AGING
1415 Truxton Avenue, Suite AB
Bakersfield, CA 93301
(805) 861-2445

COLORADO
Aging and Adult Services Division
Department of Social Services
State Social Services Bldg., 10th Floor.
1575 Sherman Street
Denver, CO 80203
(303) 866-5905

NORTHEASTERN COLORADO AREA AGENCY
ON AGING
231 Main Street
Fort Morgan, CO 80701
(303) 867-9409

LARIMER COUNTY AREA AGENCY ON AGING
Department of Human Development

525 W. Oak Street
Fort Collins, CO 80521
(303) 221-7440

WELD COUNTY AREA AGENCY ON AGING
1551 N. 17th Avenue
Greeley, CO 80632
(303) 744-1573

DRCOG AREA AGENCY ON AGING
2480 West 26th Street, Suite 200B
Denver, CO 80211
(303) 455-1000

PACG/COUNCIL OF GOVERNMENTS
27 Vermijo Street
Colorado Springs, CO 80903
(303) 471-7080

EAST CENTER AREA AGENCY ON AGING
535 Main Street
Box 28
Stratton, CO 80836
(303) 348-5562

LOWER ARKANSAS AREA AGENCY ON AGING
Ottero County Courthouse
P.O. Box 494
La Junta, CO 81050
(303) 384-8165

PUEBLO AREA AGENCY ON AGING
1120 Court Street
Pueblo, CO 81003
(303) 544-4307

S. CENTRAL COLORADO SENIORS, INC.
P.O. Box 420
Alamosa, CO 81101
(303) 589-4511

SAN JUAN BASIN AREA AGENCY ON AGING
Southwest Community Resources
649 Sixth Street
Durango, CO 81301
(303) 259-1967

DISTRICT X REGIONAL PLANNING COMMIS-
SION
301-B N. Cascade
Drawer 849
Montrose, CO 81402
(303) 249-2436

ASSOCIATED GOVERNMENTS OF NORTHWEST
COLORADO
202 Railroad Avenue
P.O. Box 351
Rifle, CO 81650
(303) 625-1723

SKYLINE SIX AREA AGENCY ON AGING
409 Main Street, Suite 209
Box 739
Frisco, CO 80443
(303) 668-5445

UPPER ARKANSAS AREA AGENCY ON AGING
1310 East Rainbow Blvd., No. 17
Salida, CO 81201
(303) 275-8350

HUERFANO/LAS ANIMAS AREA AGENCY ON
AGING
Council of Governments
Room 201
Courthouse
Trinidad, CO 81082
(303) 846-4401

CONNECTICUT
Department on Aging
175 Main Street
Hartford, CT 06106
(203) 566-3238

SOUTHWESTERN CONNECTICUT AREA AGENCY
276 Park Avenue
Bridgeport, CT 06604
(203) 333-9288

S. CENTRAL CONNECTICUT AREA AGENCY ON
AGING
201 Noble Street

West Haven, CT 06516
(203) 933-5431

E. CONNECTICUT AREA AGENCY ON AGING
16 Franklin Street, Room 214
Norwich, CT 06360
(203) 278-2044

N. CENTRAL AREA AGENCY ON AGING
999 Asylum Avenue
Hartford, CT 06105
(203) 278-2044

WESTERN AREA AGENCY ON AGING
20 E. Main Street, Suite 324
Waterbury, CT 06702
(203) 757-5449

DELEWARE
Division on Aging
Department of Health and Social Services
1901 North DuPont Highway
New Castle, DE 19720
(302) 421-6791

DISTRICT OF COLUMBIA
D.C. Office on Aging
1424 K Street, NW, 2nd Floor
Washington, DC 20011
(202) 724-5622

FLORIDA
Program Office of Aging and Adult Services
Department of Health and Rehabilitation Services
1317 Winewood Blvd.
Tallahassee, FL 32301
(904) 488-8922

NORTHWEST FLORIDA AREA AGENCY ON AGING
24 W. Chase Street, Suite A,
Pensacola, FL 32501
(909) 436-5224

AREA AGENCY ON AGING
2639 North Monroe Street, Suite 145B

Box 12
Tallahassee, FL 32303
(904) 488-0055

MID-FLORIDA AREA AGENCY ON AGING
5700 S.W. 34th Street, Suite 222
Gainesville, FL 32608
(908) 378-6649

NORTHEAST FLORIDA AREA AGENCY ON AGING
2227 Riverside Avenue
P.O. Box 43187
Jacksonville, FL 32204
(904) 388-6495

TAMPA BAY REGIONAL PLANNING COUNCIL
9455 Koger Blvd.
St. Petersburg, FL 33702
(813) 577-5151

WEST CENTRAL FLORIDA AGENCY ON AGING
1419 W. Waters Avenue
Tampa, FL 33604
(813) 933-5945

EAST CENTRAL FLORIDA AREA AGENCY ON AGING
1011 Wymore Road, Room 105
Winter Park, FL 32789
(305) 645-3339

AREA AGENCY ON AGING
8895 N. Military Trail
Palm Beach Gardens, FL 33410

AREA AGENCY ON AGING
1400-01 Jackson Street
Fort Myers, FL 33901
(813) 332-4233

AREA AGENCY ON AGING OF BROWARD COUNTY
5345 NW 35th Avenue
Ft. Lauderdale, FL 33309
(305) 485-6370

ALLIANCE FOR AGING, INC.
9100 S. Dadeland Blvd.
Miami, FL 33156
(305) 670-6500

GEORGIA
Office of Aging
878 Peachtree Street, NE, Room 632
Atlanta, GA 30309
(404) 894-5333

ALTAMAHA GEORGIA AREA PLANNING AND
DEVELOPMENT COMMISSION
505 W. Parker Street
P.O. Box 328
Baxley, GA 31513
(912) 367-3648

ATLANTA REGIONAL COMMISSION
3715 Northside Parkway
Atlanta, GA 30327
(404) 364-2500

CENTRAL SAVANNAH RIVER AREA PLANNING
AND DEVELOPMENT COMMISSION
2123 Wrightsbond Road
P.O. Box 2800
Augusta, GA 30914
(404) 737-1823

CHATTAHOOCHEE FLINT AREA PLANNING AND
DEVELOPMENT COMMISSION
Rte. 1, Hwy 34 East
P.O. Box 110
Franklin, GA 30217

COASTAL AREA PLANNING AND DEVELOP-
MENT COMMISSION
127 F Street
P.O. Box 1917
Brunswick, GA 31521
(912) 264-7363

SOUTH GEORGIA AREA PLANNING AND DEVEL-
OPMENT COMMISSION
327 W. Savannah Avenue
P.O. Box 1223

Valdosta, GA 31063
(912) 333-5277

COOSA VALLEY AREA PLANNING AND DEVEL-
OPMENT COMMISSION
P.O. Drawer H
Rome, GA 30162
(404) 295-6485

GEORGIA MOUNTAINS AREA PLANNING AND
DEVELOPMENT COMMISSION
1010 Ridge Road
P.O. Box 1720
Gainesville, GA 30501
(404) 536-3431

HEART OF GEORGIA COUNCIL ON AGING
118 S. Second Avenue
P.O. Box 503
McRae, GA 31055
(912) 868-5917

LOWER CHATTAHOOCHEE AREA PLANNING
AND DEVELOPMENT COMMISSION
930 S. Second Street
P.O. Box 1908
Columbus, GA 31994
(404) 324-4221

MCINTOSH TRAIL AREA PLANNING AND DEVEL-
OPMENT COMMISSION
408 Thomaston Street
P.O. Drawer A
Barnesville, GA 30204
(404) 358-3647

MIDDLE FLINT AREA PLANNING AND DEVELOP-
MENT COMMISSION
203 E. College Street
P.O. Box 6
Ellaville, GA 31806
(912) 937-2561

MIDDLE GEORGIA AREA PLANNING AND DE-
VELOPMENT COMMISSION
600 Grand Building

Macon, GA 31201
(912) 751-6160

NORTH GEORGIA AREA PLANNING AND DEVEL-
OPMENT COMMISSION
503 W. Waugh Street
Dalton, GA 30720
(404) 272-2300

NORTHEAST GEORGIA PLANNING AND DEVEL-
OPMENT COMMISSION
305 Research Road
Athens, GA 30610
(404) 548-3141

OCONEE AREA PLANNING AND DEVELOPMENT
COMMISSION
3014 Heritage Road
P.O. Box 707
Milledgeville, GA 31601
(912) 453-5327

SOWEGA COUNCIL ON AGING
309 Pine Avenue
P.O. Box 3149
Albany, GA 31701
(912) 432-1124

SOUTHEAST GEORGIA PLANNING AND DEVEL-
OPMENT COMMISSION
3995 Harris Road
Waycross, GA 31501
(912) 285-6096

HAWAII
Executive Office on Aging
Office of the Governor
335 Merchant Street, Room 241
Honolulu, HI 96813
(808) 548-2593

KAUAI COUNTY OFFICE OF ELDERLY AFFAIRS
4193 Hardy Street
Lihue, Hawaii 96766
(808) 245-4737

ELDERLY AFFAIRS DIVISION
Office of Human Resources
650 S. King Street
Honolulu Municipal Building
Honolulu, HI 96813
(808) 523-4361

MAUI COUNTY COMMITTEE ON AGING
200 South High Street
Wailuku, Hawaii 96793
(808) 244-7837

HAWAII COUNTY OFFICE OF AGING
101 Aupuni Street
Hilo, HI 96720
(808) 961-3794

IDAHO
Office on Aging
Room 108-Statehouse
Boise, ID 83720
(208) 334-3833

AID
1000 W. Garden Avenue
Coeur D'Alene, ID 83814
(208) 772-4096

AREA II AGENCY ON AGING
1448 G. Street
Lewiston, ID 83501
(208) 743-5580

IDA-ORE PLANNING AND DEVELOPMENT ASSO-
CIATION
25 W. Idaho
P.O. Box 311
Weiser, ID 83672
(208) 549-2411

COLLEGE OF SOUTH IDAHO
315 Falls Avenue
P.O. Box 1238
Twin Falls, ID 83301
(208) 733-9554

SOUTHEAST IDAHO COUNCIL OF GOVERN-MENTS
1651 Alvin Ricken Drive
Pocatello, ID 83201
(208) 233-4032

EAST IDAHO SPECIAL SERVICES
P.O. Box 51098
Idaho Falls, ID 83408
(208) 522-5391

ILLINOIS
Department on Aging
421 East Capitol Avenue
Springfield, IL 62701
(217) 785-2870

NORTHWESTERN ILLINOIS AREA AGENCY ON AGING
638 Hollister Avenue
Rockford, IL 61108
(815) 226-4901

REGION II AREA AGENCY ON AGING
Community College W. Campus
Building 5
P.O. Box 809
Kankakee, IL 60901
(815) 939-0727

WESTERN ILLINOIS AREA AGENCY ON AGING
729 34th Avenue
Rock Island, IL 61201
(309) 793-6800

CENTRAL ILLINOIS AREA AGENCY ON AGING
700 Hamilton Blvd.
Peoria, IL 61603
(309) 674-2071

EAST CENTRAL ILLINOIS AREA AGENCY ON AGING
1003 Maple Hill Road
Bloomington, IL 61704
(309) 829-2065

WEST CENTRAL ILLINOIS AREA AGENCY ON AGING
P.O. Box 428
1125 Hampshire Street
Quincy, IL 62306
(217) 223-7904

PROJECT LIFE AREA AGENCY ON AGING
2815 West Washington Street, Suite 220
Springfield, IL 62702
(217) 787-9234

SOUTHWESTERN ILLINOIS AREA AGENCY ON AGING
333 Salem Place, Suite 225
Fairview Heights, IL 62208
(618) 632-1323

MIDLAND AREA AGENCY ON AGING
Shawnee Road
P.O. Box 1420
Centralia, IL 62801
(618) 532-1853

SOUTHEASTERN ILLINOIS AREA AGENCY ON AGING
109 W. 6th Street
Mount Carmel, IL 62863
(618) 262-8001

EGYPTIAN AREA AGENCY ON AGING
108 South Division Street
Carterville, IL 62918
(618) 985-8311

DEPARTMENT ON AGING AND DISABILITY
510 N. Peshtigo Court, 3rd Floor
Chicago, IL 60611
(312) 744-5775

SUBURBAN COOK COUNTY AREA AGENCY ON AGING
600 West Jackson, Suite 600
Chicago, IL 60606
(312) 559-0616

INDIANA
Department of Aging and Community Service
251 North Illinois Street
P.O. Box 7083
Indianapolis, IN 46207
(317) 232-7000

LAKE COUNTY ECONOMIC OPPORTUNITY
COUNCIL
5518 Calumet Avenue
Hammond, IN 46320
(219) 937-3500

AREA 2 COUNCIL ON AGING
REAL Services
622 N. Michigan Avenue
P.O. Box 1835
South Bend, IN 46634
(219) 233-8205

NORTHEAST AREA 3 COUNCIL ON AGING
5720 St. Joe Road
Ft. Wayne, IN 46835
(219) 485-4026
(800) 552-3662

AREA 4 AGENCY ON AGING AND COMMUNITY
SERVICES
660 N. 36th Street
Lafayette, IN 47905
(317) 447-7683
(800) 382-7556

AREA 5 COUNCIL ON AGING AND COMMU-
NITY SERVICES
3001 U.S. 24 East
Logansport, IN 46947
(219) 722-4451

AREA 6 COUNCIL ON AGING
2100 N. Granville Avenue
Muncie, IN 47308

WEST CENTRAL INDIANA ECONOMIC DEVELOP-
MENT DISTRICT
1718 Wabash
P.O. Box 359

Terre Haute, IN 47808
(812) 238-1561
(800) 742-0804

CENTRAL INDIANA COUNCIL ON AGING
4755 Kingsway Drive
Indianapolis, IN 46205
(317) 254-5465

AREA 9 AGENCY ON AGING
Indiana University East
303 South A Street
Richmond, IN 47374
(317) 966-1795

AREA 10 AGENCY ON AGING
9350 Yost Avenue
Bloomington, IN 47401
(812) 334-1769

AREA 11 AGENCY ON AGING
1635 N. National Road
P.O. Box 904
Columbus, IN 47202
(812) 343-4992

AREA 12 COUNCIL ON AGING
P.O. Box 97
Dillsboro, IN 47018
(812) 432-5215

AREA 13A COUNCIL ON AGING
Vincennes University
P.O. Box 314
Vincennes, IN 47591
(812) 885-4292

SOUTHWEST INDIANA COUNCIL ON AGING
7 SE 7th Street
Evansville, IN 47708
(812) 464-7800

SOUTH CENTRAL COUNCIL ON AGING AND
AGED
134 E. Main
New Albany, IN 47150
(812) 948-9161

AREA 15 AGENCY ON AGING
Hoosier Uplands Economic Corp.
521 Main Street
Mitchell, IN 47446
(812) 849-4457

IOWA
Department of Elder Affairs
Suite 236, Jewett Building
914 Grand Avenue
Des Moines, IA 50319
(515) 281-5187

AREA 1 AREA AGENCY ON AGING
808 River Street
Decorah, IA 52101
(319) 382-2941

AREA AGENCY ON AGING OF NORTH CENTRAL
IOWA
22 N. Georgia
Mason City, IA 50401
(515) 424-0678

IOWA LAKES AREA AGENCY ON AGING
2 Grand Avenue
P.O. Box 3010
Spencer, IA 51301
(712) 262-1775

AREA 4 AREA AGENCY ON AGING
508 Francis Bldg.
Sioux City, IA 51101

HAWKEYE VALLEY AREA AGENCY
620 Mulberry Street
P.O. Box 2576
Waterloo, IA 50704
(319) 233-5214

SCENIC VALLEY AREA AGENCY ON AGING
2013 Central
Dubuque, IA 52001
(319) 588-3970

GREAT RIVER BEND BI-STATE METROPOLITAN
PLANNING COMMISSION
P.O. Box 3008
Davenport, IA 52808

HERITAGE AREA AGENCY ON AGING
6301 Kirkwood Blvd., SW
Cedar Rapids, IA 51102
(319) 398-5559

CROSSROADS OF IOWA AREA AGENCY ON
AGING
921 6th Avenue
Des Moines, IA 50309
(515) 244-4046

S.W. EIGHT AREA XIII AREA AGENCY ON AGING
3319 Nebraska Avenue
P.O. Box 368
Council Bluffs, IA 51502
(712) 328-2540

AREA XIV AREA AGENCY ON AGING
228 North Pine
Creston, IA 50801
(515) 782-4040

SIEDA AREA AGENCY ON AGING
228 E. Second
P.O. Box 1546
Ottumwa, IA 52501
(515) 682-8741

SOUTHWEST IOWA AREA AGENCY ON AGING
510 Jefferson Street
Burlington, IA 52601
(319) 752-5433

KANSAS
Department on Aging
915 S.W. Harrison
Topeka, KS 66612
(913) 296-4986

WYANDOTTE-LEAVENWORTH COUNTY AREA
AGENCY ON AGING
9400 State Avenue
Kansas City, KS 66112
(913) 788-7820

CENTRAL PLANS AREA AGENCY ON AGING
510 N. Main Street
Wichita, KS 67203
(316) 268-7298

NORTHWEST KANSAS AREA AGENCY ON
AGING
301 West 13th, Room 306
Hays, KS 67601
(913) 628-8204

JAYHAWK AREA AGENCY ON AGING
1195 Buchanan, No. 103
Topeka, KS 66604
(913) 235-1367

SOUTHEAST KANSAS AREA AGENCY ON AGING
1500 W. 7th Street
Box 269
Chanute, KS 66720
(316) 431-2980

SOUTHWEST KANSAS AREA AGENCY ON AGING
108 North 14th
P.O. Box 1636
Dodge City, KS 67801
(316) 225-0510

MID-AMERICA COUNCIL ON AGING
132 South Main
Ottawa, KS 66067
(913) 242-7200

NORTH CENTRAL FLINT HILLS AREA AGENCY
ON AGING
437 Houston Street
Manhattan, KS 66502
(913) 776-9294

NORTHEAST KANSAS AREA AGENCY ON AGING
107 Oregon West
Hiawatha, KS 66434
(913) 742-7152

SOUTH CENTRAL KANSAS AREA AGENCY ON
AGING
P.O. Box 1122
Arkansas City, KS 67005
(316) 442-0268

HUMAN RESOURCES AND AGING DEPART-
MENT
301-A S. Clairborne
Olathe, KS 66062
(316) 442-0268

KENTUCKY
Division for Aging Services
Department of Human Resources
DHR Building-6th Floor
275 East Main Street
Frankfort, KY 40621
(502) 564-6930

PURCHASE AREA DEVELOPMENT DISTRICT
U.S. Highway 45 N.
P.O. Box 588
Mayfield, KY 42066
(502) 247-7171

PENNYRILE AREA DEVELOPMENT DISTRICT
300 Hamond Drive
Hopkinsville, KY 42240
(502) 886-9484

GREEN RIVER AREA AGENCY ON AGING
3860 U.S. Highway 60 West
Owensboro, KY 42301
(502) 926-4433

BARREN RIVER DEVELOPMENT DISTRICT
740 E. 10th Street
P.O. Box 90005
Bowling Green, KY 42102
(502) 781-2381

LINCOLN TRAIL AREA DEVELOPMENT DISTRICT
702 College Street
Elizabethtown, KY 42701
(502) 769-2393

KENTUCKIANA REGIONAL PLANNING AND DE-
VELOPMENT AGENCY
11520 Commonwealth Drive
Louisville, KY 40299
(502) 266-6084

NORTHERN KENTUCKY AREA DEVELOPMENT
DISTRICT
7505 Sussex Drive, Suite 8
Florence, KY 41042
(606) 283-1885

BUFFALO TRACE AREA DEVELOPMENT DISTRICT
327 West Second Street
Maysville, KY 41056
(606) 564-6894

GATEWAY AREA DEVELOPMENT DISTRICT
Main and State Streets
P.O. Box 1070
Owingsville, KY 40360
(606) 739-5191

FIVCO AREA AGENCY ON AGING
3000 Louisa Street
Box 636
Catlettsburg, KY 41129
(606) 739-5191

BIG SANDY AREA DEVELOPMENT DISTRICT
Municipal Building
Lake Shore Drive, 2nd Floor
Prestonburg, KY 41653
(606) 886-2374

KENTUCKY RIVER AREA AGENCY ON AGING
381 Percy Park Road
Hazard, KY 41701

CUMBERLAND VALLEY AREA AGENCY ON
AGING
CVADD Building

100 State Police Road
London, KY 40741
(606) 864-7391

LAKE CUMBERLAND AREA DEVELOPMENT DIS-
TRICT
P.O. Box 570
Russell Springs, KY 42642
(502) 343-3154

BLUEGRASS AREA AGENCY ON AGING
3220 Nicholasville Road
Lexington, KY 40503
(606) 272-6656

LOUISIANA
Office of Elderly Affairs
P.O. Box 80374
Baton Rouge, LA 70898
(504) 925-1700

ALLEN COUNCIL ON AGING
Drawer E-L
600 East 7th Avenue
Oakdale, LA 71463
(318) 335-3195

BEAUREGARD COUNCIL ON AGING
P.O. Drawer 534
104 Port Street
DeRidder, LA 71634
(318) 463-6578

BIENVILLE COUNCIL ON AGING
112 Courthouse
Arcadia, LA 71001
(318) 263-8936

BOSSIER COUNCIL ON AGING
P.O. Box 5606
701 Coleman
Bossier City, LA 71111
(318) 742-8993

CADDO COUNCIL ON AGING
4015 Greenwood Road

Shreveport, LA 71109
(318) 636-7956

CALCASIEU COUNCIL ON AGING
P.O. Box 6403
Lake Charles, LA 70606
(318) 433-1627

CALDWELL COUNCIL ON AGING
P.O. Box 1498
Main Street
Columbia, LA 71418
(318) 649-2584

CAMERON COUNCIL ON AGING
P.O. Box 421
D Street
Cameron, LA 70631
(318) 775-5668

CLAUBORNE COUNCIL ON AGING
608 East 4th Street
Homer, LA 71040
(318) 927-6922

DESOTO COUNCIL ON AGING
P.O. Box 1003
1004 Polk Street
Mansfield, LA 71052
(318) 872-2691

EAST BATON ROUGE COUNCIL ON AGING
2905 Fairfields Avenue
Baton Rouge, LA 70802
(504) 389-4916

JEFFERSON COUNCIL ON AGING
P.O. Box 6878
4425 Utica Street
Metaire, LA 70009
(504) 888-5880

LAFOURCHE COUNCIL ON AGING
710 Church Street
P.O. Box 187
Lockport, LA 70374
(504) 532-2381

LINCOLN COUNCIL ON AGING
109 South Sparta
Ruston, LA 71270
(318) 255-5070

MADISON COUNCIL ON AGING
211 S. Chestnut Street
P.O. Drawer 352
Tallulah, LA 71282
(318) 574-4101

MOREHOUSE COUNCIL ON AGING
P.O. Box 1471
Elm Street
Bastrop, LA 71221
(318) 281-6127

NATCHITOCHES COUNCIL ON AGING
P.O. Box 566
220 East 5th Street
Natchitoches, LA 71457
(318) 352-8490

NEW ORLEANS COUNCIL ON AGING
P.O. Box 19067
2400 Canal Street
New Orleans, LA 70179
(504) 821-4121

OUCHITA COUNCIL ON AGING
1209 Oliver Road
Monroe, LA 71207
(318) 387-0535

PLAQUEMINES COUNCIL ON AGING
P.O. Box 189
Highway 23
Port Sulphur, LA 70083
(504) 564-3220

RED RIVER COUNCIL ON AGING
P.O. Box 688
1825 Front Street
Coushatta, LA 71019
(318) 932-5419

SABINE COUNCIL ON AGING
750 Railroad Avenue
Many, LA 71449
(318) 256-5278

ST. BERNARD COUNCIL ON AGING
1818 Center Street
Arabi, LA 70032
(504) 279-0444

ST. CHARLES COUNCIL ON AGING
5940 Pine Street
Hahnville, LA 70057

ST. JAMES AREA AGENCY ON AGING
P.O. Box 87
St. James Parish Courthouse
Department of Human Services
Convent, LA 70723
(504) 562-2300

ST. JOHN COUNCIL ON AGING
P.O. Drawer H
1805 W. Airline Highway
Laplace, LA 70068
(504) 652-3660

ST. TAMMANY COUNCIL ON AGING
328 East Boston
P.O. Box 171
Covington, LA 70434
(504) 892-0377

TENSAS COUNCIL ON AGING
104 Panola
P.O. Box 726
St. Joseph, LA 71366
(318) 766-3770

TERREBONNE COUNCIL ON AGING
P.O. Box 10066
Station 1
Houma, LA 70360
(504) 868-7701

WEBSTER COUNCIL ON AGING
P.O. Box 913

316 McIntyre
Minden, LA 71055
(318) 377-0141

WEST CARROLL COUNCIL ON AGING
207 East Jefferson
P.O. Box 1058
Oak Grove, LA 71263
(318) 428-4217

CAPITAL AREA AGENCY ON AGING
P.O. Box 86430
11861 Coursey Blvd.
Baton Rouge, LA 70879
(504) 296-0266

KISATCHIE DELTA REGIONAL PLANNING AND
DEVELOPMENT DISTRICT
P.O. Box 12248
Alexandria, LA 71315
(318) 487-5454

CAJUN AREA AGENCY ON AGING
1304 Betrand Drive, Suite F-6
Lafayette, LA 70506
(318) 237-7744

NORTH DELTA PLANNING AND DEVELOPMENT
DISTRICT
2115 Justice Street
Monroe, LA 71201
(318) 387-2572

MAINE
Bureau of Maine's Elderly
Department of Human Services
State House-Station No. 11
Augusta, ME 04333
(207) 289-2561

ARROSTOCK AREA AGENCY ON AGING
33 Davis Street
P.O. Box 1288
Presque Isle, ME 04769
(207) 764-3396

EASTERN AREA AGENCY ON AGING
Twin City Shopping Plaza
238 State Street
Brewer, ME 04412
(207) 941-2865

SENIOR SPECTRUM
51 Maine Avenue
P.O. Box 248
Gardince ME 04345
(207) 582-8000

WEST AREA AGENCY ON AGING
465 Main Street
P.O. Box 659
Lewiston, ME 04240
(207) 784-8797

SOUTHERN MAINE AREA AGENCY ON AGING
237 Oxford Street
P.O. Box 10480
Portland, ME 04104
(207) 775-6503

MARYLAND
Office on Aging
State Office Building
301 West Preston Street, Room 1004
Baltimore, MD 21201
(301) 225-1106

GARRETT COUNTY AREA AGENCY ON AGING
360 W. Liberty Street
P.O. Box 449
Oakland, MD 21550
(301) 334-9431

ALLEGANY COUNTY AREA AGENCY ON AGING
19 Frederick Street
Cumberland, MD 21502
(301) 777-5970

WASHINGTON COUNTY AREA AGENCY ON
AGING
9 Public Square
Alexander House

Hagerstown, MD 21740
(301) 790-0275

FREDERICK COUNTY COMMISSION ON AGING
520 N. Market Street
Frederick MD 21701
(301) 694-1604

CARROLL COUNTY OFFICE ON AGING
West End School
Schoolhouse Avenue
Westminster, MD 21157
(301) 875-3342

BALTIMORE COUNTY DEPARTMENT OF AGING
611 Central Avenue
Towson, MD 21204
(301) 494-2107

BALTIMORE CITY AREA AGENCY ON AGING
222 E. Saratoga Street
Baltimore, MD 21202
(301) 396-5780

HARFORD COUNTY AREA AGENCY ON AGING
Equitable Building
145 North Hickory Avenue
Bel Air, MD 21014
(301) 879-2000

AREA AGENCY ON AGING
101 Monroe Street
Rockville, MD 20850
(301) 279-1920

HOWARD COUNTY OFFICE ON AGING
John Carroll Building, 1st Floor
3450 Courthouse Drive
Ellicott City, MD 21043
(301) 992-2327

ANNE ARUNDEL COUNTY AREA AGENCY ON
AGING
Anne Arundel Center North
101 N. Crain Highway
Glen Burnie, MD 21061
(301) 787-6707

PRINCE GEORGES' COUNTY AREA AGENCY ON AGING
County Services Building
5012 Rhode Island Avenue
Hyattsville, MD 20781
(301) 699-2797

CALVERT COUNTY OFFICE ON AGING
450 West Dares Beach Road
P.O. Box 221
Prince Frederick, MD 20678
(301) 535-4606

CHARLES COUNTY AGING SERVCIES
Rt.1, P.O. Box 1144
Port Tobacco, MD 20677

ST. MARYS COUNTY OFFICE ON AGING
245 N. Washington Street
Governmental Center
P.O. Box 653
Leonardtown, MD 20650
(301) 475-5621

UPPER SHORE AGING, INC.
400 High Street, 2nd Floor
Chestertown, MD 21620
(301) 778-6000

QUEEN ANNE'S COUNTY OFFICE ON AGING
County Annex Building
P.O. Box 20
208 N. Commerce Street
Centreville, MD 21617
(301) 758-0848

MAC, INC., AREA AGENCY ON AGING
1504 Riverside Drive
Salisbury, MD 21801
(301) 742-0505

MASSACHUSETTS
Executive Office of Elder Affairs
38 Chauncy Street
Boston, MA 02111
(617) 727-7750

ELDER SERVICES OF BERKSHIRE COUNTY, INC.
100 North Street
Pittsfield, MA 01201
(413) 499-1353

FRANKLIN COUNTY HOME CARE CORP.
Central Street
Turners Falls, MA 01376
(413) 863-9565

HIGHLAND VALLEY ELDER SERVICES CENTER
320 Riverside Drive
Northamptom, MA 01060
(413) 586-2000

HOLYOKE/CHICOPEE HOME CARE
198 High Street
Holyoke, MA 01040
(413) 538-9020

GREATER SPRINGFIELD SENIOR SERVICES
66 Industry Avenue
Springfield, MA 01104
(413) 781-8800

CENTRAL MASSACHUSETTS AGENCY ON AGING
306 W. Boylston Street
W. Boylston, MA 01583

SENIOR HOME CARE SERVICES
2 Main Street
Glouceser, MA 01930
(617) 281-1750

NORTH SHORE ELDER SERVICES
152 Sylvan Street
Danvers, MA 01923

GREATER LYNN SENIOR SERVICES
8 Silsbee Street
Lynn, MA 01902
(617) 599-0110

CALSEA/REVERE/WINTHROP HOME CARE CENTER
300 Broadway
P.O. Box 189

Revere, MA 02151
(617) 286-0550

MYSTIC VALLEY ELDER HOME CARE
661 Main Street, Suite 110
Malden, MA 02148
(617) 324-7705

SOMERVILLE/CAMBRIDGE HOME CARE CORP.
1 Davis Square
Somerville, MA 02144
(617) 628-2601

MINUTEMAN HOME CARE
24 Third Avenue
Burlington, MA 01803

WEST SUBURBAN ELDER SERVICES
124 Watertown Street
Parker Office Building
Watertown, MA 02173
(617) 926-4100

BAYPATH SENIOR CITIZENS SERVICES
P.O. Box 2625
Building 13
Cushing Hospital
Framingham, MA 01701
(617) 620-0840

HEALTH AND SOCIAL SERVICES CONSORTIUM
IGO Building
Carpenter Street
Foxboro, MA 02035
(617) 543-2611

SOUTH SHORE HOME CARE SERVICES
639 Granite Street
P.O. Box 367
Braintree, MA 02184
(617) 848-3910

OLD COLONY ELDERLY SERVICES
70 School Street
Brockton, MA 02401
(617) 584-1561

BRISTOL ELDER SERVICES
182 N. Main Street
Fall River, MA 02720
(617) 675-2101

COAST LINE ELDER SERVICES
106 Huttleston Avenue
Fairhaven, MA 02719
(617) 999-6400

ELDER SERVICES OF CAPE COD AND ISLANDS
68 Route 134
South Dennis, MA 02660
(617) 394-4630

ELDER SERVICES OF THE MERRIMACK VALLEY
360 Merrimack Street
Lawrence, MA 01843
(617) 683-7747

BOSTON COMMISSION ON AFFAIRS OF THE EL-
DERLY
1 City Hall Square, Room 271
Boston, MA 02201
(617) 725-4366

MICHIGAN
Office of Services to the Aging
P.O. Box 30026
Lansing, MI 48909
(517) 373-8230

DETROIT AREA AGENCY ON AGING
1100 Michigan Bldg.
220 Bagley Avenue
Detroit, MI 48226
(313) 222-5330

REGION I-B AREA AGENCY ON AGING
29508 Southfield Road, Suite 100
Southfield, MI 48076
(313) 569-0333

THE SENIOR ALLIANCE
3850 2nd Street, Suite 160
Wayne, MI 48184
(313) 722-2830

REGION II COMMISSION ON AGING
3221 North Adrian Drive
P.O. Box 646
Adrian, MI 49221
(517) 265-7881

SOUTHCENTRAL MICHIGAN COMMISSION ON
AGING
8135 Cox's Drive, Suite 1-C
Portage, MI 49002
(616) 343-4996

REGION IV AREA AGENCY ON AGING
2919 Division Street
St. Joseph, MI 49085
(616) 983-0177

VALLEY AREA AGENCY ON AGING
708 Root Street, Room 110
Flint, MI 48503
(313) 239-7671

TRI-COUNTY OFFICE ON AGING
500 West Washtenaw
Lansing, MI 48933
(517) 483-4150

REGION VII AREA AGENCY ON AGING
126 Washington Avenue
Bay City, MI 48708
(517) 893-4506

AREA AGENCY ON AGING OF WESTERN MICHI-
GAN
540 Two Fountain Place
Grand Rapids, MI 49504
(616) 456-5664

NORTHEAST MICHIGAN COMMUNITY SER-
VICES
2373 Gordon Road
P.O. Box 1038
Alpena, MI 49707
(517) 356-3474

NORTHWEST MICHIGAN AREA AGENCY ON
AGING
1609 Park Drive
P.O. Box 2010
Traverse City, MI 49685
(616) 947-8920

REGION XI AREA AGENCY ON AGING
UPCAP Services
118 North 22nd Street
Escanaba, MI 49829
(906) 786-4701

REGION XIV AREA PLANNING COUNCIL ON
AGING
255 W. Sherman Blvd.
Muskegon Hts., MI 49444

MINNESOTA
Board on Aging
Human Services Bldg.
444 Lafayette Blvd.
St. Paul MN 55155
(612) 296-2544

NORTHWEST REGIONAL DEVELOPMENT COM-
MISSION
P.O. Box E
Brooks Avenue South
Thick River Falls, MN 56701
(218) 281-1396

REGION II AREA AGENCY ON AGING
Headwater Regional Development Commission
722 15th Street
Box 906
Bemidji, MN 56601
(218) 751-3108

ARROWHEAD AREA AGENCY ON AGING
330 Canal Park Drive
Duluth, MN 55802
(218) 722-5545

WEST CENTRAL AREA AGENCY ON AGING
P.O. Box 726
112 West Washington Avenue
Fergus Falls, MN 56537
(218) 739-4617

REGION V AREA AGENCY ON AGING
Region V Regional Development Commission
611 Iowa Avenue
Staples, MN 56479
(218) 894-3233

MID-MINNESOTA REGIONAL DEVELOPMENT
COMMISSION
333 West 6th Street
Willmar, MN 56201
(612) 235-8504

REGION VI, WEST AREA AGENCY ON AGING
Upper Minnesota Valley Regional Development Commission
323 W. Schlieman
Appleton, MN 56208
(612) 289-1981

REGION VII AREA AGENCY ON AGING
100 South Park Street
Mora, MN 55051
(612) 679-4065

CENTRAL MINNESOTA COUNCIL ON AGING
600 25th Avenue S.
St. Cloud, MN 56301
(612) 253-9349

SOUTHWEST REGIONAL DEVELOPMENT COM-
MISSION'S AGING PROGRAM
2425 Broadway
Box 265
Slayton, MN 56172
(507) 836-8549

REGION NINE AREA AGENCY ON AGING
410 South 5th Street
Box 3367

Mankato, MN 56001
(507) 387-5643

SOUTHEASTERN MINNESOTA AREA AGENCY
ON AGING
121 North Broadway, Room 302
Rochester, MN 55904
(507) 288-6944

METROPOLITAN AREA AGENCY ON AGING
Mearsburg Park Center
230 E. 5th Street
St. Paul, MN 55101
(612) 291-6497

MINNESOTA CHIPEWA TRIBE
Area Agency on Aging
P.O. Box 217
Cass Lake, MN 56633
(218) 335-2252

MISSISSIPPI
Council on Aging
301 West Pearl Street
Jackson, MS 39203
(601) 949-2013

NORTH DELTA AREA AGENCY ON AGING
P.O. Box 1244
130 Lafleur Avenue
Clarksdale, MS 38614
(601) 627-3401

SOUTH DELTA AREA AGENCY ON AGING
P.O. Box 1776
124 South Broadway
Greenville, MS 38702
(601) 378-3831

NORTH CENTRAL PLANNING AND DEVELOP-
MENT DISTRICT
Aging Division
P.O. Box 668
Highway 51 South
Winona, MS 38967
(601) 283-2675

GOLDEN TRIANGLE PLANNING AND DEVELOP-
MENT DISTRICT
Aging Division
P.O. Drawer DN
Memorial Hall, Room 215
Mississippi State, MS 39762
(601) 325-3855

THREE RIVERS PLANNING AND DEVELOPMENT
DISTRICT
Aging Division
75 South Main
P.O. Drawer B
Pontotoc, MS 38863
(601) 489-2415

NORTH EAST PLANNING AND DEVELOPMENT
DISTRICT
Aging Division
Highway 4 N. 30 Bypass
P.O. Box 600
Booneville, MS 38829
(601) 728-6248

CENTRAL MISSISSIPPI AREA AGENCY ON AGING
2675 River Ridge Road
Jackson, MS 39216
(601) 981-1511

EAST CENTRAL PLANNING AND DEVELOPMENT
DISTRICT
410 Decatur Street
P.O. Box 499
Newton, MS 39345
(601) 683-2007

SOUTHERN MISSISSIPPI AREA AGENCY ON
AGING
1020 32nd Avenue
Gulfport, MS 39501
(601) 868-2311
(800) 222-9504

SOUTHWEST MISSISSIPPI AREA AGENCY ON
AGING
110 S. Wall Street
Natchez, MS 39120

MISSOURI
Division on Aging
Department of Social Services
P.O. Box 1337
Jefferson City, MO 65102
(314) 751-3082

SOUTHWEST MISSOURI AREA AGENCY ON
AGING
P.O. Box 50805
317 Park Central E.
Springfield, MO 65805
(417) 862-0762

SOUTHEAST MISSOURI AREA AGENCY ON
AGING
121 S. Broadview
Cape Girardeau, MO 63701
(314) 335-3331

DISTRICT III AREA AGENCY ON AGING
604 N. McGuire
P.O. Box 1078
Warrensburg, MO 64093
(816) 747-3107

NORTH MISSOURI AREA AGENCY ON AGING
P.O. Drawer G
106 S. Smith
Albany, MO 64402
(816) 762-3800

NORTHEAST MISSOURI AREA AGENCY ON
AGING
2412 S. Business 63
P.O. Box 1067
Kirksville, MO 63501
(816) 665-4682

CENTRAL MISSOURI AREA AGENCY ON AGING
601 Business Loop 70 West
Columbia, MO 65203
(314) 443-5823

MID-AMERICA REGIONAL AREA AGENCY ON
AGING
300 Rivergate Center
600 Broadway

Kansas City, MO 64105
(816) 474-4240

MID-EAST AREA AGENCY ON AGING
2510 S. Brentwood, Room 215
Brentwood, MO 63144
(314) 962-0808

MAYOR'S OFFICE ON AGING
Courts Building
10 N. Tucker, 12th Floor
St. Louis, MO 63101
(314) 622-3201

REGION 10 AREA AGENCY ON AGING
1710 E. 32nd Street
Joplin, MO 64804
(417) 781-7562

MONTANA
Family Services Division
P.O. Box 8005
Helena, MT 59601
(406) 444-5900

AREA AGENCY ON AGING
111 W. Bell
Glendive, MT 59330
(406) 365-3364

AREA AGENCY ON AGING
236 Main Street
Roundup, MT 59072
(406) 323-1320

NORTH CENTRAL AREA AGENCY ON AGING
323 S. Main Street
Conrad, MT 59425
(406) 278-5662

ROCKY MOUNTAIN DEVELOPMENT COUNCIL
Area Agency on Aging
201 South Main
P.O. Box 721
Helena, MT 59624
(406) 442-1552

AREA AGENCY ON AGING
115 East Pennsylvania Avenue
Anaconda, MT 59711
(406) 563-3110

WESTERN MONTANA AREA AGENCY ON AGING
802 Main Street
Polson, MT 59860
(406) 833-6211

TRIBAL ELDERS PROGRAM
Area Agency on Aging
P.O. Box 21838
1445 Avenue B
Billings, MT 59104
(406) 652-3113

CASCADE COUNTY COUNCIL ON AGING
1601 2nd Avenue North
Great Falls, MT 59401
(406) 761-1919

FLATHEAD COUNTY COUNCIL ON AGING
723 5th Avenue East
Kalispell, MT 59901
(406) 752-5300

HILL COUNTY COUNCIL ON AGING
2 West 2nd Street
Havre, MT 59501
(406) 265-5464

MISSOULA COUNTY COUNCIL ON AGING
227 W. Front Street
Missoula, MT 59802
(406) 728-7682

NEBRASKA
Department on Aging
P.O. Box 95044
301 Centennial Mall South
Lincoln, NE 68509
(402) 471-2306

EASTERN NEBRASKA OFFICE ON AGING
885 South 72nd Street

Omaha, NE 68114
(402) 444-6536

LINCOLN AREA AGENCY ON AGING
129 N. 10th Street, Room 241
Lincoln, NE 68508
(402) 471-7022

NORTHEAST NEBRASKA AREA AGENCY ON
AGING
North Stone Building
Regional Center Grounds
P.O. Box 1447
Norfolk, NE 68701
(402) 371-7454

SOUTH CENTRAL NEBRASKA AREA AGENCY ON
AGING
124 West 46th Street
Kearney, NE 68847
(308) 234-1851

MIDLAND AREA AGENCY ON AGING
305 N. Hastings
P.O. Box 905
Hastings, NE 68902
(402) 463-4565

BLUE RIVERS AREA AGENCY ON AGING
Gage County Courthouse, Room 24
Beatrice, NE 68310
(402) 223-3124

WEST CENTRAL NEBRASKA AREA AGENCY ON
AGING
200 South Silber Avenue
North Platte, NE 69101
(308) 534-6780

AGING OFFICE OF WESTERN NEBRASKA
4502 Avenue I
Scottsbluff, NE 69361
(308) 635-0851

NEVADA
Division on Aging
Department of Human Resources
505 East King Street

Kinkead Building, Room 101
Carson City, NV 89710
(702) 885-4210
(800) 992-0900 (NV)

NEW HAMPSHIRE
Division of Elderly & Adult Services
6 Hazen Drive
Concord, NH 03301
(603) 271-4680

NEW JERSEY
Division on Aging
Department of Community Affairs
C N 807
Trenton, NJ 08625
(609) 292-4833

ATLANTIC COUNTY DIVISION ON AGING
1333 Atlantic Avenue
Atlantic City, NJ 08401
(609) 345-6700

BERGEN COUNTY OFFICE ON AGING
Court Plaza South, 21 Main Street
Hackensack, NJ 07601
(201) 646-2625

BURLINGTON COUNTY OFFICE ON AGING
49 Rancocas Road
Mounty Holly, NJ 08060
(609) 265-5000

CAMDEN COUNTY OFFICE ON AGING
120 White Horse Pike, Suite 103
Haddon Heights, NJ 08035
(609) 546-6404

CAPE MAY COUNTY OFFICE ON AGING
P.O. Box 222
Social Services Building
Rio Grande, NJ 08242
(609) 886-2784

CUMBERLAND COUNTY OFFICE ON AGING
Administration Building
790 East Commerce Street

Bridgeton, NJ 08302
(609) 451-8000

ESSEX COUNTY OFFICE ON AGING
15 South Munn Avenue
East Orange, NJ 07018
(201) 678-9700

GLOUCESTER COUNTY DEPARTMENT ON
AGING
Budd Blvd. & State Hwy. #45
Woodbury, NJ 08096
(609) 853-3312

HUDSON COUNTY OFFICE ON AGING
114 Clifton Place
Murdock Hall
Jersey City, NJ 07304
(201) 434-6900

HUNTERDON COUNTY OFFICE ON AGING
6 Gauntt Place
Flemington, NJ 08822
(201) 788-1362

MERCER COUNTY OFFICE ON AGING
Mercer County Administration Building
640 S. Broad Street
P.O. Box 8068
Trenton, NJ 08650
(609) 989-6661

MIDDLESEX COUNTY OFFICE ON AGING
841 Georges Road
North Brunswick, NJ 08902
(201) 745-3293

MONMOUTH COUNTY OFFICE ON AGING
Hall of Records Annex
E. Main Street
Freehold, NJ 07728
(201) 431-7450

MORRIS COUNTY OFFICE ON AGING
CN 900
Morristown, NJ 07960
(201) 829-8539

OCEAN COUNTY OFFICE ON AGING
CN-2191
Toms River, NJ 08754
(201) 244-2121

PASSAIC COUNTY OFFICE ON AGING
675 Goffle Road
Hawthorne, NJ 07506
(201) 881-4850

SALEM COUNTY OFFICE ON AGING
Lakeview Complex
P.O. Box 276
Woodstown, NJ 08098
(201) 769-4150

SOMERSET COUNTY OFFICE ON AGING
Box 3000
Somerville, NJ 08876
(201) 231-7175

SUSSEX COUNTY OFFICE ON AGING
175 High Street
Newton, NJ 07860
(201) 383-5098

UNION COUNTY DIVISION ON AGING
County Administration Building, 4th Floor
Elizabethtown Plaza
Elizabeth, NJ 07207
(201) 527-4866

WARREN COUNTY OFFICE ON AGING
Wayne Dumont Jr. Administration Building
Belvidere, NJ 07823
(201) 475-8000

NEW MEXICO
State Agency on Aging
224 East Palace Avenue, 4th Floor
La Villa Rivera Building
Santa Fe, NM 87501
(505) 827-7640

CITY OF ALBUQUERQUE ADMINISTRATOR
714 7th Street, SW

Albuquerque, NM 87102
(505) 764-6488

DISTRICT II AREA AGENCY ON AGING
P.O. Box 5115
Santa Fe, NM 87504
(505) 983-3621

EASTERN NEW MEXICO AREA AGENCY ON
AGING
901 West 13th Street
Clovis, NM 88101
(505) 769-1613

SOUTHWESTERN NEW MEXICO AREA AGENCY
ON AGING
Mesilla Community Center
P.O. Box 822
Mesilla, NM 88046
(505) 525-0352

NEW YORK
Office for the Aging
New York State Executive Department
Empire State Plaza, Agency Building No. 2
Albany, NY 12223
(518) 474-4425
(800) 342-9871 (NY)

ALBANY COUNTY DEPARTMENT FOR AGING
AND HANDICAPPED
112 State Street, Room 710
Albany, NY 12207
(518) 447-7180

ALLEGANY COUNTY OFFICE FOR AGING
17 Court Street
Belmont, NY 14813
(716) 268-9390

BROOME COUNTY OFFICE FOR AGING
County Office Building
Government Plaza
Binghamton, NY 13902
(607) 772-2411

CATTARAUGUS COUNTY OFFICE FOR AGING
1701 Lincoln Avenue

Olean, NY 14760
(716) 375-4114

CAYUGA COUNTY OFFICE FOR AGING
160 Genessee Street
County Office Building
Auburn, NY 13021
(315) 253-1226

CHAUTAUQUA COUNTY OFFICE FOR AGING
Hall R. Clothier Building
Mayville, NY 14757
(716) 753-4417

CHEMUNG COUNTY OFFICE FOR AGING
425-447 Pennsylvania Avenue
Elmira, NY 14904
(607) 737-5520

CHENANGO COUNTY OFFICE FOR AGING
County Office Building
5 Court Street
Norwich, NY 13815
(607) 335-4624

CLINTON COUNTY OFFICE FOR AGING
137 Margaret Street
Plattsburgh, NY 12901
(518) 565-4620

COLUMBIA COUNTY OFFICE FOR AGING
71 North 3rd Street
Hudson, NY 12534
(518) 828-4258

CORTLAND COUNTY OFFICE FOR AGING
County Office Building
60 Central Avenue
P.O. Box 5590
Cortland, NY 13045
(607) 753-5060

DELAWARE COUNTY OFFICE FOR AGING
6 Court Street
Delhi, NY 13753
(607) 746-6333

DUTCHESS COUNTY OFFICE FOR AGING
488 Main Street
Poughkeepsie, NY 12601
(914) 431-2465

ERIE COUNTY DEPARTMENT OF SENIOR SERVICES
95 Franklin Street
Buffalo, NY 14202
(716) 846-6046

ESSEX COUNTY OFFICE FOR AGING
Church Street
Elizabethtown, NY 12932
(518) 873-6301

FRANKLIN COUNTY OFFICE FOR AGING
County Court House
89 West Main Street
Malone, NY 12953
(518) 483-6767

FULTON COUNTY OFFICE FOR AGING
1 E. Montgomery Street
Johnstown, NY 12095
(518) 762-0650

GENESEE COUNTY OFFICE FOR AGING
Batavia Genesee Senior Center
2 Bank Street
Batavia, NY 14020
(716) 343-1611

GREEN COUNTY DEPARTMENT FOR THE AGING
19 S. Jefferson Avenue
P.O. Box 392
Catskill, NY 12414
(518) 943-5332

HERKIMER COUNTY OFFICE FOR AGING
County Office Building
Mary Street
Herkimer, NY 13350
(315) 867-1121

JEFFERSON COUNTY OFFICE FOR AGING
250 Arsenal Street

Watertown, NY 13601
(315) 782-9100

LEWIS COUNTY OFFICE FOR AGING
Lewis County Office Building
P.O. Box 408
Lowville, NY 13367
(315) 376-5313

LIVINGSTON COUNTY OFFICE FOR AGING
Livingston County Campus, Building 1
Mount Morris, NY 14510
(716) 658-2881

MADISON COUNTY OFFICE FOR AGING
43 E. Main Street
Box 250, Rt. 20
Morrisville, NY 13408
(315) 684-9424

MONROE COUNTY OFFICE FOR AGING
375 Westfall Road
Rochester, NY 14620
(716) 442-6350

MONTGOMERY COUNTYWIDE OFFICE FOR THE AGING
21 New Street
Amsterdam, NY 12010
(518) 843-2300

NASSAU COUNTY DEPARTMENT OF SENIOR CITIZENS AFFAIRS
400 County Seat Drive
Mineola, NY 11501
(516) 535-5990

NIAGARA COUNTY OFFICE FOR AGING
Switzer Building
100 Davidson Road
Lockport, NY 14094
(716) 439-6044

ONEIDA COUNTY OFFICE FOR AGING
County Office Building
800 Park Avenue

Utica, NY 13501
(315) 798-5771

METROPOLITAN COMMISSION ON AGING
421 Montgomery Street
Civic Center, 13th Floor
Syracuse, NY 13202
(315) 425-2362

ONTARIO COUNTY OFFICE FOR AGING
3871 County Road #46
Canandaigua, NY 14424
(716) 396-4040

ORANGE COUNTY OFFICE FOR AGING
60 Erie Street, 3rd Floor
Goshen, NY 10924
(914) 294-5151

ORLEANS COUNTY OFFICE FOR AGING
Orleans County Administration Building
14016 Route 31
Albion, NY 14411
(716) 589-5673

OSWEGO COUNTY OFFICE FOR AGING
County Office Complex
70 Bunner Street
P.O. Box 3080
Oswego, NY 13126
(315) 349-3484

OTSEGO COUNTY OFFICE FOR AGING
County Office Building
Cooperstown, NY 13326
(607) 547-4233

PUTNAM COUNTY OFFICE FOR AGING
110 Old Route 6, Building A
Carmel, NY 10512
(914) 225-1034

RENSSELAER COUNTY DEPARTMENT FOR THE
AGING
1600 7th Avenue
Troy, NY 12180
(518) 270-2730

ROCKLAND COUNTY OFFICE FOR AGING
Health and Social Services Complex
Building B
Pomona, NY 10970
(914) 354-0200

ST. LAWRENCE COUNTY OFFICE FOR AGING
Sheriff's Annex, Covet House
Canton, NY 13617
(315) 379-2204

SARATOGA COUNTY OFFICE FOR AGING
40 South Street
Ballston Spa, NY 12020
(518) 885-2212

SCHENECTADY COUNTY OFFICE FOR AGING
117 Nott Terrace
Schenectady, NY 12308
(518) 382-8481

SCHOHARIE COUNTY OFFICE FOR AGING
122 E. Main Street
Cobleskill, NY 12043
(518) 234-4219

SCHUYLER COUNTY OFFICE FOR AGING
336-338 West Main Street
Montour Falls, NY 14865
(607) 535-7108

SENECA COUNTY OFFICE FOR AGING
1 DiPronio Drive
Waterloo, NY 13165

STEUBEN COUNTY OFFICE FOR THE AGING
c/o The Infirmary
P.O. Box 697
Bath, NY 14810
(607) 776-7651

SUFFOLK COUNTY OFFICE FOR THE AGING
395 Oser Avenue
Hauppauge, NY 11788
(516) 348-5310

SULLIVAN COUNTY OFFICE FOR THE AGING
County Government Center
100 N Street
Monticello, NY 12701
(914) 794-3000

TIOGA COUNTY OFFICE FOR THE AGING
231 Main Street
Oswego, NY 13827
(607) 687-4120

TOMPKINS COUNTY OFFICE FOR THE AGING
309 N. Tioga Street
Ithaca, NY 14850
(607) 274-5427

ULSTER COUNTY OFFICE FOR THE AGING
1 Albany Avenue
Box 1800
Kingston, NY 12401
(914) 331-9300

WARREN/HAMILTON COUNTY OFFICE FOR
THE AGING
Warren County Municipal Center
Lake George, NY 12845
(518) 761-6347

WASHINGTON COUNTY OFFICE FOR THE
AGING
Grays Corners Road
P.O. Box 58
Whitehall, NY 12887
(518) 499-2468

WAYNE COUNTY AREA AGENCY ON AGING
16 Williams Street
Lyons, NY 14489
(315) 946-4163

WESTCHESTER COUNTY OFFICE FOR THE
AGING
214 Central Avenue, Room 938
White Plains, NY 10601
(914) 682-3045

WYOMING COUNTY OFFICE FOR THE AGING
76 North Main Street
Warsaw, NY 14569
(716) 786-3144

YATES COUNTY AREA AGENCY ON AGING
5 Collins Avenue
Penn Yan, NY 14527
(315) 536-2368

NEW YORK CITY DEPARTMENT FOR THE AGING
2 Lafayette Street
New York, NY 10007
(212) 577-0848

ST. REGIS-MOHAWK OFFICE FOR THE AGING
St. Regis-Mohawk Indian Reservation
Hogansburg, NY 13655
(518) 358-2272

SENECA NATION OF INDIANS OFFICE FOR THE
AGING
1500 Route 438
Irving, NY 14081
(716) 532-5777

NORTH CAROLINA
Division on Aging
1985 Umpstead Drive, Kirby Building
Raleigh, NC 27603
(919) 733-3983

SOUTHWESTERN NORTH CAROLINA PLAN-
NING AND ECONOMIC DEVELOPMENT COM-
MISSION
P.O. Box 850
Bryson City, NC 28713
(714) 488-9211

LAND OF SKY REGIONAL COUNCIL
25 Heritage Drive
Asheville, NC 28806
(704) 254-8131

ISOTHERMAL PLANNING AND DEVELOPMENT
COMMUNITY
101 West Court Street

P.O. Box 841
Rutherfordton, NC 28139
(704) 287-2281

REGION D COUNCIL OF GOVERNMENTS
P.O. Box 1820
Executive Arts Building
Furman Road
Boone, NC 28607
(704) 264-5558

WESTERN PIEDMONT COUNCIL OF GOVERN-
MENTS
317 First Avenue, NW
Hickory, NC 28601
(704) 322-9191

CENTRALINA COUNCIL OF GOVERNMENTS
1300 Baxter Street
P.O. Box 35008
Charlottetown Center
Charlotte, NC 28235
(704) 372-2416

PIEDMONT TRIAD COUNCIL OF GOVERN-
MENTS
Kroger Center
Wilmington Building, Suite 201
2216 West Meadowview Road
Greensboro, NC 27407
(919) 294-4950

PEE DEE COUNCIL OF GOVERNMENTS
302 Leak Street
P.O. Drawer 1417
Rockingham, NC 28379
(919) 895-6306

TRIANGLE J COUNCIL OF GOVERNMENTS
P.O. Box 12276
100 Park Drive
Research Triangle Park, NC 27709
(919) 549-0551

KERR TAR REGIONAL COUNCIL OF GOVERN-
MENTS
238 Orange Street

P.O. Box 709
Henderson, NC 27536
(919) 492-8561

REGION L COUNCIL OF GOVERNMENTS
1309 South Wesleyan Blvd.
P.O. Box 2748
Rocky Mount, NC 27802
(919) 446-0411

REGION M COUNCIL OF GOVERNMENTS
130 Gillespie Street
P.O. Drawer 1510
Fayetteville, NC 28302
(919) 323-4191

LUMBER RIVER COUNCIL OF GOVERNMENTS
4721 Fayetteville Road
P.O. Drawer 1529
Lumberton, NC 28359
(919) 738-8104

CAPE FEAR COUNCIL OF GOVERNMENTS
321 North Front Street
P.O. Box 1491
Wilmington, NC 28402
(919) 763-0191

NUESE RIVER COUNCIL OF GOVERNMENTS
233 Middle Street
P.O. Box 1717
New Bern, NC 28560
(919) 638-3185

MID-EAST DEVELOPMENT COMMISSION
1 Harding Square
P.O. Box 1787
Washington, NC 27889
(919) 946-8043

ALBEMARLE REGIONAL PLANNING AND DEVEL-
OPMENT COMMISSION
P.O. Box 646
Hertford, NC 27944
(919) 426-5753

NORTHWEST PIEDMONT COUNCIL OF GOV-
ERNMENTS
280 South Liberty Street
Winston-Salem, NC 27101
(919) 722-9346

NORTH DAKOTA
Aging Services
Department of Human Services
State Capitol Building
Bismarck, ND 58505
(701) 224-2577

OHIO
Department on Aging
50 West Broad Street, 9th Floor
Columbus, OH 43266
(614) 466-5500

COUNCIL ON AGING OF THE CINCINNATI AREA
601 Provident Bank Building
7th and Vine
Cincinnati, OH 45202
(513) 721-1025

AREA AGENCY ON AGING
6 S. Patterson Blvd.
Dayton, OH 45402
(513) 225-3027

PSA 3 AREA AGENCY ON AGING
311 Building, Suite 201
311 E. Market Street
Lima OH 45801
(419) 222-7723

AREA OFFICE ON AGING OF NORTHWESTERN
OHIO
Executive Office Building
2155 Arlington Avenue
Toledo, OH 45809
(419) 382-0624

DISTRICT 5 AREA AGENCY ON AGING
P.O. Box 1978
Mansfield, OH 44901
(419) 524-4144

CENTRAL OHIO AREA AGENCY ON AGING
272 S. Gift Street
Columbus, OH 43215
(614) 222-7250

AREA AGENCY ON AGING
P.O. Box 978
Rio Grande College
Rio Grande, OH 45674
(614) 245-5306

BUCKEYE HILLS-HOCKING VALLEY REGIONAL
DEVELOPMENT DISTRICT
Rte. 1, Box 299D
Marietta, OH 45750
(614) 374-9436

AREA AGENCY ON AGING
Box 429
117 S. 11th Street
Cambridge, OH 43725
(614) 439-4478

WESTERN RESERVE AREA AGENCY ON AGING
1030 Euclid Avenue
Cleveland, OH 44115
(216) 621-8010

AREA OFFICE ON AGING
411 Wolf Lodges Parkway
Akron, OH 44311
(216) 376-9172

DISTRICT 11 AREA AGENCY ON AGING
Ohio One Building
25 E. Boardman Street
Youngstown, OH 44503
(216) 746-2938

OKLAHOMA
Special Unit on Aging
Department of Human Services
P.O. Box 253532
Oklahoma City, OK 73125
(405) 521-2327

GRAND GATEWAY EDA AREA AGENCY ON AGING
P.O. Box 330
320 S. Wilson
Vinita, OK 74301
(918) 256-6478

EODD AREA AGENCY ON AGING
P.O. Box 1367
Muskogee, OK 74402
(918) 682-7891

KEDDO AREA AGENCY ON AGING
Highway 2, North
P.O. Box 638
Wilburton, OK 74578
(918) 465-2367

SODA AREA AGENCY ON AGING
P.O. Box 848
Admore, OK 73402
(405) 226-2250

COEDD AREA AGENCY ON AGING
400 N. Bell
Shawnee, OK 74801
(405) 273-6410

TULSA AREA AGENCY ON AGING
200 Civic Center, Room 1022
Tulsa, OK 74103
(918) 529-7688

NODA AREA AGENCY ON AGING
1216 W. Willow
Enid, OK 73703
(405) 237-4810

AREAWIDE AGENCY ON AGING
3200 N.W. 48th Street
Oklahoma City, OK 73112
(405) 236-2426

ASCOG AREA AGENCY ON AGING
802 Main Street
P.O. Box 1647
Duncan, OK 73534
(405) 252-0595

SWODA AREA AGENCY ON AGING
P.O. Box 569
Burns Flat, OK 73624
(405) 562-4886

OEDA AREA AGENCY ON AGING
330 Douglas Avenue
P.O. Box 668
Beaver, OK 73932
(405) 625-4531

OREGON
Senior Services Division
313 Public Service Building
Salem, OR 97310
(503) 378-4728
(800) 232-3020 (OR)

DISTRICT 1 AREA AGENCY ON AGING
1065 Hemlock Street
P.O. Box 488
Cannon Beach, OR 97110
(503) 436-1156

CLACKAMAS AREA AGENCY ON AGING
821 Main Street
Oregon City, OR 97045
(503) 655-8200

COLUMBIA COUNCIL OF SENIOR CITIZENS
11 Plaza
P.O. Box 141
St. Helens, OR 97204
(503) 397-4000

WASHINGTON COUNTY AGING PROGRAM
180 E. Main Street
Hillsboro, OR 97123
(503) 640-3489

AGING SERVICES DIVISION
426 SW Stark, 5th Floor
B 160
Portland, OR 97204
(503) 248-3646

MID-WILLAMETTE VALLEY SENIOR SERVICES
AGENCY
2450 Lancaster N.E.
P.O. Box 12189
Salem, OR 97309
(503) 371-1313

SENIOR AND DISABLED ADULT SERVICES
408 S.W. Monroe
Corvallis, OR 97333
(503) 757-6851

DISTRICT 5 AREA AGENCY ON AGING
1025 Willamette Street
Eugene, OR 97401
(503) 687-4283

DOUGLAS COUNTY SENIOR SERVICES
621 W. Madrone
Roseburg, OR 97470
(503) 440-3601

DISTRICT 7 AREA AGENCY ON AGING
295 S. 10th Street
Coos Bay, OR 97420
(503) 756-2563

DISTRICT 8 AREA AGENCY ON AGING
Rouge Valley Council of Governments
155 S. 2nd Street, Room 200
P.O. Box 3275
Central Point, OR 97502
(503) 664-6674

MID-COLUMBIA AREA AGENCY ON AGING
P.O. Box 988
700 Union Street, Room 233
The Dallas, OR 97058
(503) 298-4101

CENTRAL OREGON COUNCIL ON AGING
2303 S.W. 1st Street
Redmond, OR 97756

KLAMATH BASIN SENIOR CITIZENS COUNCIL
2045 Arthur Street

Klamath Falls, OR 97603
(503) 882-4098

EAST CENTRAL OREGON ASSOCIATION OF
COUNTIES AREA AGENCY ON AGING
17 SW Frazer
P.O. Box 1207
Pendleton, OR 97801
(503) 276-6732

HELP
104 Elm Street
LaGrande, OR 97850
(503) 963-3186

MALHEUR COUNCIL ON AGING
Box 937
1309 NW 16th Avenue
Ontario, OR 97914
(503) 889-7651

HARNEY COUNTY SENIOR CITIZENS
17 South Alder Street
Burns, OR 97720
(503) 573-6024

PENNSYLVANIA
Department of Aging
231 State Street
Harrisburg, PA 17101
(717) 783-1550

ERIE COUNTY AREA AGENCY ON AGING
Greater Erie Community Action Commission
18 West 9th Street
Erie, PA 16501
(814) 459-4581

ACTIVE AGING, INC.
1034 Park Avenue
Meadville, PA 16335
(814) 336-1792

NORTH CENTRAL PENNSYLVANIA OFFICE OF
HUMAN SERVICES
108 Center Street
P.O. Box A

Ridgway, PA 15853
(814) 776-2191

BEAVER COUNTY OFFICE ON AGING
500 Market Street, W.B. 202
Beaver, PA 15009
(412) 728-5700

AGING SERVICES OF INDIANA COUNTY
201 Airport Offices and Professional Center
RD 3
Indiana, PA 15701
(412) 349-4500

ALLEGHENY COUNTY AREA AGENCY ON
AGING
441 Smithfield Street
Pittsburgh, PA 15222
(412) 355-4234

WESTMORELAND COUNTY AREA AGENCY ON
AGING
2482 South Grande Blvd.
Greensburg, PA 15601
(412) 836-1111

SOUTHWESTERN PENNSYLVANIA AREA
AGENCY ON AGING
Eastgate 8
Monessen, PA 15062
(412) 684-9000

AREA AGENCY ON AGING OF SOMERSET
COUNTY
132 E. Catherine Street
Somerset, PA 15501
(814) 443-2681

CAMBRIA COUNTY AREA AGENCY ON AGING
P.O. Box 88
Ebensburg, PA 15931
(814) 472-5580

BLAIR SENIOR SERVICES
1404 Eleventh Avenue
Altoona, PA 16601
(814) 946-1235

HUNTINGDON/BEDFORD/FULTON AREA
AGENCY ON AGING
240 Wood Street
P.O. Box 46
Bedford, PA 15522
(814) 623-8149

CENTRE COUNTY AREA AGENCY ON AGING
Willowbank Building
Homes and Valentine Streets
Bellefonte, PA 16823
(814) 355-6716

BI-COUNTY OFFICE ON AGING
P.O. Box 770
352 East Water Street
Lock Haven, PA 17745
(717) 748-8665

COLUMBIA/MONTOUR AREA AGENCY ON
AGING
15 Peery Avenue
Bloomsburg, PA 17815
(717) 784-9272

NOTHUMBERLAND COUNTY AREA AGENCY
ON AGING
RD 1, Box 943
State Route 225
Shamokin, PA 17872
(717) 644-4545

UNION/SNYDER COUNTY OFFICE ON AGING
116 N. Second Street
Lewisburg, PA 17837
(717) 837-0675

MIFFLIN-JUNIATA AREA AGENCY ON AGING
P.O. Box 750
Buena Vista Circle
Lewistown, PA 17044
(717) 242-0315

FRANKLIN COUNTY OFFICE FOR THE AGING
50 N. Duke Street
Chambersburg, PA 17201
(717) 263-2153

ADAMS COUNTY AREA AGENCY ON AGING
220 Baltimore Street
Gettysburg, PA 17325
(717) 334-9296

CUMBERLAND COUNTY OFFICE ON AGING
Rm. 111R-East Wing Courthouse
Carlisle, PA 17013
(717) 243-8442

PERRY COUNTY OFFICE FOR THE AGING
Courthouse Annex
South Carlisle Street
New Bloomfield, PA 17068
(717) 582-2131

DAUPHIN COUNTY AREA AGENCY ON AGING
25 S. Front Streets
Harrisburg, PA 17101
(717) 255-2790

POTTER COUNTY AREA AGENCY ON AGING
Mapleview Health Center
Route 872
Coudersport, PA 16915

LEBANON COUNTY AREA AGENCY ON AGING
710 Maple Street, Room 209
Senior Center
Lebanon, PA 17042
(717) 273-9262

YORK COUNTY AREA AGENCY ON AGING
141 West Market Street
York, PA 17401
(717) 771-9610

LANCASTER COUNTY OFFICE ON AGING
50 North Duke Street
Lancaster, PA 17602
(717) 299-7979

CHESTER COUNTY SERVICES FOR SENIOR CITI-
ZENS
10 N. Church Street
West Chester, PA 19380
(215) 431-6350

MONTGOMERY COUNTY OFFICE ON AGING
AND ADULT SERVICES
Montgomery County Courthouse
Norristown, PA 19404
(215) 278-3601

BUCKS COUNTY AREA AGENCY ON AGING
30 E. Oakland Avenue
Doylestown, PA 18901
(215) 348-0510

DELAWARE COUNTY SERVICES FOR THE AGING
Second and Orange Streets
Government Center
Media, PA 19063
(215) 891-4455

PHILADELPHIA CORPORATION FOR AGING
642 N. Broad Street
Philadelphia, PA 19130
(215) 765-9000

BERKS COUNTY AREA AGENCY ON AGING
15 South 8th Street
Reading, PA 19602
(215) 378-8808

LEHIGH COUNTY AREA AGENCY ON AGING
Courthouse Annex
523 Hamilton Street
Allentown, PA 18101
(215) 820-3248

NORTHAMPTON COUNTY AREA AGENCY ON
AGING
Gracedale-South-West Ground
Gracedale Avenue
Nazareth, PA 18064
(215) 759-7970

WAYNE/PIKE AREA AGENCY ON AGING
Pike County Program Office
106 Broad Street
Milford, PA 18337
(717) 296-7813

AREA AGENCY ON AGING FOR THE COUNTIES OF BRADFORD, SULLIVAN, SUSQUEHANNA AND TIOGA
701 Main Street
Towanda, PA 18848
(717) 265-6121

LUZERNE/WYOMING COUNTIES BUREAU FOR THE AGING
111 North Pennsylvania Blvd.
Wilkes-Barre, PA 18701
(717) 822-1158

LACKAWANNA COUNTY AREA AGENCY ON AGING
200 Adams Avenue
Scranton, PA 18503
(717) 963-6740

CARBON COUNTY AREA AGENCY ON AGING
COURT HOUSE ANNEX
P.O. Box 251
Jim Thorpe, PA 18229
(717) 325-2726

SCHUYLKILL COUNTY AREA AGENCY ON AGING
13-15 North Centre Street
Pottsville, PA 17901
(717) 622-3103

CLEARFIELD COUNTY AREA AGENCY ON AGING
103 N. Front Street
P.O. Box 550
Clearfield, PA 16830
(814) 765-2696

JEFFERSON COUNTY AREA AGENCY ON AGING
Jefferson County Service Center
RD 5
Brookville, PA 15825
(814) 849-3096

EXPERIENCE, INC. AREA AGENCY ON AGING
514 West Third Avenue
P.O. Box 886
Warren, PA 16365
(814) 726-1700

VANANGO COUNTY AREA AGENCY ON AGING
P.O. Box 1130
Franklin, PA 16323
(814) 437-6871

ARMSTRONG COUNTY AREA AGENCY ON AGING
125 Queen Street
Kittanning, PA 16201
(412) 548-7516

LAWRENCE COUNTY AREA AGENCY ON AGING
15 W. Washington Street
New Castle, PA 16101
(412) 658-5661

MERCER COUNTY AREA AGENCY ON AGING
404 Mercer County Courthouse
Mercer, PA 16125
(412) 662-3800

MONROE COUNTY AREA AGENCY ON AGING
62 Analomink Street
East Stroudsburg, PA 18301
(717) 424-5290

CLARION COUNTY AREA AGENCY ON AGING
12 Grant Street
Clarion, PA 16214
(814) 226-4640

BUTLER COUNTY AREA AGENCY ON AGING
111 Sunnyview Circle
Butler, PA 16001
(412) 282-3008

RHODE ISLAND
Department of Elderly Affairs
79 Washington Street
Providence, RI 02903
(401) 277-2858

SOUTH CAROLINA
Commission on Aging
915 Main Street
Columbia, SC 29201
(803) 783-3203

APPALACHIAN COUNCIL OF GOVERNMENTS
P.O. Drawer 6668
50 Grand Avenue
Greenville, SC 29606
(803) 242-9733

EDGEFIELD SENIOR CITIZENS COUNCIL
400 Church Street
P.O. Box 510
Edgefield, SC 29824
(803) 637-5326

GREENWOOD COUNTY COUNCIL ON AGING
123 Bailey Circle
P.O. Box 997
Greenwood, SC 29648
(803) 223-0164

LAURENS COUNTY COUNCIL FOR SENIOR CITI-
ZENS PROGRAMS
P.O. Box 777
Laurens, SC 29360
(803) 984-4572

MCCORMICK COUNTY SENIOR CITIZENS PRO-
GRAMS
407 Augusta Street
P.O. Box 684
McCormick, SC 29835
(803) 465-2626

SALUDA COUNTY COUNCIL ON AGING
104 W. Church Street
P.O. Box 507
Saluda, SC 29138
(803) 445-2175

CATAWBA REGIONAL PLANNING COUNCIL
2424 India Hook Road
P.O. Box 450
Rock Hill, SC 29732
(803) 327-9041

CENTRAL MIDLANDS REGIONAL PLANNING
COUNCIL
800 Dutch Square Blvd., No. 155

Columbia, SC 29210
(803) 798-1243

LOWER SAVANNAH COUNCIL OF GOVERN-
MENTS
Highway 302 North
P.O. Box 850
Aiken, SC 29802
(803) 649-7981

SANTEE-LYNCHES REGIONAL COUNCIL
Box 1837
Sumter, SC 29150
(803) 775-7382

PEE DEE COUNCIL OF GOVERNMENTS
P.O. Box 5719
Florence-Darlington Highway
Florence, SC 29502
(803) 669-3138

TRIDENT AREA AGENCY ON AGING
P.O. Box 2696
1069 King Street
Charleston, SC 29403
(803) 723-1676

LOW COUNTRY COUNCIL OF GOVERNMENTS
Interstate 95
U.S. 17
P.O. Box 98
Yemeassee, SC 29945
(803) 726-5536

SOUTH DAKOTA
Office of Adult Services and Aging
700 Governor's Drive
Kneip Building
Pierre, SD 57501
(605) 773-3656

TENNESSEE
Commission on Aging
706 Church Street, Suite 201
Nashville, TN 37219
(615) 741-2056

FIRST TENNESSEE AREA AGENCY ON AGING
207 North Boone, Suite 800
Johnson City, TN 37604
(615) 928-0224

AREA AGENCY ON AGING
East Tennessee Human Resource Agency
408 N. Cedar Bluff Road
Knoxville, TN 37923
(615) 691-2551

CARCOG/SOUTHEAST TENNESSEE DEVELOP-
MENT DISTRICT
216 West 8th Street, Suite 300
Chattanooga, TN 37402
(615) 266-5781

UPPER CUMBERLAND PLANNING AND SERVICE
AREA
1225 Burgess Falls Road
Cookeville, TN 38501
(615) 432-4111

MID-CUMBERLAND DEVELOPMENT DISTRICT
211 Union Street
Box 233
Nashville, TN 37201
(615) 259-5491

SOUTH CENTRAL TENNESSEE DEVELOPMENT
DISTRICT
815 South Main Street
P.O. Box 1346
Columbia, TN 38401
(615) 381-2040

NORTHWEST PLANNING AND SERVICE AREA
P.O. Box 63
Weldon Drive
Martin, TN 38237
(901) 587-4215

SOUTHWEST TENNESSEE DEVELOPMENT DIS-
TRICT
416 East Lafayette Street
Jackson, TN 38301
(901) 422-4041

DELTA COMMISSION ON AGING
City Hall, Room 419
125 N. Mid-Amer Hall
Memphis, TN 38103
(901) 528-2600

TEXAS
Department on Aging
P.O. Box 12786 Capitol Station
1949 IH 35
South Austin, TX 78741
(512) 444-2727
(800) 252-9240 (TX)

PANHANDLE REGION PLANNING COUNCIL
AREA AGENCY ON AGING
P.O. Box 9257
2736 W. 10th
Amarillo, TX 79105
(806) 372-3381

SOUTH PLAINS ASSOCIATION OF GOVERN-
MENTS
1323 58th Street
Lubbock, TX 79452
(806) 762-8721

NORTEX REGIONAL PLANNING COMMISSION
P.O. Box 5144
2101 Kemp Blvd.
Wichita Falls, TX 76307
(817) 322-5281

NORTH CENTRAL TEXAS COUNCIL OF GOVERN-
MENT
Area Agency on Aging
616 Six Flags Drive, Center Point 2
P.O. Drawer COG
Arlington, TX 76005
(817) 322-5281

COMMUNITY COUNCIL OF GREATER DALLAS
2121 Main Street, Suite 500
Dallas, TX 75201
(214) 741-5851

TARRANT COUNTY AREA AGENCY ON AGING
201 E. Ninth Street
Fort Worth, TX 76102
(817) 335-3473

ARK-TEX AREA COG
911 Loop 151
Suite 100, Building A
P.O. Box 5307
Texarkana, TX 75505
(501) 774-3481

EAST TEXAS AREA AGENCY ON AGING
3800 Stone Road
Kilgore, TX 75662
(214) 984-8641

WEST CENTRAL TEXAS AREA AGENCY ON AGING
1025 East North 10th
P.O. Box 3195
Abilene, TX 79604
(915) 672-8544

WEST TEXAS COG AREA AGENCY ON AGING
1014 W. Stanton
El Paso, TX 79902
(915) 541-4681

PERMIAN BASIN REGIONAL PLANNING COMMISSION
P.O. Box 6391
Midland, TX 79711
(915) 563-1061

CONCHO VALLEY AREA AGENCY ON AGING
P.O. Box 60050
5002 Knickerbocker Road
San Angelo, TX 76906
(915) 944-9666

HEART OF TEXAS COG AREA AGENCY ON AGING
320 Franklin Avenue
Waco, TX 76701
(817) 756-6631

CAPITAL AREA AGENCY ON AGING
2520 Interstate Highway 355 South
Suite 100
Austin, TX 78704
(512) 443-7653

BRAZOS VALLEY DEVELOPMENT COUNCIL AREA AGENCY ON AGING
P.O. Drawer 4128
Bryan, TX 77805
(713) 822-7421

DEEP EAST TEXAS AREA AGENCY ON AGING
203-A S. Main Street
Jasper, TX 75951
(713) 384-5704

SOUTH EAST TEXAS AREA AGENCY ON AGING
P.O. Drawer 1387
Neperland, TX 77627

HOUSTON-GALVESTON AREA AGENCY ON AGING
3550 Timmons, Suite 500
P.O. Box 22777
Houston, TX 77227
(713) 627-3200

HOUSTON-HARRIS COUNTY AREA AGENCY ON AGING
800 Stadium Drive
Houston, TX 77054
(713) 236-7700

GOLDEN CRESCENT REGIONAL PLANNING COMMISSION
Area Agency on Aging
P.O. Box 2028
Victoria Regional Airport Building 102
Victoria, TX 77902
(512) 578-1587

ALAMO AREA AGENCY ON AGING
118 Broadway, Suite 400
San Antonio, TX 78205
(512) 225-5201

BEXAR COUNTY AREA AGENCY ON AGING
118 Broadway, Suite 400
San Antonio, TX 78205
(512) 225-5201

SOUTH TEXAS AREA AGENCY ON AGING
600 South Sandman
P.O. Box 2187
Laredo, TX 78044
(512) 722-3995

COASTAL BEND AREA AGENCY ON AGING
2910 Leopard Street
P.O. Box 1909
Corpus Christi, TX 78469
(512) 883-5743

LOWER RIO GRANDE VALLEY AREA AGENCY ON
AGING
4900 N. 23rd Street
McAllen, TX 78504
(512) 682-3481

TEXOMA AREA AGENCY ON AGING
10000 Grayson Drive
Denison, TX 75020
(214) 786-2955

CENTRAL TEXAS COG AREA AGENCY ON AGING
302 East Central
P.O. Box 729
Belton, TX 76513
(817) 939-1886

MIDDLE RIO GRANDE VALLEY AREA AGENCY
ON AGING
403 East Nopal
P.O. Box 1199
Carrizo Spring, TX 78834
(512) 876-3533

UTAH
Division of Aging and Adult Services
Department of Social Services
Social Services Bldg.
120 North, 200 West

Salt Lake City, UT 84145
(801) 538-3910

BEAR RIVER AREA AGENCY ON AGING
170 N. Main Street
Logan, UT 84321
(801) 752-7242

WEBER COUNTY DEPARTMENT OF AGING
2650 Lincoln, Room 268
Ogden, UT 84401
(801) 399-8840

SALT LAKE COUNTY AGING SERVICES
2001 South State, Suite S-1500
Salt Lake City, UT 84190
(801) 468-2454

DAVIS COUNTY COUNCIL ON AGING
Davis County Courthouse Annex
28 East State Street
P.O. Box 618
Farmington, UT 84025
(801) 451-3370

TOOELE AREA AGENCY ON AGING
59 East Vine
P.O. Box 477
Tooele, UT 84074
(801) 882-2870

MOUNTAINLAND AREA AGENCY ON AGING
2545 North Canyon Road
Provo, UT 84604
(801) 377-2262

AGING SERVICES DISTRICT IV
P.O. Box 788
Sevier County Courthouse
Richfield, UT 84701
(801) 896-9222

FIVE COUNTY AREA AGENCY ON AGING
237 N. Bluff
P.O. Box 1550
St. George, UT 84770
(801) 673-3548

UINTAH BASIN AREA AGENCY ON AGING
120 South 100 East, Nos. 43-4
Roosevelt, UT 84066
(801) 722-4518

UINTAH COUNTY AREA AGENCY ON AGING
155 South 100 West
Vernal, UT 84078
(801) 789-2169

SOUTHEAST UTAH AREA AGENCY ON AGING
Industrial Park
P.O. Drawer 1106
Price, UT 84501
(801) 637-4268

SAN JUAN AREA AGENCY ON AGING
117 S. Main
P.O. Box 9
Monticello, UT 84535
(801) 587-2231

VERMONT
Office on Aging
103 South Main Street
Waterbury, VT 05676
(802) 241-2400

CHAMPLAIN VALLEY AREA AGENCY ON AGING
P.O. Box 158
Winooski, VT 05404
(802) 655-0084

CENTRAL VERMONT COUNCIL ON AGING
18 South Main Street
Barre, VT 05641
(802) 479-0531

AREA AGENCY ON AGING FOR NORTHERN VER-
MONT
44 Main Street
P.O. Box 640
St. Johnsbury, VT 05819
(802) 748-5182

SOUTHWESTERN VERMONT AREA AGENCY ON
AGING
142 Merchants Row
Rutland, VT 05701
(802) 775-0486

COUNCIL ON AGING FOR SOUTHEASTERN VER-
MONT
139 Main Street
P.O. Box 818
Brattleboro, VT 05301
(802) 257-0569

VIRGINIA
Department on Aging
700 Franklin Street
Richmond, VA 23219
(804) 225-2271

MOUNTAIN EMPIRE OLDER CITIZENS GROUP
330 Norton Road
P.O. Box 1097
Wise, VA 24293
(703) 328-2302

APPALACHIAN AGENCY ON SENIOR CITIZENS
Box SVCC
Richlands, VA 23641
(703) 964-4915

DISTRICT III GOVERNMENT COOPERATIVE
305 S. Park Street
Marion, VA 24354
(703) 783-8158

NEW RIVER VALLEY AGENCY ON AGING
143 3rd Street, NW
Pulaski, VA 24301
(703) 980-8888

LEAGUE OF OLDER AMERICANS
P.O. Box 14205
Roanoke, VA 24038
(703) 345-0451

VALLEY PROGRAM FOR AGING SERVICES
352 Pine Avenue
P.O. Box 817
Waynesboro, VA 22980
(703) 949-7141

SHENANDOAH AREA AGENCY ON AGING
15 North Royal Avenue
Front Royal, VA 22630
(703) 635-7141

DISTRICT OFFICE ON AGING
2525 Mt. Vernon Avenue, Unit 5
Alexandria VA 22301
(703) 838-4822

ARLINGTON AREA AGENCY ON AGING
1801 N. George Mason Drive
Arlington, VA 22207
(703) 558-2341

FAIRFAX COUNTY AREA AGENCY ON AGING
11242 Waples Mill Road
Fairfax, VA 22030
(703) 691-3384

LOUDOUN COUNTY AREA AGENCY ON AGING
751 Miller Drive, S.E.
Leesburg, VA 22075
(703) 777-0257

PRINCE WILLIAM AREA AGENCY ON AGING
7987 Ashton Avenue
Manassas, VA 22110
(703) 335-6400

RAPPAHANNOCK-RAPIDAN AREA AGENCY ON
AGING
401 South Main Street
Culpeper, VA 22701
(703) 825-6494

JEFFERSON AREA AGENCY ON AGING
2300 Commonwealth Drive
Charlottesville, VA 22901
(804) 977-3444

CENTRAL VIRGINIA COMMISSION ON AGING
2511 Memorial Avenue
Lynchburg, VA 25401
(804) 384-0372

SOUTHERN AREA AGENCY ON AGING
433 Commonwealth Avenue
Martinsville, VA 24112
(703) 632-6442

LAKE COUNTY COMMISSION ON AGING
1105 West Danville Street
South Hill, VA 23970
(804) 447-7661

PIEDMONT SENIOR RESOURCES
Area Agency on Aging
Piedmont Hospital Building, Room 228
P.O. Box 398
Burkeville, VA 23922
(804) 767-5588

CAPITAL AREA AGENCY ON AGING
316 E. Clay Street
Richmond, VA 23219
(804) 648-8381

RAPPAHANNOCK AREA AGENCY ON AGING
204 Thompson Avenue
Fredericksburg, VA 22405
(703) 371-3375

NORTHERN NECK-MIDDLE PENINSULA AREA
AGENCY ON AGING
Virginia Street
P.O. Box 610
Urbana, VA 23175
(804) 758-2386

CRATER DISTRICT AREA AGENCY ON AGING
23 Seyler Drive
Petersburg, VA 23805
(804) 732-7020

SOUTHEASTERN VIRGINIA AREAWIDE MODEL
PROGRAM
7 Koger Executive Center, Suite 100
Norfolk, VA 23502
(804) 461-9481

PENINSULA AGENCY ON AGING
1010 Old Denbigh Road
Newport News, VA 23602
(804) 874-2495

EASTERN SHORE COMMUNITY DEVELOPMENT
GROUP
54 Market Street
P.O. Box 8
Onancock, VA 23417
(804) 787-3532

WASHINGTON
Aging and Adult Services Administration
Department of Social and Health Services
OB-44A
Olympia, WA 98504
(206) 586-3768

OLYMPIC AREA AGENCY ON AGING
P.O. Box 1072
423 Washington
Port Townsend, WA 98368
(206) 385-2564

NORTHWEST WASHINGTON AREA AGENCY ON
AGING
1800 James Street
Belingham, WA 98225
(206) 676-6749

SNOHOMISH COUNTY DIVISION OF AGING
DHA
2722 Colby
Everett, WA 98201
(206) 259-9586

KING COUNTY AREA AGENCY ON AGING
110 Prefontaine Place
Seattle, WA 98104
(206) 625-4711

PIERCE COUNTY AREA AGENCY ON AGING
8811 S. Tacoma Way
Tacoma, WA 98499
(206) 593-4828

LEWIS/MASON/THURSTON AREA AGENCY ON
AGING
503 W. Fourth Avenue
Olympia, WA 98501
(206) 786-5579

SOUTHWEST WASHINGTON AREA AGENCY ON
AGING
1703 Main Street
P.O. Box 425
Vancouver, WA 98666
(206) 694-6577

COLUMBIA RIVER AREA AGENCY ON AGING
230 N. Georgia
East Wenatchee, WA 98802
(509) 662-1651

YAKIMA/SOUTHEAST WASHINGTON AREA
AGENCY ON AGING
2009 South 64th Avenue
Yakima, WA 98903
(509) 575-4226

YAKIMA INDIAN NATION AREA AGENCY ON
AGING
P.O. Box 151
Toppenish, WA 98948
(509) 865-5121

EASTERN WASHINGTON AREA AGENCY ON
AGING
West 1101 College Avenue, Room 365
Spokane, WA 99201
(509) 458-2509

COLVILLE CONFEDERATED TRIBES
P.O. Box 150
Nespelem, WA 99155
(509) 634-4761

KITSAP COUNTY AREA AGENCY ON AGING
Kitsap County Courthouse
614 Division Street
Port Orchard, WA 98366
(206) 876-7068

WEST VIRGINIA
Commission on Aging
Holly Grove—State Capitol
Charleston, WV 25305
(304) 348-3317
(800) 642-3671 (WV)

REGION 1 PLANNING AND DEVELOPMENT
COUNCIL
P.O. Box 1432
Princeton, WV 24740
(304) 425-9508

REGION II PLANNING AND DEVELOPMENT
COUNCIL
P.O. Box 939
1221 6th Avenue
Huntington, WV 25712
(304) 529-3357

COMMUNITY COUNCIL OF KANAWHA VALLEY
702 1/2 Lee Street East
Box 2711
Charleston, WV 25330
(304) 340-3515

EASTERN HIGHLANDS AREA AGENCY ON
AGING
500-B Main Street
Summersville, WV 26651
(304) 872-4970

MID-OHIO REGIONAL COUNCIL
925 Market Street
P.O. Box 247
Parkersburg, WV 26102
(304) 422-0522

REGION VI AREA AGENCY ON AGING
200 Adams Street

Fairmont, WV 26554
(304) 366-5693

CENTRAL WEST VIRGINIA AREA AGENCY ON
AGING
5 S. Florida Street
P.O. Box 186
Buckhannon, WV 26201
(304) 472-0395

UPPER POTOMAC AREA AGENCY ON AGING
Airport Road
P.O. Box 869
Petersburg, WV 26847
(304) 257-1221

NORTHERN PANHANDLE AREA AGENCY ON
AGING
2177 National Road
Wheeling, WV 26003
(304) 242-1800

WISCONSIN
Bureau of Aging
Division of Community Services
P.O. Box 7851
Madison, WI 53702
(608) 266-2536

AREA AGENCY ON AGING
3601 Memorial Drive
Madison, WI 53704
(608) 249-0441

AREA AGENCY ON AGING
235 W. Galena Street
Milwaukee, WI 53212
(414) 289-5950

SOUTHEAST WISCONSIN AREA AGENCY ON
AGING
W25S-N499 Grandview Blvd.
Waukesha, WI 53188
(414) 521-5420

LAKE MICHIGAN-WINNEBAGO AREA AGENCY
ON AGING
850-C Lombardi Avenue
Green Bay, WI 54304
(414) 465-1662

WESTERN WISCONSIN AREA AGENCY ON
AGING
505 Dewey Street S., Room 207
Eau Claire, WI 54701
(715) 836-4105

DISTRICT VII NORTHERN CENTRAL AREA
AGENCY ON AGING
P.O. Box 1028
1835 N. Stevens
Rhinelander, WI 54501
(715) 362-7800

WYOMING
Commission on Aging
Hathaway Building-Room 139
Cheyenne, WY 82002
(307) 777-7986

LOCAL AREA SENIOR GAMES CENTERS

ALABAMA

SPORTS FESTIVAL
GCPF&S
560 S. McDonough Street
Montgomery, AL 36130
(205) 261-4496

ARIZONA

ARIZONA SENIOR OLYMPICS
1201 N. 3rd Street
Phoenix, AZ 85004
(602) 495-5490

ARKANSAS

ARKANSAS SENIOR OLYMPICS
P.O. Box 1795
Harrison, AR 72601
(501) 741-1144

CALIFORNIA

NORTHERN CALIFORNIA SENIOR OLYMPICS
Oakland Office of Parks and Recreation
1520 Lakeside Drive
Oakland, CA 94612
(415) 3896

SOUTHERN CALIFORNIA SENIOR OLYMPICS
Leisure Services Manager
Administrative Office
City of Palm Springs
P.O. Box 1786
Palm Springs, CA 92263
(619) 323-8274

COLORADO

ROCKY MOUNTAIN SENIOR GAMES
City of Lakewood
1580 Yarrow Street
Lakewood, CO 80215
(303) 235-6717

CONNECTICUT
Senior Olympics
Arnold College
University of Bridgeport
Bridgeport, CT 06601
(203) 576-4722

DELAWARE

FIRST STATE GAMES
P.O.Box 9998
Newark, DE 19714
(302) 239-3200

DISTRICT OF COLUMBIA

DC SENIOR OLYMPICS
1230 Taylor Street, NW
Washington, DC 20011
(202) 673-6973

DC SENIOR GAMES
6062 Arlington Blvd.
Falls Church, VA 22044
(202) 530-4140

FLORIDA

BIG SUN SENIOR GAMES
Central Florida Community College
P.O. Box 1388
Ocala, FL 32674

FT. MYERS SENIOR GAMES
Recreation Department
City of Ft. Myers
P.O. Drawer 2217
Ft. Myers, FL 33902

NORTH FLORIDA SENIOR GAMES
Area Agency on Aging, Suite 145-B
2639 N. Monroe Street
Tallahassee, FL 32303

GOOD LIFE GAMES SENIOR OLYMPICS
P.O.Box 12288
St. Petersburg, FL 33733

SENIOR OLYMPICS
Methodist Hospital
Public Relations Department
580 W. Eighth Street
Jacksonville, FL 32209

TAMPA BAY SENIOR GAMES
Department of Aging
700 Twigg Street, Suite 804
Tampa, FL 33601

U.S. SENIOR ATHLETIC GAMES
200 Castlewood Drive
North Palm Beach, FL 33408

MARGATE SENIOR GAMES
Northwest Focal Point Senior Center
5750 Park Drive
Margate, FL 33063

PLANTATION SENIOR OLYMPICS
Plantation Central Park
9151 N.W. Second Avenue
Plantation, FL 33324

SOUTH FLORIDA SENIOR SPORTS FEST
10776 N. Kendall Drive, Suite F11
Miami, FL 33176

SENIOR OLYMPICS OF CHARLOTTE COUNTY
660 Albany Avenue
Port Charlotte, FL 33952

GEORGIA

GOLDEN OLYMPICS
P.O. Box 1340
Columbus, GA 31993
(404) 571-5886

VALDOSTA GOLDEN OLYMPICS
P.O. Box 1746
Valdosta, GA 31603
(912) 333-1817

GA SOUTHERN
P.O. Box 8073
Georgia Southern College
Statesboro, GA 30460
(912) 681-5462

GEORGIA GOLDEN OLYMPICS
878 Peachtree Street, NE, Room 102
Atlanta, GA 30309
(404) 894-4451

SOUTHEAST GEORGIA GOLDEN OLYMPICS
P.O. Box 1965

21 Riverside Drive
Waycross, GA 31501

HAWAII

HAWAII SENIOR OLYMPICS
2164 Halekoa Drive
Honolulu, HI 96821
(808) 734-8450

ILLINOIS

ILLINOIS SENIOR OLYMPICS
1415 N. Grand Avenue, E
Springfield, IL 62702
(217) 789-2284

MT. VERNON SENIOR OLYMPICS
707 Maple Street
Mt. Vernon, IL 62864
(618) 242-1566

SOUTHWESTERN ILLINOIS REGIONAL SENIOR
OLYMPICS
Southern Illinois University
Box 1084
Edwardsville, IL 62026
(618) 692-3209

INDIANA

INDY SENIOR CLASSIC
1426 W. 29th Street
Indianapolis, IN 46208
(317) 636-1802

INDIANA SENIOR GAMES
7 S.E. 7th Street
Evansville, IN 47708
(812) 464-7800

INDIANA SENIOR GAMES
(217) 237-7191

SENIOR GAMES OF INDIANA
211 N. St. Louis Blvd.

South Bend, IN 46617
(219) 234-2961

IOWA

IOWA SENIOR OLYMPICS
713 8th Street
West Des Moines, IA 50265
(515) 277-6026

BURLINGTON SENIOR GAMES
509 Jefferson Street
Burlington, IA 52601
(319) 752-54433

KANSAS

PARKS AND RECREATION OLYMPICS
1534 SW Clay
Topeka, KS 66604
(913) 232-9665

JILL HOWELL
HCA Wesley Medical Center
550 N. Hillside
Wichita, KS 67214
(313) 688-3144

KENTUCKY

KENTUCKY SENIOR GAMES
c/o Green River Aging Services
1650 W. 2nd, Suite 106
Owensboro, KY 42301
(502) 926-0787

KENTUCKY SENIOR GAMES
228 Bridgett Drive
Mt. Sterling, KY 40353
(606) 674-6355

LOUISIANA

LOUISIANA SENIOR OLYMPICS
P.O. Box 14748
Baton Rouge, LA 70898
(504) 925-1700

MAINE

MAINE SENIOR GAMES
University of South Maine
96 Felma Street
Portland, ME 04103
(207) 780-4573

MARYLAND

MARYLAND SENIOR OLYMPICS
Towson State University
Physical Education Department
Towson, MD 21204
(301) 321-31632

MASSACHUSETTS

NATIONAL CONGRESS OF STATE GAMES
P.O. Box 8336
Boston, MA 02114
(617) 727-3227

MICHIGAN

MICHIGAN SENIOR OLYMPICS
34299 Claudia Court
Westland, MI 48185

W. MICHIGAN GOLDEN GAMES
Wyoming Senior Center
2380 DeHoop
Wyoming, MI 49509

OLDER PERSONS COMMISSION
312 Woodward
Rochester, MI 48063
(313) 656-1403, ext. 27

GREAT LAKES STATE GAMES
Mayland Hall
Northern Michigan University
Marquette, MI 49855
(906) 227-2888

MINNESOTA

STATE OF MINNESOTA SENIOR OLYMPICS
303 City Hall
Duluth, MN 55802
(218) 723-3662

MINNESOTA SENIOR SPORTS-A-RAMA
Bloomington Parks and Recreation
2215 W. Old Shakopee Road
Bloomington, MN 55431
(612) 887-9601

MISSISSIPPI

MISSISSIPPI SENIOR OLYMPICS
P.O. Drawer B
Pontotoc, MS 38863
(601) 489-2415

MISSOURI

MID-SOUTH SENIOR OLYMPICS
P.O. Box 1407
Popular Bluff, MO 63901
(314) 785-6760

UNIVERSITY OF MISSOURI—COLUMBIA
410 Turner Avenue
624 Clark Hall
Columbia, MO 65211

ST. LOUIS SENIOR OLYMPICS
2 Millstone Campus
St. Louis, MO 63146
(314) 432-5700

MONTANA

MONTANTA SENIOR OLYMPICS
Division of HPER
Eastern Montana College
1500 N. 30th Street
Billings, MT 59101
(406) 657-2370

NEBRASKA

NEBRASKA LAND DAYS SENIOR OLYMPICS
RSVP
211 W. 3rd Street
North Platte, NE 69101
(308) 534-7212

SENIOR OLYMPICS
Ashland Senior Center
123 N. 14th Street
Ashland, NE 68003
(402) 944-7627

SENIOR GAMES
c/o RSVP
129 N. 10th, Room 230
Lincoln, NE 68508
(402) 471-7026

NEBRASKA SENIOR GAMES
201 N. 8th Street, Suite 219
Lincoln, NE 68508
(402) 476-3852

NEVADA

NEVADA SENIOR GAMES
P.O. Box 70863
Las Vegas, NV 89170
(702) 739-3157

NEW HAMPSHIRE

GOLDEN AGE OLYMPICS NORTH
70 Temple Street
Nashua, NH 03060
(603) 889-6155

GRANITE STATE SENIOR OLYMPICS
Division of Elderly and Adult Services
6 Hazen Drive
Concord, NH 03301
(603) 271-4642

NEW JERSEY

RAYMOND FUNDHOUSER
Harborside Financial Center
200 Plaza 3
Jersey City, NJ 07311
(201) 432-5530

NEW MEXICO

NEW MEXICO SENIOR CITIZEN OLYMPICS
Room 129, Federal Building
108 Cathedral Place
Sante Fe, NM 87501
(505) 988-6577

NEW YORK

NEW YORK STATE SENIOR GAMES
Parks and Recreation
Empire State Plaza
Agency Building 1, 12th Floor
Albany, NY 12238
(518) 474-2324

NORTH CAROLINA

NORTH CAROLINA SENIOR GAMES
P.O. Box 33590
Raleigh, NC 27636
(919) 851-5456

OHIO

OHIO STATE SENIOR OLYMPICS
University of Akron
Akron, OH 44325
(216) 375-7473

COLUMBUS SENIOR OLYMPICS
1125 College Avenue
Columbus, OH 43209
(614) 231-2731

OKLAHOMA

OKLAHOMA SENIOR OLYMPICS
Tulsa Parks and Recreation Department
707 S. Houston, Suite 201
Tulsa, OK 74127
(918) 592-7877

OREGON

SENIOR GAMES OF OREGON
State Games of Oregon
P.O. Box 400
Lake Oswego, OR 97034
(503) 775-0522

PENNYSLVANIA

PENNSYLVANIA SENIOR GAMES
P.O. Box 568
Harrisburg, PA 17108
(717) 783-1549

JOHN KELLY
County Chester Services for Senior Citizens
Administrative Offices
10 N. Church Street
West Chester, PA 19380
(215) 431-6200

RHODE ISLAND

RHODE ISLAND SENIOR OLYMPICS
Department of Elderly Affairs
79 Washington Street
Providence, RI 02903
(401) 277-6880

SOUTH CAROLINA

SOUTH CAROLINA SENIOR SPORTS CLASSIC
P.O. Box 1476
Florence, SC 29503
(803) 665-3253

SOUTH CAROLINA SENIOR CLASSIC
Parks/Recreation/Tourism, Recreation Division

1205 Pendleton Street
Columbia, SC 29201
(803) 734-0141

TENNESSEE

TENNESSEE SENIOR OLYMPICS
2599 Avery
Memphis, TN 38112
(901) 454-5750

UTAH

WORLD SENIOR GAMES
1291 S. Wasatch Drive
Salt Lake City, UT 84108
(801) 583-6231

VERMONT

GREEN MOUNTAIN SENIOR GAMES
R1, Box 93
Weston, VT 05161
(802) 824-6521

VIRGINIA

GOLDEN OLYMPICS
Belmont Park
1600 Hilliard Road
Richmond, VA 23228
(804) 262-4728

HENRICO SENIOR OLYMPICS
Division of Recreation and Parks
P.O. Box 27032
Richmond, VA 23273
(804) 649-0566

WASHINGTON

SENIOR SPORTS FEST
100 Dexter Avenue N.
Seattle, WA 98109
(206) 684-4951

WEST VIRGINIA

PUTNAM COUNTY PARKS AND RECREATION
COMMISSION
P.O. Box 4145
Winfield, WV 25213
(304) 757-6511

WISCONSIN

WISCONSIN SENIOR OLYMPICS
Washington Park Senior Center
4420 Vliet Street
Milwaukee, WI 53208
(414) 933-2332

MIDDLETOWN SENIOR OLYMPICS
1811 Parmenter Street
Middleton, WI 53562
(608) 831-2373

WYOMING

WYOMING SENIOR OLYMPICS
Recreation Coordinator—City of Casper
1801 E. 4th Street
Casper, WY 82601
(307) 235-8403

INFORMATION AND CONSUMER SERVICES

GENERAL INFORMATION AND REFERRAL SERVICES

In many communities across the country, the United Way has established special services that maintain information and provide referrals to all kinds of community programs and services, including health services, financial assistance, housing, recreation, transportation, family counseling, legal aid, and educational programs. For example, you can find out:

- How to get "Meals on Wheels" delivered to your home
- The address of a support group after the death of a spouse
- Where to apply for food stamps
- When and where arts and crafts classes meet

ALABAMA

Anniston	(205) 237-4636
Birmingham	(205) 323-0000
Decatur	(205) 255-5465
Gadsden	(205) 546-0446
Huntsville	(205) 534-1779
Mobile	(205) 433-3524
Montgomery	(205) 284-0006
Tuscaloosa	(205) 345-7775

ARIZONA

Mesa	(602) 834-7777
Phoenix	(602) 263-8856
Tucson	(602) 323-1303

ARKANSAS

Jonesboro	(501) 932-5555
Little Rock	(501) 376-4567

CALIFORNIA

Bakersfield	(415) 325-9423
Danville	(415) 837-8235
El Monte	(818) 350-1841
Monterey	(408) 646-4636
Newbury Park	(805) 498-6643
Riverside	(714) 686-4402
Sacramento	(916) 446-4483
San Diego	(619) 292-4777
San Francisco	(415) 772-4444
Santa Barbara	(805) 682-2727
Santa Clara	(408) 248-4636

Santa Rosa	(707) 527-2783			
Santa Rosa	(707) 525-0143			
Stockton	(208) 948-1200			
Sunnyvale	(408) 738-4321			

COLORADO

Boulder	(303) 449-2255
Colorado Springs	(303) 632-1543
Englewood	(303) 837-9999
Fort Collins	(303) 493-3888
Grand Junction	(303) 242-4636
Greeley	(303) 352-9477
Pueblo	(303) 542-6814

CONNECTICUT

Danielson	(203) 456-8886
Greenwich	(203) 622-7979
Hartford	(203) 249-6850
Hartford	(203) 522-4636
New Haven	(203) 624-4143
Norwalk	(203) 853-2525
Norwich	(203) 886-0516
Waterbury	(203) 753-0171

DELAWARE

Wilmington	(302) 656-4630

FLORIDA

Bradenton	(813) 758-9999
Cocoa	(305) 631-2747
Daytona Beach	(904) 253-0564
Ft. Lauderdale	(305) 467-6333
Ft. Myers	(813) 334-1685
Gainesville	(904) 375-4636
Jacksonville	(904) 384-4357
Lakeland	(813) 688-5739
Leesburg	(904) 787-9945
Miami	(305) 579-2200
Orlando	(305) 894-1441
Sarasota	(813) 366-5025
St. Petersburg	(813) 536-9464
Tallahassee	(904) 224-6333
Tampa	(813) 272-6666
Vero Beach	(305) 569-8118
West Palm Beach	(305) 686-4000

GEORGIA

Athens	(404) 353-1313
Atlanta	(404) 522-7370
Augusta	(404) 724-4357
Columbus	(404) 324-0487
Dalton	(404) 226-4357
Macon	(912) 745-9292
Rome	(404) 232-4636
Savannah	(912) 234-1636

HAWAII

Honolulu	(808) 521-4566
Wailuku	(808) 244-7405

IDAHO

Boise	(208) 378-0111
Idaho Falls	(208) 524-2433
Pocatello	(208) 232-1114

ILLINOIS

Alton	(618) 462-1234
Belleville	(618) 397-0963
Chicago	(312) 580-2850
Geneva	(312) 232-9100
Granite City	(618) 877-6780
Joliet	(815) 744-5280
Kankakee	(815) 932-7477
Libertyville	(312) 367-1080
Peoria	(309) 674-5181
Quincy	(217) 224-1223
Rockford	(815) 968-5400
Springfield	(217) 789-7000
Urbana	(217) 384-4357

INDIANA

Anderson	(317) 649-4939
Columbus	(812) 376-3001
Dillsboro	(812) 432-5000
Elkhart	(219) 293-8671
Evansville	(812) 423-4245
Ft. Wayne	(219) 426-4357
Griffith	(219) 738-2524
Indianapolis	(317) 923-1466
Kokomo	(317) 457-4357
Lafayette	(317) 742-2077
South Bend	(219) 232-2522
Terre Haute	(812) 235-8333

Valparaiso	(219) 464-3583
Washington	(812) 254-4886

IOWA

Ames	(515) 292-7000
Burlington	(319) 752-7831
Cedar Rapids	(319) 398-5364
Clinton	(319) 243-7712
Davenport	(319) 324-0625
Des Moines	(515) 244-8646
Dubuque	(319) 557-8331
Marshaltown	(515) 752-7162
Sioux City	(712) 252-1861
Waterloo	(319) 233-8484
Waterloo	(319) 233-2273

KANSAS

Hutchinson	(316) 669-0159
Lawrence	(913) 841-2345
Salina	(913) 827-4747
Topeka	(913) 273-4804
Topeka	(913) 232-9065
Wichita	(316) 267-4327

KENTUCKY

Hopkinsville	(502) 886-0222
Lexington	(606) 255-2374
Louisville	(502) 589-4313
Owensboro	(502) 684-9466

LOUISIANA

Alexandria	(318) 443-7203
Lafayette	(318) 232-4357
Lake Charles	(318) 433-1088
Monroe	(318) 387-0535
New Orleans	(504) 488-4636
Shreveport	(318) 869-2352

MAINE

Portland	(207) 773-4830

MARYLAND

Baltimore	(301) 685-0525
Frederick	(301) 663-4235
Rockville	(301) 279-1904

MASSACHUSETTS

Amherst	(413) 256-0121
Boston	(617) 482-1454
Brockton	(617) 584-4357
Fall River	(617) 674-1100
Marlboro	(617) 485-9300
North Adams	(413) 663-5244
Springfield	(413) 737-2691
Worcester	(617) 755-1233

MICHIGAN

Ann Arbor	(313) 971-8200
Battle Creek	(616) 968-2294
Detroit	(313) 833-0622
Flint	(313) 767-0500
Grand Rapids	(616) 459-2255
Holland	(616) 396-2301
Jackson	(517) 783-2861
Lansing	(517) 482-7355
Monroe	(313) 242-1331
Mt. Pleasant	(517) 772-2918
Pontiac	(313) 456-8800
Port Huron	(313) 985-7161
Saginaw	(517) 755-0457
St. Joseph	(616) 983-3511
Traverse City	(616) 947-3200

MINNESOTA

Alexandria	(612) 763-6638
Duluth	(218) 726-4775
Grand Rapids	(218) 326-8565
Hastings	(612) 437-7134
Minneapolis	(612) 340-7431
New Ulm	(507) 354-8515
Owatonna	(507) 451-9100
St. Paul	(612) 291-4666

MISSISSIPPI

Bay St. Louis	(601) 467-9292
Columbus	(601) 328-0200
Gulfport	(601) 863-4890
Hattiesburg	(601) 544-4357
Jackson	(601) 352-4357
Pascagoula	(601) 762-8557
Tupelo	(601) 842-0681

MISSOURI

Columbia	(314) 874-2273
Fulton	(314) 642-6388
Kansas City	(816) 421-4980
Springfield	(417) 866-2707
St. Joseph	(816) 364-1131
St. Louis	(314) 421-0700

MONTANA

Great Falls	(406) 453-6511
Helena	(406) 442-6800
Kalispell	(406) 752-8181
Kalispell	(406) 752-7273
Missoula	(406) 543-8277

NEBRASKA

Grand Island	(308) 384-8170
Omaha	(402) 444-6666

NEVADA

Las Vegas	(702) 382-4357
Reno	(702) 329-4630

NEW HAMPSHIRE

Claremont	(603) 543-0121
Concord	(603) 225-9000
Keene	(603) 352-1999
Laconia	(603) 524-8811
Lebanon	(603) 448-4400
Manchester	(603) 668-8600
Nashua	(603) 883-9330
Rockingham County	(800) 582-7214

NEW JERSEY

Cape May Courthouse	(609) 465-5300
Elizabeth	(201) 353-7171
Farmingdale	(201) 938-2250
Hackensack	(201) 343-6543
Jersey City	(201) 434-2628
Milltown	(201) 247-3727
Montclair	(201) 746-1871
Morrestown	(609) 234-8808
Morristown	(201) 898-0550
Newark	(201) 624-8300
Princeton	(609) 924-5865
Somerville	(201) 725-6640

Toms River	(201) 341-5322
Totowa	(201) 790-3900
Trenton	(609) 896-1912
Washington	(609) 689-7335
Woodbury	(609) 845-4308

NEW MEXICO

Albuquerque	(505) 247-3671
Farmington	(505) 326-4345

NEW YORK

Binghamton	(607) 729-2592
Buffalo	(716) 887-2631
Dansville	(716) 335-3500
Fredonia	(716) 673-3133
Elmira	(607) 737-2077
Glens Falls	(518) 793-3817
Goshen	(914) 294-7411
Jamestown	(716) 483-1562
Melville	(516) 483-1110
Nassau County	(516) 249-1100
New York	(212) 557-1050
Potsdam	(315) 265-2422
Plattsburgh	(518) 561-4441
Poughkeepsie	(914) 473-1500
Rochester	(716) 275-5151
Rome	(315) 336-5638
Syracuse	(315) 474-7011
White Plains	(914) 997-6750

NORTH CAROLINA

Asheville	(704) 252-8102
Burlington	(919) 227-2096
Charlotte	(704) 373-0982
Concord	(704) 788-1156
Gastonia	(704) 864-5788
Raleigh	(919) 755-6089
Wentworth	(919) 342-3331
Wilmington	(919) 762-5252
Wilson	(919) 237-5156
Winston-Salem	(919) 727-8100

NORTH DAKOTA

Fargo	(701) 293-6450
Grandforks	(701) 775-0671

OHIO		Medford	(503) 779-4357
Akron	(216) 376-6660	Portland	(503) 222-5555
Astabula	(216) 798-2609		
Canton	(216) 453-9172	PENNSYLVANIA	
Carey	(419) 396-6276	Allentown	(215) 435-7111
Cinncinnati	(513) 721-7900	Beaver	(412) 728-3900
Cleveland	(216) 696-4262	Chambersburg	(717) 264-7799
Chardon	(216) 834-4165	Clearfield	(814) 765-6157
Dolumbus	(614) 221-6766	Erie	(814) 453-5656
Coshocton	(614) 622-3457	Harrisburg	(717) 652-4400
Dayton	(513) 225-3101	Johnstown	(814) 322-4847
Delaware	(614) 369-3316	Lancaster	(717) 299-2821
Fostoria	(419) 435-4357	Lebanon	(717) 274-3363
Fremont	(419) 334-2720	Lewistown	(717) 248-9636
Fremont	(419) 334-8939	Mansfield	(717) 662-4466
Hamilton	(513) 893-1234	Media	(215) 566-8604
Lancaster	(614) 687-0500	Philadelphia	(215) 568-3750
Lima	(419) 228-6575	Pittsburgh	(412) 255-1155
Lorain	(216) 233-8575	Pottstown	(215) 323-9000
Marion	(614) 382-4357	Scranton	(717) 961-1234
Mentor	(216) 951-3646	Souderton	(215) 723-5430
Napoleon	(419) 592-3577	Tannersville	(717) 629-5658
New Philadelphia	(216) 343-7771	West Chester	(215) 436-4040
Newark	(614) 345-5353	Wilkes-Barre	(717) 829-1341
Ravenna	(216) 678-8820	Williamsport	(717) 323-8555
Springfield	(513) 323-1400	York	(717) 755-1000
Steubenville	(614) 282-6880		
Tiffin	(419) 448-0585	RHODE ISLAND	
Toledo	(419) 244-3728	Providence	(401) 351-6500
Van Wert	(419) 238-4357		
Warren	(219) 395-5255	SOUTH CAROLINA	
Wooster	(216) 264-9473	Beaufort	(803) 524-4357
Zanesville	(614) 454-6872	Charleston	(803) 723-1676
		Greenville	(803) 233-4357
		Spartenburg	(803) 582-7556
OKLAHOMA		Sumter	(803) 775-9424
Blackwell	(405) 363-1738		
Lawton	(405) 357-0605	SOUTH DAKOTA	
Norman	(405) 364-3800	Aberdeen	(605) 226-1212
Oklahoma City	(405) 236-8441	Sioux Falls	(605) 339-4357
Ponca City	(405) 765-5551		
Tulsa	(918) 583-4357	TENNESSEE	
		Chattanooga	(615) 265-8000
		Fayetteville	(615) 433-5561
OREGON		Memphis	(901) 725-8895
Albany	(503) 967-3800	Pigeon Forge	(615) 453-4261
Coos Bay	(503) 269-5910	Rogersville	(615) 272-2830
Grants Pass	(503) 479-2349		

TEXAS

Abilene	(915) 673-8211
Amarillo	(806) 373-2662
Angelton	(409) 849-4404
Arlington	(817) 274-2534
Austin	(512) 926-7080
Bay City	(713) 245-5852
Baytown	(713) 422-6793
Beaumont	(409) 835-3886
Bryan	(409) 823-5226
Corpus Christi	(512) 993-7411
Dallas	(214) 747-3711
El Paso	(915) 779-7130
Ft. Worth	(817) 335-3473
Galveston	(409) 766-2248
Houston	(713) 527-0222
Lubbock	(806) 765-6262
Plano	(214) 422-1850
San Angelo	(915) 942-7670
San Antonio	(512) 227-4357
Sherman	(214) 868-1551
Temple	(817) 773-0221
The Woodlands	(800) 392-6744
Waco	(817) 752-8355
Wichita Falls	(817) 322-8638

UTAH

Farmington	(801) 451-5151
Porvo	(801) 374-2588
Salt Lake City	(801) 487-4716

VIRGINIA

Bristol	(703) 466-2312
Charlottesville	(804) 979-1903
Hampton	(804) 827-0327
Lebanon	(703) 889-8042
Lynchburg	(804) 845-8016
Norfolk	(804) 625-4543
Petersburg	(804) 733-4357
Richmond	(804) 275-2000
Roanoke	(703) 982-2345

WASHINGTON

Bremerton	(206) 373-5031
Ellensburg	(509) 925-4168
Everett	(206) 258-4357
Mount Vernon	(206) 336-2442
Olympia	(206) 352-2211
Pullman	(509) 332-1505
Richland	(509) 946-0486
Seattle	(206) 447-3215
Spokane	(509) 624-2277
Tacoma	(206) 383-3414
Vancouver	(206) 694-8899
Walla Walla	(509) 529-3377

WEST VIRGINIA

Charleston	(304) 342-5109
Clarksburg	(304) 623-6681
Morgantown	(304) 293-6819
Parkersburg	(304) 485-5574
Wheeling	(304) 232-4625

WISCONSIN

Appleton	(414) 735-5803
Eau Claire	(715) 834-8781
Green Bay	(414) 497-6222
Janesville	(608) 752-3100
Kenosha	(414) 658-4104
La Crosse	(608) 782-8010
Madison	(608) 246-4357
Milwaukee	(414) 276-0760
Stevens Point	(715) 345-5380
Waukesha	(414) 547-3388
Wausau	(715) 842-5152

WYOMING

Casper	(307) 234-6715

FEDERAL INFORMATION CENTERS

The U.S. government has established Federal Information Centers across the country to answer any questions about federal services, programs, and regulations, and to direct you to the federal agency that can provide the assistance you need to solve a wide variety of problems.

For example, you can call your nearest federal information center to find out:

- The address and telephone number of the nearest Social Security office
- Where you can attend auctions of government surplus property
- How to get tickets for White House tours
- How to replace a lost Medicare card
- How to get in touch with your Congressman or Senator

The Federal Information Centers are:

ALABAMA
Birmingham	(205) 322-8591
Mobile	(205) 438-1421

ALASKA
Anchorage	(907) 271-2898

ARIZONA
Phoenix	(602) 261-3313

CALIFORNIA
Los Angeles	(213) 894-3800
San Diego	(619) 557-6030
San Francisco	(415) 556-6600
Santa Ana	(714) 836-2386

COLORADO
Colorado Springs	(303) 471-9491
Denver	(303) 844-6575
Pueblo	(303) 544-9523

CONNECTICUT
Hartford	(203) 527-2617
New Haven	(203) 624-4720

FLORIDA
Ft. Lauderdale	(305) 522-8531
Jacksonville	(904) 354-4756
Miami	(305) 536-4155
Orlando	(305) 422-1800
St. Petersburg	(813) 893-3495
Tampa	(813) 229-7911
West Palm Beach	(305) 833-7566

GEORGIA
Atlanta	(404) 331-6891

HAWAII
Honolulu	(808) 551-1365

ILLINOIS
Chicago	(312) 353-4242

INDIANA
Gary	(219) 883-4110
Indianapolis	(317) 269-7373

IOWA
All points	(800) 532-1556

KANSAS
All points	(800) 432-2934

KENTUCKY
Louisville	(502) 582-6261

LOUISIANA
New Orleans	(504) 589-6696

MARYLAND
Baltimore	(301) 962-4980

MASSACHUSETTS
Boston	(617) 565-8121

MICHIGAN
Detroit	(313) 226-7016
Grand Rapids	(616) 732-2739

MINNESOTA
Minneapolis	(612) 370-3333

MISSOURI
St. Louis	(314) 539-2106
All other points	(800) 392-7711

NEBRASKA		PENNSYLVANIA	
Omaha	(402) 221-3353	Philadelphia	(215) 597-7042
All other points	(800) 642-8383	Pittsburgh	(412) 644-3456
NEW JERSEY		RHODE ISLAND	
Newark	(201) 645-3600	Providence	(401) 331-5565
Trenton	(609) 396-4400		
NEW MEXICO		TENNESSEE	
Albuquerque	(505) 766-3091	Chattanooga	(615) 265-8231
		Memphis	(901) 521-3285
NEW YORK		Nashville	(615) 242-5056
Albany	(518) 463-4421		
Buffalo	(716) 846-4010	TEXAS	
New York	(212) 264-4464	Austin	(512) 472-5494
Rochester	(716) 546-5075	Dallas	(214) 767-8585
Syracuse	(315) 476-8545	Fort Worth	(817) 334-3624
		Houston	(713) 653-3025
NORTH CAROLINA		San Antonio	(512) 224-4471
Charlotte	(704) 376-3600		
		UTAH	
OHIO		Salt Lake City	(801) 524-5353
Akron	(216) 375-5638		
Cincinnati	(513) 684-2801	VIRGINIA	
Cleveland	(216) 522-4040	Norfolk	(804) 441-3101
Columbus	(614) 221-1014	Richmond	(804) 643-4920
Dayton	(513) 223-7377	Roanoke	(703) 982-8591
Toledo	(419) 241-3223		
		WASHINGTON	
OKLAHOMA		Seattle	(206) 442-0570
Oklahoma City	(405) 231-4868	Tacoma	(206) 383-7970
Tulsa	(918) 584-4193		
		WISCONSIN	
OREGON		Milwaukee	(414) 271-2273
Portland	(503) 326-2222		

STATE GOVERNMENT INFORMATION SERVICES

Throughout this book, we have discussed the many valuable services and programs provided by most state governments. For example:

- Your state employment service has special job-training and placement services

- Your state insurance department has information to help you purchase the best policies from the most financially stable companies

- Your state utility commission has information on special discounts, rebates, and energy conservation programs

If you can't find the number of the appropriate agency in your local telephone directory, you can get it easily by calling your state government information service. In addition, your state information service can answer questions and direct you to the appropriate agencies to solve many other kinds of problems—from complaining about snow clearance on a state highway to obtaining permits to camp in state parks.

The state government information services are:

ALABAMA
(205) 261-2500

ALASKA
(907) 466-2111

ARIZONA
(602) 255-4900

ARKANSAS
(501) 371-3000

CALIFORNIA
(916) 322-9900

COLORADO
(303) 866-5000

CONNECTICUT
(203) 566-2211

DELAWARE
(302) 736-4000

DISTRICT OF COLUMBIA
(202) 727-1006

FLORIDA
(904) 488-1234

GEORGIA
(404) 656-2000

HAWAII
(808) 548-2211

IDAHO
(208) 334-2411

ILLINOIS
(217) 782-2000

INDIANA
(317) 232-3140

IOWA
(515) 281-5011

KANSAS
(913) 296-0111

KENTUCKY
(502) 564-2500

LOUISIANA
(504) 342-6600

MAINE
(207) 289-1110

MARYLAND
(301) 974-2000

MASSACHUSETTS
(617) 727-2121

MICHIGAN
(517) 373-1837

MINNESOTA
(612) 296-6013

MISSISSIPPI
(601) 354-7011

MISSOURI
(314) 751-2000

MONTANA
(406) 444-2511

NEBRASKA
(402) 471-2311

NEVADA
(702) 885-5000

NEW HAMPSHIRE
(603) 271-1110

NEW JERSEY
(609) 292-2121

NEW MEXICO
(505) 827-4011

NEW YORK
(518) 474-2121

NORTH CAROLINA
(919) 733-1110

NORTH DAKOTA
(701) 224-2000

OHIO
(614) 466-2000

OKLAHOMA
(405) 521-2011

OREGON
(503) 378-3131

PENNSYLVANIA
(717) 787-2121

RHODE ISLAND
(401) 277-2000

SOUTH CAROLINA
(803) 734-1000

SOUTH DAKOTA
(605) 773-3011

TENNESSEE
(615) 741-3011

TEXAS
(512) 463-4630

UTAH
(801) 538-3000

VERMONT
(802) 828-1110

VIRGINIA
(804) 786-0000

WASHINGTON
(206) 753-5000

WEST VIRGINIA
(304) 348-3456

WISCONSIN
(608) 266-2211

WYOMING
(307) 777-7220

STATE AND LOCAL CONSUMER PROTECTION OFFICES

All states and many local governments have established Consumer Protection Offices. Among the services these offices offer are:

- Pamphlets, fact sheets, and other information on products and services that you should read before you make a major purchase. This includes information on state and local business and consumer laws.

- Information on the business practices and complaint record of firms doing business in that state.
- Mediation for resolving consumer complaints.
- Intervention to enforce consumer protection laws and to prosecute fraud cases.

While all Consumer Protection Offices will provide information over the phone, some require that complaints and related documentation be submitted in writing. Below, we have provided the telephone numbers and addresses of all state Consumer Protection Agencies. These state agencies can direct you, where appropriate, to local Consumer Protection Agencies.

ALABAMA

CONSUMER PROTECTION DIVISION
Office of the Attorney General
11 South Union Street
Montgomery AL 36130
(800) 392-5658 (AL)
(205) 261-7334

ALASKA

CONSUMER PROTECTION SECF ON
Office of the Attorney General
1031 West Fourth Avenue, Suite 110-B
Anchorage AK 99501
(907) 279-0428

OFFICE OF THE ATTORNEY GENERAL
100 Cushman Street, Suite 400
Fairbanks, AK 99701
(907) 456-8588

ARIZONA

FINANCIAL FRAUD DIVISION
Office of the Attorney General
1275 West Washington Street
Phoenix AZ 85007
(800) 352-8431 (AZ)
(602) 255-3702 (fraud only)

FINANCIAL FRAUD DIVISION
Office of Attorney General
402 West Congress Street, Suite 315
Tucson, AZ 85701
(602) 628-5501

ARKANSAS

CONSUMER PROTECTION DIVISION
Office of the Attorney General
200 Tower BLDG. 4th & Center Streets
Little Rock AR 72201
(800) 482-8982 (AR)
(501) 682-2007

CALIFORNIA

CALIFORNIA DEPARTMENT OF CONSUMER AFFAIRS
1020 N Street
Sacramento CA 95814
(916) 445-0660 (complaint assistance)
(916) 445-1254 (consumer information)

PUBLIC INQUIRY UNIT
Office of Attorney General
1515 K Street, Suite 511
P.O. Box 944255
Sacramento, CA 94244
(800) 952-5225 (CA)
(916) 322-3360

BUREAU OF AUTOMOTIVE REPAIR
California Department of Consumer Affairs
10240 Systems Parkway
Sacramento, CA 95827

(800) 952-5210 (CA)
(916) 366-5100

COLORADO

CONSUMER PROTECTION UNIT
Office of Attorney General
1525 Sherman Street, 3rd Floor
Denver CO 80203
(303) 866-5167

CONSUMER AND FOOD SPECIALIST
Department of Agriculture
1525 Sherman Street, 4th Floor
Denver, CO 80203
(303) 866-3561

CONNECTICUT

DEPARTMENT OF CONSUMER PROTECTION
State Office Building
165 Capitol Avenue
Hartford CT 06106
(800) 842-2649 (CT)
(203) 566-4999

ANTITRUST/CONSUMER PROTECTION
Office of Attorney General
110 Sherman Street
Hartford, CT 06105
(203) 566-5374

DELAWARE

DIVISION OF CONSUMER AFFAIRS
Department of Community Affairs
820 N. French Street, 4th Floor
Wilmington DE 19801
(302) 571-3250

ECONOMIC CRIME/CONSUMER RIGHTS DIVISION
Office of Attorney General
820 North French Street
Wilmington, DE 19801
(302) 571-3849

DISTRICT OF COLUMBIA

DEPARTMENT OF CONSUMER AND REGULATORY AFFAIRS
614 H Street, NW
Washington DC 20001
(202) 727-7000

FLORIDA

DIVISION OF CONSUMER SERVICES
218 Mayo Bldg.
Tallahassee FL 32399
(800) 327-3382 (FL)
(904) 488-2226

CONSUMER PROTECTION DIVISION
Office of Attorney General
401 NW Second Avenue, Suite 450
Miami, FL 33128
(305) 377-5619

GEORGIA

GOVERNOR'S OFFICE OF CONSUMER AFFAIRS
2 Martin Luther King Drive, SE
Plaza Level, East Tower
Atlanta GA 30334
(800) 282-5808 (GA)
(404) 656-7000

HAWAII

OFFICE OF CONSUMER PROTECTION
Department of Commerce and Consumer Affairs
P.O. Box 3767
Honolulu HI 96812
(808) 548-2560 (administration and legal)
(808) 548-2540 (complaints)

OFFICE OF CONSUMER PROTECTION
Department of Commerce and Consumer Affairs
75 Aupuni Street
Hilo, HI 96720
(808) 961-7433

OFFICE OF CONSUMER PROTECTION
Department of Commerce and Consumer Affairs
3060 Elwa Street
Lihue, HI 96766
(808) 245-4365

OFFICE OF CONSUMER PROTECTION
Department of Commerce and Consumer Affairs
54 High Street
P.O. Box 1098
Wailuku, HI 96793
(808) 244-4387

ILLINOIS

GOVERNOR'S OFFICE OF CITIZENS ASSISTANCE
201 West Monroe Street
Springfield IL 62706
(800) 642-3112 (IL)
(217) 782-0244

CONSUMER PROTECTION DIVISION
Office of Attorney General
100 West Randolph, 12th Floor
Chicago, IL 60601
(312) 917-3580

DEPARTMENT OF CITIZEN'S RIGHTS
100 West Randolph, 12th Floor
Chicago, IL 60601
(312) 917-3289

INDIANA

CONSUMER PROTECTION DIVISION
Office of Attorney General
219 State House
Indianapolis IN 46204
(800) 382-5516 (IN)
(317) 232-6330

IOWA

IOWA CITIZENS' AIDE/OMBUDSMAN
515 East 12th Street

Des Moines IA 50319
(800) 358-5510 (IA)
(515) 281-3592

CONSUMER PROTECTION DIVISION
Office of Attorney General
1300 East Walnut Street, 2nd Floor
Des Moines, IA 50319
(515) 261-5926

KANSAS

CONSUMER PROTECTION DIVISION
Office of Attorney General
Kansas Judicial Center, 2nd Floor
Topeka KS 66612
(800) 432-2310 (KS)
(913) 296-3751

KENTUCKY

CONSUMER PROTECTION DIVISION
Office of Attorney General
209 Saint Clair Street
Frankfort KY 40601
(800) 432-9257 (KY)
(502) 564-2200

CONSUMER PROTECTION DIVISION
Office of Attorney General
107 S. 4th Street
Louisville, KY 40202
(502) 588-3262

LOUISIANA

CONSUMER PROTECTION DIVISION
Office of Attorney General
P.O. Box 94005
Baton Rouge LA 70804
(504) 342-7013

OFFICE OF AGRO-CONSUMER SERVICES
Department of Agriculture
325 Loyola Avenue, Room 317
New Orleans, LA 70112
(504) 568-5472

MAINE

BUREAU OF CONSUMER CREDIT PROTECTION
State House Station No. 35
Augusta ME 04333
(207) 582-8718

CONSUMER AND ANTITRUST DIVISION
Office of Attorney General
State House Station No. 6
Augusta, ME 04333
(207) 289-3716

MEDIATION CONSUMER SERVICE
Office of Attorney General
991 Forest Avenue
Portland, ME 04104
(207) 797-8978

MARYLAND

CONSUMER PROTECTION DIVISION
Office of Attorney General
7 North Calvert Street
Baltimore MD 21202
(800) 492-2114
(301) 528-8662

LICENSING AND CONSUMER SERVICES
Motor Vehicle Administration
6601 Ritchie Highway, NE
Glen Burnie, MD 21062
(301) 768-7420

EASTERN SHORE BRANCH OFFICE
Consumer Protection Division
Office of Attorney General
State Office Complex
Route 50 and Cypress Street
Salisbury, MD 21801
(301) 543-6620

WESTERN MARYLAND BRANCH OFFICE
Consumer Protection Division
Office of Attorney General
138 East Antietam Street, Suite 210

Hagerstown, MD 21740
(301) 791-4780

MASSACHUSETTS

CONSUMER PROTECTION DIVISION
Department of Attorney General
131 Tremont Street
Boston MA 02111
(617) 727-8400 (information and referral)

CONSUMER AFFAIRS AND BUSINESS REGULA-
TION
One Ashburton Plaza, Room 1411
Boston, MA 02108
(617) 727-7780 (information and referral)

CONSUMER PROTECTION DIVISION
Department of Attorney General
436 Dwight Street
Springfield, MA 01103
(413) 784-1240

MICHIGAN

MICHIGAN CONSUMERS COUNCIL
414 Holister Building
106 West Allegan Street
Lansing MI 48933
(517) 373-0947

CONSUMER PROTECTION DIVISION
Office of Attorney General
670 Law Building
Lansing, MI 48913
(517) 373-1140

BUREAU OF AUTOMOTIVE REGULATION
Michigan Department of State
Lansing, MI 48918
(800) 292-4204 (MI)
(517) 373-7858

MINNESOTA

OFFICE OF CONSUMER SERVICES
Office of Attorney General

117 University Avenue
Street Paul MN 55155
(612) 296-2331

CONSUMER SERVICES DIVISION
Office of Attorney General
320 West Second Street
Duluth, MN 55802
(218) 723-4891

MISSISSIPPI

OFFICE OF CONSUMER SERVICES
Office of Attorney General
P.O. Box 220
Jackson MS 39205
(601) 354-6018

REGULATORY SERVICES
Department of Agriculture and Commerce
High and Presidents Streets
P.O. Box 1609
Jackson, MS 39215
(601) 354-7063

MISSOURI

TRADE OFFENSE DIVISION
Office of Attorney General
P.O. Box 899
Jefferson City MO 65102
(800) 392-8222 (MO)
(314) 751-2616

DEPARTMENT OF ECONOMIC DEVELOPMENT
P.O. Box 1157
Jefferson City, MO 65102
(314) 751-4962

MONTANA

CONSUMER AFFAIRS UNIT
Department of Commerce
1424 Ninth Avenue
Helena MT 59620
(406) 444-4312

NEBRASKA

CONSUMER PROTECTION DIVISION
Department of Justice
P.O. Box 98920
Lincoln NE 68509
(402) 471-4723

NEVADA

CONSUMER AFFAIRS DIVISION
Department of Commerce
201 Nye Building, Capitol Complex
Carson City NV 86710
(702) 885-4340

COMMISSIONER OF CONSUMER AFFAIRS
Department of Commerce
State Mail Room Complex
Las Vegas, NV 89158
(702) 486-4150

NEW HAMPSHIRE

CONSUMER PROTECTION DIVISION
Office of Attorney General
State House Annex
Concord NH 03301
(603) 271-3641

NEW JERSEY

DIVISION OF CONSUMER AFFAIRS
1100 Raymond Boulevard, Room 504
Newark NJ 07102
(201) 648-4010

DEPARTMENT OF PUBLIC ADVOCATE
CN850, Justice Complex
Trenton, NJ 08625
(800) 792-8600 (NJ)
(609) 292-7087

NEW MEXICO

CONSUMER AND ECONOMIC CRIME DIVISION
Office of Attorney General

P.O. Drawer 1508
Santa Fe NM 87504
(800) 432-2070 (NM)
(505) 872-6910

NEW YORK

NEW YORK STATE CONSUMER PROTECTION
BOARD
99 Washington Avenue
Albany NY 12210
(518) 474-8583

BUREAU OF CONSUMER FRAUDS AND PROTEC-
TION
Office of Attorney General
State Capitol
Albany, NY 12224
(518) 474-5481

NEW YORK STATE CONSUMER PROTECTION
BOARD
250 Broadway, 17th Floor
New York, NY 10007
(212) 587-4908

BUREAU OF CONSUMER FRAUDS AND PROTEC-
TION
Office of Attorney General
120 Broadway
New York, NY 10271
(212) 341-2300

NORTH CAROLINA

CONSUMER PROTECTION SERVICE
Office of Attorney General
P.O. Box 629
Raleigh NC 27602
(919) 733-7741

NORTH DAKOTA

CONSUMER FRAUD DIVISION
Office of Attorney General
State Capitol Building
Bismark ND 58505

(800) 472-2600 (ND)
(701) 224-3404

OHIO

CONSUMER FRAUDS AND CRIMES SECTION
Office of Attorney General
30 East Broad Street
Columbus OH 43266
(800) 282-0515 (OH)
(614) 466-4986

CONSUMERS' COUNSEL
137 East State Street
Columbus, OH 43215
(800) 282-9448 (OH)
(614) 466-9605

OKLAHOMA

CONSUMER AFFAIRS
Office of Attorney General
112 State Capitol Building
Oklahoma City OK 73105
(405) 521-3921

DEPARTMENT OF CONSUMER CREDIT
4545 Lincoln Blvd.
Oklahoma City, OK 73105
(405) 521-3653

OREGON

FINANCIAL FRAUD SECTION
Department of Justice
Justice Building
Salem OR 97310
(503) 378-4320

PENNSYLVANIA

BUREAU OF CONSUMER PROTECTION
Office of Attorney General
Strawberry Square, 14th Floor
Harrisburg PA 17120
(800) 441-2555 (PA)
(717) 787-9707

OFFICE OF CONSUMER ADVOCATE-UTILITIES
Office of Attorney General
Strawberry Square, 14th Floor
Harrisburg, PA 17120
(717) 783-5048

BUREAU OF CONSUMER PROTECTION
Office of Attorney General
27 North Seventh Street
Allentown, PA 18101
(215) 821-6690

BUREAU OF CONSUMER PROTECTION
Office of Attorney General
Strawberry Square, 14th Floor
Harrisburg, PA 17120
(717) 787-7109

BUREAU OF CONSUMER PROTECTION
Office of Attorney General
1009 State Office Building
1400 West Spring Garden Street
Philadelphia, PA 19130
(215) 560-2414

BUREAU OF CONSUMER PROTECTION
Office of Attorney General
Manor Building, 4th Floor
564 Forbes Avenue
Pittsburg, PA 15219
(412) 565-5135

BUREAU OF CONSUMER PROTECTION
Office of Attorney General
State Office Building, Room 358
100 Lackawanna Avenue
Scranton, PA 18503
(717) 963-4913

RHODE ISLAND

CONSUMER PROTECTION DIVISION
Department of Attorney General
72 Pine Street
Providence, RI 02903
(800) 852-7776 (RI)
(401) 277-2104

RHODE ISLAND CONSUMERS' COUNCIL
365 Broadway
Providence, RI 02909
(401) 277-2764

SOUTH CAROLINA

DEPARTMENT OF CONSUMER AFFAIRS
P.O. Box 5757
Columbia SC 29250
(800) 922-1594 (SC)
(803) 734-9452

CONSUMER FRAUD AND ANTITRUST SECTION
Office of Attorney General
P.O. Box 11549
Columbia, SC 29211
(803) 734-3970

STATE OMBUDSMAN
Office of Executive Policy and Program
1205 Pendelton Street, Room 412
Columbia, SC 29201
(803) 734-0457

SOUTH DAKOTA

DIVISION OF CONSUMER AFFAIRS
Office of Attorney General
Anderson Building
Pierre SD 57501
(605) 773-4400

TENNESSEE

DIVISION OF COMMUNITY AFFAIRS
Department of Commerce and Insurance
500 James Robertson Parkway
Nashville TN 37219
(800) 342-8385 (TN)
(615) 741-4737

ANTITRUST AND CONSUMER PROTECTION DIVISION
Office of Attorney General
450 James Robertson Parkway

Nashville, TN 37219
(615) 741-2672

TEXAS

CONSUMER PROTECTION DIVISION
Office of Attorney General
Capitol Station, P.O. Box 12548
Austin, TX 78711
(512) 463-2070

CONSUMER PROTECTION DIVISION
Office of Attorney General
Renaissance Place, 7th Floor
714 Jackson Street
Dallas, TX 75202
(214) 742-8944

CONSUMER PROTECTION DIVISION
Office of Attorney General
4824 Alberta Street, Suite 160
El Paso, TX 79905

CONSUMER PROTECTION DIVISION
Office of Attorney General
1001 Texas Avenue, Suite 700
Houston, TX 77022
(713) 223-5886

CONSUMER PROTECTION DIVISION
Office of Attorney General
1208 14th Street
Lubbock, TX 79401
(806) 747-5238

CONSUMER PROTECTION DIVISION
Office of Attorney General
3600 N. 23rd Street
McAllen, TX 78501
(512) 682-4547

CONSUMER PROTECTION DIVISION
Office of Attorney General
200 Main Plaza, Suite 400
San Antonio, TX 78205
(512) 225-4191

UTAH

DIVISION OF CONSUMER PROTECTION
Department of Business Regulation
160 East 3rd. South
P.O. Box 45802
Salt Lake City, UT 84145
(801) 530-6601

CONSUMER AFFAIRS
Office of Attorney General
115 State Capitol
Salt Lake City, UT 84114
(801) 538-1331

VERMONT

PUBLIC PROTECTION DIVISION
Office of Attorney General
109 State Street
Montpelier, VT 05602
(802) 828-3171

VIRGINIA

OFFICE OF CONSUMER AFFAIRS
Department of Agriculture and Consumer Services
Room 101, Washington Building
1100 Bank Street
Richmond, VA 23219
(800) 552-9963 (VA)
(804) 786-2042

DIVISION OF CONSUMER COUNSEL
Office of Attorney General
Supreme Court Building
101 North Eighth Street
Richmond, VA 23219
(800) 451-1525 (VA)
(804) 786-2116

NORTHERN VIRGINIA BRANCH
Office of Consumer Affairs
Department of Agriculture and Consumer Services
100 North Washington Street, Suite 412

Falls Church, VA 22048
(703) 532-1613

WASHINGTON

CONSUMER AND BUSINESS FAIR PRACTICES DIVISION
Office of Attorney General
710 Second Ave.
Seattle, WA 98104
(800) 551-4636 (WA)
(206) 464-7744

CONSUMER AND BUSINESS FAIR PRACTICES DIVISION
Office of Attorney General
North 121 Capitol Way
Olympia, WA 98501
(206) 753-6210

CONSUMER AND BUSINESS FAIR PRACTICES DIVISION
Office of Attorney General
West 116 Riverside Avenue
Spokane, WA 99201
(509) 456-3123

CONSUMER AND BUSINESS FAIR PRACTICES DIVISION
Office of Attorney General
1019 Pacific Avenue

Tacoma, WA 98402
(206) 593-2904

WEST VIRGINIA

CONSUMER PROTECTION DIVISION
Office of Attorney General
812 Quarrier Street, 6th Floor
Charleston, WV 25301
(800) 368-8808 (WV)
(304) 348-8986

WEIGHTS AND MEASURES
Department of Labor
1800 Washington St. East
Charleston, WV 25305
(304) 348-7890

WISCONSIN

OFFICE OF CONSUMER PROTECTION
Department of Justice
P.O. Box 7856
Madison, WI 53707
(800) 362-8189 (WI)
(608) 266-1852

WYOMING

OFFICE OF ATTORNEY GENERAL
123 State Capitol Building
Cheyenne, WY 82002
(307) 777-7841

BETTER BUSINESS BUREAUS

The Better Business Bureaus are nonprofit organizations sponsored by local businesses. These bureaus produce consumer education materials and programs, and engage as well in activities that foster ethical conduct in business. To you, the consumer, they are perhaps most valuable as a resource when you're considering purchasing a product or service, are involved in a dispute with a company that sold you a product or service, or are asked to donate to a charitable organization. Each Better Business Bureau:

- Provides general information on companies and charitable organizations
- Maintains a file of past complaints about individual companies and charitable organizations

- Receives complaints from consumers and attempts to mediate disputes

ALABAMA

- 1214 S. 20th Street
Birmingham, AL 35205
(205) 558-2222
- P.O. Box 383
Huntsville, AL 35804
(205) 533-1640
- 707 Van Antwerp Building
Mobile, AL 36602
(205) 433-5494
- Union Bank Building
Commerce Street, Suite 810
Montgomery, AL 36104
(205) 262-5606

ALASKA

- 3380 C Street, Suite 100
Anchorage, AL 99503
(907) 562-0704

ARIZONA

- 4428 North 12th Street
Phoenix, AZ 85014
(602) 264-1721
- 50 West Drachman Street, Suite 103
Tucson, AZ 85705
(602) 622-7651

ARKANSAS

- 1415 South University
Little Rock, AR 72204
(501) 664-7274

CALIFORNIA

- 705 Eighteenth Street
Bakersfield, CA 93301
(805) 322-2074
- P.O. Box 970
Colton, CA 92324
(714) 825-7280
- 6101 Ball Road, Suite 309
Cypress, CA 90630
(714) 527-0680
- 5070 North Sixth, Suite 176
Fresno, CA 93710
(209) 222-8111
- 510 16th Street, Suite 550
Oakland, CA 94612
(415) 839-5900
- 400 S Street
Sacramento, CA 95814
(916) 443-6843
- Union Bank Building, Suite 301
525 B Street
San Diego, CA 92101
(619) 234-0966
- 33 New Montgomery Tower
San Francisco, CA 94105
(415) 243-9999
- 1505 Meridian Avenue
San Jose, CA 95125
(408) 978-8700
- 20 North San Mateo Drive
P.O. Box 294
San Mateo, CA 94401
(415) 347-1251
- P.O. Box 746
Santa Barbara, CA 93102
(805) 963-8657
- 1111 North Center Street
Stockton, CA 95202
(209) 948-4880

COLORADO

- P.O. Box 7970
Colorado Springs, CO 80933
(303) 636-1155
- 1780 South Bellaire, Suite 700
Denver, CO 80222
(303) 758-2180
- 1730 S. College Avenue, Suite 700
Fort Collins, CO 80525
(303) 484-1348
- 432 Broadway
Pueblo, CO 81004
(303) 542-6464

CONNECTICUT

- Fairfield Woods Plaza
2345 Black Rock Turnpike

Fairfield, CT 06430
(203) 374-6161
- 2080 Silas Deane Highway
Rocky Hill, CT 06067
(203) 529-3575
- 100 South Turnpike Road
Wallingford, CT 06492
(203) 269-2700

DELAWARE
- 20 South Walnut Street
P.O. Box 300
Milford, DE 19963
(302) 856-6969 (Sussex)
(302) 422-6300 (Kent)
- P.O Box 5361
Wilmington, DE 19808
(302) 996-9200

DISTRICT OF COLUMBIA
- 1012 14th Street, NW
Washington, DC 20005
(202) 393-8000

FLORIDA
- 13770 58th Street North, Suite 309
Clearwater, FL 34620
(813) 535-5522
- 2976-E Cleveland Avenue
Fort Myers, FL 33901
(813) 334-7331
- 3100 University Blvd., S., #23
Jacksonville, FL 32216
(909) 721-2288
- 2605 Maitland Center Parkway
Maitland, FL 32751
(407) 660-9500
- 16291 North West 57th Avenue
Miami, FL 33014
(305) 524-2803
- 250 School Road
New Port Richey, FL 33652
(813) 842-5459
- P.O. Box 1511
Pensacola, FL 32597
(904) 433-6111

- 1950 Port St. Lucie Blvd.
Port St. Lucie, FL 34952
(407) 878-2010
- 1111 N. Westshore Blvd.
Tampa, FL 33607
(813) 875-6200
- 3015 Exchange Court
West Palm Beach, FL 33409
(305) 686-2200

GEORGIA
- 1319-B Dawson Road
Albany, GA 31707
(912) 883-0744
- 100 Edgewood Avenue, Suite 1012
Atlanta, GA 30303
(404) 688-4910
- P.O. Box 2085
August, GA 30903
(404) 722-1574
- P.O. Box 2587
Columbus, GA 31902
(404) 324-0712
- 6606 Abercorn Street
Savannah, GA 31416
(912) 354-7521

HAWAII
- 1600 Kapiolani Blvd., Suite 714
Honolulu, HI 96813
(808) 942-2355

IDAHO
- 409 West Jefferson
Boise, ID 83702
(208) 342-4649
- 545 Shoup
Idaho Falls, ID 83402
(208) 523-9754

ILLINOIS
- 211 West Wacker Drive
Chicago, IL 60606
(312) 444-1188
- 109 Southwest Jefferson Street
Peoria, IL 61602
(309) 673-5194

INDIANA

- P.O. Box 405
  Elkhart, IN 46518
  (219) 262-8996
- 119 Southeast Fourth Street
  Evansville, IN 47708
  (812) 422-6879
- 1203 Webster Street
  Fort Wayne, IN 46802
  (219) 423-4433
- 4231 Cleveland Street
  Gary, IN 46408
  (219) 980-1511
- Victoria Centre
  22 East Washington Street, Suite 310
  Indianapolis, IN 46204
  (317) 637-0197
- 204 Iroquois Building
  Marion, IN 46952
  (317) 668-8954
- Ball State University BBB
  Whitinger Building, Room 160
  Muncie, IN 47306
  (317) 285-5668
- 509-85 U.S. 33 North
  South Bend, IN 46637
  (219) 277-9121

IOWA

- 2435 Kimberly Road, Suite 110N
  Bettendorf, IA 52722
  (319) 355-6344
- 1500 2nd Avenue, SE, Suite 212
  Cedar Rapids, IA 52403
  (319) 366-5401
- 615 Insurance Exchange Building
  Des Moines, IA 50309
  (515) 243-8137
- 318 Badgerow Building
  Sioux City, IA 51101
  (712) 252-4501

KANSAS

- 501 Jefferson, Suite 24
  Topeka, KS 66607
  (913) 232-0455

- 300 Kaufman Building
  Wichita, KS 66607
  (913) 263-3146

KENTUCKY

- 154 Patchen Drive
  Lexington, KY 40502
  (606) 268-4128
- 844 South Fourth Street
  Louisville, KY 40203
  (502) 583-6546

LOUISIANA

- 1605 Murray Street, Suite 117
  Alexandria, VA 71301
  (318) 473-4494
- 2055 Wooddale Blvd.
  Baton Rouge, LA 70806
  (504) 926-3010
- 300 Bond Street
  Houma, LA 70306
  (504) 868-3456
- P.O. Box 30297
  Lafayette, LA 70361
  (318) 234-8341
- 1413 Ryan Street, Suite C
  P.O. Box 1681
  Lake Charles, LA 70602
  (318) 433-1633
- 141 De Slard Street, Suite 114
  Monroe, LA 71201
  (318) 387-4600
- 1539 Jackson Avenue
  New Orleans, LA 70136
  (504) 581-6222
- 1401 North Market Street
  Shreveport, LA 71107
  (318) 221-8352

MAINE

- 812 Stevens Avenue
  Portland, ME 04103
  (207) 878-2715

MARYLAND

- 2100 Huntingdon Avenue
  Baltimore, MD 21211
  (301) 347-3990

MASSACHUSETTS

- 8 Winter Street, 6th Floor
  Boston, MA 02108
  (617) 482-9151
- 106 State Road, Suite 4
  Darmouth, MA 02747
  (617) 999-6060
- 1 Kendall Street, Suite 307
  Framingham, MA 01701
  (617) 872-5585
- 78 North Street
  Hyannis, MA 02601
  (617) 771-3022
- 316 Essex Street
  Lawrence, MA 01840
  (617) 687-7666
- 293 Bridge Street, Suite 324
  Sprinfgield, MA 01103
  (413) 734-3114
- P.O. Box 379
  Worcester, MA 01608
  (617) 755-2548

MICHIGAN

- 150 Michigan Avenue
  Detroit, MI 48226
  (313) 962-7566
- 620 Trust Building
  Grand Rapids, MI 49503
  (616) 774-8236

MINNESOTA

- 1745 University Avenue
  St. Paul, MN 55104
  (612) 646-7700

MISSISSIPPI

- 2917 West Beach Blvd.
  Biloxi, MS 39531
  (601) 374-2222
- 105 Fifth Avenue
  Columbus, MS 39701
  (601) 327-8594
- P.O. Box 390
  Jackson, MS 39205
  (601) 948-8222

MISSOURI

- 306 East 12th Street
  Kansas City, MO 64106
  (816) 421-7800
- 5100 Oakland, Suite 200
  St. Louis, MO 63110
  (314) 531-3300
- 205 Park Central East, Room 312
  Springfield, MO 65806
  (417) 862-9231

NEBRASKA

- 719 North 48th Street
  Lincoln, NE 68504
  (402) 467-5261
- 417 Farnam Building
  1613 Farnam Street
  Omaha, NE 68102
  (402) 346-3033

NEVADA

- 1022 E. Sahara Avenue
  Las Vegas, NV 89104
  (702) 735-6900
- P.O. Box 21269
  Reno, NV 89505
  (702) 322-0657

NEW HAMPSHIRE

- 410 S. Main Street
  Concord, NH 03301
  (603) 224-1991
  (800) 852-3737 (NH)

NEW JERSEY

- 690 Whitehead Road
  Lawrenceville, NJ 08648
  (609) 396-1199 (Mercer County)
  (201) 536-6306 (Monmouth County)
  (201) 329-6855 (Middlesex, Somerset, and
  Underston Counties)
- 34 Park Place
  Newark, NJ 07102
  (201) 643-3025
- 2 Forest Avenue
  Paramus, NJ 07652
  (201) 845-4044

- 1721 Route 37 East
  Toms River, NJ 08753
  (201) 270-5577
- 16 Maple Avenue, Box 303
  Westmont, NJ 08108
  (609) 854-8467

NEW MEXICO
- 4600-A Montgomery, NE
  Albuquerque, NM 87109
  (505) 884-0500
- 308 North Locke
  Farmington, NM 87401
  (505) 326-6501
- 1210 Louisa Street, Suite 5
  Santa Fe, NM 87502
  (505) 988-3648

NEW YORK
- 775 Main Street, Suite 401
  Buffalo, NY 14203
  (716) 856-7180
- 266 Main Street
  Farmingdale, NY 11735
  (516) 420-0500
- 257 Park Avenue South
  New York, NY 10010
  (212) 533-6200
- 1122 Sibley Tower
  Rochester, NY 14604
  (716) 546-6776
- 200 University Building
  Syracuse, NY 13202
  (315) 479-6635
- 258 Genessee Street
  Utica, NY 13502
  (315) 724-3129
- 120 East Main
  Wappinger Falls, NY 12590
  (914) 297-6550
- One Brockway Place
  White Plains, NY 10601
  (914) 428-1230

NORTH CAROLINA
- 29½ Page Avenue
  Ashville, NC 28801
  (714) 253-2392

- 1130 East 3rd Street, Suite 400
  Charlotte, NC 28204
  (714) 332-7151
- 3608 West Friendly Avenue
  Greensboro, NC 27410
  (919) 852-4240
  (919) 889-4297 (High Point)
- P.O. Box 425
  Newton, NC 28658
  (714) 464-0372
- 3120 Poplarwood Drive, Suite G-1
  Raleigh, NC 27604
  (919) 872-9240
- 2110 Cloverdale Avenue, Suite 2-B
  Winston-Salem, NC 27103
  (919) 725-8348

OHIO
- P.O. Box 596
  Akron, OH 44308
  (216) 253-4590
- 1434 Cleveland Avenue North
  Canton, OH 44703
  (216) 454-9401
- 898 Walnut Street
  Cincinnati, OH 45202
  (513) 421-3015
- 527 South High Street
  Columbus, OH 43215
  (614) 221-6336
- 40 West Fourth Street, Suite 280
  Dayton, OH 45402
  (513) 222-5825
- P.O. Box 1706
  Mansfield, OH 44901
  (419) 522-1700
- 425 Jefferson Avenue, Suite 909
  Toledo, OH 43604
  (419) 241-6276
- 311 Mahoning Bank Building
  P.O. Box 1495
  Youngstown, OH 44501
  (216) 744-3111

OKLAHOMA
- 17 South Dewey
  Oklahoma City, OK 73102
  (405) 239-6081

- 4833 South Sheridan, Suite 412
  Tulsa, OK 74145
  (918) 664-1266

OREGON
- 520 South West 6th Avenue, Suite 600
  Portland, OR 97204
  (503) 226-3981

PENNSYLVANIA
- 528 North New Street
  Bethelem, PA 18018
  (215) 866-8780
- 53 North Duke Street
  Lancaster, PA 17602
  (717) 291-1151
  (717) 232-2800 (Harrisburg)
  (717) 846-2700 (York County)
- 511 North Broad Street
  Philadelphia, PA 19123
  (215) 574-3600
- 610 Smithfield Street
  Pittsburg, PA 15222
  (412) 456-2700
- 601 Connell Building, 6th Floor
  Scranton, PA 18503
  (717) 342-9129

RHODE ISLAND
- 270 Weybosset Street
  Providence, RI 02903
  (401) 272-9800

SOUTH CAROLINA
- 1338 Main Street, Suite 500
  Columbia, SC 29201
  (803) 254-2525
- 311 Pettigru Street
  Greenville, SC 29601
  (803) 242-5052

TENNESSEE
- 1010 Market Street, Suite 200
  Chattanooga, TN 37402
  (615) 266-6144

- P.O. Box 3608
  Knoxville, TN 37927
  (615) 522-1300
- 1835 Union, Suite 312
  Memphis, TN 38104
  (901) 272-9641
- 506 Nashville City Bank Building
  Nashville, TN 37201
  (615) 254-5872

TEXAS
- Bank of Commerce Building
  Suite 320
  Abilene, TX 79605
  (915) 691-1533
- 1008 West 10th
  Amarillo, TX 79101
  (806) 374-3735
- 1005 M Bank Plaza
  Austin, TX 78701
  (512) 476-6943
- P.O. Box 2988
  Beaumont, TX 77704
  (409) 835-5348
- 202 Varisco Building
  Bryan, TX 77803
  (409) 823-8148
- 109 North Cappareal, Suite 101
  Corpus Christi, TX 78401
  (512) 888-5555
- 2001 Bryan Street, Suite 850
  Dallas, TX 75201
- 6024 Gateway East, Suite 1-C
  El Paso, TX 79905
  (915) 778-7000
- 709 Sinclair Building
  106 West 5th Street
  Fort Worth, TX 76102
  (817) 332-7585
- 2707 North Loop West, Suite 900
  Houston, TX 77008
  (713) 868-9500
- 1015 15th Street
  Lubbock, TX 97408
  (806) 763-0459
- Airport 20 Road
  P.O. Box 6006

Midland, TX 79711
(915) 563-1880
- 115 South Randolph
San Angelo, TX 76903
(915) 653-2318
- 1800 Northeast Loop 410
San Antonio, TX 78217
(512) 828-9441
- 6801 Sanger, Suite 125
Weslaco, TX 78596
(512) 968-3678
- 1106 Brook Avenue
Wichita Falls, TX 76301
(817) 723-5526

UTAH
- 385 24th Street, Suite 717
Ogden, UT 84401
(801) 399-4701
- 1588 South Main Street
Salt Lake City, UT 84115
(801) 487-4656

VIRGINIA
- 105 East Annandale Road, Suite 210
Falls Church, VA 22046
(703) 533-1900
- 2019 Llewellyn Avenue
P.O. Box 11133
Norfolk, VA 23517

(804) 627-5651
(804) 851-9101 (Peninsula area)
- 701 East Franklin Street, Suite 712
Richmond, VA 23219
(804) 648-0016
- 151 W. Campbell Avenue, SW
Roanoke, VA 24011
(703) 342-3455

WASHINGTON
- 127 West Canal Drive
Kennewick, WA 99336
(509) 582-0222
- 2200 Sixth Avenue
Seattle, WA 98121
(206) 448-8888
- South 176 Stevens
Spokane, WA 98121
(509) 747-1155
- 1101 Fawcett Avenue, Suite 222
Tacoma, WA 98402
(206) 383-5561
- P.O. Box 1584
Yakima, WA 98907
(509) 248-1326

WISCONSIN
- 740 N. Plankinton Avenue
Milwaukee, WI 53203
(414) 273-1600

OBTAINING VITAL RECORDS

Certificates of birth, death, marriage, and divorce are necessary for a wide variety of reasons, from applying for Social Security to collecting life insurance benefits. As we discussed previously in this book, everyone should keep these vital records, along with other important documents, in a vital papers file, the existence of which is known to loved ones. However, since none of us are perfect, we are likely to find ourselves in the position of having to obtain new copies of the vital records of ourselves or our relatives.

The majority of states have made this task relatively simple by collecting recent vital records in a central office. Below we list (by state):

- The address of the central office for each state
- The type of certificates available from that office
- A telephone number to call for information about current fees and methods of

payment accepted (for example, personal check, money order, etc.)

When writing for vital records, you should include the following information:

Birth or death record

1. Full name of person whose record is being requested
2. Sex of person
3. Parents' names, including mother's maiden name
4. Month, day, and year of birth or death
5. City, county, and state where birth or death took place, including name of hospital, if known
6. Purpose for which copy is needed
7. Your relationship to person whose record is being requested

Marriage record

1. Full names of bride and groom
2. Month, day, and year of marriage
3. City, county, and state where marriage took place
4. Purpose for which copy is needed
5. Your relationship to person whose record is being requested

Divorce record

1. Full names of husband and wife
2. Date of divorce or annulment
3. Place of divorce or annulment
4. Type of final decree
5. Purpose for which copy is needed
6. Your relationship to person whose record is being requested

In some states, marriage and divorce records, as well as older birth and death records,

have to be obtained from county clerks or other local officials. For more complete information about obtaining these records:

Publication: *Where to Write for Vital Records*
Cost: $1.50
From: Consumer Information Center
P.O. Box 100
Pueblo, CO 81002

The following list contains state offices of Vital Statistics:

ALABAMA (BIRTH, DEATH, MARRIAGE, DIVORCE)

BUREAU OF VITAL STATISTICS
State Department of Public Health
Montgomery, AL 36130
(205) 261-5033

ALASKA (BIRTH, DEATH, MARRIAGE, DIVORCE)

DEPARTMENT OF HEALTH AND SOCIAL SERVICES
Bureau of Vital Statistics
P.O. Box H-02G
Juneau, AK 99811
(907) 465-3391

ARIZONA (BIRTH, DEATH)

VITAL RECORDS SECTION
Arizona Department of Health Services
P.O. Box 3887
Phoenix, AZ 85030
(602) 255-1080

ARKANSAS (BIRTH, DEATH, MARRIAGE, DIVORCE)

DIVISION OF VITAL RECORDS
Arkansas Department of Health
4815 West Markham Street
Little Rock, AR 72201
(501) 661-2336

CALIFORNIA (BIRTH, DEATH, MARRIAGE, DI-
VORCE)

VITAL STATISTICS SECTION
Department of Health Services
410 N. Street
Sacramento, CA 95814
(916) 445-2684

COLORADO (BIRTH, DEATH, MARRIAGE, DI-
VORCE)

VITAL RECORDS SECTION
Colorado Department of Health
4210 East 11th Avenue
Denver, CO 80220
(303) 320-8674

CONNECTICUT (BIRTH, DEATH, MARRIAGE, DI-
VORCE)

VITAL RECORDS SECTION
Division of Health Statistics
State Department of Health
150 Washington Street
Hartford, CT 06106
(203) 566-1124

DELAWARE (BIRTH, DEATH, MARRIAGE, DI-
VORCE)

OFFICE OF VITAL STATISTICS
Division of Public Health
P.O. Box 6378
Dover, DE 19903
(302) 736-4721

DISTRICT OF COLUMBIA (BIRTH, DEATH)

VITAL RECORDS BRANCH
425 I Street, NW, Room 3009
Washington, DC 20001
(202) 727-5316

FLORIDA (BIRTH, DEATH, MARRIAGE, DIVORCE)

DEPARTMENT OF HEALTH AND REHABILITA-
TIVE SERVICES
Office of Vital Statistics
P.O. Box 210
Tallahassee, FL 32231
(904) 359-6900

GEORGIA (BIRTH, DEATH, MARRIAGE, DI-
VORCE)

GEORGIA DEPARTMENT OF HUMAN RE-
SOURCES
Vital Records Unit
Room 217-H
47 Trinity Avenue, SW
Atlanta, GA 30334
(404) 656-4900

HAWAII (BIRTH, DEATH, MARRIAGE, DIVORCE)

RESEARCH AND STATISTICS OFFICE
State Department of Health
P.O. Box 3378
Honolulu, HI 96801
(808) 548-5819

IDAHO (BIRTH, DEATH, MARRIAGE, DIVORCE)

BUREAU OF VITAL STATISTICS
State Department of Health and Welfare
Statehouse
Boise, ID 83720
(208) 334-5988

ILLINOIS (BIRTH, DEATH, MARRIAGE, DIVORCE)

DIVISION OF VITAL RECORDS
State Department of Health
605 West Jefferson Street
Springfield, IL 62702
(217) 782-6553

INDIANA (BIRTH, DEATH, MARRIAGE)

DIVISION OF VITAL RECORDS
State Board of Health
1330 West Michigan Street

P.O. Box 1964
Indianapolis, IN 46206
(317) 633-0274

IOWA (BIRTH, DEATH, MARRIAGE, DIVORCE)

IOWA DEPARTMENT OF PUBLIC HEALTH
Vital Records Section
Lucas Office Building
Des Moines, IA 50319
(515) 281-5871

KANSAS (BIRTH, DEATH, MARRIAGE, DIVORCE)

OFFICE OF VITAL STATISTICS
Kansas State Department of Health and Environment
900 Jackson Street
Topeka, KS 66612
(913) 298-1400

KENTUCKY (BIRTH, DEATH, MARRIAGE, DIVORCE)

OFFICE OF VITAL STATISTICS
Department of Health Services
275 East Main Street
Frankfort, KY 40621
(502) 564-4212

LOUISIANA (BIRTH, DEATH)

DIVISION OF VITAL RECORDS
Office of Health Services and Environmental Quality
P.O. Box 60630
New Orleans, LA 70160
(504) 568-5175

MAINE (BIRTH, DEATH, MARRIAGE, DIVORCE)

OFFICE OF VITAL RECORDS
Human Services Building
State House Station No. 11
Augusta, ME 04333
(207) 289-3181

MARYLAND (BIRTH, DEATH, MARRIAGE, DIVORCE)

DIVISION OF VITAL RECORDS
State Department of Health and Mental Hygiene
State Office Building
P.O. Box 13146
201 West Preston Street
Baltimore, MD 21203
(301) 225-5988

MASSACHUSETTS (BIRTH, DEATH, MARRIAGE, DIVORCE)

REGISTRY OF VITAL RECORDS AND STATISTICS
150 Tremont Street, Room B-3
Boston, MA 02111
(617) 727-0110

MICHIGAN (BIRTH, DEATH, MARRIAGE, DIVORCE)

OFFICE OF THE STATE REGISTAR AND CENTER FOR HEALTH STATISTICS
Michigan Department of Public Health
3500 North Logan Street
Lansing, MI 48909
(517) 335-8655

MINNESOTA (BIRTH, DEATH, MARRIAGE, DIVORCE)

MINNESOTA DEPARTMENT OF HEALTH
Section of Vital Statistics
717 Delaware Street, SE
P.O. Box 9441
St. Paul, MN 55101
(612) 623-5121

MISSISSIPPI (BIRTH, DEATH, MARRIAGE, DIVORCE)

VITAL RECORDS
State Board of Health
P.O. Box 1700
Jackson, MS 39215
(601) 354-6606

MISSOURI (BIRTH, DEATH, MARRIAGE, DI-
VORCE)

DEPARTMENT OF HEALTH
Bureau of Vital Records
P.O. Box 570
Jefferson City, MO 65102
(314) 751-6387

MONTANA (BIRTH, DEATH, MARRIAGE, DI-
VORCE)

BUREAU OF RECORDS AND STATISTICS
State Department of Health and Environmental
Sciences
Helena, MT 59620
(406) 444-2614

NEBRASKA (BIRTH, DEATH, MARRIAGE, DI-
VORCE)

BUREAU OF VITAL STATISTICS
State Department of Health
301 Centennial Mall, South
P.O. Box 95007
Lincoln, NE 68509
(402) 471-2871

NEVADA (BIRTH, DEATH, MARRIAGE, DIVORCE)

DIVISION OF HEALTH—VITAL STATISTICS
Capitol Complex
Carson City, NV 89710
(702) 885-4480

NEW HAMPSHIRE (BIRTH, DEATH, MARRIAGE,
DIVORCE)

BUREAU OF VITAL RECORDS
Health and Human Services Building
6 Hazen Drive
Concord, NH 03301
(603) 271-4654

NEW JERSEY (BIRTH, DEATH, MARRIAGE)

STATE DEPARTMENT OF HEALTH
Bureau of Vital Statistics
CN 360

Trenton, NJ 08625
(609) 292-4087

NEW MEXICO (BIRTH, DEATH)

VITAL STATISTICS BUREAU
New Mexico Health Services Division
P.O. Box 968
Santa Fe, NM 87504
(505) 827-2338

NEW YORK (EX. NEW YORK CITY) (BIRTH,
DEATH, MARRIAGE, DIVORCE)

BUREAU OF PUBLIC RECORDS
State Department of Health
Empire State Plaza
Tower Building
Albany, NY 12237
(518) 474-3075

NEW YORK CITY (BIRTH, DEATH)

BUREAU OF VITAL RECORDS
Department of Health of New York City
125 Worth Street
New York, NY 10013
(212) 619-4530

NORTH CAROLINA (BIRTH, DEATH, MARRIAGE,
DIVORCE)

DEPARTMENT OF HUMAN RESOURCES
Division of Health Services
Vital Records Branch
P.O. Box 2091
Raleigh, NC 27602
(919) 733-3526

NORTH DAKOTA (BIRTH, DEATH, MARRIAGE,
DIVORCE)

DIVISION OF VITAL RECORDS
State Department of Health
Office of Statistical Services
Bismarck, ND 58505
(701) 224-2360

OHIO (BIRTH, DEATH, MARRIAGE, DIVORCE)

DIVISION OF VITAL STATISTICS
State Department of Health
G-20, Ohio Department Building
65 South Front Street
Columbus, OH 43266
(614) 466-2531

OKLAHOMA (BIRTH, DEATH)

VITAL RECORDS SECTION
State Department of Health
Northeast 10th Street and Stonewall
P.O. Box 53551
Oklahoma City, OK 73152
(405) 271-4040

OREGON (BIRTH, DEATH, MARRIAGE, DIVORCE)

OREGON STATE HEALTH DIVISION
Vital Statistics Section
P.O. Box 116
Portland, OR 97207
(503) 229-5710

PENNSYLVANIA (BIRTH, DEATH, MARRIAGE, DI-
VORCE)

DIVISION OF VITAL RECORDS
State Department of Health
Central Building
101 South Mercer Street
P.O. Box 1528
New Castle, PA 16103
(412) 656-3100

RHODE ISLAND (BIRTH, DEATH, MARRIAGE)

DIVISION OF VITAL STATISTICS
State Health Department
Room 101, Cannon Building
75 Davis Street
Providence, RI 02908
(401) 277-2811

SOUTH CAROLINA (BIRTH, DEATH, MARRIAGE,
DIVORCE)

OFFICE OF VITAL RECORDS AND PUBLIC
HEALTH STATISTICS
SC Department of Health and Environmental
Control
2600 Bull Street
Columbia, SC 29201
(803) 734-4830

SOUTH DAKOTA (BIRTH, DEATH, MARRIAGE,
DIVORCE)

STATE DEPARTMENT OF HEALTH
Center for Health Policy and Statistics
Vital Records
523 E. Capitol
Pierre, SD 57501
(605) 773-3355

TENNESSEE (BIRTH, DEATH, MARRIAGE, DI-
VORCE)

TENNESSEE VITAL RECORDS
Department of Health and Environment
Cordell Hull Building
Nashville, TN 37219
(615) 741-1763
(800) 423-1901 (TN)

TEXAS (BIRTH, DEATH, MARRIAGE, DIVORCE)

BUREAU OF VITAL STATISTICS
Texas Department of Health
110 West 49th Street
Austin, TX 78756
(512) 458-7380

UTAH (BIRTH, DEATH, MARRIAGE, DIVORCE)

BUREAU OF VITAL RECORDS
Utah Department of Health
288 North 1480 West
P.O. Box 16700
Salt Lake City, UT 84116
(801) 538-6105

VERMONT (BIRTH, DEATH, MARRIAGE, DIVORCE)

VERMONT DEPARTMENT OF HEALTH
Vital Records Section
Box 70
60 Main Street
Burlington, VT 05402
(802) 863-7275

VIRGINIA (BIRTH, DEATH, MARRIAGE, DIVORCE)

DIVISION OF VITAL RECORDS
State Health Department
P.O. Box 1000
Richmond, VA 23208
(804) 786-6228

WASHINGTON (BIRTH, DEATH, MARRIAGE, DIVORCE)

VITAL RECORDS
P.O. Box 9709, ET-11
Olympia, WA 98504
(800) 551-0562 (Ex. WA)
(800) 331-0680 (WA)

WEST VIRGINIA (BIRTH, DEATH, MARRIAGE, DIVORCE)

DIVISION OF VITAL STATISTICS
State Department of Health
State Office Building No. 3
Charleston, WV 25305
(304) 348-2931

WISCONSIN (BIRTH, DEATH, MARRIAGE, DIVORCE)

BUREAU OF HEALTH STATISTICS
Wisconsin Division of Health
P.O. Box 309
Madison, WI 53701
(608) 266-1371

WYOMING (BIRTH, DEATH, MARRIAGE, DIVORCE)

VITAL RECORDS SERVICES
Division of Health and Medical Services
Hathaway Building
Cheyenne, WY 82002
(307) 777-7591

Individuals may contact the following office for birth and death records of U.S. citizens in foreign countries:

PASSPORT SERVICES
Correspondence Branch
U.S. Department of State
Washington, DC 20524

Death records of servicemen who died in foreign countries may be obtained from:

SECRETARY OF DEFENSE (FOR MEMBERS OF THE ARMY, NAVY, OR AIR FORCE)
Washington, DC 20301

COMMANDANT, P.S. (FOR MEMBERS OF THE COAST GUARD)
U.S. Coast Guard
Washington, DC 20226

Records of births or deaths occurring on vessels or aircrafts on the high seas can be obtained from:

U.S. DEPARTMENT OF STATE
Washington, DC 20520

Most, but not all, foreign countries record births and deaths. U.S. citizens who need a copy of a foreign birth or death certificate can obtain assistance by writing:

OFFICE OF OVERSEAS CITIZEN SERVICES
U.S. Department of State
Washington, DC 20520

You may also find yourself needing the following types of vital records:

- Records of military service (for records of Army, Navy, Marine Corps, and Air Force)

NATIONAL PERSONNEL RECORDS CENTER
9700 Page Blvd. St. Louis, MO 63132

- For records of the Coast Guard

GENERAL ARCHIVES DIVISION (WNRC)
Washington, DC 20409

- Naturalization records or birth records of alien children adopted by U.S. citizens:

IMMIGRATION AND NATURALIZATION SERVICE
Washington, DC 20536

TOURIST BUREAUS

U.S. TOURIST INFORMATION BUREAUS

We have listed below the addresses and telephone numbers for all state tourist information offices. You can obtain a listing of all local tourist information sources in a specific state when you contact the state tourist office.

ALABAMA

BUREAU OF TOURISM AND TRAVEL
532 South Perry Street
Montgomery AL 36104
(800) 252-2262
(205) 261-4169

ALASKA

DIVISION OF TOURISM
P.O. Box E
Juneau, AL 99811
(907) 465-2010

ARIZONA

OFFICE OF TOURISM
1100 W. Washington Street
Phoenix AZ 85007
(602) 542-3618

ARKANSAS

DEPARTMENT OF PARKS AND TOURISM
One Capitol Mall
Little Rock AR 72201
(800) 643-8383 (Ex. AR)
(800) 482-8999 (AR)

CALIFORNIA

OFFICE OF TOURISM
1121 L Street, Suite 103
Sacramento CA 95814
(800) 862-2543 (Ex. CA)
(916) 322-2881 (CA)

COLORADO

TOURISM BOARD
P.O. Box 38700
Denver CO 80238
(800) 433-2656 (Ex. CO)
(303) 592-5410

CONNECTICUT

DEPARTMENT OF ECONOMIC DEVELOPMENT
210 Washington Street
Hartford CT 06106
(800) 243-1685 (Ex. CT)
(800) 566-3385 (CT)

DELAWARE

TOURISM OFFICE
99 Kings Highway
P.O. Box 1401
Dover DE 19903
(800) 441-8846 (Ex. DE)
(800) 282-8667 (DE)

DISTRICT OF COLUMBIA (WASHINGTON, DC)

DC CONVENTION AND VISITORS ASSOCIATION
1575 Eye Street, NW, Suite 250
Washington DC 20005
(202) 789-7000

FLORIDA

DIVISION OF TOURISM
107 W. Gaines Street, Suite 509
Tallahassee FL 32301
(904) 488-5606

GEORGIA

TOURIST DIVISION
230 Peachtree Street, Suite 605
Atlanta GA 30303
(404) 656-3553

HAWAII

VISITORS BUREAU
220 S. King Street
Honolulu HI 96813
(808) 548-3958

IDAHO

DIVISION OF TRAVEL PROMOTION
The Statehouse, Room 108
Boise ID 83720
(208) 334-2017

ILLINOIS

STATE OF ILLINOIS CENTER
100 W. Randolph, Suite 3-400
Chicago IL 60601
(312) 917-4732

INDIANA

DEPARTMENT OF COMMERCE
Tourism Development Division
One N. Capitol Avenue, Suite 700
Indianapolis IN 46204
(317) 232-8860

IOWA

TOURISM OFFICE
Iowa Department of Economic Development
200 East Grand Avenue
Des Moines IA 50309
(800) 345-4692
(515) 281-3100

KANSAS

DIVISION OF TRAVEL AND TOURISM DEVELOP-
MENT
400 W. Eighth Street, 5th Floor
Topeka, KS 66603
(913) 296-2009

KENTUCKY

DEPARTMENT OF TRAVEL DEVELOPMENT
Capitol Tower Plaza, 22nd Floor
Frankfort KY 40601
(800) 225-8747 (Ex. KY)
(502) 564-4930

LOUISIANA

OFFICE OF TOURISM
900 Riverside Hall N.
Baton Rouge LA 70804
(800) 535-8388 (Ex. LA)
(504) 342-8119

MAINE

VACATION INFORMATION
189 State Street
Augusta, ME 04333
(207) 289-5710

MARYLAND

OFFICE OF TOURISM DEVELOPMENT
217 E. Redmond Street
Baltimore, MD 21202
(301) 333-6611

MASSACHUSETTS

DIVISION OF TOURISM
100 Cambridge Street
Boston MA 02202
(617) 727-3205
(800) 447-6277 (Ex. MA)

MICHIGAN

TRAVEL BUREAU
P.O. Box 30226
Lansing MI 48909
(800) 543-2937 (Ex. MI)
(517) 373-0676

MINNESOTA

OFFICE OF TOURISM
375 Jackson Street
250 Skyway Level
St. Paul, MN 55101
(800) 328-1461 (Ex. MN)
(800) 652-9747 (MN)

MISSISSIPPI

DIVISION OF TOURISM
P.O. Box 22825
Jackson MS 39205
(800) 647-2290 (Ex. MS)
(601) 359-3414

MISSOURI

DIVISION OF TOURISM
P.O. Box 1055
Jefferson City, MO 65102
(314) 751-4133

MONTANA

TRAVEL PROMOTION
1424 Ninth Avenue
Helena MT 59601
(800) 548-3390 (Ex. MT)
(406) 444-2654

NEBRASKA

DIVISION OF TRAVEL AND TOURISM
P.O. Box 94666
Lincoln NE 68509
(800) 228-4307
(402) 471-3796

NEVADA

COMMISSION ON TOURISM
Capitol Complex
Carson City NV 89710
(800) 638-2328 (Ex. NV)
(702) 885-4322

NEW HAMPSHIRE

OFFICE OF VACATION TRAVEL
105 Loudon Road
P.O. Box 856
Concord NH 03301
(603) 271-2666

NEW JERSEY

DIVISION OF TRAVEL AND TOURISM
CN-826
Trenton NJ 08625
(609) 292-2496
(800) 537-7397 (Ex. NJ)

NEW MEXICO

TOURISM AND TRAVEL DIVISION
Joseph Montoya Building
1100 St. Francis Drive
Santa Fe NM 87503
(800) 545-2040
(505) 827-0291

NEW YORK

STATE DIVISION OF TOURISM
230 Park Avenue, Suite 866
New York NY 10169
(800) 225-5697 (Ex. NY)
(518) 473-0715

NORTH CAROLINA

DIVISION OF TRAVEL AND TOURISM
430 N. Salisbury Street
Raleigh NC 27603
(800) 847-4862
(919) 733-4171

NORTH DAKOTA

TOURISM PROMOTION
Liberty Memorial Building
Bismark ND 58505
(701) 224-2525

OHIO

OFFICE OF TRAVEL AND TOURISM
P.O. Box 1001
Columbus OH 43266
(800) 282-5393 (Ex. OH)
(614) (466-8844)

OKLAHOMA

TOURISM AND RECREATION DEPARTMENT
Division of Marketing Services
505 Will Rogers Building
Oklahoma City, OK 73105
(800) 652-6552 (Ex. OK)
(405) 521-2413

OREGON

TOURISM DIVISION
595 Cottage Street NW
Salem OR 97310
(800) 547-7842 (Ex. OR)
(800) 233-3306 (OR)

PENNSYLVANIA

BUREAU OF TRAVEL DEVELOPMENT
453 Forum Building
Harrisburg PA 17120
(800) 237-4363 (Ex. PA)
(717) 787-5453

RHODE ISLAND

TOURISM DIVISION
7 Jackson Walkway
Providence RI 02903
(401) 277-2601

SOUTH CAROLINA

DEPARTMENT OF PARKS, RECREATION AND
TOURISM
1205 Pendleton Street Suite 106
Columbia SC 29201
(803) 734-0135

SOUTH DAKOTA

DEPARTMENT OF TOURISM
Capitol Lake Plaza
711 Wells Avenue
Pierre SD 57501
(605) 773-3301

TENNESSEE

DEPARTMENT OF TOURIST DEVELOPMENT
320 Sixth Avenue North, Suite 500
Nashville TN 37219
(615) 741-2159

TEXAS

DEPARTMENT OF COMMERCE
Tourism Division
816 Congress
Austin TX 78701
(512) 472-5059

UTAH

TRAVEL COUNCIL
Council Hall/Capitol Hill
Salt Lake City UT 84114
(801) 538-1030

VERMONT

TRAVEL DIVISION
134 State Street
Montpelier VT 05602
(802) 828-3236

VIRGINIA

DIVISION OF TOURISM
202 N. Ninth Street, Suite 500

Richmond VA 23219
(804) 786-2051

WASHINGTON

STATE TOURISM DIVISION
101 General Administration Building
Olympia WA 98504
(206) 753-5600

WEST VIRGINIA

DEPARTMENT OF COMMERCE
Division of Tourism
2101 Washington Street E
Charleston WV 25305
(800) 225-2982 (Ex. WV)
(304) 348-2200

WISCONSIN

DIVISION OF TOURISM DEVELOPMENT
123 W. Washington Avenue
Madison WI 53702
(608) 266-2147

WYOMING

TRAVEL COMMISSION
I-25 at College Drive
Cheyenne WY 82002
(800) 225-5996 (Ex. WY)
(307) 777-7777

FOREIGN TOURIST INFORMATION BUREAUS

Almost every major foreign tourist destination maintains at least one tourist information bureau in the United States. Most of these bureaus have elaborate publications describing their countries as well as tour packages offered by national airlines and other companies. These tourist information offices can also provide information about visas, currency exchange, and a host of other specific questions for tourists as well as business travelers.

By region of the world, these agencies are:

CANADA

CANADIAN GOVERNMENT OFFICE OF TOURISM
1251 Avenue of the Americas

New York, NY 10020
(212) 757-4917

CANADIAN GOVERNMENT OFFICE OF TOUR-
ISM
235 Queen Street East
Ottawa, Ontario K1A 0H6
Canada
(613) 954-3829

PROVINCIAL TOURIST OFFICES

TRAVEL ALBERTA
10025 Jasper Avenue
Edmonton, Alberta T5J 3Z3
Canada
(800) 661-8888
(403) 427-4321

TOURISM BRITISH COLUMBIA
562 Burrard Street, Suite 802
Vancouver, BC V6C 2J6
Canada
(604) 683-2000

TRAVEL MANITOBA
155 Carlton Street
Winnipeg, Manitoba R3C 3H8
Canada
(800) 665-0040
(204) 945-3777

TOURISM NEW BRUNSWICK
P.O. Box 12345
Fredericton, NB E3B 5C3
Canada
(800) 561-0123
(506) 453-2444

NEWFOUNDLAND TOURISM DIVISION
Department of Development
P.O. Box 2016
St. John's, Newfoundland A1C 5R8
Canada
(800) 563-6353
(709) 576-2830

NOVA SCOTIA DEPARTMENT OF TOURISM
P.O. Box 456
Halifax, NC B3J 2R5
Canada
(800) 341-6096
(902) 424-5000

ONTARIO MINISTRY OF TOURISM AND RECREA-
TION
Queens Park
Toronto, Ontario M7A 2E5
Canada
(800) 268-3735
(416) 965-4008

PRINCE EDWARD ISLAND VISITOR SERVICES
P.O. Box 940
Charlottetown, Prince Edward Island C1A
7M5
Canada
(800) 565-9060
(902) 368-4444

TOURISM QUEBEC
P.O. Box 20,000
Quebec City, Quebec G1K 7X2
Canada
(800) 443-7000
(514) 873-2025

SASKATCHEWAN TOURISM DEPARTMENT
2103 11th Avenue
Regina, Saskatchewan S4P 3V7
Canada
(800) 667-7191
(306) 787-2300

CARIBBEAN

ANGUILLA TOURIST INFORMATION OFFICE
1208 Washington Drive
Centerport, NY 11721
(212) 869-0402
(516) 673-0150

ANTIGUA DEPARTMENT OF TOURISM
610 Fifth Avenue
New York, NY 10020
(212) 541-4117

ARUBA TOURIST BUREAU
521 5th Avenue
New York, NY 10020
(800) 862-7822 (Ex. NY)
(212) 557-1585 (NY)

BAHAMAS TOURIST OFFICE
150 East 52nd Street
New York, NY 10022
(212) 757-1611

BARBADOS BOARD OF TOURISM
800 Second Avenue
New York, NY 10017
(800) 221-9831 (Ex. NY)
(212) 986-6516 (NY)

BERMUDA DEPARTMENT OF TOURISM
310 Madison Avenue
New York, NY 10017
(800) 223-6106 (Ex. NY)
(800) 223-6107 (NY)

BONAIRE GOVERNMENT TOURIST OFFICE
275 Seventh Avenue
New York, NY 10001
(212) 242-7707

BRITISH VIRGIN ISLANDS TOURIST BOARD
370 Lexington Avenue
New York, NY 10017
(212) 696-0400

CARIBBEAN TOURISM ASSOCIATION
3166 S. River Road
Des Plains, IL 60018
(800) 621-1270

CAYMAN ISLANDS TOURIST BOARD
420 Lexington Avenue
New York, NY 10170
(212) 682-5582

CURACAO TOURIST BOARD
400 Madison Avenue, Suite 311
New York, NY 10017
(212) 751-8266

DOMINICA
c/o Caribbean Tourism Association
20 East 46th Street
New York, NY 10017
(212) 682-0435

DOMINICAN REPUBLIC TOURIST INFORMA-
TION CENTER
485 Madison Avenue
New York, NY 10022
(212) 826-0750

FRENCH WEST INDIES TOURIST BOARD
610 Fifth Avenue
New York, NY 10020
(212) 757-1125

GRENADA DEPARTMENT OF TOURISM
141 East 44th Street
New York, NY 10017
(212) 687-9554

GUADELOUPE
c/o French West Indies Tourist Board
610 Fifth Avenue
New York, NY 10020
(212) 757-1125

HAITI TOURIST OFFICE
18 E. 41 Street
New York, NY 10017
(212) 779-7177

JAMAICA TOURIST BOARD
866 Second Avenue
New York, NY 10017
(800) 223-5225 (Ex. NY)
(212) 688-7650 (NY)

MARTINIQUE
c/o French West Indies Tourist Board
610 Fifth Avenue

New York, NY 10020
(212) 757-1125

COMMONWEALTH OF PUERTO RICO TOURISM
COMPANY
1290 Avenue of the Americas
New York, NY 10020
(800) 443-0266
(212) 599-6262

ST. BARTHELEMY
c/o French West Indies Tourist Board
610 Fifth Avenue
New York, NY 10020
(212) 757-1125

ST. CROIX
c/o U.S. Virgin Islands Division of Tourism
1270 Avenue of the Americas
New York, NY 10020
(212) 582-4520

ST. JOHN
c/o U.S. Virgin Islands Division of Tourism
1270 Avenue of the Americas
New York, NY 10020
(212) 582-4520

ST. LUCIA TOURIST BOARD
820 Second Avenue
New York, NY 10017
(212) 867-2950

ST. MAARTEN-SABA-ST. EUSTATIUS TOURIST IN-
FORMATION OFFICE
275 Seventh Avenue
New York, NY 10001
(212) 989-0000

ST. MARTIN
c/o French West Indies Tourist Board
610 Fifth Avenue
New York, NY 10020
(212) 757-1125

ST. THOMAS
c/o U.S. Virgin Islands Division of Tourism
1270 Avenue of the Americas

New York, NY 10020
(212) 582-4520

ST. VINCENT AND THE GRENADINES TOURIST
OFFICE
801 Second Avenue, 21st Floor
New York, NY 10017
(212) 687-4981

TOBAGO
c/o Trinidad and Tobago Tourist Board
118-35 Queens Boulevard
Forest Hills, NY 11375
(800) 232-0082
(718) 575-3909

TORTOLA
c/o British Virgin Islands Tourist Board
370 Lexington Avenue
New York, NY 10017
(212) 696-0400

TRINIDAD
c/o Trinidad and Tobago Tourist Board
118-35 Queens Boulevard
Forest Hills, NY 11375
(800) 232-0082
(718) 575-3909

U.S. VIRGIN ISLANDS DIVISION OF TOURISM
1270 Avenue of the Americas
New York, NY 10020
(212) 582-4520

VIRGIN GORDA
c/o British Virgin Islands Tourist Board
370 Lexington Avenue
New York, NY 10017
(212) 696-0400

EUROPE

AUSTRIAN NATIONAL TOURIST OFFICE
500 Fifth Avenue
New York, NY 10110
(800) 223-0284
(212) 944-6880

BELGIAN NATIONAL TOURIST OFFICE
745 Fifth Avenue, Suite 714
New York, NY 10151
(212) 758-8130

BRITISH TOURIST AUTHORITY
40 West 57th Street
New York, NY 10019
(212) 581-4708

BULGARIAN TOURIST OFFICE
121 E. 62nd. St.
New York, NY 10028
(212) 935-4646

CYPRUS TOURIST OFFICE
13 East 40th Street
New York, NY 10016
(212) 213-9100

CZECHOSLOVAK TRAVEL BUREAU
10 East 40th Street
New York, NY 10016
(212) 689-9720

DANISH NATIONAL TOURIST OFFICE
655 Third Avenue
New York, NY 10017
(212) 949-2333

FINNISH TOURIST BOARD
655 Third Avenue
New York, NY 10017
(212) 949-2333

FRENCH GOVERNMENT TOURIST OFFICE
610 Fifth Avenue
New York, NY 10020
(212) 757-1125

GERMAN TOURIST INFORMATION OFFICE
747 Third Avenue
New York, NY 10017
(212) 308-3300

GREEK NATIONAL TOURIST ORGANIZATION
645 Fifth Avenue, Olympic Tower
New York, NY 10022
(212) 421-5777

HUNGARIAN TRAVEL BUREAU
1602 2nd Avenue
New York, NY 10111
(212) 249-9342

ICELANDIC NATIONAL TOURIST OFFICE
655 Third Avenue
New York, NY 10017
(212) 949-2333

IRISH TOURIST BOARD
757 Third Avenue
New York, NY 10017
(212) 418-0800
(800) 223-6470 (Ex. NY)

ITALIAN GOVERNMENT TRAVEL OFFICE
630 Fifth Avenue
New York, NY 10111
(212) 245-4822

LUXEMBOURG TOURIST INFORMATION OFFICE
801 Second Avenue
New York, NY 10017
(212) 370-9850

MALTESE CONSULATE
249 East 35th Street
New York, NY 10016
(212) 725-2345

MONACO GOVERNMENT TOURIST OFFICE
845 Third Avenue
New York, NY 10022
(212) 759-5227

THE NETHERLANDS BOARD OF TOURISM
355 Lexington Avenue
New York, NY 10017
(212) 370-7367

NORWEGIAN NATIONAL TOURIST OFFICE
655 Third Avenue
New York, NY 10017
(212) 949-2333

POLISH NATIONAL TOURIST OFFICE
333 N. Michigan Avenue
Chicago, IL 60601
(312) 236-9013

PORTUGUESE TOURIST AND INFORMATION
OFFICE
590 Fifth Avenue
New York, NY 10036
(212) 354-4403

ROMANIAN NATIONAL TOURIST OFFICE
573 Third Avenue
New York, NY 10016
(212) 697-6971

SPANISH NATIONAL TOURIST OFFICE
665 Fifth Avenue
New York, NY 10022
(212) 759-8822

SWEDISH NATIONAL TOURIST OFFICE
655 Third Avenue
New York, NY 10017
(212) 949-2333

SWISS NATIONAL TOURIST OFFICE
608 Fifth Avenue
New York, NY 10020
(212) 757-5944

TURKISH TOURISM AND INFORMATION OFFICE
821 UN Plaza
New York, NY 10017
(212) 687-2194

USSR
c/o Intertourist
630 Fifth Avenue
New York, NY 10111
(212) 757-3884

YUGOSLAV NATIONAL TOURIST OFFICE
630 Fifth Avenue, Suite 280
New York, NY 10111
(212) 757-2801

CENTRAL AND SOUTH AMERICA AND MEXICO

EMBASSY OF BELIZE
1575 Eye Street, NW, Suite 695
Washington, DC 20005
(202) 289-1416

BOLIVIAN CONSULATE
3014 Massachusetts Avenue, NW
Washington, DC 20008
(202) 483-4410

BRAZILIAN TOURISM CENTER
2 W. 45th Street, Suite 1409
New York, NY 10036
(212) 840-3320

CHILEAN CONSULATE
809 United Nations Plaza
New York, NY 10017
(212) 687-7547

COLUMBIAN GOVERNMENT TOURIST OFFICE
140 East 57th Street
New York, NY 10022
(212) 688-0151

COSTA RICA TOURIST BOARD
200 S.E. First Street
Miami, FL 33131

ECUADOR TOURIST OFFICE
18 E. 41st Street
New York, NY 10017
(212) 547-0711

EMBASSY OF EL SALVADOR
2308 California Street, NW
Washington, DC 20008
(202) 265-3480

GUATEMALA CONSULATE
57 Park Avenue
New York, NY 10017
(212) 686-3837

MEXICAN NATIONAL TOURIST COUNCIL
405 Park Avenue
New York, NY 10022
(212) 755-7261

PANAMA MISSION TO THE UN
866 United Nations Plaza
New York, NY 10017
(212) 421-5420

PARAGUAY MISSION TO THE UN
211 East 43rd Street
New York, NY 10017
(212) 687-3490

PERUVIAN MISSION TO THE UN
820 Second Avenue
New York, NY 10017
(212) 687-3336

CONSULATE OF URUGUAY
747 3rd Avenue
New York, NY 10017
(212) 752-8240

VENEZUELAN GOVERNMENT TOURIST BUREAU
7 East 51st Street
New York, NY 10022
(212) 826-1660

ASIA AND THE PACIFIC

AUSTRALIA TOURISM OFFICE
289 5th Avenue
New York, NY 10017
(212) 687-6300

EMBASSY OF BANGLADESH
2201 Wisconsin Avenue, NW
Washington, DC 20007
(202) 342-0741

BURMA MISSION TO THE UN
10 East 77th Street
New York, NY 10021
(212) 535-1310

CHINA NATIONAL TOURIST OFFICE
60 E. 42nd Street
New York, NY 10165
(212) 867-0271

FIJI MISSION TO THE UN
New York, NY 10017
(212) 355-7316

HONG KONG TOURIST ASSOCIATION
P.O. Box 7720
Itasca, IL 60143

INDIA TOURIST OFFICE
30 Rockefeller Plaza
New York, NY 10112
(212) 586-4901

INDONESIA MISSION TO THE UN
325 E. 38th Street
New York, NY 10016

JAPAN NATIONAL TOURIST ORGANIZATION
630 Fifth Avenue
New York, NY 10111
(212) 757-5640

MALAYSIAN TOURIST CENTER
420 Lexington Avenue
New York, NY 10017
(212) 697-8995

NEW ZEALAND TOURIST OFFICE
10960 Wilshire Blvd.
Los Angeles, CA 90024

PAKISTAN MISSION TO THE UN
8 East 65th Street
New York, NY 10021

PHILIPPINES TRAVEL CENTER
556 Fifth Avenue
New York, NY 10021
(212) 575-7915

CONSULATE OF WESTERN SAMOA
820 Second Avenue
New York, NY 10017

SINGAPORE TOURIST PROMOTION BOARD
590 Fifth Avenue
New York, NY 10021
(212) 302-4861

SRI LANKA MISSION TO THE UN
630 Third Avenue
New York, NY 10017

TAHITI TOURIST BOARD
12233 W. Olympic Blvd.
Los Angeles, CA 90064

TOURISM AUTHORITY OF THAILAND
5 World Trade Center
New York, NY 10048
(212) 432-0433

AFRICA AND MIDDLE EAST

ALGERIAN EMBASSY
2118 Kalorama Road, NW
Washington, DC 20008

ANGOLAN PERMANENT REPRESENTATIVE TO
THE UN
747 Third Avenue, 18th Floor
New York, NY 10017

BAHRAIN MISSION TO THE UN
2 UN Plaza
New York, NY 10017
(212) 223-6200

EMBASSY OF THE REPUBLIC OF BOTSWANA
WASHINGTON, DC 20008
(202) 244-4990

EMBASSY OF BRUNEI
2600 Virginia Avenue, NW, Suite 300
Washington, DC 20037

EMBASSY OF BURKINA FASO
Washington, DC 20008
(202) 332-5577

EMBASSY OF CAMEROON
Washington, DC 20008
(202) 265-8790

EMBASSY OF THE CENTRAL AFRICAN REPUBLIC
Washington, DC 20008
(202) 483-7800

EMBASSY OF CHAD
Washington, DC 20009
(202) 462-4009

PEOPLE'S REPUBLIC OF THE CONGO MISSION
TO THE UN
New York, NY 10021

EMBASSY OF COTÉ DIVOIRE (IVORY COAST)
2424 Massachusetts Avenue, NW
Washington, DC 20008
(202) 483-2400

EGYPTIAN GOVERNMENT TOURIST OFFICE
630 Fifth Avenue
New York, NY 10111
(212) 246-6960

ETHIOPIAN EMBASSY
2134 Kalorama Road, NW
Washington, DC 20008
(202) 234-2281

EMBASSY OF GABON
Washington, DC 20009
(202) 797-1000

GAMBIA MISSION TO THE UN
19 East 47th Street
New York, NY 10017

GHANA MISSION TO THE UN
19 East 47th Street
New York, NY 10017

EMBASSY OF GUINEA
Washington, DC 20009
(202) 797-1000

IRAN
c/o Embassy of Algeria
Iranian Interests Section
Washington, DC 20007

IRAQ
c/o Embassy of India
Iraqi Interests Section
1801 P Street, NW
Washington, DC 200036

ISRAEL GOVERNMENT TOURIST OFFICE
350 Fifth Avenue
New York, NY 10118
(212) 560-0650

JORDAN MISSION TO THE UN
866 United Nations Plaza
New York, NY 10017

KENYA TOURIST OFFICE
424 Madison Avenue
New York, NY 10022
(212) 486-1300

CONSULATE OF KUWAIT
801 Second Avenue
New York, NY 10017
(212) 973-4318

LEBANON MISSION TO THE UN
866 United Nations Plaza
New York, NY 10017

EMBASSY OF LESOTHO
1430 K Street, NW
Washington, DC 20005
(202) 628-4833

EMBASSY OF LIBERIA
5201 16th Street, NW
Washington, DC 20011

MADAGASCAR MISSION TO THE UN
New York, NY 10017
(212) 968-9491

MALAWI MISSION TO THE UN
600 Third Avenue
New York, NY 10016
(212) 949-0180

EMBASSY OF MALI
Washington, DC 20008
(202) 332-2249

EMBASSY OF MAURITANIA
Washington, DC 20008
(202) 232-5700

MOROCCAN NATIONAL TOURIST OFFICE
20 East 46th Street
New York, NY 10017
(212) 557-2520

MOZAMBIQUE MISSION TO THE UN
70 East 79th Street
New York, NY 10021

EMBASSY OF NIGER
Washington, DC 20008
(202) 483-4224

NIGERIAN CONSULATE
417 East 50th Street
New York, NY 10019

EMBASSY OF THE SULTANATE OF OMAN
Washington, DC 20008
(202) 387-1980

EMBASSY OF THE STATE OF QATAR
Washington, DC 20037
(202) 338-0111

EMBASSY OF RWANDA
Washington, DC 20009
(202) 232-2882

SAUDI ARABIAN CONSULATE
866 United Nations Plaza
New York, NY 10017

EMBASSY OF SENEGAL
Washington, DC 20008
(202) 234-0540

EMBASSY OF SIERRA LEONE
Washington, DC 20009
(202) 939-9261

EMBASSY OF SOMALI
Washington, DC 20037
(202) 342-1575

SOUTH AFRICA TOURIST CORPORATION
747 Third Avenue
New York, NY 10017
(212) 838-8841

SUDAN MISSION TO THE UN
210 East 49th Street
New York, NY 10017

SYRIAN EMBASSY
2215 Wyoming Avenue, NW
Washington, DC 20008

EMBASSY OF SWAZILAND
Washington, DC 20008
(202) 362-6683

EMBASSY OF TANZANIA
Washington, DC 20008
(202) 939-6125

EMBASSY OF TOGO
Washington, DC 20008
(202) 234-4212

TUNISIAN MISSION TO THE UN
405 Lexington Avenue
New York, NY 10174

UGANDA MISSION TO THE UN
New York, NY 10017

EMBASSY OF THE REPUBLIC OF ZAIRE
1800 N. Hampshire Avenue, NW
Washington, DC 20009

MISSION OF ZAMBIA TO THE UN
New York, NY 10022

EMBASSY OF ZIMBABWE
Washington, DC 20008
(202) 332-7100

Index

The letter "t" following a number indicates that the information is contained in a table.

The letter "t" following a number indicates that the information is contained in a table.

The letter "t" following a number indicates that the information is contained in a table.

The letter "t" following a number indicates that the information is contained in a table.

The letter "t" following a number indicates that the information is contained in a table.

The letter "t" following a number indicates that the information is contained in a table.

The letter "t" following a number indicates that the information is contained in a table.

The letter "t" following a number indicates that the information is contained in a table.

The letter "t" following a number indicates that the information is contained in a table.

The letter "t" following a number indicates that the information is contained in a table.

The letter "t" following a number indicates that the information is contained in a table.

The letter "t" following a number indicates that the information is contained in a table.

The letter "t" following a number indicates that the information is contained in a table.

The letter "t" following a number indicates that the information is contained in a table.

Warrants, 65–66
Warts, 212–213
Watch collecting, 382
Water, 130
Weight
    losing, 132t, 133
    normal ranges, 132t, 133
Wills, 292–293
Wine, collecting, 382
Women
    credit rights for, 31–32

Women *(cont.)*
    divorce and, 292
    employment rights for, 255
    health concerns, 226–228
    insuring your equal right to credit, 31–32
    outdoor activities for, 356
    pension rights for, 18–19
    Social Security benefits and, 11, 13
    spouse abuse, 288–291
Work, 256–258. *See also* Employment

YMCAs
    swimming programs at, 361
    travel accommodations at, 338–339
YWCAs, swimming programs at, 361

Zero coupon bonds, 58–59
    advantages of, 59
    degree of investment risk, 39
    disadvantages of, 59

The letter "t" following a number indicates that the information is contained in a table.